AF556217

HEAT AND MASS TRANSFER

A Transport Phenomena Approach

HEAT AND MASS TRANSFER

A Transport Phenomena Approach

Preparation of this book was assisted by a grant from the Department of Science & Technology, Government of India, New Delhi

K.S. Gandhi
Department of Chemical Engineering
Indian Institute of Science
Bangalore, Karnataka

PUBLISHING FOR ONE WORLD

NEW AGE INTERNATIONAL (P) LIMITED, PUBLISHERS
New Delhi • Bangalore • Chennai • Cochin • Guwahati • Hyderabad
Jalandhar • Kolkata • Lucknow • Mumbai • Ranchi
Visit us at www.newagepublishers.com

Published by New Age International (P) Ltd., Publishers
First Edition: 2011

Branches:

- 37/10, 8th Cross (Near Hanuman Temple), Azad Nagar, Chamarajpet, **Bangalore**-560 018. Tel.: (080) 2675 6823 Telefax: 2675 6820, E-mail: bangalore@newagepublishers.com
- 26, Damodaran Street, T. Nagar, **Chennai**-600 017. Tel.: (044) 24353401, Telefax: 24351463 E-mail: chennai@newagepublishers.com
- CC-39/1016, Carrier Station Road, Ernakulam South, **Cochin**-682 016. Tel.: (0484) 2377004, Telefax: 4051303 E-mail: cochin@newagepublishers.com
- Hemsen Complex, Mohd. Shah Road, Paltan Bazar, Near Starline Hotel, **Guwahati**-781 008. Tel.: (0361) 2513881 Telefax: 2543669, E-mail: guwahati@newagepublishers.com
- 105, 1st Floor, Madhiray Kaveri Tower, 3-2-19, Azam Jahi Road, Nimboliadda, **Hyderabad**-500 027 Tel.: (040) 24652456, Telefax: 24652457, E-mail: hyderabad@newagepublishers.com
- RDB Chambers (Formerly Lotus Cinema)106A, 1st Floor, S.N. Banerjee Road, **Kolkata**-700 014 Tel.: (033) 22273773, Telefax: 22275247, E-mail: kolkata@newagepublishers.com
- 16-A, Jopling Road, **Lucknow**-226 001. Tel.: (0522) 2209578, 4045297, Telefax: 2204098 E-mail: lucknow@newagepublishers.com
- 142C, Victor House, Ground Floor, N.M. Joshi Marg, Lower Parel, **Mumbai**-400 013. Tel.: (022) 24927869 Telefax: 24915415, E-mail: mumbai@newagepublishers.com
- 22, Golden House, Daryaganj, **New Delhi**-110 002. Tel.: (011) 23262370, 23262368, Telefax: 43551305 E-mail: sales@newagepublishers.com

---

ISBN : 978-81-224-3277-0

₹ 495.00

C-11-05-5567

Printed in India at Glorious Printers, Delhi.
Typeset by Author.

PUBLISHING FOR ONE WORLD
NEW AGE INTERNATIONAL (P) LIMITED, PUBLISHERS
4835/24, Ansari Road, Daryaganj, New Delhi-110002
Visit us at **www.newagepublishers.com**

Dedicated to

my parents
Sri Kandukuri Virabhadra Rao
Srimati Kandukuri Bhramaramba Lalita
and
my mother's siblings
Sri Mallampalli Somasekhara Sarma
Srimati Kandukuri Sundaramma
Sri Mallampalli Umamaheswara Rao

Preface

Publication of the classic text *Transport Phenomena* by Bird, Stewart and Lightfoot, affectionately known as BSL, started a revolution in chemical engineering. Prior to that, chemical engineering surely was quantitative, but largely empirical. BSL started the strong analytical trend which swept chemical engineering education. I was introduced to it in 1963 and learnt the beautiful foundations on which Unit Operations could be based. Many texts on Transport Phenomena have come since BSL, but it always remained, and remains unique. The natural question that arises in the minds of admirers of BSL like me is about the need for another text. BSL lays out derivations with clarity, selects examples highly illustrative of principles, and poses intellectually teasing problems to be solved. Interpretation of results, possible applications, and potential extensions are left to be dealt with by the teacher, and that is how a book ought to be planned in general. After years of teaching however, I felt that the deliberate gap left by BSL remains unbridged in India. The reason is easy to see. With the rapid expansion of engineering education in India, there has always been a shortage of able teachers, and teaching of Transport Phenomena has suffered especially due to this. My first aim in writing this text has been to help alleviate this difficulty faced by Indian students. However, I always tell my students that while they use my class notes, which formed the starting point for this text, they should read BSL. I have left out fluid mechanics from this text and my reason is the availability of books on this subject in large numbers and in a wide variety. Just as with BSL, I suggest to my students that they should read the classic *Introduction to fluid dynamics* by Batchelor. Radiation is an omission. I feel that as it is so very different from the rest of the transport processes, its inclusion is more for completeness rather than for pedagogical value.

Chemical engineering is going through a phase of expansion and diversification. Chemical engineers are well poised for this phase with their strong connection to mathematics and physics, umbilical binding to chemistry, and natural entry into biology based on these. Several pleas have been made to introduce into textbooks newer applications, which chemical engineers are helping to develop. My second aim has been to do this. However, newer applications have a context and its exposition does eat into the space normally devoted to expounding the basics. A balance is always needed. I introduce applications in processing of materials and fuel cells, normally not found in a text on Transport Phenomena, to fulfil this aim. I must say that many other areas are left out, *e.g.*, biomedical applications on which excellent texts are available, many more separation processes other than the membrane based ones, making of electronic devices, polymer processing, *etc.* This omission is entirely due to limitations imposed by my knowledge base!

My other aims have been dictated by my biases. Computations have made significant impact on not education alone but on life itself. I feel that numerical solutions of transport phenomena problems, commonly referred to as CFD, has to be known to every chemical engineer. 'There are beautiful or useful solutions' that summarizes my attitude. With this as the goal, while keeping a few exact solutions, a chapter on CFD was introduced. In the same vein, the chapter on turbulence and turbulence modeling mainly emphasizes Kolmogorov's theory.

I adopted a style of presentation very much under the influence of the brilliant book *How to solve it?* by Polya. There he presents a systematic approach to solving problems which consists of understanding the problem, hypothesizing an approach to solve it, solution of the problem itself and digesting the results by checking for consistencies. In this text, the first two were combined into *problem identification*, and the last was renamed as *looking at the results*. Hopefully, the last step builds intuition while the first trains in posing well defined problems by suitable physical approximations. I have deliberately laid less emphasis on solution procedures, and the problems at the end of the chapter which do not ask for solutions should make this abundantly clear. This has been prompted by my belief in the great value of teaching to correctly frame problems and relying upon computers to get results.

The three transport processes are similar but not identical, and I tried to emphasize both the similarities and differences in this text. My teaching experience indicated that chemical engineers understand and visualize heat transfer more easily than mass transfer. I, therefore, feel that it is best to teach these subjects in series than in parallel. The book is structured in that way. I begin with heat transfer and shell balances. Shell balances give a physical feel while intuition is developed on the basis of heat transfer. Advantage is taken of the experience gained in heat transfer and the problems selected for mass transfer are more complex than the corresponding ones in heat transfer. The same applies for topics selected in the chapters on advanced topics.

I feel that the text is suitable for first year post-graduate students of India. To do justice, two semester long courses will be needed to teach Transport phenomena. It then seems reasonable that only a part of this text can be taught in a semester. I feel that, after laying the basics contained in the first two chapters, third and fourth chapters and a selection of topics from the fifth and sixth chapters will form a good coverage of heat transfer. Seventh and eighth chapters and a selection of topics from the ninth and tenth chapters will give a good view of mass transfer. The chapter on turbulence can be covered, perhaps leaving out the material on spectrum. The last chapter on CFD can be taught in full.

I now have the pleasant task of acknowledging the contributions of my colleagues. Material covered in my classes has formed the basis for this text. I am very grateful to my students who have given valuable feed back. Professor Raj Chhabra of Indian Institute of Technology, Kanpur has patiently read the entire text and his suggestions have helped greatly improve the presentation. Dr. Srinivasa Mohan of Fluent, and Ms. Akila Harith of Mechanical Engineering, Indian Institute of Science read the chapter on CFD; Professors V Shankar and Raj Pala of Indian Institute of Technology, Kanpur, K. Kesava Rao and S. Venugopal of Indian Institute of Science have read parts of the text and the kind words from all these were encouraging. My understanding and teaching of topics covered in this text was enriched by discussions with many colleagues of Indian Institute of Science, in particular Professor K. Kesava Rao, and I acknowledge these inputs. Finally, I would like to acknowledge the support lent for writing of this book by the Department of Science & Technology through the USERS scheme. While I tried to make the book error free, I am sure there will be many left. I would be grateful to all readers who find errors in the book if they can kindly communicate those to me.

K.S. Gandhi

Contents

Chapter 1

INTRODUCTION

```
We discuss the scope of transport processes,
           the causes for heat and mass transfer,
           the fundamental ideas and methods that
           are used in  transport processes.
We examine the motivation for studying transport processes.
```

An engine can be defined as a device made to achieve some change: an agent of change. In a broad sense, a steam turbine changes heat into mechanical energy. Petrochemical plants change crude oil into more useful chemicals. Engineers invent, design, make and operate engines to achieve a purpose and engineering is a discipline that trains them. Chemical Engineering, in particular is concerned with managing chemical and physical changes to manufacture products safely, reproducibly, efficiently, and economically. In chemical plants, one is interested in various kinds of chemical changes. For example, in a petroleum industry, one is interested in converting the large molecules that are naturally found in crude oil into smaller ones, changing the alkane characteristics into aromatic character, *etc.* Physical changes are also of equal interest in chemical plants. Changing the temperature in a reactor or altering the concentration of species in a stream or pumping ('changing the location') products into storage tanks are some examples. One question that we might ask is whether the desired changes are likely to occur, so to speak, by themselves or they have to be 'forced' to change? One part of this question is addressed by thermodynamics.

1.1 DRIVING FORCES OF CHANGE

Thermodynamics considers closed systems[1] and specifies conditions under which their *state* remains unaltered or they exist in *equilibrium*. A system not in equilibrium is expected to evolve[2] to attain equilibrium, and conversely, if a change in a closed system in equilibrium is desired, it has to be forced by some means. One form of condition for equilibrium specifies that, if the entropy of a closed system at constant energy and volume is a maximum, the system will be in a state of equilibrium. It can be mathematically stated as:

$$(\delta S)_{U,V} \leq 0$$

where δS is the difference in the entropy of *any*[3] and the current state of the system, and U and V the internal energy and volume of the system respectively. A system at constant volume and energy is in an equilibrium state if entropy of any other state is less or entropy is maximum for an equilibrium state. If the above criterion is satisfied, the system is in equilibrium and therefore, will not move from its current state. As noted earlier, if the above condition is not satisfied the system will move away from its current state to some new state. Thus, if a change in the state of the system increases its entropy from its current state, the system will change to some new state by itself or the change occurs 'spontaneously'[4]. The criterion can be applied to the new state as well. If the criterion is not satisfied, the state of the system continues to change till the criterion is satisfied, *i.e.*, till equilibrium is reached. Consider the following example: two closed systems in equilibrium but at two different temperatures will continue to exist in their states. Thus, a change in the state of any one of the two systems can only be forced. Suppose they are 'forced' by bringing them into contact[5] with each other and insulating them from the surroundings. Together, they form a closed system and thermodynamics predicts from the above criterion that, 'heat' flows from the hotter body to the colder body and, the temperatures of both bodies will be equal when equilibrium is attained. Another *equivalent* condition of equilibrium states that change is feasible if Gibbs free energy of the system decreases [6],

$$(dG)_{T,P} < 0$$

where G, T and P are the Gibbs free energy, temperature and pressure respectively. Alternatively, the free energy is a minimum at equilibrium:

$$(dG)_{T,P} \geq 0$$

This particular form of the equilibrium criterion predicts that when two solutions containing a solute at different concentrations are brought into contact, mass of solute transfers from a region of higher concentration to that of a lower concentration so that chemical potential, and hence concentration in this example, is the same everywhere in the final mixture.

The criteria discussed above can be understood in a more useful way. In a system, there could be different parts or regions which are not in the same state (*e.g.*, not having the same S or G). Then changes will occur in the system. The entire system changes in a direction so as to reach a *homogeneous* and *minimal (or maximal)* state according to the above criteria. In all such processes involving a change, a 'difference', *e.g.*, a difference in the free energy, characterizing the inhomogeneity between the different regions, is identifiable. In specific instances, it can be related to easily measurable quantities. In heat transfer it is the difference in temperature. In mass transfer, it is the difference in the chemical potential, which is proportional to the difference in concentration. Thus, due to the spatial variation of these characteristic differences, commonly referred to as *driving forces*, transport of heat and mass occurs. The direction of transport is such that the system tends to move towards a state of equilibrium. The argument can be reversed and it follows that heat and or mass transfer is achieved by applying suitable driving forces.

Heat and mass transfer are two kinds of physical changes in the state of a system. These two processes form the basis of many Unit Operations. Although it is not apparent from the commonly-used texts on Unit Operations, the flow of fluids can be identified with transfer of momentum. The three processes of momentum, heat and mass transfer are commonly referred to as **transport**

processes, and most physical changes are a result of transport processes. Unit Operations are about engineering different types of physical changes and therefore, transport processes constitute the knowledge base of Unit Operations. In this sense, understanding transport processes is, *in principle*, equivalent to understanding the fundamentals of all Unit Operations[7] An understanding of transport processes enables us to engineer desired physical changes by applying suitable driving forces.

1.2 RATE OF A PROCESS

In the previous section, we pointed out that thermodynamics can identify criteria for a change to occur *spontaneously*. However, the word spontaneous as used in thermodynamics does not imply that rate of change is fast! In fact, thermodynamics is silent about the rate at which the change will occur. An important question is about the rate of change or rate of the process. In thermodynamics, the differences in functions, *e.g.,* internal energy, between two states are calculated by imagining a *reversible process* that takes the system from one state to another. In such a process, changes occur in infinitesimal increments. Correspondingly, the driving forces are also infinitesimal in magnitude. Intuitively, it appears that the rate of such a process is also infinitesimally small. Reversible processes have the maximum efficiency because they do not cause an increase in the entropy of the universe. The reversible path, though it is the most efficient one, has to be abandoned if the process is to be carried out at a rate that is practically useful. It is expected that the rate of a process increases when the magnitude of the driving force is increased. However, any process carried out with a finite driving force is irreversible. Such processes are commonly referred to as **irreversible** or **dissipative processes**[8]. As the processes occur at a finite rate, they are also known as **rate processes**. The rate processes involving transport of momentum, heat and mass are also referred to as transport phenomena.

1.2.1 Flux is a measure of rate

It is now worthwhile to think a little more to sharpen the idea of rate of a process. As we referred to earlier, when two bodies at different temperatures are brought into contact, heat flows from the one at a higher temperature into the one at a lower temperature. Similarly, if a temperature gradient exists in a body, heat will flow from regions of higher temperature into those at lower temperatures. The quantity of interest is then the rate of transfer of heat. By considering examples of mass transfer of solutes from regions of higher chemical potential into those at lower chemical potential, we can conclude that the rate of transfer of mass of solute is the quantity of interest. As the transfer is from one body to the other or from one part of a body to another, it has to go through the surface of one and enter the other. We propose that the fundamental quantity defining the rate of a transport process is the rate of transfer per unit area or *flux*. Thus, we could have heat flux or mass flux.

1.2.2 Convection and diffusion

Now we need to distinguish carefully between the causes that create a flux. Heat or mass of a solute can be transported from place to place in two ways. In the first, these could be transported by bulk flow. All have experienced cool air flowing out of an air conditioner or fragrance of a flower being brought over by wind. This is referred to as transport due to **convection.** As fluid flows, it brings energy along with it as reflected by its temperature, or a solute as reflected by the concentration of solute in it. If $\mathbf{v}$ is the velocity in the medium and its temperature was T, the convective heat flux is given by $\rho\hat{C}_pT\mathbf{v}$ where $\rho\hat{C}_p$ is the heat capacity per unit volume. Similarly, if C_i is the mass concentration of some solute, the mass flux is given by $C_i\mathbf{v}$. There is a very important characteristic of convective flux; homogeneity at molecular level characterizes equilibrium and *convection does not achieve this*. Consider once again example of the air conditioner blowing cool air into a room full of hot air. If the cold and hot air do not mix at the molecular level, the room will contain only a mixture of packets, perhaps tiny in size, of hot and cold air.

The mechanisms by which homogeneity at molecular level is achieved are broadly referred to as *diffusive* processes. The random motion of molecules causes mixing at the molecular level. This is characterized as mass transfer by diffusion of species. Exchange of energy and momentum through collisions between molecules or through other molecular interactions causes exchange of energy and momentum. These processes are referred to as heat transfer by conduction[9] and momentum transfer by viscous action. Rates of all these processes are characterized by diffusive fluxes. It is the diffusive fluxes that drive a system towards thermodynamic equilibrium. One of the main questions that needs to be answered in the study of transport processes is: 'What is the dependence of the rate of a diffusive transport process on the driving force?' The relationships between the rate of a process and the driving force are referred to as **constitutive relationships** or **rate laws**.

A very important aspect of diffusive flux is that it is connected with random molecular motions. Hence *diffusive fluxes are present at all times and at every place* till equilibrium is achieved. In contrast, convection is present only if flow is there. In particular, convective transfer is absent in solids.

Both diffusive flux and convective flux play a role in transport processes. We will illustrate this in greater detail in chapters on mechanisms of heat and mass transfer.

1.3 BALANCE QUANTIFIES CHANGE

Any process is aimed at carrying out a change. It is expected that if the extent of change to be brought about is known, the rate law would provide an estimate of the time required to accomplish the change. Consider a simple example. Suppose 10 kg of water is available at 10°C. Call this the input state. Say, we desire to raise its temperature to 50°C. Call this the desired or output state. The 'extent' of 'change in enthalpy (or thermal energy)' required is the difference in the enthalpy of the output and input states. In the present example, it is approximately equal to 1600 kJ. If we are able to supply heat at a constant rate (an unrealistic rate law as it turns out) of 1 kW, it would require 1600 s to do the job. Real processes are very complex: they may be batch, semi-batch or continuous; they may operate under steady state or unsteady conditions. Hence, an accurate accounting is required to assess the extent of desired change. **Balance laws** provide the accounting procedures that accurately characterize the extent of change required to reach the output state from the input state. The simple example mentioned depicts how balance laws are combined with a constitutive relationship to provide answers to practical questions. One would clearly expect more fundamental formulations of constitutive relationships.

1.4 TRANSPORT PHENOMENA APPROACH

The approach of transport phenomena towards describing physical changes can now be summarized as follows: Balance laws are applied to *every point*[10] in space of any equipment or region of space of interest at every instant of its operation. Clearly, this is the most detailed description one can ask for. *Formulating the balance laws in generality is one of the fundamental steps in the study of transport processes.* Formulating and simplifying them to specific examples is one of our major learning objectives of this book. *Balance laws have to be combined with constitutive relationships to obtain equations of change.* The equations of change are then solved along with boundary conditions to obtain answers to practically important questions. Several simple examples of combining balance laws with constitutive relationships and solving the resultant equations of change will be considered in this book. These form the basis to develop a 'physical feel' for real and complex problems, which is essential to develop an ability to analyze more complex problems. Study of development of constitutive relationships is important to understand the characteristics of transport processes. In this text, however we consider origins of only the simple relationships.

1.5 SIMILARITY OF TRANSPORT PROCESSES

The molecular mechanisms underlying the three transport processes: momentum, energy and mass, turn out to be similar. As a result, the transport processes themselves show analogous, but not identical, behavior on macroscopic level as well. The similarity between heat and mass transfer is more pronounced than with momentum transfer. For this reason, it is advantageous to study them together. The present text is an introduction to the study of heat and mass transfer from a transport phenomena approach. Before we move into the study of transport processes, let us examine the reasons to adopt this approach.

1.6 WHY TRANSPORT PHENOMENA APPROACH?

Earlier, it was mentioned that studying Transport Processes in principle is same as studying Unit Operations. We also noted that transport phenomena approach gives a description of physical changes at every point in an equipment at every instant. This is clearly more complex than that attempted in Unit Operations. It is but natural to ask if there are any advantages in studying transport phenomena over and above Unit Operations. We attempt to answer this question in this section.

1.6.1 Unification advances knowledge

A bit of history will help to provide an answer to this question. As we know, the discipline of chemical engineering arose out of a need for skilled persons trained to combine chemistry with engineering. Such persons had to discipline their minds to think in both chemical and engineering idioms. For training to be of general and wider value, it cannot be confined to a particular chemical industry. The pioneers of chemical engineering education thought about what could form a program to develop the new discipline. A dissection of the various physical changes occurring in any chemical industry revealed many commonalities. If raw materials are solids, they had to be *crushed* and *ground* to reduce their physical size, and perhaps *leached* with suitable liquors to extract products.

Sluggishly reactive raw materials had to be *heated* and *pumped* into reactors. Products invariably were present as mixtures in solvents and with reactants and side products. Separation could be done by removing solvent by *evaporation*. Separation from other undesirable compounds could be done by *distillation* or *extraction* and so on. These diverse operations leading to physical changes were common to all industries and any chemical industry can be thought of as made up of these Unit Operations. Thus, the dissection led to unity, progress and birth of a new discipline: chemical engineering. It is but natural to think if further dissection[11] leading to a new unity is possible. We have alluded to the idea that all Unit Operations can also be thought of as a combination of the three transport processes. Pumps, packed and fluidized beds, settlers and so on are examples of momentum transfer. Heat exchangers are an example of heat transfer. Evaporation is an example of both heat and mass transfer where the solvent has to diffuse to the interface and escape into the vapor phase. Distillation is another example where the more volatile component diffuses to the vapor–liquid interface and further on into the vapor phase. It therefore appears that a unification of Unit Operations is possible through a study of transport processes.

Unification of diverse ideas through a few laws drives progress in science. Newton's laws are a great example of this. Thus, trying to tie up the knowledge in diverse Unit Operations through the idiom of Transport Processes will lead to progress.

1.6.2 Computing as a driving force

Fundamental descriptions of transport processes are old, as old as chemical engineering, if not older: Stokes, Fourier and Fick are names that are historical and established in the early twentieth century. These are names intimately linked with fluid flow, heat transfer and mass transfer. Why did the pioneers of chemical engineering not start with transport processes? Why did they take the semi-empirical approach of correlations to develop Unit Operations? History often shows that there is a time, a place and men & women for events to occur. As we mentioned earlier, transport phenomena attempts to describe temporal changes at every point in a region of space of interest. As we will find in subsequent chapters, such description is embedded in partial differential equations. These, except in simple situations, are difficult to solve. Thus, though the equations were known, their utility in complex settings encountered in chemical process equipment was minimal. It is for this reason that the approach was not adopted earlier. The advances in computing have been very rapid in the recent times and numerical solution of the complex partial differential equations has become feasible. This approach is commonly referred to as *computational fluid dynamics*[12] or CFD. The main driving force for making transport phenomena approach–timely now and too early some fifty years ago– is the suitable advances in computing have become available now. Even today however, there are many problems where CFD cannot be applied and the empirical approaches of Unit Operations will have to be employed.

1.6.3 Basic question on Unit Operations approach

In this section, we show that the combination of balances with rate laws is also the foundation of Unit Operations. We however point out the limitations of the Unit Operations approach.

Macroscopic balances

Mass and energy balances are very familiar to chemical engineers. Procedures to make these balances are "given" in many undergraduate books on Unit Operations. Sometimes, they are derived using some intuitive arguments. Making such balances is intimately connected with the subject of Transport Processes. We start with the balance laws as written in Unit Operations books, and raise questions about their origins. These questions would concretely illustrate the need for a fundamental outlook and provide motivation for studying Transport Processes.

Mass balance: A domain of interest is known as **control volume**. Consider any equipment through which material is flowing. It could be a storage vessel (see Figure 1.1). We show the control volume by a boundary marked by dotted lines. We write mass balance equation for the control volume in the following form:

Rate of accumulation of total mass in the CV = **Rate of input of total mass into the CV by convection** − **Rate of output of total mass into the CV by convection** + **Rate of generation of total mass in the CV**

If we are interested in making a mass balance at steady state[13], the accumulation term is zero. Now we assert that, according to **the law of conservation of mass**, mass can neither be created nor destroyed. Hence the last term is equal to zero. Thus for the storage vessel

$$\dot{m}_{in} = \dot{m}_{out}$$

However, the law of conservation of mass is valid for a system[14], and the above is an intuitive generalization of the law to a *control volume* or to an *open system*. How is the generalization done precisely?

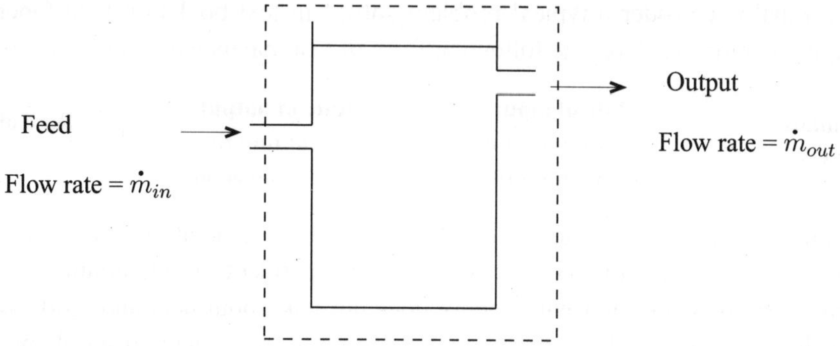

Figure 1.1. Mass balance around an equipment. Control volume is marked by dotted line.

Energy balance: Though this example is from fluid mechanics, we use it here to show that the questions we are raising are general. Engineering Bernoulli equation is commonly used in fluid mechanics. It is written as:

$$\left(\frac{v^2}{2}+\frac{P}{\rho}+gz\right)_{in}=\left(\frac{v^2}{2}+\frac{P}{\rho}+gz\right)_{out}+\text{Frictional losses}-\text{Work done on the control volume}$$

This is a very important and useful equation. Why is it valid? All of us are familiar with the law of conservation of energy or the first law of thermodynamics. As with the previous example, it is also valid for closed systems only. An intuitive generalization of the first law is seen in books on thermodynamics, where losses are attributed to the irreversible nature of the process. Those generalizations also have a term dealing with the rate of supply of heat. Does this mean that the Bernoulli equation is a version of the first law of thermodynamics for isothermal systems where heat is not being supplied? Is pressure divided by density a form of energy or is it mechanical ($p\,dV$) work? May we separate heat and work terms like that? What should be done for non-isothermal systems?

Further, Unit Operations books give expressions for losses. For example, when a fluid flows at an average velocity v in a pipe of length L and diameter d,

$$\text{Head loss due to friction}=\frac{4fLv^2}{2d}$$

where f is the friction factor. This has its origins in Newton's laws, and some books do contain a derivation. Why does the Bernoulli equation itself not follow from Newton's laws? Or does it? How do we know that losses are given by this expression? Almost all Unit Operations books show that velocity varies with position in a tube *i.e.,* a *velocity profile* exists in a tube, and that it is parabolic in laminar flow. Then, should we use the square of the average velocity or the average of the square of velocity in the above expression?

Heat balance: Finally, consider a typical problem solved in text books on Unit Operations: heat transfer through a composite slab. The following form of heat balance on a thin slice is used there:

Rate of accumulation of heat in the CV = **Rate of input of heat into the CV by convection** − **Rate of output of heat into the CV by convection** + **Rate of generation heat in the CV**

We simplify this for steady state and, in the absence of heat generation, show that temperature profiles are linear provided thermal conductivities are independent of temperature. Again, is it not strange that the first law connected with energy does not talk about heat and work separately and yet we talk of 'heat balance'? Although this may be justified in conduction problems, where work terms are absent, we also use heat balances in other equipment where flow occurs. When is the use of heat balances justified?

1.6.4 Limitations of Unit Operations

In this section, we review solutions of a few problems illustrating the typical approach of Unit Operations, and show the limitations of this approach. These limitations can be overcome by using transport phenomena approach.

Heat exchanger design

Consider the familiar problem of determining the length of a double-pipe heat exchanger required to effect a certain amount of heat exchange. Let quantities with subscript c refer to cold fluid and those with subscript h refer to hot fluid. Let $\dot{m}$ be the flow rate. We consider a thin slice of a heat exchanger as shown in Figure 1.2. By mass balance over this section we get

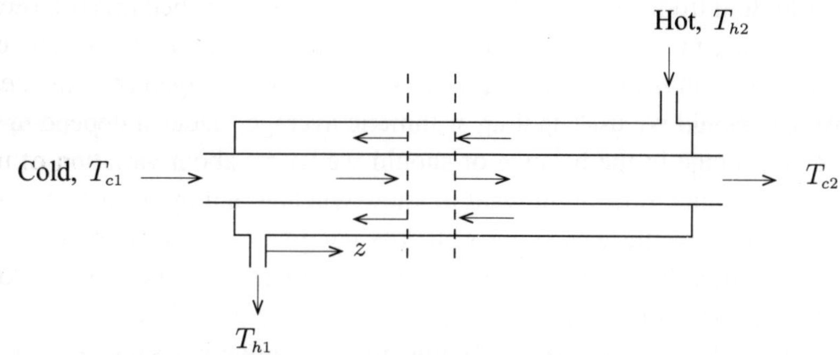

Figure 1.2. Double pipe heat exchanger.

$$\dot{m}_c|_z - \dot{m}_c|_{z+\Delta z} = 0$$

or $\dot{m}_c$ is constant. Similarly we can show that w_h is also constant. Heat balance over only the cold fluid we get

$$(\dot{m}_c \hat{C}_{pc} T_c)|_z - (\dot{m}_c \hat{C}_{pc} T_c)|_{z+\Delta z} = \text{Rate at which heat is lost from it} = U_h \pi d \Delta z (T_c - T_h)$$

where U_h is the overall heat transfer coefficient. Dividing by Δz and taking the limit as $\Delta z \to 0$,

$$-\dot{m}_c \hat{C}_{pc} \frac{dT_c}{dz} = U_h \pi d (T_c - T_h)$$

Notice that this is a *combination of balance law with rate law* where the overall heat transfer coefficient is being used to describe the *rate* of the process. A heat balance over both the streams put together yields

$$(\dot{m}_c \hat{C}_{pc} T_c)|_z - (\dot{m}_c \hat{C}_{pc} T_c)|_{z+\Delta z} - (\dot{m}_h \hat{C}_{ph} T_h)|_z + (\dot{m}_h \hat{C}_{ph} T_h)|_{z+\Delta z} = 0$$

Dividing by Δz and taking the limit as $\Delta z \to 0$,

$$-\dot{m}_c \hat{C}_{pc} \frac{dT_c}{dz} + \dot{m}_h \hat{C}_{ph} \frac{dT_h}{dz} = 0$$

This can be integrated along with the boundary conditions to get

$$\dot{m}_c \hat{C}_{pc} (T_{c2} - T_c) = \dot{m}_h \hat{C}_{ph} (T_{h2} - T_h)$$

The above can be used to solve for T_h in terms of T_c, and the result substituted in the differential equation derived for T_c. The differential equation can then be integrated to get the famous formula

$$\dot{m}_c\, C_{pc}(T_{c2} - T_{c1}) = U_h \pi d L\, (\Delta T)_{lm}$$

where $(\Delta T)_{lm}$ is the log mean temperature difference. It can be used to find the length of the pipe required to heat the cold fluid from a temperature of T_{c1} to T_{c2}. We described this briefly to illustrate that Unit Operations also use the approach of combining balances with rate laws. The temperature used in the above equation is an *average* value for the stream. It is averaged over the cross section, but what kind of average should we use? Is it an arithmetic average? Does it depend upon velocity profile? Can we use an average in the balance or should we worry about variation of temperature across the cross section? Further, one might want to know whether and by what extent temperature varies along the cross section and the above approach does not given any indication of this. Consider a few examples. Viscosity of a fluid is a strong function of temperature. The viscosity of fluid near hotter walls will be lower and affects the heat transfer rate. Empirical correlations do indicate that ignoring this might not be always correct. Temperature sensitive materials are often used in a reactor. These could be –products or temperature sensitive catalysts– and these will degrade in the hotter zones. Knowing temperature distribution is necessary to answer these questions and we need a more fundamental understanding to do this.

Consider a shell-and-tube heat exchanger. The following formula is used to relate the heat load $\dot{Q}$ to the area necessary for the required heat transfer rate:

$$\dot{Q} = U_h A F (\Delta T)_{lm}$$

where F is a correction factor to the log mean temperature difference. In a shell-and-tube heat exchanger, the flow of the tube-side and shell-side fluids is neither counter current nor co-current. The factor F accounts for the non–ideal behavior. Of course its value is read off charts. How are the charts prepared? In general, how can the effect of any kind of convection be taken into account?

Correlations for heat and mass transfer coefficients

We raise a different type of question in this section. Consider convective heat transfer in laminar flow in a tube. Here we imagine that a fluid is flowing through a pipe whose walls are wound with a heating coil. Suppose the velocity profile is parabolic when the fluid enters the pipe. The following expression can then be used for predicting the heat transfer coefficient, h:

$$\frac{hd}{k} \sim \left(\frac{d}{L}\mathrm{Re\ Pr}\right)^{0.33}$$

But for the same flow, at large distances from the entrance, the heat transfer coefficient becomes a constant! Notice the differences in the effect of velocity and viscosity. Are these correct? If they are, why do these differences arise? Yet another example is the correlation for laminar natural convection past a vertical hot plate:

$$h \sim (\Delta T)^{0.25}$$

Here the heat transfer coefficient is dependent on the driving force, in contrast to the forced convection heat transfer. This is to be expected since the flow itself is created by the temperature difference. But, why is there a dependence on the 0.25 power of temperature difference, *i.e.*, why is the power not equal to 0.5?

A more fundamental question is the origin of correlations. As will be seen in later chapters, need for correlations does not exist if the balance equations can be solved along with the rate laws. It is not yet possible to achieve this in *all* situations, though it is possible in several instances.

Correction for diffusion in a stagnant film

Consider gas A dissolving from its mixture in gas B into a solvent. Suppose B is insoluble in solvent. In gas absorber design, the following expression is used for calculating the mass flux across the gas–liquid interface:

$$N_A = K_m P \frac{y_{Ag} - y^*_{Al}}{P_B|_{lm}}$$

where K_m is the overall mass transfer coefficient, and y^*_{Al} is the mole fraction in a gas phase that would have been in equilibrium with the liquid phase. Notice that in case of heat transfer the driving force, *i.e.*, temperature difference was used directly to calculate the flux. Here, the driving force, $P(y_{Ag} - y^*_{Al})$ is being corrected by the factor $P_B|_{lm}$ to account for the fact that gas B is 'stagnant' since it cannot dissolve in the solvent. Suppose we have a three component mixture instead of binary: gases A, B and C. Suppose both B and C are insoluble. Is the above expression valid if we use the sum of the partial pressures of B and C instead of B alone?

Beyond Unit Operations

Chemical engineering is diversifying and developing borders with many disciplines. New demands are made on chemical engineers. Many have written about it and Danckwerts memorial lecture by Masehlkar [2] is an excellent source to get an idea of the changes demanded of the profession. These demands cannot always be met in the Unit Operations paradigm. The following examples illustrate this:

1. Scales of production become small in case of high value, small volume products. Similar could be the case where inventory has to be reduced. Micro reactors, mixers, *etc* are used in such cases. Shapes used in these equipments are varied. Transport phenomena approach is ideally suited to deal with such situations.

2. Microwave processing has become common. This operation does not fall into any of the known Unit Operations. Yet, it is possible to integrate the effect of electromagnetic waves into transport phenomena approach to describe microwave processing.

3. Chromatography has become a common means of separation. Once again, analysis of performance of chromatographic columns is easily done in the transport phenomena approach. Within this approach, it is possible to analyze even more complex methods such as separation by molecular recognition.

Dimensional analysis

In this section, we consider another popular method of solving engineering problems and consider its links with transport phenomena approach. Dimensional analysis is widely used in Unit Operations. To apply this type of analysis, *all* the variables important to the problem have to be *guessed* at first. It is expected that the variables are related to each other through some equation, which of course is not known, and that is why dimensional analysis is attempted. However, such an equation must be dimensionally consistent, *i.e.,* its left and right hand sides must have the same units. The units that commonly appear in chemical engineering problems are mass, length, time, and temperature. If four suitable variables are selected from the set guessed, all the other variables of the set can be rendered dimensionless in terms of the selected variables. Thus, a set of dimensionless groups are arrived at. The equation that relates all the guessed variables is equivalent to a relationship[15] between the dimensionless groups.

Let us take an example. Suppose we are interested in calculating the drag force F on a sphere while a liquid flows past it with a velocity v. In applying dimensional analysis, *we have to guess* the variables that are important. We would expect that the frictional force exerted by the liquid would depend upon its viscosity μ, and upon the area of contact between the sphere and the liquid. The latter depends upon the diameter of the sphere D. Hence we expect F to be related to v, d and μ through some complex equation:

$$F = \mathcal{F}(v, d, \mu)$$

The particular function is not known.

Force has dimensions of mass multiplied by acceleration. The latter has units of length divided by the square of time. We now select the variables from those that we thought were important to represent the dimensions of mass, length and time, and write force in terms of these. We can select diameter to represent length:

$$\text{Length} \leftrightarrow d$$

Velocity has units of length divided by time. Let us then use diameter and velocity to represent the units of time:

$$\text{Time} \leftrightarrow \frac{d}{v}$$

Viscosity has units of mass divided by the product of length and time. Therefore we can use viscosity to represent the unit of mass:

$$\text{Mass} \leftrightarrow \mu\frac{d^2}{v}$$

Hence,

$$F \leftrightarrow \text{Mass. Length/square of Time} \leftrightarrow \mu d v$$

The unknown equation that was written earlier for F can now be written as

$$\frac{F}{\mu d v} = \frac{\mathcal{F}(v, d, \mu)}{v d \mu}$$

However, the left hand side is dimensionless, *i.e.,* it has no units. The right hand side also must have no dimensions and the only possibility is that it is a constant[16]. Thus,

$$\frac{F}{\mu d v} = \text{constant}$$

This, you would recognize, is Stokes law. Of course the constant is not known. The constant must be determined experimentally. However, it is easily seen that the effects of μ, d and v need not be investigated separately, and the extent of experimentation required to determine the constant is reduced considerably.

You also know that this is not the complete story. We know that this is true only for creeping flow. So where did we go wrong? The error crept in while making the list of variables that are important in the problem. Suppose we thought that the inertia or the acceleration of the fluid as it goes around the sphere is also important. Then we must include the density of the fluid ρ, in the list. Now we can replace the dimensions of density as follows:

$$\rho \leftrightarrow \text{Mass/cube of Length} \leftrightarrow \frac{\mu}{vd}$$

and we get another ratio[17]:

$$\frac{dv\rho}{\mu}$$

which is the Reynolds number. Dimensional analysis would indicate that we should expect a relation like

$$\frac{F}{\mu d v} = \text{Function of (Re)}$$

Reynolds number is the ratio of inertial to viscous forces. When the flow is slow, inertial forces and Reynolds number will be small. Hence, based on the previous analysis, the right hand side can be expected to become a constant as Reynolds number becomes small. Notice how the "meaning" assigned to Reynolds number helps us in arriving at this conclusion.

One question that would arise in our minds is, how do we guess the right number and the correct variables? Further, how do we assign meaning to the dimensionless groups? As we shall see later, transport phenomena approach throws significant light on this question.

1.6.5 Conclusion

We provided motivation for adopting transport phenomena approach. Unification of concepts into a more compact formulation drives progress in science and transport phenomena is such a unifying idiom for Unit Operations. Several basic questions about the approach used in Unit Operations and its limitations have been raised here to make the case for Transport Processes paradigm. out. Those can be answered only after a study of Transport Processes.

Appendix

1.A Continuum Model

One possible way of solving problems in transport processes is to apply Newton's laws of motion to a collection of molecules. Such a procedure is known as molecular dynamics simulation. To get the ideas clear, consider a single component system. We can write an equation of motion for each molecule provided we know the forces experienced by them. All molecules move under the combined influence of various external forces, such as gravitational field. In addition, each molecule exerts an attractive or repulsive force on the others depending upon the distance between them. The forces are attractive when the molecules are far apart. When they come very close, their electron clouds overlap and the forces become repulsive, and we need an expression to calculate the forces. For example, gradient of the Lennard Jones potential gives intermolecular forces between a pair of non-polar molecules. Let $\mathbf{x}_i$ be the position of each molecule in some reference frame. Let $\mathbf{F}_i(\mathrm{r}_{ij})$ be the force exerted by jth molecule on the ith molecule, where we have assumed that it depends *only* upon the distances between the two molecules, r_{ij}. Thus, we can write Newton's second law for the ith molecule:

$$m\frac{d^2\mathbf{x}_i}{dt^2} = \sum_j \mathbf{F}_i(r_{ij})$$

There will be very many equations of course because there are 6×10^{23} molecules in each mole, which translates to that many molecules in just 18 cm^3 of water! Clearly the computational difficulties are unsurmountable at this time when the scale of the system is macroscopic in size. Hence, we need an alternative model and that is the continuum model[18].

Continuum model proposes that in view of the large number of molecules present in a small volume, the discrete nature of matter can be ignored and matter can be treated as continuous. As space is continuous, continuum model implies that matter is also present at every *point*[19] in space. Matter has properties. Hence, in the continuum model, we can assign *values to a property at every point in space*. Thus, we refer to temperature, velocity, *etc.* at a point. Models where we assign a value to quantities such as temperature, velocity, *etc.* at every point in space are called **continuum models** [20]. Temperature and velocity are terms which refer to the state of matter. Temperature is proportional to the mean kinetic energy per unit mass. Similarly, velocity is the mean momentum per unit mass. In other words they can be related to only the material present. A point on the other hand has neither volume nor mass: it is a mathematical idealization. So, how can a value of temperature, velocity, *etc.* be attributed to a point?

1.A.1 Point quantities and volume averaging

The continuum model proposes that a limiting process can be used to define point quantities unambiguously. Suppose we are able to determine positions and velocities of all molecules in a region of interest at some time. Now consider any point, P. Consider concentric spheres of decreasing radius r centered around the point P. Since the positions of all molecules are known, it is possible to determine the total mass, m of all the molecules contained in each sphere. Because the volume of each of the spheres is known, we can determine the ratio m/V in each of them. Continuum model proposes that the point density ρ can be defined as a limit

$$\rho = \lim_{r\to 0}\frac{\sum_i m_i}{V} = \lim_{r\to 0}\frac{m}{V} \tag{A1.1}$$

We can extract this limit by plotting the values of m/V against r. (See figure 1.3). Clearly, when r approaches the molecular dimensions, the ratio m/V will fluctuate a great deal, and would not even be continuous. It is therefore not shown in the figure. Thus, the limit does not exist in a mathematical sense. Continuum model

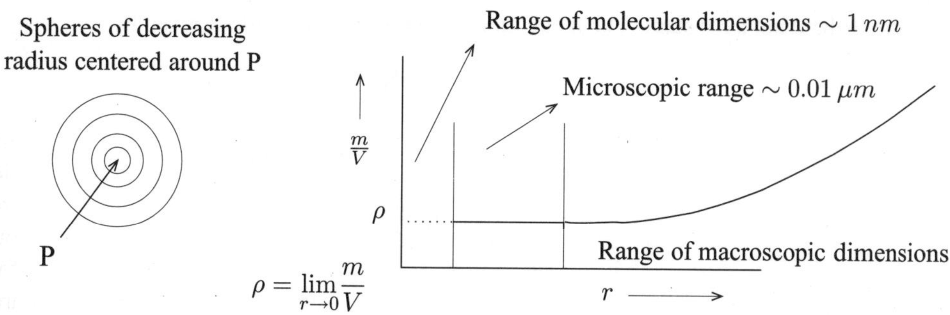

Figure 1.3. Graph showing the limiting process to obtain a volume average. The volume is shrunk around the point by taking spheres centered around the point and decreasing their radius.

hypothesizes that there is a sufficiently broad range of size, *larger than molecular dimensions and smaller than the macroscopic dimensions*, over which the ratio m/V will be constant, and that can be taken as the limit. These features are shown in Figure 1.3 where the dotted line shows the value accepted to be the result of the limiting process.

It is important to note that the radius is decreased around a selected point, and hence the limit evaluated can be uniquely assigned to that point.

The procedure can be used to determine fractions of molecules with certain properties too. A familiar example is the fraction of molecules of a particular type in a mixture, *i.e,* mole fraction of species. Following the procedure described above, a mole fraction can be assigned to every point. Another type of fraction is of immediate interest. In a single component system, it is known that molecules move with different velocities. We can ask what fraction of molecules, f_i possess a velocity[21] $\mathbf{v}_i$. Let there be N_i number of molecules in a volume V with velocity $\mathbf{v}_i$. The fraction of these in the total number of molecules will be

$$\frac{N_i}{\sum_i N_i}$$

Therefore, it is expected that in the limit, f_i can also be defined as the fraction of molecules with velocity $\mathbf{v}_i$:

$$f_i = \lim_{r\to 0} \frac{N_i/V}{\sum_i N_i/V} = \frac{\lim_{r\to 0} (N_i/V)}{C}$$

where C is the number of molecules per unit volume. Hence

$$Cf_i = \lim_{r\to 0} \frac{N_i}{V}$$

Let us use this definition to evaluate temperature, another important point quantity. Temperature is defined as the mean kinetic energy per molecule:

$$\text{mean kinetic energy} = \frac{3k_B T}{2}$$

where k_B is the Boltzmann's constant. The mean kinetic energy per molecule is given by

$$\begin{aligned}\text{mean kinetic energy} &= \lim_{r\to 0}\frac{\sum_i (N_i/V)mv_i^2/2}{\sum_i N_i/V} \\ &= \frac{\sum_i Cf_i mv_i^2/2}{C} \\ &= \frac{m}{2}\sum_i f_i v_i^2 \end{aligned} \tag{A1.2}$$

Thus,

$$T = \frac{m}{3k_B}\sum_i f_i v_i^2$$

Similarly,

$$\mathbf{v} = \lim_{r\to 0}\frac{\sum_i (N_i/V)\mathbf{v}_i}{\sum N_i/V} \tag{A1.3}$$

Thus, the continuum model hypothesizes that although matter is discrete in nature, unambiguous point quantities varying in space with time can be defined. Thus, we can define $\rho(x, y, z; t), T(x, y, z; t), \mathbf{v}(x, y, z; t)$, *etc.* Such point quantities that depend on time and location are referred to as 'fields', *e.g.,* velocity field. Transport processes deal with these fields and try to predict how these fields behave under a variety of conditions using the known laws of physics.

1.A.2 Point quantities and area averaging

Each of the above limits can be thought of as **volume averaged quantities**[22]. For example, in the case of mass, we determined the average mass per unit volume for different sizes of concentric spheres, and density is the limit of this averaged quantity as the size is gradually decreased to zero. Another type of limit we come across is the limit obtained by averaging over an area. Suppose we are interested in a quantity that depends upon the area, such as the mass of molecules crossing a surface per unit time. We expect this quantity to depend upon both area and the surface chosen. Thus, if we consider a domain that is cylindrical in cross section and of some length, the mass of molecules crossing per unit area will depend upon whether we chose the circular planes or the curved cylindrical surface. Further, it might even change from point to point on the surface. Thus, at a point we could think of limits of quantities *per unit area.* Such limits are obtained by considering what happens on an area in the limit of the area going to zero.

Refer to Figure 1.4. Consider an area δA. Since the area is small, it can be considered as planar. We could

ask the question: How much mass crosses the plane per unit time and per unit area? Only those molecules having a velocity component normal[23] to the plane will cross it. The normal component of the velocity of the ith molecule is $\mathbf{v}_i.\mathbf{n}$, where $\mathbf{v}_i$ is a velocity vector and $\mathbf{n}$ is the unit vector normal to the plane. Consider a

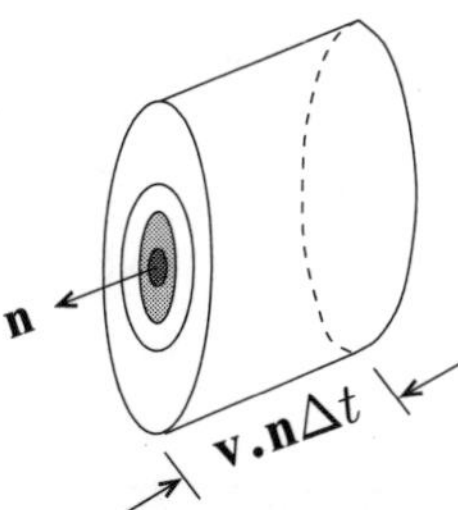

Figure 1.4. Limiting process in area averaging. The rings show the successively smaller areas while the direction of the normal vector is kept constant.

small time interval Δt. A molecule with velocity $\mathbf{v}_i$ will not travel in the direction dictated by the velocity for the *entire* duration of Δt as it may collide with others and change direction. However, in the limit of $\Delta t \to 0$ it will move in the direction of $\mathbf{v}_i$. Such a molecule will move a distance $\mathbf{v}_i.\mathbf{n}\Delta t$ towards the plane during the small time interval. Thus, in a cylinder of length $\mathbf{v}_i.\mathbf{n}\Delta t$ and area δA, shown in Figure1.4, there are Cf_i number of molecules with velocity $\mathbf{v}_i$, and all of them will cross the plane during time Δt. The area averaged mass flux across the plane is given by

$$\begin{aligned}\text{Average mass flux} &= \lim_{(\delta A \text{ and } \Delta t)\to 0} \frac{\sum_i Cf_i m\mathbf{v}_i.\mathbf{n}\delta A\Delta t}{\delta A\Delta t} \\ &= \lim_{(\delta A \text{ and } \Delta t)\to 0} \frac{\rho\mathbf{v}.\mathbf{n}\delta A\Delta t}{\delta A\Delta t} \\ &= \rho\mathbf{v}.\mathbf{n}\end{aligned} \qquad \text{(A1.4)}$$

Thus, in the limit of Δt and δA tending to zero, the mass of molecules crossing the plane per unit time per unit area is given by $\rho\mathbf{v}.\mathbf{n}$.

Here it is important to note that in the limiting process of area going to zero, the direction of $\mathbf{n}$ is kept constant. In other words, to obtain the limit, the area is being shrunk in a particular way, *i.e.,* by keeping the direction of its unit normal constant. Note that the above formula can be broken up as the dot product of two vectors: the flux vector $\rho\mathbf{v}$ and the normal vector to a plane of differential area. Therefore, once the normal vector is constructed and the point values of ρ and $\mathbf{v}$ are known, the mass crossing *any* differential area per unit time and unit area can be calculated and is given by $\rho\mathbf{v}.\mathbf{n}$. Later we will see more of this type of decomposition and limiting processes on area.

1.A.3 Derivatives of point quantities

In future we will be interested in the temporal and spatial changes of the point quantities we have just defined. Derivatives are defined as the limit of the ratio of change in the quantity to the corresponding change in the independent variable. As the point quantities have been unambiguously defined in terms of volume averaging, it is not difficult to define derivatives with respect to spatial variations. In continuum models, it is assumed that such spatial derivatives exist.

Now let us consider the time derivative. As matter is composed of molecules, there is a time scale of dynamics of molecules. In the case of gases, it could be the mean time interval between collisions. Therefore, there is an intrinsic time scale in which quantities could be changing abruptly. It can be anticipated that mathematical difficulties exist in determining time derivatives by calculating the limit as time interval between observations goes to zero. Recall that point quantities were defined as averages over a *finite* volume, and that the limiting process has not been taken all the way to zero volume. In considering the limiting process with respect to time interval here as well, the continuum model hypothesizes that even though the limit of the ratio of change in any point quantity to the time interval in which the change occurred may not exist as the time interval actually goes to zero, a range of sufficiently small but finite time intervals exist over which the ratio remains constant. Such a constant value obtained is taken to be the time derivative *at that instant of time*.

1.B Dimensional Analysis

One way of understanding the argument of dimensional analysis is as follows: Suppose one set of people are using MKS system of units. Another set of people, as in USA and UK, could be using FPS system. We expect that any system of units must obey the following restriction. If two masses m_1 and m_2, are weighed by the followers of the two systems, they should find the *same* value for the *ratio* m_1/m_2. Similar restriction follows for length and time. This is possible only if the two units are related to each other by a *constant value*. Thus, a one meter long scale has 3.28 feet in it. It is convenient to think of change of units as change of *scale* used to make measurement, and the *conversion* factor as the *scale factor*. Thus we have four fundamental scale factors for each system of units: one each for mass, length, time and temperature. Note that the ratios we considered had no units or were *dimensionless* and are independent of the unit of measurement.

We come across several quantities other than mass, length and time, *e.g.*, force. Units of such quantities are derived from the fundamental units, *e.g.,* Newton from kg, m and s. The scale factors to convert units of such derived quantities from one system to another are not independent and can be obtained from the three fundamental scale factors. It follows that units of derived quantities in different systems are also related to each other by a *constant* scale factor, and that ratios of derived quantities will also be independent of the system of units. Thus, if two forces, F_1 and F_2 were measured in two different units, the ratio F_1/F_2 will be dimensionless and is independent of the system of units. One more important result also follows. Any quantity, which is formed by several quantities but is dimensionless, will also have values independent of the system of units. In other words, *dimensionless quantities are independent of scale of measurement.*

Now consider the ratio $F/\mu DV$. This quantity is dimensionless and hence must be independent of the scale of measurement. Now consider the function $\mathcal{F}(V, D, \mu)$. The numerical values of V, D and μ will be different in different system of units. When these values are substituted, the numerical value of $\mathcal{F}$ may be different. However, $\mathcal{F}(V, D, \mu)/V D\mu$ must be independent of the system of units, and hence must be equal to a constant. Further, a quantity like $\mathcal{F}(V, D, \mu, \pi_1, \pi_2, \ldots)/(V\ D\,\mu)$, where $\pi_1, \pi_2, \ldots$ are dimensionless groups, must be independent of the system of units and hence, at best, be a function of $\pi_1, \pi_2, \ldots$ as these are independent of the system of units.

Notes

[1]We follow the nomenclature of Denbigh [1]. An isolated system does not permit both mass and energy exchange. A closed system permits only energy exchange.

[2]There could be internally imposed constraints that prevent change. Equilibrium can be reached only when these constraints are removed.

[3]Such a new state can be purely imaginary. If the new state imagined has internal restraints, attainment of equilibrium is possible only when they are relaxed.

[4]The word 'spontaneously' *does not mean* that the change will occur instantaneously. Thermodynamics predicts only the direction of change and not its rate.

[5]If an insulating barrier exists between them, it poses an internal restraint preventing attainment of equilibrium.

[6]It is being assumed that extraction of any forms of useful work other than mechanical is absent.

[7]Please do note the accent on 'in principle'. The peculiarities and differences between various equipment and the detailed knowledge required to design and operate them are important. Thus, it is said that physics forms a basis for understanding chemistry but that does not mean knowing physics implies knowing chemistry. Understanding from a

fundamental view point helps in general, and in fact, in appreciating the similarities as well as the differences between phenomena.

[8]An irreversible process is accompanied by a finite free energy change which could have been used to produce useful 'work' had a reversible path been followed. In this sense, the process has 'dissipated' the driving potential. In momentum transfer (and to a smaller extent, in mass transfer) heat is produced as the final result of the dissipative nature of the irreversible process. Heat transfer results in an increase in entropy or in dissipation of the organized nature of thermal energy.

[9]Radiative heat transfer is a molecular phenomena and can lead to homogeneity at molecular level.

[10]Matter is composed of molecules. Thus, any quantity associated with matter can be defined at a point only as an average. This approach is defined as *continuum approach*. Appendix to this chapter describes this idea in brief.

[11]Every idea contains its own seed of destruction!

[12]Though it is called computational fluid dynamics, the subject also includes heat and mass transfer.

[13]A process is said to be in a steady state if none of the variables characterizing it change with time. Same is the case with an equilibrium state, but it is distinguished from steady state by the absence of 'driving forces' or that it has no potential for change.

[14]We use the following nomenclature throughout this book: We use the word *system* to mean the same as *closed system* in Thermodynamics. Thus, a set of objects of the world selected for observation is referred to as a system. The system, by definition then, always consists of the **same set of objects.** Hence objects are not exchanged between the system and surroundings. The law of conservation of mass states that the mass of a closed system, or system according to our nomenclature, is constant.

[15]The equation that relates the dimensionless groups to each other is still not known. However, this procedure has two advantages. Firstly, we get an idea of how to plan experiments as we can often assign 'meaning' to dimensionless groups. For example, we interpret the Reynolds number to be the ratio of inertial to viscous forces. Secondly, it combines the effect of several variables and hence each of the variables need not be investigated separately for its effect. Thus, if we want to ascertain the effect of velocity and viscosity on the pressure drop in a pipe, dimensional analysis tells us that it is sufficient to investigate the effect of the group $dv\rho/\mu$.

[16]See Appendix for this longer footnote.

[17]Different groups arise depending on the variables chosen to represent the basic dimensions. The Buckingham-Pi theorem tells us how many *independent* groups will be obtained from the kind of analysis carried out.

[18]We mention a couple of interesting things here. Suppose we make a change of variable from t to $-t$. The aforementioned equations remain unaltered. Hence the equations cannot tell whether the system is moving forward or backward in time. In this sense the system of equations is reversible. Irreversibility has to be introduced into the system through a hypothesis and that is one of the puzzling aspects of this approach. Irreversibility is often introduced through the assumption of molecular chaos, *i.e.,* randomizing the outcomes of collisions between molecules. Semi-empirical methods, referred to as Lattice Boltzmann methods, based on kinetic theory approach, are being increasingly and widely used to solve problems of transport processes as they are able to incorporate characteristics of molecules.

[19]Points do not occupy any volume and so cannot contain matter. Other concepts, density in this particular instance, have to be introduced to "mimic" reality. That is why this is termed a 'model'.

[20]The name arises because they treat matter composed of discrete entities (molecules) as a continuous medium or *continuum.*

[21]We are adopting a discrete description for simplicity. It should be described as a continuous distribution. Interested readers can refer to any book on kinetic theory, like the book by Present[3] or by Sears and Salinger[4]

[22]Volume averaged quantities are also defined in the context of porous media. Though the process is the same, there one is concerned with deriving volume averaged equations.

[23]As in any other language, English has the delightful and sometimes annoying feature of having several meanings for the same word. It is this that lends color to the language, allows poets to invoke many images with the same words, and of course allows a jester to pun. Normal here is not being used in its normal sense. 'Normal' here means perpendicular. Is it the normal behavior of Indians to be normal to each other?

References

[1] K.G. Denbigh. *The principles of chemical equilibrium*. Cambridge University Press, 3 edition, 1971.

[2] R.A. Mashelkar. Seamless chemical engineering: An emerging paradigm. *Chem. Engg Sci.*, 50:1–22, 1994.

[3] R.D. Present. *Kinetic theory of gases*. McGraw Hill, 1958.

[4] F.W. Sears and G.L. Salinger. *Thermodynamics, kinetic theory and statistical thermodynamics*. Narosa, 3 edition, 1986.

Chapter 2

PHYSICAL LAWS & OPEN SYSTEMS

```
We show the use of
   Reynolds transport theorem
   to derive physical laws for open systems
```

Many of the questions we encountered in the previous chapters were concerned with the following basic difficulty: the laws of physics are stated for closed systems but we need to apply them to open systems, *i.e.,* equipment through which fluids flow in and out. Resolution of this difficulty is presented in a very elegant way in the article by Truesdell and Toupin [1]. Here we give an intuitive treatment to provide a physical picture.

The basic difficulty has two parts. The first is to find a way of identifying a *system* in a continuum where, unlike in solids, there does not exist an obvious boundary demarcating the system from the rest of the world. The second is to connect the performance of equipment of interest and the results of application physical laws to a system.

In this chapter, we will restrict ourselves to a fluid system composed of a single component. We will generalize this to multicomponent systems later.

2.1 FLUID DOMAINS MOVE AND DEFORM

The subject matter of transport processes is concerned mainly with fluids[1]. Unlike solids, fluids (*e.g.,* water and air) do not possess distinct and identifiable shapes. When a bullet travels in air, it is clear where its center of mass is because its boundaries are easily identified. This is true of the entire bullet as well as of any arbitrary part of the bullet that we chose. The boundary of the part we choose also remains identifiable even when the bullet is in motion. In contrast, a fluid or a part of it, does not present such a clear boundary. Look at a river. Except for floating solid bodies, it is difficult to clearly demarcate a part of the fluid and to follow it. Suppose, through some device, at some instant, we manage to mark all the matter in a chosen domain of the river and make it visible. Then the domain, contents and its surface become identifiable, and their course at subsequent times can be followed. If we managed to do this, we would find that, unlike in solids, the shape of the marked domain can change considerably as it flows[2]. This is easy to understand. Because *the surface of the domain has the same velocity as the fluid on the surface and the velocity on different parts of the surface can be different, the shape of the domain can constantly change.* The surface of the domain constitutes a moving boundary as shown in Figure 2.1.

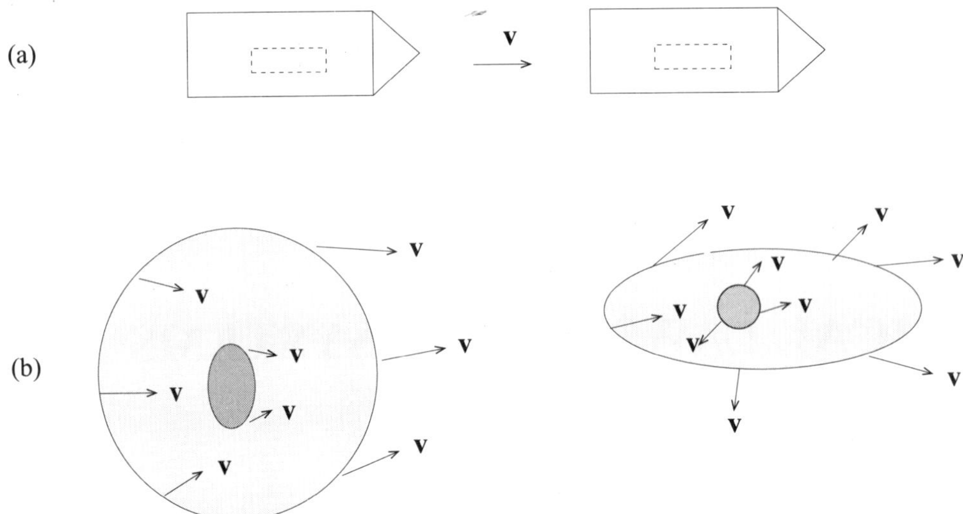

Figure 2.1. Closed systems in solids and fluids. (a) A travelling bullet. The rectangle with the dotted boundary is the system. Its shape and volume do not change while the bullet moves. (b) A marked and travelling fluid packet and a part inside it. Notice both change shape and the changes can be different. This is because the velocities at different points can be different.

2.2 A SYSTEM IN A CONTINUUM OF FLUID

Consider an imaginary domain marked in a fluid. Now, an object can cross a moving boundary only if it has a relative velocity with respect to the boundary. Hence, there is one important property of the domain so marked; as its surface has the same velocity as the fluid there, *no fluid can cross its boundary*. Thus, the domain which we have marked in imagination, constitutes a closed system[3]. Clearly, we can apply all the laws of physics to the contents of this imaginary domain, whose boundaries are moving with the velocity of the fluid.

There are other important differences between the closed system of a fluid and a part of a moving solid. All the fluid inside a system may not travel with the same velocity but the solid moves like a rigid body. The density of a fluid may vary from point to point in the system while such is not the case, to a very good approximation at least, for solids. Hence, while dealing with fluid systems we must account for variation of properties with time and from point to point in the systems.

2.3 REYNOLDS TRANSPORT THEOREM

Application of the laws of physics to a closed system often needs calculation of an extensive property of the entire system. For example, to apply the law of conservation of mass, we need to calculate the total mass contained in the system. For a solid, we easily calculate it because its volume and shape remain constant. It might not be so for a closed system of fluid since density in it can change from point to point, and with time. Further, its volume and shape can also change. Thus, we need to know how to compute the properties of a system whose boundary is moving. Almost always, these properties are obtained by integrating an intensive quantity, defined per unit volume, over the volume occupied by the system. Thus, integration of density gives the mass of the system, integration of the product of density and velocity gives the momentum of the system, *etc.* Let ϕ be any entity defined per unit volume. Let it be a function of both time and spatial location. Thus, $\phi = \phi(\mathbf{x}, t)$. Then the total 'quantity' of that entity in the system, Φ, is given by

$$\Phi(t) = \int\limits_{V_s(t)} \phi(\mathbf{x}, t) dV$$

where $V_s(t)$ is the volume occupied by the system at time t.

Many physical laws of interest in irreversible processes are about the rate of change of a property. For example, the law of conservation of mass states that mass can neither be created nor destroyed and hence the rate of change of mass in a closed system is zero. Similarly, Newton's second law states that the rate of change of momentum of a closed system is equal to the sum of forces acting on it. Thus, to apply these laws, we need to know how to evaluate the derivative of a quantity, such as Φ, with respect to time. In the instances of interest to us, Φ is an integral over a domain whose boundaries are moving with time. Finding the derivative of Φ with respect to time is equivalent to differentiating an integral whose limits are a function of time. Leibniz theorem on the differentiation of an integral when its limits are a function of the integration variable, is an example of such a calculation. Leibniz theorem states

$$\frac{d}{dt} \int\limits_{x=g(t)}^{x=f(t)} \mathcal{R}(x, t) dx = \int\limits_{x=g(t)}^{x=f(t)} \frac{\partial \mathcal{R}(x, t)}{\partial t} dx + \mathcal{R}(f(t), t) \frac{df}{dt} - \mathcal{R}(g(t), t) \frac{dg}{dt} \tag{2.1}$$

This is a theorem for an integral in one dimension, if we consider x to be a space dimension and t to be time. Let us examine the significance of the various terms on the right side. One is familiar with differentiation of an integral over immobile domains. There only the first term of the above equation would appear. The first term therefore represents total temporal change over the domain due to changes in the value of $\mathcal{R}(x, t)$ with time inside the domain. We can interpret df/dt and dg/dt as the "velocities" of the "upper" and "lower" boundaries of the system. The last two terms represent corrections to the first term as the system is occupying or vacating locations in physical space where *properties can be different.*

For our purposes we need a generalization of the Leibniz theorem in three dimensions. This is referred to as the **Reynolds Transport Theorem**. It is given by

$$\frac{d}{dt} \int\limits_{V_s(t)} \phi(\mathbf{x}, t) = \int\limits_{V_s(t)} \frac{\partial \phi(\mathbf{x}, t)}{\partial t} dV + \int\limits_{A_s(t)} \mathbf{n}.\mathbf{v} \phi(\mathbf{x}, t) dA \tag{2.2}$$

where $\mathbf{n}$ is the **outward normal** to the boundary of the system domain, and $\mathbf{v}$ is the velocity of fluid particles. The outward normal to a volume is defined as the normal that points away from the volume. See Figure 2.2.

One important aspect of the above theorem should be noted. The theorem relates the rate of change of any extensive property of the entire system to the point quantities both *in* the domain of the volume currently occupied by the system, and *on* the surface of that volume.

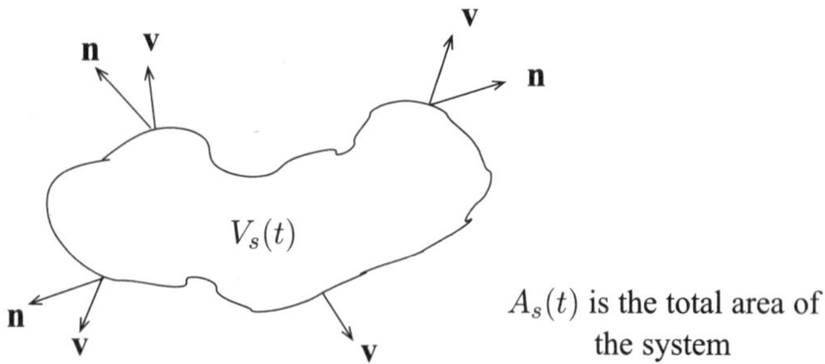

Figure 2.2. The Reynolds Transport Theorem.

2.4 APPLICATION OF PHYSICAL LAWS

We begin our discussion with a familiar example of how laws of nature are applied. The dynamics of rigid bodies are familiar to all of us. Suppose we want to calculate the path of a ball. It can be calculated if the velocity of the ball is known as by definition

$$\frac{d\mathbf{x}}{dt} = \mathbf{v}$$

where $\mathbf{x}$ and $\mathbf{v}$ are the position and the velocity of the ball respectively. Momentum of the ball is equal to the mass of the ball times its velocity, $\mathbf{v}$. We apply Newton's second law to calculate the velocity:

$$\frac{d}{dt}(\text{Momentum of the ball}) = \text{ Forces acting on it} \tag{2.3}$$

This can be used to calculate the path once the forces are identified. We would like to derive similar equations for fluids also. These equations can be used to calculate the velocity in a fluid as a function of forces acting, and also the path of a "fluid particle" as it flows into and out of an equipment.

The Reynolds Transport Theorem tells us how to calculate the rate of change with time of some quantity for a system composed of a fluid. Thus, when we consider the dynamics of fluids, we can use the transport theorem to calculate a term similar to the one on the left hand side of eq. 2.3. We should also show how to apply physical laws, Newton's second law in this example, to open systems. We want to do this in a way that is applicable to any arbitrarily chosen quantity, not just momentum. We would like to check if the intuitive generalizations of "balance" laws used in Unit Operations do arise from this exact approach.

2.5 CONTROL VOLUME AND SYSTEM

But today he only saw one of the river's secrets....
He saw that the water continually flowed and flowed
and yet it was always there;
it was always the same
and yet every moment it was new.

From *Siddhartha* by Hesse

Consider a volume in space of interest to us. We restrict ourselves to the case when this volume

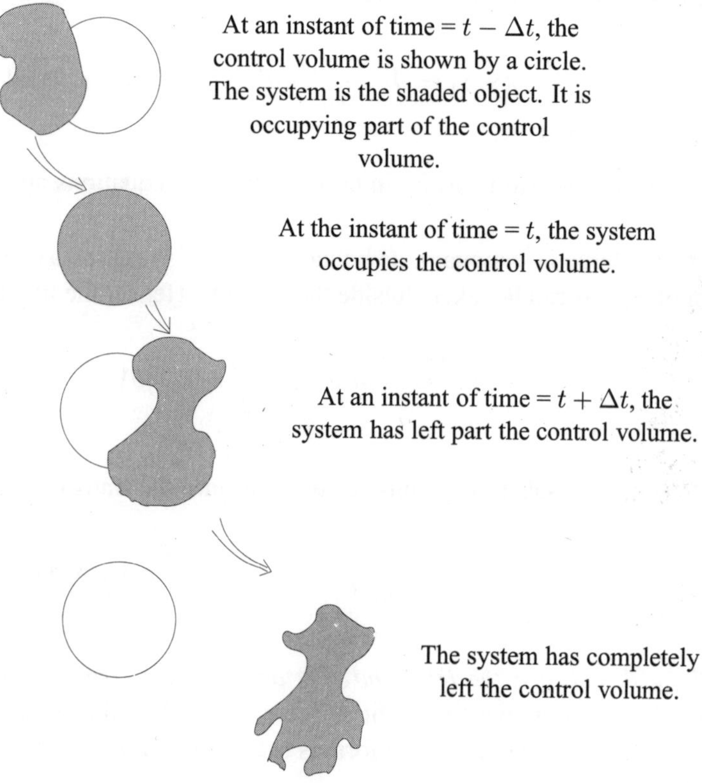

Figure 2.3. A system moving in and out of control volume of interest.

is stationary, *i.e.*, to *a stationary control volume*, referred to as CV for short. It could be part of an equipment through which a fluid is flowing. Thus, even though the control volume is stationary, fluid could be moving through it. A CV is therefore an open system. At a given instant of time, this control volume is filled with a packet of fluid or a (closed) system. This packet passes through the control volume[4], coming from somewhere and going somewhere else. At the instant of time being considered, however, the boundaries of the control volume and this fluid packet coincide (see Figure 2.3). Thus, if we choose that particular packet of fluid as the system, at the instant of time when the system occupies the control volume, we have

$$\begin{aligned}\frac{d}{dt}\int_{V_s(t)} \phi(\mathbf{x},t) &= \int_{V_s(t)} \frac{\partial \phi(\mathbf{x},t)}{\partial t} dV + \int_{A_s(t)} \mathbf{n.v}\phi(\mathbf{x},t)dA \\ &= \int_V \frac{\partial \phi(\mathbf{x},t)}{\partial t} dV + \int_A \mathbf{n.v}\phi(\mathbf{x},t)dA \end{aligned} \tag{2.4}$$

where V and A are the volume and the area of the *control volume* respectively.

Very often we use another form of above equation which involves only the volume. The second term on its right hand side can be converted into a volume integral by using Gauss's theorem to obtain

$$\frac{d}{dt}\int\limits_{V_s(t)} \phi(\mathbf{x},t) = \int\limits_{V} \frac{\partial \phi(\mathbf{x},t)}{\partial t} dV + \int\limits_{V} \nabla.(\mathbf{v}\phi(\mathbf{x},t))dV \tag{2.5}$$

It turns out that the above form is useful in deriving balance equations applicable at every point in space.

As the control volume is stationary, its boundaries are also stationary, the differential with time in the first term of eq. 2.4 can be taken outside the integral. Hence, the first term can be rewritten as

$$\int\limits_{V} \frac{\partial \phi(\mathbf{x},t)}{\partial t} dV = \frac{d}{dt}\int\limits_{V} \phi(\mathbf{x},t)dV$$

The equation obtained by substituting this relationship into the transport theorem gives a different form:

$$\frac{d}{dt}\int\limits_{V_s(t)} \phi(\mathbf{x},t) = \frac{d}{dt}\int\limits_{V} \phi(\mathbf{x},t)dV + \int\limits_{A} \mathbf{n.v}\phi(\mathbf{x},t)dA \tag{2.6}$$

Carefully distinguish between the left hand side and the first term on the right hand side. The first is the time derivative as we follow the system while the other is the time derivative on the control volume. It turns out that the above form is useful for making balances over the entire control volumes or *integral balances.*

Equations 2.5 and 2.6 are different forms of what is referred to as the *transport theorem for stationary control volumes*. Transport theorem for stationary control volumes allows us to relate the rate of change of total quantity Φ of the system *at any instant* to the distribution of ϕ in the control volume and its boundaries *at that instant.*

2.6 PHYSICAL LAWS APPLIED TO A CONTROL VOLUME

Now we are ready to show how to apply the laws of nature to control volumes. We take the law of conservation of mass as an example. The total mass of a system is given by

$$\text{Total mass of a system} = \int\limits_{V_s(t)} \rho(\mathbf{x},t)dV$$

The rate of change of mass of the system is given by

$$\frac{d}{dt}\int\limits_{V_s(t)} \rho(\mathbf{x},t)dV$$

According to the law of conservation of mass, the rate of change of mass of a system is zero. Hence, we have

$$\text{Rate of change of mass of a system} = \frac{d}{dt}\int\limits_{V_s(t)} \rho(\mathbf{x},t)dV$$
$$= 0$$

or

$$\frac{d}{dt}\int\limits_{V_s(t)} \rho(\mathbf{x},t) = 0$$

The above equation follows from a physical law. We now use the transport theorem to derive this law for a control volume. By applying eq. 2.6 to replace the left hand side, we have

$$\frac{d}{dt}\int\limits_{V} \rho(\mathbf{x},t)dV + \int\limits_{A} \mathbf{n.v}\rho(\mathbf{x},t)dA = 0$$

Consider the application of this to the flow of a fluid in a tube of circular cross-section. See Figure 2.4. The first term is obviously the rate of change of mass in the control volume, *i.e.*, the rate

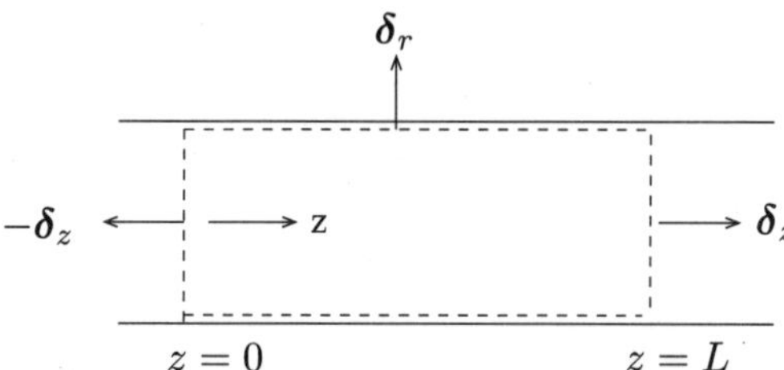

Figure 2.4. Mass balance on a control volume for flow in a pipe. Control volume is shown by dotted lines. Outward unit normal vectors are shown. The flow is from left to right.

of accumulation of mass. As the pipe wall is non-porous, the surface integral vanishes on the cylindrical surface. Only the surface integrals on the circular faces at $z = 0$ and $z = L$ are not zero. These surface integrals give the volumetric flow rates. The word "inlet" implies that fluid enters the CV. Hence, there the velocity and the outward normal to the control surface are in opposite directions. On the other hand, the outward normal and velocity will be parallel to each other at the outlet. Thus, the sum of the two area integrals is equal to the flow rate through the outlet or output flow rate minus the flow rate into the input or input flow rate. Hence, the above equation reduces to the familiar rule we have always applied:

Rate of accumulation of total mass in the CV	=	**Rate of input of total mass into the CV by convection**	−	**Rate of output of total mass into the CV by convection**	+	**Rate of generation of total mass in the CV**

This is exactly the form that is used for mass balance in Unit Operations.

The procedure we followed is absolutely general and will be followed in subsequent chapters to derive balance laws for control volumes. The first step is to apply a physical law to a system. In general it will have integrals to evaluate rate of change of the relevant total property of the system with time. Those terms are converted to integrals over a control volume using the transport theorem for stationary control volumes. We now turn to heat transfer and apply this procedure to apply first law of thermodynamics to a control volume.

Notes

[1]Transport of heat and mass in solids is also of interest.

[2]In making this statement, small changes that occur in the shape of a solid due to elasticity are being ignored as they usually are negligible.

[3]For simplicity we will sometimes refer to such a marked domain as a *system*.

[4]Imagine trains passing through a station without halting, so that no one is getting off or into the train. The trains are closed systems. The station is a control volume.

Reference

[1] C.A. Truesdell and R. Toupin. *Handbuch der Physik*, chapter III/1. Springer-Verlag, Berlin, 1960.

Chapter 3

FUNDAMENTALS OF HEAT TRANSFER

```
We apply first law of thermodynamics to control volumes.
Under some assumptions, above gives the usual 'heat' balance.
Development of temperature profiles is described to gain
   physical feel.
Boundary conditions used in  heat transfer are explained.
```

SINGLE PHASE & SINGLE COMPONENT SYSTEMS

In this chapter we will derive equations of energy balance and enthalpy balances applicable to control volumes. *All the equations are applicable to single phase systems*[1], and we should keep that in mind. We shall restrict our self to single component systems in this chapter but we will generalize these results to multicomponent systems in chapter 7. Though the equations derived are for a single phase, problems involving multiple phases can be solved by applying the equations separately to each phase. In such instances, we need conditions that prevail at the boundary between the phases. These are referred to as **boundary conditions.** We will discuss these towards the end of this chapter.

3.1 THERMODYNAMICS & HEAT BALANCE

Thermodynamics is the most fundamental science dealing with energy. First law of thermodynamics is an important law dealing with energy conversions. It plays a similar role that Newton's second law of motion does in determining the motion of fluids and solids. *Heat* is one but very common form of energy *in motion or transit* and application of heat into or removal of heat from an equipment is an important aspect of chemical processes. Thus, it is necessary to know the effects of such operations. Temperature is the most common variable used to characterize the effects of addition or removal of heat. Thus, it is often desired that the temperature distribution in an equipment be known. In this chapter, balance laws are used to develop equations that allow calculation of temperature profiles. As mentioned earlier, heat is only one form of energy and in this chapter we wish to develop rules which permit us to focus on the effects of heat. However, the only law we have is the first law concerning the *total* energy. The other common form of input or output of energy is mechanical energy. We need to find a way to separate the effects of input of heat and mechanical energy. *Work* is mechanical energy in motion and is a result of forces acting on the system. The equation describing the dynamical effects of work on a system is referred to as the equation of mechanical energy. It can be derived from equation of motion, and such a derivation is given in books on fluid mechanics, for example in the text by Bird *et al.* [1]. It will be derived in the appendix of chapter 5. In this chapter, for convenience, we take the result to achieve this.

3.1.1 First law of thermodynamics

First law of thermodynamics can be thought of as a law of *conservation of energy*. It states that, in a process, the change in the internal energy of a closed system is equal to the heat supplied to it plus the *work done on it by the surroundings* during the process:

$$\Delta U = Q + W$$

Confusion lingers when new concepts are encountered, and that is natural. Its more common source is notation, and it is terrible! It is as if *When I use a word, it means just what I choose it to mean neither more nor less*[2]. We are following the notation that work done on the system is considered to be positive, and hence the plus sign in front of the work term in the above equation. We are following that because we refer you throughout this book on matters thermodynamic to the excellent book by Denbigh [2]. If you considered work done by the system to be positive, you would have a negative sign, and this is also used in many books. There will be more such confusions to follow, and we will warn you at the appropriate places. Be careful therefore in using equations either from this text or others!

The above formulation is applied to changes between two *equilibrium* states of the system, and internal energy is a property of a material at equilibrium. We are interested in non-equilibrium systems where other forms of energy[3] are encountered. In many chemical engineering operations, flow is present and thus kinetic energy[4] of matter in motion is of great interest. The first law is then restated by joining kinetic energy with the internal energy. Thus, it is proposed that the change in internal[5] energy and kinetic energy is equal to the heat supplied to it plus the work done on it by the surroundings:

$$\Delta(U + \text{ Kinetic energy}) = Q + W$$

If the processes causing the changes occur over a small time interval Δt, the above equation can be divided by the time interval and, in the limit of the $\Delta t \to 0$, obtain an equation in terms of derivatives of the left and right hand sides with respect to time. Thus, the first law of thermodynamics can be reformulated as follows:

The rate of change in the internal energy plus the kinetic energy of a closed system is equal to the rate at which heat is supplied to it plus the rate at which work is done by the surroundings on it.

3.1.2 First law and closed systems

Rate of change of energy

Let $\hat{U}$ be the internal energy per unit mass of the system. The total internal plus kinetic energy of a closed system is given by

$$\int\limits_{V_s(t)} \rho(\hat{U} + \frac{1}{2}v^2)dV$$

The rate of change of this is given by

$$\frac{d}{dt}\int_{V_s(t)} \rho(\hat{U} + \frac{1}{2}v^2)dV$$

Rate of work done

Both body and surface forces act on the system. The work done by these has to be calculated. Consider the work done by body forces. A little volume dV inside the system has a mass of ρdV. The body force on it is $\rho\mathbf{g}dV$. When it moves with a velocity $\mathbf{v}$, work is done *by* the body forces at a rate given by $\rho\mathbf{g}.\mathbf{v}dV$. Thus, the rate of work done by the body forces *on* the entire system can be written as

$$\text{Rate at which work is done by body forces} = \int_{V_s(t)} \rho\mathbf{g}.\mathbf{v}dV$$

The surface forces can be calculated from the stress tensor. *Here is another matter concerning notation*[6] . The force exerted by the surroundings on a little area dA of the system is $\mathbf{n}.(-P\boldsymbol{I} + \boldsymbol{\tau})dA$. If the velocity on the surface is $\mathbf{v}$, then the rate at which work is done *by* the surface forces on the little area is given by $\mathbf{n}.(-P\boldsymbol{I} + \boldsymbol{\tau}).\mathbf{v}dA$. Thus, the rate at which work is done by the surface forces *on* the entire system is given by

$$\text{Rate at which work is done by surface forces} = \int_{A_s(t)} \mathbf{n}.(-P\boldsymbol{I} + \boldsymbol{\tau}).\mathbf{v}dA$$

Rate of heat supplied

Heat can be supplied to the system in two ways. It can be supplied inside the system throughout its volume. For example, it can be due to absorption of radiant energy. Another way heat could be supplied is by passage of electricity, *i.e.*, ohmic conversion of electrical energy into heat. Yet another way heat could be 'supplied', generated is a better description, is by conducting chemical reactions[7]. All these processes supplying heat *occur throughout the volume*, and are similar to body forces in momentum transfer. They are referred to as **volumetric sources**. Let us denote the rate of heat supplied per unit volume by the symbol $\dot{Q}_v$. The rate at which heat is supplied to the system is then given by

$$\int_{V_s(t)} \dot{Q}_v \, dV$$

The second way in which heat can be supplied to the system is through its surface. We have mentioned in chapter 1 that heat can be transported by molecular motion or by conduction and by convection. We are applying the first law to a *closed system*. Mass does not cross the boundaries of a closed system. Hence, heat cannot enter the closed system by convection. Heat can only be redistributed inside the closed system by convection. Heat can be supplied to a closed system through conduction as molecular mechanisms do not require macroscopic motion. We expect the rate of heat transfer across any surface by conduction to be proportional to the surface area. Thus we, also expect it to depend upon the direction of the area chosen[8]. Hence, the rate of heat supplied per unit area by conduction should be a vector. Let us denote the *conduction heat flux* by $\mathbf{q}$. Then the rate at which heat is supplied to the system through its surfaces is given by

$$-\int_{A_s(t)} \mathbf{n.q}dA$$

You will note that this is entirely similar to the calculation of surface forces encountered in momentum balance. There, a stress *tensor* was needed to calculate the *force*. The tensorial order of force is one less than that of the stress tensor. The rate of supply of heat is a *scalar*. Thus, to calculate this, we have to use the heat flux vector, a quantity which is one greater in tensorial order than the scalar.

Putting all this information together, the mathematical statement of the first law is therefore given by

$$\frac{d}{dt}\int_{V_s(t)} \rho(\hat{U}+\frac{1}{2}v^2)dV = \int_{V_s(t)} \dot{Q}_v\, dV - \int_{A_s(t)} \mathbf{n.q}dA + \int_{A_s(t)} \mathbf{n.}(-P\boldsymbol{I}+\boldsymbol{\tau})\mathbf{.v}dA + \int_{V_s(t)} \rho\mathbf{g.v}dV \tag{3.1}$$

Let us quickly recap what each of these terms mean. The left hand side is the rate of change of total internal energy plus kinetic energy of the system. The right hand side lists all the reasons for its increase. It could be due to any heat liberated in the system which is the first term. The second term represents the total heat supplied to it through its surfaces. The fourth term represents work done on its surfaces by the surroundings. The last term represents the work done on it by body forces.

3.1.3 Equation of mechanical energy balance

Equation 3.1 is a statement of conservation of three forms of energy: internal, heat and kinetic. As mentioned in the beginning of this chapter, we are interested in the effects of addition or removal of thermal energy or heat only. Rate at which work is done is related to application of force and the velocity created in response. The effect of the work done could be to increase the kinetic energy or increase the gravitational potential energy and so on. An 'account' of the effects of work done is given by the *mechanical energy balance.* This can be derived from the equation of motion of fluids. It is derived in many standard texts such as the one by Bird *et al.* [1]. The equation of mechanical energy balance will be derived in the appendix to chapter 5. It is reproduced below:

$$\frac{\partial}{\partial t}\left(\frac{1}{2}\rho v^2\right) + \nabla\mathbf{.v}\left(\frac{1}{2}\rho v^2\right) = \rho\mathbf{g.v} - \nabla.P\mathbf{v} + p\nabla\mathbf{.v} + \nabla.\boldsymbol{\tau}\mathbf{.v} - \boldsymbol{\tau} : \nabla\mathbf{v} \tag{A5.32}$$

Let us reinforce the meaning of the last two terms of eq. A5.32. The fourth term on the right hand side is the rate at which work is done by surface or viscous forces. *Viscous forces arise from friction.* Hence, some of the work done by viscous forces has to result in heat generation. The last term represents the rate of heat generation due to friction. It is referred to as *viscous dissipation.*

Thus, the sum of the fourth and the fifth terms is the work done by viscous forces minus the rate at which it is lost into heat. The entire equation then represents the mechanical energy balance: *when work is done, a fraction of it is lost in heat, the rest goes into raising the kinetic and potential energy of the system and or storing energy in the form of a more compressed state.*

The equation of mechanical energy balance is valid at each and every point in the fluid and therefore is valid in the entire domain of the system. Thus, if we integrate this equation over the entire domain of the system it will still be valid. Carrying this out and using Gauss's divergence theorem we get

$$\int_{V_s(t)} \frac{\partial}{\partial t}\left(\frac{1}{2}\rho v^2\right) dV + \int_{A_s(t)} \mathbf{n}.\mathbf{v}\frac{1}{2}\rho v^2 dA =$$
$$\int_{V_s(t)} \rho\mathbf{g}.\mathbf{v}dV - \int_{A_s(t)} P\mathbf{n}.\mathbf{v}dA + \int_{A_s(t)} \mathbf{n}.\boldsymbol{\tau}.\mathbf{v}dA + \int_{V_s(t)} P\nabla.\mathbf{v}dV - \int_{V_s(t)} \boldsymbol{\tau}:\nabla\mathbf{v}dV \quad (3.2)$$

Let us use the first part of transport theorem given by eq. 2.4, but in the reverse, to convert the left hand side into a total derivative. Equation 3.2 can then be rewritten as

$$\frac{d}{dt}\int_{V_s(t)} \frac{1}{2}\rho v^2 dV = \int_{V_s(t)} \rho\mathbf{g}.\mathbf{v}dV - \int_{A_s(t)} P\mathbf{n}.\mathbf{v}dA + \int_{A_s(t)} \mathbf{n}.\boldsymbol{\tau}.\mathbf{v}dA + \int_{V_s(t)} P\nabla.\mathbf{v}dV - \int_{V_s(t)} \boldsymbol{\tau}:\nabla\mathbf{v}dV \quad (3.3)$$

3.1.4 Enthalpy balance equation for a closed system

We subtract eq. 3.3 from eq. 3.1 which was obtained by applying the first law to a closed system. The resulting equation is about the effects of heat and gives an equation that balances internal energy:

$$\frac{d}{dt}\int_{V_s(t)} \rho\hat{U}dV = \int_{V_s(t)} \dot{Q}_v\, dV - \int_{A_s(t)} \mathbf{n}.\mathbf{q}dA - \int_{V_s(t)} P\nabla.\mathbf{v}dV + \int_{V_s(t)} \boldsymbol{\tau}:\nabla\mathbf{v}dV \quad (3.4)$$

Equation 3.4 is enough for our purposes. However, for incompressible fluids, it is more convenient to put the equation in terms of enthalpy. Let $\hat{H}$ be the enthalpy per unit volume. Then,

$$\hat{H} = \hat{U} + \frac{P}{\rho}$$

Thus,

$$\frac{d}{dt}\int_{V_s(t)} \rho\hat{U}dV = \frac{d}{dt}\int_{V_s(t)} \rho\hat{H}dV - \frac{d}{dt}\int_{V_s(t)} PdV$$

The term containing integral of pressure is not in a convenient form. It is generally converted into integrals over a volume or surface. By applying transport theorem given by eq. 2.4, the pressure term can be written as

$$\frac{d}{dt}\int\limits_{V_s(t)} PdV = \int\limits_{V_s(t)} \frac{\partial P}{\partial t} + \int\limits_{A_s(t)} \mathbf{n.v}PdA = \int\limits_{V_s(t)} \left(\frac{\partial P}{\partial t} + \nabla.P\mathbf{v}\right) dV$$

where we have used Gauss's divergence theorem. Dp/Dt is the substantial derivative of P and is defined as

$$\frac{DP}{Dt} = \frac{\partial P}{\partial t} + \mathbf{v}.\nabla P$$

Substituting this definition into the above, we can rewrite it as

$$\frac{d}{dt}\int\limits_{V_s(t)} PdV = \int\limits_{V_s(t)} \left(\frac{DP}{Dt} + P\nabla.\mathbf{v}\right) dV$$

Using all these results, we can write eq. 3.4 in terms of enthalpy to obtain the following enthalpy balance equation:

$$\frac{d}{dt}\int\limits_{V_s} \rho\hat{H}dV = \int\limits_{V_s} \dot{Q}_v\, dV - \int\limits_{A_s} \mathbf{n.q}dA + \int\limits_{V_s} \frac{DP}{Dt}dV + \int\limits_{V_s} \boldsymbol{\tau}:\nabla\mathbf{v}dV \tag{3.5}$$

3.1.5 Enthalpy balance over a control volume

The balance equations derived for system were converted to those useful for stationary control volumes. This was done by applying them to a system which occupies the control volume of interest at the instant of interest and using the transport theorem for stationary control volumes. Thus, applying eq. 2.6, we note that the left hand side of eq. 3.5 is equal to

$$\frac{d}{dt}\int\limits_{V} \rho\hat{H}dV + \int\limits_{A} (\rho\mathbf{n.v}\hat{H})dA$$

Substituting these results into the thermal energy balance and noting that the integrals over the volume and surface of the system and control volume are the same at the time of interest, we obtain

$$\frac{d}{dt}\int\limits_{V} \rho\hat{H}dV = -\int\limits_{A} (\rho\mathbf{n.v}\hat{H})dA + \int\limits_{V} \dot{Q}_v\, dV - \int\limits_{A} \mathbf{n.q}dA + \int\limits_{V} \boldsymbol{\tau}:\nabla\mathbf{v}dV + \int\limits_{V} \frac{DP}{Dt}dV \tag{3.6}$$

This equation is easily interpreted. The rate of accumulation of enthalpy of a control volume is equal to the rate of net input of enthalpy into the control volume by convection plus the rate at which heat is being generated in the control volume plus the rate at which heat is being supplied through its surfaces plus the rate at which heat is being generated due to viscous dissipation in the control volume minus a correction due to compressibility effects. Usually, the compressibility effects are small when we deal with liquids, and can be neglected. If we do so, this statement can be written for the control volume as:

Rate of accumulation of enthalpy in the CV	=	Net rate of input of enthalpy into the CV by convection	+	Rate of input of heat through control surfaces by conduction	+	Rate of generation of heat in the CV due to chemical reactions, *etc.*	+	Rate of heat generation in the CV due to viscous dissipation

It is with this form that you might be familiar with from your study of books on Unit Operations. It is this form that we will also use in making balances over control volumes.

3.1.6 Heat flux through boundaries

The above balance equation contains **q**, the conductive heat flux through boundaries. This is similar to the surface forces encountered in momentum balance. Recall that an expression for the stress tensor was needed before the equation of motion could be solved. In chapter 1, we stated that random molecular motions is the mechanism by which heat is transported by conduction through the surfaces. Conduction flux is always present in any medium. We need a *constitutive relationship* for the conductive heat flux. The mechanisms that cause heat flux and the constitutive relationships will form the subject of our discussion in the section that follows.

3.1.7 Connection to temperature

In the beginning of the chapter, we mentioned that one of our objectives here is to ascertain the effects of heat transfer on the system and to relate it to variations in temperature in the system. The enthalpy balance equation meets the first objective. The next step is to relate this to temperature.

It was mentioned earlier in the chapter that, as long as the system is not far from equilibrium, it can be assumed that the thermodynamic state functions like enthalpy, internal energy, *etc.* and state variables like temperature, pressure, *etc,* can be assumed to exist and relations between them are the *same* as those obtained under conditions of equilibrium. Hence, for a single component system,

$$\hat{H} = \hat{H}(T, P)$$

Further, other thermodynamic relationships derived to relate changes in enthalpy to temperature are also valid. Hence,

$$\begin{aligned} d\hat{H} &= \left(\frac{\partial \hat{H}}{\partial T}\right)_P dT + \left(\frac{\partial \hat{H}}{\partial p}\right)_T dP \\ &= \hat{C}_p dT + \left(\frac{\partial \hat{H}}{\partial P}\right)_T dP \end{aligned}$$

Thus, it can be seen how the thermal energy balance can be related to temperature by using such relationships. Further simplifications are made by relating the changes in enthalpy, due to changes in pressure, to changes in density. We show it here to emphasize once again the idea that thermodynamic relationships are used in 'non-equilibrium' situations. Thus,

$$d\hat{H} = Td\hat{S} + \frac{1}{\rho} dP$$

Hence

$$\begin{aligned}\left(\frac{\partial \hat{H}}{\partial P}\right)_T &= \frac{1}{\rho} + T\left(\frac{\partial \hat{S}}{\partial P}\right)_T \\ &= \frac{1}{\rho} - T\left(\frac{\partial}{\partial T}\frac{1}{\rho}\right)_P \\ &= \frac{1}{\rho}\left[1 + \left(\frac{\partial \ln \rho}{\partial \ln T}\right)_P\right]\end{aligned}$$

where we have used a Maxwell relationship to derive the second equation from the first.

Substituting this we get the following equation for $d\hat{H}$,

$$d\hat{H} = \hat{C}_p dT + \frac{1}{\rho}\left[1 + \left(\frac{\partial \ln \rho}{\partial \ln T}\right)_P\right] dP \qquad (3.7)$$

When this is substituted into the enthalpy balance equation, we get an equation that can be used to calculate changes in temperature as a result of addition of heat and or work done on the system by the surroundings. As the balance equation is in an integral form, we can only indicate the idea here and its use will be exemplified in later chapters.

3.2 MECHANISMS OF HEAT TRANSFER

In the previous section, enthalpy balance for control volumes was derived. Its connection to temperature was also established. Heat flux vector due to conduction appeared in the balance equation. Its relationship to temperature is needed before we can solve the enthalpy balance to determine the effects of addition of heat and input of work into a control volume on the temperature distribution. Development of constitutive relationship for conductive heat flux is the topic of discussion in this section.

3.2.1 Conductive Heat Flux Vector

Energy and temperature are concepts well grounded in Thermodynamics. Heat can be thought of as energy in motion. A system absorbs heat from surroundings which are at a temperature higher than itself. Consequently its internal energy increases. Here, heat is said to flow *through the boundaries* separating the system and surroundings. As heat flows through surfaces, it is natural to assume that the flow rate of heat will be proportional to the area of the boundary. Hence **heat flux**, *i.e.,* the rate of flow of heat per unit area, will be an important quantity to understand. Any moving quantity will have a direction and hence will be a vector. We designate conduction heat flux vector by $\mathbf{q}$. We now discuss mechanisms of heat transfer by conduction and a constitutive equation for it.

Direction of heat flow by conduction

Suppose two blocks, 1 and 2, of equal mass of the same material but at different temperatures are brought into contact with each other at constant pressure, and insulated from the surroundings. Let their initial temperatures be T_1 and T_2. After some time, they will attain thermal equilibrium and will be at the same temperature. As the sum of energies of the two blocks must remain constant, temperature of one block must decrease and the other must increase. We want to know the direction of heat transfer or, in other words, which of the two blocks will cool. The condition of equilibrium for isolated systems (*i.e.,* constant mass and energy) is

$$(\delta S)_{U,\rho} \leq 0$$

Thus, any process for which

$$(\delta S)_{U,\rho} > 0$$

is feasible and will occur leading to equilibration. We will use this criterion to evaluate the direction of heat transfer.

Suppose a small amount of heat flows from block 1 into block 2. Denote it by $\delta q_{1\to 2}$. Let the temperature of block 1 change by δT. By conservation of energy, the temperature of block 2 will change by $-\delta T$. The change in entropy of the system for this process is

$$\delta S = -\frac{\delta q_{1\to 2}}{T_1} + \frac{\delta q_{1\to 2}}{T_2} = \frac{\delta q_{1\to 2}}{T_1 T_2}(T_1 - T_2)$$

But for this process to occur, $\delta S > 0$. Thus, if $\delta q_{1\to 2} > 0$ then $T_1 > T_2$, and if $\delta q_{1\to 2} < 0$ then $T_2 > T_1$. Hence, the criterion that dictates feasibility of a process implies that heat will flow when the temperatures of the two bodies are not equal and that heat must flow from regions of higher temperature to those at a lower temperature.

3.2.2 Heat Conduction

As mentioned in chapter 1, equilibration and homogeneity at a molecular level are achieved by heat conduction. Matter is composed of molecules which are in random motion. As molecules execute random motion, they interact with each other through intermolecular forces and exchange energy. In gases this can occur through collisions between molecules. It is these processes occurring at a molecular level that lead to equilibration. It is through these processes that energy is conducted from location to location. Thus, *heat can be conducted only through matter*. Simple models based on kinetic theory give a good picture of how heat is transported through conduction in gases. Heat conduction in solids occurs by more complex mechanisms and interested readers may refer to these in the text by Bird *et al.* [1].

3.2.3 Fourier's law of heat conduction

As heat flux is zero when there exists no temperature difference, we expect it to be proportional to the temperature differences. We can therefore think of the temperature difference to be the driving force for heat transfer. As heat flux is a vector, we expect it to be related to a vector connected to temperature difference in space and to the direction of its difference. Intuitively, it can be seen that temperature gradient satisfies these requirements. Fourier formulated the relationship between the heat flux vector and the temperature gradient, and in his honor, it is known as Fourier's law of heat conduction:

$$\mathbf{q} = -k\nabla T$$

Here, k is the thermal conductivity and is a property of the material. Fourier's law is the *constitutive relationship* for conduction heat transfer. Thus, Fourier's law is analogous to the Newton–Stokes law of viscosity. **Fourier's law is the constitutive relationship for heat conduction.** The relationship depends upon the *constitution* of the material, *e.g.,* its chemical composition, physical state, *etc.* All known homogeneous and isotropic materials satisfy Fourier's law of heat conduction. This is in contrast to the situation in momentum transfer, where a large class of materials *e.g.*, polymers[9], do not satisfy the Newton–Stokes law of viscosity.

A comment about the negative sign is in order. Heat should flow from regions of higher temperature to those of lower temperature, and the negative sign ensures this. Consider the x component of the Fourier's law:

$$q_x = -k\frac{\partial T}{\partial x}$$

If the temperature decreases in the positive x direction, heat should flow in the positive x direction or q_x should be positive. If temperature decreases in the positive x direction, then $\partial T/\partial x$ is negative, then q_x is positive according to Fourier's law, and that is consistent.

Materials that are more complex and have intrinsic structure will not obey Fourier's law of heat conduction. For such materials, the conductivity in different directions can be different. For composite materials, Fourier's law of heat conduction may not be applicable. But, if it is applicable, it will be necessary to use an effective thermal conductivity. It can be calculated by solving enthalpy balance for such mixtures if one of the components is present to a small extent. These aspects are discussed by Bird *et al.* in chapter 9 of their text [1].

Direction of heat flux vector

Here we want to further consider the relationship between the heat flux vector and isotherms to gain some insights. If $\delta\mathbf{r}$ is an infinitesimal length vector, change in temperature ΔT along the direction pointed by the infinitesimal vector is given by

$$\Delta T = \delta\mathbf{r}.\nabla T$$

Take a reference point on an isothermal surface, and let $\mathbf{t}$ be the tangent vector to the surface at that point. Consider another point on the surface away from it by a small length δs, and along the tangential direction to the isothermal surface. The temperature difference between the two points is given by

$$\Delta T = (\delta s)\mathbf{t}.\nabla T$$

But as both the points are on the isothermal surface, *i.e.,* the surface on which temperature remains constant, $\Delta T = 0$. Hence,

$$\mathbf{t}.\nabla T = 0$$

Hence

$$\mathbf{q}.\mathbf{t} = 0$$

Hence, $\mathbf{q}$ is perpendicular or normal to the isothermal surfaces. In other words, heat flux takes the direction of steepest temperature change.

3.2.4 Radiation

Radiation is of molecular origin. When a downward change in any of the rotational, vibrational and electronic energy states of a molecule occurs, electromagnetic radiation is emitted. This is the source of radiation from materials. When a body emits radiation, it loses energy and its temperature can fall. When radiation falls on a material's surface, it is absorbed by molecules and their rotational, vibrational and electronic energy levels are altered. Due to collisions or other means of molecular interactions, the absorbed energy gets partitioned into translational energy. Thus, the temperature of the material can rise. Unlike the conduction mechanism, radiation does not need any medium for it to propagate and carry energy. Molecular states are continually undergoing transitions, and hence a body always emits radiation. Thus, if its temperature has to remain constant, it must receive heat from other sources.

Bodies radiate energy flux depending on their temperature. The maximum energy that can be emitted by a body can be derived from laws of thermodynamics, statistical mechanics and quantum mechanics. A **black body** (a hypothetical body) is defined as that which radiates energy at the maximum rate at a given temperature. The energy flux emitted by a black body is given by Stefan–Boltzmann law

$$q_r = \sigma T^4$$

Here, σ is the Stefan–Boltzmann constant and is equal to 5.67×10^{-8} W/(m^2 K^4), and T is *absolute temperature* in K. Bodies however emit radiation at a lesser rate, though the dependence on temperature remains the same. Due to the strong dependence on temperature, radiation becomes a dominant mechanism of heat transfer at high temperatures and or when other mechanisms of heat transfer are weak. Radiation falling on the surface of a body can be partly reflected, and the rest can pass through the body, and while it does so, can be absorbed. We do not consider this topic any more and for details, one can refer to chapter 15 of the text by Bird *et al.* [1] or other standard texts, *e.g.* by Siegel and Howell [4].

3.2.5 Convection

Convection is another way in which heat can be transported from place to place though it does not lead to homogeneity at the molecular level. Fluid can move from one place to another and of course it carries energy with it too. It is this *mode* of heat transport that is represented by the term

$$\int_S \mathbf{n.v}\rho\hat{H}dA$$

in the thermal energy balance which was derived in the previous chapter. This is the *convective heat flux*. It was also used in making a heat balance for a double pipe heat exchanger in section 1.6.

As fluid moves from one place to another, it can encounter environment at different temperatures. Then it will exchange energy with the environment and energy transfer occurs. The intimate exchange leading to spatial homogenization of temperature over length scales of molecular dimensions still has to occur by conduction. Thus, if we had 'fluid particles' of zero thermal conductivity, they would not exchange energy even when they pass through zones at different temperatures due to convection. In this sense there is some difference in the way energy can be transported by convection as opposed to by conduction. As thermal conductivity is not identically zero for any fluid, energy transfer occurs by convection simultaneously with conduction.

Convection depends upon motion. So, energy transfer by convection depends upon flow conditions also. This feature *links calculation of the rate of energy transfer with the equations of motion.* It is this aspect, especially if the flow is turbulent, that makes calculation of temperature profiles difficult. Correlations are needed for such conditions though computational fluid dynamics (CFD) has been a very useful way of making these calculations.

A fluid can move due to the action of an external agency: a pump or a blower or a fan, *etc.* Heat transfer accompanied by such motion created (or forced) by an external agency is defined as **forced** convection. Motion can also be created due to a combination of gravity and density differences. The condition where a heavier fluid is situated on 'top'[10] of a lighter fluid is unstable and fluids will move in an attempt to attain a more stable configuration. Such an instability can occur when a fluid is heated. Depending on where heating is carried out, it is possible that hotter, and hence necessarily less dense fluid, is below the colder or more dense fluid. Then motion is created 'naturally' when the system attempts to reach a more stable state. Heat transfer accompanied by such motion is defined as **natural** convection.

3.2.6 Classification of heat transfer problems

Heat transfer problems can be broadly classified into two categories. If there is *no flow or motion* in the control volume of interest, the only means of heat transfer is by conduction. Such problems are referred to as heat **conduction problems**. Certainly such is the case with heat transfer in solids. If heat transfer occurs in a fluid in such a manner that natural convection is avoided and there is no external agency causing motion, only conduction is left as a mechanism of heat transfer. Analysis of such problems is similar to heat transfer in solids.

As opposed to conduction heat transfer, flow is present in **convective heat transfer**. Convection problems can further be classified as *natural* or *forced* depending on the absence or presence of an external agency that creates flow. More detailed classification can carried out based on whether flow is laminar or turbulent, flow is fully developed or developing. These categories will be defined and considered in the following chapters.

3.2.7 Comparison of momentum & heat transfer problems

Conduction mechanism of heat transfer is similar to the mechanism by which momentum is transferred by viscous action in fluid motion. Just as viscous momentum flux depends upon velocity gradients, conductive heat flux depends upon the temperature gradient. Thus, the Fourier's law of heat conduction is similar to the Newton's law of viscosity. Conductive heat flux is similar to the viscous momentum flux. Velocity is similar to temperature. They are only similar and not identical, *e.g.* temperature is a scalar while velocity is a vector, heat flux is only a vector while momentum flux is a second order tensor. A major difference is with non-Newtonian materials. Fortunately, no non-Fourier materials have been found. Thus, there is no similarity between momentum transfer and heat transfer in this respect. This does not mean that momentum is one up on heat transfer. Heat can be transferred by radiation, and there is no analogue of this kind of mechanism in momentum transfer.

Thus, we can expect similarities between the problems of heat transfer and momentum transfer in Newtonian fluids. Thinking about analogous problems between the two deepens the understanding of both.

3.3 PHYSICS OF HEAT TRANSFER

In this section we consider a few simple situations involving heat transfer and focus on describing the development of temperature profiles to get a physical feel. A temperature gradient must exist before heat transfer can occur. The temperature gradients usually come into being when two phases at different temperatures are brought into contact. Consider a simple example. Suppose a pan of water is to be heated. This can be done by placing an electrical immersion heater into it. As current is passed in the heater, the surface of the heater becomes hot. The water however is at room temperature. A temperature gradient is then setup and heat flows from the hot surface of heater to the water. A description of development of the temperature profile in water is possible when the thermal energy balance equation is solved with suitable boundary conditions. All types of boundary conditions used in the context of heat transfer will be stated a little later but one of them, which is needed to discuss qualitatively the development of temperature profiles, is stated here: temperature is continuous across the interface between two phases.

3.3.1 Development of temperature profile: Constant temperature case

Let us reconsider the example of heating of water by an immersion heater. For convenience, let us approximate the immersion heater by a plane. We will also assume that the heater is being controlled in such a manner that its surface temperature remains constant. Let us also assume that water extends to infinity in the direction perpendicular to the plane which approximates the heater. Let us assume that soon after the current is switched on, the surface of the heater attains the desired constant temperature. The temperature of the fluid adjoining is however unchanged, except next to the heater surface. The fluid temperature at the fluid–heater interface, according to the boundary condition stated, must be the same. Hence, a large temperature gradient is established in the fluid phase and heat will be transferred from the heater surface to the fluid, the rate of which is dictated by Fourier's law of heat conduction. Part of the heat coming in will be absorbed and raise the temperature of the fluid layers adjoining the heater surface while the rest will be conducted to the next layers. Enthalpy balance will dictate the amounts that are absorbed and conducted. Due to heat being conducted to the next layers, the temperature increase will percolate deeper into the interior of the fluid phase. Thus, heat flux will be established into deeper and deeper regions of the fluid. It is easily seen that this process leads to a temperature profile decreasing away from the surface of the heater because heat can only flow down a temperature gradient. As layers continue to receive heat, their temperature will continue to increase with time. As the temperature approaches the heater's surface temperature, the temperature gradient will decrease with time. All this is shown in figure 3.1. Let us emphasize that in drawing this plot *we assumed that a controller maintains the temperature of the heater constant, and that fluid will remain stagnant.* We will discuss more of these aspects shortly. In this problem, the heater is a source of heat. The domain of heat transfer

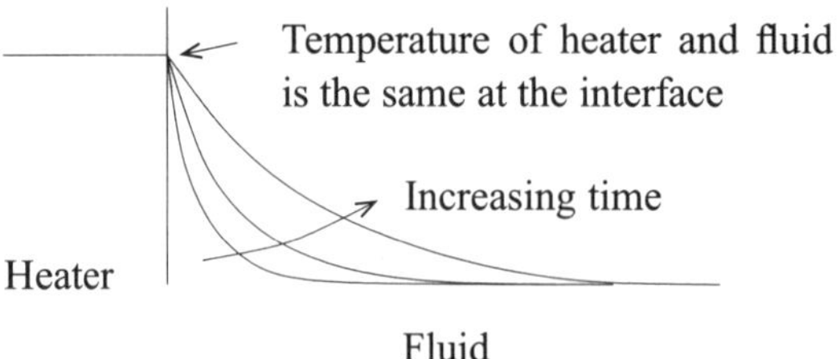

Figure 3.1. Development of temperature profile.

extends to infinity and hence a heat sink is not present. Thus, the temperature profiles will never reach a steady state. Suppose the fluid was placed between a hot and a cold plate. In this instance, the cold plate will act as a sink and steady state will be reached when the heat flowing from the hot plate is equal to that removed from the cold plate.

It is worthwhile to notice the similarities between these problems and the fluid mechanics problems. The boundary condition of constant temperature is similar to the no–slip boundary condition, in particular, the constant velocity boundary condition imposed by a moving plate. The problem of a heater in an infinitely large fluid is then similar to the problem of an infinitely wide plate suddenly set in motion in an otherwise quiescent fluid of infinite extent. The problem of fluid in between a hot and a cold plate is equivalent to the Couette flow between parallel plates.

From figure 3.1, it is seen that the temperature gradient decreases with time. Hence the heat flux decreases according to Fourier's law. Thus, as mentioned earlier, a controller is needed to regulate the heat flux to keep the temperature of the surface constant. It is possible to imagine that we have a surface which can deliver a specified or programmed heat flux too. Analysis of such problems will need more general boundary conditions, and we will discuss this now.

3.4 BOUNDARY CONDITIONS

3.4.1 Role of boundary conditions

We will jump slightly ahead and cursorily discuss the issue of specifying boundary conditions here. As mentioned in chapter 1, transport phenomena approach gives us information at every point in the control volume. As can be anticipated from a knowledge of fluid mechanics, such information will be contained in the balances on very small control volumes which will be converted into differential equations. We will discuss this in detail in chapter 5. Earlier, we mentioned that the *equations derived to obtain information at every point are valid only for a single phase.* We will discuss this point also in detail in chapter 5. Validity of the differential balance equations to a single phase implies that we will encounter boundaries in which the control volume is enclosed. For example, a control volume could be the fluid phase in a stirred vessel contained in or enclosed by solid walls. Another example is fluid flowing in a pipe, where the fluid phase is surrounded or enclosed by solid walls. In general, boundaries of domains of interest are encountered between phases. We *exert control on the domain of interest by imposing conditions on the boundaries* in order to get desired performance. Thus, we exert pressure gradient across the boundaries of a fluid to make it flow at a desired rate or heat the walls of a stirred vessel to raise the temperature of the fluid in it and so on. Thus, *boundary conditions are imposed by us*[11] and the system responds to them. *The balance equations along with the rate laws describe the performance of the control volume in response to the boundary conditions imposed on it.* It is this response that is of great interest to engineers.

3.4.2 Types of boundaries

We will mention one more concept here. The domain of interest may consist of several phases[12]. However, all the boundaries between phases might not be *accessible* to us. We also refer to them as *internal* boundaries since they may be located inside the overall control volume of interest and hence inaccessible. Clearly, only the accessible boundaries are open to control. Consider the well known example of a series of slabs through which heat is conducted due to a temperature difference. Only the external boundaries are accessible and the internal ones are not. So control can be exercised only on the accessible or external boundaries. However, *boundary conditions have to be specified at all boundaries.*

3.4.3 Velocity boundary conditions

We will now formally state the boundary conditions generally used, and illustrate their use with a few examples. Refer to figure 3.2. Let $\boldsymbol{\xi}$ be the unit normal to the interface pointing from phase II to

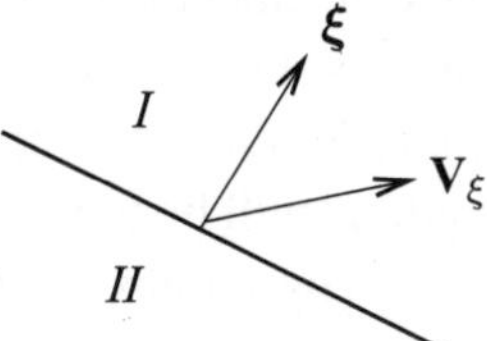

Figure 3.2. Figure giving notation to specify boundary conditions. It applies to both heat and mass transfer.

I. *Note that construction of the unit normal at an interface is arbitrary, and it is necessary to specify its direction*[13]. We let the phase boundary move with a velocity [14] $\mathbf{V}_\xi$. The important aspect here is that the *velocity of the interface can be different from the velocity in either phase* at the interface. Such a situation arises, for example, when water is heated and it vaporizes. We will examine this shortly.

Let us consider a mass balance made by an observer sitting on the interface[15]. Let us consider a single component system, and we will generalize this for multicomponent systems, thereby permitting interfacial reactions, in section 7.6. Consider a little area δA on the interface. The rate at which mass reaches the interface from phase I is given by

$$-\rho^I(\mathbf{v}^I - \mathbf{V}_\xi).\boldsymbol{\xi}\delta A$$

The velocity must have a component in the negative $\boldsymbol{\xi}$ direction in order to reach the interface from phase I. Hence the minus sign in the above expression. Mass that reaches from phase II is equal to

$$\rho^{II}(\mathbf{v}^{II} - \mathbf{V}_\xi).\boldsymbol{\xi}\delta A$$

As interface has no capacity, the rate of accumulation of mass must be zero. Hence,

$$-\left[\rho^I(\mathbf{v}^I - \mathbf{V}_\xi) - \rho^{II}(\mathbf{v}^{II} + \mathbf{V}_\xi)\right].\boldsymbol{\xi}\delta A = 0$$

This is valid at every part of the interface. Thus, in the limit of area tending to zero, the term in the brackets itself must be zero. Hence,

$$\rho^I(\mathbf{v}^I - \mathbf{V}_\xi).\boldsymbol{\xi} = \rho^{II}(\mathbf{v}^{II} - \mathbf{V}_\xi).\boldsymbol{\xi} = \dot{m}_b \tag{3.8}$$

This constitutes the velocity continuity boundary condition in a direction normal to the interface. This equation can be interpreted as follows: Either side of the above equation is equal to the net mass flux crossing the moving boundary, $\dot{m}_b$ from phase II to phase I. The above equation suggests that the mass flux must be continuous across the interface as mass is not generated at the interface. If it is known that mass flux is zero, then the velocity component normal to the interface in both the phases is equal to the velocity of the interface, and that is the condition of velocity continuity generally used in fluid mechanics. The above condition indicates that the normal components of the velocities in the two phases, relative to the phase boundary, are *not* continuous if there is a net flux of mass across the boundary. Suppose vaporization occurs at the interface. Then $\dot{m}_b$ is not zero. Then, normal components of the relative velocities will not be equal as the mass flux is continuous while the densities in the two phases are different. In the case of vaporization, as liquid density is thousand times more than that of vapor, we can expect the relative velocity in the vapor phase to be thousand times more than in the liquid phase. Note that *this condition is a consequence of the mass conservation and it is not some thing that can be subject to our control.*

The tangential velocity boundary conditions will be identical to those generally used in momentum transfer, *i.e.*, tangential velocities will be continuous. This is the no–slip condition. It appears that this is also a consequence of molecular nature of interactions although off and on questions are raised regarding its validity. Now consider this condition as applied between a solid wall and a fluid wall. No–slip condition dictates that the tangential velocity is continuous. However, it is up to us to move the solid wall at a velocity of choice, if that wall is accessible to us. It is in this sense that we referred to exertion of control on the domain of interest.

3.4.4 Boundary conditions on temperature

Now let us turn to the boundary conditions relevant to energy transfer. A basic hypothesis made in solving heat transfer problems is that the interface between two phases is always at thermodynamic equilibrium[16]. Thus, the temperature in the two phases at the interface is the same or it is continuous across the phase boundary. This is one of the boundary conditions for heat transfer problems. Consider once again the example of heating of water by an immersion heater. The boundary condition states that the surface of the heater and water adjacent to it are at the same temperature. *It is worthwhile to note the analogy between this boundary condition and the no–slip condition, i.e., boundary condition of continuity of velocity across fluid–fluid or fluid-solid interfaces.* Figure 3.2 shows the interface between phases I and II. The condition of thermal equilibrium at the interface or continuity of temperature specifies that

$$T^I = T^{II} \tag{3.9}$$

As this is a consequence of thermodynamic equilibrium prevailing at the interface and hence is not subject to our control. However, as discussed with the heater example, as the heater is accessible to us, we can control its temperature and hence impose control on the fluid domain of interest to us. In other words, the temperature of the accessible surface can be controlled but the condition of continuity of temperature is not subject to control.

3.4.5 Heat flux boundary conditions

Boundary conditions pertaining to stress appear in momentum balance. But stress is same as momentum flux due to viscous action. Conditions in heat transfer analogous to stress conditions are boundary conditions pertaining to heat flux. We follow a procedure similar to the one followed for mass balance. Consider a little area δA on the interface. The rate at which energy[17] reaches the interface from phase I is given by

$$-\left[\mathbf{q}^I + (\mathbf{v}^I - \mathbf{V}_\xi)\rho^I \hat{H}^I\right].\boldsymbol{\xi}\delta A$$

while that reaching from phase II is equal to

$$\left[\mathbf{q}^{II} + (\mathbf{v}^{II} - \mathbf{V}_\xi)\rho^{II} \hat{H}^{II}\right].\boldsymbol{\xi}\delta A$$

Here, we have accounted for conduction and convection. Additionally, there could be radiative heat flux that is absorbed, and there could be heat generated due to reactions occurring on the surface, *e.g.* catalytic reactions. Let us denote the former by $\dot{Q}_{s,rad}$. We will consider the reaction terms in detail later. For the moment let us denote the heat generated per unit area per unit time due to reactions by $\dot{Q}_{s,rea}$. As the interface has no capacity, it cannot accumulate energy. Hence the energy balance on a small area of interface must be given by

$$(\mathbf{q}^{II} - \mathbf{q}^I).\boldsymbol{\xi} + \dot{Q}_{s,rad} + \dot{Q}_{s,rea} = \dot{m}_b\,(\hat{H}^I - \hat{H}^{II}) \tag{3.10}$$

where we have used the boundary condition on the normal component of the velocity. The above boundary condition can be interpreted as follows: $\dot{m}_b$ is the net mass flux leaving the interface. It comes from phase II and enters phase I. Hence, the term on the right hand side is equal to the net convective energy flux leaving the interface due to net mass exchange. The first term on the left hand side is equal to the net conduction heat flux arriving at the phase boundary. The other two terms are the radiative heat flux absorbed plus the heat generated per unit area due to reactions. As there is no accumulation, it must equal the net convective energy flux leaving the interface. This boundary condition is a consequence of energy balance and hence not subject to any control.

Several simplified forms of the above condition are of interest. Suppose that there is no mass transfer across the boundary and that the radiative and reactive terms are zero. Then, the above boundary condition reduces to continuity of normal component of the conductive flux in the two phases:

$$(\mathbf{q}^{II} - \mathbf{q}^I).\boldsymbol{\xi} = 0$$

It is this form that we will encounter most often. Note that one of the heat fluxes could be controlled as discussed in the example of heater. Once again, as pointed out with respect to the condition of continuity of temperature, condition dictated by energy balance is not subject to control, but a flux supplied by an accessible surface can be controlled. You should note that this condition is similar to the continuity of stress vector in momentum transfer.

From the above discussion, it is clear that in specifying boundary conditions to solve heat transfer problems, we should identify the accessible boundaries and the ones which are not accessible. The problem statement should contain what is being controlled at the accessible boundaries and that should give the clue to formulating the boundary conditions there.

3.4.6 Heat transfer coefficient

Very often, heat flux into a *fluid phase* at the interface between a wall and a fluid phase is characterized by the well known heat transfer coefficient. *The heat transfer coefficient is used to calculate the heat flux due to convection.* It is therefore used only for the phase in which convection is present. As we shall demonstrate in later chapters, heat transfer coefficient can be calculated *only* for simple flows and geometries. Thus, the use of heat transfer coefficient in a boundary condition is especially useful when heat transfer coefficient cannot be computed and the effect of a fluid phase is accounted for in a lumped manner. Such is the case when flow becomes turbulent, and under these conditions, heat transfer coefficient cannot be computed but has to be correlated. One must rely on experimental results that often form the basis of such correlations. One can define a heat transfer coefficient in general at any interface, *e.g.* fluid–fluid interfaces also. We will illustrate the use of boundary condition that uses heat transfer coefficient with an example.

Solid–fluid interface:

Refer to Figure 3.2. Let phase II be an inert solid and phase I be a fluid phase. As the solid is inert, there will not be any mass exchange across the interface. Hence $\mathbf{v}^I = \mathbf{v}^{II} = \mathbf{V}_\xi$. Hence in the absence of radiation and reactions, the boundary condition at the interface is given by

$$\mathbf{q}^I.\boldsymbol{\xi} = \mathbf{q}^{II}.\boldsymbol{\xi}$$

It is customary to define the normal component of the heat flux *into* the fluid phase using a heat transfer coefficient:

$$\mathbf{q}^I.\boldsymbol{\xi} \equiv h(T - T_b)$$

where T is the temperature at the interface and T_b is the bulk temperature of the fluid[18]. Here $(T - T_b)$ is considered as the *driving force* for heat transfer in the *fluid phase*.

Heat transfer coefficient depends upon the hydrodynamic conditions. Thus, even if the solid was active in the sense that it may sublime or melt and create some mass transfer across the interface, if the sublimation or melting does not influence hydrodynamic conditions appreciably, the *same* heat transfer coefficient measured for an inert solid can be used. Thus, the boundary condition given by eq. 3.10 is now given by

$$\mathbf{q}^{II}.\boldsymbol{\xi} - h(T - T_b) + \dot{Q}_{s,rad} + \dot{Q}_{s,rea} = \dot{m}_b\,(\hat{H}^I - \hat{H}^{II})$$

Similar ideas can be used for fluid–fluid interfaces as well. In such a case, two heat transfer coefficients, one for each phase, are needed.

3.4.7 Development of temperature profile: Constant flux case

Now that we are familiar with the heat flux boundary condition, let us return to our problem of heating water to see how the development is altered if the boundary condition is changed. Let us re-examine the temperature profiles obtained earlier where the temperature of the surface of heater was assumed to remain constant. Under that assumption, the temperature of the water increases with time, and the temperature gradients decrease with time. Now we will examine what happens if the heater supplies a heat at a constant rate. There is no mass exchange between the heater phase and water. There are no reactions and radiative effects. Now the heat flux boundary condition will warrant that the normal component of heat flux from the heater must equal to the heat flux into the water. The boundary condition now becomes

$$\text{Heat flux from heater} = -k\frac{\partial T}{\partial x} + \rho \hat{C}_p v_x T$$

where x is the coordinate normal to the heater surface. As heater is not moving, v_x is zero. Hence the heat flux from heater is equal to the conductive flux into water, and it must remain constant. This implies that the temperature gradient in the fluid at the interface must remain constant. The temperature of water will still increase with time due to heating, and this will tend to decrease the temperature gradient. Hence, the temperature of the phase boundary must increase in such a way that the gradient remains constant with time. This is shown in figure 3.3. Clearly, if temperature of

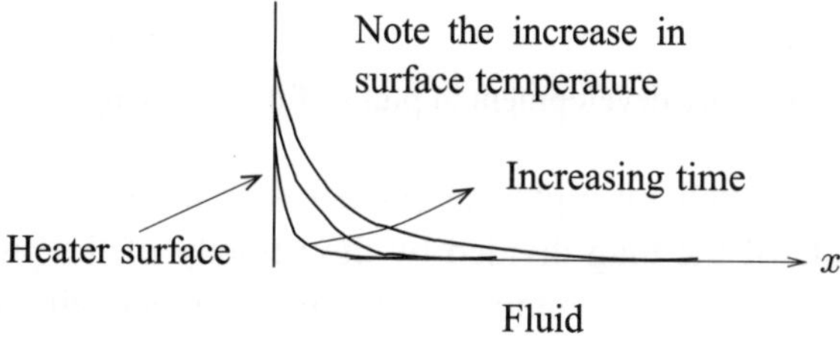

Figure 3.3. Temperature development with constant wall flux.

the surface increases beyond the melting point of the heating material, the heater will melt. This is how an electrical fuse works.

3.5 ONSET OF NATURAL CONVECTION

We have assumed in the previous discussion, and in the discussion on temperature development in constant wall temperature case that the fluid will remain stagnant. Whether motion will begin or not depends upon the stability of the static condition of fluid in the presence of temperature gradients. Suppose a fluid in a container is being heated from the bottom. As the temperature profiles develop, fluid at the bottom becomes hotter, and hence lighter than the fluid at the top. Such a configuration is inherently unstable. As a result, the fluid begins to move to attain a stable configuration, whereby the hotter fluid rises and the colder fluid descends. This is how *natural convection* starts. Description of the velocity profiles that develop in natural convection is one of the interesting problems in heat transfer and we will discuss this in more detail later.

On the other hand, if the fluid is heated on its top surface, natural convection is not expected and heat transfer will only be by conduction.

3.6 CONVECTIVE HEAT TRANSFER

Convection in general increases the heat transfer. The extent of increase in heat transfer depends on many factors, and that can be found only by solving the enthalpy balance equation together with appropriate boundary conditions. Here we want to qualitatively explain as to why heat transfer rate increases due to convection. Consider a simple case where plugs of fluid move past a hot surface. In this way it is similar to the problem we recently discussed. To make things easy to understand, let us also assume that the plugs do not exchange heat between each other by conduction. See Figure 3.4. Since they do not exchange heat with each other, the temperature profiles in each slab will be identical to those obtained for a plug in contact with a hot surface when the contact time is equal to the y coordinate of the plug divided by the velocity of the plug. Thus, they will look like those shown in Figure 3.4. If only conduction was taking place, all the plugs would have been in contact with the hot surface for the same duration, and hence all of them would have had the same temperature gradient. However, since the plugs are moving now, almost all plugs would be in contact with the hot surface for a shorter time, and hence have steeper temperature gradients in them. Thus, heat flux to the plugs would be more. Thus, convection leads to a larger heat transfer rate as compared to conduction.

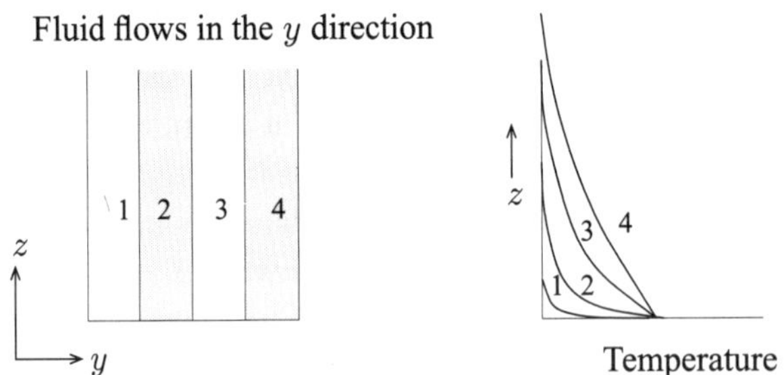

Figure 3.4. Temperature development in plugs of fluid moving past a hot surface.

Another way of thinking about this is as follows: Fluid next to a hot (or cold) wall is stagnant and it receives heat by conduction alone. Fluid away from the wall moves and hence its "contact time" with hot elements will be less than that if it were stagnant. As a result it will be colder (or hotter) than when it is stagnant. This difference increases with distance from the stagnant wall. As a result, at any given cross section, the temperature gradients become steeper, and hence, the heat transfer rate increases. The underlying feature is the movement of "fresh fluid" into what might have been stagnant otherwise. This movement accounts for enhanced heat transfer.

3.7 SOLUTION OF HEAT TRANSFER PROBLEMS

We have discussed the basic features of heat transfer. The next step for us would be to calculate the rate of heat transfer and temperature profiles in a given situation. The procedures are outlined here and examples of the solution are presented in the next chapter.

The procedure adopted in this book for teaching a student to set up heat transfer problems is as follows. We learn the basic ideas through shell balances. Here a thermal energy balance is made on a shell of small dimensions, and then the constitutive equation is substituted into it. The resulting balance is converted into a differential equation by obtaining the limit as the shell volume decreases to zero. The differential equation is solved along with the boundary conditions. As the problems are simple in nature, considerable physical insight can be obtained from these. After that we derive general differential equations that represent the thermal energy balance and which form the starting point to solve the problems of heat transfer. These will be similar to the Navier–Stokes equation. In problems involving convection, it is easily seen that we need velocity profiles. Hence, in general, the Navier–Stokes equations have to be solved simultaneously with the equation of thermal energy. Often we can decouple them under fairly general simplifying assumptions. The case where this is not possible is where the thermo-physical properties show appreciable dependence on temperature, and of course significantly, where natural convection occurs. Thus, the discussion of natural convection forms an important special category of problems in heat transfer. We cover a few problems that use this approach of starting from the general differential equations of balances. It is this experience that prepares one to use CFD. This then forms the menu for the next few chapters on heat transfer.

Problems for Chapter 3.

3.1 Derive the jump conditions for the following problem at the liquid–solid interface. It would help if you first sketch the possible temperature profiles. A liquid initially at $T_o > T_{m.p.}$ (melting temperature) is brought into contact with a cold wall which is maintained at $T_w < T_{m.p.}$

3.2 If thermal conductivity is a very complicated but non-negative function of temperature, is the profile shown in the figure possible to be reached in the following two cases? (a) Temperature depends only on x. (b) Temperature profile shown is at some time t.

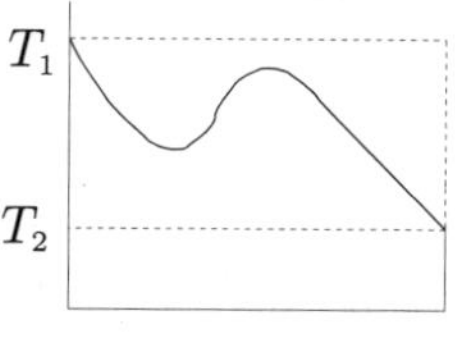

Figure for problem 3.2.

3.3 The diagram shows lines to which heat flux vector is tangential everywhere. The direction of heat flux is also shown. Plot the isotherms and indicate the direction in which the temperature decreases.

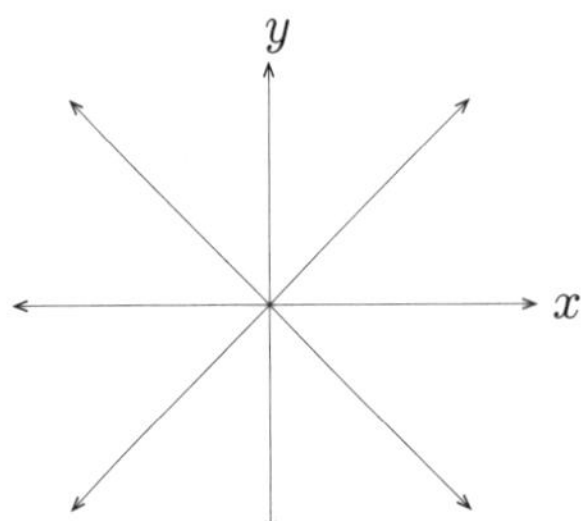

Figure for problem 3.3.

3.4 A rectangular block is shown with two of its parallel faces maintained at T_1 while the other two parallel faces are maintained at T_2. Sketch (qualitatively) the isotherms at steady state.

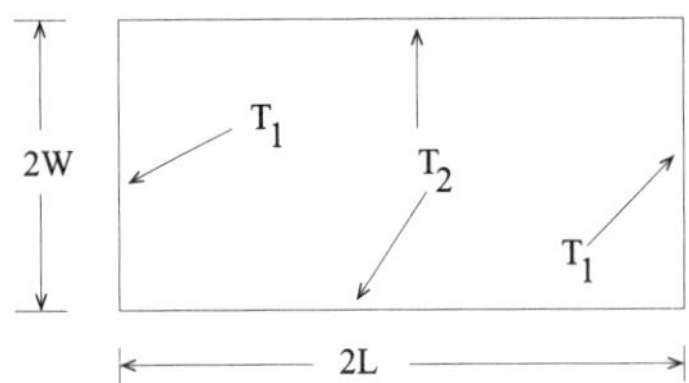

Figure for problem 3.4.

Notes

[1]In the following we will use variables like velocity, internal energy, stress tensor, *etc*. These might not be continuous across different phases. As we use integration and differentiation, we restrict ourselves by claiming applicability to only a single phase.

[2]Refer to the classic sentence written by Lewis Carroll in his book Through the Looking Glass: "When I use a word," Humpty Dumpty said, in a rather a scornful tone, "it means just what I choose it to mean neither more nor less." Notation is like that, and so we have to find out what the author means by his symbols!

[3]Conservation of energy is a difficult and subtle subject since energy can exist in many forms and one form of energy can be converted into another. Kinetic energy can be attributed to motion, potential energy to gravitation for example, electrical energy, elastic energy, *etc.* All these forms will have to be included in case they are relevant to the problem at hand. Historically, forms of energy have been invented assuming that energy is conserved. Such is the faith in this particular law of conservation. The subject is delightfully discussed by Feynman [3].

[4]We are referring to motion at the macroscopic level and not at the molecular level.

[5]Internal energy is a thermodynamic function and is not defined for a non-equilibrium process. It is assumed that if the system is not very far from equilibrium, the functions as defined in thermodynamics can be used. Thus, temperature can also be defined, and the relationship between it and the internal energy is the same as that found in equilibrium systems. What is meant by far from equilibrium is dealt with more precisely in books on irreversible thermodynamics. High speed flow is an example of the exception. It is sufficient to mention that almost all situations normally encountered in chemical engineering are *not very far* from equilibrium.

[6]We are using a convention of definition of pressure and stress tensor commonly used in texts on fluid mechanics. In our notation compressive pressure exerted on the system is positive. Similarly, stress tensor is defined such that its dot product with the *unit outward normal* gives the force per unit area, exerted *by the surroundings on the system.* However, other texts, in particular the one by Bird *et al.* [1], use a different convention. You must check this carefully before using formulae given in different books.

[7]We need not write this separately if we consider that chemical reactions generate several species and carry out the analysis for multicomponent systems, as we shall do in later chapters. For the moment we are restricting ourselves to single component systems. Due to this we have to add this in an *ad hoc* manner.

[8]Recall the area averaging discussed in the appendix to chapter 1.

[9]It must be said that polymers in flow are not isotropic.

[10]Gravity is being assumed to act 'downward'.

[11]Sometimes, the conditions at boundaries may not be in our control. We will discuss this later.

[12]In that case, balance equations will have to be solved in each phase separately.

[13]It is uniquely constructed only when we have a body since we specify it to be the outward normal.

[14]We are giving the boundary condition for a moving boundary here. The boundary conditions for momentum transfer are however, generally specified for stationary boundary as it requires more 'machinery' to set them up. Readers interested in this can refer to the book by Slattery [5].

[15]Interface is a mathematical surface, has no volume or capacity to hold anything, and therefore it has zero-cross sectional area. Hence, there can only be mass flux in a direction perpendicular to the interface.

[16]If a barrier preventing equilibration exists, this would not be correct. For example, a few molecules thick layer of oxide on the surface of metal could be one such barrier.

[17]One should apply first law to interface. In writing this we are neglecting kinetic energy and work terms. They are generally small.

[18]The averaging process to obtain the bulk temperature will be discussed in later chapters.

References

[1] R.B. Bird, W.E. Stewart, and E.N. Lightfoot. *Transport Phenomena.* John Wiley, 2 edition, 2002.

[2] K.G. Denbigh. *The principles of chemical equilibrium.* Cambridge University Press, 3 edition, 1971.

[3] R.P. Feynman. *The Character of Physical Law.* MIT Pres, 1967.

[4] R. Siegel and J.R. Howell. *Thermal Radiation Heat Transfer.* Taylor & Francis, 4 edition, 2002.

[5] J.C. Slattery. *Momentum, energy and mass transfer in continua.* McGraw Hill, 1971.

Chapter 4

SHELL BALANCES IN HEAT TRANSFER

```
We give examples of application of shell balances to solve
    heat transfer problems.
These illustrate identification of the problem to be solved
   from a situation encountered in practice. Application of
   boundary conditions at external and internal boundaries
   is another concept demonstrated.
An example of calculation of heat transfer coefficient in
  forced convection is considered.
Problems dealing with volumetric heat sources are illustrated.
```

This chapter demonstrates how to use shell balances in solving heat transfer problems. We start with a description of a complex problem normally encountered in practice and think of simplifications that reduce the problem to a level where it can be solved simply. We refer this to as problem identification[1]. The first two problems are familiar to all as they are part of the bread and butter of Unit Operations. We use these problems to illustrate the way boundary conditions are applied at internal and external boundaries. We then move on to a problem in convection. This example is used to illustrate the concept of *heat transfer coefficient*, and has to be studied with care because it has many features that are often encountered in convective heat transfer. The last problem is an example of volumetric heat source: heat dissipated due to viscous friction in bearings, or viscous dissipation.

Velocity profile is usually the first to be calculated in problems of fluid mechanics. In heat transfer, it is the *temperature profile* that has to be determined. To do this, a shell heat balance is made to *develop a differential equation* with temperature as the dependent variable. Then *boundary conditions are specified as dictated by the problem statement.* The differential equation is then solved with the boundary conditions to obtain the temperature profile. Problems can be solved in this fashion only in simple situations, *i.e.*, where several simplifications can be made and for simple geometries[2]. However, using shell balances before launching into the general balance equations is like learning to walk before we run. There is gain too. Considerable physical feel can be developed by solving such problems.

In fluid mechanics, frictional force exerted by a fluid on solids, fluid on another fluid phase, *etc.*, is calculated once the velocity profile is known. That information is "summarized" in the form of friction factors or drag coefficients, *etc.* These coefficients along with knowledge of some *average velocity* can then be used to calculate frictional forces. Similarly, in *convective* heat transfer problems, heat flux into a fluid phase from a solid *at their interface* is calculated from the temperature profiles obtained in the fluid phase. That information is summarized in the form of heat transfer coefficient. The heat transfer coefficient along with knowledge of a *difference between the interface temperature and some average temperature of the fluid* can be used to calculate the heat flux from the solid phase into the fluid phase. Thus, heat transfer coefficient is analogous to friction factor or drag coefficient. It may be noted that one can calculate heat transfer coefficients between fluid–fluid phases also. In such a case, there will be two heat transfer coefficients, one for each fluid phase.

4.1 HEAT CONDUCTION THROUGH SLABS IN SERIES

4.1.1 Problem identification

Consider a stack of slabs of different materials. The surface at one end of the stack is being maintained at a constant temperature, T_o while the surface at the other end of the stack is being maintained at a constant temperature T_e. Let us assume that the other surfaces of the stack are insulated. The geometry of the arrangement is shown in figure 4.1. This kind of situation prevails when equipments are insulated, *e.g.* furnaces, heat exchangers, *etc.* The objective in the present problem is to calculate the rate of heat loss through the stack of slabs *at steady state*. As we shall soon observe, this requires calculation of the temperature profile.

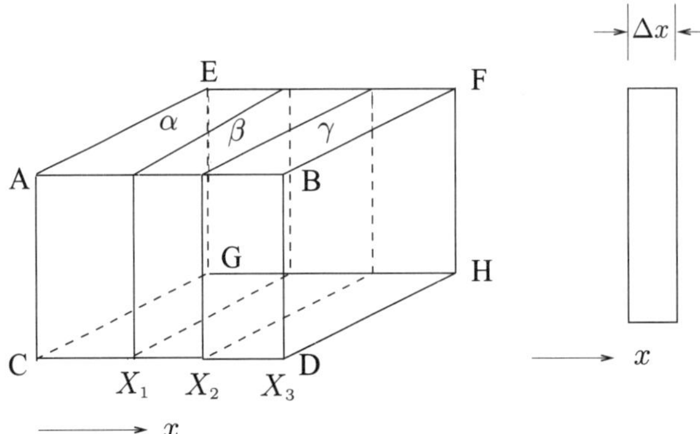

Figure 4.1. Slabs in series. The faces ABDC, EFHG, ABEF, and CDGH are insulated. A small control volume of thickness Δx is shown on the right side.

Simplifications and assumptions

Cartesian coordinate system is selected as it is best suited to describe the geometry of slabs. The slabs are solid, and hence convection is absent[3]. Thus, only conduction heat transfer is important. All faces except those perpendicular to the x axis are insulated. Further, the faces ACGE and BDHF are at different but constant temperatures, *i.e.,* in a homogeneous condition. Thus, we do not expect much variation in the y and z directions. Let us then simplify and assume that only heat flux in the x direction can be expected to be non-zero. All physical properties are assumed to be constant, in particular, they do not change due to variation in temperature. We have solid phases in contact. It is assumed that surfaces are in perfect contact, and hence surface resistance to heat transfer is absent.

4.1.2 Heat balance over a control volume

As only heat flux in the x direction is non-zero, by Fourier's law dT/dx is not zero. Hence, we need to determine temperature variation in the x direction. So, we select a control volume of thickness Δx and with area (of the x plane) same as the slabs. Let the area be a. The heat balance is written as (refer to section 3.1)

Rate of accumulation of enthalpy in the CV	=	Net rate of input of enthalpy into the CV by convection	+	Rate of input of heat through control surfaces by conduction	+	Rate of generation of heat in the CV due to chemical reactions, *etc.*	+	Rate of heat generation in the CV due to viscous dissipation

According to the statement of the problem, steady state prevails. Thus, the accumulation term can be set to zero. As there is no flow, the convective terms and the viscous dissipation term are zero. In the system, there are no known sources of heat, *e.g.* chemical reactions, ohmic heating, *etc.* Hence, heat generation due to these effects is also zero. The only control surfaces in the control volume through which heat flows are at x and $x + \Delta x$. Thus, the heat balance yields

$$(a\, q_x)\,|_x - (a\, q_x)\,|_{x+\Delta x} = 0$$

Now a systematic procedure is followed to obtain a differential equation. The above heat balance is converted into "per unit volume basis" by dividing it with $a\Delta x$ and the limit of the resulting equation is evaluated as the differential quantity, Δx tends to zero. The following differential equation is then obtained:

$$\frac{dq_x}{dx} = 0$$

This represents heat balance per unit volume *at every point* in the system. This equation has a simple interpretation: the heat flux remains constant. This is justified as heat flux has to remain constant in view of the conservation of energy, constancy of the area through which heat flows, and because accumulation and generation are absent. Notice the similarity between this equation and the equation of continuity for an incompressible fluid in one dimensional flow. The similarity is to be expected because both describe the behavior of a conserved quantity: mass or energy.

4.1.3 Combining rate law with heat balance

It is easily seen that the above equation cannot be solved to obtain the temperature profile unless heat flux can be related to temperature. As mentioned in chapter 1, the balance laws have to be combined with the rate laws. A similar situation is encountered in solving fluid mechanics problems, where progress could not be made unless stress tensor is related to velocity. The constitutive relationship, namely the Newton–Stokes law, is used there to achieve the link. Here, similar role is played by the Fourier's law of heat conduction. Fourier's law of heat conduction is the rate law or the constitutive equation that has to be combined with the energy balance. After substituting the Fourier's law, the balance equation then becomes,

$$\frac{d}{dx}\left(k\frac{dT}{dx}\right) = 0$$

where we dropped the negative sign as the term is equal to zero. As all physical properties were assumed to be independent of temperature, the thermal conductivity can be removed from the above equation to obtain the final form of the heat balance equation:

$$\frac{d^2T}{dx^2} = 0 \tag{4.1}$$

As the balance is perfectly general, this is valid in all the three slabs, but with three separate temperatures, *i.e.,* dependent variables, one for each phase or slab. Let us denote the temperatures in the three slabs by T_α,T_β and T_γ.

4.1.4 Boundary conditions

The three second order differential equations derived in the previous sub-section have to be solved and it requires a total of six boundary conditions. As discussed in section 3.3, the boundary conditions have to be specified at the phase boundaries, *i.e.,* the interfaces of the slabs. There are four interfaces, two at the ends of the stack and two in between the three materials. First consider the end at $x = 0$. It is given in the problem statement that the temperature is being maintained constant at T_o. This forms the boundary condition:

$$T_\alpha = T_o \qquad\qquad x = 0 \tag{4.2}$$

Consider next the interface between slab α and β. Let it be located at X_1. At this interface, neither the heat flux nor the temperature are specified. This is typical of situation at inaccessible or internal boundaries[4]. *At such boundaries, we apply all possible boundary conditions.* Thus, both types of boundary conditions, namely continuity of temperature and energy balance, will be used. This is reminiscent of boundary conditions between fluid–fluid interfaces in fluid mechanics where both velocity and stress continuity are used. Now refer to eq. 3.9. The boundary condition states that the temperature is continuous across the boundary. Thus,

$$T_\alpha = T_\beta \qquad\qquad x = X_1 \tag{4.3}$$

The other condition is an equation for energy balance given by eq. 3.10. All the interfaces under consideration are stationary and hence $\mathbf{V}_\xi = 0$ for all boundaries. There is no heat generation due to reactions and radiation is absent. Further, velocity is zero because solid phases are being considered. Thus, all the terms in eq. 3.10 are zero except the conduction terms. Thus the boundary condition implies that heat flux is continuous at this boundary:

$$q_{x,\alpha} = q_{x,\beta} \qquad \text{at} \quad x = X_1$$

After substituting the constitutive relationship into the above, it yields

$$k_\alpha \frac{dT_\alpha}{dx} = k_\beta \frac{dT_\beta}{dx} \qquad \text{at} \quad x = X_1 \tag{4.4}$$

Let the other boundary between β and γ phase be located at $x = X_2$. Application of similar ideas gives the following boundary conditions:

$$T_\beta = T_\gamma \qquad \text{at} \quad x = X_2 \tag{4.5}$$

$$k_\beta \frac{dT_\beta}{dx} = k_\gamma \frac{dT_\gamma}{dx} \qquad \text{at} \quad x = X_2 \tag{4.6}$$

Finally, consider the end face of the stack. Let it be located at $x = X_3$. According to the problem statement it is being maintained at a constant temperature of T_e. Hence

$$T_\gamma = T_e \qquad \text{at} \quad x = X_3 \tag{4.7}$$

These six equations constitute the required boundary conditions.

4.1.5 Scaling

In section 1.6, we mentioned that the transport phenomena approach helps in dimensional analysis. In this section, this is what we will demonstrate. We look for quantities with which we can form dimensionless entities of the various dependent and independent variables that appear in the differential equation and boundary conditions. The quantities used to do this are like *scales*, units that are used to measure. This entire procedure is referred to as *scaling analysis* or simply scaling. The scaling here is simple. We can use one of the temperatures as a scale. But the physical situation tells us that for heat transfer to occur, temperature differences are crucial rather than temperature itself. This is clearly indicated by Fourier's law. Thus, *we select the temperature difference, $T_o - T_e$, for making temperature non-dimensional.* Hence, a non-dimensional temperature difference can be defined in each phase. Thus[5],

$$\theta_\alpha = \frac{T_o - T_\alpha}{T_o - T_e}, \; \theta_\beta = \frac{T_o - T_\beta}{T_o - T_e}, \; \theta_\gamma = \frac{T_o - T_\gamma}{T_o - T_e},$$

A characteristic length is also available in each phase. A different characteristic length can be used in each phase. It is also possible to use the total length of slabs. As can be easily observed, the form of the differential equations would not change. However, it would be difficult to implement boundary conditions if different lengths are chosen for each phase. Let us choose the thickness of the α slab, X_1 for scaling the length. Let $\xi = x/X_1$. Skipping all the algebra, we list the differential equations and the boundary conditions in non-dimensional form:

$$\frac{d^2\theta_\alpha}{d\xi^2} = 0, \; \frac{d^2\theta_\beta}{d\xi^2} = 0, \; \frac{d^2\theta_\gamma}{d\xi^2} = 0$$

in the respective regions.

$$\theta_\alpha = 0 \qquad \text{at} \quad \xi = 0$$

$$\theta_\alpha = \theta_\beta, \; \frac{d\theta_\alpha}{d\xi} = \frac{k_\beta}{k_\alpha}\frac{d\theta_\beta}{d\xi} \qquad \text{at} \quad \xi = 1$$

$$\theta_\beta = \theta_\gamma, \quad \frac{d\theta_\beta}{d\xi} = \frac{k_\gamma}{k_\beta}\frac{d\theta_\gamma}{d\xi} \qquad \text{at} \quad \xi = \frac{X_2}{X_1}$$

$$\theta_\gamma = 1 \qquad \text{at} \quad \xi = \frac{X_3}{X_1}$$

Note the various dimensionless quantities that have appeared after scaling *both in the differential equation and the boundary conditions*. They are $\theta_\alpha, \theta_\beta$ and θ_α, which are the quantities of interest. The others are related to properties and dimensions of the apparatus. They are $X_2/X_1, X_3/X_1, k_\beta/k_\alpha$ and k_γ/k_β. It is easy to observe that if we solved the differential equations along with the boundary conditions, we would obtain a solution which would be of the form:

$$\theta_\alpha = \theta_\alpha\left(\xi, \frac{X_2}{X_1}, \frac{X_3}{X_1}, \frac{k_\beta}{k_\alpha}, \frac{k_\gamma}{k_\beta}\right)$$

and similar forms for θ_β and θ_γ. Note that the *solution depends upon the dimensionless groups that appear in the differential equations as well as in the boundary conditions*. The quantity of interest is the heat flux, Q through the slabs. It is same through all the slabs as is easily inferred from energy balance and the boundary conditions. Thus, we can calculate heat flux at any plane, and hence

$$Q = -k_\alpha \frac{dT_\alpha}{dx} \qquad \text{at} \quad x = 0$$

Substituting the form we obtained here, we would find that

$$\frac{QX_1}{k_\alpha(T_o - T_e)} = \mathcal{F}\left(\frac{X_2}{X_1}, \frac{X_3}{X_1}, \frac{k_\beta}{k_\alpha}, \frac{k_\gamma}{k_\beta}\right)$$

We conclude that there are five dimensionless groups in the problem from the scaling analysis. We went through this in great detail to illustrate how transport phenomena approach helps in selection of the quantities of importance to the problem and reduces the guess work normally involved in using Buckingham's π theorem.

4.1.6 Temperature profile

We will not pursue the dimensionless approach any further because the problem is very simple. The solution to the differential equations and boundary conditions is well known and is given by

$$\frac{T_o - T_\alpha}{T_o - T_e} = \frac{1}{R}\frac{X_1}{k_\alpha}\frac{x}{X_1} \qquad 0 \le x \le X_1 \tag{4.8}$$

$$\frac{T_o - T_\beta}{T_o - T_e} = \frac{R_\alpha}{R} + \frac{1}{R}\frac{k_\beta}{X_2 - X_1}\frac{x - X_1}{X_2 - X_1} \qquad X_1 \le x \le X_2 \tag{4.9}$$

$$\frac{T_o - T_\gamma}{T_o - T_e} = \frac{R_\alpha + R_\beta}{R} + \frac{k_\gamma}{X_3 - X_2}\frac{x - X_2}{X_3 - X_2} \qquad X_2 < x \le X_3 \tag{4.10}$$

where

$$R = R_\alpha + R_\beta + R_\gamma = \frac{X_1}{k_\alpha} + \frac{X_2 - X_1}{k_\beta} + \frac{X_3 - X_2}{k_\gamma} = \frac{k_\alpha}{X_1}\left(1 + \frac{k_\beta}{k_\alpha}\frac{X_2 - X_1}{X_1} + \frac{k_\gamma}{k_\alpha}\frac{X_3 - X_2}{X_1}\right)$$

The heat flux is easily calculated as:

$$Q = \frac{T_o - T_e}{R}$$

4.1.7 Look at the results

The results are well known to all chemical engineers and are easily interpreted. Each slab offers a 'conduction resistance', given by the ratio of thickness to thermal conductivity. Since the slabs are in series, the total resistance of the slabs, R, is the sum of all these. The heat flux, analogous to electric current, is given by the ratio of the driving force to the resistance. The driving force is the total temperature difference. As expected the heat flux should increase as driving force increases and resistance decreases.

By the same analogy, the total temperature difference is the sum of 'temperature drops' across each slab. This feature is easily noticed in the equation for flux. For example, the second equation shows that the temperature is given by the drop in the first slab, $X_1/(Rk_\alpha)$ plus the drop corresponding to the thickness up to the location of interest in the second slab. The temperature drop is proportional to the resistance of the slab. The resistance is inversely proportional to the conductivity and directly proportional to the thickness. Thus, the temperature drop in a more conducting material will be smaller than in a less conducting material provided, if both are of the same thickness. Thus, a small thickness of an insulating material is effective, and convenient to use in preventing heat loss.

The solution shows that the temperature drops linearly in the slabs. This is a consequence of thermal conductivity being constant and heat flux remaining constant. Heat flux remains a constant because the area through which heat flows remains constant. These are expected and of course agree with the formulae derived in Unit Operations books.

Transport phenomena approach gives rise to dimensionless groups in a natural way eliminating some of the need to make guesses unlike with the approach of Π theorem.

4.2 TEMPERATURE DISTRIBUTION IN A HEATED WIRE

4.2.1 Problem identification

Consider a long wire through which current is passing. The wire is insulated. The surface of the insulation is being maintained at a constant temperature, T_o. The geometry of the arrangement is shown in figure 4.2. Obviously, this problem is only a prototype of many instances where heat is generated inside a body from where heat loss has to be minimized for the sake of energy efficiency. The most familiar example is human body in cold weather! It could be a reactor where exothermic reaction occurs and it is planned to recover heat. Or, it could even be an apparatus from where heat has to be removed[6]. In these problems, the temperature profile inside the solid is of interest, mainly with a view to know the maximum temperature reached inside it. It will be assumed that steady state has been reached.

Simplifications and assumptions

Cylindrical coordinates are selected as they are ideally suited to describe the geometry of a wire. As steady state is being considered, temperature is not a function of time. As the wire is very long,

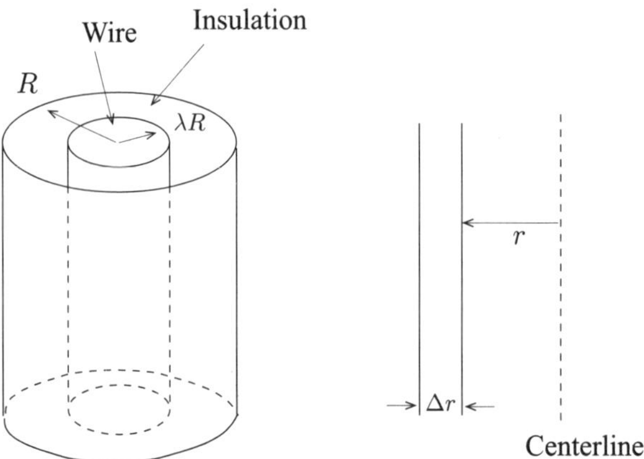

Figure 4.2. Insulated and heated wire. A control volume is shown on the left.

end effects can be neglected and this implies that the temperature profile is not a function of z or the axial coordinate. If the wire and the insulation are perfectly circular, symmetry around the z axis can be expected and hence temperature will not be a function of θ. Can real wires be perfectly symmetric? But let us assume this to be the case! Thus, $T = T(r)$ only.

4.2.2 Heat balance over a control volume

A control volume of thickness Δr and of unit length is selected for making heat balance. Since the temperature is only a function of radius, length does not play any role and in the end the heat loss *per unit length* is calculated. The heat balance is written as (refer to section 3.1)

Rate of accumulation of enthalpy in the CV	=	**Net rate of input of enthalpy into the CV by convection**	+	**Rate of input of heat through control surfaces by conduction**	+	**Rate of generation of heat in the CV due to chemical reactions,** ***etc.***	+	**Rate of heat generation in the CV due to viscous dissipation**

As steady state prevails, the accumulation term is set to zero. As there is no flow, convective and the viscous dissipation terms are zero. As no chemical reactions are occurring in the system, heat generation due to these is zero. Heat is generated only due to the ohmic losses. Using the notation adopted earlier, let the heat generated per unit volume be $\dot{Q}_v$. Let i be the current passing through the wire. Let the electrical conductivity of the material of the wire be k_e. If a is the area of cross section and l is the length of the material through which current is passing, the resistance of the electrical path is given by $l/(ak_e)$. Hence,

$$
\begin{aligned}
a\,l\left(\dot{Q}_v\right) &= i^2(\text{Resistance}) \\
&= \frac{li^2}{ak_e}
\end{aligned}
$$

or

$$\dot{Q}_v = \frac{I^2}{k_e}$$

where I is the current density, i/a.

Like before, effects of radiation are absent and heat flux is only due to conduction. As temperature is only a function of radius, the control volume selected is differential in that direction, as shown in figure 4.2. The control surfaces through which heat flows in the control volume are the cylindrical surfaces at r and $r + \Delta r$. Thus, the heat balance over unit length yields

$$(2\pi r q_r)|_r - (2\pi r q_r)|_{r+\Delta r} + 2\pi r \Delta r \stackrel{\bullet}{Q}_v = 0$$

Following a procedure identical to that followed in the previous section, this equation is converted per unit volume basis by dividing it by $2\pi r\Delta r$, and the limit of the resulting equation is evaluated as Δr tends to zero to obtain

$$\frac{1}{r}\frac{d}{dr}(rq_r) = \stackrel{\bullet}{Q}_v$$

Note that difference in rq_r across a shell of small thickness is proportional to the net *heat flowing* out of the shell in the radial direction per unit length. Similarly rdr is proportional to the volume of the shell. Thus, the equation is easily interpreted: the net heat flowing out of the control volume is equal to heat generated in the control volume, both quantities being calculated on *per unit volume basis*. This equation is valid both in the wire and also in the insulating phase, except that $\stackrel{\bullet}{Q}_v$ is zero in the insulating phase. Once again, note the similarity between the left hand side of this equation and the equation of continuity in cylindrical coordinates.

4.2.3 Combining rate law with heat balance

We substitute the Fourier's law of heat conduction into the heat balance. Then we have the following equations to solve, where subscript w is used for the wire and i for the insulation:

$$\rho \stackrel{\bullet}{Q}_v = -k_w \frac{1}{r}\frac{d}{dr}\left(r\frac{dT_w}{dr}\right) \tag{4.11}$$

$$0 = -k_i \frac{1}{r}\frac{d}{dr}\left(r\frac{dT_i}{dr}\right) \tag{4.12}$$

where, as in the previous section, it has been assumed that the thermal conductivities of both materials are independent of temperature.

4.2.4 Scaling

The equations have to be non-dimensionalized. The length scale can be selected to be R. One could also select two length scales, λR in the wire and $R(1 - \lambda)$ in the insulation phase. As discussed in the context of the previous problem, it does not change much, but it would be very inconvenient to implement boundary conditions. Thus, R is selected to be the length scale, and non-dimensional length ξ is defined as

$$\xi = \frac{r}{R}$$

T_o is the temperature at the periphery of the insulation and off-hand one might think that it can be used to scale temperature. This, however is unphysical as discussed in the previous example since conduction mechanism of heat transfer depends upon *temperature differences.* Thus, the temperature differences have to be scaled. In the present problem, a characteristic temperature difference has to be found to scale the temperature difference $(T_o - T)$. In the present problem, the total heat to be lost through the insulation is known since it is equal to the total heat generated in the wire. Therefore, it seems appropriate to build up a characteristic temperature difference from this quantity.

4.2.5 Scaling: general concepts

We now introduce one more concept important in selecting scales. It is generally desired that non-dimensional quantities be of the order of unity. Note that this was satisfied by the scales chosen in the previous sections. This has obvious advantages in numerical solutions but we set aside that for the moment. Unlike in the simple problems we are considering presently, there will be more complex problems to be dealt with later. When the dimensions of a term are removed using a *scale*, it will appear as a product of the scale and the non-dimensional term. Thus, r in this example will appear as $R\xi$. If ξ is of the order of unity, then the magnitude of the original term is approximately equal to R. After the whole equation is non-dimensionalized, various non-dimensional terms will be found to be multiplied by *dimensionless groups or numbers made up of the scales used* since the whole equation is dimension-free. The magnitude of various terms then is indicated by the dimensionless number multiplying it, *if scales were chosen correctly such that the order of magnitude of the dimensionless quantities is of the order of unity.* The magnitude of the dimensionless number is known because the scales are chosen by us. Thus, we can compare the importance of various terms in the dimensionless equations by comparing the dimensionless numbers multiplying them. This is a very important concept and should be understood carefully.

Returning to the example of heated wire, the characteristic temperature difference chosen should be realistic and also the largest possible, since only then the non-dimensional quantities would be of the order of unity. Such a characteristic temperature difference can be estimated as follows: A temperature difference is needed to lose all the heat being generated. The largest estimate of it would be that which is required to lose the heat through the material of the smallest conductivity. In the present problem it is the insulating material. Thus, if $(\Delta T)_c$ is the characteristic temperature difference

$$\dot{Q}_v = \text{Total heat to be dissipated per unit volume} \sim k_i \frac{(\Delta T)_c}{R^2}$$

or

$$(\Delta T)_c = \frac{\dot{Q}_v\, R^2}{k_i}$$

The non-dimensional temperature differences can then be defined as

$$\theta_w = \frac{k_i(T_w - T_o)}{\dot{Q}_v\, R^2} \quad \text{and} \quad \theta_i = \frac{k_i(T_i - T_o)}{\dot{Q}_v\, R^2}$$

In terms of the non-dimensional quantities, the differential equations take the form:

$$\begin{aligned}\frac{1}{\xi}\frac{d}{d\xi}\left(\xi\frac{d\theta_w}{d\xi}\right)+\frac{k_i}{k_w} &= 0, \qquad 0\le\xi\le\lambda \\ \frac{1}{\xi}\frac{d}{d\xi}\left(\xi\frac{d\theta_i}{d\xi}\right) &= 0, \qquad \lambda\le\xi\le 1\end{aligned} \tag{4.13}$$

4.2.6 Boundary conditions

To solve the two second order differential equations obtained above, four boundary conditions are required. The boundary between the insulation and the wire is an internal boundary. There, drawing from the experience of the previous problem, both the temperature continuity condition and the heat balance will have to be used. The temperature of the boundary at $r = R$ is being maintained constant at temperature, T_o, and that forms the boundary condition. The *line* $r = 0$ forms another boundary and it is also an inaccessible boundary. But this line is special as it is a line of symmetry. At such a boundary, either the gradients are set to zero or it is demanded that the dependent variable itself must be bounded. This is similar to the boundary condition used in solving for the velocity profile in a pipe. The boundary conditions are summarized below:

$$\begin{aligned}\frac{dT_w}{dr} &= 0 &&\text{at}\quad r=0\\ T_w &= T_i &&\text{at}\quad r=kR\\ k_w\frac{dT_w}{dr} &= k_i\frac{dT_i}{dr} &&\text{at}\quad r=\lambda R\\ T_i &= T_o &&\text{at}\quad r=R\end{aligned}$$

It may be mentioned that T_w must remain finite can be an alternative to the first equation. In terms of non-dimensional variables

$$\frac{d\theta_w}{d\xi} = 0 \qquad \text{at}\quad \xi=0 \tag{4.14}$$

$$T_w = T_i \qquad \text{at}\quad \xi=\lambda \tag{4.15}$$

$$\frac{d\theta_w}{d\xi} = \frac{k_i}{k_w}\frac{d\theta_i}{d\xi} \qquad \text{at}\quad \xi=\lambda \tag{4.16}$$

$$\theta_i = 0 \qquad \text{at}\quad \xi=1 \tag{4.17}$$

4.2.7 Temperature profile

The solution to the problem is given by

$$\theta_w = -\frac{k_i}{k_w}\frac{\xi^2-\lambda^2}{4}-\frac{\lambda^2}{2}\ln\lambda \tag{4.18}$$

$$\theta_i = -\frac{\lambda^2}{2}\ln\xi \tag{4.19}$$

4.2.8 Look at the results

From the temperature profiles, it is clear that the maximum temperature is generated at the center of the wire and the temperature profile in the wire is parabolic. Equation 4.13 is very similar to the equation of motion for laminar flow in a pipe under applied pressure gradient. There, the equation of motion represents the balance between pressure forces and the viscous forces. The latter are due to diffusion of momentum. However, forces can also be thought of as sources of momentum. Thus, eq. 4.13 which is a balance between heat generation and diffusion, is similar to equation of motion for flow in a pipe. Therefore, a parabolic temperature profile can be expected in this problem! It is always worthwhile to think in terms of analogy between heat transfer and fluid mechanics because experience in one area can help in the other. Figure 4.3 shows the temperature profile. Note the

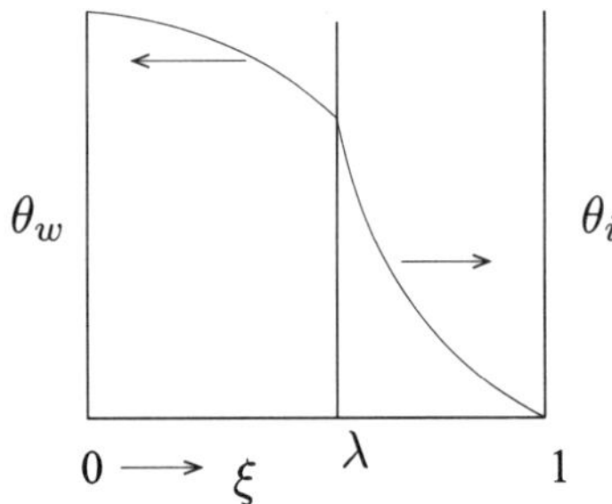

Figure 4.3. Temperature profile in a heated insulated wire.

continuity of temperature at the interface between wire and the insulation. Also note that since the conductivity of the insulation is less than that of the wire, the temperature gradient at the interface in the insulation has to be more steep than that in the wire for the heat flux to remain constant.

The maximum temperature is expected to increase with $\dot{Q}_v$ or current density and with decreasing thermal conductivity of the insulation, and expected to decrease as the ratio of the thermal conductivity of wire to that of the insulation increases. As the radius of the wire increases, the heat generated increases as square of radius while the area available through which it can be lost increases only linearly as the radius. Further, the gradients tend to decrease with increasing radius. Thus, the maximum temperature can be expected to increase with the radius. The maximum temperature is calculated from the solution to be

$$T_{max} - T_o = \frac{\dot{Q}_v R^2}{k_i} \left(\frac{k_i}{k_w} \frac{\lambda^2}{4} - \frac{\lambda^2}{2} \ln \lambda \right)$$

It can be seen that all these expectations are borne out by the expression for T_{max}. The second term in the bracket is the temperature drop in the insulation while the first is the drop in the wire. The temperature drop in the wire becomes negligible as the thermal conductivity of the wire increases, which is also expected. If the thermal conductivity of the insulation goes to infinity, which is not expected in this application, only the first term remains, once again as expected. The wire will melt if the maximum temperature reached exceeds its melting point, and this is the principle on which a fuse works. A fuse is expected to 'blow' if current density exceeds a critical value or equivalently when the heat generation exceeds a critical value. One can calculate the maximum heat generated an arrangement can withstand from the temperature profile. It must be remembered that this might not be accurate because we assumed physical properties to be constant.

4.3 HEAT TRANSFER COEFFICIENT

A detour is needed before shell balances in forced convection can be discussed. Two concepts, that of *bulk temperature* and *heat transfer coefficient* have to be introduced.

4.3.1 Bulk temperature

The rate at which enthalpy is carried by a flowing stream of fluid across an area is given by

$$\int_{A_s} \rho \hat{H} \mathbf{v.n} dA$$

This book deals with mostly incompressible *fluids*. Thus, the previous expression is equal to

$$\int_{A_s} \rho \hat{C}_p (T - T_r) \mathbf{v.n} dA$$

where T_r is some reference temperature. It is often convenient to define a **mean or bulk temperature**, T_b of a stream such that, when multiplied by the mass flow rate and specific heat, it gives the total enthalpy carried by the stream per unit time. Hence,

$$(T_b - T_r) \int_{A_s} \rho \hat{C}_p \mathbf{v.n} dA \equiv \int_{A_s} \rho \hat{C}_p (T - T_r) \mathbf{v.n} dA$$

If properties do not change over the cross section, this equation can be written as

$$T_b = \frac{\int_{A_s} T \mathbf{v.n} dA}{\int_{A_s} \mathbf{v.n} dA} \tag{4.20}$$

This equation is easily linked to measurements. If liquid coming out of cross section is collected in a cup[7] for some duration of time, Δt the amount of mass collected in it will be

$$\Delta t \, \rho \int_{A_s} \mathbf{v.n} dA$$

If specific heat is assumed to be independent of temperature, the heat capacity of the mass collected is

$$\Delta t \, \rho \hat{C}_p \int_{A_s} \mathbf{v.n} dA$$

If the mass collected is well stirred or *mixed* perfectly, it will attain a uniform temperature, T_{cup}. Hence, the total enthalpy of the stream collected is

$$(T_{cup} - T_r)\Delta t\, \rho\hat{C}_p \int_{A_s} \mathbf{v.n}dA$$

However, this must also equal the enthalpy of the liquid collected:

$$\Delta t\, \rho\hat{C}_p \int_{A_s} (T - T_r)\mathbf{v.n}dA$$

Thus, it is easily seen that the bulk temperature is identical to the uniform temperature reached by the stream if it were well-stirred. Hence, it is also referred to as *cup mixing temperature* in the text by Bird *et al.* [1].

4.3.2 Heat transfer coefficient

We briefly discussed the heat transfer coefficient in section 3.3. We now elaborate a little more on that. In case of fluid mechanics, where possible, the velocity profiles are obtained first. They are used to calculate the drag forces, pressure drops, *etc.* The results of those calculations are summarized as plots of drag coefficient (C_D) or friction factor (f). These plots contain *all* the information needed to calculate forces, rate of work done, *etc.* They are sufficient if one is interested only in those quantities, which is usually the case in applications. Similar is the case in heat transfer, where usually the rate of heat transfer between two phases is the main quantity of interest. Thus, it appears that if a quantity similar to drag coefficient or friction factor is defined for heat transfer problems, it would be of great practical value. The corresponding factor is **heat transfer coefficient**. It is defined such that use of heat transfer coefficient, along with the driving forces, allows calculation of the heat flux into a stream of *flowing* fluid from an interface between two phases. In this sense, it is similar to friction factor or drag coefficient.

The heat transfer coefficient is defined as follows. Let a normal be constructed from an interface *pointing into the fluid* phase of interest. Notice that the normal is located at an interface: fluid–fluid or solid–fluid, usually the latter is most commonly encountered. The heat transfer coefficient, h is defined such that *the heat flux into the fluid from the interface* is given by

$$\mathbf{q.n} \equiv h(T_w - T_b) \tag{4.21}$$

where T_w is the temperature [8] of the interface. This is of course the definition that is widely used in Unit Operations. It is also commonly referred to as Newton's law of cooling. Notice however, that we have *precisely defined the temperature of the fluid to be used: it is the bulk temperature.* This definition makes sense since we are often interested in calculating changes in the total enthalpy of flowing fluid streams, which is related to the bulk temperature of the stream. The above definition of heat transfer coefficient allows us to link the rate of heat transfer to the bulk temperature. It will be beneficial if you go back and refer to the heat exchanger problem dealt with in section 1.6 to once again to understand this aspect.

Note that as soon as the heat transfer coefficient to a fluid stream is known, the heat flux into that stream can be calculated. No more information is required to make overall enthalpy balances. The main objective of solving convective heat transfer problems then is to *calculate the heat transfer coefficient*. This, in turn allows calculation of rate of heat transfer into flowing fluid streams. This is similar to the situation in fluid mechanics. The idea of solving fluid mechanics problems from a fundamental view point is to *calculate* the friction factors, and drag coefficients. If the friction factor or the drag coefficient is known, the drag forces, the power requirements, *etc.* can be calculated. In fluid mechanics, it is found that the objective of calculation of friction factors is only partly fulfilled, because such calculation is not possible when flow becomes turbulent. Similar is the situation in heat transfer. When flow becomes turbulent, heat transfer coefficients also cannot be calculated, but have to be measured. However, a lot of insight can be gained by learning how to calculate heat transfer coefficients where it can be done.

4.4 LAMINAR FORCED CONVECTION

4.4.1 Problem identification

Consider a *liquid* flowing through a tube due to a pressure gradient. Let the conditions be such that *laminar flow* prevails. The fluid enters the tube at a uniform temperature of T_i. The beginning portion of the tube is at the same temperature T_i. But after some length, the tube is being heated and the arrangement is such that the *heat flux to the wall, q_w is constant.* The overall arrangement is shown in figure 4.4. Suppose the process has been in progress for long. This permits us to assume

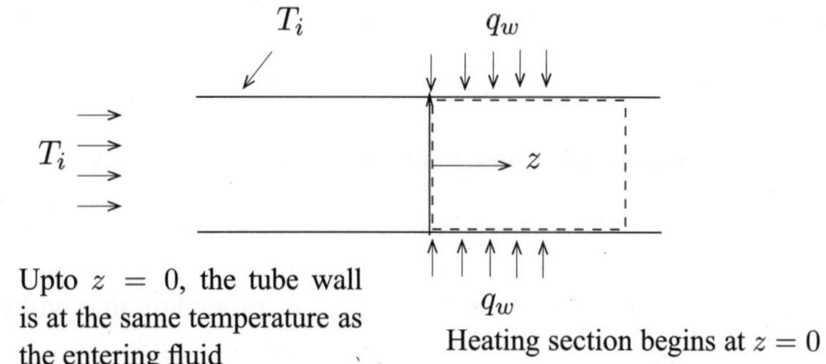

Figure 4.4. Overall flow arrangement. The control volume shown in dotted line will be referred to later.

that steady state has been reached. As it turns out, it is difficult to solve this problem in its full complexity. Therefore, different zones of the pipe are considered for solution. In a later chapter, we will consider solving the problem in the entry zone. In this section, we will consider solving the problem in a zone far away from the entrance. The objective is to calculate the temperature in the fluid as a function of radius and axial position in the tube, and of course, the heat transfer coefficient.

4.4.2 Heat balance over a control volume

We start in this problem with a heat balance, instead of the usual statements of hypotheses, because it is the best way to show the kind of simplifications that are made in convection problems. The heat balance over the control volume can be written as

$$\begin{array}{c} \textbf{Rate of accumulation} \\ \textbf{of enthalpy in the CV} \end{array} = \begin{array}{c} \textbf{Net rate of input} \\ \textbf{of enthalpy into} \\ \textbf{the CV by convection} \end{array} + \begin{array}{c} \textbf{Rate of input of} \\ \textbf{heat through} \\ \textbf{control surfaces} \\ \textbf{by conduction} \end{array} + \begin{array}{c} \textbf{Rate of generation} \\ \textbf{of heat in the CV} \\ \textbf{due to chemical} \\ \textbf{reactions}, \textit{etc.} \end{array} + \begin{array}{c} \textbf{Rate of heat} \\ \textbf{generation in} \\ \textbf{the CV due to} \\ \textbf{viscous dissipation} \end{array}$$

We choose cylindrical coordinates as they are the most convenient to describe problems in pipes. In this problem, we expect temperature to vary in the radial direction since heat has to percolate from the wall into the interior of the fluid. We also expect it to change along the axial direction because the fluid is getting heated as it flows. As we will explain shortly, we do not expect any variation along the circumferential direction or we expect symmetry around the axis of the pipe. So we choose a control volume with differentially small dimensions in the radial and axial directions. A part of the tube, as shown in figure 4.5, is chosen to be the control volume.

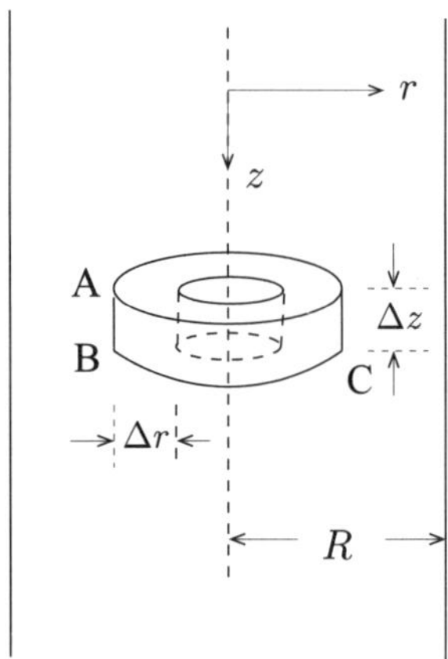

Figure 4.5. Control volume in pipe for heat balance.

Let us examine the individual terms in the heat balance. As this is a *steady state* problem, the accumulation term can be set to zero. No chemical reactions are occurring in the system, and the generation of heat due to this need not be considered. The procedure that will be useful in estimating the magnitude of heat generated due to viscous dissipation is considered in the next section. But for the moment, it will be assumed that it is negligible. We introduce one assumption. In view of the uniformity of boundary conditions on the circumference of the tube, axisymmetry is assumed, *i.e.,* $\partial/\partial\theta = 0$.

The control volume has two cylindrical surfaces. One is at $r + \Delta r$, shown as ABC, and the other at r. It also has two annular circular faces. One is at z and is shown shaded in Figure 4.5. The other is directly below it, at $z + \Delta z$. The rate of input of enthalpy across any interface of area A and in the direction of the normal $\mathbf{n}$ to it is given by

$$-\int_A \rho \hat{H} \mathbf{v}.\mathbf{n} dA$$

Thus, the net rate of input of enthalpy into the control volume through all the control surfaces is equal to

$$(2\pi r \Delta z v_r \rho \hat{H})|_r - (2\pi r \Delta z v_r \rho \hat{H})|_{(r+\Delta r)} + (2\pi r \Delta r v_z \rho \hat{H})|_z - (2\pi r \Delta r v_z \rho \hat{H})|_{(z+\Delta z)}$$

The heat flux through the surfaces can be by conduction and radiation. Let us assume that radiation is absent. Thus, heat flux is given by $\mathbf{q}$, and the net rate of *input* of heat by conduction through the control surfaces is given by

$$-\int_{A_s} \mathbf{q}.\mathbf{n} dA = (2\pi r \Delta z q_r)|_r - (2\pi r \Delta z q_r)|_{(r+\Delta r)} + (2\pi r \Delta r q_z)|_z - (2\pi r \Delta r q_z)|_{(z+\Delta z)}$$

As in the previous examples, these results are substituted into the heat balance, the resulting equation divided by $2\pi r \Delta r \Delta z$ to convert it into per unit volume basis, and the limit of this equation as $\Delta r \Delta z$ tends to zero, is evaluated. The following differential equation will then be obtained:

$$\frac{1}{r}\frac{\partial}{\partial r}(r v_r \hat{H}) + \frac{\partial}{\partial z}(v_z \hat{H}) = -\frac{1}{r}\frac{\partial}{\partial r}(r q_r) - \frac{\partial q_z}{\partial z}$$

4.4.3 Coupling to fluid mechanics

The first thing to be noticed is that the above equation cannot be solved unless the velocity profiles are known. *Thus, the equations of convective heat transfer are coupled to the equation of continuity and motion.* The natural question to ask is under what conditions, if at all such exist, the equation of motion can be solved independent of the heat balance equation, *i.e.,* conditions under which they can be decoupled. The Navier–Stokes equations were derived by assuming that physical properties, specifically viscosity and density, remain constant. But these are affected by temperature. *Thus, unless some simplifications are made, the equation of motion and the thermal energy balance equation cannot be decoupled.* This is obvious in natural convection but is true even for forced convection problems.

In general, a simplification is made in case of *liquids*. Mass conservation implies that velocities should change as density varies. Thus, for ideal gases, the density varies significantly with temperature, and these effects can be significant. However, the variation in density with temperature is not so important for liquids. Thus, variations in velocity caused by the small changes in density are also small and are not expected to have important effect on the momentum balance. Hence, unless necessary density is assumed to be constant. *One instance where such an approximation cannot be made is natural convection.* Natural convection is driven by buoyancy forces created by density differences caused by variation in temperature. If density variation is neglected, the very force that drives motion also gets thrown out! But density can be assumed to remain constant in *forced* convection problems.

One more simplification, though difficult to justify, is also made for the sake of obtaining simple solutions. Thus, it is assumed that *viscosity also remains constant*! Usually, this is a significant error and needs to be corrected for practical applications. This is the origin of the wall correction applied in calculating heat transfer coefficients for designing heat exchangers.

Thus, if both density and viscosity are assumed to be constant, the heat balance equation is decoupled from the equations of continuity and motion, and can be solved independently. In the present text also, it will be assumed that both density and viscosity remain constant in dealing with forced convection problems.

4.4.4 Simplifications and assumptions

As stated, it will be assumed that the physical properties remain constant. This permits solution of the equation of motion without having to solve the heat transfer equation. As fluid flows through the tube, the velocity profile develops as a result of the imbalance between the pressure and viscous forces. If the length prior to where heating begins is long enough, then the flow can be expected to be *fully developed* before the fluid reaches the heated section. Further, it is given that the flow is laminar. Hence, the velocity profile is given by

$$v_r = 0 \text{ and } v_z = 2V\left(1 - \frac{r^2}{R^2}\right)$$

where V is the average velocity of the fluid.

It was briefly mentioned in section 3.2 that heat transfer problems are classified using several criteria. One of them is about the state of flow. Thus, the present problem comes under the category of heat transfer in laminar and fully developed flows.

Link to thermodynamics

In section 3.1 the issue of relating enthalpy to temperature and pressure was briefly discussed. Thus, if it is assumed, as it will be here, that the state of the fluid is not far from equilibrium, thermodynamic relationships can be applied. In the present problem, as mentioned earlier, incompressibility or constancy of density is assumed. Thus,

$$d\hat{H} = \hat{C}_p dT$$

In the spirit of the spate of constancies being assumed, let $\hat{C}_p$ also join the list. Substituting all these results and assumptions into the enthalpy balance gives

$$2\rho\hat{C}_p V\left(1 - \frac{r^2}{R^2}\right)\frac{\partial T}{\partial z} = -\frac{1}{r}\frac{\partial}{\partial r}(rq_r) - \frac{\partial q_z}{\partial z}$$

It may be noted that the equation of continuity was used to effect algebraic simplifications.

4.4.5 Combining rate law with balance

Fourier's law of heat conduction is then substituted into the balance equation to obtain

$$2\rho\hat{C}_p V\left(1 - \frac{r^2}{R^2}\right)\frac{\partial T}{\partial z} = k\frac{1}{r}\frac{\partial}{\partial r}\left(r\frac{\partial T}{\partial r}\right) + k\frac{\partial^2 T}{\partial z^2}$$

where, in the same spirit as the other ones, thermal conductivity was also assumed to remain constant.

4.4.6 Scaling

The appropriate length scale in the r direction is the radius of the pipe, R. Let ξ be the non-dimensional radius:

$$\xi = \frac{r}{R}$$

However, there are no obvious characteristic quantities for temperature and the length along the axial direction. As mentioned in the discussion of the previous problem, selection of T_i as a scale temperature is unphysical, and a characteristic temperature difference is needed to scale $(T - T_i)$. In the present problem, the heat flux is specified. Thus, in a manner similar to what was done in the section dealing with a heated wire, the scale for the temperature difference could be derived from the heat flux. The heat flux is supplied at the wall, where velocity is zero by no–slip condition. Hence, right at the wall, the heat must be removed into the interior of the fluid by conduction. A good scale for a characteristic *temperature difference*, ΔT_c is obtained by using Fourier's law of conduction as the basis for scaling, *i.e.*, $q_w \sim k\Delta T_c/R$. Use this to define non-dimensional temperature difference:

$$\theta = \frac{(T - T_i)}{Rq_w/k} = \frac{k(T - T_i)}{Rq_w}$$

A length scale in the axial direction is not there in the problem, but we will first illustrate a point by assuming that one is available. Let it be L. Let the non-dimensional length be $\tilde{z} = z/L$. Substituting all these, the following non-dimensional equation is obtained:

$$2\frac{\rho\hat{C}_p VL}{k}\left(\frac{R}{L}\right)^2(1-\xi^2)\frac{\partial\theta}{\partial\tilde{z}} = \frac{1}{\xi}\frac{\partial}{\partial\xi}\left(\xi\frac{\partial\theta}{\partial\xi}\right) + \frac{R^2}{L^2}\frac{\partial^2\theta}{\partial\tilde{z}^2}$$

Now we will make use of the point we made in section 4.2 on magnitude of dimensionless groups and relative magnitude of terms. We begin this discussion with the similarity between momentum transfer and heat transfer. During flow in a pipe, as the velocity profile develops into parabolic shape, momentum diffuses from bulk towards the wall. There, in the beginning portions of entry zone, a boundary layer develops near the wall, and the velocity gradients are confined to the wall. However, when the thickness of the boundary layer increases along the length of the pipe, velocity gradients percolate all the way to the center. After the boundary layer extends up to the center of the tube, the velocity profile further changes until it achieves the fully developed parabolic shape. Thus, flow becomes fully developed only at some considerable distance from the entry. Similarly, in the case of heat transfer also, temperature gradients are confined to a layer near the wall region in the beginning portions of the entry zone. Further downstream, this layer thickens, and the temperature gradients reach the center. The temperature profile further changes along the length. Now consider a location L from the entry into the tube where the gradients have already percolated into the center. There, R^2/L^2 is expected to be small. If our scaling is correct, *the non-dimensional terms are of the order of unity and hence the magnitude of the axial conduction term is of the order of* $(R/L)^2$. Thus, *if we are interested in heat transfer in regions of pipe far into the tube and away from the entrance, the second term in the right hand side of the equation of heat balance can be neglected.* It appears that by the same argument, the entire left hand side of the equation also should be put to zero! This is unrealistic as the term being neglected is the convection term, which is the heart of the present problem. It appears therefore that it should be kept, and for this to be logical, the following condition[9] must be valid:

$$\frac{\rho \hat{C}_p V R}{k} \frac{R}{L} \sim 1$$

The point to be noted is that scaling arguments will have to be consistent. The consistency requirement throws up another combination, $\rho \hat{C}_p V R/k$, which also determines scaling considerations. As it turns out, this provides a clue to the length scale for the axial coordinate.

More insight can be gained by recognizing that a length scale for axial distance has to be built, much the same way a characteristic temperature difference was derived, because a natural length scale is not available in the axial direction. This is also reminiscent of the experience with similarity solutions of fluid mechanics. The central issue here is to find when convective terms in the axial direction are comparable to conduction terms in the radial direction since only then they can be retained. One way is to compare the heat transferred by conduction and convection while following the fluid element. Thus, the time scale for convection can be compared with the time scale of conduction. At any z, the time scale of convection is z/V. The conduction (or diffusion[10]) time scale is $R^2 \rho \hat{C}_p/k$. Thus,

$$\zeta = \frac{zk}{\rho \hat{C}_p V R^2}$$

is the ratio of convective time scale over length z to diffusive time scale over length scale R. If we use this ratio and remove dimensions of axial length, we can use a criteria that this ratio be at least of the order of unity for convective terms to be as important as radial conduction terms. Yet another way to think about this is to construct a length scale for axial distance, *the direction of convection,* by combining velocity with (since we want the convective terms to be comparable to the diffusion terms) the radial diffusion time scale. Thus, as long as ζ is *at least of the order of unity*, the convective heat transfer remains important. With these variables the non-dimensional equation is given by

$$2(1-\xi^2)\frac{\partial \theta}{\partial \zeta} = \frac{1}{\xi}\frac{\partial}{\partial \xi}\left(\xi \frac{\partial \theta}{\partial \xi}\right) + \left(\frac{k}{\rho \hat{C}_p V R}\right)^2 \frac{\partial^2 \theta}{\partial \zeta^2}$$

The group

$$\frac{\rho \hat{C}_p V R}{k}$$

is called the Peclet number, Pe. From our earlier efforts to find the scale for axial length, the number is easily interpreted as the ratio of the conduction (or thermal diffusion) time scale to the *convection time scale for a length of* R. Now, it can be seen from the non-dimensional equation that axial conduction can be neglected compared to the radial conduction term if Pe is large. Further, even if z/R is large, we cannot neglect axial convection term if $z/(R\,Pe)$ it is of the order of unity or greater, which is possible if Pe is large. This resolves our question regarding retention of convective terms while neglecting axial conduction term based only on the magnitude of z/R.

Thus, we finally have the equation we are looking for:

$$2(1-\xi^2)\frac{\partial \theta}{\partial \zeta} = \frac{1}{\xi}\frac{\partial}{\partial \xi}\left(\xi \frac{\partial \theta}{\partial \xi}\right) \tag{4.22}$$

4.4.7 Boundary conditions

The above is a partial differential equation, first order with respect to ζ and second order with respect to ξ. Solution of the equation therefore, needs one boundary condition in ζ coordinate and two in ξ coordinate. The boundary conditions at $z = 0$ and at the center of the tube are easily specified. These correspond to $\theta = 0$ and the gradient of temperature equal to zero, respectively:

$$\frac{\partial \theta}{\partial \xi} = 0 \qquad \text{at} \quad \xi{=}0 \tag{4.23}$$

$$\theta = 0, \qquad \text{at} \quad \zeta{=}0 \tag{4.24}$$

Now consider the boundary at the wall. Denote wall as phase I and the fluid as phase II. Application of the temperature boundary condition suggests that the wall temperature and the fluid temperature are equal. While this is correct, it does not help us because the wall temperature is not known. The other boundary condition concerns continuity of heat flux. Refer to eq. 3.10. The wall–fluid boundary is fixed, and hence its velocity is zero. Take the unit normal to be $\boldsymbol{\delta}_r$. There is no mass flux across the interface, and and all other effects like radiation influx, heat released due to surface reactions, *etc.* are absent. Thus, the boundary condition reduces to

$$(\mathbf{q}^{\mathbf{II}} - \mathbf{q}^{\mathbf{I}}).\boldsymbol{\delta}_r = 0$$

However, $-\mathbf{q}^{\mathbf{I}}.\boldsymbol{\delta}_r$ is the heat supplied *to* the wall, q_w. The boundary condition then reduces to

$$k\frac{\partial T}{\partial r} = q_w \qquad \text{at} \quad r{=}R,$$

$$\text{or} \quad \frac{\partial \theta}{\partial \xi} = 1 \qquad \text{at} \quad \xi{=}1 \tag{4.25}$$

4.4.8 Temperature profile

The partial differential equation, eq. 4.22 can be solved by using separation of variables[11]. The whole solution is not of interest to us at the present, and so we give a quick outline to justify the special solution which is the focus here. Let us assume

$$\theta = \chi(\zeta)\Xi(\xi) + \mathcal{F}(\zeta) + \mathcal{R}(\xi)$$

After substituting the assumed solution and separating variables, we will obtain:

$$\frac{d\mathcal{F}}{d\zeta} = \frac{1}{2(1-\xi^2)}\frac{1}{\xi}\frac{d}{d\xi}\left(\xi\frac{d\mathcal{R}}{d\xi}\right)$$

$$\frac{1}{\chi}\frac{d\chi}{d\zeta} = \frac{1}{2(1-\xi^2)}\frac{1}{\Xi}\frac{1}{\xi}\frac{d}{d\xi}\left(\xi\frac{d\Xi}{d\xi}\right)$$

As the left hand side of both equations is a function of only ζ while the right hand side is a function of only ξ, both must be equal to a constant. Let the constant in the first equation be β, while that in the second is λ. Then

$$\mathcal{F} = \beta\zeta$$

and

$$\mathcal{R} = 2\beta\left(\frac{\xi^2}{4} - \frac{\xi^4}{16}\right) + C_1 \ln\xi + C_2$$

From the second equation

$$\chi \sim e^{\lambda\zeta}$$

However, as heat is being supplied at a constant rate, the temperature might be expected to increase linearly but we do not expect the temperature to blow up *exponentially*. Thus, λ has to be negative, which is conveniently rewritten as $-\lambda^2$. Thus, the total solution can be written as a sum of solutions:

$$\theta = \beta\zeta + \mathcal{R} + e^{-\lambda^2\zeta}\Xi(\lambda, \xi)$$

Recall that the formulation of the problem focused at large lengths into the pipe. Under those conditions, the last term decays to zero leaving only the first two terms.

$$\theta = \beta\zeta + 2\beta\left(\frac{\xi^2}{4} - \frac{\xi^4}{16}\right) + C_1 \ln\xi + C_2$$

The boundary conditions have to be used to determine the various constants. The boundary condition at the center of the tube implies that C_1 is zero. The boundary condition at the wall gives $\beta = 2$. A problem occurs in implementing the boundary condition at $\zeta = 0$. It is easily found that the above solution cannot satisfy the boundary condition at $\zeta = 0$. The above solution represents the form in the limit of large lengths, and it does make sense that the boundary condition is not satisfied by it. Thus, in order to incorporate the boundary condition, an integral form of heat balance is used. The total heat supplied into the tube *from the beginning*[12] *up to some length*, should be carried outward by the fluid at that location. This is same as heat balance over the control volume shown by dotted line in figure 4.4. After noting that we have neglected axial conduction, the heat balance gives

$$2\pi Rzq_w = 2V\int_0^{2\pi}\int_0^{R}\rho\hat{C}_p\left(1 - \frac{r^2}{R^2}\right)(T - T_i)rdrd\phi$$

In non-dimensional form, this reduces to

$$\zeta = 2\int_0^1 \theta(1-\xi^2)\xi d\xi \tag{4.26}$$

in view of the axisymmetry. This condition can be used to determine C_2.

The final solution is found to be

$$\theta = 2\zeta + \xi^2 - \frac{\xi^4}{4} - \frac{7}{24} \tag{4.27}$$

This is exact in the limit $\zeta \to \infty$. Surprisingly, as Bird *et al.* [1] note, it is accurate to 2% for $\zeta > 0.1$! Usually, limiting solutions are good, even when the limit is far away! This is yet another reason to attempt to find limiting solutions.

4.4.9 Look at the results

The temperature profile obtained does make intuitive sense. The temperature of the fluid increases above the its inlet temperature proportionately to the increase in wall flux. The temperature of the fluid is expected to rise *linearly* along the length of the tube as heat is being supplied at a constant rate and the residence time of fluid increases linearly with length. However, no one could have guessed that this is valid at *every radial position*. This is also a gain from the solution. The radial gradients decrease as conductivity increases. This is to be expected because heat flux is a constant. The solution also implies that the wall temperature increases along the length of the tube. This was also expected. As the fluid gets heated, its temperature rises. Thus, to supply heat at a constant rate, as dictated by the boundary condition, the wall temperature also has to rise.

This example has to be studied carefully. Ideas regarding heat balances in the context of convection, the coupling between fluid mechanics and heat balances, the approximations made to effect decoupling, and evaluation of heat transfer coefficient have been illustrated in this example. Heat transfer coefficient plays the same role as friction factor does in fluid mechanics. It is sufficient to know only the heat transfer coefficient to tackle problems in the manner of Unit Operations. The example here illustrates that, in some cases at least, heat transfer coefficient itself can be *calculated.* Often temperature profiles are also required. Unit Operations approach cannot provide such information. The example considered shows that with the fundamental approach, such information can also be obtained.

4.4.10 Bulk temperature

The bulk temperature is easily calculated by using the definition:

$$T_b - T_i = \frac{2V\displaystyle\int_0^{2\pi}\int_0^R \rho\hat{C}_p\left(1-\frac{r^2}{R^2}\right)(T-T_i)rdrd\phi}{2V\displaystyle\int_0^{2\pi}\int_0^R \rho\hat{C}_p\left(1-\frac{r^2}{R^2}\right)rdrd\phi}$$

where T_i has been used as the reference temperature. The denominator is equal to the mass flow rate multiplied by the specific heat. The numerator, according to the integral boundary condition just derived, is equal to $2\pi Rzq_w$. After substituting all these into the equation defining the bulk temperature, it is found that

$$T_b - T_i = 2\frac{q_w R}{k}\zeta$$

As expected, this shows that the bulk temperature increases *linearly* with the length of the tube.

4.4.11 Heat transfer coefficient

It has been mentioned earlier that the results of the temperature profiles are summarized in the form of heat transfer coefficient. The heat transfer coefficient is defined as

$$q_w = h\left[T(R,z) - T_b(z)\right]$$

But from the temperature profiles,

$$T(R,z) - T_i = \frac{q_w R}{k}\theta(\xi = 1) = \frac{q_w R}{k}\left(2\zeta + \frac{11}{24}\right)$$

Substituting this equation and the equation for the bulk temperature into the defining equation, it is found that

$$\frac{hd}{k} = \frac{48}{11}$$

where d is the diameter of the tube. The group

$$\frac{hd}{k}$$

is the well known Nusselt number. We draw your attention to the fact that the Nusselt number and hence the heat transfer coefficient is a constant. This idea is discussed in detail later. It turns out that this is the property of *fully developed temperature profiles.* Note in particular that Nusselt number is not a function of Reynolds number.

4.5 CONVECTIVE HEAT TRANSFER TO SLABS

We have mentioned that if heat transfer coefficient is given, problems involving convective heat transfer can be calculated without needing any more information. Let us illustrate this by returning to the problem of heat transfer to slabs in series. Refer to figure 4.1. Let a fluid at a bulk temperature of T_o flow at a fast rate parallel to the face $ACGE$. Similarly let another fluid at a bulk temperature of T_e flow at a fast rate parallel to the face $BDHF$. This is equivalent to flow of air past the inside and outside surfaces of the walls of a room. The fluids will gain or lose heat and their temperature should change as they flow past the surface. But if the flow rate is sufficiently large, the temperature of the fluid will not change significantly. The earlier solution to this problem indicates that the heat flux through the slabs can be calculated once the surface temperatures are known. The first thought that comes to our mind is that a shell balance in the fluid has to be made and coupled to heat transfer in the solids to determine the required surface temperatures. However, the heat transfer coefficient neatly contains *all* the information needed for calculating the heat fluxes, and that permits us to bypass the shell balance in the fluid. Let us illustrate this, which of course is already well known to you!

The possible boundary conditions at $x = 0$ are the temperature continuity and flux continuity. The former cannot be implemented because only the *bulk* temperature of the fluid is known. Thus, we can try the flux continuity and it reads

$$q_x = h_\alpha(T_o - T_\alpha) = -k_\alpha \frac{dT_\alpha}{dx}, \quad \text{at} \quad x{=}0$$

Similar boundary condition is written at the other face:

$$q_x = h_\gamma(T_\gamma - T_e) = -k_\gamma \frac{dT_\gamma}{dx}, \quad \text{at} \quad x{=}X_3$$

The problem can now be solved. The solution is well known, and is given by

$$\frac{T_o - T_\alpha}{T_o - T_e} = \frac{1}{Rh_\alpha} + \frac{1}{R}\frac{X_1}{k_\alpha}\frac{x}{X_1} \qquad \text{for} \quad 0 \leq x \leq X_1$$

$$\frac{T_o - T_\beta}{T_o - T_e} = \frac{1}{Rh_\alpha} + \frac{1}{R}\frac{X_1}{k_\alpha} + \frac{1}{R}\frac{X_2 - X_1}{k_\beta}\frac{x - X_1}{X_2 - X_1} \qquad \text{for} \quad X_1 \leq x \leq X_2$$

$$\frac{T_o - T_\gamma}{T_o - T_e} = \frac{1}{Rh_\alpha} + \frac{1}{R}\frac{X_1}{k_\alpha} + \frac{1}{R}\frac{X_2 - X_1}{k_\beta} + \frac{1}{R}\frac{X_3 - X_2}{k_\gamma}\frac{x - X_2}{X_3 - X_2} \qquad \text{for} \quad X_2 \leq x \leq X_3$$

where

$$R = \frac{1}{h_\alpha} + \frac{X_1}{k_\alpha} + \frac{X_2 - X_1}{k_\beta} + \frac{X_3 - X_2}{k_\gamma} + \frac{1}{h_\gamma}$$

4.5.1 Look at the results

Two new resistances have arisen, one each due to the resistance offered by *convecting* fluid. The resistance offered by convection to heat transfer is given by the inverse of heat transfer coefficient. Thus, two new dimensionless groups will emerge. These will evolve out of the boundary conditions at the two phases. Without going into details, it is easy to see that these are given by $h_\alpha X_1/k_\alpha$ and $h_\gamma X_1/k_\gamma$. These are called *Biot numbers*. They reflect a comparison between conduction resistance[13] to convection resistance. If heat transfer coefficient is large, the convection resistance is zero and the difference between the fluid temperature and the temperature of the solid surface adjoining the fluid vanishes.

The main point we wanted to illustrate is that all the vital information about fluid and convection in it is contained in the heat transfer coefficient. Once it is known, the equations for the fluid phase can be ignored as far as heat flux calculations are concerned.

4.6 HEAT REMOVAL FROM A BEARING

Bearings float on a fluid film and their carrying capacity depends upon viscosity, and the gap between the rotor and stator. The fluid mechanics of these films is referred to as *lubrication* theory.

Usually gaps are small, the fluids used are viscous, and the work done to overcome the friction to keep the rotor moving is large. The work done is dissipated as heat in the fluid, and is referred to as *viscous dissipation*. If it is large, there could be a large variation in the temperature and hence viscosity. Thus, the carrying capacity of the bearing could be effected by the temperature distribution. In the example to be considered, the density and viscosity are assumed to be constant to make an estimate of the maximum temperature in the bearing. It gives an idea of the kind of effects one can expect, and whether it is necessary to account for viscous heat generation in various cases. A more exact solution of course is required where it is important to account for viscous dissipation as well as property variation. We consider an axle rotating in a circular housing. The gap between them is filled with the lubricating fluid. The axle is slightly eccentric with respect to the housing when it rotates in order to support the weight on the axle. But for the purposes of the present analysis, where heat transfer is the focus, it is assumed that the axle and the housing are concentric.

4.6.1 Problem identification

Consider a concentric set of cylinders. The gap between them is filled with a Newtonian fluid. The gap is small compared to the radius of the cylinders. The outer cylinder is stationary while the inner one rotates at a constant speed. Though the speed of rotation may be large, the gaps are small. Due to this, the flow can be assumed to be laminar. Let the outer cylinder be maintained at a constant temperature T_1. Let us also assume that the inner cylinder is being maintained at a constant temperature T_o. The objective is to calculate the maximum temperature produced in the fluid at steady state.

Simplifications and approximations

To keep the analysis simple, we neglect the small variation in temperature and velocities in the axial direction. This would be valid if the length of the cylinder is large compared to the radius. All quantities, namely temperatures and velocities, are being maintained constant on the surfaces of the cylinders. Hence, we expect variation in the fluid only in the radial direction, or axisymmetry can be expected to prevail. The flow is given to be laminar and hence v_θ is the only non-zero component of the velocity. Thus,

$$v_\theta = v_\theta(r) \quad \text{and} \quad T = T(r)$$

In the spirit of obtaining the first approximation, all physical properties are assumed to be independent of temperature. This decouples the fluid mechanics problem from the heat transfer problem, and the velocity profile can be determined immediately.

Velocity profile

The velocity profile for this geometry can be obtained by solving the equation of motion. Interested readers can look this up in the text by Bird *et al.* [1]. If the gap is small, as in bearings, the velocity profile is nearly linear:

$$v_\theta = \lambda\omega\frac{R-r}{1-\lambda}$$

where ω is the rotational velocity of the inner cylinder, and λ is the ratio of the radii of inner and outer cylinders.

The annular geometry can be replaced by a parallel plate geometry, if the gap is small. This is shown in figure 4.6. Cartesian coordinates can then be used. Thus, the radial direction can coincide with one of the coordinates, say x. The angular direction coincides with another coordinate, say y. The z coordinate coincides with the axial direction of the concentric cylinders. The control volume

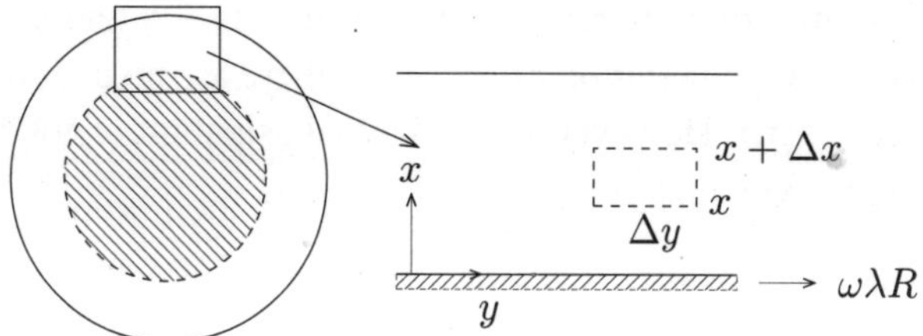

Figure 4.6. Coordinate system and geometry for the bearing and control volume.

is shown in figure 4.6. Thus

$$x = r - \lambda R$$

The angular rotational velocity becomes the y component of the velocity and the velocity at the inner cylinder is now written as:

$$v_y = \omega\lambda R \text{ at } x = 0$$

This problem is now identical to Couette flow, and the velocity profile is given by

$$v_y = \omega\lambda R\left[1 - \frac{x}{R(1-\lambda)}\right]$$

In cylindrical coordinates, axial symmetry implied that all variables like temperature, and velocity are independent of θ, the angular coordinate. An important thing here is to translate this condition also into Cartesian coordinates. It is easy to see that this condition is equivalent to

$$\frac{\partial}{\partial y} = 0$$

4.6.2 Heat balance

The control volume has four surfaces: two each perpendicular to the x and y axes. Convection is only in the y direction. The net rate of input of enthalpy by convection through the surfaces perpendicular to the y surface is given by

$$\left(\rho\hat{H}v_y\Delta x\right)\Big|_y - \left(\rho\hat{H}v_y\Delta x\right)\Big|_{y+\Delta y}$$

This can be written in terms of temperature as discussed in the previous section:

$$\left(\rho\hat{C}_pTv_y\Delta x\right)\Big|_y - \left(\rho\hat{C}_pTv_y\Delta x\right)\Big|_{y+\Delta y}$$

y direction is same as the angular direction. Because of axisymmetry, there is no variation in the angular direction. Therefore, there is no variation in y direction, and the above sum is equal to zero. The heat flux through the y surfaces can also be by conduction while that through the x surface is only by conduction. Thus, The net rate of input of heat by conduction through the control surfaces is given by

$$(q_y \Delta y)|_y - (q_y \Delta x)|_{y+\Delta y} + (q_x \Delta y)|_x - (q_x \Delta y)|_{x+\Delta x}$$

Once again, as there is no variation with respect to y, the terms at y and $y + \Delta y$ are equal.

As stated earlier, effects due to radiation are absent. There are no chemical reactions and so heat liberated due to that cause is zero. However, the viscous dissipation is not zero. The rate of viscous dissipation per unit volume is given by

$$\boldsymbol{\tau}:\nabla \mathbf{v}$$

For this example, it is equal to

$$\tau_{xy} \frac{dv_y}{dx}$$

The fluid is Newtonian. Thus, the above is equal to

$$\mu \left(\frac{dv_y}{dx} \right)^2 = \mu \left(\frac{\omega \lambda}{1 - \lambda} \right)^2$$

Thus, the rate of viscous heat dissipation in the control volume is obtained by multiplying the above by $\Delta x \Delta y$.

All these results are substituted into the heat balance, and the limit of the resulting equation, after dividing by $\Delta x \Delta y$ is evaluated as $\Delta x \Delta y$ tends to zero. The result is

$$0 = -\frac{dq_x}{dx} + \mu \left(\frac{\omega \lambda}{1 - \lambda} \right)^2$$

4.6.3 Combining rate law with heat balance

The conductive heat flux is given by the Fourier's law of heat conduction. When it is substituted into the heat balance, the following equation is obtained for determining the radial variation of temperature

$$0 = k \frac{d^2 T}{dx^2} + \mu \left(\frac{\omega \lambda}{1 - \lambda} \right)^2$$

where the thermal conductivity has also been assumed to be independent of temperature.

The above equation is easily interpreted. The first term represents the net heat flux out from a small volume and the second is the heat generated by viscous dissipation, both per unit volume basis. The two balance each other. This suggests that temperature profile will remain unaltered because generation is balancing the out flux. Thus, even in a rectangular channel, it is possible that the temperature profile will remain unaltered *in the flow direction*, after some distance downstream, if the heat generated can be conducted away through the walls.

4.6.4 Boundary conditions

The temperature is being maintained constant at the boundaries of both the cylinders. Thus,

$$T = T_o \quad \text{at} \quad x = 0$$
$$T = T_1 \quad \text{at} \quad x = (1-\lambda)R$$

4.6.5 Scaling

The x coordinate can obviously be scaled with $(1-\lambda)R$. A characteristic temperature difference is available in this problem: $(T_1 - T_o)$. Thus, the following non-dimensional variables can be defined

$$\xi = \frac{x}{(1-\lambda)R}, \qquad \theta = \frac{T - T_o}{T_1 - T_o}$$

The non-dimensional differential equation is then given by

$$\frac{d^2\theta}{d\xi^2} + Br = 0 \tag{4.28}$$

where Br is known as the *Brinkman* number and is given by

$$Br = \frac{(1-\lambda)^2 R^2}{k(T_1 - T_o)}\mu\left(\frac{\omega\lambda}{1-\lambda}\right)^2 = \frac{\mu(\lambda R\omega)^2}{k(T_1 - T_o)}$$

The factor

$$\frac{(1-\lambda)R^2}{k}\mu\left(\frac{\omega\lambda}{1-\lambda}\right)^2$$

can be thought of as the temperature difference that is *required* to lose the heat generated through the walls. Hence, Brinkman number is the ratio of the temperature difference required to remove the dissipation to that available. If Brinkman number is small, viscous dissipation is small and the available temperature difference is enough to remove the heat generated. Thus, there will be little temperature rise above T_1 or T_o in the bearing. Viewed differently, the heat flux created by the imposed temperature difference is much larger than the heat generated by viscous dissipation. Under these conditions, the problem reduces to that of heat conduction in a slab and the temperature profile is linear. If the rate of viscous dissipation is large, the available driving force or temperature difference is not enough to remove the heat generated, and the fluid temperature will have to increase. Thus, large viscous dissipation will increase the temperature beyond larger of the two temperatures T_1 and T_o. Thus, Brinkman number is an estimate of the rise in fluid temperature one can expect due to viscous heat dissipation.

4.6.6 Temperature profiles

The solution of the above equation with the boundary conditions is given by

$$\theta = \frac{Br}{2}\xi(1-\xi) + \xi \tag{4.29}$$

If $Br << 1$, the source term is zero, the quadratic part of the solution is insignificant and the linear part is the solution. In other words, the only heat flux is due to conduction. The maximum temperature is given by

$$\theta_{max} = \frac{Br}{2}\left(\frac{1}{4} - \frac{1}{Br^2}\right) + \frac{1}{2} + \frac{1}{Br}$$

It occurs at

$$\xi = \frac{1}{2} + \frac{1}{Br}$$

There will not be a maximum if $\xi > 1$, which can happen only if Br is small. For large values of Br the maximum occurs at the middle since the maximum temperature will be much larger than the temperature of either wall. An estimate of the maximum temperature produced at large Br is $Br/8$, a tenth of the Brinkman number.

4.6.7 Look at results

The effects due to viscous dissipation should increase with increasing viscosity and rotational speed, and decrease with increasing thermal conductivity and gap between the cylinders. The Brinkman number has all these characteristics. The maximum in the temperature increases with increasing Brinkman number confirming all our expectations. If viscous dissipation is very large, $Br >> 1$, the conduction term is insignificant. Then equal heat is lost through both the walls, and the maximum in the temperature occurs in the middle. This is confirmed by the equation for the maximum temperature.

4.7 FULLY DEVELOPED TEMPERATURE PROFILE

In the previous section, we found that temperature itself does not change in the flow direction even though heat is being generated. It is because heat generated was balanced by conduction. It is reminiscent of fully developed velocity profiles. We have mentioned earlier that applied forces can be thought of generators of momentum. Velocity profile becomes fully developed, *i.e.,* does not change in the direction of flow, when the momentum generated is balanced by conduction of momentum by viscous action. It naturally raises questions regarding possibility of temperature profiles becoming fully developed. However, convective heat transfer problems exhibit a more complex pattern depending on the geometry and boundary conditions.

Let us reconsider the problem on convective heat transfer of the previous section. Heat is being supplied at a constant rate and we can ask "is it possible for the temperature profile to become fully developed?" However, as the geometry is circular, it is seen that heat supplied can not be removed at some other wall, *i.e.*, heat supplied cannot be removed by conduction. However, there are other interesting features of temperature profiles which permit an extended definition of a fully developed temperature profile. We found in the previous section that

$$T_b - T_i = 2\frac{q_w R}{k}\zeta$$

and that

$$\theta = \frac{k(T - T_i)}{Rq_w} = 2\zeta + \xi^2 - \frac{\xi^4}{4} - \frac{7}{24}$$

Combining the two, we find that

$$k\frac{T - T_b}{Rq_w} \sim \xi^2 - \frac{\xi^4}{4}$$

which does not change in the flow direction. Thus, we can define a non-dimensional *temperature profile*, that does not change in the flow direction. This is a useful concept, reminiscent of the fully developed velocity profile.

Consider heating of a fluid flowing in a duct. A non-dimensional temperature can be defined as follows:

$$\theta = \frac{T - T_w}{T_b - T_w}$$

where T_w is the temperature of the wall of the duct, *which need not be a constant*. This definition is like the non-dimensional velocity in a tube. T_b and T_w are similar to the average velocity, and velocity at the wall, respectively. Thus, we can define the **temperature profile to be fully developed** for a flow in z direction if

$$\frac{\partial \theta}{\partial z} = 0$$

We leave it to you to get the same results for Nusselt number if you follow this approach in the convection problem considered in the previous section.

If the flow is fully developed, friction factors do not depend upon the flow direction. By analogy it is easy to show that if the temperature profiles are fully developed heat transfer coefficients also do not vary in the direction of flow. This is the case in most practical applications. For example, correlations for Nusselt number in turbulent flow indicate that it depends only on Reynolds number and Prandtl number, and do not vary in the direction of flow. However, there will be exceptions too, *e.g.* flow in short dies which are used to extrude polymers.

Problems for Chapter 4.

4.1 A liquid at its melting point T_m is brought in contact with a large mass of a highly conducting solid at $T_o < T_m$. a) Plot the expected temperature profile as a function of distance and time?

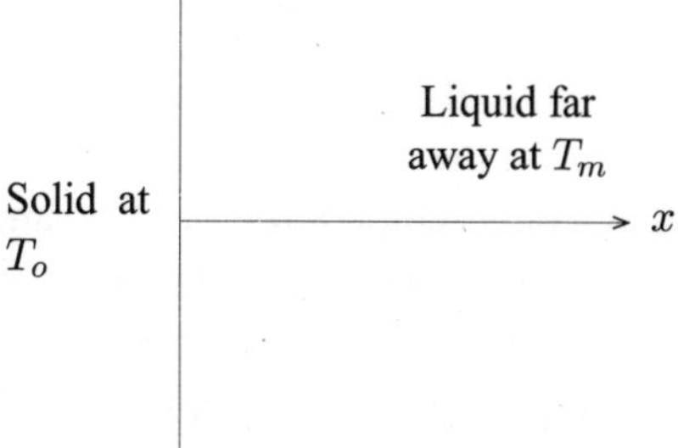

Figure for problem 4.1.

b) What is the jump boundary condition at the liquid-solid boundary? c) If $T_m - T_o$ is small, the rate of freezing will be low. Under those conditions the temperature profiles in the solid can be assumed to be linear. Obtain a simple expression for the rate of freezing.

4.2 If we tried to use simple minded selection of variables to apply conventional dimensional analysis, we might have chosen one of the temperatures. Suppose the quantity of interest is the heat flux through slabs in series. Use the Buckingham's π theorem and find the dimensionless groups. Compare this with the result we have in the chapter.

4.3 Infinitely long bars of rectangular cross section of two solid materials A and B are in perfect contact with each other as shown in the figure. The thermal conductivities of the two materials are constant and denoted by k_A and k_B. The surfaces at $x = 0$ and $x = L$ are maintained at T_1 and T_2. The surfaces at $y = W_A$ and $y = -W_B$ are insulated. Under steady conditions: a) Is the temperature a function of x only or of both x and y? Does this depend upon whether the thickness of the solids A and B are the same or not? b) Specify the boundary conditions. c) Determine the temperature profiles and the rate of heat transfer.

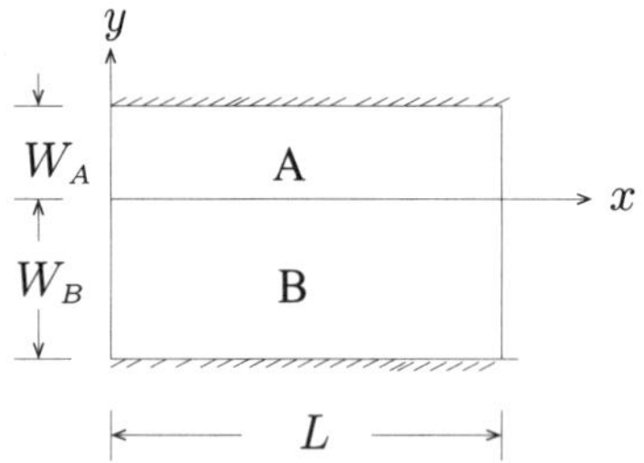

Figure for problem 4.3.

4.4 An infinitely long bar shown in the figure has the following properties: $\rho = 3000\ kg/m^3$, C_p

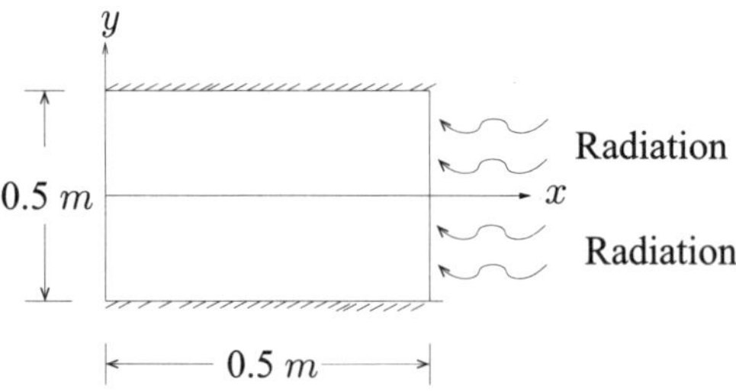

Figure for problem 4.4.

$= 1\ kJ/(kg\,C)$, $k = 300\ W/(m\,C)$. It absorbs all the radiative flux falling on its surface at $x = 0.5\ m$ (shown by curly arrows) at the rate of 500 w/m^2. Further, the surface at $x = 0.5\ m$ is exposed to a flowing liquid at a bulk temperature of 50°C and with a heat transfer coefficient of $h = 50\ W/(m^2\,°C)$. The face at $x = 0$ is exposed to a flowing fluid at 100 C and with a heat transfer coefficient of $h = 100\ W/(m^2\,°C)$. The surfaces at $y \pm 0.25\,m$ are insulated. Under steady conditions, in which direction is the heat flowing in the solid, $+x$ or $-x$? Calculate the heat flux at the $x = 0$ face.

4.5 We are interested in finding the *steady* temperature profiles in a body of trapezoidal cross section shown in the figure. The body extends to infinity in the z direction. The surfaces at $x = 0$ and $x = L$ are maintained at constant temperatures T_o and T_1, respectively. The other surfaces are insulated. (i) *Assume* that temperature is *not* a function of y. *Choose an appropriate control volume* and make a shell thermal energy balance to derive the relevant differential equation for temperature. Specify the boundary conditions needed. Solve the equation and find the temperature profile. (ii) Is it correct to assume that temperature is not a function of y? Specify the *exact* boundary condition on the insulated surface.

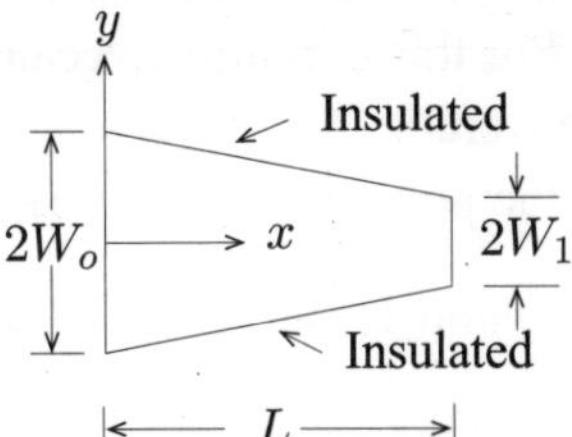

Figure for problem 4.5.

4.6 A very long nuclear fuel element is shaped in the form of a very thick walled tube. A fluid

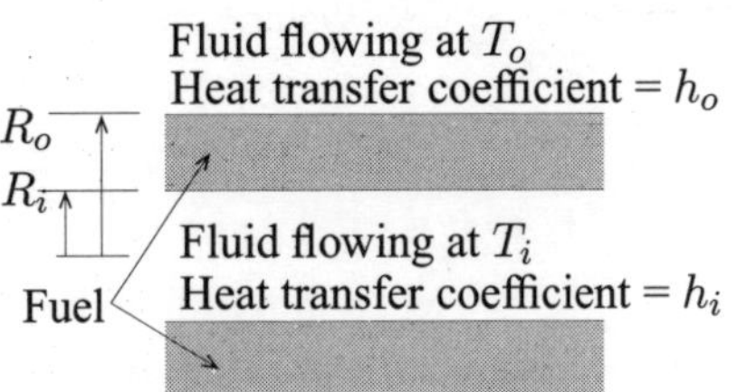

Figure for problem 4.6.

at constant temperature T_i is flowing through the inner tubular space, and the heat transfer coefficient is h_i. Another fluid at constant temperature T_o is flowing over the outer side of the fuel element, and the heat transfer coefficient is h_o. Heat is generated inside the fuel and it is given that $\hat{q}_G = A/r$. (i) Make a shell balance to derive the thermal energy balance equation for finding the steady state temperature profile in the fuel element. The thermal conductivity of the fuel can be denoted by k. (ii) Specify the boundary conditions. (iii) Find the temperature profile.

4.7 **Heat Recovery from a Solar Pond**: A solar pond is a large lake of water. The bottom of the lake is made of a black surface so as to absorb all the radiation that falls on it. Sun's radiation falls on the surface of water, and passes through the body of water and is absorbed at the bottom. Very little of the Sun's radiation is absorbed in the body of water itself. At the bottom of the lake and beneath the black surface, provision is made to remove heat. The sides of the pond are insulated and can be assumed to lose little heat. However, the pond loses heat from the top surface of water by natural convection. Suppose that the radiant heat flux from Sun reaching the surface of the pond is given by 800 w/m^2. Consider a pond 3 m in depth.

a) The heat transfer coefficient for natural convection through the top surface of water is equal to 10 $w/(m^2\,K)$ (a reasonable value for natural convection to gases). Assume that the water in the pond is stagnant. The thermal conductivity of water is equal to 0.6 $w/(m\,K)$. If the bottom is being maintained at 90°C and the ambient temperature is 27°C, how much of the radiant energy is being recovered?
b) Is it reasonable to assume that the water in the pond will be stationary, and that there will be no convective heat transfer from the bottom surface and water?
c) Suppose that the pond becomes 'unstable' and the heat transfer coefficient from the bottom surface to water is 60 $W/(m^2\,K)$ (a reasonable value for turbulent natural convection heat transfer coefficient in liquids). For this condition, recalculate the temperature attained by the bottom surface and the heat recovered.
d) What are the ways in which the pond can be stabilized?

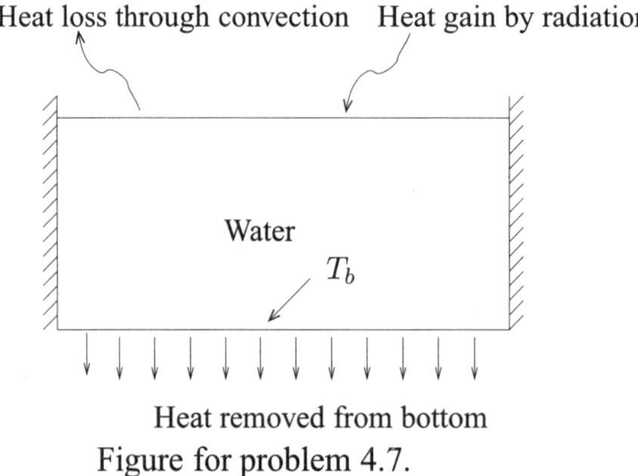

Figure for problem 4.7.

4.8 a) Consider a circular rod being used as a fin. The radius of the rod is R while its length is L. The heat transfer coefficient between the fin and the ambient is h. Suppose the thermal conductivity of the rod is infinitely large. Make suitable shell balance and derive an expression for the rate of loss of heat from the entire fin. A fin with infinite thermal conductivity is referred to as an **ideal fin**.
b) Even when the fin has finite thermal conductivity, the resistance to heat transfer in the

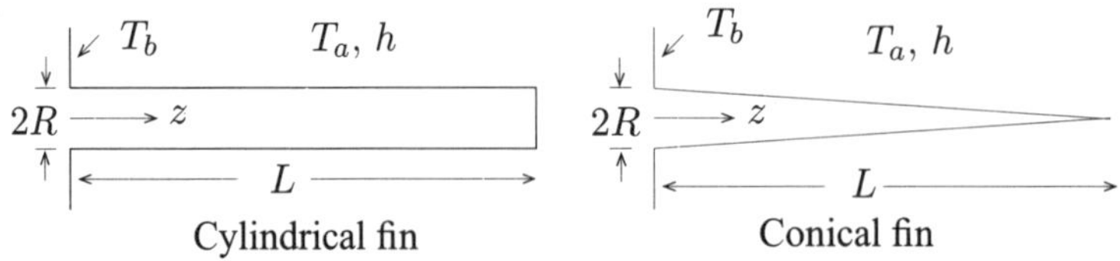

Figure for problem 4.8.

radial direction is usually dominated by the film. *Thus, the radial gradients in the fin are negligible.* This is a *one-dimensional approximation.* Make suitable shell balance and derive an expression for the rate of loss of heat from the entire fin. Fin efficiency is defined as the ratio of the rate of heat loss in the fin to the rate of heat loss from an ideal fin. Derive an

expression for the fin efficiency.
c) Suppose we use a cone of length L with the base radius being equal to R in place of the rod. Derive an expression for the fin efficiency. This leads to Bessel equation, and you might refer to the text *Applied Mathematics in Chemical Engineering* by Mickley, Sherwood and Reid or any other book.
d) Which of the two shapes is better per unit weight of the fin?

4.9 A cylindrical fin of diameter D is made of two materials. The two pieces are of the same length. The thermal conductivities of the two materials are k_1 and k_2. The fin is attached to a hot surface maintained at a temperature of T_o. The fin loses heat to the surroundings at a temperature of T_a and the heat transfer coefficient is given by h. Heat loss at circular surface at the end of the second piece is negligible. *In the following use one-dimensional approximation for the fin.* (i) What are the simplified energy equations for the fin? What are the boundary conditions? Solve these to derive an expression for heat loss through the fin. (ii) To obtain **greater** fin efficiency, which material should be put near the hot surface: one with greater conductivity or smaller conductivity? Give reasons.

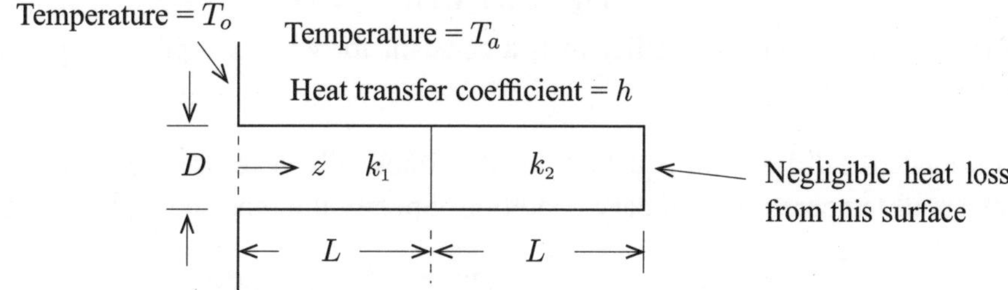

Figure for problem 4.9.

4.10 Sun is very hot because of thermonuclear reactions taking place inside. We wish to calculate the temperature at Sun's surface by treating him as a sphere with heat generation inside. We will assume that Sun is at steady state. (This is not correct because it is going to die. But don't worry since it will live for another 5 billion years.)

Assume that heat transfer occurs inside the Sun by only **conduction**. (Of course it is a bad assumption as there are other mechanisms of heat transfer.) The thermal conductivity (k) however is a very strong function of temperature. This dependence can be approximated by treating k as a function of radial position (r) inside the Sun: $k = 1.5 \times 10^7 (R^2/r^2)$, $W/(m°C)$. Here R is the radius of the Sun and is equal to $7 \times 10^8 m$.

The heat generation is also a function of temperature and it also can be approximated by treating it as a function of radial position: $\dot{Q}_v = 0.1\,(R^2/r^2)$, W/m^3 (This is a cooked up value!). Sun loses heat from its surface by radiation to the outer space which can be assumed to be at 0 K. (a) Calculate the surface temperature of the Sun. (b) Simplify the energy equation inside the Sun. What are the boundary conditions? (c) Solve the equation and find the temperature at the center. The 'observed' value is 2×10^7K. Compare the calculated value with this and give your comments.

4.11 A water vapor bubble is growing in an infinitely large pool of super-heated water. Denote the boiling point by T_B and that of the super-heated liquid far away from the bubble by T_∞. a) Show that if the liquid can be assumed to be of constant density, the velocity in the liquid (v_r) created due to the growth of the bubble is given by $r^2\, v_r \;=\; R^2\;\dot{R}$ where R is the radius of the bubble and $\dot{R}$ is the rate of growth of the bubble. b) For small values of super-heat $\Delta T \;=\; T_\infty \;-\; T_B$, the growth rate can be expected to be small and the processes can be analyzed by assuming *pseudo steady state* to prevail. For these conditions, make an appropriate shell balance find the temperature profile in the liquid. What will be the temperature profile in the bubble? Specify the boundary conditions. c) Solve the equations to find the heat transfer coefficient. d) Derive an expression for $\dot{R}$ in terms of $\Delta\, T$.

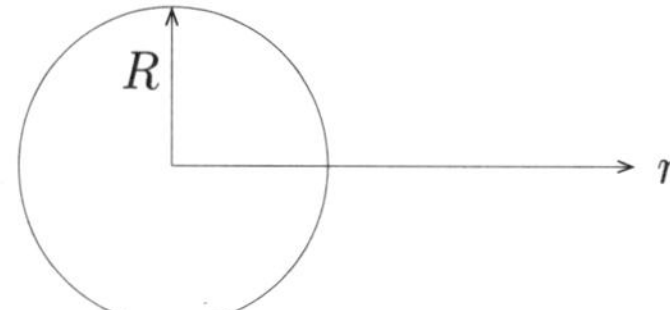

Figure for 4.11.

4.12 Show that heat transfer coefficient is a constant for when temperature profile is fully developed.

4.13 Formulate the differential equation that describes fully developed temperature profile for constant wall temperature boundary condition. Specify the other boundary conditions.

4.14 The velocity profile for fully developed laminar flow of a power-law fluid in a tube of circular cross section is given by

$$v_z(r) \;=\; \frac{1+3n}{1+n}V\left[1 \;-\; \left(\frac{r}{R}\right)^{1+\frac{1}{n}}\right]$$

where V is the average velocity. Derive the expression for Nusselt number for thermally fully developed conditions for constant wall heat flux boundary conditions.

4.15 Consider fully developed laminar flow of a Newtonian incompressible liquid in a tube of circular cross section. The wall temperature is maintained as a linearly increasing function of the axial distance. Consider the portion where thermally fully developed profile exists.

a) Derive a relationship between $\dfrac{dT_b}{dz}$ and $\dfrac{dT_w}{dz}$ where T_b is the bulk temperature.
b) Derive an expression for Nusselt number

4.16 A fluid is flowing between two infinitely wide parallel plates in the x direction. The two plates are separated by a distance b in the y direction. The velocity profile is fully developed and is given by $v_x = V\dfrac{y}{b}$. This is known as Couette flow.

i) The plate at $y = 0$ is receiving a constant heat flux q_w while the plate at $y = b$ is insulated. Calculate the Nusselt number if the temperature is fully developed.

ii) Determine the Nusselt number(s) if both walls are being supplied different but constant heat fluxes?

4.17 A fluid is flowing in an **insulated** cylindrical tube of radius R. The flow is fully developed and laminar. Heat is being generated in the tube at a constant rate per unit volume, $\dot{Q}_v$. Neglect heat generation by viscous dissipation.

i) Do you think that the temperature will be independent of r?

ii) Is it possible for the temperature profile to become fully developed?

4.18 Fermi is one of the great physicists of our times. He went to the hospital where his friend was recovering from a heart attack. (Story taken from *Physics Today*, page 43, June 2002.) His friend complained that he was being given too little to eat, 1500 calories per day. Fermi asked his friend "You are a great lover of detective stories. How long does it take for a corpse to cool to, say, a degree above room temperature?" His friend replied "About four hours." After some thought, Fermi concluded that his friend will not survive if he continued to get only that much food. Is he right?

4.19 Solve the problem of viscous dissipation but in cylindrical coordinates without assuming that the gap is small. The inner wall is stationary and its radius is κR while that of the outer wall is R. The outer wall rotates with an angular velocity of Ω. The velocity profile is given by

$$v_\theta(r) = \Omega R \frac{\kappa R/r - r/\kappa R}{\kappa - 1\kappa}$$

The formula for shear stress can be taken from the appendix at the end of the text. Further, implement the following change in boundary condition. The velocity profile is given by Consider that the inner cylinder is insulated. Define a suitable non-dimensional temperature. Define a Brinkman number. Interpret it.

Notes

[1]Science deals with complex universe. A complete description of it is perhaps impossible. The genius of a scientist lies in finding simplified and elegant versions but those that can also be solved. That is why science has been described by Medawar[2] as the 'Art of the soluble'.

[2]Heat and mass balances can be made in shells that use curvilinear coordinates since heat and mass are scalars. However, one must be careful in making shell balances on vector quantities, notably momentum, since unit vectors are not constant in curvilinear systems.

[3]If the layers are made of fluid, and if the direction of the temperature gradient is such that natural convection is not generated, results of this section will be applicable there also.

[4]As mentioned in section 3.3, a boundary condition can be imposed only on physically accessible boundaries. In this problem, these are the ends of the stack of the slabs. The other boundaries are internal boundaries.

[5]We are graduating to higher levels! Instead of starred English letters for non-dimensional quantities, we have now gone to Greek. The latest trend is to use the same symbols after giving the scales. It does save a lot of trouble to printers, but often creates confusion.

[6]It might sound odd that we insulate while desiring to remove heat! The need may arise since it may be necessary to protect the cooling medium from exposure to very high temperature or for safety reasons, *e.g.* a nuclear reactor.

[7]Figuratively speaking of course, since we may need a big cup.

[8]The subscript w is being used since the most common interface is a solid wall.

[9]If the ratio is very large, the convective terms dominate radial conduction as well. However, if radial conduction is neglected, there is no heat transfer from the wall! Thus, our scaling of radius with R is wrong. This will be the issue dealt with in section 5.11 on heat transfer in entry zone and in section 6.2 on boundary layers.

[10]Remember that $k/\rho\hat{C}_p$ is the thermal diffusivity. We are jumping slightly ahead. But, this is apparent from dimensions of diffusivity, which are "length square per time". A keenly interested reader might refer to our discussion of Brownian motion in section 7.3.

[11]A brief summary of the method of separation of variables is given in the appendix to chapter 5.

[12]This is how the entry temperature enters the problem.

[13]A more 'physical' Biot number for the last slab would be $h_\gamma(X_3 - X_2)/k_\gamma$.

References

[1] R.B. Bird, W.E. Stewart, and E.N. Lightfoot. *Transport Phenomena.* John Wiley, 2 edition, 2002.

[2] P. B. Medawar. *The art of the soluble.* Basic books, 1967.

Chapter 5

CONSERVATION EQUATIONS FOR SINGLE COMPONENT SYSTEMS

```
The general form of conservation equations that predict
  temperature profiles are derived.
The use of these equations is demonstrated for conduction
  and convection problems. Calculation of temperature
  profiles in unsteady state and in developing flows are new.
```

So far we have dealt with finding temperature profiles in non-isothermal single component systems by making shell balances. Based on (your) past experience with fluid mechanics where Navier–Stokes equations were formulated, one will naturally expect that procedures of shell balances can be systematized, and equations applicable in general can be derived. These will be, like Navier–Stokes equations, partial differential equations. As explained in chapter 1, such partial differential equations will give information *at every point* of a volume of interest at *all times*, and so these are central to the transport phenomena approach. Derivation of the general balance equations is the topic of this chapter. Navier–Stokes equations are commonly derived by making a momentum balance over a *stationary* parallelepiped and applying the transport theorem for a stationary control volume. To break the monotony, and to show a different way, a slightly different procedure is followed here. In the new procedure, balances are made on a closed system itself. This gives rise to the general equations of thermal energy balance.

After deriving the enthalpy balance equation, we consider some examples of its solution. The general procedure is as follows. After examining the problem posed, we make some physically sound hypotheses regarding the variation of the dependent variable on the independent variables, *e.g.* steady state implies that variation with the independent variable time will be zero. These hypotheses are used to simplify the general balance equations. The problem is examined once again to specify the required and relevant boundary conditions. The simplified balance equations are solved along with the boundary conditions to determine the temperature profiles.

5.1 BALANCES ON A SYSTEM

Recall the transport theorem derived for a system:

$$\frac{d}{dt}\int_{V_s(t)} \phi(\mathbf{x},t) = \int_{V_s(t)} \frac{\partial \phi(\mathbf{x},t)}{\partial t} dV + \int_{A_s(t)} \mathbf{n.v}\phi(\mathbf{x},t)dA \tag{2.2}$$

The system moves through a fluid, and as it moves its properties change. The rate of change of any property is given by the transport theorem. Properties change due to some external actions. Its momentum would change since forces are acting on it. Similarly, the sum of its kinetic and internal energies change because of work done on it and heat supplied to it, and we turn to this now.

5.2 ENTHALPY BALANCE ON A SYSTEM

The basic steps in deriving the thermal enthalpy balance are the same as those followed in section 3.1. We briefly recall the earlier steps. First, we stated the first law of thermodynamics, modified to take into account the kinetic energy, as:

The rate of change in the internal energy plus the kinetic energy of a closed system is equal to the rate at which heat is supplied to it plus the rate at which work is done by the surroundings on it.

This was applied to a system to obtain:

$$\frac{d}{dt}\int_{V_s(t)} \rho(\hat{U}+\frac{1}{2}v^2)dV = \int_{V_s(t)} \dot{Q}_v\, dV - \int_{A_s(t)} \mathbf{n.q}dA + \int_{A_s(t)} \mathbf{n.}(-P\boldsymbol{I}+\boldsymbol{\tau})\mathbf{.v}dA + \int_{V_s(t)} \rho\mathbf{g.v}dV \tag{3.1}$$

For convenience, we want an equation separating the unsteady and convection effects. We do this by applying the transport theorem to the left hand side of equation, 3.1. This gives us the following integral form:

$$\int_{V_s(t)} \frac{\partial}{\partial t}\left(\rho\hat{U}+\frac{\rho}{2}v^2\right) dV + \int_{A_s(t)} \mathbf{n.v}\rho(\hat{U}+\frac{1}{2}v^2)dA =$$

$$\int_{V_s(t)} \dot{Q}_v\, dV - \int_{A_s(t)} \mathbf{n.q}dA + \int_{A_s(t)} \mathbf{n.}(-P\boldsymbol{I}+\boldsymbol{\tau})\mathbf{.v}dA + \int_{V_s(t)} \rho\mathbf{g.v}dV \tag{5.1}$$

As the focus is on thermal energy, the contributions from mechanical work and kinetic energy have to be removed from the above equation. Conversion of work into kinetic energy and *vice-versa* is related to the creation of velocity under the action of forces. The equation for kinetic energy can be derived by taking a dot product of the equation of motion with velocity. We derive the equation of motion in the appendix to this chapter. We show the derivation of *mechanical energy balance* equation also in the appendix. It is given by

$$\frac{\partial}{\partial t}\left(\frac{1}{2}\rho v^2\right) + \nabla\mathbf{.v}\left(\frac{1}{2}\rho v^2\right) = \rho\mathbf{g.v} - \nabla.P\mathbf{v} + p\nabla\mathbf{.v} + \nabla.\boldsymbol{\tau}\mathbf{.v} - \boldsymbol{\tau}:\nabla\mathbf{v} \tag{A5.32}$$

We want an integral form applicable to a system. We therefore integrate eq. A5.32 over the volume of the system to obtain

$$\int\limits_{V_s(t)} \frac{\partial}{\partial t}\left(\frac{1}{2}\rho v^2\right) dV + \int\limits_{A_s(t)} \mathbf{n.v}\frac{1}{2}\rho v^2 dA =$$

$$\int\limits_{V_s(t)} \rho\mathbf{g.v}dV - \int\limits_{A_s(t)} p\mathbf{n.v}dA + \int\limits_{A_s(t)} \mathbf{n.}\boldsymbol{\tau}\mathbf{.v}dA + \int\limits_{V_s(t)} P\nabla\mathbf{.v}dV - \int\limits_{V_s(t)} \boldsymbol{\tau}:\nabla\mathbf{v}dV \tag{3.2}$$

When eq. 3.2 is subtracted from eq. 5.1, which is representation of the first law of thermodynamics, the equation for the balance of internal energy can be obtained:

$$\int\limits_{V_s(t)} \frac{\partial}{\partial t}\rho\hat{U}dV + \int\limits_{A_s(t)} \mathbf{n.v}\rho\hat{U}dA = \int\limits_{V_s(t)} \dot{Q}_v\, dV - \int\limits_{A_s(t)} \mathbf{n.q}dA - \int\limits_{V_s(t)} P\nabla\mathbf{.v}dV + \int\limits_{V_s(t)} \boldsymbol{\tau}:\nabla\mathbf{v}dV \tag{5.2}$$

The internal energy is eliminated from eq. 5.2 in favour of enthalpy anticipating the convenience it offers for incompressible fluids. Definition of enthalpy was used earlier, and will be used now, for that purpose:

$$\hat{U} = \hat{H} - \frac{P}{\rho}$$

The equation in terms of enthalpy is obtained as:

$$\int\limits_{V_s(t)} \frac{\partial}{\partial t}\rho\hat{H}dV + \int\limits_{A_s(t)} \mathbf{n.v}\rho\hat{H}dA - \int\limits_{V_s(t)} \frac{\partial P}{\partial t}dV - \int\limits_{A_s(t)} \mathbf{n.v}PdA \tag{5.3}$$

$$= \int\limits_{V_s} \dot{Q}_v\, dV - \int\limits_{A_s} \mathbf{n.q}dA - \int\limits_{V_s(t)} P\nabla\mathbf{.v}dV + \int\limits_{V_s} \boldsymbol{\tau}:\nabla\mathbf{v}dV \tag{5.4}$$

This is the general enthalpy balance for a system. Now, we have to find a procedure to derive the general enthalpy balance equation applicable at every point.

5.2.1 Divergence theorem

We hope that this can be achieved if an equation valid over any arbitrary volume can be derived. To derive such an equation, we apply the divergence theorem to the integrals on the area of the system in eq. 5.4 to convert those into an integral over volume of the system. We then get

$$\int\limits_{V_s} \frac{\partial}{\partial t}(\rho\hat{H})dV + \int\limits_{V_s} \nabla.(\rho\mathbf{v}\hat{H})dV = \int\limits_{V_s} \dot{Q}_v\, dV - \int\limits_{A_s} \nabla\mathbf{.q}dA + \int\limits_{V_s} \frac{DP}{Dt}dV + \int\limits_{V_s} \boldsymbol{\tau}:\nabla\mathbf{v}dV$$

where we used the definition of the total or substantial derivative:

$$\frac{D}{Dt} = \frac{\partial}{\partial t} + \mathbf{v}.\nabla$$

Collecting all terms on one side, it can be rewritten as

$$\int_{V_s} dV \left(\frac{\partial}{\partial t}(\rho \hat{H}) + \nabla.(\rho \mathbf{v} \hat{H}) dV - \dot{Q}_v + \nabla.\mathbf{q} - \frac{DP}{Dt} - \boldsymbol{\tau}:\nabla \mathbf{v} \right) = 0 \tag{5.5}$$

5.3 APPLICATION TO ARBITRARY SYSTEM

Equation 5.5 suggests that the integral of sum of certain terms, collectively referred to as the integrand, should equal zero. The system that was selected was arbitrary. Suppose that initially system A occupying a volume V_{as} was selected. The integral of the integrand over V_{as} must be equal to zero. Suppose we selected initially a system which was a part of system A. Call it system B, and let its volume be V_{bs}. System B will be contained in system A. But the above equation says that the integral of the integrand over V_{bs} should also be zero. In other words, the integral is zero over a part of the volume V_{as}. The argument can be generalized and it can be argued that the integral must be zero over any *arbitrary* part of V_{as}. In fact, V_{as} itself is arbitrary. The only way the integral over any arbitrary part of any system is equal to zero is that the integrand itself be equal to zero or there exist a finite number of compensating discontinuities in the integrand. However, discontinuities are not expected *if we restrict ourselves to a control volume composed of a single phase*. Thus, the integrand must be equal to zero *everywhere*. In other words

$$\frac{\partial}{\partial t}(\rho \hat{H}) - \nabla.(\rho \mathbf{v} \hat{H}) - \dot{Q}_v + \nabla.\mathbf{q} - \frac{DP}{Dt} - \boldsymbol{\tau}:\nabla \mathbf{v} = 0$$

The equation can be rearranged to put it in the form of a conservation equation like the Cauchy's equation of motion:

$$\frac{\partial}{\partial t}(\rho \hat{H}) + \nabla.(\rho \mathbf{v} \hat{H}) = -\nabla.\mathbf{q} + \frac{DP}{Dt} + \boldsymbol{\tau}:\nabla \mathbf{v} + \dot{Q}_v$$

Left hand side of the above equation can be expressed as

$$\rho \frac{\partial \hat{H}}{\partial t} + \rho \mathbf{v}.\nabla \hat{H} + \hat{H} \left(\frac{\partial \rho}{\partial t} + \nabla.(\rho \mathbf{v}) \right)$$

But the last term is equal to zero by application of equation of continuity. The thermal energy balance can then be written as

$$\rho \frac{\partial \hat{H}}{\partial t} + \rho \mathbf{v}.\nabla \hat{H} = -\nabla.\mathbf{q} + \frac{DP}{Dt} + \boldsymbol{\tau}:\nabla \mathbf{v} + \dot{Q}_v$$

The right hand side is the substantial derivative of enthalpy. Thus, the equation can be written in compact form as

$$\rho \frac{D\hat{H}}{Dt} = -\nabla.\mathbf{q} + \frac{DP}{Dt} + \boldsymbol{\tau}:\nabla \mathbf{v} + \dot{Q}_v \tag{5.6}$$

The above equation is known as *differential enthalpy balance*.

5.4 EQUATION OF CHANGE OF TEMPERATURE

Let us recall that our original objective stated in chapter 1 was to predict the changes in temperature when various equipments are heated or cooled. This is because temperature is directly measurable while enthalpy is not. Hence, the differential enthalpy balance equation is more useful in terms of temperature. This was discussed in section 3.1. There it was shown that

$$d\hat{H} = \hat{C}_p dT + \frac{1}{\rho}\left[1 + \left(\frac{\partial \ln \rho}{\partial \ln T}\right)_P\right] dP \tag{3.7}$$

Substituting this relationship into the differential thermal balance, we get

$$\rho \hat{C}_p \frac{DT}{Dt} + \frac{DP}{Dt}\left(\frac{\partial \ln \rho}{\partial \ln T}\right)_p = -\nabla.\mathbf{q} + \boldsymbol{\tau}{:}\nabla\mathbf{v} + \dot{Q}_v$$

At this stage, the above equation is similar to the *Cauchy's equation of motion.*

5.4.1 Constitutive equation

The equation is still not entirely in terms of temperature. The heat flux vector has to be replaced by a suitable constitutive equation, in this case, Fourier's law of heat conduction. Substituting this, the final form is obtained:

$$\rho \hat{C}_p \frac{DT}{Dt} + \frac{DP}{Dt}\left(\frac{\partial \ln \rho}{\partial \ln T}\right)_p = \nabla.k\,\nabla T + \boldsymbol{\tau}{:}\nabla\mathbf{v} + \dot{Q}_v \tag{5.7}$$

This equation is *similar* to the Navier–Stokes equation. It is generally assumed that properties are constant, except where it is important to account for variation with temperature, *e.g.,* natural convection. Under such restrictive assumptions, the following widely used form of equation of change of temperature is obtained:

$$\rho \hat{C}_p \frac{DT}{Dt} = k\nabla^2 T + \boldsymbol{\tau}{:}\nabla\mathbf{v} + \dot{Q}_v \tag{5.8}$$

This equation is the analog of the Navier–Stokes equation and will be the most used in this text.

It is easy to interpret this equation. The left hand side is the rate of increase in the enthalpy content per unit volume as observed when moving with the fluid. Enthalpy increases due to net heat conducted into the volume, which is represented by the first term on the right hand side. The second term represents irreversible conversion of mechanical work due to friction into heat or viscous dissipation. The last term accounts for heat generated per unit volume per unit time by other causes.

5.5 BOUNDARY CONDITIONS

The boundary conditions have already been discussed earlier in section 3.4. Once again recall that the general balance equations are restricted to a single phase. Hence, boundaries are at the surfaces between homogeneous phases. The balance equations are applicable in each phase and the boundary conditions are applicable at the boundary. These are the continuity of temperature and heat fluxes. The heat flux continuity should in general include rate of heat generation *per unit area*, by any mechanism. Very common ones are by radiation, $\dot{Q}_{s,rad}$ and by reactions, $\dot{Q}_{s,rea}$. Consider the boundary between two phases I and II and let $\boldsymbol{\xi}$ be the normal pointing from phase II to phase I. See figure 3.2. As discussed earlier, the boundary conditions will be given by

$$T^I = T^{II} \tag{3.9}$$

$$(\mathbf{q}^{\mathbf{II}} - \mathbf{q}^{\mathbf{I}}).\boldsymbol{\xi} + \dot{Q}_{s,rad} + \dot{Q}_{s,rea} = \dot{m}_b\,(\hat{H}^I - \hat{H}^{II}) \tag{3.10}$$

where $\dot{m}_b$ is the net mass transferred from phase II to phase I.

5.6 COORDINATE SYSTEMS

The equation of change of temperature and the boundary conditions are equations that involve vector operators. The components of the gradient and divergence operators are needed to solve those equations. It is likely that different coordinate systems are used to solve the equations, *e.g.* we used cylindrical coordinates in section 4.2. Thus, they need to be decomposed into components in the commonly used coordinate systems for use. Many texts present tables for this purpose and we give them in an appendix at the end of the text.

5.7 SOLUTION METHODOLOGY

The equation of change of temperature is a *scalar* equation. Thus, it is simpler to solve than the equations of motion. However, it is coupled to the equations of motion since velocity appears in it. Thus, the equations of motion and the equation of change of temperature have to be solved *simultaneously*. This aspect has already been discussed in chapter 4, and will be mentioned only briefly here. Natural convection and cases where the physical properties are a sensitive function of temperature are obvious instances where simultaneous solution is required. In other instances, it is customary to assume that the physical properties, in particular density and viscosity, remain constant. Then, the equations of motion are *decoupled* from the equation of thermal energy balance. This is the most common procedure[1] that is used.

The solution method is same as adopted with the Navier–Stokes equations. A suitable coordinate system is selected once the problem is specified. Depending upon the problem and the level of complexity of solution required, assumptions are made. The assumptions are translated into mathematical terms, in particular about the various derivatives that vanish. The resulting ordinary or partial differential equations are solved along with the boundary conditions.

5.8 OLD WINE IN NEW BOTTLES

Formulation of problems solved earlier using shell balances will be reconsidered in the following sections in light of the generalized procedure.

5.8.1 Heat conduction through slabs in series

Refer to figure 4.1. The slabs are rectangular in cross section. Hence, the Cartesian coordinate system is chosen. The length and height of the slabs are very large compared to their thicknesses. From shell balance problems, we have learnt that resistance to conduction increases with length of the medium. In view of it, it is assumed that the conduction occurs only in the direction of least thickness or in the x direction. If heat is not conducted in the perpendicular directions, from Fourier's law, we do not expect gradients of temperature to exist in those directions:

$$\frac{\partial T}{\partial y} = \frac{\partial T}{\partial z} = 0$$

The heat transfer occurs at steady state, and hence $\partial T/\partial t = 0$. Heat transfer occurs through solids and so convection is absent or $\mathbf{v}$ is zero. Further heat generation is absent and hence $\dot{Q}_v$ is equal to zero. After these assumptions are incorporated, the equation of change of temperature in rectangular coordinates, eq. I.1 (Note that equation numbers starting with I refer to the equations in the appendix at the end of the chapter.) simplifies to

$$\frac{d^2T_i}{dx^2} = 0, \quad i = \alpha, \beta, \gamma$$

which are identical to those derived earlier. The boundary conditions are to be applied at the boundary of solid α and surroundings, interfaces between the solids, and finally between boundary of solid γ and surroundings. Temperature of the surface of solid α at $x = 0$ is being maintained at T_o. Thus it forms a boundary condition. The unit normal vector to the interfaces between the solids is $\mathbf{i}$. At the *inner* interfaces between the solids, the continuity of temperatures and x component of the heat fluxes apply. No heat is being generated at the boundaries, and so $\dot{Q}_{s,rea}$ is equal to zero. Mass is not being exchanged across the boundaries either, and hence $\dot{m}_b$ is equal to zero. Thus, the boundary conditions are given by

$$T_\alpha = T_\beta, \text{ and } q_{x,\alpha} = q_{x,\beta}, \text{ at } x = X_1$$

These are identical to the ones derived earlier. The other boundaries are treated similarly to arrive at the same equations as before. We do not solve this as the solution was already obtained.

5.8.2 Temperature distribution in a heated wire

The problem is of determining the temperature distribution in a electrically heated wire at steady state. Cylindrical coordinates are the correct choice. The heating is uniform and hence axisymmetry is expected. As the length of the wire is very large compared to its radius, heat loss in the axial direction, and hence the temperature gradients in the axial direction are expected to be small. Thus,

$$\frac{\partial T}{\partial \theta} = \frac{\partial T}{\partial z} = \frac{\partial T}{\partial t} = 0$$

The heat generation occurs in the entire volume, and is given by

$$\dot{Q}_v = \frac{I^2}{k_e}$$

where I is the current density, i/a. Heat transfer occurs in the solid and hence convection is absent. When these hypotheses are inserted, the equation of change of temperature given by eq. I.3 simplifies to

$$0 = k_w \frac{1}{r}\frac{d}{dr}(r\frac{dT_w}{dr}) + \frac{I^2}{k_e}$$

Heat generation is absent in the insulation and hence, in that phase, the equation of change of temperature simplifies to

$$0 = k_i \frac{1}{r}\frac{d}{dr}\left(r\frac{dT_i}{dr}\right)$$

The boundary condition at the center is one of symmetry or that temperature must be finite. The unit normal vector to the interface between the insulation and the wire be $\boldsymbol{\delta}_r$. There are no interfacial heat sources. Hence, the temperature and the radial component of the heat fluxes must be continuous at the interface between the wire and the insulation. Finally the surface of the insulation is kept at temperature T_o. These give the same boundary conditions as before:

$$\begin{aligned}
\frac{dT_w}{dr} &= 0, \text{ or } T_w \text{ is finite} && \text{at } r = 0 \\
T_w &= T_i && \text{at } r = kR \\
k_w\frac{dT_w}{dr} &= k_i\frac{dT_i}{dr} && \text{at } r = \lambda R \\
T_i &= T_o && \text{at } r = R
\end{aligned}$$

Solution to the equations for the boundary conditions has already been given, and hence is not repeated here.

5.8.3 Laminar forced convection

In this problem, steady state heat transfer to a fluid flowing through a tube under laminar flow conditions is examined. Cylindrical coordinates are the correct choice. The flow is fully developed and hence only $v_z(r)$ is non-zero and the profile is parabolic. As the wall of the tube is being heated at a constant rate, the temperature profiles are expected to be axisymmetric. Thus,

$$\frac{\partial T}{\partial \theta} = \frac{\partial T}{\partial t} = 0$$

The following equation is obtained from the equation of change of temperature when the above simplifications are used:

$$\rho\hat{C}_p\left(1 - \frac{r^2}{R^2}\right)\frac{\partial T}{\partial z} = k\frac{1}{r}\frac{\partial}{\partial r}\left(r\frac{\partial T}{\partial r}\right) + k\frac{\partial^2 T}{\partial z^2}$$

which is identical to the one obtained earlier. One of the boundary conditions is heat flux continuity at the interface between the wall and the fluid. Let the unit normal to the wall–fluid interface be $\boldsymbol{\delta}_r$ to formulate the flux continuity boundary condition. The boundary condition is then given by

$$\text{At } r = R, \qquad k\frac{\partial T}{\partial r} = q_w$$

Another boundary condition is the symmetry at the center of the tube:

$$\text{At } r = R, \qquad k\frac{\partial T}{\partial r} = 0$$

or finiteness of temperature can also be used equivalently. These are identical to those used earlier. The solution to the equation was discussed in great detail earlier.

By now, the methodology of using generalized balance equations might have become old hat for you! Let us turn out attention therefore to some **new wine in old bottles**! Let us consider a few more complex problems. As you will notice some of them have great similarity to fluid mechanics problems and have the same significance.

5.9 VISCOUS HEATING IN COUETTE FLOW

5.9.1 Problem identification

Consider flow in a wide but narrow channel. Let the top plate move parallel to itself with a constant velocity while the bottom plate remains stationary. If the top plate moves with a fairly large velocity and if the gap is small, we would expect the viscous dissipation to be large. Let the two plates be maintained at a constant temperature of T_o. Therefore, the heat generated will mostly be removed through the walls. We are interested in calculating the steady and *fully developed temperature profile* after assuming that physical properties remain constant. See figure 5.1.

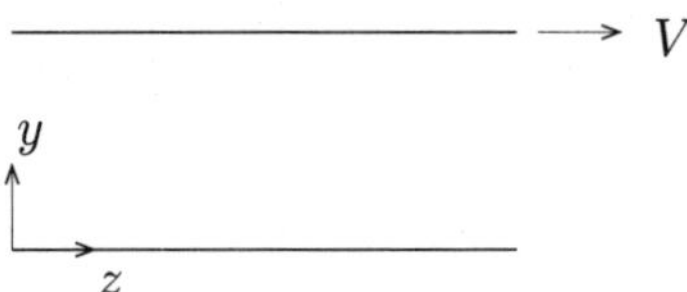

Figure 5.1. Viscous heating in Couette flow.

Velocity profile

Temperature profiles cannot be fully developed unless the velocity profiles are fully developed. Thus, we have

$$\frac{\partial v_z}{\partial z} = 0$$

As the channel is wide but narrow, we can approximate the flow by that between two infinitely wide parallel plates with the gap separating them, δ, being very small. Thus, $v_y = v_x = 0$. Navier–Stokes equations can be solved easily and the velocity profile is found to be linear: $v_z = V(y/\delta)$.

Fully developed temperature profile

Refer to our discussion in section 4.7 on fully developed temperature profile. If a temperature profile is fully developed, it implies that the profile does not change in the flow direction. Let us examine whether this is possible or not in the present problem. If the heat being liberated due to viscous dissipation is removed through the walls, we can expect the bulk temperature not to change when the two balance exactly. Thus, no heat is transported by convection, and the viscous heat dissipation is removed entirely by conduction in the y direction. But, as the rate of viscous dissipation is constant, the temperature profile can remain unchanged in the flow direction. We are looking for such a solution and it is likely to be reached at a long distance from the entry to the channel. According to the definition of fully developed temperature profile used in section 4.7

$$\frac{d}{dz}\frac{T-T_o}{T_b-T_o}=0$$

where we substituted $T_w = T_o$. But, as we argued, T_b is constant and the wall temperature is being maintained constant. Hence, if the temperature profile is fully developed, then

$$\frac{\partial T}{\partial z} = 0$$

As the channel is very wide compared to the thickness, we can assume that

$$\frac{\partial T}{\partial x} = 0$$

Equation of change of temperature

Substituting these assumptions and results into the equation of change of temperature in rectangular coordinates, we obtain

$$0 = k\frac{d^2T}{dy^2} + \Phi_v$$

But, $\Phi_v = \boldsymbol{\tau}{:}(\nabla \mathbf{v})$. For the Couette flow, the rate of viscous dissipation is given by $\mu(\partial v_x/\partial y)^2$. Thus, the final form of equation of change of temperature is given by

$$0 = k\frac{d^2T}{dy^2} + \mu\left(\frac{V}{\delta}\right)^2$$

Boundary conditions

The above is a second order differential equation and its solution requires two boundary conditions. They are given by

$$T = T_o \text{ at } y = 0 \text{ and at } y = \delta$$

5.9.2 Scaling

Characteristic length scale is δ.

$$\xi = \frac{y}{\delta}$$

A characteristic temperature difference is not available. We use the procedure used in finding temperature profiles in a heated wire to generate one. Thus, the characteristic temperature difference is that which is required to conduct away the viscous dissipation. Thus,

$$\mu \left(\frac{V}{\delta} \right)^2 \sim k \frac{(\Delta T)_c}{\delta^2}$$

We define non-dimensional temperature difference as

$$\theta = \frac{k(T - T_o)}{\mu V^2}$$

Dimensionless equations

The equation of change of temperature and boundary conditions can now be written in terms of the non-dimensional variables:

$$0 = \frac{d^2\theta}{d\xi^2} + 1 \tag{5.9}$$

The boundary conditions are given by

$$\theta = 0, \text{ at } \xi = 0, \quad \theta = 0, \text{ at } \xi = 1$$

5.9.3 Temperature profile

The solution is given by

$$\theta = \frac{Br}{2} (\xi - \xi^2)$$

where Br is Brinkman number and is given by

$$Br = \frac{\mu V^2}{k T_o}$$

5.9.4 Look at the results

The results are expectedly similar to those obtained in section 4.6. We therefore do not discuss the results any further and look at a different aspect.

Similarity to momentum transfer

It is always good to always ask "which problem in fluid mechanics is similar to this?" And *vice versa*! This kind of exercise helps build intuition and also creates an ability to translate experience in one transfer process into the other. Equation 5.9 indicates that the heat generated is 'conducted' away. Moreover, the heat generated is uniform throughout the domain. This kind of balance, translated into momentum balance, should read that momentum generated is being diffused away. Forces generate momentum while viscous action diffuses the momentum away. We need uniform generation to find similarity. Therefore, the force must be uniform in the entire body, and so the force must be a body force. The problem of fluid film falling under the influence of gravity is identical to the present heat transfer problem since gravity is a body force that acts equally on all parts of the fluid. Laminar flow in a pipe under the influence of gravity and or pressure gradient is similar, but not identical, since the problem uses a different coordinate system.

Now if we refer to the classical problem of a film of fluid falling down a *single* wall solved in the text by Bird *et al.* [2], we see that the equations are identical but boundary conditions are different. The surface at $y = \delta$ is exposed to atmosphere (air) and therefore is at zero shear stress or that velocity gradient was equal to zero. This would correspond in the present problem to the top surface being insulated. However, as both plates are at the same temperature, the middle plane must be a plane of symmetry or the temperature gradient must be equal to zero on that plane. Thus, we can reduce the problem, *in all respects*, to the falling film problem by using the middle plane as the "top surface" of the falling film problem. This is accomplished by letting

$$\xi' = 2\xi$$

Then,

$$\theta \sim 2\xi' - (\xi')^2 \sim \left[1 - (1 - \xi')^2\right]$$

which is identical to the equation for velocity profile for a film falling down a single wall given in the text by Bird *et al.* [2].

5.10 HEAT TRANSFER IN A RADIAL FLOW REACTOR

5.10.1 Problem identification

In a radial catalytic flow reactor, the catalyst is shaped like a ring. Reactants flow in the radial direction entering the inner side of the ring. Reactants and products flow out at the far side. As the flow is outward and radial, velocity decreases in the direction of flow. Therefore, the contact time increases as the reactants flow through the reactor. This can compensate to some extent for the decreasing concentration of reactants and attain higher reaction rates compared to a packed bed reactor. See figure 5.2. Clearly, cylindrical coordinates are the appropriate choice for this problem.

Velocity profile

Typically, plug flow can be assumed to occur in porous catalyst beds. The velocity profile is therefore easy to compute from equation of continuity and pressure drop can be computed by substituting

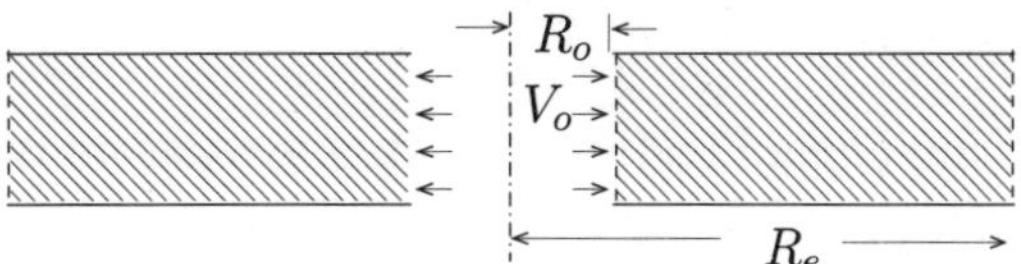

Figure 5.2. Schematic of a radial flow reactor.

this into the equation of motion. Equation of continuity can be used to show that rv_r is a constant. Thus, we have

$$v_r = V_o \frac{R_o}{r}$$

where V_o is the velocity at the inner ring.

Equation of change of temperature

We can expect axial symmetry in this problem and hence $\partial T/\partial \theta = 0$. Let us assume that the top and bottom walls of the reactor are insulated, which implies that heat loss in that direction is negligible and hence temperature is not a function of z. Thus, temperature is only a function of radius at steady state. Assuming that physical properties are constant, the energy balance equation simplifies to

$$\rho \hat{C}_p V_o \frac{R_o}{r}\frac{dT}{dr} = k\frac{1}{r}\frac{d}{dr}\left(r\frac{dT}{dr}\right) + \dot{Q}_v$$

where we have substituted the equation derived for the radial velocity profile in the equation of change of temperature. The rate at which heat is liberated depends upon the rate of reaction and the enthalpy change of the reaction. Thus, the energy balance has to be solved simultaneously with a species balance equation, which we have not yet derived. So, to make matters simple, let us assume that $\dot{Q}_v$ remains constant. This implies that rate of reaction must remain constant. Despite the explanation offered regarding the usefulness of radial reactors, this of course is an overly simplified choice since reaction rate, and hence heat liberated, are expected to have different dependencies on temperature and concentration. But our idea here is to illustrate solution of simple problems which can offer some insight.

Boundary conditions

Let us assume that we are maintaining the inlet to the reactor at a constant temperature of T_i while the outlet is being maintained[2] at a constant temperature of T_e.

5.10.2 Scaling

The radial coordinate can be scaled with the radius of the inlet. Let the temperature difference be scaled with the temperature difference between the outlet and the inlet. Thus,

$$\xi = \frac{r}{R_o}, \text{ and } \theta = \frac{T - T_o}{T_e - T_o}$$

Dimensionless equations

The equation of change of temperature and the boundary conditions are rewritten in terms of the non-dimensional variables as follows:

$$Pe\frac{1}{\xi}\frac{d\theta}{d\xi} = \frac{1}{\xi}\frac{d}{d\xi}\left(\xi\frac{d\theta}{d\xi}\right) + \mathcal{Q} \tag{5.10}$$

where Pe is the Peclet number. The non-dimensional parameters appearing in the above equation are given by

$$Pe = \frac{V_o R_o}{\alpha}, \quad \alpha = \frac{k}{\rho \hat{C}_p}, \quad \text{and } \mathcal{Q} = \frac{\dot{Q}_v\, R_o^2}{k(T_e - T_o)}$$

It is easy to interpret these parameters. $\mathcal{Q}$ is the ratio of rate at which heat is liberated to the rate at which it can be conducted away given the temperature difference being maintained. You would observe that it is similar to Brinkman number. Pe is the ratio of the rate of heat removal by convection to that by conduction. If $\mathcal{Q}$ is positive, heat is liberated due to reaction, and it has to be removed by conduction and or by convection both in the radial direction. We can expect convection to dominate if Pe is large.

The non-dimensional boundary conditions are given by

$$\theta = 0 \quad \text{at} \quad \xi = 1, \quad \theta = 1 \quad \text{at} \quad \xi = \frac{R_e}{R_o} \equiv \gamma$$

Temperature profile in radial reactor

The solution to the non-dimensional equation of change of temperature is given by

$$\theta = \frac{\xi^{Pe} - 1}{\gamma^{Pe} - 1} + \frac{(\gamma^2 - 1)\mathcal{Q}}{2(2 - Pe)}\left(\frac{\xi^{Pe} - 1}{\gamma^{Pe} - 1} - \frac{\xi^2 - 1}{\gamma^2 - 1}\right) \tag{5.11}$$

5.10.3 Look at the results

Figure 5.3 shows temperature profiles for $\mathcal{Q} = 7.5$ and for Peclet numbers of 0.1 and 3. Since $\mathcal{Q}$ is positive, heat is liberated. At low Peclet numbers, convection is ineffective. The solution for Peclet number = 0.1 is mostly represented by the quadratic terms in ξ in eq. 5.11. As heat liberated is large and since the end temperatures are fixed, a maximum in temperature is produced in the reactor. As the radial gradient of temperature is positive at the inlet but it is negative at the outlet, heat is lost by conduction through both the inner and the outer surfaces. As Peclet number is increased, the sign of the temperature gradients is unaltered, but the gradient at the inlet is now smaller. Convection brings in heat at the inlet and removes it at the outlet. The former is less because the temperature at the inlet is smaller. Thus, at larger Peclet numbers, more heat is swept out of the reactor due to convection while the heat liberated remains the same. Therefore, the heat lost through the inner surface can now be less and this is reflected by the reduced gradients there. As convection is effective and sweeps more heat out in the radial direction, temperatures inside the reactor are reduced from what they would have been had conduction been the only mechanism of removal of heat. As heat liberated is large, a maximum is still present. But one can expect it to disappear if Peclet number is increased further, and very steep radial temperature gradients to appear at the outlet.

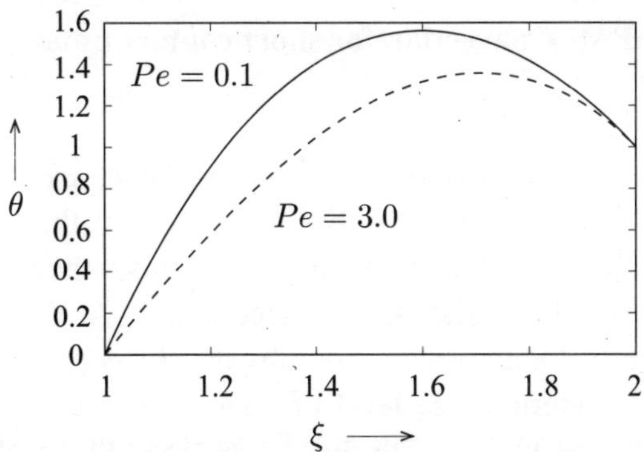

Figure 5.3. Temperature profiles in radial flow reactor.

Limiting cases

There are a few limiting cases of the above solution that are of interest.

1. If Q is zero, the problem is referred to as *transpiration cooling*[3]. Suppose that $T_e > T_o$. The situation is similar to that of a refrigerator. Heat would "leak" from the outer surface into the ring and finally into the domain of the inside cylinder. Convection opposes the heat leak and so reduces its magnitude. This helps in keeping the temperature low and hence refrigeration. In an earthen pot, convection is created by evaporation of water through the pores of the pot. Evaporation cools water and convection reduces heat leak to keep water cool in hot summer. The ratio of heat leak with and without transpiration is an indicator of the effectiveness of transpiration. The temperature profiles are plotted for a few values of Pe. Figure 5.4 shows temperature profiles in the absence of heat generation. Notice how the temperature gradients become less steep at the inlet as Pe increases and hence heat leak is reduced into the inner ring.

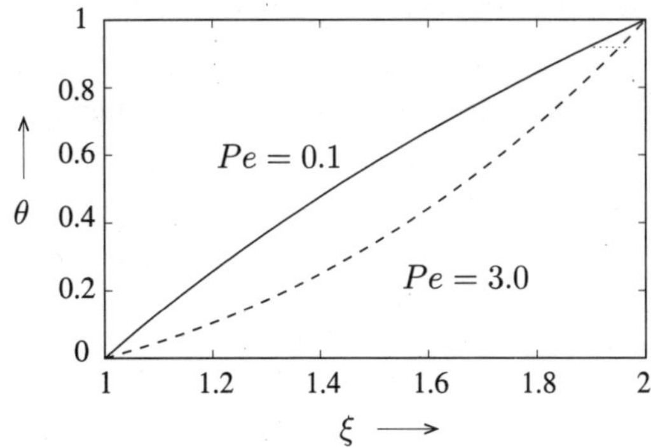

Figure 5.4. Temperature profiles in transpiration cooling.

2. If thermal conductivity is very large, $Pe = 0$, even though Q can still be large due to large heat liberation. The problem reduces to that of a pure conduction problem and is identical to the problem of conduction in a heated annulus.

5.11 LEVEQUE PROBLEM: Convection for short contact times

5.11.1 Problem identification

Let us consider heating of a cold fluid when it enters a hot tube, and the flow is laminar. Let the process be at steady state. Here, three possibilities exist. One of them is that the flow as well as the temperature profiles are fully developed. A problem of this nature, but with constant wall flux boundary condition, has already been discussed in section 4.4. At the other extreme lies the case where neither temperature nor velocity profiles are fully developed, and we will consider a problem of this nature in section 6.2. Intermediate level of complexity arises if only the velocity profile is fully developed, and this is the topic of the present section. Physically this occurs if fluid first enters a *long* inlet section which is at the same temperature as that of fluid before encountering the hot portion. See figure 5.5. Thus, flow is fully developed when it reaches $z = 0$ and it is at a temperature T_o. It remains at the temperature it entered with as the wall is also at the temperature T_o. However, the pipe wall is at a temperature T_w for $z > 0$. The fluid will then get heated for $z > 0$ assuming that $T_w > T_o$. If one observes at locations where z is very large, the temperature profiles will be found to be fully developed. But as mentioned earlier in this section, we are interested in the temperature profiles for small values of z, *i.e.*, in the section just after the heated portion. If we

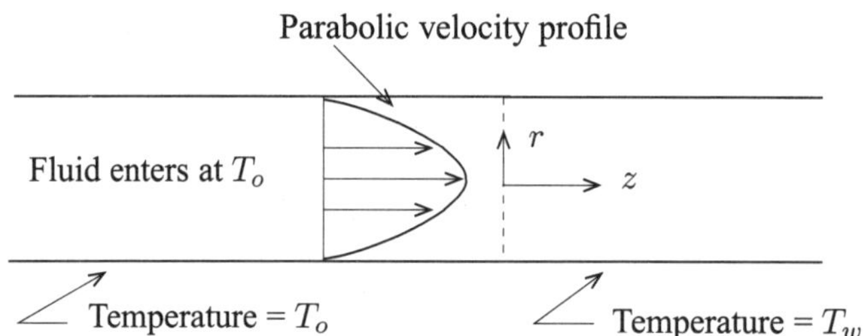

Figure 5.5. Schematic of fully developed flow entering a heated pipe.

were to move with the fluid, we would observe that, in this region of the pipe, the fluid has flown past the hot wall only for a short time. In chemical reaction engineering, we would have stated that the residence time is small. Hence, the title contains the words "short contact times".

If certain simplifying assumptions are made, the present problem offers a beautiful mathematical solution which is a classic. It was obtained by Leveque and hence the name. Such solutions offer insight into practical problems, and are an important part of the tools of an engineer. The simplifications invoked are towards preparation to find the elegant solution.

Velocity profile

We assume that physical properties remain constant. Hence, the equation of motion is decoupled from the energy balance. Because the flow is fully developed, only axial component of the velocity vector is not zero and it is a function of only the radial coordinate, r. Hence, the velocity profile is parabolic:

$$v_z = 2V\left(1 - \frac{r^2}{R^2}\right)$$

where R is the radius of the tube, and V is the average velocity.

Equation of change of temperature

Cylindrical coordinates are appropriate for this problem. Due to circular geometry of the tube and boundary conditions being independent of the angle, we expect axisymmetry. Temperature is not a function of the angle, θ. The temperature has to be a function of radius, r, as the fluid receives heat from the wall. It has to be a function of the axial distance, z, because it gets heated as it travels downstream. After substituting these hypothesized dependencies into the equation of change of temperature, the following partial differential equation is obtained:

$$2\rho\hat{C}_p V\left(1-\frac{r^2}{R^2}\right)\frac{\partial T}{\partial z} = k\left[\frac{1}{r}\frac{\partial}{\partial r}\left(r\frac{\partial T}{\partial r}\right)\right] + k\frac{\partial^2 T}{\partial z^2}$$

Boundary conditions

Fluid is assumed to enter at a uniform temperature, T_o. Further, the temperature profile must be axisymmetric, and hence the temperature gradient in the radial direction must be zero at the center of the tube. Thus, the following boundary conditions can be written:

$$\begin{aligned} T(r,z) &= T_o \quad \text{at} \quad z=0 \\ T(r,z) &= T_w \quad \text{at} \quad r=R \\ \frac{\partial T}{\partial r} &= 0 \quad \text{at} \quad r=0 \end{aligned}$$

As second derivative of the temperature with respect to z appears in the equation of change of temperature, we should require one more boundary condition. We will discuss this in greater detail a little later.

5.11.2 Scaling

Characteristic values for dimension and temperature difference are available which can be used to non-dimensionalize radius and temperature difference:

$$\theta = \frac{T-T_o}{T_w-T_o}, \quad \xi = \frac{r}{R}$$

Dimensionless equations

After introducing these variables, the equation of change of temperature reads

$$2\frac{\rho\hat{C}_p}{k}VR^2\left(1-\xi^2\right)\frac{\partial\theta}{\partial z} = \frac{1}{\xi}\frac{\partial}{\partial\xi}\left(\xi\frac{\partial\theta}{\partial\xi}\right) + R^2\frac{\partial^2\theta}{\partial z^2}$$

Short contact time approximation

Let us non-dimensionalize z with length L from the entrance. After some rearrangement, the non-dimensional equation will be given by

$$\frac{R^2}{L^2}\left(-\frac{\partial^2\theta}{\partial\tilde{z}^2}+2\frac{\rho\hat{C}_pLV}{k}\left(1-\xi^2\right)\frac{\partial\theta}{\partial\tilde{z}}\right)=\frac{1}{\xi}\frac{\partial}{\partial\xi}\left(\xi\frac{\partial\theta}{\partial\xi}\right)$$

L is expected to be small as we are interested in small axial distances from the beginning of the heated part of the wall. The group $\rho\hat{C}_pLV/k$ is the axial Peclet number. Thermal diffusivities of typical liquids are of the order of $10^{-4}m^2/s$. Therefore, even if the velocity is as small as $10^{-2}m/s$, the axial Peclet number will be of the order of unity for lengths as small as a centimeter. Thus, the axial diffusion term will be negligible compared to convection term except very near the beginning of the heated portion. The non-dimensional equation now simplifies to

$$2\frac{R^2}{L^2}\frac{\rho\hat{C}_pL}{k}\left(1-\xi^2\right)\frac{\partial\theta}{\partial\tilde{z}}=\frac{1}{\xi}\frac{\partial}{\partial\xi}\left(\xi\frac{\partial\theta}{\partial\xi}\right)$$

If we naively take the limit of the above equation as L becomes small, we would end up with neglecting the conduction term itself! This problem arises since the characteristic length we chose for radius is not correct for short contact times. As the distance the fluid travelled into the tube is small, or the contact time is short, we expect changes in temperature to be confined to small distances *in the radial direction* from the wall, and R is an incorrect choice for non-dimensionalizing the radial coordinate. We rework the problem by taking notice of the small depths of penetration of heat into the pipe.

We start with

$$2\frac{\rho\hat{C}_pR^2}{k}\left(1-\xi^2\right)\frac{\partial\theta}{\partial z}=\frac{1}{\xi}\frac{\partial}{\partial\xi}\left(\xi\frac{\partial\theta}{\partial\xi}\right)$$

The domain of interest in the radial direction is confined to values of ξ less than unity but very close to unity. Thus, the effects of curvature of the wall can be expected to be not important, *i.e.*, we expect to approximate the important zone as a thin flat layer of fluid. We implement this idea mathematically as follows. Let us now define a non-dimensional distance from the wall

$$y=1-\xi,\quad\frac{\partial}{\partial\xi}=-\frac{\partial}{\partial y}$$

where the above follow from the definition of y itself. But since $\xi\sim 1$, or $y\sim 0$, we write

$$\xi\frac{\partial}{\partial\xi}=-(1-y)\frac{\partial}{\partial y}\sim-\frac{\partial}{\partial y}$$

and hence

$$\frac{\partial}{\partial\xi}\left(\xi\frac{\partial}{\partial\xi}\right)=\frac{\partial^2}{\partial y^2}$$

We see that the radial conduction term changes to a form as if we are in Cartesian coordinates. It makes sense since the basic idea is that curvature effects are not important since the temperature gradients do not penetrate very much into the fluid and are confined to a very thin layer near the wall. Using the same argument, the velocity profile *in the zone of interest* can be approximated using Taylor's series by

$$v_z(y) = v_z(y=0) + y \left. \frac{dv_z}{dy} \right|_{y=0} = 4Vy$$

that is, the velocity profile near the wall is being approximated by a linear profile. Substituting these results into the equation of change of temperature, we get

$$4 \frac{\rho \hat{C}_p}{k} V R^2 y \frac{\partial \theta}{\partial z} = \frac{\partial^2 \theta}{\partial y^2} + R^2 \frac{\partial^2 \theta}{\partial z^2}$$

It is easy to judge the relative importance of the two conduction terms on the right hand side. As long as we are interested in much smaller lengths in the y direction compared to those in the z direction, *i.e.*, $Ry << z$, the conduction term in the z direction is negligible compared to that in the y direction. This approximation breaks down near the edge around $z \sim 0$, but will be valid further down. The equation can be recast after accepting this approximation to obtain

$$4 \frac{\rho \hat{C}_p}{k} V R^2 y \frac{\partial \theta}{\partial z} = \frac{\partial^2 \theta}{\partial y^2}$$

The second derivative in z direction has been "lost", so one boundary condition is enough! Physically, this means that the "end" of the tube is so far away from the zone of interest that the effects of what is maintained there do not affect the zone of interest.

5.11.3 Similarity transformation

A length scale is still not apparent in the z direction. As we are interested in short lengths, the end of the tube can be considered as being very far away or that z can take on very large values. Of course, we will use the solution, when we obtain one, only for small values of z. If z is considered to be infinitely long, a characteristic length is absent in one direction. In such problems where some characteristic quantities are 'missing', one can make them up using other properties and *independent* variables of the problem. In this sense different independent variables become 'similar', and a variable formulated by combining independent variables is known as the **similarity variable**. Transforming the equations in terms of similarity variable is known as the **similarity transformation**. Before we try this, for the sake of convenience, let us non-dimensionalize the z coordinate by a length scale obtained in terms of conduction time scale and velocity:

$$\zeta = \frac{z}{V} \frac{\alpha}{4R^2}$$

where α is the thermal diffusivity. The equation of change of temperature reduces to

$$y \frac{\partial \theta}{\partial \zeta} = \frac{\partial^2 \theta}{\partial y^2}$$

Similarity variable

Discovery of the form of a similarity variable is by trial and error. Let us try the following form for a similarity variable

$$\eta = Cy^m\zeta^n$$

where C, m and n are constants. We are expecting that only the similarity variable will be the independent variable in the problem. Hence, a similarity transformation is said to "work" if the partial differential equation is reduced to an ordinary differential equation in terms of *only* the similarity variable, and the boundary conditions can also be stated in terms of only the similarity variable. Substituting the assumed form of the similarity variable, and a bit of manipulation, the equation of change of temperature is converted to

$$n\frac{d\theta}{d\eta} = m(m-1)\frac{\zeta}{y^3}\frac{d\theta}{d\eta} + m^2\eta\frac{\zeta}{y^3}\frac{d^2\theta}{d\eta^2}$$

It is easy to observe that, for the similarity transformation to work, we need $n/m = -1/3$. The equation will also take a simple form if we choose $m = 1$. Hence

$$\eta \sim \frac{y}{\zeta^{1/3}}$$

Test of similarity variable

The equation of change of temperature now simplifies to

$$-\frac{1}{3C^3}\eta^2\frac{d\theta}{d\eta} = \frac{d^2\theta}{d\eta^2}$$

The equation will simplify to the following convenient form

$$\frac{d^2\theta}{d\eta^2} + 3\eta^2\frac{d\theta}{d\eta} = 0$$

if we choose

$$C^3 = \frac{1}{9}$$

This is equivalent to defining the similarity variable as

$$\eta = y\left(\frac{1}{9\zeta}\right)^{1/3}$$

As required, the partial differential equation has reduced to an ordinary differential equation in terms of only the similarity variable. Note that the differential equation is a second order and hence would need only *two* boundary conditions. Thus, we still need to examine whether the three boundary conditions will 'collapse' into two.

The boundary conditions are given by

$$T(y,\zeta) = T_o \quad \text{at} \quad \zeta = 0$$
$$T(y,\zeta) = T_w \quad \text{at} \quad y = 0$$
$$\frac{\partial T}{\partial y} = 0 \quad \text{at} \quad y = 1$$

It is easy to see that the three boundary conditions would not reduce in number to two. Keeping in mind that we are dealing with small penetration depths or that the range of y of interest is much smaller than R, the temperature there is likely to be equal to the inlet value. Hence, the last boundary condition is modified as

$$T(y \to \infty, \zeta) = T_o$$

In terms of the non-dimensional temperature, the boundary conditions are given by

$$\theta(y,0) = 0, \; \theta(0,\zeta) = 1, \text{ and } \theta(y \to \infty, \zeta) = 0$$

These can be rewritten in terms of the similarity variable as

$$\theta(\eta \to \infty) = 0, \; \theta(0) = 1, \; \text{ and } \theta(\eta \to \infty) = 0$$

The last and the first boundary conditions have now "collapsed" into one and thus we can conclude that the similarity transformation will work. Now the equation of change of temperature and boundary conditions can be written in terms of the similarity variable as

$$\frac{d^2\theta}{d\eta^2} + 3\eta^2 \frac{d\theta}{d\eta} = 0 \tag{5.12}$$

$$\theta(0) = 1, \quad \theta(\eta \to \infty) = 0 \tag{5.13}$$

5.11.4 Temperature profile

Solution to eq. 5.12 is found to be

$$\theta = \frac{\displaystyle\int_\eta^\infty \exp(-x^3)dx}{\displaystyle\int_0^\infty \exp(-x^3)dx} \equiv \frac{\displaystyle\int_\eta^\infty \exp(-x^3)dx}{\Gamma\left(\dfrac{4}{3}\right)} \tag{5.14}$$

Heat flux

The major quantity of interest is the heat flux into the fluid. As velocity is zero at the wall, the heat flux is only by conduction, and it is in the $-r$ direction. Hence,

$$-q_r(r = R) \equiv q_w = -k\frac{1}{R}\frac{\partial T}{\partial y}\bigg|_{y=0} = -k(T_w - T_o)\frac{1}{R}\left(\frac{1}{9\zeta}\right)^{(1/3)}\frac{d\theta}{d\eta}\bigg|_{\eta=0}$$

The derivative can be evaluated from eq. 5.14 and the heat flux can be evaluated to be

$$q_w = k(T_w - T_o)\frac{1}{R}\left(\frac{1}{9\zeta}\right)^{(1/3)}\frac{1}{\Gamma\left(\frac{4}{3}\right)} \tag{5.15}$$

5.11.5 Heat transfer coefficient

As discussed in chapter 4 and section 4.3, the heat transfer coefficient is sufficient to calculate changes in the average enthalpy of a stream due to heating or cooling. Thus, it alone is sufficient for the practically useful engineering calculations. One therefore summarizes the detailed calculations on temperature profiles by calculating the heat transfer coefficient. The heat transfer coefficient is defined as

$$\mathbf{n.q} = h(T_w - T_b)$$

where **n** is the unit normal and the temperature difference is taken in its direction. Further, T_b is the bulk temperature. For the present problem, then, $\mathbf{n} = -\boldsymbol{\delta}_r$. Hence,

$$q_w = h_{loc}(z)\,(T_w - T_b(z))$$

where h_{loc} is the heat transfer coefficient at a given value of z. As the fluid extends to infinity, the value of T_b will be the same as the entry temperature or T_o. Thus,

$$h_{loc} = k\frac{1}{R}\left(\frac{1}{9\zeta}\right)^{1/3}\frac{1}{\Gamma\left(\frac{4}{3}\right)}$$

or

$$\frac{2h_{loc}R}{k} \equiv Nu_{loc} = 2\left(\frac{1}{9}\frac{2VR}{\mu}\frac{\mu}{\alpha}\frac{2R}{z}\right)^{1/3} = \left(\frac{8}{9}\right)^{1/3}\left(Re\,Pr\,\frac{D}{z}\right)^{1/3} \tag{5.16}$$

where D, Nu, Re and Pr are diameter of the tube, Nusselt, Reynolds, and Prandtl numbers respectively. Some times, results are also reported as the average Nusselt number which is defined as

$$\bar{h}(z) = \frac{1}{z}\int_0^z h_{loc}(x)dx$$

which can be easily calculated by using eq. 5.16.

5.11.6 Look at the results

The temperature profiles are plotted in figure 5.6. As expected, the non-dimensional temperature is only a function of the similarity variable, η. The left panel shows the temperature profile in terms of the similarity variable. It is seen that the temperature decreases from the value at the wall to the value at the entrance as distance from the wall increases or into the interior of the pipe. We can easily plot the profiles at different axial distances from the entry to the tube. These are shown in

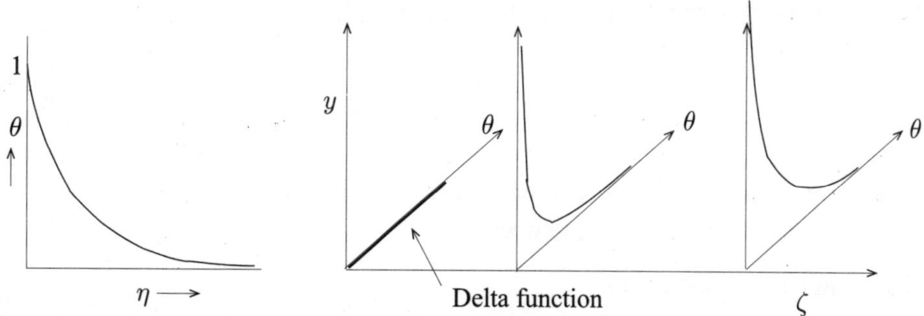

Figure 5.6. Temperature profiles in entry zone of pipe with constant wall temperature and fully developed flow. The left panel shows it as a function of similarity variable. The right panel shows it as a function of axial distance from the entry.

the right panel. It is seen that the temperature gradients are sharper at locations nearer to the entry. This is to be expected since the fluid gets hotter as it flows downstream into the tube. The same is indicated by the equation for the heat flux, eq. 5.15. It also can be seen from the same equation that the heat flux is infinitely large at the leading edge. It is because the temperature gradient in the y direction suffers a jump[4] at $\zeta = O^+$.

Due to the decreasing values of heat flux with axial distance, the heat transfer coefficient must also decrease.

Graetz–Nusselt–Leveque solution

It is possible to solve the equation of change of temperature exactly but after neglecting the axial conduction term by the technique of separation of variables. Such a solution is referred to as Graetz–

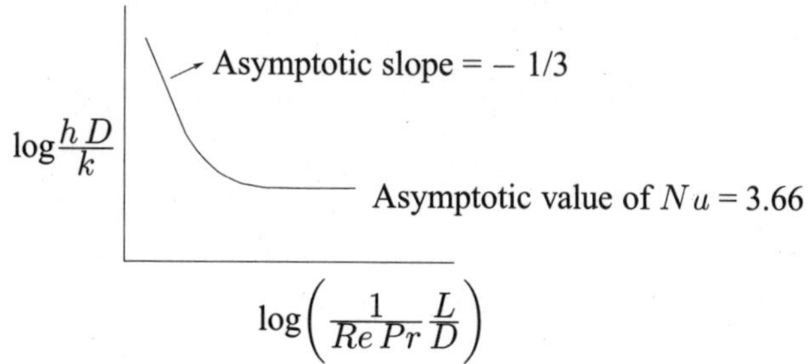

Figure 5.7. Schematic of Nusselt number for fully developed laminar flow entering a heated pipe: Constant wall temperature case.

Nusselt–Leveque solution. The similarity solution and the fully developed temperature profile for large z form the asymptotes of the more complete solution. The latter gives a constant value of 3.66 for the Nusselt number. A sketch of the entire solution is shown in figure 5.7.

Note the value of the two 'limiting' cases corresponding to short contact times, and long contact times when temperature profile is fully developed. The in-between solution is complex, though it can be obtained in this particular case. However, the two limiting solutions do provide bounds and characteristic behavior which can be used to make estimates for what happens in between.

5.12 HEAT TRANSFER TO A SEMI-INFINITE SLAB

5.12.1 Problem identification

Consider a semi-infinite solid slab initially at a temperature T_i. Suppose that its surface temperature is raised to T_o at $t = 0$ and kept constant at that value thereafter. The temperature in the slab will now change with time and the change will be different at different locations. We want to calculate the spatial and temporal variation of the temperature.

Equation of change of temperature

Let the slab be semi-infinite in the x direction and as it is infinite in extent in the other two directions, *i.e.*, the slab occupies the domain, $0 \leq x < \infty$, $0 - \infty < y < \infty$, and $-\infty < z < \infty$. In view of the infinite extent of the body in the y and z directions and that the entire surface of the body at x =0 is being maintained at the same temperature T_o, we do not expect temperature to depend upon y and z coordinates. Thus, we expect the dependence to be $T(x, t)$. As the body is a solid, convection is absent. Let us assume that physical properties remain constant. Cartesian coordinates are suitable for this problem and the equation of change of temperature in these coordinates simplifies to

$$\frac{\partial T}{\partial t} = \alpha \frac{\partial^2 T}{\partial x^2}$$

Initial and boundary conditions

As the partial differential equation is first order with respect to time and second order with respect to space. Hence, we need one condition in time. This is the condition from where we start analysing the problem, commonly known as the *initial condition.* As the slab was at temperature T_i before its surface was raised to a higher temperature, the initial condition is given by

$$T(x, 0) = T_i$$

The surface at $x = 0$ is being maintained at T_o. Hence, the boundary condition there is given by

$$T(0, t) = T_o$$

No heat will reach from a hot surface to an infinitely large distance. Thus, the temperature infinitely far away from a hot surface will continue to remain at whichever level it was. Thus,

$$T(x \to \infty, t) = T_i$$

5.12.2 Scaling

The temperature can be non-dimensionalized with the characteristic temperature difference available:

$$\theta = \frac{T - T_i}{T_o - T_i}$$

The initial and boundary conditions in terms of the non-dimensional temperature are given by

$$\theta(x, 0) = 0, \;\; \theta(0, t) = 1, \;\; \text{and,} \;\; \theta(x \to \infty, t) = 0$$

5.12.3 Similarity transformation

Note that a characteristic variable does not exist for either of the coordinates, t and x, and we may expect a similarity solution. One can try the procedure given in the previous section. Without repeating those details, let us state that the problem admits a similarity solution and the *similarity variable* is given by

$$\eta = \sqrt{\frac{x^2}{4\alpha t}}$$

The differential equation reduces to

$$\frac{d^2\theta}{d\eta^2} + 2\eta\frac{d\theta}{d\eta} = 0 \tag{5.17}$$

The initial and boundary conditions of the original problem reduce to two boundary conditions in terms of the similarity variable and are given by

$$\theta(0) = 1, \quad \text{and } \theta(\eta \to \infty) \to 0$$

Note that this problem turns out to be identical to the problem of a plate, immersed in a stationary Newtonian fluid, dragged suddenly with a constant velocity because the energy equation is identical to the equation that describes that flow. The initial and boundary conditions for that problem are identical to the initial and boundary conditions here. Thus, the solution must also be identical[5]. We could have drawn inspiration to find the similarity solution from there!

5.12.4 Temperature profile

The solution is given by

$$\theta = 1 - \text{erf}(\eta)$$

where erf is the error function. It is defined as

$$\text{erf}(\eta) = \frac{2}{\sqrt{\pi}} \int_0^{\eta} e^{-a^2}\, da$$

where a is a dummy integration variable. Those who have studied this problem in fluid mechanics will realize that all one had to do was to replace ν by α! Thus, while momentum diffusion is characterized by ν, heat conduction (or diffusion of heat) is governed by α.

5.12.5 Look at the results

The temperature profile is given by figure 5.8. The temperature decreases with increasing η as heat flows into the body from the surface at $x = 0$, and hence temperature must decrease in that direction. Similar to what was done in the earlier section, we can plot these as a function of x at different times. We will leave that to you, and introduce some new and valuable concepts.

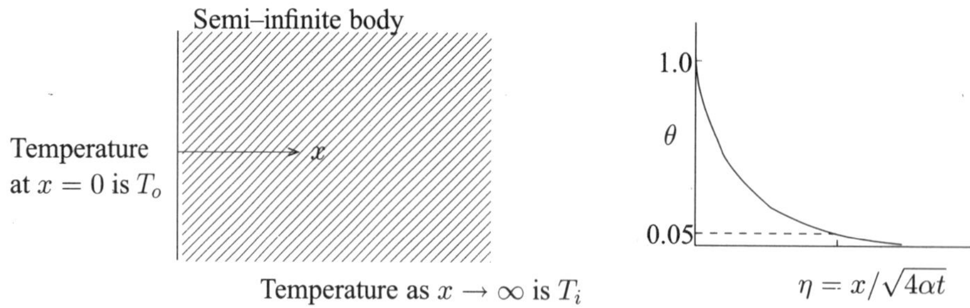

Figure 5.8. Temperature profiles in a semi-infinite slab whose surface is suddenly raised to a constant value different from its initial value.

Penetration times and depths

Note that the temperature profile is a function of only η, and so in some ways, time and distance have similar effects. We can think of time required for the heat to reach a certain location or the depth to which heat will penetrate after some time has elapsed. These ideas lead us to define two quantities: **penetration time** and **penetration distance**[6]. Penetration time, τ_p, is the time required for the effects of heat conduction to be felt *at a specified distance*. Similarly penetration depth, δ_p is the depth up to which the effects of heat conduction are felt by a *specified time*. We of course have to specify what we mean by the term 'the effects are felt'. It is arbitrary and we can say that the effects are *not* felt when the non-dimensional temperature at the location and time specified is less than 5% of that imposed by the boundary, *i.e.,* $\theta < 0.05$. Conversely, the effects are deemed to be felt when $\theta > 0.05$. The absolute number we calculate will therefore be arbitrary but the numbers will allow us to compare different situations. In our problem, the value of η is fixed since we chose $\theta = 0.05$. Hence

$$\delta_p \sim \sqrt{\alpha t} \quad \text{and} \quad \tau_p \sim \frac{x^2}{\alpha}$$

Thermal diffusivity is the "diffusion coefficient" for heat. Thus, penetration depth should increase, and penetration time decrease with an increase in thermal diffusivity. These are confirmed by the expressions given.

Suppose we had a slab of thickness L instead of the semi-infinite slab. We can then guess that the effect of changed boundary temperature will not be felt up to the thickness L for a time less than L^2/α and for times much smaller than this, the solution we derived can be used, even though the slab is *not* semi-infinite in extent. Thus, we see that ideas of penetration time and depth have enormous value in thinking about limiting solutions.

Heat flux

Heat is lost into the body from the hot surface. Hence, heat has to be supplied to keep the surface at $x = 0$ at the constant temperature of T_o. The heat to be supplied is equal to the heat flux from the surface into the body. The latter heat flux is through conduction. It is given by

$$q_x(0,t) \;=\; -k\frac{\partial T}{\partial x}\bigg|_{x=0}$$

If you recall the solution to the corresponding momentum transfer problem, heat flux is seen to be *similar* to the drag force. It is easily calculated to be

$$q_x(0,t) = \frac{k(T_o - T_i)}{\sqrt{\pi \alpha t}}$$

As expected, heat flux increases with thermal conductivity but is proportional to its square root. As time progresses, temperature of the solid increases and hence the temperature gradients decrease. Consequently, the heat flux decreases with time.

Heat flux and velocity gradients

Suppose we had plug flow, instead of laminar flow with parabolic velocity profile as was the case in the problem worked out in the previous section, the solution of the present section can be directly applied. All one needs to do is to replace the time with residence time or $t = z/V$ where V is the z component of the velocity of the plug. Thus, as velocity profile changes from the parabolic to plug flow, the dependence of heat flux on thermal diffusivity will change from the 0.66 power to 0.5. Similarly, the heat flux decreases more rapidly as $z^{-0.5}$ in plug flow compared to $z^{-0.33}$ in laminar flow. Hence, one can see that, not only velocities, but velocity gradients have a significant influence on rates of heat and mass transfer.

5.13 HEAT CONDUCTION IN A FINITE SLAB

5.13.1 Problem identification

Consider another problem in heat conduction. Suppose a slab bound by the planes $x = 0$ and $x = L$ is initially at T_i. Now let the surface at $x = 0$ be maintained at T_i. Let the surface at $x = L$ be exposed to a fluid at a bulk temperature T_b flowing past it. If the flow rate is large, the fluid can be assumed to remain at T_a despite the heat flux from or to the slab. The conditions are such that the heat transfer coefficient is given by h. See figure 5.9. Once again, as with the previous problem, the

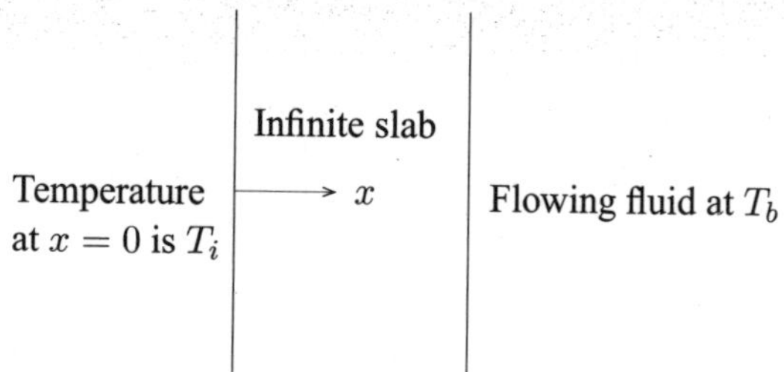

Figure 5.9. Infinite slab being heated by convection.

temperature will change with time and position and we are interested in calculating this dependence.

Equation of change of temperature

As the slab extends to infinity in the y and z directions, and because both the x faces are maintained at a uniform condition, temperature is not expected to depend upon the y and z coordinates. Thus,

$T = T(x,t)$. Convection is absent as the slab is solid. Cartesian coordinates are suitable for this problem and the equation of change of temperature in these coordinates simplifies to

$$\frac{\partial T}{\partial t} = \alpha \frac{\partial^2 T}{\partial y^2}$$

Initial and boundary conditions

As with the problem on heating of a semi-infinite slab, we need an initial condition and two boundary conditions. The initial and boundary condition at $x = 0$ are respectively given by

$$T(x,t) = T_i \quad \text{at} \quad t = 0 \quad \text{and for all } x$$
$$T(x,t) = T_i \quad \text{at} \quad x = 0 \quad \text{and for all } t$$

We need one more boundary condition at $x = L$. There are two *possible* boundary conditions at $x = L$. One is temperature continuity. However, only the bulk temperature of the fluid, and not the temperature at $x = L$, is known. Thus, we have to apply the other possible boundary condition, namely the energy balance at the interface:

$$(\mathbf{q}^{\mathbf{II}} - \mathbf{q}^{\mathbf{I}}).\boldsymbol{\xi} + \dot{Q}_{s,rad} + \dot{Q}_{s,rea} = \dot{m}_b\,(\hat{H}^I - \hat{H}^{II}) \tag{3.10}$$

The heat generation terms at the surface are zero and there is no mass flux across the interface. $\boldsymbol{\xi}$ can be taken to be the unit normal in the x direction. Then

$$q_x(x = L^-) = q_x(x = L^+)$$

But heat is lost by convection into the fluid, and hence

$$q_x(x = L^+) = h\,(T(L,t) - T_b)$$

Note that we *have* used the temperature continuity in writing the above expression. It may also be noted that once the heat transfer coefficient is given, analysis of fluid phase is unnecessary. All the heat transfer characteristics are contained in the heat transfer coefficient. Substituting Fourier's law for heat flux in the solid, we get

$$-k\left.\frac{\partial T}{\partial x}\right|_{x=L} = h\,(T(L,t) - T_b)$$

5.13.2 Scaling

We do have a characteristic length, L, and it can be used as the length scale. Similarly, we do have a characteristic temperature difference, $(T_a - T_i)$ which can be used to non-dimensionalize temperature A. We do not have a definite time scale, but we expect it to be of the order of the *penetration time* over a length L and it is given by L^2/α. It can be used to non-dimensionalize time. Thus, we have the following non-dimensional variables:

$$\xi = \frac{x}{L}, \quad \tau = \frac{\alpha t}{L^2}, \quad \theta = \frac{T - T_i}{T_b - T_i}$$

Dimensionless equations

The equation of change of temperature can be written in terms of the non-dimensional variables as

$$\frac{\partial \theta}{\partial \tau} = \frac{\partial^2 \theta}{\partial \xi^2} \tag{5.18}$$

and, the initial condition and the boundary conditions can be written as

$$\theta(\xi, 0) = 0, \ \theta(0, \tau) = 0, \ -\left.\frac{\partial \theta}{\partial \xi}\right|_{\xi=1} = Bi(\theta(1, \tau) - 1), \text{ where } Bi = \frac{hL}{k} \tag{5.19}$$

In the above, Bi is the Biot number which is the ratio of resistance to conduction in the slab to the resistance due to convection at the $x = L$ plane.

5.13.3 Temperature profile

The solution to the above equation is obtained by separation of variables. Let us assume that $\theta = \Xi(\xi)\Phi(\tau)$. Substituting this into eq. 5.18, and separating variables

$$\frac{1}{\Phi}\frac{d\Phi}{d\tau} = \frac{1}{\Xi}\frac{d^2\Xi}{d\xi^2} = C$$

where C can be a constant or constants[7]. The first equation can be solved to get

$$\Phi \sim \exp(C\tau)$$

The temperature does not diverge with time, and hence we know $C \leq 0$. If $C = 0$, the dependence of time vanishes. Hence, the solution corresponding to $C = 0$ is the *steady state* solution. Let it be denoted by θ_s. The entire solution can then be written as[8]

$$\theta = \theta_u + \theta_s \tag{5.20}$$

θ_s satisfies the *steady state heat conduction equation*,

$$\frac{d^2\theta_s}{d\xi^2} = 0$$

The boundary conditions are the same at steady state and hence remain the same as specified in eq. 5.19. Using these boundary conditions, the steady state solution is easily found and is given by

$$\theta_s = \frac{Bi}{Bi + 1}\xi$$

Now let us turn our attention to θ_u. By substituting eq. 5.20 into eq. 5.18, it can be shown that θ_u satisfies

$$\frac{\partial \theta_u}{\partial \tau} = \frac{\partial^2 \theta_u}{\partial \xi^2}$$

The boundary and initial conditions for θ are known. But $\theta = \theta_u + \theta_s$. The boundary and initial conditions for θ_u are therefore obtained by subtracting the ones for θ_s from those for θ. The boundary and initial conditions for θ_u are found in this manner to be

$$\theta_u(\xi, 0) = -\theta_s(\xi), \; \theta_u(0, \tau) = 0, \; -\left.\frac{\partial \theta_u}{\partial \xi}\right|_{\xi=1} = Bi\theta_u(1, \tau)$$

Now we separate variables and write $\theta_u = \mathcal{T}(\tau)\mathcal{Z}(\xi)$. Repeating the procedure adopted earlier, we get

$$\frac{1}{\mathcal{T}}\frac{d\mathcal{T}}{d\tau} = \frac{1}{\mathcal{Z}}\frac{d^2\mathcal{Z}}{d\xi^2} = -\lambda^2$$

where we have used the idea that the separation constants must be negative as we have already accounted for the zero value. The above equations are easily solved and substituted into the assumed product form for θ_u to obtain

$$\theta_u = \exp(-\lambda^2\tau)\left[C_1 \sin(\lambda\xi) + C_2 \cos(\lambda\xi)\right]$$

In view of the boundary condition at $\xi = 0$, C_2 must be equal to zero. The boundary condition at $\xi = 1$ gives

$$\lambda \cos\lambda = -Bi \sin\lambda, \quad \text{or,} \quad \tan\lambda = -\frac{\lambda}{Bi}$$

There are several values of λ that can satisfy the this equation. The initial condition that has to be satisfied is

$$C_1 \sin(\lambda\xi) = -\theta_s(\xi) = -\frac{Bi}{Bi+1}\xi$$

Clearly the given condition cannot be satisfied with any single value of λ. Looking at the expression given, we need to express the function on the right hand side in terms of the "eigen functions" that have arisen out of solution by separation of variables. Sturm–Liouville theory[9] guarantees that this is possible, and tells that the eigen functions are "complete" and any arbitrary function can be expressed in terms of the eigen functions. Thus, we write

$$\mathcal{Z}(\xi) = \sum_{n=-\infty}^{\infty} C_n \sin(\lambda_n\xi)$$

The eigen values are obtained by solving the transcendental equation

$$\tan\lambda_n = -\frac{\lambda_n}{Bi} \tag{5.21}$$

The roots of this equation are shown graphically in figure 5.10 There are infinite number of roots and can be determined numerically. First, we notice from eq. 5.21 that since $\tan\lambda = -\tan(-\lambda)$, $\lambda_n = -\lambda_{-n}$. Further sine is an odd function. Hence, the solution can be written as

$$\mathcal{Z}(\xi) = \sum_{n=1}^{\infty}(C_n - C_{-n})\sin(\lambda_n\xi) = \sum_{n=1}^{\infty} C'_n \sin(\lambda_n\xi)$$

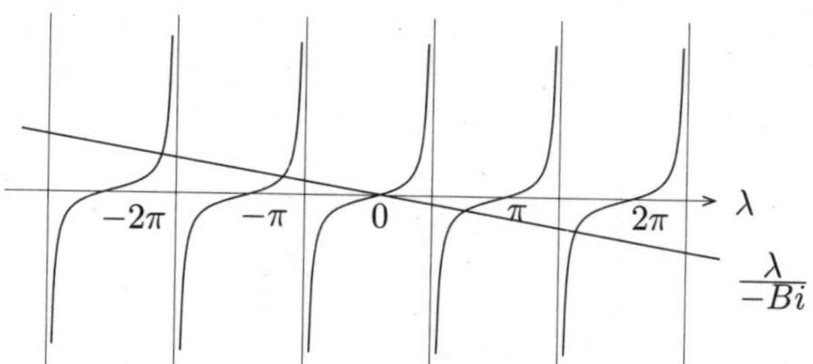

Figure 5.10. Roots of the equation $\tan\lambda_n = -\lambda_n/Bi$. The curves are plots of tan of angle. The straight line is the plot of$-\lambda_n/Bi$. Points of intersection give the roots.

and the positive roots are sufficient for description. Then, the initial condition requires that

$$-\frac{Bi}{Bi+1}\xi = \sum_{n=1}^{\infty} C'_n \sin(\lambda_n \xi)$$

The constants can be found from the initial condition using the orthogonal property of sines. It gives

$$C'_n = -\frac{Bi}{Bi+1}\frac{\int_0^1 x\sin(\lambda_n x)dx}{\int_0^1 \sin^2(\lambda_n x)dx}$$

The entire solution can now be written as

$$\frac{T-T_i}{T_b-T_i} = \frac{Bi}{Bi+1}\xi + \sum_{n=1}^{\infty} C_n \exp(-\lambda_n^2\tau)\sin(\lambda_n\xi)$$

5.13.4 Look at the results

Initially, the second term on the right hand side is equal and opposite in sign to the first term, because that is what we used to determine the constants, and hence $T = T_i$. The solution shows that as time increases, the second term on the right hand side decreases and goes to zero. The solution as $\tau \to \infty$ corresponds to that of steady state. τ is proportional to α/L^2. Thus, for a given thickness L, the exponential terms decrease more rapidly for materials with greater thermal diffusivity. This makes sense since greater thermal conductivity and or smaller heat capacities enable the material to respond faster to the changes in the environment. Similarly, for a given α, steady state is reached faster as L decreases. This also makes sense because resistance to conduction has reduced and the slab should adjust more quickly to environmental changes. These trends are as expected. Figure 5.11 shows qualitatively the temperature profiles as a function of time.

If the heat transfer coefficient increases, Bi increases. The slope of the straight line used to determine eigen values in figure 5.11 decreases as can be seen from the figure. Thus, λ_n values increase and the response is faster. This is to be expected since increasing heat transfer coefficient decreases the resistance due to convection.

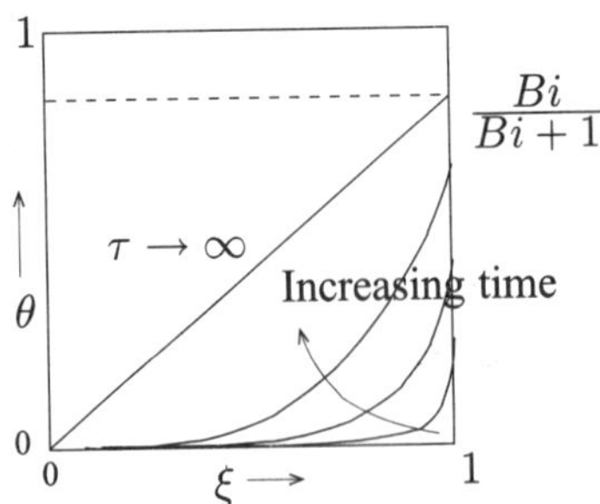

Figure 5.11. Qualitative trends in the temperature profiles in a slab exposed to hot fluid. Bi is constant.

Limiting cases

If $Bi \to \infty$, resistance due to convection is negligible. Here, the surface temperature should equal T_b. It can be seen from Figure 5.10 that as $Bi \to \infty$, the roots will tend to $n\pi$, and hence the surface temperature does equal T_b. If $Bi \to 0$, convection resistance dominates and hence the temperature in the slab will be uniform. This corresponds to $k \to \infty$ and $\partial T/\partial x \to 0$, but their product, which is the heat flux, will be finite because the temperature of the fluid and the slab are different. In particular, the heat flux into the slab at $x = L$ is given by $h(T_b - T)$. The equation for the change of temperature in the slab is obtained by shell balance and is given by

$$\rho \hat{C}_p L \frac{dT}{dt} = h(T_b - T)$$

We will leave it for you to show that the same can be obtained by integrating (over x) the original equation for change of temperature.

5.14 HEAT TRANSFER TO A RECTANGULAR SOLID

5.14.1 Problem identification

Let us next consider a two-dimensional problem but at steady state. Imagine a rectangular slab extending to infinity in the z direction, but its thicknesses in the other two dimensions are comparable. Let the solid occupy the domain $0 \leq x \leq a$ and $-b \leq y \leq b$. See figure 5.12. Suppose the

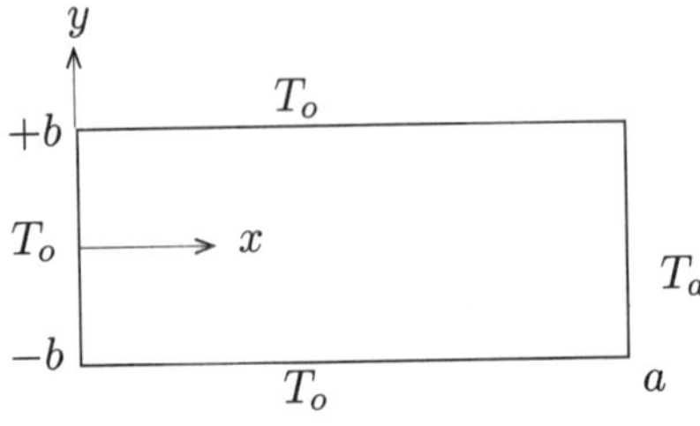

Figure 5.12. Sketch of a two dimensional slab showing boundary conditions.

surface at $x = 0$ is maintained at a constant temperature T_o while that at $x = a$ is maintained at a constant temperature T_a. Further suppose that the surfaces at $y = \pm b$ are maintained at a constant temperature T_o. Now it is desired to calculate the *steady* temperature distribution in the solid. It is similar to what one encounters with a door to a hot furnace, the inside wall is at one temperature while the other walls are at ambient.

Equation of change of temperature

As the solid extends to infinity in z direction, temperature does not depend on z. Temperature is not a function of time since steady state prevails. Thus, $T = T(x, y)$. Rectangular coordinates are the natural choice. The equation of change of temperature in these coordinates, with the usual assumptions of constant physical properties, no sources, *etc.* simplifies to

$$\frac{\partial^2 T}{\partial x^2} + \frac{\partial^2 T}{\partial y^2} = 0$$

Boundary conditions

We have a second order partial differential equation in x and y. We need two boundary conditions for each of the dimensions. The temperatures are being kept constant in each of the four surfaces. The boundary conditions are then given by

$$\begin{aligned} T(x,y) &= T_o \quad \text{at} \quad x = 0 \quad \text{and for all } y \\ T(x,y) &= T_a \quad \text{at} \quad x = a \quad \text{and for all } y \\ T(x,y) &= T_o \quad \text{at} \quad y = \pm b \quad \text{and for all } x \end{aligned}$$

5.14.2 Scaling

The temperature difference $(T_a - T_o)$ can be used to scale the temperature. There are two length scales, and either of them can be used. Let us select a. Thus,

$$\theta = \frac{T - T_o}{T_a - T_o}, \ \xi = \frac{x}{a}, \ \zeta = \frac{y}{a}$$

Dimensionless equations

The equation of change of temperature and the boundary conditions can be written in terms of the dimensionless variables as

$$\frac{\partial^2 \theta}{\partial \xi^2} + w^2 \frac{\partial^2 \theta}{\partial \zeta^2} = 0 \tag{5.22}$$

where w is the aspect ratio equal to a/b, and

$$\theta(0, \zeta) = 0, \ \theta(\xi, \pm 1) = 0, \ \theta(1, \zeta) = 1 \tag{5.23}$$

5.14.3 Temperature profile

We attempt to solve this equation by separation of variables:

$$\theta = \mathcal{X}(\xi)\mathcal{Y}(\zeta)$$

After substituting the assumed form into the equation of change of temperature and separating variables, we get

$$\frac{1}{\mathcal{X}}\frac{d^2\mathcal{X}}{d\xi^2} = -w^2\frac{1}{\mathcal{Y}}\frac{d^2\mathcal{Y}}{d\zeta^2} = C$$

where C is a constant. In the previous section, we chose the *sign* of the constant by using the idea that solution must remain finite as time tends to infinity. Here we use the *requirement* of the nature of Sturm–Liouville theory. Refer to the appendix of this chapter. Based on the experience of the previous section, we would expect C to turn out to be eigen values. Sturm–Liouville theory guarantees complete set of eigen functions and a solution when the boundary conditions are homogeneous. Thus, to obtain eigen functions, we should be focusing on the boundary conditions in ζ. The differential equation in ζ is given by

$$\frac{d^2\mathcal{Y}}{d\zeta^2} + \frac{C}{w^2}\mathcal{Y} = 0$$

Solution corresponding to $C = 0$ would not satisfy the boundary conditions. Now suppose that $C < 0$. The solutions are exponential in ζ, and the solutions for $\mathcal{X}$ are sines and cosines. The latter can be eigen functions. But, as the boundary conditions in ξ are not homogeneous, we should not expect to get a complete set of eigen functions. In contrast, if $C > 0$, sines and cosines are the solutions for $\mathcal{Y}$, and we will get eigen functions because the boundary conditions in ζ are homogeneous. Thus, let $C = \lambda^2$. Hence,

$$\mathcal{Y} = A_1 \cos\left(\frac{\lambda}{w}\zeta\right) + A_2 \sin\left(\frac{\lambda}{w}\zeta\right)$$

The boundary condition dictates symmetry in ζ. Thus, we choose cosines as the solution. Then, we require that

$$\mathcal{X}\mathcal{Y}(\pm 1) = 0,$$

This can only be satisfied if

$$\mathcal{Y}(\pm 1) = A_1 \cos\left(\frac{\pm\lambda}{w}\right) = 0$$

This gives the eigen values:

$$\lambda_n = \frac{(2n+1)\pi}{2}w, \; n = 0, 1, 2 \ldots$$

The differential equation for $\mathcal{X}$ is given by

$$\frac{d^2\mathcal{X}}{d\xi^2} - \lambda_n^2\mathcal{X} = 0$$

and the solution is

$$\mathcal{X} = E_n \sinh(\lambda_n\xi), + D_n \cosh(\lambda_n\xi)$$

The solution can now be written as

$$\theta = \sum_{n=0}^{\infty} [a_n \sinh(\lambda_n \xi) + b_n \cosh(\lambda_n \xi)] \cos\left(\frac{(2n+1)\pi}{2}\zeta\right)$$

The boundary conditions require that

$$\theta(0, \zeta) = 0$$

which is satisfied by setting b_n to zero. The other boundary condition requires

$$\theta(1, \zeta) = 1$$

and hence

$$\sum_{n=0}^{\infty} a_n \sinh(\lambda_n) \cos\left(\frac{(2n+1)\pi}{2}\zeta\right) = 1$$

Using the orthogonal properties of the cosine functions,

$$\begin{aligned} a_n \sinh(\lambda_n) &= \frac{\displaystyle\int_{-1}^{1} \cos\left(\frac{(2n+1)\pi}{2}\zeta\right) d\zeta}{\displaystyle\int_{-1}^{1} \cos^2\left(\frac{(2n+1)\pi}{2}\zeta\right) d\zeta} \\ &= (-1)^n \frac{4}{(2n+1)\pi} \end{aligned}$$

Summarizing

$$\theta = \sum_{n=0}^{\infty} (-1)^n \frac{4}{(2n+1)\pi} \frac{\sinh(\lambda_n \xi)}{\sinh(\lambda_n)} \cos\left(\frac{(2n+1)\pi}{2}\zeta\right) \tag{5.24}$$

5.14.4 Look at the results

The isotherms obtained from the solution are sketched in figure 5.13. Isotherm of $\theta = 0$ are the

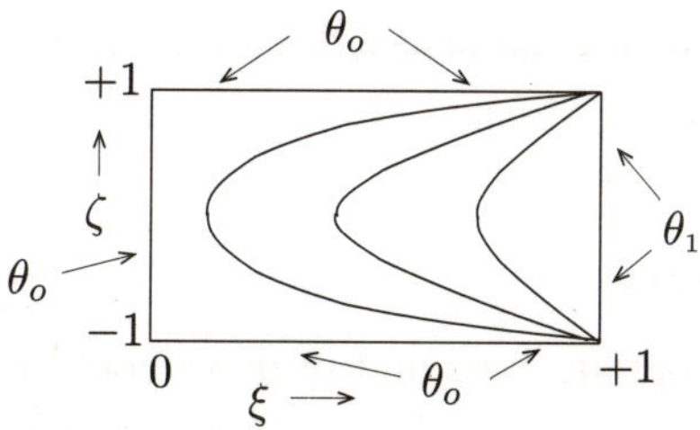

Figure 5.13. Temperature profiles in a two-dimensional slab. The isotherms are marked. The $\theta = 1$ isotherm is the face at $\xi = 1$. The other faces coincide with the $\theta = 0$ isotherms. The curves are for intermediate values of θ.

lines corresponding to $\xi = 0$ and $\zeta = \pm 1$. Isotherm of $\theta = 1$ is the line corresponding to $\xi = 1$. Temperature falls gradually. Lines orthogonal to the isotherms show the lines along which heat flows. It is easily seen that heat flows from right wall to the side walls as well as to the opposite wall. Note the symmetry. The heat loss from the right wall can be computed from

$$\text{Heat loss, per unit width, from the wall} = \int_{-1}^{1} k \left.\frac{\partial T}{\partial x}\right|_{x=a} dy$$

It can be seen that the temperature profiles are independent of thermal conductivity and that only the heat loss increases with the conductivity. This is because the equation of change of temperature and the boundary conditions do not contain the thermal conductivity. The temperature profile is solely determined by the geometry.

5.15 HEAT DISSIPATION FROM A SOURCE

We illustrate a solution of a different type from those involving eigen values and similarity solution. Imagine an instantaneous heat source left in an infinitely large space. It will lose heat to the surroundings and the temperature of the surroundings will change with location and time. We are interested in calculating the temporal temperature distribution in space. The problem is solved in a somewhat round about way. First we solve the problem of how an arbitrary initial temperature distribution in infinitely large medium changes with time. Then we imagine a small spherical region into which the heat source is put suddenly, the spherical region itself being part of an infinite medium. The temperature of the sphere will rise, and we calculate how it decreases using the results obtained from our results on temperature redistribution in an infinite medium. Limit of this result as the radius of sphere goes to zero gives the desired result! Though complicated, this path requires mathematics only at an ordinary level.

5.15.1 Problem identification: Redistribution of initial temperature profile

Imagine an infinitely large solid. Suppose, its initial temperature distribution was non-uniform. We would like to know how it will reach a uniform temperature eventually. We will take a simple case where the initial temperature distribution is only a function of x. Since, temperature is not uniform, heat will flow from regions of higher to lower temperatures, and the temperature distribution will evolve with time. It is this that we would like to calculate. As the initial temperature distribution is not a function of y and z coordinates, no heat will flow in those directions, and temperature will continue to not depend upon those coordinates. Thus, $T = T(x, t)$. Convection is absent and there are no heat sources.

Equation of change of temperature

Rectangular coordinates are appropriate here and in these coordinates, the equation of change of temperature simplifies to

$$\frac{\partial T}{\partial t} = \alpha \frac{\partial^2 T}{\partial x^2}$$

Initial condition

As the solid is infinite, there are no boundary conditions. Let the initial condition be

$$T(x,0) = f(x) \quad -\infty < x < \infty$$

5.15.2 Separation of variables

Neither a length scale nor a time scale nor a temperature difference is available. Thus, we attempt a solution and do not look for scaling. If at all a similarity solution works, the similarity variable would be given by

$$\eta \sim \frac{x}{\sqrt{\alpha t}}$$

For similarity solution to work, we know that the temperature must be same at $t = 0$, and as $x \to \infty$ since both correspond to $\eta \to \infty$. But this is not the case in the present problem and we know that similarity solution will not work. We try separation of variables. Let us try

$$T = \mathcal{X}(x)\tau(t)$$

Substituting this into the equation of change of temperature and separating variables, we get

$$\frac{1}{\tau}\frac{d\tau}{dt} = \frac{1}{\mathcal{X}}\frac{d^2\mathcal{X}}{dx^2} = -\gamma^2$$

where we chose a negative constant since temperature cannot increase indefinitely with time. Thus, the solution is given by

$$T = \exp^{-\alpha\gamma^2 t}\left(A\cos\gamma x + B\sin\gamma x\right)$$

The initial condition demands that

$$f(x) = \left(A\cos\gamma x + B\sin\gamma x\right)$$

A single value of γ is not enough to satisfy the initial condition. When there was a finite length scale, we got infinite number of *discrete* values for γ. These are specific values and hence, they are referred to as eigen values, eigen being a German word for specific. The present situation is resolved by letting γ be continuous. An arbitrary function could be expanded in terms of a complete set of eigen functions. The corresponding theorem for the present situation is the Fourier's integral. Fourier's integral[10] states that any arbitrary function of x can be expanded in terms of cosines as follows:

$$f(x) = \frac{1}{\pi}\int_0^{\infty} d\gamma \int_{-\infty}^{\infty} d\lambda f(\lambda)\cos\gamma(\lambda - x)$$

After noting that

$$\cos\gamma(\lambda - x) = \cos\gamma\lambda\cos\gamma x + \sin\gamma\lambda\sin\gamma x$$

and comparing the initial condition with the Fourier's integral, we can solve for A and B as

$$A = \frac{1}{\pi}\int_{-\infty}^{\infty} d\lambda f(\lambda)\cos\gamma\lambda$$

$$B = \frac{1}{\pi} \int_{-\infty}^{\infty} d\lambda f(\lambda) \sin \gamma\lambda$$

Substituting these results, we find the solution to be

$$T = \frac{1}{\pi} \int_{-\infty}^{\infty} d\lambda f(\lambda) \int_{0}^{\infty} d\gamma \text{exp}^{-\alpha\gamma^2 t} \cos \gamma(\lambda - x)$$

You need the value of a definite integral to simplify further. You can look it up in some table of integrals and is given by

$$\int_{0}^{\infty} da \text{exp}^{-m^2 a^2} \cos na = \frac{\sqrt{\pi}}{2m} \text{exp} {-n^2/(4m^2)}$$

where a is a dummy variable of integration. This can be used to simplify our solution to

$$T(x,t) = \frac{1}{\sqrt{4\alpha\pi t}} \int_{-\infty}^{\infty} d\lambda f(\lambda) \text{exp}^{-(\lambda-x)^2/(4\alpha t)}$$

which can be rewritten as

$$T(x,t) = \frac{1}{\sqrt{4\alpha\pi t}} \int_{0}^{\infty} d\lambda f(\lambda) \left(\text{exp}^{-(\lambda-x)^2/(4\alpha t)} - \text{exp}^{-(\lambda+x)^2/(4\alpha t)} \right) \tag{5.25}$$

5.15.3 Problem identification: Heat loss from hot sphere

Let us now proceed to the next step. Consider the following problem. Let us imagine we have an infinitely large solid. Let us suppose its temperature was zero. Let us select a spherical region of radius R in this body. Suppose, somehow, we suddenly released Q amount of energy only in that sphere. Further suppose that all the heat went into raising the temperature of the sphere only. Its temperature would rise and will be given by

$$T(r) = \frac{3Q}{4\pi R^3 \rho \hat{C}_p} \quad 0 \leq r \leq R$$

Now as a starting point, we have an infinite solid with the above initial distribution in the region $0 < r < R$ and zero everywhere else. The spherical region will now lose heat into the rest of the infinitely large body surrounding it, and we want to calculate the dynamics of the temperature redistribution. This problem can be solved by applying the results obtained in the previous section, but the problem has to be solved in spherical coordinates. We proceed to show how this is done.

Equation of change of temperature

Convection and heat sources are absent. Spherical coordinates are appropriate for this problem. Radial symmetry can be expected here and the equation of change of temperature simplifies to

$$\frac{\partial T}{\partial t} = \alpha \frac{1}{r^2} \frac{\partial}{\partial r} \left(r^2 \frac{\partial T}{\partial r} \right)$$

The initial condition is

$$\begin{aligned} T(r,0) &= \frac{3Q}{4\pi R^3 \rho \hat{C}_p} \qquad 0 \le r \le R \\ &= 0 \qquad\qquad r > R \end{aligned}$$

By using the substitution $u = Tr$, it turns out that the equation of change of temperature can also be written as

$$\frac{\partial u}{\partial t} = \alpha \frac{\partial^2 u}{\partial r^2}$$

The initial condition now is given by

$$\begin{aligned} u(r,0) &= \frac{3Q}{4\pi R^3 \rho \hat{C}_p} r \qquad 0 \le r \le R \\ &= 0 \qquad\qquad r > R \end{aligned}$$

The equations now look like those in Cartesian coordinates and we can apply eq. 5.25. The result is

$$u(r,t) = \frac{1}{\sqrt{4\alpha\pi t}} \int_0^R d\lambda \frac{3Q}{4\pi R^3 \rho \hat{C}_p} \lambda \left(\exp^{-(\lambda - r)^2/(4\alpha t)} - \exp^{-(\lambda + r)^2/(4\alpha t)} \right)$$

It can be rewritten as

$$u(r,t) = \frac{1}{\sqrt{4\alpha\pi t}} \int_0^R d\lambda \frac{3Q}{4\pi R^3 \rho \hat{C}_p} \lambda \exp^{-r^2/(4\alpha t)} \left(\exp^{-(\lambda^2 - 2\lambda r)/(4\alpha t)} - \exp^{-(\lambda^2 + 2\lambda r)/(4\alpha t)} \right)$$

Now we are ready to take the last step. Let us recall that we are actually interested in how an instantaneous point source spreads. Result for a point source is obtained by letting $R \to 0$. When this limit is being taken, the value of λ will be very small. Keeping this in mind, we can expand the exponentials and retain linear terms in λ to obtain

$$\begin{aligned} u(r,t) &= \frac{1}{\sqrt{4\alpha\pi t}} \int_0^R d\lambda \frac{3Q}{4\pi R^3 \rho \hat{C}_p} \lambda \exp^{-r^2/(4\alpha t)} (4\lambda r)/(4\alpha t) \\ &= \frac{1}{\sqrt{4\alpha\pi t}} \frac{Q}{4\pi \rho \hat{C}_p} \frac{r}{4\alpha t} \exp^{-r^2/(4\alpha t)} \end{aligned}$$

We can now write the expression for the temperature as

$$\rho \hat{C}_p T(r,t) = Q \left(\frac{1}{\sqrt{4\alpha t}} \right)^3 \exp^{-\frac{r^2}{4\alpha t}} \tag{5.26}$$

We have written the left hand side as the energy density. As expected, temperature far away from the source will be zero. The temperature at the location of the source is infinitely large initially since a finite source was released into zero volume. But temperature decreases with time as heat flows away. We alluded to diffusion and heat transfer being similar. It is easier to visualize the problem we posed in the context of mass transfer. Imagine a bottle of perfume opened in the middle of a room, and we can ask how the perfume spreads into the room. A more unpleasant situation would be about a sudden release of a pollutant into atmosphere. These problems will be more complex in reality since convection is likely to be present as well.

Appendix

5.A Equations of fluid mechanics

In this and the next chapters, we consider application of the balance laws for energy and mass of individual species. As mentioned in chapter 1, convection is one mode of transferring mass and heat. Convection exists if there is motion at a macroscopic level. Hence, velocity distribution or velocities at every point is needed to deal with convection. In this section, we give a quick account of this. For a more detailed discussion, readers should refer to books on fluid mechanics[11]

5.A.1 Equation of continuity

We consider the balance of total mass in an open system. Apply eq. 2.5 to the system by replacing ϕ by ρ. This will give the equation for conservation of total mass:

$$\begin{aligned}\frac{d}{dt}\int_{V_s(t)} \rho(\mathbf{x},t) &= \int_V \frac{\partial \rho(\mathbf{x},t)}{\partial t} dV + \int_V \nabla.(\mathbf{v}\rho(\mathbf{x},t))dV \\ &= \int_V \left(\frac{\partial \rho(\mathbf{x},t)}{\partial t} + \nabla.(\rho(\mathbf{x},t)\mathbf{v})\right) dV\end{aligned}$$

The left hand side is zero by law of conservation of mass. Hence

$$0 = \int_V \left(\frac{\partial \rho(\mathbf{x},t)}{\partial t} + \nabla(.\rho(\mathbf{x},t)\mathbf{v})\right) dV$$

The integral should vanish not only on the control volume chosen, but in any portion of it also since the choice of the control volume is arbitrary. One way the integral can vanish on any arbitrary control volume is if there are mutually compensating discontinuities in the domain of interest. However, this would not be possible *if we are to restrict ourselves to a control volume composed of a single phase*. Then, the integral can vanish for any arbitrary control volume only if the integrand itself is equal to zero. Thus,

$$\frac{\partial \rho(\mathbf{x},t)}{\partial t} + \nabla.(\rho(\mathbf{x},t)\mathbf{v}) = 0 \tag{A5.27}$$

If ρ is assumed to be constant, the above reduces to the commonly used equation

$$\nabla.\mathbf{v} = 0 \tag{A5.28}$$

5.A.2 Cauchy's equation of motion

We consider the balance of total linear momentum in an open system. First for simplicity, consider balance of x-momentum. Apply eq. 2.5 to the system by replacing ϕ by ρv_x. For simplicity, we do not indicate the explicit dependence of all variables on $\mathbf{x}, t$. Then,

$$\begin{aligned}\frac{d}{dt}\int_{V_s(t)} \rho v_x \, dV &= \int_V \frac{(\partial \rho v_x)}{\partial t} dV + \int_V \nabla.(\mathbf{v}\rho v_x)dV \\ &= \int_V \left(\frac{\partial(\rho v_x)}{\partial t} + \nabla.(\rho\mathbf{v}v_x)\right) dV\end{aligned}$$

$$= \boxed{\int\limits_V v_x \left(\frac{\partial \rho}{\partial t} + \nabla.(\rho \mathbf{v}) \right) dV} + \int\limits_V \left(\rho \frac{\partial v_x}{\partial t} + (\rho \mathbf{v}.\nabla) v_x \right) dV$$

$$= \int\limits_V \rho \left(\frac{\partial v_x}{\partial t} + (\mathbf{v}.\nabla) v_x \right) dV$$

The last equation is obtained after setting the boxed term to zero by applying equation of continuity to it. From Newton's second law, the rate of change of x-momentum of a body is equal to the sum of x-components of forces acting on it:

$$\text{Sum of x-components of forces acting on the CV} = \int\limits_V \rho \left(\frac{\partial v_x}{\partial t} + (\mathbf{v}.\nabla) v_x \right) dV$$

$$= \int\limits_V \rho \left(\frac{\partial \mathbf{v}}{\partial t} + (\mathbf{v}.\nabla) \mathbf{v} \right) .\mathbf{i} dV$$

where $\mathbf{i}$ is the unit vector in the x direction. If $\mathbf{g}$ is the body force acting per unit mass of the fluid and $\mathbf{T}$ is the total stress tensor corresponding to surface forces, the left hand side is given by

$$\int\limits_V \rho \mathbf{g}.\mathbf{i} dV + \int\limits_A \mathbf{n}.\mathbf{T}.\mathbf{i} dA = \int\limits_V (\rho \mathbf{g} + \nabla.\mathbf{T}) .\mathbf{i} dV$$

where the last transformation follows by application of Gauss's theorem. Substituting this in the momentum balance, we obtain

$$\int\limits_V (\rho \mathbf{g} + \nabla.\mathbf{T}) .\mathbf{i} dV = \int\limits_V \rho \left(\frac{\partial \mathbf{v}}{\partial t} + (\mathbf{v}.\nabla) \mathbf{v} \right) .\mathbf{i} dV$$

Generalizing the above into a vector equation and applying the argument about integrand having to be zero for integral on any arbitrary control volume to vanish, we obtain Cauchy's equation of motion:

$$\rho \frac{\partial \mathbf{v}}{\partial t} + \rho (\mathbf{v}.\nabla) \mathbf{v} = \rho \mathbf{g} + \nabla.\mathbf{T}$$

If the total stress tensor is written as a sum of isotropic compressive pressure p, and deviatoric stress tensor $\boldsymbol{\tau}$, we get

$$\rho \frac{\partial \mathbf{v}}{\partial t} + \rho (\mathbf{v}.\nabla) \mathbf{v} = \rho \mathbf{g} - \nabla p + \nabla.\boldsymbol{\tau} \qquad \text{(A5.29)}$$

5.A.3 Navier–Stokes equation

Newton–Stokes law of viscosity states that

$$\boldsymbol{\tau} = \mu \left(\nabla \mathbf{v} + (\nabla \mathbf{v})^t \right) - \frac{2}{3} \mu \mathbf{I} \nabla.v \qquad \text{(A5.30)}$$

where superscript t stands for transpose, and $\mathbf{I}$ is the identity matrix. If this is substituted into Cauchy's equation of motion, and ρ and μ are assumed to be constant, we get the Navier–Stokes equation:

$$\rho \frac{\partial \mathbf{v}}{\partial t} + \rho (\mathbf{v}.\nabla) \mathbf{v} = -\nabla p + \mu \nabla^2 \mathbf{v} + \rho \mathbf{g} \qquad \text{(A5.31)}$$

Solutions to problems in fluid mechanics are obtained by solving eq. A5.28 and eq. A5.31 along with the relevant boundary conditions. *We remind ourselves that we have to solve the equations in a domain consisting of a single phase.* When dealing with practical problems however, we will encounter boundaries between phases. For example, the domain of interest in flow of a gas in a pipe will be bounded by a solid–fluid interface. Boundary conditions have to be selected to deal with these interfaces. The boundary conditions commonly used are selected as appropriate from

1. No slip boundary condition at fluid–solid and fluid–fluid interfaces
2. Stress continuity condition at fluid–fluid interfaces
3. Specified stress condition at fluid–solid interfaces
4. Negligible shear stress condition at gas–liquid interfaces

5.A.4 Equation of mechanical energy balance

Cauchy's equation of motion is the equivalent of Newton's second law for fluids. It can be used to calculate the motion created as a result of application of forces. Rate at which work is done is related to application of force and the velocity created in response. Equation of motion describes the response of fluid to applied forces. Thus, it should be possible to derive an equation for the work done, and its effects, from the equation of motion. The effect of work done on a body could be to increase its kinetic energy or increase its gravitational potential energy and so on. An 'account' of the effects of work done can be thought of as *mechanical energy balance*. The rate of work done *by* a force is equal to the dot product of the force and the velocity created. Thus, if we obtain the dot product of the equation of motion with velocity, we can derive an equation of mechanical energy balance. A dot product of that equation with velocity vector gives a balance of mechanical energy: conversion of work done into kinetic energy and other forms of energy. The result is derived in many books on fluid mechanics and is given here for further reference:

$$\frac{\partial}{\partial t}(\frac{1}{2}\rho v^2) + \nabla.\mathbf{v}(\frac{1}{2}\rho v^2) = \rho\mathbf{g}.\mathbf{v} - \nabla.p\mathbf{v} + p\nabla.\mathbf{v} + \nabla.\boldsymbol{\tau}.\mathbf{v} - \boldsymbol{\tau} : \nabla\mathbf{v} \tag{A5.32}$$

This equation is interpreted as follows. The first term on the right hand side is the work done by body forces on the fluid particles. The second term is the work done by pressure forces. The third term is that part of the work done by pressure forces which is reversible and goes into compressing the fluid. The fourth term is the work done by viscous forces. The last term represents that part of work done by viscous forces that goes into heat due to the irreversible nature of the viscous forces or their frictional aspects. Thus, the difference between the total work done on the fluid and the work that has been stored as compression of fluid and lost as heat goes towards increasing the kinetic energy of the fluid, which is represented by the left hand side.

5.B Separation of variables

Several linear partial differential equations will be encountered in this text. This section of the appendix gives examples of the type of equations we encounter in the text, and the theory relevant to solving them. For more detail, the reader should refer to standard texts on partial differential equations. We can often solve them by using the technique of separation of variables. The idea is as follows.

Suppose we are dealing with the coordinate system y_1, y_2, y_3. Consider some dependent variable $C(y_1, y_2, y_3, t)$. Suppose it obeys an equation of the form

$$C(y_i, t) = T(t)Y_1(y_1)Y_2(y_2)Y_3(y_3)$$

When we substitute the assumed form into the partial differential equation obeyed by C, it is found that the partial differential equation is made up of the sum of *ordinary* differential equations, one each for T and Y_i. Let us represent these ordinary differential equations by $f_1(T, T^{(n)}, t)$, $f_i(Y_i, Y_i^{(n)}, y_i)$ where the superscript n indicates the nth derivative. It often turns out that the original partial differential equation as represented by sum of *ordinary* differential equations, one each for T and Y_i can be rearranged to get

$$f_1(T, T^{(n)}, t) = \sum_i f_i(Y_i, Y_i^{(n)}, y_i), \quad f_i(Y_i, Y_i^{(n)}, y_i) = \sum_{j \neq i} f_j(Y_j, Y_j^{(n)}, y_j)$$

Because each is a function of a single *independent* variable, the only way by which the equations given can be satisfied is that they all must equal a constant. Then each of these differential equations is solved to construct the desired solution.

Consider the following partial differential equation in Cartesian coordinates:

$$\frac{\partial C}{\partial t} = \frac{\partial^2 C}{\partial x^2} + \frac{\partial^2 C}{\partial y^2}$$

Assume that $C = T(t)X(x)Y(Y)$. Substituting this we find that the partial differential equation is equivalent to

$$XY\frac{dT}{dt} = TY\frac{d^2X}{dx^2} + TX\frac{d^2Y}{dy^2}$$

Dividing by TXY we find

$$\frac{1}{T}\frac{dT}{dt} = \frac{1}{X}\frac{d^2X}{dx^2} + \frac{1}{Y}\frac{d^2Y}{dy^2}$$

The left hand side is only a function of t while the right hand side is a function of x and y. Hence both must be equal to a constant, say $-\lambda$. Hence we have

$$\frac{1}{T}\frac{dT}{dt} = -\lambda$$

and

$$\lambda = -\frac{1}{X}\frac{d^2X}{dx^2} + \frac{1}{Y}\frac{d^2Y}{dy^2}$$

The first equation is a differential equation for T and can be solved. The second equation can be rearranged to get

$$\frac{1}{X}\frac{d^2X}{dx^2} + \lambda = \frac{1}{Y}\frac{d^2Y}{dy^2}$$

Once again while the left hand side is a function of x only, the right hand side is a function of y. Hence both sides must be equal to another constant, say α. Hence we have

$$\frac{1}{Y}\frac{d^2Y}{dy^2} = \alpha$$

and

$$\frac{1}{X}\frac{d^2X}{dx^2} = \alpha - \lambda$$

These two are ordinary differential equations that can be solved. We find the solution that satisfies the boundary conditions by **choosing** the constants α and λ.

Separation of partial differential equations in curvilinear coordinates can be done in a similar way and you should refer to a book to see how it is done.

5.B.1 Sturm–Liouville problems

A concept that is invariably associated with the technique of separation of variables is the idea that any arbitrary function can be 'expanded' in terms of a **set of complete** orthogonal functions. This set is referred to as a (complete) **basis** set. This is similar to the idea of Fourier series with which you are already familiar, *i.e.* any arbitrary function of an independent variable, x, $0 < x < 2\pi$ can be expanded in terms of sine and cosine functions of x. In a broad manner, it is similar to any arbitrary vector in space being expanded in terms of the basis vectors, *i.e.,* the unit vectors.

The main point to note is that such basis functions have to come from solving ordinary differential equations of the type that arise when a partial differential equation is separated.

The Sturm–Liouville theory[12] gives mathematical conditions, which when satisfied, assure that a set orthogonal and complete basis functions arise while solving ordinary differential equations along with boundary conditions.

Consider a homogeneous differential equation of the form

$$[r(x)X'(x)]' + [q(x) + \lambda p(x)]X = 0 \tag{A5.33}$$

where superscript prime refers to differentiation with respect to x. Let $a \leq x \leq b$ be the domain of interest. Suppose we need to find a solution subject to the boundary conditions

$$a_1 X(a) + a_2 X'(a) = 0 \tag{A5.34}$$

and

$$b_1 X(b) + b_2 X'(b) = 0 \tag{A5.35}$$

The following are the results of theory by Sturm and Liouville.

5.B.2 Regular Sturm–Liouville problem

If $p, q, r,$ and r' are real, continuous and $p > 0$ as well as $q > 0$, the problem is called a regular Sturm-Liouville problem.

1. A regular Sturm–Liouville problem has non-trivial solutions for infinite number of real values of λ_n, $n = 1, 2, 3, \ldots$, called **eigen values** or **spectrum of eigen values**.
2. The function X_n obtained by solving the differential equation for each eigen value is called an **eigen function**.
3. The eigen functions corresponding to two distinct eigen values are orthogonal to each other, *i.e.,*

$$\int_a^b p(x) X_m X_n dx = \text{Constant } \delta_{mn}$$

4. The eigen functions are unique and complete.
5. The 'completeness' of the eigen functions assures that any arbitrary function $f(x)$ in the domain of $a \leq x \leq b$ can be expanded in terms of X_n:

$$f(x) = \sum_n f_n X_n$$

where f_n are constants. They can be determined using the orthogonal property of the eigen functions:

$$f_n = \frac{\int_a^b f(x) X(x) dx}{\int_a^b X^2(x) dx}$$

5.B.3 Singular Sturm–Liouville problem

If any of the conditions imposed upon p, q and r are not satisfied, the problem is called a singular Sturm–Liouville problem. We discuss only one case that is of interest in the present context because it arises in curvilinear coordinates where r vanishes either at a or at b. In this case also the results stated for the regular Sturm–Liouville problem are valid provided p, r and r' are continuous in the closed interval $a \leq x \leq b$, and q is continuous in the open interval $a < x < b$. However, the boundary conditions at a or b have to be dropped or modified as follows:

1. $r(a) = 0$, eq. A5.34 is dropped
2. $r(b) = 0$, eq. A5.35 is dropped
3. $r(a) = r(b)$, the boundary conditions have to be altered to $X(a) = X(b)$ and $X'(a) = X'(b)$

An example is the Bessel's equation which arises in cylindrical coordinates. When boundary conditions are dropped, that the function must be bounded or be finite is required for physical reasons. This is the case with solutions involving Bessel functions, Legendre functions, *etc.*

Problems for Chapter 5.

5.1 (a) Solve for the temperature profiles in a radial reactor in the limit of large Peclet numbers. Be careful in working the problem since the differential equation can become first order if you are not careful. You might wonder what this means. Can there be a minimum temperature in the reactor? Explain.

(b) Rework the problem of temperature profiles in a radial reactor with Danckwerts boundary conditions. Comment upon the differences between the two solutions.

5.2 A semi-infinite slab initially at T_i is suddenly exposed to a fluid at T_f. The heat transfer coefficient is h while the thermal conductivity is k.

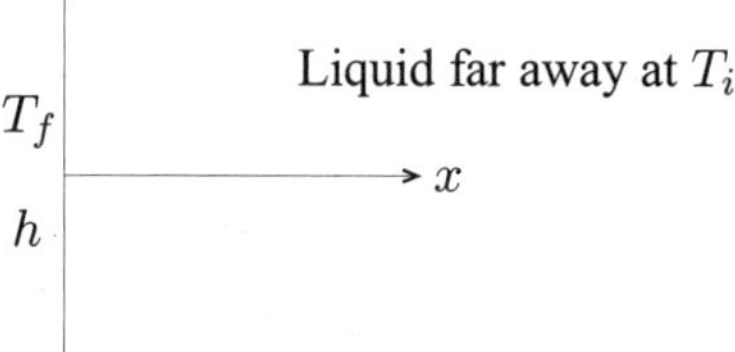

Figure for problem 5.2.

(i) Sketch how temperature profiles will change with time and distance. Show the effect of small and large h in a qualitative but comparative manner. (ii) Formulate the unsteady state conduction equation and specify the initial and boundary conditions. (iii) Define non-dimensional temperature, and a new dependent variable

$$\theta = \frac{T - T_f}{T_i - T_f} \quad \phi = \theta - \frac{k}{h}\frac{\partial \theta}{\partial x}$$

We now look for a similarity solution for ϕ in terms of the similarity variable $\eta = \sqrt{\frac{x^2}{4\alpha t}}$ Show that ϕ satisfies the same partial differential equation as θ. Show that partial differential equation for ϕ does admit a similarity solution with η as a similarity variable. What are the initial and boundary conditions for ϕ? Solve the equation to find ϕ. (iv) Derive an expression for θ.

5.3 Consider a semi-infinite body occupying the positive half of the x axis. It is initially at a temperature of T_o. For $t > 0$, the face at $x = 0$ is supplied with a periodically varying heat flux given by $q_m \cos \omega t$. Determine the *steady* periodic temperature profile created. Hint: You may try to solve it using complex variables.

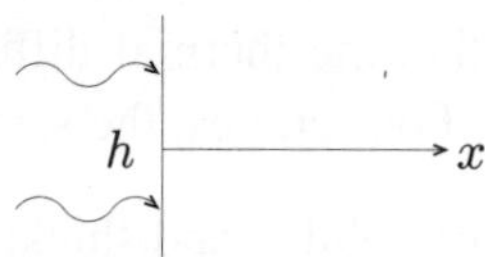

Figure for problem 5.3.

5.4 Consider a solid bounded by two planes at $x = 0$ and $x = l$. The solid is initially at a uniform temperature of T_o. At $t > 0$, the surface at $x = l$ is maintained at $T_s \cos\omega t$ while the surface at $x = 0$ is maintained at T_o itself. (a) Find the steady periodic temperature reached in the body. (b) Which problem of fluid mechanics is this analogous to?

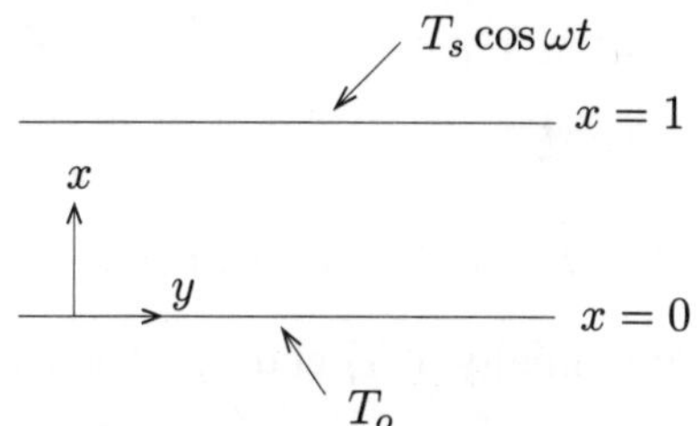

Figure for problem 5.4.

5.5 Consider a solid bounded by two planes at $x = 0$ and $x = l$. The solid is initially at a uniform

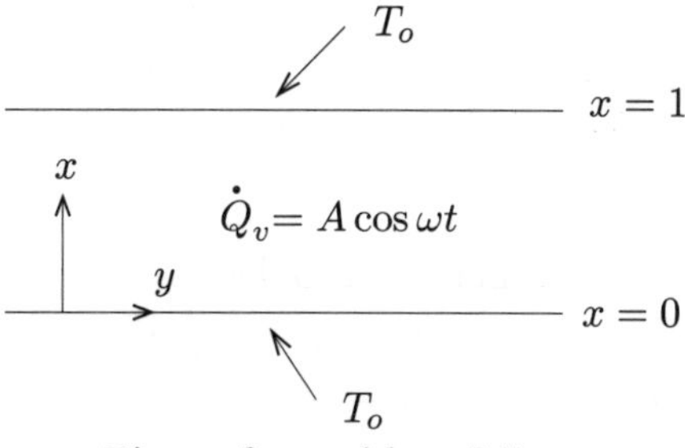

Figure for problem 5.5.

temperature of T_o. At $t > 0$, heat is generated uniformly inside the body at a rate given by $\dot{Q}_v = A \cos\omega t$. Both the surfaces at $x = l$ and at $x = 0$ are maintained at T_o itself. (a) Find the steady periodic temperature reached in the body. (b) Which problem of fluid mechanics is this analogous to?

5.6 It is known that near the surface of the earth, the temperature (averaged over long periods of time, e.g., a year) increases with depth. It is referred to as geothermal gradient and is measured (in the recent times) to be $0.04°C/m$. We wish to estimate the age of earth from this measurement.

Suppose that, at its time of birth, earth was a solid mass at its melting point: $3500°C$. Since its birth, it has been losing heat to the outer space. This cooling process can be approximated by assuming that the surface of the earth is at a constant temperature of $0°C$. It is also known that, even now, the depth of penetration is very small compared to the diameter of the earth. Estimate the age of earth given that the thermal diffusivity of earth is $10^{-6}m^2/s$. (If you don't like this problem, curse Mr. Fourier, yes, the same fellow.)

5.7 Consider an infinitely long slab of solid 1 and thickness L in perfect contact with a semi-infinite solid 2. Both solids are initially at T_i. At $t = 0$, the temperature of the free surface of solid 1 is raised to T_o. Simplify the thermal energy balance for this situation. Specify the initial and boundary conditions. Solve the problem using Laplace transformation.

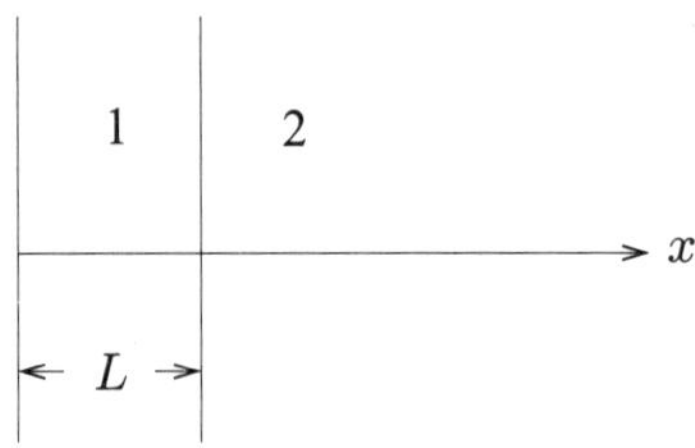

Figure for problem 5.7.

5.8 Two semi-infinite bodies are initially at T_l and T_r. Their thermal diffusivities are α_l and α_r

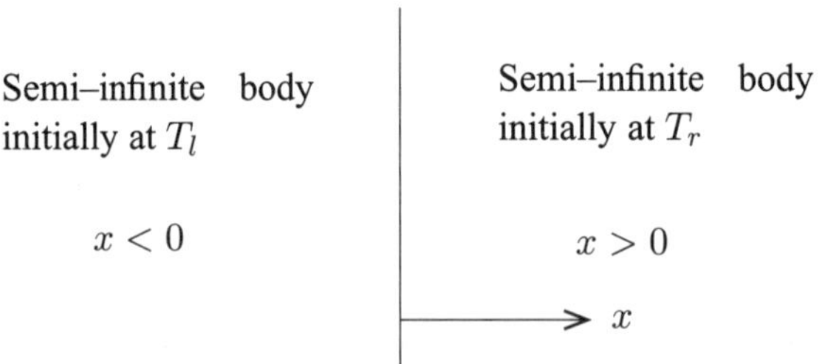

Figure for problem 5.8.

respectively. Their thermal conductivities are k_l and k_r respectively. They are brought into contact with each other at $t = 0$. The temperature profiles in both bodies are expected to obey similarity solution, i.e.,

$$T = A + B \int exp(-\eta^2)d\eta, \text{ and } \eta = \frac{x}{\sqrt{4\alpha t}}$$

where A and B are constants. (i) Find the temperature profiles in both the solids as a function of time. You will need the Leibnitz formula for differentiating an integral. (ii) Sketch the temperature profiles for $t = 0$, $t = t_1$ and t_2 where $t_1 > t_2$. (iii) What is the value of the interface temperature? (iv) When you touch a metal or wood, both at the same temperature but lower than the body temperature, your hand **instantaneously** feels colder with metal rather than wood. Can you explain why?

5.9 Find the steady state two-dimensional temperature distribution in an infinitely long rectangular solid. The surfaces at $y = \pm B$ are exposed to a flowing fluid at a temperature of T_a and the heat transfer coefficient is h. The surface at $x = 0$ is being maintained at T_o while the surface at $x = L$ is being maintained at T_1.

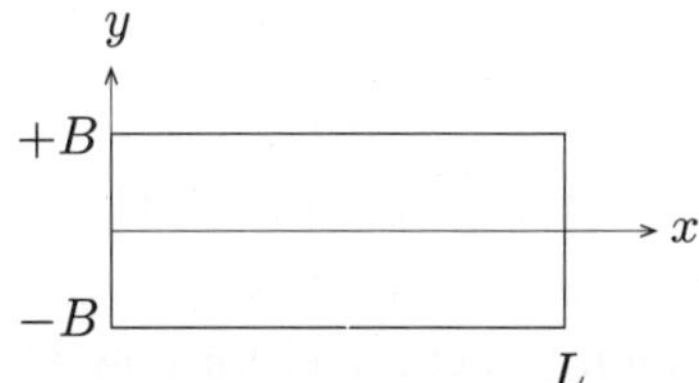

Figure for problem 5.9.

5.10 Consider an infinite slab of thickness L. It is initially at temperature T_o. From $t > 0$, the face at $x = 0$ is being supplied with a **constant** heat flux q_o while the other face is being maintained at T_o. We are interested in finding the unsteady temperature profile $T(x, t)$. (i) Find the temperature profile at *steady state*, T_s. (ii) What is the energy equation for unsteady state? What are the boundary conditions? (iii) Are the boundary conditions in form required by Sturm–Liouville theory? (iv) Define $\theta = T - T_s$. Substitute this form in the energy equation and derive the equation for θ. What are the boundary conditions for θ? Are the boundary conditions in form required by Sturm–Liouville theory? (v) Find the unsteady temperature profile.

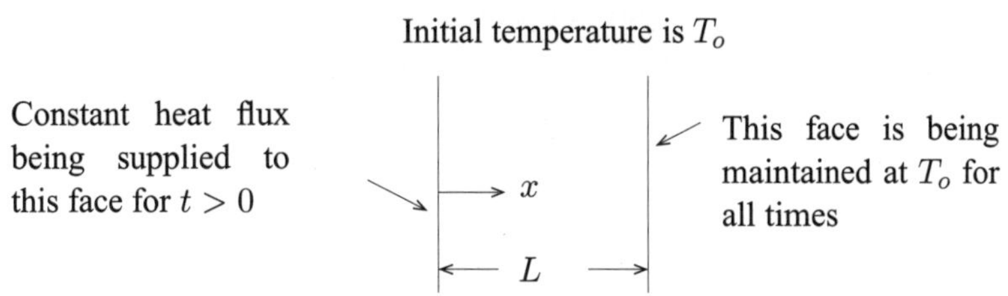

Figure for problem 5.10.

5.11 Find the steady state temperature profile in the solids shown in the figures.
a) An infinitely long rectangular block of dimensions $2M$ by $2L$. The faces whose lengths are $2L$ are insulated. One of the faces measuring $2M$ is maintained at non-dimensional temperature of 0 while the other has a temperature profile varying linearly from 0 to 1 with length along the side.
b) An infinitely long cylindrical arc. The non-dimensional temperature on both the edges of

the arc are 0.5, and one of the circular faces is being maintained at 0 while the other is being maintained at 1.

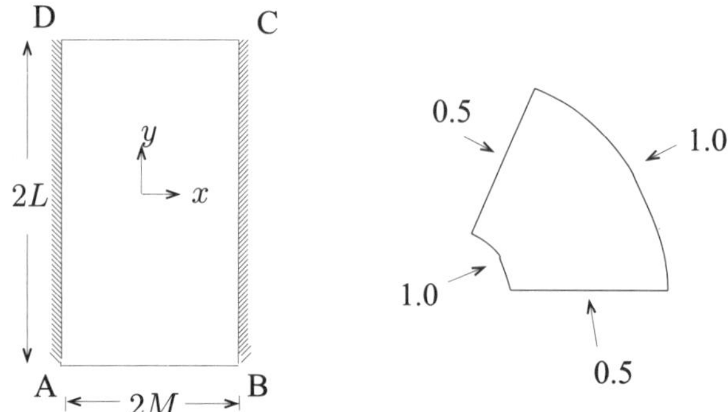

Figure for problem 5.11.

5.12 The one-dimensional approximation for fin has been considered in many books. It can be compared with the exact solution to get a feel for how the approximation works. (a) Write down the two-dimensional heat conduction equation for the fin shown in the diagram. (b) Specify the boundary conditions. (c) Solve the equation by using the separation of variables technique. (d) Does the two-dimensional solution reduce to the one-dimensional approximation when $\dfrac{hW}{k} << 1$ and $\dfrac{hL^2}{kW} << 1$? The latter is usually used in obtaining one dimensional solution.

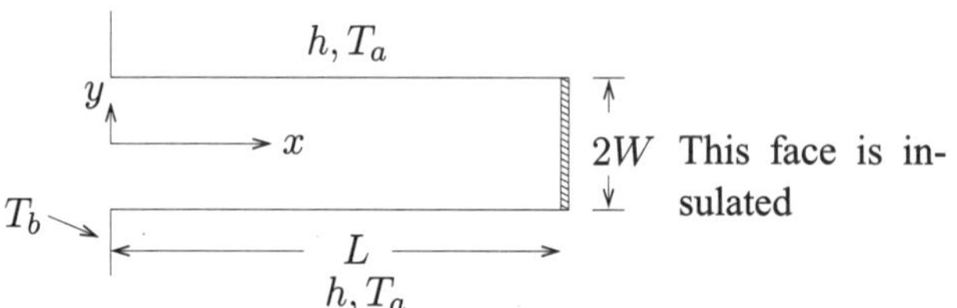

Figure for problem 5.12.

5.13 Two parallel faces of an infinitely long rectangular bar are maintained at T_o while the other

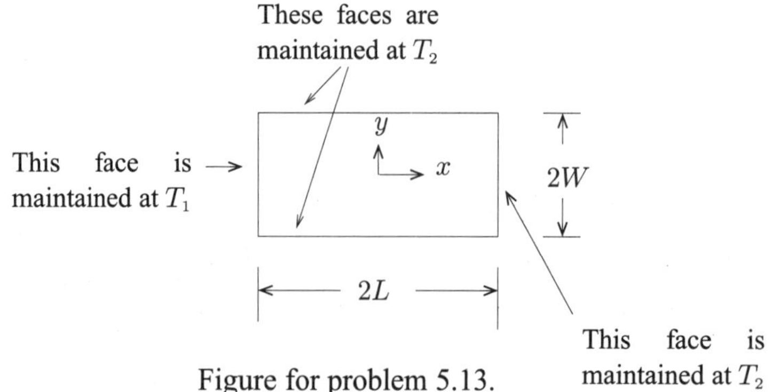

Figure for problem 5.13.

two perpendicular faces are maintained at T_1 and T_2. See the attached figure. (i) Derive an expression for the steady temperature profiles. (ii) Draw a few heat flux lines. Draw on a separate figure isotherms corresponding to T_o, T_1, and T_2 given $T_1 > T_o > T_2$.

5.14 Consider fully developed laminar axial flow of a Newtonian incompressible liquid in an annulus. The velocity profile is given by

$$v_z = v_{z,max}\left(1 - \frac{r}{R}^2 + \frac{1-\kappa^2}{\ln(1/\kappa)}\ln(r/R)\right)$$

Derive expressions for Nusselt numbers for the inner wall and outer wall for constant wall temperature boundary condition in the entry zone, i.e., the temperature profile is developing.

5.15 For fully developed temperature profile conditions, derive expressions for Nusselt number for constant wall flux boundary condition for laminar flow in ducts of isoscles triangular cross section of side a. For a Cartesian coordinate system set up with origin at the centroid of the triangle, the z component velocity profile is given by

$$v_z = -\frac{1}{2\mu}\frac{dP}{dz}\left[\frac{1}{2}(x^2+y^2) - \frac{1}{2}(x^3 - 3xy^2) - \frac{2a^2}{27}\right]$$

This problem is to be setup only as it cannot be solved in closed form.

5.16 An ideal gas bubble is placed in an infinite extent of a Newtonian liquid. The solubility of the gas in the liquid is negligible. The initial radius of the bubble is R_o, and is in equilibrium with the liquid surrounding it. Initially, the pressure in the liquid is $p_{L\infty}$ and the temperature of the liquid is $T_{L\infty}$. The surface tension of the liquid is σ.

a) Determine the initial pressure p_B and temperature T_B in the bubble.
b) For $t > 0$, heat is generated in the bubble at a uniform rate. The rate of generation in the entire bubble is $\dot{Q}_B$. Will the bubble expand or contract?
c) Assume the pressure and temperature of the bubble to be uniform. Simplify the necessary balance equations and boundary conditions to determine the radius of the bubble as a function of time. State any assumptions that you make.

5.17 Nylon fibers are made by extruding a molten filament of radius R_o at a velocity V_o. The filament is wound at a higher speed, and hence the radius of the filament, R, reduces. The z component velocity as a function of the distance from the point where nylon comes out, z, can be found by solving equation of motion and is given by

$$v_z = V_o D_R e^{(z/L)}$$

where D_R and L are constants related to operating conditions. The radius at the corresponding point can therefore be found by mass conservation

$$v_z R^2(z) = V_o R_o^2$$

Let the temperature of the filament at $z = 0$ be T_o. As it is being wound in ambient conditions, the filament cools. It is desired to calculate the temperature as a function of the distance from the point it comes out into the room. The following data are given: $R_o = 100\mu$ m, $D_R = 100$, $R_L = 10\mu$ m, L = 3 m, k of air = 0.025 w/(m C), k of molten nylon = 0.3 w/(m C), thermal diffusivity of nylon = 10^{-7} m^2/s, h between air and nylon = 4 w/(m^2 C). (i) What are the non-zero velocities? Simplify the thermal energy balance equation neglecting viscous dissipation as well as axial conduction, and specify the boundary conditions needed to solve it. (ii) We wish to calculate the way temperature of the fibre falls as a function of z in a simple way. Assume that the variation of temperature in the radial direction in the fiber is negligible. Simplify the equation obtained in (i) to derive a differential equation for the temperature of the fiber as a function of z. (iii) Are we justified in assuming that there is no variation of temperature in the radial direction in the fiber?

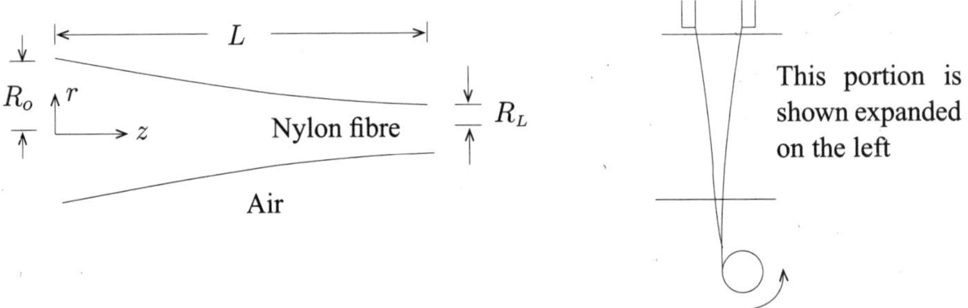

Figure for problem 5.17

5.18 Two large plates (extending to infinity in the x and y directions) are separated by distance L, and the gap is filled with a fluid (with properties k_f, ρ_f and C_{pf}. $Pr >> 1$). The two plates are being maintained at constant temperatures, the left one at T_L and the right one at T_R. **Assume that natural convection is not present in answering the following**. Steady state is allowed to reach in the system.

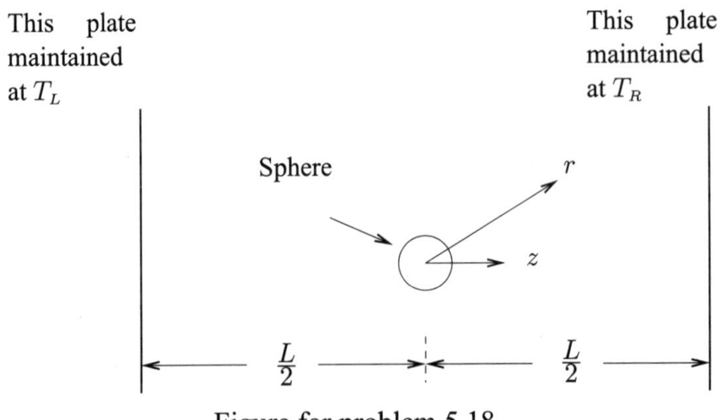

Figure for problem 5.18

(a) What is the temperature profile at steady state? (b) A solid sphere of radius R (with properties k_s, ρ_s and C_{ps}) at a uniform temperature of T_o is placed and held stationary (at $z = 0$) in the middle of the gap between the plates. **It is given that** $R <<< L$. Use spherical coordinates to do the following: (i) simplify the relevant energy equations needed to determine the temperature profiles in the fluid and the solid, (ii) specify the boundary conditions needed to solve the resulting equations. (c) Suppose that the solid sphere (instead of being held stationary) is moved with a constant velocity $-V_\infty$ in the z direction (*i.e.,* moves with a velocity V_∞ in the negative z direction) such that $RV_\infty/\nu << 1$. As $Pr >> 1$, velocities in the fluid can be described by the steady Stokes profiles *in a frame moving with the sphere.* They are given by

$$v_r = V_\infty \left[1 - \frac{3}{2}\frac{R}{r} + \frac{3}{2}\left(\frac{R}{r}\right)^3\right] \cos\theta$$

and

$$v_\theta = V_\infty \left[-1 + \frac{3}{4}\frac{R}{r} + \frac{1}{4}\left(\frac{R}{r}\right)^3\right] \sin\theta$$

Use spherical coordinates moving with the sphere to do the following:(i) simplify the relevant energy equations needed to determine the temperature profiles in the fluid and the solid, (ii) specify the boundary conditions needed to solve the resulting equations.

5.19 Fluid at T_∞ approaches a long cylinder, perpendicular to its axis, with a uniform velocity V_∞. The surface of the cylinder is being maintained at a constant temperature, T_w. Reynolds number of the flow is small and the velocity profiles near the cylinder are given by

$$v_r = \frac{V_\infty R \cos\theta}{2S}\left(\frac{1}{R}(2\ln\frac{r}{R} - 1) + \frac{R}{r^2}\right)$$

$$v_\theta = -\frac{V_\infty R \sin\theta}{2S}\left(\frac{1}{R}(2\ln\frac{r}{R} - 1) + \frac{2}{R} - \frac{R}{r^2}\right)$$

We are interested in "short contact time" solution for heat transfer to the cylinder. Simplify the convection equations for this case and specify the boundary conditions.

5.20 A fluid enters an annulus at temperature T_o. The radius of the inner wall is R_i while that of

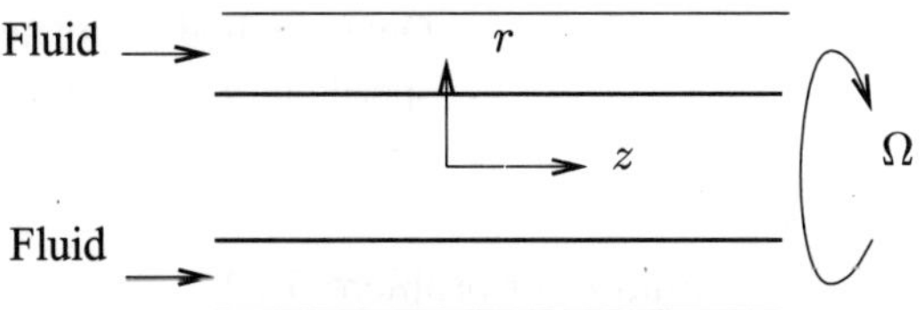

Inner cylinder rotates with constant speed

Figure for problem 5.20

the outer wall is R_o. The flow is laminar, fully developed and steady. A constant pressure gradient is applied in the axial direction. Only the inner cylinder is rotating with a constant speed Ω. The fluid is being heated since the inner wall is maintained at constant temperature T_o for $z < 0$ and T_w for $z > 0$. The outer wall is insulated. (i) Specify a convenient coordinate system that you will use to solve the problem, (ii) specify the non-zero velocities, (iii) specify the coordinates on which temperature of fluid depends. (iv) simplify the thermal energy balance equation, (v) specify the boundary conditions needed for solving the energy balance equation.

5.21 An ideal gas bubble is placed in an infinite extent of a Newtonian liquid. The solubility of the gas in the liquid is negligible. The initial radius of the bubble is R_o, and is in equilibrium with the liquid surrounding it. Initially, the pressure in the liquid is $p_{L\infty}$ and the temperature of the liquid is $T_{L\infty}$. The surface tension of the liquid is σ. (a) Determine the initial pressure p_B and temperature T_B in the bubble. (b) For $t > 0$, heat is generated in the bubble at a uniform rate. The rate of generation in the entire bubble is $\dot{Q}_B$. Will the bubble expand or contract? (c) Assume the pressure and temperature of the bubble to be uniform. Simplify the necessary balance equations and boundary conditions to determine the radius of the bubble as a function of time. State any assumptions that you make.

5.22 The annular space in an infinitely long concentric cylindrical annulus is filled with a liquid. The outer cylinder is rotating at a constant velocity, Ω while the inner cylinder is stationary. The outer wall is being maintained at a constant temperature of T_o while the inner wall is stationary. Heat is being generated in the annular space at a constant rate per unit volume, $\dot{Q}_v$. Neglect heat generation by viscous dissipation. The velocity profile is given by:

$$v_r = 0, \quad v_\theta = \Omega R_o \frac{r - \kappa R_o}{R_o - \kappa R_o}, \quad v_z = 0$$

where R_o is the radius of the outer wall while κR_o is the radius of the inner wall. Simplify the thermal energy balance for this situation. Specify the boundary conditions. Determine the temperature profile.

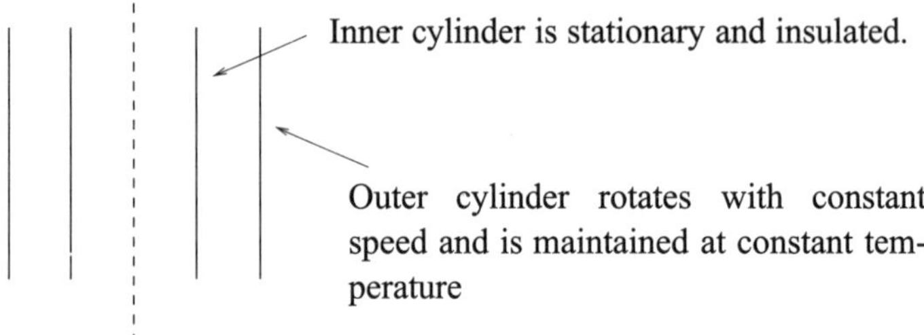

Figure for problem 5.22

5.23 *Scaling arguments in Leveque problem.* We wish to show a different method to solve Leveque problem. Let $y = R - r$ and as mentioned we expect $y/R << 1$. Let us therefore non-dimensionalize y as $\tilde{y} = y/\epsilon(z)R$ where $\epsilon(z)$ is a suitably small parameter. Show that the equation of change of temperature is now given by

$$\frac{4\rho\hat{C}_p V R^2}{k}\epsilon^3(z)\frac{\partial\theta}{\partial z} = \frac{\partial^2\theta}{\partial\tilde{y}^2}$$

As y is scaled now correctly, derivatives of temperature with $\tilde{y}$ will all be of the order of unity. How should $\epsilon(z)$ depend upon z and other parameters so that the left hand side is also of the order of unity? Use this result to show that

$$\frac{hD}{k} \sim \left(\frac{z}{D}\frac{1}{RePe}\right)^{-1/3}$$

The proportionality constant can only be obtained from the similarity solution.

Notes

[1] It must be emphasized that all these assumptions are **not needed** when numerical solutions are sought. Such is the case with using CFD approaches to problem solving.

[2] Alternatively, we could use so called Danckwerts boundary condition.

[3] Refer to text by Bird *et al.* [2] for this problem

[4] The jump occurs because we neglected axial heat conduction. If that term is included, a more realistic solution will be obtained. However, the present solution is fairly accurate except when z is very close to zero.

[5] To quote Feynman, "the same equations have the same solutions!"

[6] In the modern parlance, these are referred to as diffusion time scale and diffusion length scale

[7] Does the word "eigenvalues" ring a bell?

[8] The method is reminiscent of the way we solved the unsteady flow of a Newtonian fluid in a pipe. It is being done here in a slightly different way to illustrate the idea that zero eigen value corresponds to steady state.

[9] Refer to this theory given in the appendix.

[10] More advanced readers will recognize that the method we are using is the Fourier transform.

[11] An excellent but slightly advanced text is by Batchelor [1]. The book by Bird *et al.* [2] also has a good coverage of these topics.

[12] This is a brief summary culled from the book by Churchill and Brown [3].

References

[1] G.K. Batchelor. *Introduction to fluid dynamics*. Cambridge University Press, 1 edition, 1967.

[2] R.B. Bird, W.E. Stewart, and E.N. Lightfoot. *Transport Phenomena*. John Wiley, 2 edition, 2002.

[3] R.V. Churchill and J.W. Brown. *Fourier series and boundary value problems*. McGraw Hill, 4 edition, 1987.

Chapter 6

ADVANCED TOPICS IN HEAT TRANSFER

```
Superficial neglect of conduction in convection dominated
   flows leads to a contradiction and the discovery of
   boundary layers where conduction can never be neglected.
Natural convection is where solution of equation of motion
   has to be simultaneous with that of energy balance.
Change in phase can occur when heat is supplied, and both
   rates are related.
```

In this chapter, we consider three topics which are advanced in nature. In section 4.4, we considered heat transfer where convection and conduction were equally important. We briefly alluded to what might happen in case convection is dominant, and referred you to this chapter. Superficial neglect of conduction in convection dominated flows leads to a conclusion that there should be no heat transfer even when common sense dictates that there should be! It requires careful analysis, and leads to the conclusion that there will always be thin layers where conduction is of equal importance as convection no matter how large convection is. These thin layers are referred to as boundary layers. We begin with a brief review of momentum boundary layers in the first section, and we study heat transfer in a boundary layer in the next section. In the problems considered in chapter 5, the equations of motion were not solved. However, this is not possible when we consider problems in natural convection, and that is the topic of the third section. Evaporation and melting are caused by supplying heat and these problems are referred to as phase change problems. The relation between the rate of change of phase and heat supplied is analyzed in the last section.

6.1 MOMENTUM BOUNDARY LAYER

6.1.1 Introduction

Let a fluid approach a stationary flat plate with a uniform velocity of V_∞ in a direction parallel to the plate. Due to the no-slip boundary condition, it slows down near the wall too. Thus, both temperature and velocity profiles develop as fluid flows downstream. See figure 6.1. This kind of problem is encountered not just in free stream flows like the one just described. Consider uniform flow, such as that from a large reservoir, entering a pipe. Just past the entrance, we expect velocity gradients to be confined to a zone near the wall, and the effects of the finiteness of the flow domain would not have been felt. Hence, flow in the entry zones to equipments will be similar to the flow

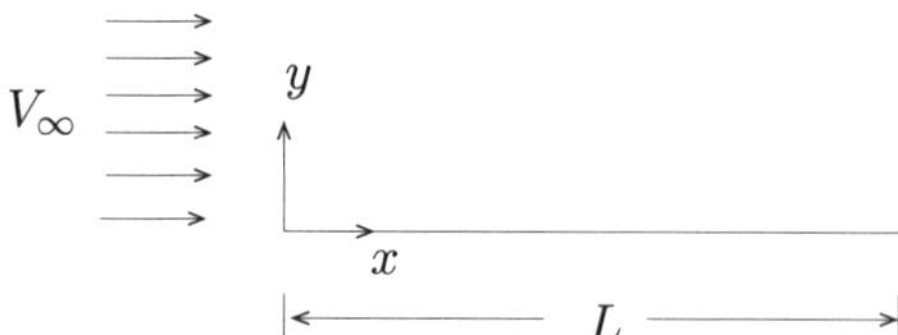

Figure 6.1. Fluid with a uniform x component velocity and temperature approaches a stationary plate but at a temperature different from the fluid.

being considered here. Another set of examples come from flow past bodies like spheres, cylinders, *etc* at high Reynolds numbers. Here also, flow of the kind being considered develops in the front side of the body.

6.1.2 Fluid mechanics

Usually, these problems are important when the velocity is large, *or when convection is dominant.* You might be familiar with the idea of a boundary layer from fluid mechanics. For the sake of completeness, we will cover both fluid mechanics and heat transfer in this chapter. Consider parallel flow past a plate. Refer to figure 6.2. Length of the plate is the only *apparent* length scale available

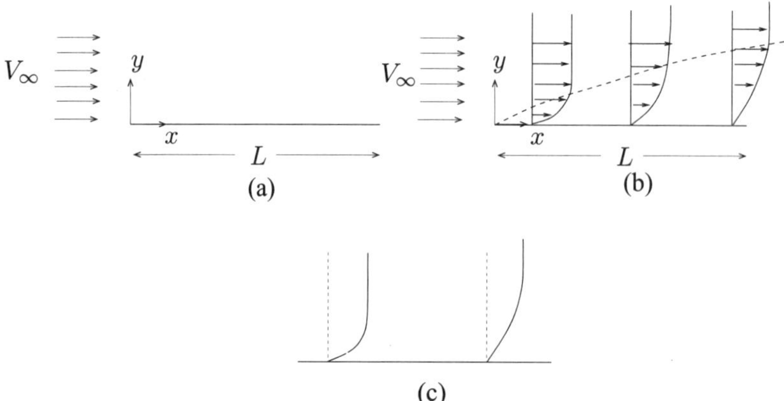

Figure 6.2. (a) Uniform flow past a flat plate. (b) The velocity profiles at different locations. Notice that the boundary layer thickness increases along the plate. (c) The expected results of the experiment discussed in the text.

and is used as the characteristic length. The free stream velocity is high and hence Reynolds number is large. It is found that if the length of the plate is used as the characteristic length, the terms containing the second derivatives of velocity, or the viscous forces, vanish. This lowers the order of the differential equation. This is equivalent to the neglect of conduction terms in relation to convection terms. This has two consequences. First, the viscous forces shearing the fluid in flow direction are being neglected. Second, it does not allow enforcing the no-slip condition on the surface of the plate. This is equivalent to not being able to enforce condition of thermal equilibrium at the wall–fluid interface. If one persists and solves the equations of motion, the drag force is found to be zero, clearly an unrealistic result. This is equivalent to heat not being transferred between wall and fluid even though they are at different temperatures. Prandtl[1] resolved this controversy based on brilliant experiments and intuitive arguments, but well supported by theory. It is this theory that we will now summarize first.

Boundary layer

No-slip condition forces the velocity to be zero on the surface of the plate, and creates a velocity gradient in the y direction. Therefore, x component of momentum, while being simultaneously convected in the x direction, diffuses in the y direction from the regions far away from the plate to regions near the surface of the plate where velocities are smaller. Far away from the plate, convection dominates while diffusion is also important near the plate. This gives rise to an estimate of distance[2] from the plate up to where effects of momentum diffusion can be felt. Momentum diffusion is equivalent to viscous processes. The estimate then is also the distance from the plate up to where viscous forces are comparable to the inertial forces. Thus, as long as no-slip condition is valid, and typically it occurs near a solid *boundary* in relative motion with respect to the fluid, there will always be a *layer* of fluid, where viscous forces will be comparable to inertial forces. This is the concept of *boundary layer*.

This can be demonstrated with an experiment. A line of dye can be inserted perpendicular to the plate before starting the flow. The line deforms soon after the flow is started according to the velocity profile while *remaining anchored to the plate*. The shape will show that velocity rises from zero to the free stream value over a short distance perpendicular to the plate. The length scale is very small, and hence, viscous forces are large, and comparable to the inertial forces. It is the appropriate length scale for non-dimensionalization[3]. It had to be discovered and hence was not an "obvious" choice. Let us now consider how the *hidden* length scale is discovered.

Boundary layer thickness

Consider uniform flow shown in figure 6.2. Fluid particles coming into contact with the plate have to come to a halt due to the no-slip condition. *Thus, a velocity gradient is established in the y direction.* Thus, a drag force in the negative y direction is exerted by layers near to the plate surface on those further away. The effect will be felt only up to some distance away from the plate. Beyond that distance, the velocity will approach V_∞, the free stream velocity. At very small values of x, the effect will be felt to a smaller depth. At larger values of x, because fluid elements have been under the influence of the drag forces for a longer time, the effect will be felt to a greater depth. Thus, there is a layer adjoining the plate, growing in thickness in the flow direction, and the velocity gradients are confined to it.

There is yet another way of looking at it. The phenomena is equivalent to diffusion of x momentum from fluid layers far away from the plate towards the plate or in the negative y direction. As momentum diffuses, it is also convected away in the x direction. Thus, momentum will be able to reach the plate only after reaching a closer distance to the plate, where convection begins to be less dominant due to slowing down of fluid enforced by the no-slip condition. Once again, diffusion occurs due to velocity gradients and hence they are confined to this distance.

We therefore postulate that there is a characteristic length $\delta(x)$ to represent these processes. The processes we discussed pertain to diffusion of momentum in the y direction or alternatively, concern viscous forces caused due to velocity gradients in the y direction. Hence, we use $\delta(x)$ as the characteristic length in that direction. This is the thickness of the layer to which velocity gradients are entirely confined to. The layer is called the *boundary layer*, and $\delta(x)$ is referred to as *boundary layer thickness*. The next task is to determine its value if possible or at least its functional dependence.

Boundary layer equations

The equation of continuity is given by

$$\frac{\partial v_x}{\partial x} + \frac{\partial v_y}{\partial y} = 0$$

The free stream velocity can be used as a characteristic velocity for the x *component of velocity.* We first note that if v_y is zero, v_x does not change in the flow direction. This does not agree with the experiment described in figure 6.2. We can also rationalize this as follows. Since v_x is zero at the surface of the plate, flow is slowing down and, in order to satisfy mass conservation, some fluid must flow in the y direction, *i.e.*, v_y will not be equal to zero everywhere. But we do not know what is the characteristic velocity for the y component. Let it be $v_{y,ch}$. L is the characteristic length in the x direction. We have postulated that δ is the characteristic length in the y direction. The following non-dimensional quantities can be defined:

$$\tilde{v}_x = v_/V_\infty,\ \tilde{x} = x/L,\ \tilde{v}_y = v_y/v_{y,ch},\ \tilde{y} = y/\delta$$

Let us substitute these in the equation of continuity:

$$\frac{V_\infty}{L}\frac{\partial \tilde{v}_x}{\partial \tilde{x}} + \frac{v_{y,ch}}{\delta}\frac{\partial \tilde{v}_y}{\partial \tilde{y}} = 0$$

The non-dimensional quantities are all of order unity or $\mathcal{O}(1)$. Hence, if the term containing y component velocity has to be retained, then

$$v_{y,ch} \sim \frac{\delta}{L}V_\infty$$

Thus, we have a result. The characteristic velocity is proportional to the free stream velocity, but small since the proportionality constant is equal to the ratio of boundary layer thickness (at the end of the plate) to the plate length. With this characteristic velocity, the non-dimensional equation of continuity for a boundary layer is given by

$$\frac{\partial \tilde{v}_x}{\partial \tilde{x}} + \frac{\partial \tilde{v}_y}{\partial \tilde{y}} = 0$$

Now let us consider the x momentum equation. It is given by

$$v_x\frac{\partial v_x}{\partial x} + v_y\frac{\partial v_x}{\partial y} = -\frac{1}{\rho}\frac{\partial P}{\partial x} + \nu\left(\frac{\partial^2 v_x}{\partial x^2} + \frac{\partial^2 v_x}{\partial y^2}\right)$$

We have not included gravity just to emphasize the boundary layer aspects. We need a characteristic pressure. As the flow is fast, inertial forces are the correct ones to non-dimensionalize pressure:

$$\tilde{P} = \frac{P}{\rho V_\infty^2}$$

Substituting all these and using the result that $v_{y,ch} \sim v_\infty \delta / L$, we get

$$\tilde{v}_x \frac{\partial \tilde{v}_x}{\partial \tilde{x}} + \tilde{v}_y \frac{\partial \tilde{v}_x}{\partial \tilde{y}} = -\frac{\partial \tilde{P}}{\partial \tilde{x}} + \frac{1}{Re} \frac{\partial^2 \tilde{v}_x}{\partial \tilde{x}^2} + \frac{L^2}{\delta^2} \frac{1}{Re} \frac{\partial^2 \tilde{v}_x}{\partial \tilde{y}^2}$$

where $Re = LV_\infty/\nu$. If we now let Reynolds number take on large values, we see that while the first term in the viscous forces vanishes, the other will not go to zero if

$$\frac{\delta^2}{L^2} \sim \frac{1}{Re}$$

Thus, if the boundary layer thickness is small and is inversely proportional to the square root of Reynolds number, the viscous forces will not vanish no matter how large the Reynolds number is. But we *do know* that viscous forces do not vanish. Hence we have another result. The boundary layer thickness δ at L is $\sim 1/\sqrt{Re(L)}$. We now can state both the results in a more general way:

$$\frac{\delta(x)}{x} \sim \sqrt{\frac{\nu}{v_\infty x}}, \quad v_{y,ch} \sim \frac{\delta(x)}{x} V_\infty$$

With these non-dimensionalization factors, the x component equation of motion reads

$$\tilde{v}_x \frac{\partial \tilde{v}_x}{\partial \tilde{x}} + \tilde{v}_y \frac{\partial \tilde{v}_x}{\partial \tilde{y}} = -\frac{\partial \tilde{p}}{\partial \tilde{x}} + \frac{\partial^2 \tilde{v}_x}{\partial \tilde{y}^2}$$

Physical interpretation: We now try to physically justify the observed dependence of boundary layer thickness on various parameters. The viscous forces and inertial forces inside the boundary layer are of similar order of magnitude. As free stream velocity increases, inertial forces increase as the square of the velocity. The boundary layer thickness must therefore decrease so that viscous forces, which increase linearly with free stream velocity, can increase. If the plate length is increased or if we interpret L as a particular point along a long plate, fluid would have been in contact with the plate for a longer period. The effects of drag force have therefore been felt by a fluid package for a longer period. Hence, the depth into the free stream up to which the fluid would have slowed down is greater. Thus, boundary layer thickness increases. An increase in kinematic viscosity is equivalent to increasing momentum diffusivity, and hence boundary layer thickness increases. As a whole, the dependence of non-dimensional boundary layer thickness is an inverse dependence on the square root of Reynolds number. That is characteristic of *laminar*[4] *boundary layers*.

A look at the terms: It is illustrative to understand why certain terms are retained while some others are dropped in the above equations. We note that the inertial terms or the terms representing convection of momentum contain both the x and y component of velocity while the terms representing viscous forces have only the gradients of x component velocity in the y direction. The boundary layer thickness is small and hence the y component velocity is small. Thus, superficial inspection would suggest that convection in the y direction should be small. However, the magnitude of convection also depends upon the extent of change in that direction. As the x component of velocity changes rapidly in the y direction, the net convection in y direction is not negligible. In contrast, the changes of x component of velocity in the x direction are small. However, the x component of velocity, namely the convecting velocity, is large. Hence that term is also not negligible. However, in the viscous terms, the gradients of x component of velocity in the y direction are so large compared to those in the x direction, that only the former are retained. This kind of arguments will often be used in heat and mass transfer also and are very useful.

Equation for the y component

The y component equation of motion is non-dimensionalized to get

$$\frac{\delta^2}{L^2}\left(\tilde{v}_x\frac{\partial \tilde{v}_y}{\partial \tilde{x}} + \tilde{v}_y\frac{\partial \tilde{v}_y}{\partial \tilde{y}}\right) = -\frac{\partial \tilde{P}}{\partial \tilde{y}} + \frac{1}{Re}\left(\frac{\delta^2}{L^2}\frac{\partial^2 \tilde{v}_y}{\partial \tilde{x}^2} + \frac{\partial^2 \tilde{v}_y}{\partial \tilde{y}^2}\right)$$

From the above equation, it appears that the inertial terms and the viscous terms are of the order of $1/Re$. Thus, one has to conclude that the pressure terms are also of the same order. In the limit of high Re, hence, the pressure gradient in the y direction is zero. One of the confusing things about this equation is that its non-dimensional quantities are unity in order of magnitude. Thus, $\partial \tilde{P} \partial \tilde{y}$ must be of the order of unity, yet we seem to conclude that it is zero! It must be concluded that *pressure changes* in y direction are much smaller and should not be scaled with inertial terms.

Final equations

In summary, the boundary layer equations in dimensional form are written as

$$\begin{aligned} \frac{\partial v_x}{\partial x} + \frac{\partial v_y}{\partial y} &= 0 \\ v_x\frac{\partial v_x}{\partial x} + v_y\frac{\partial v_y}{\partial y} &= -\frac{\partial p}{\partial x} + \nu\frac{\partial^2 v_x}{\partial y^2} \\ 0 &= -\frac{\partial p}{\partial y} \end{aligned} \tag{6.1}$$

6.1.3 Boundary layer on an infinitely long plate

The boundary layer equations are non-linear and so a general solution cannot be found. In his revolutionary paper on boundary layer theory, Prandtl considered flow past an infinitely long plate, and solved it approximately. We consider that solution here as it gives an excellent feel for the behavior. Consider a uniform parallel flow approaching an infinitely long plate aligned with the flow. The same coordinate system shown in figure 6.2 is used here as well.

Pressure on the boundary layer

First we solve the y component equation of motion! This gives that pressure is constant in the y direction. Thus, pressure at the plate surface, that is inside the boundary layer and that far away from it are equal. Flow far away from the plate is inviscid as it is outside the boundary layer. Hence, pressure is obtained by solving the Euler's equation. In this sense, it is said that pressure is *impressed* on the boundary layer by the *inviscid* flow outside it. In the particular case we are considering, the flow outside the boundary layer is given by uniform flow. By applying Bernoulli's equation, we therefore conclude that pressure remains constant outside the boundary layer[5]. Hence, the pressure gradient in x direction is zero in the boundary layer as well. The boundary layer equations for uniform flow past a flat plate are then given by

$$\begin{aligned} \frac{\partial v_x}{\partial x} + \frac{\partial v_y}{\partial y} &= 0 \\ v_x \frac{\partial v_x}{\partial x} + v_y \frac{\partial v_y}{\partial y} &= \nu \frac{\partial^2 v_x}{\partial y^2} \end{aligned}$$

Similarity variable

As we are considering an infinitely long plate, there now is no characteristic length scale in the x direction. Prandtl proposed that a similarity solution can be found for the *boundary layer*[6] equations. He proposed that

$$\eta = y\sqrt{\frac{V_\infty}{\nu x}}, \; \frac{v_x}{V_\infty} = \frac{df(\eta)}{d\eta}$$

Now recall the similarity solution for an impulsively started plate in a quiescent fluid. There the similarity variable was $y/\sqrt{4\nu t}$. If we interpret x/V_∞ as the "time" for which a fluid packet has been in "contact" with the plate, the two similarity variables become similar!

First we should check if similarity solution can exist, *i.e.,* the equations will depend only upon η when the assumed forms are substituted. First let us consider the equation of continuity. It can be solved to obtain v_y:

$$\begin{aligned} v_y &= -\int_0^y \frac{\partial v_x}{\partial x} dy \\ &= -V_\infty \int_0^\eta \frac{d^2 f}{d\eta^2} \frac{\partial \eta}{\partial x} \sqrt{\frac{\nu x}{V_\infty}} d\eta \end{aligned}$$

or

$$\begin{aligned} \frac{v_y}{V_\infty} &= \frac{1}{2}\sqrt{\frac{\nu}{x V_\infty}} \int_0^\eta f'' \eta d\eta \\ &= \frac{1}{2}\sqrt{\frac{\nu}{x V_\infty}} \left(f'\eta - f\right) \end{aligned}$$

where we have used the condition[7] that $f = 0$ at $\eta = 0$. We seem to be in trouble since v_y is turning out to be a function of x. As it turns out, similarity solution will be found to work if we persist. If it were not so, we would not be writing about this here! However, we wish to deviate a little to demonstrate another way of deriving the assumed *form* for the velocity.

Stream function is used for solving two-dimensional flows. Let v_x be a function of similarity variable η. However, v_x is also given by the y derivative of stream function. Hence, it is not necessary that stream function be dependent only on the similarity variable. Let $\psi = g(x)f(\eta)$. Then

$$v_x \sim g(x)f'\sqrt{\frac{V_\infty}{\nu x}}$$

But v_x can be only a function of η if $g(x) \sim \sqrt{x}$. If we let

$$\psi = \sqrt{\nu x V_\infty} f(\eta)$$

then,

$$\frac{v_x}{V_\infty} = f'(\eta)$$

Now we proceed to convert the x component of equation of motion, in terms of the similarity variable and to verify that the form derived earlier for v_y does not vitiate similarity solution. The various terms of the equation are evaluated as follows.

$$v_x \frac{\partial v_x}{\partial x} = V_\infty^2 f' f'' \frac{\partial \eta}{\partial x} = -\frac{V_\infty^2}{2x}\eta f' f''$$

$$v_y \frac{\partial v_x}{\partial y} = V_\infty^2 \frac{1}{2}\sqrt{\frac{\nu}{x V_\infty}}(f'\eta - f) f'' \frac{\partial \eta}{\partial y} = V_\infty^2 \frac{1}{2x}(f'\eta - f) f''$$

$$\frac{\partial v_x}{\partial y} = V_\infty f'' \sqrt{\frac{V_\infty}{\nu x}}$$

$$\nu \frac{\partial^2 v_x}{\partial y^2} = V_\infty^2 \frac{1}{x} f'''$$

Substituting all these terms into the x component of equation of motion, we obtain

$$2f''' + f f'' = 0 \tag{6.2}$$

The equation collapsed into an equation in terms of the similarity variable. Now let us look at the boundary conditions. The no-slip condition and the condition of uniform velocity far away from the plate read in terms of the similarity variable

$$f' = 0 \text{ at } \eta = 0, \text{ and } f' = 1 \text{ as } \eta \to \infty,$$

We had one more condition that $f = 0$ at $\eta = 0$. The three conditions are enough to solve eq. 6.2.

Similarity solution

The above equation is non-linear and hence only a numerical solution can be presented. Historically, Prandtl proposed a method of solution and Blassius obtained a power series solution[8] to it. The results are shown in figure 6.3. It is seen that when the similarity variable attains a value of about 5,

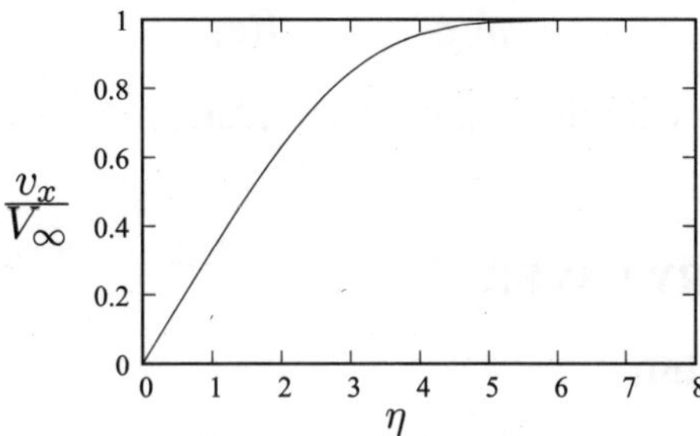

Figure 6.3. Velocity profile computed from similarity solution.

the x component of velocity has reached 99% of the free stream value, and that gradients are very small beyond that value of η. As the problem is formulated, the free stream velocity can be reached only at infinity. However, as an engineering approximation, one can say that the velocity gradients are negligible for $\eta > 5$. Hence, the layer to which viscous effects are confined is reached when $\eta \sim 5$. Thus,

$$\delta\sqrt{\frac{V_\infty}{\nu x}} = 5$$

or

$$\frac{\delta(x)}{x} = 5\sqrt{\frac{\nu}{xV_\infty}} = 5\sqrt{\frac{1}{Re_x}}$$

where Re_x is Reynolds number based on x. The similarity solution bears out the analysis done by scaling and the results obtained.

Boundary layer thickness and drag force

The numerical solution also gives the result that

$$f''(0) = 0.332$$

The shearing stress due to drag force exerted by the fluid on the plate is given by

$$\tau_w(x) = \mu\frac{\partial v_x}{\partial y}\bigg|_{y=0}$$

and can be evaluated using the value for $[f''(0)$. It is given by

$$\frac{\tau_w(x)}{\rho V_\infty^2} = 0.332\sqrt{\frac{xV_\infty}{\nu}} = \frac{0.332}{Re_x}$$

The viscous stress decreases with increasing length along the plate. This is to be expected since the velocity gradients become continually less steep along the plate due to momentum diffusion. The total drag force per unit width, over the entire length x can be found by integrating the above up to x. It is given by

$$\frac{F_d(x)}{\rho V_\infty^2} = x\,\frac{0.664}{Re_x}$$

The total drag force increases with the length of the plate, as expected. These results have been experimentally verified.

6.2 THERMAL BOUNDARY LAYER

6.2.1 Problem identification

Now let us consider the heat transfer problem. Let a fluid at a temperature of T_∞ approach a stationary flat plate with a uniform velocity of V_∞ in a direction parallel to the plate. Let the plate be maintained at a constant temperature of T_w. As the fluid flows past the plate, it gets heated if $T_w > T_\infty$. Simultaneously, it slows down near the wall too. Thus, both temperature and velocity profiles develop as fluid flows downstream. See figure 6.4

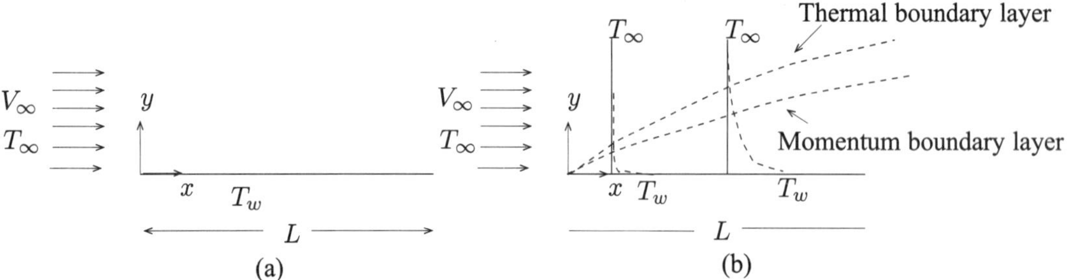

Figure 6.4. Thermal boundary layer over a heated plate with uniform flow past it. The velocity profiles and momentum boundary layer are shown in Figure 6.2. The temperature profiles at different locations are shown in (b). Note that the boundary layer thickness increases along the plate. It is being assumed that heat conduction is faster than momentum diffusion in showing that the thickness of the thermal boundary layer is greater than that of momentum boundary layer.

In chapters 4 and 5, we have considered problems where both the velocity and temperature profiles are fully developed and where the temperature profile is developing while the velocity profile is fully developed. The heating of a boundary layer is the most complex problem in this category where both velocity and temperature profiles develop simultaneously.

Equation of change of temperature

Temperature is expected to vary both in x and y directions. At steady state, the energy equation reduces to

$$v_x\frac{\partial T}{\partial x} + v_y\frac{\partial T}{\partial y} = \alpha\left(\frac{\partial^2 T}{\partial x^2} + \frac{\partial^2 T}{\partial y^2}\right)$$

where α is the thermal diffusivity. Heat diffuses into the fluid from the wall, while it is also convected away in the flow direction. Thus, based on analogy with fluid mechanics, we expect a characteristic length in the y direction different from that for the x direction. Without going through the arguments presented earlier in dealing with the momentum boundary layer, we can anticipate that the only term containing derivative with respect to y will remain from the right hand side.

Boundary conditions

The boundary conditions are

$$\begin{array}{llll} T(x,y) = T_\infty & \text{at} & x = 0 & \text{and for all } y \\ T(x,y) = T_w & \text{at} & y = 0 & \text{and for all } x \\ T(x,y) = T_\infty & \text{as} & y \to \infty & \text{and for all } x \end{array}$$

6.2.2 Scaling

Let us first define a non-dimensional temperature based on the characteristic temperature difference:

$$\theta = \frac{T - T_w}{T_\infty - T_w}$$

Similarity transformation

As no length scale exists, we can once again anticipate a similarity solution. Similarity solution for the energy balance can exist only if both velocity and temperature can be described by the same similarity variable. So let us try that. Thus,

$$\eta = y\sqrt{\frac{V_\infty}{\nu x}}$$

$$v_x \frac{\partial \theta}{\partial x} = -V_\infty \frac{f'\eta}{2x}\frac{d\theta}{d\eta}$$

$$v_y \frac{\partial \theta}{\partial y} = \frac{V_\infty}{2x}(f'\eta - f)\frac{d\theta}{d\eta}$$

$$\alpha \frac{\partial^2 \theta}{\partial y} = \alpha \frac{V_\infty}{\nu x}\frac{d^2\theta}{d\eta^2}$$

Dimensionless equations

Substituting these expressions into the energy equation we get

$$2\frac{d^2\theta}{d\eta^2} + \text{Pr} f \frac{d\theta}{d\eta} = 0$$

More similarity will become apparent between the momentum boundary layer equation and the energy equation if we replace f from eq. 6.2 to write it as

$$\frac{\theta''}{\theta'} - \text{Pr}\frac{f'''}{f''} = 0$$

The boundary conditions are similar to those for x component of velocity and will therefore reduce in terms of the similarity variable to

$$\theta(0) = 0, \quad \theta(\eta) \to 1 \text{ as } \eta \to \infty$$

6.2.3 Temperature profile

The equation of change of temperature can be formally integrated to write the following solution:

$$\theta = \frac{\displaystyle\int_o^\eta (f'')^{Pr} dz}{\displaystyle\int_o^\infty (f'')^{Pr} dz} \tag{6.3}$$

6.2.4 Look at the results

The first thing we notice is that if $Pr = 1$, the velocity profile and temperature profile are identical. This is to be expected because momentum and heat diffuse at the same rate if Prandtl number is unity. f'' is the velocity gradient and it decreases to zero as we move away from the plate. Hence, if $Pr >> 1$, $(f'')^{Pr}$ will be much less than f'' at distances away from the plate. Thus, temperature will reach the free stream value at smaller distances from the plate compared to the velocity profiles. This is also expected. If $Pr >> 1$ thermal diffusivity is smaller than kinematic viscosity, and heat diffuses slower than momentum. Thus, temperature gradients will be larger than velocity gradients for large Prandtl numbers. By similar arguments, it is easy to show that the reverse happens for small Prandtl numbers. Therefore, the thickness of thermal boundary layer, over which the temperature gradients are present depends upon Prandtl number. Thermal boundary layers are thinner than momentum boundary layers if $Pr > 1$, and *vice versa*. Expected temperature profiles and relative boundary layer thicknesses are qualitatively sketched in figure 6.4.

Heat transfer coefficient

We summarize the above results by calculating the heat transfer coefficient. The local value of heat transfer coefficient at a location x of the plate is given by

$$h_{loc}(T_w - T_b) = -k\left.\frac{dT}{dy}\right|_{y=0}$$

As the fluid is infinite in extent, T_b will be equal to T_∞. Further,

$$-k\left.\frac{dT}{dy}\right|_{y=0} = -k(T_\infty - T_w)\sqrt{\frac{V_\infty}{\nu x}}\left.\theta'\right|_{\eta=0} = -k(T_\infty - T_w)\sqrt{\frac{V_\infty}{\nu x}}\frac{(f''(0))^{Pr}}{\displaystyle\int_0^\infty (f'')^{Pr} dz}$$

Substituting this into the equation determining the heat transfer coefficient, we get

$$\frac{h_{loc}x}{k} = \sqrt{\frac{V_\infty x}{\nu}} \frac{(f''(0))^{Pr}}{\int_0^\infty (f'')^{Pr} dz}$$

where the left hand side is the local Nusselt number. In the useful range of $0.6 < Pr < 15$, the above can be approximated by

$$\frac{h_{loc}x}{k} \equiv Nu_{loc} = 0.332 Pr^{1/3} Re_x^{1/2}$$

This can be put in a form which will look familiar to those who learnt about analogies between momentum and heat transfer. The above can be written as

$$\frac{Nu_{loc}}{Pr^{1/3} Re_x} = \frac{0.332}{Re_x^{1/2}} = fr$$

where the fr on the right hand side stands for friction factor. The left hand side can be thought of as the Colburn's j-factor for boundary layers.

Note the dependence of heat transfer coefficient on Re and Pr. The powers of dependence on these numbers are different, 1/2 and 1/3, respectively. Compare this with the result in section 5.11, where the power of dependence on both the numbers was the same, and was equal to 1/3. In that problem, because flow was fully developed, only balance between heat convection and conduction was important. Hence, the dependence was on the Peclet number which is the product of Reynolds number and Prandtl number. In the present problem, momentum diffusion is also important as velocity profile is still developing. Hence, the power of dependence on Reynolds number is different.

Relative thicknesses of boundary layers: Let us now compare thicknesses of momentum and thermal boundary layers. As the temperature gradients are concentrated in the thermal boundary layer, we can infer from scaling arguments that

$$h \sim \frac{k}{\delta_T}$$

where δ_T is the thickness of the thermal boundary layer. Hence

$$\frac{hx}{k} \sim \frac{x}{\delta_T}$$

Hence, from the equation for Nusselt number

$$\frac{x}{\delta_T} \sim Pr^{1/3} Re^{1/2}$$

But

$$\frac{x}{\delta} \sim Re^{1/2}$$

Therefore, in the range of $0.6 < Pr < 15$

$$\frac{\delta_T}{\delta} \sim Pr^{-1/3}$$

This is a quantitative estimate of our earlier arguments.

6.3 NATURAL CONVECTION: INTRODUCTION

Heat transfer by natural convection is more complex to analyze than forced convection heat transfer. The reason is that a velocity scale is not available *a priori*. The motion is generated due to the buoyancy forces and hence the temperature distribution plays an important role in determining the motion. But we know that motion determines the temperature profile! Thus, the equation of motion and thermal energy balance are coupled in a way *that cannot be neglected* and have to be solved simultaneously.

6.3.1 Boussinesq approximation

Buoyancy forces are generated due to density variations produced by temperature variation. There is one more effect caused by density variation: the velocities must change to conserve mass flow rates. Boussinesq approximation suggests that the changes in velocities due to density variation are negligible.

$Coefficient\, of\, expansion$: A central parameter in all considerations regarding natural convection is the variation of density with temperature. The change of density with temperature is a physical property. It is the tendency of the fluid to expand when heated. This property is described by the coefficient of expansion, β:

$$\beta = -\frac{1}{\rho}\frac{d\rho}{dT}\bigg|_P$$

The negative sign is there for convenience to make β positive for the common case of density decreasing with increasing temperature. Hence, for not too large a change in temperature, we can write

$$\frac{\rho}{\rho_o} = 1 - \beta(T - T_o)$$

where β is evaluated at T_o, and *treated as a constant.* We will use this expression to calculate density changes in solving problems in natural convection.

Effect of conservation of mass

Now we wish to examine whether variation in velocities due to density changes will cause any significant effects. Consider flow in a pipe as an example. Suppose the average axial velocity is V. Let the temperature change be ΔT when the fluid flows over some length L. Let the reference temperature be T_o, and the density at that temperature be ρ_o. The corresponding change in density while the fluid has flowed over the length L would be proportional to $\rho_o\beta\Delta T$. Hence the velocity would have to change by a factor of $1\pm\beta\Delta T$ to keep mass flow rate the same. The change in velocity is reflected in an *additional* acceleration of fluid as it flows through the length L, and hence it affects the motion by causing inertial forces. An estimate of these additional inertial forces is of the order of $\rho_o V^2 \beta \Delta T/L$. This term will be negligible compared to the magnitude of inertial forces $\rho_o V^2/L$ as long as the temperature rise is not large. Similar is the argument about the *additional* viscous forces generated due to changes in velocities due to expansion of fluid in response to temperature variations.

The essence of Boussinesq approximation is then to ignore the effect of density variations in the equations of continuity and motion, but keep it in the latter as far as buoyancy forces are concerned.

6.3.2 Equation of motion

Thus, under the Boussinesq approximation we solve the following equations: The equation of continuity is unchanged.

$$\nabla.\mathbf{v} = 0$$

$$\rho_o \frac{D\mathbf{v}}{Dt} = -\nabla p + \mu_o \nabla^2 \mathbf{v} + \rho \mathbf{g}$$

$$\rho_o \hat{C}_p \frac{DT}{Dt} = k_o \nabla^2 T$$

where ρ is recognized to be a function of temperature. It is obvious that if it is not done so in the equation of motion, there is no buoyancy force and then occurrence of motion cannot be predicted!

6.4 NATURAL CONVECTION BETWEEN VERTICAL PLATES

6.4.1 Problem identification

As done before we can classify convection problems according to the status of 'developedness' of profiles. First we note that since temperature and velocity profiles are linked, there is no possibility of velocity profile being fully developed while the temperature profile is developing. The present section thus examines a case where both velocity and temperature profiles are fully developed.

Consider a tall and wide channel with the walls being separated by a gap b. See figure 6.5. The left wall is hotter and is being maintained at T_1 while the colder right wall is kept at T_2. Due

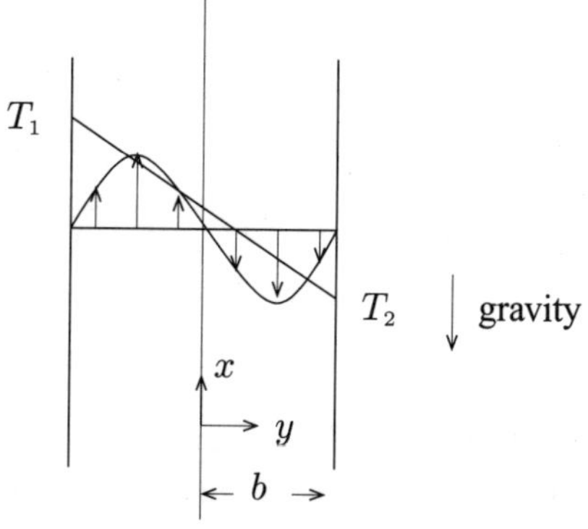

Figure 6.5. Natural convection in a vertical channel.

to buoyancy, the fluid will rise at the left wall and descend near the right wall. If the channel is sufficiently tall, then the buoyancy forces can *exactly* match the viscous forces and the flow will be fully developed. This is possible in the middle portion of the channel. The forces will not match near the end and exit of the channel, but we will restrict our analysis to the middle portion.

Equation of continuity

If the flow is fully developed we expect the x component of the velocity not to change in the x direction. As the width of the channel, *i.e.,* in the z direction is very large, we do not expect either a velocity to exist in that direction or the other dynamical quantities to depend upon that coordinate. The equation of continuity then gives, after using the idea that ρ is treated as constant in this equation,

$$\frac{\partial v_x}{\partial x} = 0$$

Hence v_x is only a function of y.

Equation of motion

Since $v_y = 0$, the y component equation of motion simply gives us the result that pressure cannot depend upon y. Hence, $P = P(x)$ only. Now we turn to the x component of the equation of motion. At steady state, it simplifies to

$$0 = -\frac{dP}{dx} + \mu\frac{\partial^2 v_x}{\partial y^2} - \rho g$$

where g is the acceleration due to gravity, and we have used the fact that $g_x = -g$. Here of course we will have to treat the density as a function of temperature. Let us take the mean of the wall temperatures as the reference temperature, T_o. Then the density can be written as

$$\rho = \rho_o\left[1 - \beta(T - T_o)\right]$$

as long as the temperature difference between the walls is not too large.

Substituting this in the equation of motion we get

$$0 = -\frac{dP}{dx} + \mu\frac{d^2 v_x}{dy^2} - \rho_o g + \rho_o g\beta(T - T_o) \tag{6.4}$$

Equation of change of temperature

Now we turn to the equation of thermal energy balance. We can simplify it to get

$$v_x\frac{\partial T}{\partial x} = \alpha\left(\frac{\partial^2 T}{\partial x^2} + \frac{\partial^2 T}{\partial y^2}\right) \tag{6.5}$$

where we have assumed that all physical properties are independent of temperature.

Fully developed temperature profile: Let us now examine the consequences of temperature profile being fully developed. For this purpose, a non-dimensional temperature can be defined using one of the wall temperatures and bulk temperature, T_b:

$$\theta_1 = \frac{T - T_1}{T_b - T_1}$$

Since the temperature profile is fully developed,

$$\frac{d\theta_1}{dx} = 0 = \frac{\partial T}{\partial x} - \theta_1 \frac{dT_b}{dx}$$

A non-dimensional temperature could have also been defined using the other wall temperatures and bulk temperature:

$$\theta_2 = \frac{T - T_2}{T_b - T_2}$$

The fully developed condition would have given the following condition:

$$\frac{d\theta_2}{dx} = 0 = \frac{\partial T}{\partial x} - \theta_2 \frac{dT_b}{dx}$$

This implies that

$$\theta_1 = \theta_2, \text{ or } \frac{T - T_1}{T - T_2} = \frac{T_b - T_1}{T_b - T_2}$$

T_b is the bulk temperature and hence can be a function of only x. Hence, the right hand side of the second equality can only be a function of x. This implies that, the left hand side, $(T - T_1)/(T - T_2)$ can also be a function of only x. Conversely, and equally important, it cannot be a function of y. But we know that T is a function of x and also y. Thus, the ratio of the temperature differences $(T - T_1)$ and $(T - T_2)$ can be independent of y only if they both have the form of y multiplied by a constant. Hence, temperature is a linear function of y. If temperature is a linear function of y, the heat supplied at one wall is equal to the heat removed at the other wall. Hence the temperature itself cannot change in the x direction. Thus, eq. 6.5 simplifies to

$$\frac{d^2T}{dy^2} = 0$$

6.4.2 Temperature profile

In this example, as it turns out, the equations of motion and change of temperature are decoupled even in natural convection. As argued earlier, the temperature profile is linear in x:

$$T = T_1 - (T_1 - T_2)\frac{x + b}{2b}$$

We can rewrite the above in terms of the mean of the temperatures of the walls, T_o as

$$\frac{T - T_o}{\Delta T} = -\frac{x}{2b}$$

where $\Delta T = T_1 - T_2$.

Velocity profile

Let us examine the equation of motion in light of these findings. We note that all terms involving velocity and temperature are only functions of y. Hence dP/dx can only be a function of y or be a constant. But we deduced from the y component equation of motion that pressure is not a function of y. Hence dP/dx can only be a constant. Now as T_o is the mean of the two wall temperatures and temperature profile is linear in x, the term $\rho_o g\beta(T - T_o)$ must be positive for negative values of x and negative for positive values of x. Thus, the terms involving velocity must change sign accordingly, and one half of fluid goes up while the other goes down. Hence, we infer that the viscous forces are balanced by the buoyancy forces, and the average weight of the fluid is balanced by pressure gradient:

$$\frac{dP}{dx} = -\rho_o g$$

and

$$\mu\frac{d^2 v_y}{dx^2} + \rho_o g\beta(T - T_o) = 0$$

6.4.3 Scaling

We have already solved for temperature profile and do not need a scale for it! We can non-dimensionalize the length with b. Let us try to get a scale for velocity. The buoyancy forces per unit volume must balance the viscous forces per unit volume. An estimate of the former is $\rho_o g\beta\Delta T$. If V_{ch} is an estimate of the characteristic velocity, an estimate of viscous forces per unit volume is given by $\mu V_{ch}/b^2$. Balancing the two forces gives an estimate of V_{ch} to be $\rho_o g b^2\beta\Delta T/\mu$. The temperature profile obtained earlier can be substituted into the equation of motion to obtain:

$$\frac{d^2\tilde{v}}{d\tilde{x}^2} - \frac{1}{2}\tilde{x} = 0$$

Velocity profile

Integrating this with the no-slip boundary conditions at the left and right walls, we get

$$v_y = \frac{1}{12}\frac{\rho_o g b^2\beta\Delta T}{\mu}\left(\tilde{x}^3 - \tilde{x}\right)$$

6.4.4 Look at the results

The velocity profile is sketched in figure 6.5. As, $\tilde{x} < 1$, $\tilde{x}^3 < \tilde{x}$. This confirms that, as expected, the flow is upward next to the hot wall where $\tilde{x} < 0$.

We were looking for a solution which allows for the velocity profile to be fully developed. By definition, velocity profile cannot change in the flow direction. But, fluid rises near the hot plate and descends near the cold one. Thus, invariance with flow direction implies that these two flows must match each other. In view of only one length scale and independence of properties on temperature, the upward and downward flow have to be mirror images. Thus, the velocity profile has a minimum and a maximum. The buoyancy forces increase with density as well as with the sensitivity of density variation with temperature. Thus, the convection velocity must increase with both these quantities. Larger imposed temperature differences increase the buoyancy forces and hence convection. Increased viscosities must have exactly the opposite effect. All these are as confirmed by the expression obtained.

Grashof number

If we formulate a Reynolds number with the estimate of characteristic velocity, we get the following ratio:

$$Gr \equiv \frac{gb^3\beta\Delta T}{\nu^2}$$

where Gr is the Grashof number. Thus, Grashof number represents the product of the ratio of buoyancy to viscous forces with the ratio of inertial to viscous forces, but based on an estimate of a characteristic velocity. Thus, the velocity profile can be written as

$$\frac{bv_y\rho_o}{\mu} = Gr\left(\tilde{x}^3 - \tilde{x}\right)$$

From the procedure we followed, the ratio $\rho_o gb^2\beta\Delta T/(\mu V_{ch})$ represents the ratio of buoyancy to viscous forces. If we multiply this ratio with a Reynolds number formulated with the characteristic velocity, we get the Grashof number. Thus, Gr can also be thought of as the ratio of product of buoyancy and inertial forces to the square of viscous forces.

Flow transitions

We have assumed that the flow is laminar. One can expect a laminar to turbulent flow transition to occur if inertial forces dominate viscous forces or if Reynolds number is large. As we discussed Grashof number is the Reynolds number for natural convection. Thus, flow transition can be expected to occur when Gr exceeds a critical value. As we shall see in a later section, a more insightful number in this regard is Rayleigh number, Ra. It is equal to the product of Grashof and Prandtl numbers. We need to pay attention to the heat transfer from the wall to the fluid element to understand this aspect. We have taken the total imposed temperature difference to evaluate the characteristic velocity. If flow becomes turbulent, it is likely that gradients of velocity and temperature are confined to layers near the walls. In such an instance, the velocity and temperature gradients can be spread over different distances from the wall depending upon Prandtl number. Thus, the selection of characteristic velocity can be expected to depend upon Prandtl number as well. It turns out that this transition occurs when $Ra = 20,000$ for flow between two vertical plates with large aspect ratio, *i.e.*, b is very small compared to the length of the plates.

6.5 NATURAL CONVECTION BOUNDARY LAYER

6.5.1 Qualitative discussion

Now we go to the next level of complexity where both the temperature and velocity profiles are developing. We deviate from the usual format of presentation in this section. We focus only on the scaling concepts because of the beautiful insights they give. This material is paraphrased from the book by Bejan [1]. A prototype of such a situation is heat transfer through boundary layers. Here we consider a hot flat plate placed vertically in an infinitely large medium. See figure 6.6.

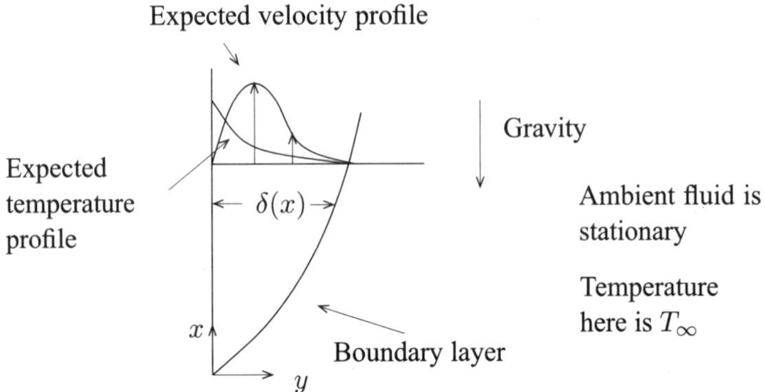

Figure 6.6. Boundary layer developing on a vertical hot plate.

The fluid adjacent to the wall gets heated and hence its temperature begins to rise. Due to conduction, heat percolates in the y direction. As the fluid next to the wall gets hot, it will rise due to buoyancy. As it moves up, it gets heated more and hence will continue to rise. This creates convection in the x direction. Hence, we expect temperature to be a function of both x and y coordinates. Far away from the plate, the temperature will remain at the undisturbed value of T_∞. Thus, we see a thermal boundary layer developing on the wall. As the fluid moves up, it continues to get hotter, and the buoyancy increases. Hence fluid elements will also accelerate. Far away from the wall, the fluid will be stationary as buoyancy forces are absent there. As a result, motion will be confined to a layer near the wall and we also see a momentum boundary layer developing. Thus, we expect that the velocity will change in both the vertical and horizontal directions.

We can qualitatively sketch the velocity and temperature profiles. The temperature is expected to monotonically change from the wall temperature to that of the ambient. The fluid far away from the plate will be stationary as buoyancy force is absent there. However, the fluid velocity must be zero at the plate due to the no-slip condition. Thus we expect the velocity profile to have a maximum. This is shown in figure 6.6.

Influence of Prandtl number

As with heat transfer to a boundary layer formed under forced convection, we expect the relative rates of diffusion of heat and momentum to influence the characteristics of heat transfer here as well.

Consider the simple case of Prandtl number being unity. Here momentum and heat diffuse at the same rate. Hence we expect the velocity to be non-zero over the same thickness to which temperature gradients are confined to. The thermal and momentum boundary layers coincide and will be of the same thickness. The buoyancy force, viscous forces, inertial forces, and heat conduction as well as convection operate on the same length scales.

Suppose Prandtl number is less than unity. Then heat diffuses faster than momentum. We get an interesting situation here. It is clear that buoyancy forces exist in the entire region where temperature gradients exist, *i.e.,* in the entire thermal boundary layer. Therefore, motion must exist throughout the thermal boundary layer. But, as momentum diffuses slower than heat, it cannot percolate throughout the thermal boundary layer. Hence, the thermal boundary layer must have two regions as far as momentum diffusion is concerned. We recall that viscous forces are important in the region where momentum diffusion is important. Thus, near the wall where viscous forces dominate due to the no-slip boundary conditions, the viscous forces must balance buoyancy forces. This region then constitutes the viscous dominated portion of the momentum boundary layer. Outside this region, motion is still present because buoyancy forces are not zero. Hence, the buoyancy forces are balanced by inertial forces. The expected velocity and temperature profiles are shown in figure 6.7.

The situation where Prandtl number is greater than unity also gives rise to an interesting situation. Here heat is diffusing slower than momentum. The buoyancy forces are created only in a region to which temperature gradients are confined to. As motion is created in this region, the momentum diffuses rapidly and causes motion outside the thermal boundary layer even though temperature gradients are absent there. Thus, inside the thermal boundary layer, the buoyancy forces are balanced by viscous forces. The momentum boundary layer thickness is determined by a balance of inertial and viscous forces. The expected velocity and temperature profiles are shown in figure 6.7.

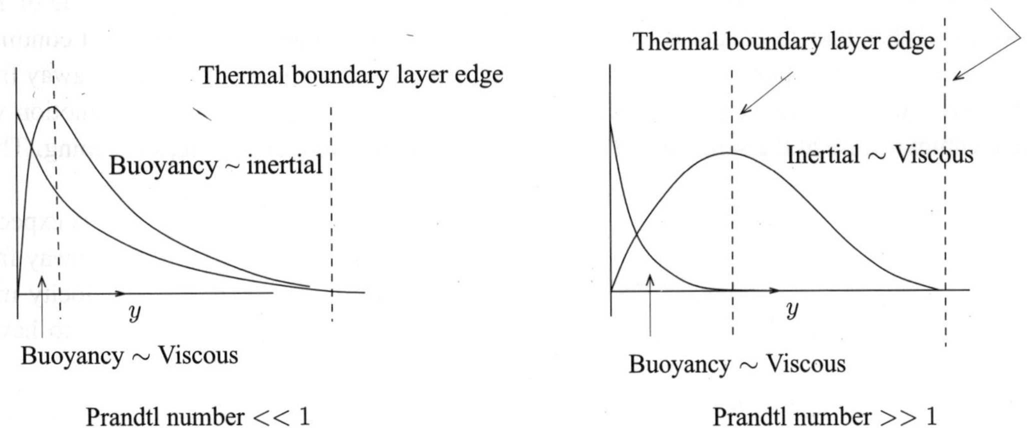

Figure 6.7. Influence of Prandtl number on force balances in boundary layer. Curves with a maximum are the expected velocity profiles.

6.5.2 Scaling in natural convection boundary layers

Here we show how far one can go based on the qualitative but deep understanding gained from the above discussion. We can get dependencies of Nusselt number on other dimensionless numbers. Heat transfer rates in natural convection boundary layers can be determined if thermal boundary layer thickness is found. The numerical values can be found only by integrating equations of motion and thermal energy balance, which we will consider a little later. Scaling arguments can be used to find the relationships between the various dynamical quantities, and we illustrate this type of argument in this section.

Estimate of buoyancy force

We take the reference temperature to be the ambient temperature, T_∞. The wall temperature is known, and hence a characteristic temperature difference is known to us. Let it be denoted by ΔT. Then an estimate of buoyancy forces per unit volume is $\rho_o \beta \Delta T g$. We use this force to estimate the characteristic velocity. The balance depends upon Prandtl number as discussed earlier.

Prandtl number is unity

Here we expect the thermal and momentum boundary layers to be of equal thickness. Let the boundary layer thickness be δ at some length L along the plate. We need characteristic velocities in both directions. In the x direction we can choose it to be the maximum velocity. Let it be represented by V_{ch}. By arguments similar to those employed in momentum boundary layer theory, using the equation of continuity, $V_{ch}\delta/L$ is estimated to be the characteristic velocity in the y direction. The buoyancy force is of the same magnitude as either the inertial or viscous forces because both these are of the same magnitude in the thermal boundary layer. The balance between the buoyancy and inertial forces gives

$$\rho_\infty \frac{V_{ch}^2}{L} \sim \rho_\infty \beta \Delta T g, \quad \text{or} \quad L V_{ch} \sim \sqrt{\beta L^3 g \Delta T}$$

Now we can either turn to equation of energy and balance magnitude of convection terms with diffusion terms or go to equation of motion and balance the viscous and inertial forces to relate the boundary layer thickness to the position along the plate. Both will give the same result as both heat and momentum diffuse at the same rate. The balance of viscous and inertial forces is given by

$$\mu \frac{V_{ch}}{\delta^2} \sim \rho_\infty \frac{V_{ch}^2}{L}$$

$$\frac{\delta}{L} \sim \sqrt{\frac{\nu}{L V_{ch}}} \sim \left(\frac{\nu^2}{\beta L^3 g \Delta T}\right)^{1/4} \sim Gr^{-.25}$$

We notice that the momentum boundary layer thickness scales with Reynolds number exactly like it does with momentum boundary layer in the absence of heat transfer. It is as expected because this dependence arises from a balance of viscous and inertial forces.

The heat transfer coefficient can be evaluated from an estimate of the heat flux by conduction at the wall:

$$k\frac{\Delta T}{\delta} \sim h\Delta T, \quad \text{or} \quad \frac{h\delta}{k} \sim 1, \quad \text{or} \quad \frac{hL}{k} \sim \frac{L}{\delta}$$

Hence we get the following scaling result

$$Nu_L = \frac{hL}{k} \sim \left(\frac{\beta L^3 g \Delta T}{\nu^2}\right)^{(1/4)} \sim Gr^{0.25}$$

This result is also presented in terms of Rayleigh number defined as

$$Ra = \frac{\beta L^3 g \Delta T}{\nu \alpha}$$

Thus

$$Nu_L \sim \left(\frac{Ra}{Pr}\right)^{0.25}.$$

Prandtl number $<< 1$

Here we expect the thermal boundary layer to be much thicker than the viscous region of the momentum boundary layer. In this region of the momentum boundary layer, both viscous and inertial forces are present and are similar in magnitude. But as the thickness of the viscous force dominated portion of the momentum boundary layer is not known, we cannot use the balance between viscous and buoyancy forces to estimate the characteristic velocity. However, inertial forces exist throughout the boundary layer. As the motion is driven by buoyancy forces, these can be balanced by inertial forces to get an estimate of the characteristic velocity. Our estimate of the characteristic velocity is then given by

$$LV_{ch} \sim \sqrt{\beta L^3 g \Delta T}$$

Now we have to look at the equation of change of temperature to estimate the thickness of the thermal boundary layer. In the thermal boundary layer, both conduction and convection are of equal importance. Thus, by balancing both, we get

$$\frac{V_{ch}\Delta T}{L} \sim \alpha \frac{\Delta T}{\delta_T^2}, \text{ or } \frac{\delta_T}{L} \sim \left(\frac{\alpha}{LV_{ch}}\right)^{0.5} \sim \left(\frac{\alpha^2}{\beta L^3 g \Delta T}\right)^{0.25}$$

Like before, the heat transfer coefficient can be evaluated from an estimate of the heat flux by conduction at the wall:

$$k\frac{\Delta T}{\delta_T} \sim h\Delta T, \text{ or } \frac{h\delta_T}{k} \sim 1, \text{ or } \frac{hL}{k} \sim \frac{L}{\delta_T}$$

Thus, we have the scaling result

$$Nu_L = \frac{hL}{k} \sim \left(\frac{\beta L^3 g \Delta T}{\alpha^2}\right)^{0.25}$$

It can be rewritten in terms of Rayleigh number as

$$Nu_L \sim (Ra\, Pr)^{0.25}$$

The thickness of the region of momentum boundary layer dominated by viscous forces, δ, can be obtained by balancing the viscous forces and inertial forces. Thus, we get

$$\frac{\delta}{L} \sim \sqrt{\frac{\nu}{LV_{ch}}} \sim \left(\frac{\nu^2}{\beta L^3 g \Delta T}\right)^{0.25} \sim Gr^{-0.25}$$

Prandtl number >> 1

Here the thermal boundary layer will be thinner than the momentum boundary layer. The buoyancy forces will be zero beyond the thermal boundary layer. Hence, the maximum in velocity can be expected to occur at the edge of the thermal boundary layer. Motion will still exist beyond the thermal boundary layer both due to diffusion and inertia. As thermal boundary layer is thinner than the momentum boundary layer, the maximum in velocity will occur close to the wall. Hence we expect the buoyancy forces to be balanced by viscous forces. Thus,

$$\mu \frac{V_{ch}}{\delta_T^2} \sim \rho_\infty \beta g \Delta T, \text{ or } V_{ch} \sim \frac{\beta g \Delta T \delta_T^2}{\nu}$$

From the balance of heat transfer by convection with diffusion, we get

$$\frac{V_{ch}}{L} \sim \frac{\alpha}{\delta_T^2}, \text{ or } \frac{\beta g \Delta T \delta_T^2}{L\nu} \sim \frac{\alpha}{\delta_T^2}$$

This can be rearranged to get

$$\frac{\delta_T}{L} \sim \left(\frac{\alpha \, \nu}{\beta g \Delta T L^3} \right)^{0.25}$$

Thus, we get

$$Nu_L = \frac{hL}{k} \sim \left(\frac{\beta g \Delta T L^3}{\alpha \, \nu} \right)^{0.25} \sim Ra^{0.25}$$

The thickness of the momentum boundary layer can be found out by balancing the inertial and viscous forces

$$\frac{\delta}{L} \sim \sqrt{\frac{\nu}{V_{ch} L}} \sim \sqrt{\frac{\nu}{\alpha}} \frac{\delta_T}{L} \sim \left(\frac{\nu^2}{\beta L^3 g \Delta T} \right)^{0.25} \sim Gr^{-0.25}$$

Heat flux in natural convection

Recall that one of the questions we raised about unit operations approach in the beginning of the course was about the non-linear dependence of heat flux on temperature difference. Now we are ready to answer this. Once the heat transfer coefficient is known, the heat flux can be calculated:

$$q_x \sim h \Delta T \sim (\Delta T)^{1.25}$$

Thus the simple analysis does show that heat flux depends non-linearly on temperature difference!

6.6 NATURAL CONVECTION ON A VERTICAL PLATE

6.6.1 Problem identification

We have seen that the results of scaling analysis give powerful insight into the relationships between various quantities. However, the numerical coefficients that appear in the relationships can only be obtained by solving the exact equations. Let us attempt this for the problem of a vertical hot plate placed in a quiescent fluid. It is not possible to obtain a simple result for a plate of finite length. An elegant similarity solution exists if the plate is assumed to be infinitely long and that the medium is unbounded. We consider this solution here. The situation is same as shown in figure 6.6. As already explained, velocity and temperature will be a function of both x and y.

Equation of motion and boundary conditions

Rectangular coordinates are the appropriate coordinates. We use the boundary layer approximations to conclude that pressure outside the boundary layer is impressed on the boundary layer. However, there is no flow outside the boundary layer and hence pressure gradient is hydrostatic. Hence,

$$\frac{\partial P}{\partial x} = \rho_o g_x$$

This is similar to what was said in the case of natural convection between parallel plates. Using this and other boundary layer approximations, the equation of motion is given by

$$v_x \frac{\partial v_x}{\partial x} + v_y \frac{\partial v_x}{\partial y} = \nu \frac{\partial^2 v_x}{\partial y^2} + g\beta(T - T_\infty)$$

The boundary conditions are given by

$$v_x(x, y) \text{ and } v_y(x, y) = 0 \text{ at } y = 0 \text{ and as } y \to \infty$$

Equation of change of temperature

The equation, after using the boundary layer approximations, simplifies to

$$v_x \frac{\partial T}{\partial x} + v_y \frac{\partial T}{\partial y} = \alpha \frac{\partial^2 T}{\partial y^2}$$

The boundary conditions are

$$T(x, 0) = T_w, \quad T(x, y) \to T_\infty \text{ as } y \to \infty$$

6.6.2 Scaling

We have a characteristic temperature difference. A non-dimensional temperature can be defined using this:

$$\theta = \frac{T - T_\infty}{T_w - T_\infty}$$

Similarity transformation

Finding similarity variable here is difficult unlike in the case of isothermal boundary layer. In that case, the characteristic velocity is a constant while in the present case, the characteristic velocity changes with distance along the plate. We may intuitively expect that the *dimensionless velocity* may depend upon y/δ since δ is a *local* characteristic length in the y direction. If such is true, we can try scaling y with δ to see if that would have lead to discovery of the similarity variable in case of isothermal boundary layer. In section 6.1, we found that

$$\frac{v_x}{V_\infty} \sim f'(\eta) \sim f'\left(y\sqrt{\frac{V_\infty}{\nu x}}\right)$$

We also found that the boundary layer thickness was given by

$$\delta \sim \sqrt{\frac{\nu x}{V_\infty}}$$

Combining these two, it appears that

$$\eta \sim \frac{y}{\delta}$$

Now, we might try if this will work in the present case also. Thus, referring to figure 6.6, we postulate that

$$\frac{v_x}{V_{ch}} = \mathcal{F}\left(\frac{y}{\delta(x)}\right)$$

Scaling analysis similar to that carried out earlier gives

$$V_{ch} \sim \sqrt{x\beta g\Delta T}$$

and

$$\frac{\delta}{x} \sim \left(\frac{\nu^2}{\beta x^3 g\Delta T}\right)^{1/4}$$

Thus, it may be expected that

$$v_x = V_{ch}\mathcal{F}\left[\frac{y}{x}\left(\frac{\beta x^3 g\Delta T}{\nu^2}\right)^{1/4}\right]$$

In other words, the argument of the function is expected to be the similarity variable

$$\eta = \frac{y}{x}\left(\frac{\beta x^3 g\Delta T}{4\nu^2}\right)^{1/4}$$

where the number four is introduced in the denominator to make the final differential equations look pretty.

The flow here is two-dimensional and hence it is more convenient to use stream function. Thus it is postulated

$$\psi = h(x)f(\eta)$$

As explained in section 6.1, $h(x)$ is introduced into this equation because we are requiring that only dimensionless velocities be a function of the similarity variable and not necessarily the stream function. However,

$$v_x = -\frac{\partial\psi}{\partial y} = -h(x)\frac{\partial\eta}{\partial y}\frac{df}{d\eta}$$

Thus, similarity hypothesis requires that v_x must equal V_{ch} multiplied by some function of only the similarity variable. Comparison with the dimensionless form gives

$$V_{ch} \sim h(x)\frac{\partial \eta}{\partial y}$$

Using our earlier estimate of the characteristic velocity gives

$$h(x) \sim (x^3\nu^2 g\beta\Delta T)^{0.25}$$

Introducing a numerical factor for reasons already mentioned, the stream function is then defined as

$$\psi = 4\nu\left(\frac{x^3 g\beta\Delta T}{4\nu^2}\right)^{0.25} f(\eta)$$

Dimensionless equations

It is postulated that non-dimensional temperature is only a function of the same similarity variable η:

$$\theta = \theta(\eta)$$

When the non-dimensional temperature and the stream function are introduced into the equation of change of temperature, it simplifies to

$$f''' + 3ff'' - 2(f')^2 + \theta = 0$$

and

$$\theta'' + 3Prf\theta' = 0$$

where prime refers to differentiation with respect to η.

Boundary conditions needed to solve this equation are given below. The no-slip velocity condition at the plate and that velocity approaches zero far away from the plate requires

$$f' = 0 \text{ at } \eta = 0 \text{ and as } \eta \to \infty$$

As stream function can be set to zero at any convenient point, the following is used

$$f = 0 \text{ at } \eta = 0$$

The non-dimensional temperature must be unity at the plate and zero far away from the plate. Thus,

$$\theta(\eta) = 0, \quad \text{and } \theta(\eta) \to 1 \text{ as } \eta \to \infty$$

6.6.3 Temperature profile

The equation of change of temperature can be integrated in terms of f:

$$\theta(\eta) = \frac{\displaystyle\int_0^{\eta} da \exp\left[-3\,Pr\mathrm{I}(0,a)\right]}{\displaystyle\int_0^{\infty} da \exp\left[-3\,Pr\mathrm{I}(0,a)\right]}$$

where

$$\mathrm{I}(0,a) \equiv \int_0^{a} f\,db$$

In the solution for the non-dimensional temperature given above, a and b are dummy integration variables. The equation of motion is non-linear and hence solutions have to be obtained numerically. We do not show the results but be assured that they follow the qualitative sketches shown in figure 6.6!

6.6.4 Look at the results

Heat transfer coefficient

Once the solutions are obtained, the heat transfer coefficient can be calculated. Thus,

$$q_y(y=0) \equiv h_{loc}(T_w - T_\infty) = -k\frac{\partial T}{\partial y}\bigg|_{y=0} = -k\frac{T_w - T_\infty}{x}\left(\frac{\beta x^3 g\Delta T}{4\nu^2}\right)^{1/4}\theta'(\eta=0)$$

or

$$Nu_x = \frac{h_{loc}x}{k} = -\left(\frac{\beta x^3 g\Delta T}{4\nu^2}\right)^{0.25}\theta'(\eta=0) = -\left(\frac{Ra_x}{Pr}\right)^{0.25}\frac{\theta'(\eta=0)}{\sqrt{2}}$$

The derivative of the non-dimensional temperature has to be evaluated numerically. It turns out that the following is a very good fit over a wide range of Prandtl numbers:

$$Nu_x = \frac{3}{4}\left(\frac{2Pr}{5(1+2\sqrt{Pr}+2Pr)}\right)^{0.25} Ra_x^{0.25}$$

As expected Nusselt number is a function of Ra and Pr. It will be interesting to see how our scale analysis compares with the exact solution. We need to only examine the factor multiplying $Ra_x^{0.25}$ for this purpose. If $Pr << 1$, the term is proportional to $Pr^{0.25}$ and hence $Nu_x \sim (Ra_x\,Pr)^{0.25}$. If $Pr >> 1$, the term is independent of Pr, and hence $Nu_x \sim Ra_x^{0.25}$. Both these are in agreement with the results of scale analysis.

Flow transitions

The flow was assumed to be laminar in the analysis presented. As discussed earlier, a flow transition can occur as velocities become larger. As buoyancy forces become larger, velocities also become greater. Inertial forces increase and the flow becomes turbulent. The transition occurs when $Ra_x \, Pr \sim 10^9$.

6.7 HEAT TRANSFER & PHASE CHANGE

6.7.1 Problem identification

We consider freezing of a liquid as an example involving phase change. Extensive literature exists on this very important subject with applications to casting and other areas. We refer the reader to the book by Davis [2] for more details. Refer to figure 6.8. Consider molten liquid at its melting

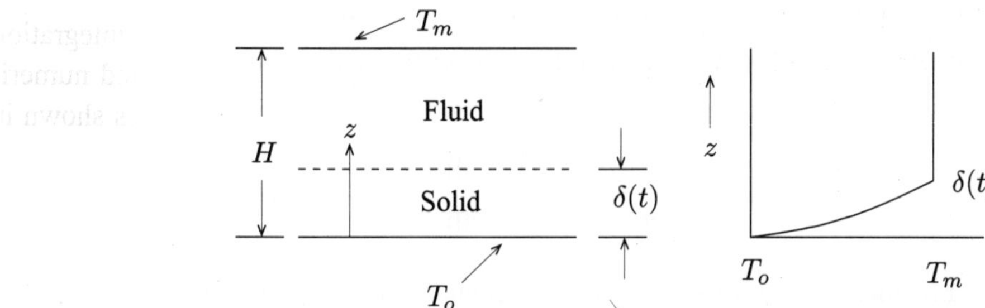

Figure 6.8. Fluid at melting point is placed between two infinitely wide plates separated by distance H. Both plates are at T_m. At $t = 0$, temperature of the bottom plate is suddenly lowered to T_o while the top plate is maintained at T_m. Freezing begins at the bottom plate and the freezing front moves up. Its location at any given time is $\delta(t)$. Expected temperature profile is shown on the right.

point, T_m, placed between two infinitely wide plates. Let both the plates be at T_m initially. At some instant, temperature of the bottom plate is lowered to T_o and is maintained there. The liquid will begin to freeze at the bottom plate and as heat is removed through it, more of the fluid will freeze. There will be a front that separates the solid and liquid regions. A special feature is that the domain of the solid keeps increasing, and the boundary separating the fluid and the solid continues to move. Such problems are therefore referred to as *moving boundary value problems.* Let the location of the front be denoted by $\delta(t)$. The objective of this section is to calculate the location of the front as a function of the difference between the temperature of the bottom plate and the melting point, and the time required for the slab to freeze.

6.7.2 Equation of change of temperature

The temperature cannot fall below T_m till freezing occurs. Hence, the liquid region between $\delta(t)$ and H will remain at T_m. The latent heat of fusion as well as sensible heat in the solid region has to be removed through the bottom plate only. Thus, the temperature will decrease from the front towards the bottom plate. The temperature in the solid region will fall from T_m at $z = \delta(t)$ to T_o at the bottom plate. As both plates are infinitely wide in x and y directions, temperature is not expected to be a function of those coordinates. Thus, $T = T(z)$ only. The expected temperature profile is shown in the right panel of figure 6.8. The problem is unsteady in nature.

We assume that the arrangement is such that natural convection is absent. Conduction then is the only relevant mechanism. The temperature of the fluid will remain constant at T_m *till the freezing front reaches* H. Hence, till the time the freezing front reaches H, energy balance in fluid phase is of no interest. Rectangular coordinates are suitable for this problem and the equation of change of temperature in those coordinates, after introduction of the hypotheses mentioned, simplifies to

$$\rho_s C_{p,s} \frac{\partial T}{\partial t} = k_s \frac{\partial^2 T}{\partial z^2} \quad 0 \le z \le \delta \tag{6.6}$$

where subscript s stands for the solid phase.

Initial and boundary conditions

As the entire fluid is at the melting point at the start, the initial condition is $T(z, 0) = T_m$. The ends of the slab are being maintained at constant temperature. Therefore, the boundary conditions are given by

$$T = T_o \quad \text{at} \quad z = 0 \quad \text{all } t \tag{6.7}$$

$$T = T_m \quad \text{at} \quad z = \delta(t) \quad \text{all } t \tag{6.8}$$

Though there are two boundary conditions available, we cannot solve the problem because $\delta(t)$ is an unknown. We need one more condition and that is provided by the energy balance at $\delta(t)$. As discussed in section 3.4, in general, we need both the mass balance and an energy balance at a boundary where phase change occurs. Mass balance at the boundary is given by eq. 3.8. Let us use the unit vector in the z direction as the unit normal $\boldsymbol{\xi}$. Thus, phase II is solid and I is liquid. The velocity of the boundary is given by

$$\dot{\delta} = \frac{d\delta(t)}{dt} = V_\xi$$

and it is in the z direction. Velocity in the solid is zero. Equation 3.8 gives the following result:

$$\rho_l(v_l - \dot{\delta}) + \rho_s \dot{\delta} = 0$$

or

$$v_l = \frac{\rho_l - \rho_s}{\rho_l} \dot{\delta}$$

As freezing proceeds, the mass of fluid converted into solid will occupy less volume if the solid is more dense. Hence, a bulk velocity must be created towards the interface. The above equation indicates that. If the top plate was free to move, it will descend with velocity v_l as there is no reason for velocity gradients to be created in bulk[9]. For simplicity, let us assume that the density differences between the solid and fluid can be neglected so that liquid also remains stationary. Hence, the boundary condition simplifies to

$$-\rho_s \dot{\delta} = \dot{m}_b \tag{6.9}$$

Now we turn to boundary condition on energy balance given by eq. 3.10. It simplifies to

$$\mathbf{q_s}.\mathbf{k} = \dot{m}_b\,(\hat{H}_l - \hat{H}_s) = -\rho_s\,\dot{\delta}\,\mathcal{L}$$

where we used the information that the temperature gradient in the liquid phase is zero and the difference between the enthalpy of fluid and solid per unit mass is equal to $\mathcal{L}$, the latent heat of melting per unit mass. Substituting Fourier's law of conduction into the above equation, it can be written as

$$k_s\frac{\partial T}{\partial z} = \rho_s\,\dot{\delta}\,\mathcal{L} \quad \text{at} \quad z = \delta(t) \tag{6.10}$$

6.7.3 Scaling

We can non-dimensionalize temperature difference using the characteristic temperature difference available:

$$\theta = \frac{T - T_o}{T_m - T_o}$$

Similarity transformation

Apparently, the problem has a length scale H. It is only superficially so because the region beyond δ is not playing any role. The thickness could as well have been infinitely large. Under such conditions, there is no time scale as well. Thus, there is no length scale and this problem is a candidate for similarity solution! The similarity variable has to be made up of independent variables and physical properties. We have seen this before and it is given by

$$\eta = \frac{z}{2\sqrt{\alpha_s t}}$$

where α_s is the thermal diffusivity of solid.

Dimensionless equations

As expected, the partial differential equation becomes an ordinary differential equation:

$$\frac{d^2\theta}{d\eta^2} + 2\eta\frac{d\theta}{d\eta} = 0$$

The initial condition does not matter because the domain has no volume initially, and we need to worry only about the boundary conditions. Equation 6.7 becomes

$$\theta(\eta) = 0$$

Equation 6.8 becomes

$$\theta(\eta) = 1 \quad \text{when} \quad \eta = \frac{\delta(t)}{2\sqrt{\alpha_s t}}$$

We can have a similarity solution only if the equations and boundary conditions are all functions of only the similarity variable. Thus, to make the given boundary condition to be a function of η only, we postulate that

$$\Gamma = \frac{\delta(t)}{2\sqrt{\alpha_s t}} = \text{Constant}$$

Similarity solution can be said to 'work' only if this postulate can be consistent for the rest of the problem too. The value of Γ is not known and has to be determined. But we have one more boundary condition, eq. 6.10. We should check if that also can be written only in terms of the similarity variable. From the definition of Γ, we have

$$\frac{d\delta(t)}{dt} = \Gamma\sqrt{\frac{\alpha_s}{t}}$$

Substituting this in eq. 6.10, and using similarity variable, we get

$$\frac{d\theta}{d\eta} = \frac{2\Gamma}{\mathsf{St}} \quad \text{at } \eta = \Gamma$$

Thus, all the conditions needed for similarity solution to exist are satisfied and we can proceed. In the above equation,

$$\mathsf{St} = \frac{C_{ps}(T_m - T_o)}{\mathcal{L}}$$

and is known as the Stefan number. It is a comparison of the latent heat of fusion to the heat capacity corresponding to the super-cooling $T_m - T_o$. Integrating the non-dimensional energy balance once gives

$$\frac{d\theta}{d\eta} = C\text{exp}^{-\eta^2}$$

We can now integrate this once more and use the boundary conditions at $\eta = 0$ and $\eta = \Gamma$ to get

$$\theta = \frac{\int_0^\eta dx \,\text{exp}^{-x^2}}{\int_0^\Gamma dx \,\text{exp}^{-x^2}} = \frac{\text{erf}(\eta)}{\text{erf}(\Gamma)}$$

We can now substitute this form in the energy balance at the moving boundary to get

$$\sqrt{\pi}\Gamma\text{erf}(\Gamma)\text{exp}^{\Gamma^2} = \mathsf{St}$$

This is a transcendental equation and has to be solved numerically to find values of Γ.

6.7.4 Look at the results

The rate of freezing depends upon the latent heat of fusion and the super-cooling. For a given super-cooling, rate of freezing is slower as latent heat becomes larger because heat to be removed is larger. Conversely, for a given latent heat, freezing is faster if the super-cooling is increased. Thus, the rate of freezing should increase when St is increased. In our expression, Γ reflects the rate of freezing and as can be seen from the transcendental equation, it increases as St is increased.

The above solution is valid till $\delta = H$. The time needed to achieve this, t_f, is the time taken for the slab to freeze. It is given by

$$t_f = \frac{H^2}{4\Gamma\alpha_s}$$

Beyond t_f, the entire slab is a solid and cools by heat conduction. The dynamics of it can be computed using unsteady state conduction equation. The 'initial' condition for that would be the temperature profile computed from the above solution.

Notes

[1]Refer to an article on Prandtl by Narasimha [3].

[2]All these arguments are being given, with hind sight after Prandtl!

[3]Here is a theme that repeats itself in transport processes. Experiments reveal phenomena that give rise to new physical insights that are very important. Many length scales and time scales may characterize a process, and it typically does happen as the complexity of the flow increases.

[4]We have implicitly assumed laminar flow in the discussion. Boundary layer flow can become turbulent.

[5]In general, this is the procedure for solving the boundary layer equations. The inviscid flow equations are solved to determine the flow and pressure outside the boundary layer. The normal component equation is solved to ascertain the pressure inside the boundary layer. In general, the pressure gradient in the flow direction would not be zero.

[6]It turns out that at small values of x the boundary layer approximations break down and hence similarity solution is not applicable at very short lengths.

[7]This is not an additional condition since we have defined v_x as a derivative and so one condition can be specified arbitrarily.

[8]It is a tricky one to obtain. As all gradients are near the wall, one would try a power series in η, and expect it to converge in a few terms. However, difficulty arises since the third boundary condition is at infinity.

[9]It is hard to imagine what will occur if the top plate was fixed. It must reduce the pressure and should lead to boiling of liquid. The resultant expansion might compensate for the reduction in volume by solidification. However, it is likely that this will lead to creation of small local temperature gradients to supply heat for vaporization!

References

[1] A. Bejan. *Convection heat transfer*. Wiley, 2 edition, 1984.

[2] S.H. Davis. *Theory of solidification*. Cambridge University Press, 2001.

[3] R. Narasimha. Divide, conquer and unify. *Nature*, 432:807, December 2004.

Chapter 7

FUNDAMENTALS OF MULTICOMPONENT SYSTEMS

The balance equations for mass of species and energy in a multicomponent system are derived by introducing the concept of a multicomponent body.
Mechanism of diffusion of species is discussed by introducing ideas of Brownian motion. We delineate the differences between diffusion and dispersion of species by convection.
We introduce boundary conditions needed for solving energy and mass transfer problems.

The law of conservation of mass for a single component (or species) has been discussed in chapter 2. Often however, chemical engineers deal with systems in which several species are present. We refer to these as multicomponent systems. It is of interest to know how to generalize the approach used to derive balance equations to multicomponent systems. An attempt to do this brings in concepts of a multicomponent body, diffusion of species and also modifications in boundary conditions for both transfer of energy and mass. Discussion of these ideas and derivation of equations of conservation of mass and energy in a multicomponent system is the focus of this chapter.

7.1 NATURE OF MULTICOMPONENT SYSTEMS

An important property of a single component system is that all fluid particles at a point move with the same velocity. There are multicomponent systems which can effectively be treated as a single component system. Consider a closed system containing many components. By definition, there is no mass exchange across the boundary of a closed system. As no mass is exchanged, the composition of such a system can remain unchanged in the absence of chemical reactions. Thus, the motion and heat transfer in such a multicomponent closed system, *i.e.,* whose composition remains unaltered, can be described by the equations of change derived earlier in section 3.1 and chapter 5 for a *single component* system. All that has to be done is to use the physical properties of the mixture of the prescribed constant composition. Pumping and or heating of a salt solution is an example of such a situation. While this idea is useful, it is too restrictive as it would not allow generalization to instances where composition in a control volume changes due to either chemical reactions or exchange of species with the surroundings caused by concentration difference between the two.

7.1.1 Species velocities

Consider a beaker of water. If we do not stir it, there would be no motion in water. Now suppose we add some sugar gently so that no motion is created. Sugar will dissolve into the bulk of the solution. Hence, sugar moves even in the absence of an external agency that can create motion or even in the absence of natural convection. This motion is caused by *diffusion*. We will study this kind of motion in greater detail in a later section in this chapter. An important point to note is that sugar and water are present at every point, and hence at every point there are two velocities: one each for water and sugar. Now suppose we also add some water soluble dye to this mixture. Both will dissolve but perhaps at different rates. Both sugar, dye and water are present at every point. Thus, now there are three velocities at every point. In general, in a system containing n species or components, there are n values of velocities. Briefly recall the approach used to identify a closed system containing only one component. A closed system in a fluid medium was tracked by imagining a domain whose surface moves with a velocity same as that of the fluid. In a multicomponent system, we cannot use this idea at a point because there is no unique value to choose for the velocity of the surface.

This situation is often encountered in science. Usually, under such circumstances, a hypothesis consistent[1] with the existing structure has to be made. The longevity of the hypothesis depends entirely on the success with which predictions based on it match the experimental observations. If it is consistently successful, it becomes part of the edifice of scientific structure. A multicomponent body has been defined in this spirit.

7.1.2 Multicomponent body

When the velocity of the surface of an imagined closed system was equated to the fluid velocity, no member of the system could cross the boundary of a system. The system became closed only because of this. Now, it is proposed that a system containing many components be *treated* as a "closed system" in a *modified* sense. In this sense, such a system will be referred to as a **multicomponent body**[2]. A collection of fluid particles is defined as a multicomponent body if **no net exchange of mass occurs** across its boundary as it moves in a continuum. In other words, in a multicomponent body, mass of some species can decrease and mass of some others can increase, but the total mass of the system remains constant. The surface of a multicomponent body can be imagined to be like a porous sieve which however manages to make sure that the mass of the body remains constant. Examine how such a "system" can be followed as it moves in a continuum. At some instant, identify some volume in the continuum, and that is the multicomponent body to be followed. Species will be crossing the boundary of the volume at that instant. Now move every part of the boundary of the identified volume by a differential amount, equal to the product of some infinitesimal time interval and a velocity, and mark the new boundary. The velocities chosen need not be constant and can vary from point to point on the boundary. This would be an "assumed" position of the multicomponent body after a small time interval since it is not known that the velocities chosen were that of the identified multicomponent body. Suppose the velocity distribution chosen was such that the mass contained in the newly marked volume is same as that in the originally marked one. Then, the newly marked space occupied by the initially identified volume is such that, on the net, no mass was exchanged across its boundary. That of course is the definition of a multicomponent body. Thus, the volume being followed is a multicomponent body. If this process of marking the position of the boundaries of the originally identified volume is continued in time, the boundary of the multicomponent closed system would have been traced. The next task then is to devise a procedure to determine the velocity distribution on the boundary of an arbitrarily chosen volume that allows us to track the multicomponent body.

Multicomponent body's surface moves with mass average velocity

It was said earlier that though individual species can have different velocities in a multicomponent body, net mass exchange cannot occur across its surface. This gives the handle needed to relate the velocities of individual species to the velocity, $\mathbf{v}$, with which every part of the boundary of a multicomponent body must move. Let $\mathbf{v}_i$ be the velocity of species i. Let the mass concentration[3] of species i be ρ_i. The rate at which mass crosses a differential area at any point on the boundary, which moves with a velocity $\mathbf{v}$, is given by

$$\sum_i \rho_i \mathbf{n}.(\mathbf{v}_i - \mathbf{v})dA$$

where $\mathbf{n}$ is the local unit normal to the surface and dA is the differential area. This must be zero for any arbitrary multicomponent body whose boundary passes through the chosen point. Surfaces of bodies arbitrarily chosen will have normal vectors pointing in arbitrary directions. Then, the only way in which the net mass flux across all arbitrarily chosen boundaries can be made zero is to equate the sum of the weighted relative velocities of the species with respect to the boundary of the multicomponent body to zero:

$$\sum_i \rho_i(\mathbf{v}_i - \mathbf{v}) = 0$$

However, $\sum_i \rho_i = \rho$, the density of the solution. Hence,

$$\mathbf{v} = \sum_i \frac{\rho_i \mathbf{v}_i}{\rho}$$

But the ratio ρ_i/ρ is equal to the mass fraction, w_i of species i. Hence

$$\mathbf{v} = \sum_i w_i \mathbf{v}_i$$

Since the velocity of each species is being weighted with the mass fraction in computing the average velocity, $\mathbf{v}$ is referred to as the **mass average velocity** [4]. *Hence, a multicomponent body can be defined as one whose boundary moves with the local mass average velocity.* As its velocity can be calculated and is unique, its contours can be traced and followed as it moves in space without any confusion.

Now it is proposed that all physical laws, namely the law of conservation of mass, Newton's laws of motion and the first law of thermodynamics are applicable to a multicomponent body. This hypothesis forms the basis for deriving the balance equations for systems containing many components.

7.1.3 Application of physical laws to a multicomponent body

Now, a brief review of the procedure of deriving the balance laws for a control volume will be useful. Consider application of law of conservation of mass. The law of conservation of mass states that the mass of a multicomponent body remains constant. Now following the approach used earlier, we can write

$$\text{Total mass of the system} = \int_{V_s} \sum_i \rho_i(\mathbf{x}, t)dV = \int_{V_s} \rho(\mathbf{x}, t)dV$$

Thus, application of law of conservation of mass to a multicomponent body gives

$$\frac{d}{dt}\int_{V_s} \rho(\mathbf{x}, t)dV = 0$$

where V_s is the volume of the multicomponent body. By applying transport theorem and specializing it to bodies occupying the control volume of interest, *i.e,* using eq. 2.6, the following result can be obtained:

$$\frac{d}{dt}\int_{V} \rho(\mathbf{x}, t)dV + \int_{A} \mathbf{n}.\mathbf{v}\rho(\mathbf{x}, t)dA = 0 \tag{7.1}$$

where V and A are the volume and surface area of the stationary control volume currently being occupied by the multicomponent body. This is identical to what was derived earlier, and is interpreted as

Rate of accumulation of total mass in the CV	−	**Net rate of input of total mass into the CV by convection**	= 0

In a similar manner, balance equations can be derived by applying Newton's second law and first law of thermodynamics. Referring back to appendix of chapter 5, it is seen that body forces and surface forces have to be redefined for a multicomponent body to apply Newton's second law of motion. This procedure is shown in the appendix to this chapter. Similarly, the heat flux across the surface of multicomponent body has to be defined. This will be considered in a later section.

However, the above discussion and equation does not throw any light on the law that governs the balance of mass of individual species in a multicomponent body, which is the focus of the next section.

7.2 LAW OF CONSERVATION OF MASS OF SPECIES

The mass of a multicomponent body remains constant by definition. However, as species can move across its boundary, the composition of the body can change. Thus, the mass of individual species present in a multicomponent body will not remain constant. Similarly, chemical reactions could be occurring and for this reason also, the mass of individual species in a multicomponent body can change. Thus, it is seen that we need a law governing changes in the mass of individual species to write an equation for balance of mass of individual species. The following hypothesis is stated for this purpose.

The rate of accumulation of mass of any species in a multicomponent body is equal to the net rate of input of mass through its boundaries plus the rate of generation of mass of species in it.

7.2.1 Diffusive flux

The boundary of a multicomponent body moves with the mass average velocity. However, as all species do not have the same velocity, some may move out of the multicomponent body while others may move in. The flux of species with respect to the mass average velocity[5] is defined as the **diffusive** mass flux. Thus, the diffusive mass flux relative to the mass average velocity is given by

$$\mathbf{j}_i = \rho_i(\mathbf{v}_i - \mathbf{v})$$

As the diffusive flux is relative to the average flux, it is clear that sum of the diffusive fluxes must be zero:

$$\sum_i \mathbf{j}_i = 0$$

Thus, in a mixture containing n components, *only* $(n-1)$ *diffusive fluxes are independent.*

Before leaving this topic, it is advantageous to give another interpretation of the expression defining the diffusive mass flux. The mass flux of species as measured by a stationary observer would be $\rho_i\mathbf{v}_i$. Suppose all species had the same velocity, $\mathbf{v}$. The mass flux of any species as measured by the observer would have been $\rho_i\mathbf{v}$. The diffusive flux is the flux over and above what is caused by the *average* motion. Thus, it is advantageous to write

$$\text{Total mass flux of species } i \equiv \mathbf{n}_i = \mathbf{j}_i + \rho_i\mathbf{v}$$

The last term is easily recognized as the usual convective flux. In this sense, it is similar to the expression describing the total heat flux at any point: $\mathbf{q} + (\rho\hat{C}_pT)\mathbf{v}$. It can therefore be seen that the diffusive mass flux is analogous to the diffusive momentum and conduction heat fluxes. Hence the same kind of molecular mechanisms can be expected to dictate the diffusive migration of species, and that a constitutive relationship would be needed to predict the magnitude of the diffusive flux.

Before the law of conservation of mass of species can be applied, an expression is needed for the rate of generation of mass of species. The most common cause of generation is chemical reactions. The notation used by Aris [1] is best suited for this purpose. Let there be N_r independent reactions occurring in the system under consideration. Let A_i represent the species involved in the reactions. The jth chemical reaction can then be represented by the equation

$$\sum_i \alpha_{ij}A_i = 0$$

where α_{ij} is the stoichiometric coefficient of ith species in the jth reaction. *The stoichiometric coefficient is positive for products by convention.* The *intrinsic rate* of jth reaction is denoted by $\dot{\mathcal{R}}_j$. It is the rate of reaction per unit volume, and is defined[6] in such a way that the rate of production of moles of ith species per unit volume due to j^{th} reaction is given by $\alpha_{ij}\,\dot{\mathcal{R}}_j$. The rate of production of moles of ith species per unit volume due to all reactions is equal to

$$\sum_{j=1}^{N_r} \alpha_{ij}\,\dot{\mathcal{R}}_j$$

Let M_i be the molecular weight of ith species. The rate of production of mass of ith species per unit volume due to all reactions is then given by

$$\sum_{j=1}^{N_r} \alpha_{ij} M_i\,\dot{\mathcal{R}}_j$$

A rate expression is needed to compute $\dot{\mathcal{R}}_j$ and it is assumed that such a "constitutive relationship" is available from the domain of chemical reaction engineering.

The balance equation for individual species in a multicomponent body can now be derived by applying the law of conservation.

$$\text{Rate of accumulation of mass of } i^{th} \text{ species} = \frac{d}{dt}\int_{V_s(t)} \rho_i(\mathbf{x},t)dV$$

By the law of conservation of mass of species, the rate of accumulation of mass of ith species is equal to the net rate of input of mass of species i through the boundaries of the multicomponent body plus the rate of generation of mass of species i in the multicomponent body due to reactions. The former of course is the diffusive flux since the surface of the multicomponent body moves with mass average velocity. Hence these two terms can be written as

$$-\int_{A_s(t)} \mathbf{n}.\mathbf{j}_i dA + \int_{V_s(t)} \sum_{j=1}^{N_r} \alpha_{ij} M_i\,\dot{\mathcal{R}}_j\, dV$$

Thus, we have

$$\frac{d}{dt}\int_{V_s(t)} \rho_i(\mathbf{x},t)dV = -\int_{A_s(t)} \mathbf{n}.\mathbf{j}_i dA + \sum_j \int_{V_s(t)} \alpha_{ij} M_i\,\dot{\mathcal{R}}_j\, dV \tag{7.2}$$

The balance equation for individual species in a stationary control volume is derived by using the same method followed earlier. Equation 7.2 is now specialized to a multicomponent body whose boundaries coincide with a stationary control volume. Thus, after using eq. 2.6, the left hand side of eq. 7.2 can be written as follows:

$$\frac{d}{dt}\int\limits_{V_s(t)} \rho_i(\mathbf{x},t) = \frac{d}{dt}\int\limits_{V} \rho_i(\mathbf{x},t)dV + \int\limits_{A} \mathbf{n}.\mathbf{v}\rho w_i(\mathbf{x},t)dA$$

Substituting this result into the mass balance for the multicomponent body and after a little rearrangement, the following equation is obtained:

$$\frac{d}{dt}\int_V \rho_i(\mathbf{x},t)dV = -\int_A \mathbf{n.v}\rho_i(\mathbf{x},t)dA - \int_A \mathbf{n.j}_i dA + \sum_{j=1}^{N_r}\int_V \alpha_{ij} M_i\, \dot{\mathcal{R}}_j\, dV$$

where V and A are the volume and surface area of the control volume. This equation is easily interpreted. $\rho_i\mathbf{n.v}$ is the outward mass flux of ith component due to the movement caused by average velocity. This is the usual *convective* term. Similarly, $\mathbf{n.j}_i$ is the outward diffusive mass flux of ith component through the control surface. Hence the above equation can be written as

Rate of accumulation of mass of ith species in the CV	=	Net rate of input of mass of ith species into the CV by convection	+	Net rate of input of mass of ith species into the CS by diffusion	+	Rate of generation of mass of ith species in the CV by homogeneous chemical reactions

We will once again emphasize that we will use these equations in future for deriving equations for domains of a single phase. Though the species balance equations are valid generally, we put in the restriction of homogeneous reactions to emphasize the general motive of using it.

Similarity to heat balance: The species balance equation is obviously similar to the heat balance equation. The terms of accumulation, and convection are identical. The conduction term in heat transfer is similar to the diffusion term here. The heat generation was due to chemical reactions or viscous dissipation. Here, it is due to chemical reactions. Hence, experience gained in solving heat transfer problems should be of great value in understanding and solving mass transfer problems.

Consistency with balance of total mass

Using the idea that no net mass crosses the boundaries of the multicomponent body, the balance equation for the total mass of the system has been derived in the previous section. It is given by

$$\frac{d}{dt}\int_V \rho(\mathbf{x},t)dV + \int_A \mathbf{n.v}\rho(\mathbf{x},t)dA = 0 \tag{7.3}$$

It would be necessary to check if the balance equation derived for individual species is consistent with this equation. The rate of change in the total mass of the system is obviously equal to sum of rates of change of mass of individual species. Thus, if the balance equations for all the individual species are summed, the previous equation must be recovered. The stoichiometric coefficients obey the following restriction:

$$\sum_i \alpha_{ij} M_i = 0$$

for all j. Further, sum of all the diffusive fluxes is zero. Thus, it is easily seen that the sum of balance equations does yield the balance equation for the total mass.

From past experience with heat transfer, it can be anticipated that if the mass balance equation for species is applied to a small volume, it would give a partial differential equation for ρ_i. If that equation is solved, the mass concentration profiles as a function of position and time in the control volume can be determined. Once again from past experience, it can be expected that a *constitutive relationship* for the diffusive mass fluxes is needed before the differential equation can be solved. These will be the topics for discussion in chapter 9.

Values of ρ_i can be calculated by solving all the n equations of balance of mass of individual species. Mathematically speaking, obtaining the solution of mass balance equations for *all* the species is equivalent to solving the overall mass balance equation and the mass balance equations for *all but any one* of the species *i.e.,* only $(n-1)$ species. As will be discussed in greater detail, it is this procedure that is followed. It is important to point out some consequences of all this discussion. Firstly, it should be noted that only $(n-1)$ constitutive constitutive relationships are needed in a multicomponent system containing n species. Secondly, the mass average velocity appears in the equation of conservation of mass of species i. The momentum balance for a multicomponent body is needed to solve for the mass average velocity and it is discussed in the appendix to this chapter. Temperature will also appear if the system is non-isothermal. Energy balance will be needed to calculate temperature changes and that is discussed at the end of this chapter.

7.2.2 Bird's eye view

It is now useful to get an overall picture of what has been done. Consider a multicomponent system. Mass averaged of velocity[7] was defined for such a system. The equation for the balance of the total mass turns out to be identical to that derived for a single component, namely the equation of continuity. In the appendix to this chapter, it is shown that the linear momentum balance for a multicomponent system is also identical to that for a single component. In other words, the mass average velocity satisfies the equation of continuity and the equations of motion[8]. Consider the system to be isothermal, *i.e.*, heat effects are not involved. Under those circumstances, the equation of continuity and the three components of equation of motion can be solved to determine the four variables P and $\mathbf{v}$. Density is given by an equation of thermodynamic state.

The other variables in the system are the mass fractions. Only $(n-1)$ of them can be considered as variables because mass fractions must add up to unity. The overall mass balance has been "used" up when the equation of continuity was solved. As was pointed out in the discussion above, for an n component mixture, only $(n-1)$ independent equations of species balances are available. That of course, is exactly the number needed to determine the $(n-1)$ mass fraction variables. Thus, if the $(n-1)$ species balance equations can be solved along with the equation of continuity and motion, the concentration distributions can be determined. The overall view remains the same even for non-isothermal systems, except that we need to solve the equation of change of temperature.

The $(n-1)$ species balance equations involve $(n-1)$ independent diffusive fluxes, $\mathbf{j}_i$. Constitutive equations are needed to predict these. The first step in this direction is to examine the mechanism of diffusion, which is the topic of the next section.

7.3 MECHANISM OF DIFFUSION

It was shown in section 7.2 that the definition of a multicomponent body, when used in the species mass balance, gave rise to flux of species with respect to the mass average velocity. The flux is referred to as diffusive flux. The mechanism of diffusion of mass of species is similar to that of heat and momentum. It is the random molecular motion that forms the basis of diffusion of mass as well. Under the influence of a concentration gradient, species acquire a macroscopic velocity as they move by diffusion. In this chapter, we use thermodynamics to draw inferences about the direction of the species velocities. The diffusive flux enters the species mass balance equation, and in order to solve it, we need a constitutive relationship for the mass flux vector. In this chapter we discuss the mechanism of diffusion and develop insights into the constitutive relationship.

7.3.1 Diffusive motion and diffusive flux

Molecules execute random motions and hence drift away from any location from which they start. This motion will be referred to as diffusive motion. However, diffusive motion alone cannot cause a flux that can be observed at a *macroscopic* level. Consider a *homogeneous* mixture of many species. Though molecules exert random motion and show a drift velocity, the drift velocity vector is randomly oriented. If we take a plane and observe drift motion of several molecules of any species, we will find that, on the average, equal number of molecules of that species move away from the plane in opposite directions. Hence, net flux in any direction will be zero. Thus, diffusive motion alone cannot cause macroscopically observable flux. A concentration gradient is needed for a *net* diffusive flux to exist.

7.3.2 Diffusive flux vector

Chemical potential is a concept from thermodynamics and is defined as

$$\mu_i = \left(\frac{\partial G}{\partial n_i}\right)_{T,P,n_{j\neq i}}$$

Thus, $\mu_i \delta n_i$ can be thought of as, δG, an increase in the free energy of the mixture when a small fraction of a mole of species i, δn_i, is added to the mixture at constant temperature and pressure. For any species, it determines the activity of a species in a mixture. Thermodynamic equilibrium prevails in a system at constant pressure and temperature when the chemical potential of the species is equal in all phases[9] present in the system. If the chemical potential of any species in different locations in a single phase is different or is different in different phases, the system is not in equilibrium and will tend to attain equilibrium by migration or diffusion of species. Just as temperature differences caused heat transfer to drive the system toward equilibrium, inequalities in chemical potential cause mass transfer so that the system moves towards a state of equilibrium. When species move, they obviously must have a direction and hence, the diffusive flux is also a vector just as heat flux is.

7.3.3 Direction of mass transfer

The direction of movement of species in the absence of equilibrium must be such that, at constant temperature and pressure, free energy of the system is reduced due to diffusion. Consider two thin slabs of a single phase of thickness Δx. See figure 7.1. Let the chemical potential of ith species in the left slab be $\mu_i(x)$ while that in the right be $\mu_i(x + \Delta x)$. Suppose the two slabs are insulated

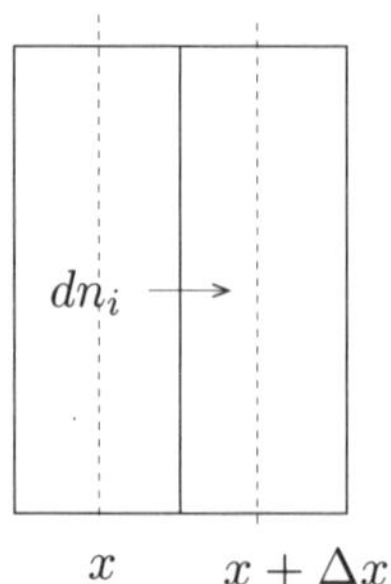

Figure 7.1. Direction of flux and gradient in chemical potential.

from the rest of the environment after they have been brought into contact and allowed to exchange mass between them. Let dn_i moles of species be transported across the interface between the slabs in the x direction, *i.e.*, if dn_i is positive, species i move in the x direction. The species leave the left slab with a chemical potential of $\mu_i(x)$, and so the Gibbs free energy of the left slab changes by $-dn_i\mu_i(x)$ due to reduction in the number of moles in the left slab. They enter right slab, and since number of moles exchanged is small, the chemical potential of the right slab will still remain at $\mu_i(x + \Delta x)$. But as the number of moles have increased, the Gibbs free energy of the right slab increases by $dn_i\mu_i(x + \Delta x)$. The change in the Gibbs free energy due to the transfer is given by

$$\big[\mu_i(x + \Delta x) - \mu_i(x)\big]dn_i$$

The change must be negative for the transfer to occur spontaneously so that the system can move in a direction to attain equilibrium. Thus, for dn_i to be positive as shown in figure 7.1, or for mass transfer to be in the positive x direction, $\mu_i(x + \Delta x)$ must be less than $\mu_i(x)$ so that the free energy decreases. Thus, mass transfer occurs in the direction of decreasing chemical potential. This is similar to heat flowing from regions at higher temperature to those at lower temperatures. The chemical potential is proportional to the concentration. Hence, we can say that the direction of mass transfer is from high concentration to low concentration. The same can be said of transfer of species between phases too.

The direction of transfer is dictated by the tendency for the free energy of the entire system to decrease. In the above derivation, we assumed that only one component moves. The derivation is not valid if many species move, as is likely in multicomponent systems. As we will see later, it is possible to have mass transfer from regions of low concentration to those at high concentration in systems containing *three or more components*. Only binary systems, the direction of mass transfer is always from high to low concentrations.

7.3.4 Rate of mass transfer by diffusion

The mechanism underlying mass transfer is the diffusive motion caused by random molecular motions, and is *similar* to the mechanism of heat conduction. Thus, we can expect a constitutive relationship similar to the Fourier's law of heat conduction. We can anticipate that the gradient of chemical potential is the driving force for mass diffusion and is related to the diffusive flux.

To get the basic ideas clearly in a simple setting, we will restrict the discussion to isothermal and isobaric two-component or *binary systems* in this chapter. In later chapters, these restrictions will be relaxed. Chemical potential gradient is the driving force for diffusion. In a binary system however, by Gibbs–Duhem equation, only one of the two chemical potential gradients is independent. Gradient of chemical potential of any one species in a binary can be used in the discussion. However, one is interested in quantities that give an indication of concentration, and chemical potential is a rather inconvenient quantity to use for this purpose. The appropriate quantities could be molar or mass concentration or mole fractions and so on. Therefore such quantities of interest are directly used in the expression for rates of diffusion.

Let the two components in a binary be denoted by A and B. For a binary system, the constitutive relationship that links diffusive flux to the concentrations is Fick's law of diffusion. It is written as

$$\mathbf{j}_A = -\rho \mathcal{D}_{AB} \nabla w_A$$

where $\mathcal{D}_{AB}$ is the binary diffusion coefficient. In a binary, $w_A + w_B = 1$. Hence, only one mass fraction gradient is independent, and this is consistent with the gradient of chemical potential of any one component being independent. By definition, $\mathbf{j}_A + \mathbf{j}_B = 0$, and only one flux is independent. Hence, only one diffusion coefficient is required to characterize diffusion in an isothermal, isobaric binary system. In other words, if we were to write Fick's law for the other component, it may look like

$$\mathbf{j}_B = -\rho \mathcal{D}_{BA} \nabla w_B$$

But when the sum of diffusive fluxes is equated to zero, we get $\mathcal{D}_{AB} = \mathcal{D}_{BA}$.

The similarity between Fick's law and Fourier's law of heat conduction is apparent. Thus, we can conclude that the diffusive mass flux vector is normal to the curves on which mass fraction remains constant, *i.e.*, mass flux is directed along the steepest gradient of mass fraction.

Alternative definitions of diffusive fluxes

We have defined diffusive flux as the macroscopic flux of species over and above that caused by the mass average velocity. This definition has arisen because we have postulated that the physical laws are applicable to a multicomponent body. However, it is possible to define different average velocities and hence different diffusive fluxes. There is no evidence to suggest whether any of these averages have an intrinsic advantage over the other or have a more fundamental significance. Different average velocities and diffusive fluxes are used based on convenience and we will define one based on molar units here. It turns out that use of molar diffusive fluxes is advantageous when dealing with gases and when chemical reactions occur. In case of gases, especially at low pressures and high temperatures, the molar density is related to the pressure and temperature by the ideal gas law and hence it is advantageous to use molar units. The rates of chemical reactions are usually related to molar concentrations, and hence once again it is better to use molar units [10]. The differences and advantages will be reiterated as and when examples are taken for study.

Molar average velocity

If the velocities of species are weighted by mole fractions, the **molar average velocity,** $\mathbf{v}^*$ is obtained.

$$\mathbf{v}^* = \sum_i y_i \mathbf{v}_i$$

The molar flux of ith species as seen by a stationary observer is given by

$$\mathbf{N}_i = C_i \mathbf{v}_i$$

where C_i is the molar concentration. If the velocity of all the species was the same, it would also be equal to the molar average velocity. The molar flux of ith species would have been $C_i\mathbf{v}^*$. The diffusive flux then is the flux over and above that due to average motion. It is given the symbols $\mathbf{J}_i^*$, and

$$\mathbf{J}_i^* = C_i(\mathbf{v}_i - \mathbf{v}^*)$$

It turns out that Fick's law for binary systems is equivalent to

$$\mathbf{J}_A^* = -C\mathcal{D}_{AB}\nabla y_A$$

where C is the molar density of the solution, y_A is the mole fraction of A. The diffusion coefficient is the *same* as that in the expression that relates $\mathbf{j}_A$ to the gradient of mass fraction.

7.3.5 Other mechanisms of diffusion

There are other mechanisms by which diffusion can occur. These are

1. *Thermal diffusion*: Temperature gradients cause diffusion and this is referred to as thermal diffusion. Isotopes are separated using this principle.

2. *Forced diffusion*: If charged species are present, they can diffuse under the influence of electrical fields. Electrolytic cells, fuel cells and batteries are important examples of this type of diffusion.

3. *Pressure diffusion*: Pressure gradients can also cause diffusion. Centrifugal separation is based on this principle.

These will be considered in greater detail in chapter 9.

Emphasis so far has been placed on binary systems so that ideas can be fixed in simpler situations first. The word 'multicomponent' customarily means more than two components. Diffusion in multicomponent systems will be considered in greater detail in chapter 9. However, it is worthwhile to note that in multicomponent systems, diffusion of a species can be influenced by gradients in the chemical potential of other species. Due to this, diffusion can occur *against the concentration gradient*, and diffusive flux can be zero even when *concentration gradient* is present!

7.4 MODELS OF DIFFUSION COEFFICIENTS

Diffusive motion is caused by random molecular motions. This is a very broad statement because details of this mechanism in solids, and fluids are different. We do not consider mechanism of diffusion in solids as it is more complex and entirely different from that in fluids. Nature of the molecular motion is different in gases and liquids. Molecules are widely separated in gases, and the average distance between molecules is much larger than their size. On the other hand, the average

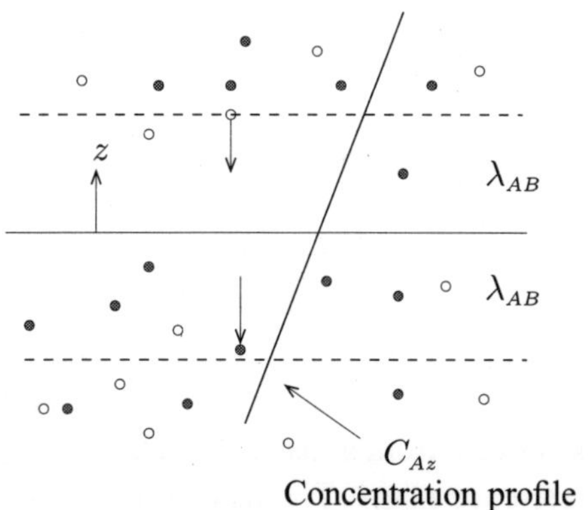

Figure 7.2. Mixture of gases A and B between two parallel planes. The concentration profile is linear. We consider one plane above and one below a reference plane. The distance of these planes from the reference planes is the mean distance travelled by molecule A before it collides with molecule B, λ_{AB}. Molecules A are represented by unhatched spheres while hatched spheres represent molecules of B.

distance between molecules in liquid phase is of the order of the size of the molecules. Thus, molecules in gas phase move considerable distances before they encounter and collide with another molecule. In hydrogen gas this is of the order of a few microns at atmospheric pressure and room temperature. In liquids, molecules can move only when other molecules, through their random motions, create a large enough void. Diffusion requires physical movement of molecules. As a result of the differences between gases and liquids we described just now, one can expect diffusion in gases to be much faster than in liquids. Typically, the diffusion coefficients in gases are of the order of $10\times^{-6}$ m^2/s while they are of the order of $10\times^{-9}$ m^2/s in liquids.

The way motion is randomized is also different in gases and liquids. As molecules are separated by large distances in gases, the intermolecular forces between them are small. So for most part, a molecule moves in a linear path till it collides with another molecule. As the number of collisions it undergoes is very large, its movement is effectively decorrelated from any initial condition. It is therefore generally assumed that molecules move in any direction with equal probability after a collision. Thus, in gases, molecular collisions cause randomization of motion. In liquids however, molecules are always under the influence of intermolecular forces exerted by the neighbors. As they jiggle in their positions and hop a distance of the order of their size when a void is created, the intermolecular forces experienced by a molecule is random in nature. It is this aspect that makes motion of molecules in liquids random. These differences need different treatments to develop models of diffusion coefficients in liquids and gases. We consider these separately in the following sub-sections.

7.4.1 Diffusion coefficients in gases

We will now try to calculate the value of a diffusion coefficient in gases. For the sake of simplicity let us consider one-dimensional diffusion. Consider a mixture of gases A and B between two parallel planes separated by a short distance. Its composition is not uniform across the distance and let the gradient of composition be linear. See figure 7.2

Diffusive flux of A

We are interested in relating the concentration gradient to the net flux of molecules of A crossing a reference plane at $z = 0$ due to random motion, and to estimate diffusion coefficient from that. We will consider a system at constant pressure and temperature. The total molar concentration is constant as total pressure and temperature are constant. We wish to calculate only diffusive flux. We therefore place the restriction that the net total flux of molecules in the system is zero. If $N_{A,z}$ and $N_{B,z}$ are the fluxes of A and B, then $N_{A,z} + N_{B,z} = 0$, and the molar average velocity is zero. Hence, any flux we calculate will only be due to diffusion. Let the concentration of A at the reference plane be C_A. Molecules starting from a distance h above the plane will come from a zone of higher concentration than the reference plane. The flux of these towards the reference plane will be $(1/2)\bar{v}_A(C_A + h(dC_A/dz))$, where $\bar{v}_A$ is the mean velocity of molecules of A. The factor of half accounts for the fact that half of the molecules starting from any plane will go up with respect to the plane while the other half go down. We can similarly calculate the flux of molecules starting from a distance h below the plane towards the reference plane. The difference between the two should give us the net flux, and it can be seen that flux will be proportional to h times the concentration gradient. But it turns out that it is not as straight forward as that. First, we have not yet specified the value of h. A molecule starting from planes very far from the reference plane will not reach it because they will collide with molecules in between and will be deflected in random directions. If it is taken to be too small, though we might avoid the problem posed by large values of h, our estimate of net flux will be too small since it is proportional to h. It is very difficult to calculate the exact distance from which A must start in order to reach the reference plane, and not suffer a collision in between. However, it can be expected that it will be of the order of the mean distance travelled by A between collisions. Before we attempt to calculate this distance, there is one more complication to be resolved. It is as follows. Suppose a molecule of A coming from above collides with a molecule of A coming from below. As a result of the collision, the two will go in different directions, and not in the same direction. But, in that event, the net flux is zero which ever way the individual molecules go. Hence, net flux will be created only by collisions[11] between molecules of A and B. The distance we are interested in is then the distance A travels before it collides with B. Let it be denoted by λ_{AB}. This is shown in figure 7.2 where two molecules of A and B are shown approaching each other so that they may collide. The net flux in the z direction is given by

$$\frac{1}{2}\bar{v}_A\left(C_A - \lambda_{AB}\frac{dC_A}{dz}\right) - \frac{1}{2}\bar{v}_A\left(C_A + \lambda_{AB}\frac{dC_A}{dz}\right) = -\bar{v}_A\lambda_{AB}\frac{dC_A}{dz}$$

Effective mean free path

Let us now calculate λ_{AB}. Suppose a molecule of A heads in some direction, and B molecules are stationary. We draw a cylinder of diameter equal to half of the sum of individual diameters, $(d_A + d_B)/2$, around its path as shown in figure 7.3. Then A has a chance to collide with any B present in that cylinder. In time interval Δt, A will travel a distance of $\bar{v}_A\Delta t$. The number of B molecules encountered by A in this interval is given by $C_B\pi(r_A + r_B)^2\bar{v}_A\Delta t$, where r_A and r_B are the radii of A and B. As A will collide with all these, it is also equal to the number of its

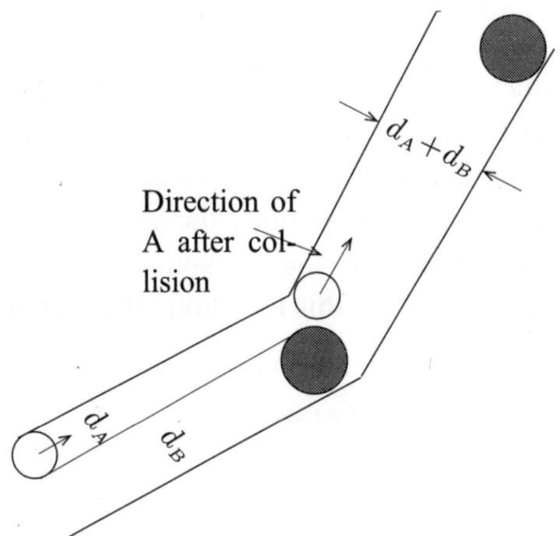

Figure 7.3. Molecule A at the bottom of figure heads in the direction shown. A cylinder of diameter $(d_A + d_B)/2$ is shown. It will collide with any B present in the cylinder. After collision, A has changed direction. We now draw another cylinder around its path. It will collide with another B if it is present in the cylinder as shown.

collisions with B. Therefore, the collision frequency between molecules of A and B is given by $C_B\pi(r_A + r_B)^2\bar{v}_A$. But B is not stationary as we assumed and we should have used some relative velocity between A and B in making this calculation. Kinetic theory of gases give the following exact result for the collision frequency between molecules of A and B:

$$\text{Collision frequency between } A \text{ and } B = C_B\pi(r_A + r_B)^2\sqrt{\bar{v}_A^2 + \bar{v}_B^2}$$

The average time interval between collision of A with B is the inverse of the collision frequency. Hence, the average distance travelled by A before it collides with a B molecule, λ_{AB}, is equal to the velocity of A multiplied by the average time interval between collision of A with B:

$$\lambda_{AB} = \frac{\bar{v}_A}{C_B\pi(r_A + r_B)^2\sqrt{\bar{v}_A^2 + \bar{v}_B^2}}$$

Now recall that the expression for the net flux of A gives

$$\text{Net flux of A in } z \text{ direction} = -\bar{v}_A\lambda_{AB}\frac{dC_A}{dz}$$

Similarly, the expression for the net flux of B would be given by

$$\text{Net flux of B in } z \text{ direction} = -\bar{v}_B\lambda_{BA}\frac{dC_B}{dz}$$

As the system is isobaric and isothermal, $C_A + C_B$ is a constant, and we can replace gradient of C_B with negative of the gradient of C_A. Hence, the net flux of B is given by

$$\text{Net flux of B in } z \text{ direction} = \bar{v}_B\lambda_{BA}\frac{dC_A}{dz}$$

Binary diffusion coefficient

As we discussed in the beginning of this section, we require that the net flux of A plus B must be zero. Looking at the expressions for the velocities of A and B and the mean distances travelled by one kind of molecule before it collides with the other kind, it is apparent that this is not satisfied by our calculation. It turns out that this is so since the calculation does not satisfy momentum balance as we could not impose the condition that pressure must remain constant. We will follow the approach of Cowling [3] and correct[12] for this by adding flux due to a uniform velocity V. Thus,

$$N_{A,z} = -\bar{v}_A \lambda_{AB} \frac{dC_A}{dz} + C_A V$$

and

$$N_{B,z} = \bar{v}_B \lambda_{BA} \frac{dC_A}{dz} + C_B V$$

We can solve for V by requiring that the net flux of A and B must equal zero. This then gives the following expression for the net flux of A:

$$N_{A,z} = -\frac{C_B \lambda_{AB} \bar{v}_A + C_A \lambda_{BA} \bar{v}_B}{C_A + C_B} \frac{dC_A}{dz}$$

Hence,

$$\mathcal{D}_{AB} = \frac{C_B \lambda_{AB} \bar{v}_A + C_A \lambda_{BA} \bar{v}_B}{C}$$

where C is the total molar concentration. Substituting the expressions for λ_{AB} and λ_{BA}, we get

$$\mathcal{D}_{AB} = \frac{\sqrt{\bar{v}_A^2 + \bar{v}_B^2}}{C(r_A + r_B)^2}$$

Noting that the kinetic energy of molecules is equal to $M\bar{v}^2$ and is proportional to the temperature T, the above can be reduced to

$$C\mathcal{D}_{AB} \sim \sqrt{T\left(\frac{1}{M_A} + \frac{1}{M_B}\right)} \frac{1}{(r_A + r_B)^2}$$

which turns out to be remarkably correct! However, exact theory requires that $(r_A + r_B)^2$ is not correct and details of collision dynamics of molecules has to considered to derive a more accurate expression.

7.4.2 Diffusion coefficient in liquids

We present two kinds of theories for diffusion coefficients in liquids. We first present one very popular correlation, more so for the insights it offers. We then consider a little more complex theory based on Brownian motion.

Stokes–Einstein relationship

In mechanics, negative gradient of a potential is often interpreted as a force. Gravity is an example. If the direction of gravity is in the negative z direction, the potential energy per unit mass due to gravity is gz where g is the magnitude of acceleration due to gravity. The force exerted by gravity per unit mass is given by $-\nabla gz = -g\mathbf{k}$. This idea can be used in diffusion as well.

In a dilute solution, solvent is the major component and all solutes are present at very low concentrations. Hence, the interactions between the solutes are very small. It is this kind of system we are considering. Apply the idea described above to calculate the driving force for diffusive motion. Since interactions between species are absent in a dilute solution, the force that drives molecular diffusive motion of a species in is the negative gradient of only its chemical potential. The force on a *mole* of species A is given by

$$\text{Force driving diffusive motion of component } A = -\nabla\mu_A$$

We imagine that as molecules move by diffusion, they will have to overcome frictional forces exerted by the medium. This is a somewhat odd because we are applying macroscopic notions of friction at a molecular level. For diffusive motion to occur, a molecule will have to overcome intermolecular attractive forces, and these can be interpreted as friction. If inertia is neglected, force due to friction is equal to the driving force, and the velocity is given by driving force times the mobility, $\mathcal{M}$:

$$\text{Velocity of component } A \text{ created by diffusion} = -\mathcal{M}_A\nabla\mu_A$$

Diffusive flux is given by concentration times the velocity. Hence

$$\mathbf{J}_A = -\mathcal{M}_A C_A \nabla\mu_A$$

If we make the approximation that $\mu_A \sim RT\ln x_A$, then

$$\mathbf{J}_A = -C\mathcal{R}T\mathcal{M}_A\nabla x_A$$

where $C, \mathcal{R}$ and T are the total concentration, universal gas constant and temperature, respectively. If we compare this with Fick's law, we get an expression for diffusivity of species A in the solvent:

$$\mathcal{D}_{A_s} = RT\mathcal{M}_A$$

If we assume that the species are spherical in shape with a diameter of d, and assume audaciously, as it turns out backed by a person no less than Einstein himself, that Stokes law can be applied to calculate the drag force on a molecule, we get:

$$\mathcal{M}_A = \frac{1}{\mathcal{N}_{avo}(3\pi\mu d)}$$

where μ is the viscosity of the solvent. Substituting this, we get

$$D_{A_s} = \frac{k_B T}{3\pi\mu d} \tag{7.4}$$

This equation is referred to as Stokes–Einstein equation and often written as

$$\frac{D_{As}\mu}{T} = \text{constant}$$

It is often used to correlate viscosity and diffusion coefficient.

The argument presented is general and is valid even if diffusive motion were to occur under the additional influence of gradient of some other potential. An instance is the diffusion of ionic species under the influence of electrical potential gradient, ϕ. The total driving force is given by the sum of the gradients of the two potentials. For this example then

$$\mathbf{J}_A = -C_A \mathcal{M}_A \left(\nabla \mu_A + z_A \nabla \phi\right)$$

where z_A is the charge of the species. We will have occasion to use this kind of expression later.

Diffusion coefficient and molecular motion in liquids

We have earlier stated that, though a molecule moves randomly, it drifts away from a position it starts from. As it turns out, this idea is also used in describing dispersion caused by random macroscopic motion of the kind observed in turbulent flows. So we will devote this section to show how to relate velocity of the drift to the diffusion coefficient.

Averaged quantities: Molecules are always in random motion, and diffusion occurs due to it. Net flux in any direction arises only when there is a concentration gradient. The objective of this section is to relate diffusion coefficient to the characteristics of the random movement. There are many ways of doing it, and we choose an intuitive development and one should refer to more advanced texts to get a more detailed treatment.

Consider the following experiment. Take a large volume of a solvent. Suppose we place N moles of some soluble species A in a tiny sphere, *a point source,* at some point. Species A will diffuse out and away from the source. If all molecules were to move with the same velocity to achieve dilution, the sphere should expand such that all the molecules will still be inside the sphere only, and there will be a sharp boundary marking the sphere. As molecular movement is a random phenomena, this is not what we would observe. Different number of molecules will move to different distances from the original location of the point source. There will be no sharp boundary. In such situations, we can only speak of the probability of finding a fraction of the species at given distance after some time period. Further, we can only predict *what happens on the average* when a collection of particles is observed. Thus, we try to derive expressions for averaged values of some quantities of interest. The average is obtained by observing many particles in the collection, or by repeated experiments on a single particle keeping all conditions of experimentation constant. We will use this argument of equivalence often.

Drift velocity: One quantity of interest is the relation between the average distance a particle moves from some initial location and the average velocity of movement or the drift speed. Let us consider the experiment described recently where a point source containing N moles of solute placed was placed at the origin, *i.e.,* $r = 0$. As there is no preferred direction to movement of particles, we expect this distribution to be radially symmetric around the origin. We could observe the distribution of their numbers as a function of time and as function of distance from the origin. This information can be recorded as the fraction of particles located in an interval Δr at different values of r. This of course is the probability distribution of the location of the particles along the r coordinate. Using the probability distribution, any average property of the particles can be found. The mean of the square of distance by which the particles have moved, or the mean of r^2, is of interest in this section.

As mentioned, we started with a source of N moles. Let $C(r,t)$ denote the number of moles per unit volume at r after some time period, t, *i.e.*, there are $4\pi r^2 C(r,t)dr$ moles of solute present per unit volume in a slice of thickness dr. Then, we have by conservation of mass

$$N = \int_0^\infty 4\pi r^2 C dr$$

The mean of the square of the distance particles have travelled from the location of the point source will not be zero and is given by

$$\overline{r^2} = \frac{1}{N}\int_0^\infty r^2 \left(4\pi r^2 C(r,t)\right) dr$$

The drift velocity is given by

$$\frac{d\sqrt{\overline{r^2}}}{dt}$$

The above tells us how to calculate the drift velocity from concentration distribution. Now we turn our attention to calculation of the concentration distribution.

Random motion and concentration distribution: In diffusion theory, the problem equivalent to the experiment we described with particles is radial diffusion from a point source of solute placed at origin. We have seen solution to the heat conduction from a point source. We have alluded to the similarity between heat and mass transfer. The energy density corresponds to concentration, and thermal and mass diffusivities similar. The concentration profile created by an instantaneous point source is therefore obtained by solving

$$\frac{\partial C}{\partial t} = \mathcal{D}\frac{1}{r^2}\frac{\partial}{\partial r}\left(r^2\frac{\partial C}{\partial r}\right) \quad 0 < r < \infty$$

with the following initial condition and boundary conditions

$$C(r,0) = N\delta(r) \text{ at } t = 0, \quad C(r \to \infty, t) = 0 \text{ for all } t$$

where δ is the Dirac delta function. The solution to this can be obtained from eq. 5.26 and is described by

$$\frac{C(r,t)}{N} = \frac{1}{8\sqrt{(\pi Dt)^3}}\exp(-\frac{r^2}{4Dt})$$

From conservation of species, it follows that

$$N = \frac{4\pi}{8\sqrt{(\pi Dt)^3}} \int_0^\infty r^2 \exp(-\frac{r^2}{4Dt})dr$$

From the definition of the mean square distance,

$$\overline{r^2} = \frac{1}{8\sqrt{(\pi Dt)^3}} \int_0^\infty 4\pi r^4 \exp(-\frac{r^2}{4Dt})dr$$

The above integral can be evaluated from differentiation of the error function integral:

$$2\sqrt{\frac{\beta}{\pi}} \int_0^\infty da e^{-\beta a^2} = 1$$

where β is a parameter and a is a dummy integration variable.

Random motion and diffusion coefficient: The mean of the square of the distance traveled by particles can be determined following this procedure, and is found to be

$$\overline{r^2} = 6Dt$$

Thus, we have this wonderful result

$$D = \frac{1}{6}\frac{d\overline{r^2}}{dt}$$

that the mean square distance travelled by particles increases linearly with time. The diffusion coefficient can therefore be evaluated by observing the rate at which the mean distance of particles from the place where they were located initially increases with time. Another equivalent way to evaluate the diffusion coefficient is to observe the distance traveled by a single particle for different intervals of time, evaluate the derivative, and average over many intervals of time. These methods are used in molecular simulations to evaluate diffusion coefficients.

Langevin equation for diffusion

We have connected diffusion coefficient to random motion of molecules. The final step is to develop a model that mimics random motion to calculate the mean square distance travelled by a molecule. This work was done by Einstein. Brown, a botanist, observed an interesting phenomena under a microscope. He found that *lifeless* particles suspended in a *stationary* liquid were moving around. This was surprising and this phenomena is referred to as Brownian motion. It is explained as follows. Particles are buffeted *on all sides* with equal probability by molecules of the liquid surrounding it. Though such interactions are random, they are *not balanced at every instant*, but are balanced on the average. Hence, particles move due to the net momentum transferred from the instantaneously imbalanced collisions. Langevin modeled the unbalanced impact of molecular collisions on the particles as a random force, $\boldsymbol{\xi}$. The following differential equation was written by him, called Langevin equation in his honor, for motion of a Brownian particle,

$$m\frac{d^2\mathbf{r}}{dt^2} = -f\frac{d\mathbf{r}}{dt} + \boldsymbol{\xi}$$

The above is easily understood. The left hand side is mass times the acceleration. It is equal to the random force acting on the particle minus the frictional force exerted by the medium on the particle. Random force is the last term on the right hand side of the above equation. Frictional force is in the opposite direction to the velocity vector. Langevin assumed a linear proportionality between force and velocity. In above f is the friction coefficient, and hence the first term on the right hand side represents the friction force exerted by the fluid on the particle. If $\mathbf{u}$ is the velocity of the particle, then the previous can be rewritten as

$$m\frac{d\mathbf{u}}{dt} = -f\mathbf{u} + \boldsymbol{\xi}$$

After noting that $d\mathbf{r}/dt = \mathbf{u}$, a dot product of this equation with the current position of the particle gives

$$m\left(\frac{d}{dt}(ru) - u^2\right) = -fru + \boldsymbol{\xi}.\mathbf{r}$$

Rearranging it, we get

$$\frac{d}{dt}(ru) + \frac{fru}{m} = u^2 + \frac{\boldsymbol{\xi}.\mathbf{r}}{m}$$

We can integrate this

$$ru - (ru)_{t=0} = e^{-ft/m}\int_0^t dt' e^{ft'/m}\left(u^2 + \frac{\xi r}{m}\right)$$

As ξ is a random force, it will not have any correlation with the location of the particle, $\mathbf{r}$. Hence, for sufficiently large times, the second term of the integral will be zero. Further, for sufficiently long times or as $t \to \infty$, we expect the mean square of velocity of the particle to reach a constant value, $\overline{U^2}$. Then, we have

$$ru - (ru)_{t=0} = \frac{m}{f}\overline{U^2}\left(1 - e^{-ft/m}\right) = \frac{m}{f}\overline{U^2}$$

for long times. If we now average over many particles, or for a single particle over several sufficiently long time intervals, as the initial velocity is not correlated with the initial position, we get

$$\overline{ru} = \frac{m}{f}\overline{U^2}$$

But

$$\overline{ru} = \frac{1}{2}\frac{d}{dt}(\overline{r^2})$$

or

$$\frac{d}{dt}(\overline{r^2}) = \frac{2m\overline{U^2}}{f}$$

Connecting this with the relation we derived between diffusion coefficient and rate of change of mean square of the distance particle travels, we have

$$\mathcal{D} = \frac{m\overline{U^2}}{3f} = \frac{1}{6}\frac{d\overline{r^2}}{dt} = \frac{\overline{ru}}{3} \tag{7.5}$$

We will have occasion to use this relation between diffusion coefficient and the correlation between position and velocity to estimate eddy diffusivity. Einstein estimated the mean velocity with which a particle moves by equating it to the thermal energy, since it is in thermal equilibrium with the surrounding fluid:

$$\frac{1}{2}m\overline{U^2} = 3\frac{k_B T}{2}$$

where k_B is the Boltzmann constant and T is the absolute temperature. Thus, he arrived at the famous result:

$$\mathcal{D} = \frac{k_B T}{3\pi\mu d}$$

where d is the diameter of the Brownian particle, and Stokes law was used[13] for calculating f. Replacing the Boltzmann's constant by the gas constant divided by the Avogadro's number, he obtained:

$$\mathcal{D} = \frac{R}{\mathcal{N}_{avo}}\frac{T}{3\pi\mu d}$$

This work was done in 1905 and, yes, at that time there were scientists who doubted the existence of molecules. The above equation permitted experimental determination of Avogadro's number as follows:

$$\frac{1}{6}\frac{d\overline{r^2}}{dt} = \mathcal{D} = \frac{R}{\mathcal{N}_{avo}}\frac{T}{3\pi\mu d}$$

The rate of movement of a Brownian particle and every other quantity, except Avogadro's number, could be experimentally measured. Hence Avogadro's number could be calculated. Einstein [4] obtained a value of 3.3×10^{23} a value remarkably close to the true value.[14] In this way, Einstein provided one proof for the existence of molecules.

Now, if one makes the audacious assumption that f is given by Stokes law for a *molecule*, we get the following

$$\mathcal{D} = \frac{k_B T}{3\pi\mu d}$$

This is well known as Stokes–Einstein equation, which we have seen before.

7.5 CONVECTION

Now we will consider other *modes* of "mass transfer". Diffusion transports mass from one location to another. Mass can be transported from place to place by convection as well[15]. We have made a distinction between diffusive flux and convective flux, and what is the difference? Convective flux is a macroscopic phenomena and random molecular motions do not play a role in convective flux. Convection moves all the species with the same velocity. Diffusive flux tends to move the system towards equilibrium or making concentrations spatially uniform or *mixed* on a molecular scale. Convective flux cannot achieve this. If a band of dye is marked in a fluid in laminar flow in a pipe, and *if diffusion were absent*, the band will stretch with flow as shown in figure 7.4. Thus, mass has moved in space, but mixing did not occur on a molecular scale. It will be noticed that area for diffusive mass transfer, if it were to occur, has increased. As packets of fluid move from

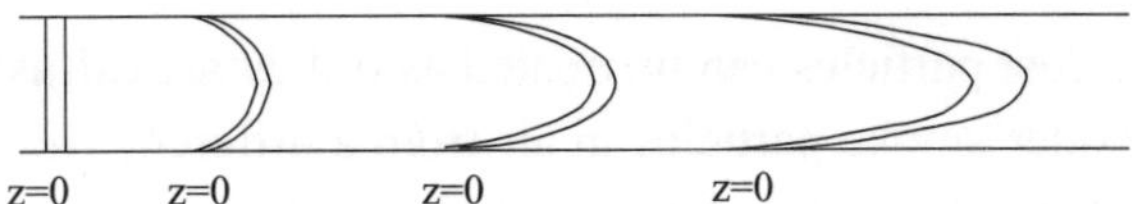

Figure 7.4. Figure shows stretching of a patch of dye introduced in laminar flow in a pipe.

one place to another, they can encounter environment at different concentrations. In such flows, as species move along with the fluid, their concentration gradients can also be enhanced. The effect of convection is to move solutes from place to place, and this can result in an increase in diffusive mass transfer due to both these effects. But in the absence of diffusion, homogenization or mixing on a molecular scale cannot occur. This is similar to the fact that heat can be transported from location to location by bulk movement of fluid since the temperature can vary from place to place. However, for temperatures to even out at molecular level, conduction has to occur. The ideas can be summarized as follows. Convection transports mass and heat, can cause an increase in area for diffusive transport, and sharpen concentration and temperature gradients. But it cannot cause homogenization at molecular level. Only diffusion and conduction can achieve this.

Convection or bulk movement of fluid caused by an external agency is forced convection. If density gradients caused by differences in the density of mixtures of different compositions coupled with gravity causes motion, it is referred to as natural convection. This nomenclature is similar to what was stated in the case of heat transfer as well.

7.5.1 Dispersion and Diffusion

Let us elaborate more on the distinction we made between the effects of convection and diffusion. We have discussed the random motion or diffusion of Brownian particles. In chemical engineering, conventionally, we talk about diffusion only in the context of molecular solutions. Thus, salt diffuses in water due to gradients in its concentration, and in this context, we are dealing with molecular solution of salt in water. What then is the difference between this and diffusion of Brownian particles? The underlying phenomena are the same, but the final state is different.

Consider smoke or very fine dust particles in air. Clearly they move randomly, *i.e.* diffuse, even in still air due to Brownian motion. Thus, if blob of smoke is left in a box full of air, smoke particles will diffuse away from their initial location. The blob spreads over larger and larger distances, and eventually, the smoke will be evenly distributed over the box. Suppose the original particles are a tenth of a micron in size. Their size remains the same after being uniformly dispersed as 'molecules' of smoke are not soluble in air. Thus, on a scale larger than tenth of a micron, say on a scale of ten microns, the number of smoke particles per unit volume will be the same everywhere in the box. The uniformity is on a scale larger than the size of the particles. On a scale only slightly larger than that of particles, the dispersion will look grainy. The same applies to molecular solution as well. Suppose we did the above experiment by placing a lump of sugar in water. Sugar will dissolve and diffuse away, and the concentration of sugar will be the same at all points in the box. The "sameness" is on a length scale larger than molecular dimensions, and graininess *will be present* on a scale comparable to molecular dimensions. In general, our interest is on a scale much larger than molecular size, and so we take it that the solution is uniform. In this sense, depending on the length scale of interest, smoke or dust particles can be treated as if they are diffusing in a medium.

Let us once again consider smoke particles in air from a different view point. The particles are usually very small and their inertia is therefore small. Thus, they will move with the local velocity of air. If there is turbulence in air, the particles will move randomly according to the velocity fluctuations in a turbulent flow field. It is the random motion of surrounding fluid that causes distribution of particles over the fluid domain, and this process where insoluble but fine particles are distributed uniformly is referred to as the *dispersion* process. This is similar to diffusion. Unlike in diffusion, which is related to random motion of molecules, here it is random motion on macroscopic scale, or convection, that causes dispersion. The problem is of immense practical value in the context of atmospheric pollution. A theory for the dispersion process is based on the same concepts used in the theory of Brownian movement. We have the following equations from eq. 7.5 of previous section:

$$\overline{ru} = \frac{1}{2}\frac{d\overline{r^2}}{dt}$$

Note that the drift velocity is that of the particles and is related to the correlation between position of the particle and its velocity or *velocity fluctuation*. The diffusivity due to random turbulent motions is referred to as the eddy diffusivity, D_t. Hence, according to eq. 7.5,

$$3D_t = \frac{1}{2}\frac{d\overline{r^2}}{dt}$$

From eq. 7.5, we also have

$$\overline{ru} = 3D_t \tag{7.6}$$

which relates eddy diffusivity to the correlation between position and velocity fluctuations. We have a very important result here. If the correlation between position and velocity fluctuation is measured, the above expression can be used to calculate turbulent diffusivity or eddy diffusivity. Taylor [7] showed how this concept can be used to obtain eddy diffusivities which can be used to understand dispersion process in turbulence. These ideas are extensively used in CFD of turbulent flows.

Macro and micromixing

Let us finally consider what happens when we stir a concentrated solution into a dilute solution. If stirring is carried out at fast speed, turbulence will be created. Turbulence will break up big lumps of concentrated solution into smaller ones and *disperses* them into the dilute solution. This is normally referred to as *macromixing* in chemical reaction engineering. As this occurs, the area for diffusion increases and the concentration gradients become steeper. Both cause mixing at molecular level. This is referred to as *micromixing* in chemical reaction engineering. Chemical reactions occur at a molecular level and hence only in micromixed regions. As micromixing can occur only after achieving macromixing, rate of macromixing is an important parameter in design of chemical reactors. Thus, the concepts of dispersion in turbulent flows are of value in chemical reaction engineering also.

7.6 PHYSICS OF MASS TRANSFER

In this section, we would like to develop a physical picture of how the effects of diffusion develop in systems. For mass transfer to occur, there must be a gradient in the chemical potential, or for simplicity, a concentration gradient. Typically, such a gradient is created by bringing two phases into contact. Consider an example. Suppose we add sugar to water. Then, as water does not contain sugar, the chemical potential of sugar in water is less than the chemical potential of solid sugar. Thus, a chemical potential difference is created and sugar begins to dissolve into water. The boundary conditions will be discussed in detail later but we will state one boundary condition that is needed to examine the development of mass transfer process in detail. As with heat transfer, thermodynamic equilibrium is assumed to prevail at the interface between two phases. In this example, this implies that the concentration of sugar in water at the sugar–water interface will be equal to its solubility in water.

7.6.1 Development of concentration profiles

Let us now consider dissolution of sugar crystals into water in detail. To simplify the issues, let us imagine that sugar is present as an infinitely wide slab and water is in contact with one side of it. Refer to figure 7.5.

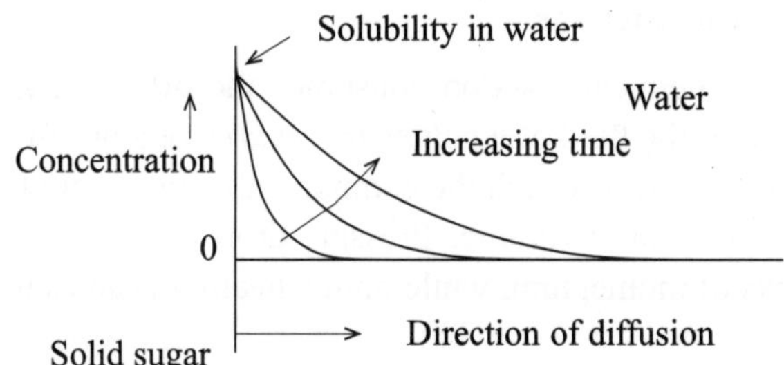

Figure 7.5. Development of concentration profiles when a slab of solid sugar is brought into contact with water.

As soon as water comes into contact with the solid sugar, because interface has no volume, the concentration in the water phase *at the interface* rises to the value of the solubility of sugar in water. However, the sugar concentration in water at all other locations is zero. Hence, a very large concentration gradient is set up at the interface. This causes a diffusive flux. The magnitude as well as direction of it is given by the Fick's law. The direction of diffusive flux is in the direction in which the concentration decreases. As the concentration decreases in the direction away from the solid–fluid interface, sugar diffuses into the bulk of the liquid phase away from the solid phase. Part of the diffusive flux increases the concentration while a part of it diffuses further according to the species mass balance. With increasing time, the diffusion causes sugar to penetrate deeper and deeper into the bulk of the liquid phase. The concentration profiles thus become less and less steep with increasing time. This is shown in figure 7.5. The example being considered is almost identical to the drag flow set up when a plate is suddenly set into motion in an infinite extent of an initially stationary fluid, and the corresponding problem of conductive heat transfer from into a semi-infinite medium.

It might be noted that though this is similar to the way velocity profiles develop in flows driven by drag forces and temperature profiles driven by conduction, there are some dissimilarities as well. Unlike with temperature profile development, as sugar molecules move into the liquid phase, they create a velocity in the liquid phase[16]. This is a complication which will be discussed in detail in the last section of this chapter. One more difference, though in detail, also exists. In the flow created between two infinitely parallel plates, where the bottom one kept stationary while the top plate is dragged with a constant velocity, the stationary plate plays the role of a 'momentum sink'. Similarly in case of heat transfer, if at some distance from a hot slab we placed a cold slab, the latter will play the role of a 'heat sink'. In both these instances, steady state can be reached when the supply from the source matches the loss at the sink. In the example we just considered, solid sugar can be considered as a source of sugar. However, steady state will not be reached since a boundary where sugar molecules can be 'consumed' is not available[17].

Another difference between mass transfer and momentum as well as heat transfer can also arise. In case of both heat and momentum transfer, problems involving specified heat or momentum flux can arise. Thus, a plate can be supplied with a constant heat flux or a plate can be dragged with a constant force. In mass transfer, such is hard to imagine, though not impossible to arrange, *e.g.* in controlled drug delivery.

Mass transfer with chemical reactions

If in the above problem, a chemical reaction consumes the diffusing species, it is equivalent to providing a sink in the *bulk* of the fluid or a *volumetric source* or sink. In such an instance, a steady state can be reached when the rate at which the component diffuses into the liquid matches the rate at which it is consumed in the entire volume. Pressure drop and body forces can be thought of as volumetric sources or sinks of momentum, while ohmic heating is an example of volumetric source in heat transfer.

7.7 BOUNDARY CONDITIONS

Boundary conditions dictate the development of concentration profiles. Let us consider the general boundary conditions for *isothermal and isobaric systems.* Generalization to non-isothermal and varying pressure conditions will be discussed later on.

7.7.1 Equilibrium at the interface

A basic hypothesis of diffusion is that thermodynamic equilibrium prevails at the interface between two phases. As with heat transfer, it is assumed that there is *no contact resistance.* Thus, chemical potential of any species which can be present in both the phases will be equal on either side of the phase boundary, *i.e.,* the chemical potential is continuous across the phase boundary. This is similar to the condition of continuity of temperature across the phase boundary. As mentioned earlier, for the sake of practical convenience, continuity of chemical potential at the interface is translated in terms of an equivalent condition involving concentration or mole fraction, *etc.* Consider once again the example of addition of solid sugar to water. The boundary condition of phase equilibrium at the interface is equivalent to stating that the concentration of sugar in water, at the interface between sugar solid and liquid phases, is equal to the solubility of sugar in water. Water is not 'soluble' in solid sugar, and hence we do not apply any equilibrium boundary condition for water. However, if water could be present in sugar, then chemical potential of water in the liquid phase and in solid phase at the interface must be equal according to the boundary condition.

The general condition is that the chemical potential of all species that can be present in both the phases must be continuous across the phase boundary. Refer to figure 7.6. The condition is stated as:

$$\mu_i^I = \mu_i^{II}$$

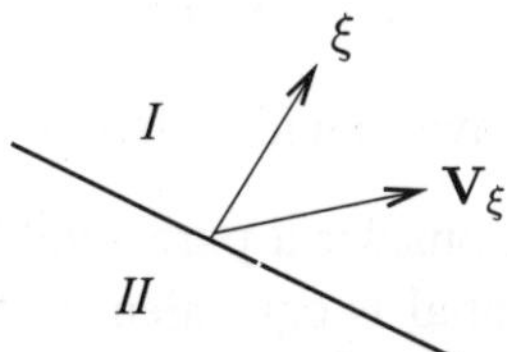

Figure 7.6. Figure giving notation to specify boundary conditions. It applies for both heat and mass transfer.

Conditions on concentration

However, as chemical potentials are not measured directly, it is more convenient to specify boundary conditions in terms of some measurable quantities. Usually, concentrations and partial pressures are used. It must be remembered that when conditions are specified in terms of these alternative measures, it is equivalent to continuity of chemical potential. These conditions, though they are very different in form, are therefore equivalent to the continuity across a phase boundary of temperature in case of heat transfer, and velocity continuity in momentum transfer.

Thermodynamics provides the relationship between the chemical potential and the concentration variables, *e.g.,* concentration or mole fraction, *etc.* Let us consider a few examples which are commonly used.

Gas – liquid interfaces: Suppose we have a gas–liquid interface. Typically, the equivalence of chemical potential is stated in the form of Henry's law. For example,

$$p_i = H_i C_i \tag{7.7}$$

where p_i is the partial pressure of the ith component in the gas phase, H_i is the Henry's law constant, and C_i is the molar concentration of the ith component in the liquid phase. This can be converted to a relationship between mole fractions of the ith component in both the phases if desired. Henry's law is commonly used in dealing with gases dissolving in non-volatile liquids.

Vapor – liquid interfaces: Suppose we have a vapor–liquid interface. Raoults law is commonly used. It is valid for ideal systems only. It states that

$$P y_i^v = P_i^s y_i^l \tag{7.8}$$

where P is the total pressure, y_i is the mole fraction of ith component, superscripts v and l refer to the vapor and liquid phases, and P_i^s is the saturation vapor pressure of ith component. For non-ideal systems, corrections through activity coefficients can be introduced to account for deviation from ideal behavior.

$Liquid - liquid\ interfaces$: When two liquid phases are brought into contact with each other, the equivalence of chemical potential is usually stated as a linear relation between the mole fractions in the two phases at equilibrium. This is highly restrictive but commonly used! The proportionality constant, m_i is referred to as the *partition coefficient*.

$$y_i^I = m_i y_i^{II} \tag{7.9}$$

where superscripts I and II refer to the two liquid phases in equilibrium.

$Solid - liquid\ interfaces$: Consider a pure solid brought in contact with a fluid. The condition of equality of chemical potential is equivalent to the concentration of the solute in the liquid phase being equal to its solubility.

$$C_i = C_i^s$$

7.7.2 Mass flux conditions

Another set of boundary conditions pertain to flux of species. Conditions on flux are equivalent to continuity of stresses and heat fluxes across phase boundaries. There however is a major difference between these and flux conditions for mass transfer. As net mass can be transferred across a phase boundary, the boundary is not made up of the 'same' particles at all times. As a result, the boundary may move with a velocity different from the mass average velocity in either phases that are in contact[18]. Consider the example of a volatile liquid placed in a beaker exposed to air. The level of the *gas–liquid interface* will fall as the liquid vaporizes at the interface and diffuses into air. The velocity in the liquid phase is 'downward'. The solute vapor will move up into the air phase due to diffusion, and the velocity in the air phase is 'upward'. Thus, velocity of the gas–liquid interface is not equal to the mass average velocity in either the gas phase or the liquid phase. In general we need boundary conditions at such an interface. Refer to figure 7.6. A very important point has to be kept in mind here. $\boldsymbol{\xi}$ is the unit normal vector and one has to clearly specify its direction. In figure 7.6, it is pointing away from phase II. Let $\mathbf{V}_\xi$ be the velocity of the interface.

The interface has no volume. Thus, the rate of accumulation of mass of any species has to be zero. The interface can be a catalytic surface in which case, chemical reactions could occur there. Thus, a mass balance of species on the interface would state that the net flux of ith species to the interface from both the phases plus the rate of generation of ith species per unit area must be equal to zero.

To implement this, we need to specify the rates of surface reactions. As with bulk chemical reactions, the overall rate of production can be specified in terms of rates of independent surface reactions. Let us follow the same methodology as with the bulk chemical reactions. Let $\dot{\mathcal{R}}_j^s$ be the intrinsic rate of jth surface reaction. It is defined as rate **per unit area**. Let α_{ij}^s be the stoichiometric coefficient of ith species in the jth surface reaction. Then the rate of generation of ith species is given by summing the rate of production of ith species due to all reactions.

Now we are in a position to write the boundary condition involving flux. Refer to figure 7.6. The mass balance states that

$$-\rho_i^I(\mathbf{v}_i^I - \mathbf{V}_\xi).\boldsymbol{\xi} + \rho_i^{II}(\mathbf{v}_i^{II} - \mathbf{V}_\xi).\boldsymbol{\xi} + M_i \sum_{j=1}^{N_r} \alpha_{ij}^s \, \dot{\mathcal{R}}_j^s = 0 \tag{7.10}$$

The rate of surface reactions has to be specified and it belongs in the domain of chemical reaction engineering.

First let us show that this gives the same condition for the overall mass balance as given earlier in eq. 3.8. We note that $\sum_{i=i}^{n} M_i \alpha_{ij}^s = 0$ for each value of j by mass conservation. Hence if the above boundary condition is summed over all possible values of i, we get

$$-\rho^I(\mathbf{v}^I - \mathbf{V}_\xi).\boldsymbol{\xi} + \rho^{II}(\mathbf{v}^{II} - \mathbf{V}_\xi).\boldsymbol{\xi} = 0$$

or

$$\rho^I(\mathbf{v^I} - \mathbf{V}_\xi).\boldsymbol{\xi} = \rho^{II}(\mathbf{v^{II}} - \mathbf{V}_\xi).\boldsymbol{\xi} = \dot{m}_b \tag{3.8}$$

which is identical to the boundary condition derived for velocity in section 3.4.

Now we give examples of use of the species flux boundary condition to make its application clear. Consider a stationary liquid–liquid interface. Since it is stationary, $\mathbf{V}_\xi = 0$. If there are no reactions occurring *at the interface*, the boundary condition gives

$$\rho_i^I \mathbf{v}_i^I.\boldsymbol{\xi} = \rho_i^{II} \mathbf{v}_i^{II}.\boldsymbol{\xi}$$

This is similar to the conditions of continuity of heat flux or of stress continuity in fluid mechanics.

Let us take a slightly more complex example. See figure 7.6. Consider a stationary impervious catalyst surface. Denote it as phase II. Let fluid phase be denoted as I. Due to impervious nature of the catalyst, $\mathbf{v}_i^{II} = 0$, and since the catalyst is stationary, $\mathbf{V}_\xi$ is also equal to zero. Let a surface reaction that is occurring be denoted by

$$A + 2B \rightarrow C \text{ or } C - A - 2B = 0$$

Note that the normal points into the fluid phase, and only it contains reactants and products. Applying the flux boundary condition we get

$$-\rho_A \mathbf{v}_A.\boldsymbol{\xi} - M_A \, \dot{\mathcal{R}}^s = 0$$

$$-\rho_B \mathbf{v}_B.\boldsymbol{\xi} - 2M_B \, \dot{\mathcal{R}}^s = 0$$

$$-\rho_C \mathbf{v}_C.\boldsymbol{\xi} + M_C \, \dot{\mathcal{R}}^s = 0$$

where the superscript corresponding to phase I was dropped for simplicity. The above conditions are rearranged sometimes to give the following equalities:

$$\frac{\rho_A \mathbf{v}_A.\boldsymbol{\xi}}{M_A} = \frac{\rho_B \mathbf{v}_B.\boldsymbol{\xi}}{2M_B} = -\frac{\rho_C \mathbf{v}_C.\boldsymbol{\xi}}{M_C}$$

This simply states that species must reach or leave the catalytic surface in appropriate stoichiometric ratio. Such equalities play an important role in solving mass transfer problems.

The stoichiometry of the reaction also suggests that $M_A + 2M_B = M_C$. Thus, by adding all the three conditions we get

$$(\rho_A \mathbf{v}_A + \rho_B \mathbf{v}_B + \rho_C \mathbf{v}_C).\boldsymbol{\xi} = \rho \mathbf{v}.\boldsymbol{\xi} = 0$$

As the catalyst surface is immobile and impervious, the mass average velocity on the surface must be zero and the boundary condition for the mass average velocity derived from those for individual species confirms this.

7.7.3 Mass transfer coefficient

Heat transfer coefficient was introduced earlier. If it is known, the heat flux from an interface into a given phase can be calculated from the driving force for heat transfer in that phase. Mass transfer coefficient is similar to the heat transfer coefficient. All the comments we made regarding heat transfer coefficient apply to mass transfer coefficient as well. It is used in presence of convection. Like heat transfer coefficient, it is also used to calculate diffusive mass flux from an interface into a fluid phase.

We illustrate the use of mass transfer coefficient in boundary conditions. The *diffusive mass flux* can be calculated using the mass transfer coefficient, and is written as the product of mass transfer coefficient and the driving force. Refer to figure 7.6. Consider fluid phase I for example. The total mass flux of species A in fluid phase I is given by

$$\rho_A^I \mathbf{v}_A^I = \mathbf{j}_A^I + \rho_A^I \mathbf{v}^I$$

The diffusive flux at the interface from the interface into the fluid phase can be calculated using the mass transfer coefficient:

$$\boldsymbol{\xi}.\mathbf{j}_A^I = k_A^I(\rho_{Ai}^I - \rho_{Ab}^I) \equiv k_A^I(\Delta\rho_A^I)$$

We should emphasize that when we use mass transfer coefficient, we calculate *only* the diffusive flux part of the total flux which may include convection. We will have more to say about this in later chapters. Note that in the above equation, $\boldsymbol{\xi}$ points from the interface into the fluid phase, ρ_{Ai}^I is the concentration at the interface in phase I, and ρ_{Ab}^I is the bulk concentration in phase I. k_A^I is the mass transfer coefficient for phase I. If it is known, then the expression

$$\rho_A^I \boldsymbol{\xi}.\mathbf{v}_A^I = k_A^I(\Delta\rho_A^I) + \rho_A^I \boldsymbol{\xi}.\mathbf{v}$$

for the *total flux* can also used as a boundary condition.

As explained in the chapters on convective heat transfer, the heat transfer coefficient can, in principle, be obtained by solving the equation of change of temperature. Similarly, the mass transfer coefficient can be obtained by solving the equations of species mass balance. However, in turbulent flows, this is not possible and hence a correlation is used to obtain the flux in the fluid phases. Under such conditions the above representation is useful. Once again, as with heat transfer, if mass transfer coefficient is given for a phase, the Navier–Stokes equations need not be solved in that phase as far as calculation of mass fluxes is concerned.

It must be mentioned that mass transfer coefficients are defined on the basis of other driving forces as well. The most common one with chemical engineers is of course based on molar concentration difference.

7.8 SPECIAL FEATURES OF MASS TRANSFER

If the sequence used in heat transfer chapters were to be followed here, shell balances should come now. Mass transfer creates some special difficulties and, unaware of these, if one proceeds to make shell balances, confusion will be the result. We will first discuss these difficulties. Unlike in heat transfer where temperature is the only dependent variable in formulating heat or thermal energy balances, more options are available in mass transfer. This is another point to be discussed later. As it turns out, due to the more complex nature of mass transfer problems, often a model is used to formulate problems. This is another idea that will also be discussed later.

7.8.1 Pure diffusion and bulk velocity

In the previous sections, it was pointed out that heat balance and mass balance equations are very similar. Heat transfer problems were classified into two categories: conduction and convection. The first attempt would then be made to classify problems in mass transfer also in a similar manner. Thus, one might expect that, similar to where heat transfer occurred only by conduction, mass transfer may also occur purely by diffusion. These class of problems are referred to as **pure diffusion problems**. Then, there can be problems where convection is present, and they can be referred to as *convection mass transfer* problems.

An important difference between pure diffusion problems and heat conduction problems exists and it has to be clearly understood. In heat conduction, there is no macroscopic[19] motion at all, as viewed from a laboratory frame. Thus, all convective terms in heat balance could be put to zero. *However, when mass transfer occurs, it is necessarily accompanied by motion.* This motion has to be distinguished from forced convection where an external agency creates motion and from natural convection where motion occurs due to buoyancy forces created through density gradients caused by mass transfer.

Species velocities and average velocity

A brief review of the concepts of velocities of species and diffusive fluxes will be of help here. Species must have a velocity if they move from one place to another. Let the velocity of species i be denoted by $\mathbf{v}_i$. A flux of species exists due to this motion. If the mass of species i per unit volume of solution, or mass concentration, is ρ_i, the flux of ith species $\mathbf{n}_i$ is given by

$$\mathbf{n}_i = \rho_i \mathbf{v}_i$$

If all species in the mixture possess the same velocity, relative motion of one species with respect to others is absent. Thus, there is only flux due to average velocity or bulk motion and it is same for all species. A *diffusive flux* exists only if there is relative motion between species. The diffusive flux is therefore defined relative to an average velocity of all the species. Average velocity can be defined by weighting the individual velocities with some property. If averaging is carried out with respect to *mass fraction*, w_i, the resulting quantity is the mass average velocity[20]:

$$\mathbf{v} = \sum_i w_i \mathbf{v}_i$$

If the species velocities are weighted with mole fraction, y_i, the molar average velocity, $\mathbf{v}^*$ is obtained:

$$\mathbf{v}^* = \sum_i y_i \mathbf{v}_i$$

The flux relative to the mass average velocity is defined as

$$\mathbf{j}_i = \rho_i \left(\mathbf{v}_i - \mathbf{v}\right) = \rho_i \mathbf{v}_i - \rho_i \mathbf{v}$$

The flux relative to the molar average velocity is defined as

$$\mathbf{J}_i^* = C_i \left(\mathbf{v}_i - \mathbf{v}^*\right) = C_i \mathbf{v}_i - C_i \mathbf{v}^*$$

where C_i is the molar concentration of species i. Thus, the fluxes over and above that caused by bulk motion are the diffusive fluxes.

Now we point out the difficulties that arise in characterizing bulk motion. If the velocities of species are different, since the molecular weights of species are different, the mass average velocity and the molar average velocity will not be equal. *In particular, if one is zero, the other need not be zero.* Another complication can also arise. Suppose that motion occurs **only** due to diffusion. In other words, there is no external agency to create motion and that motion is not due to buoyancy forces caused by density gradients. Even then it is possible that $\mathbf{v}$ is not zero. Hence macroscopic motion can be created by diffusion alone. There is no analogue of this in heat transfer.

7.8.2 Pure diffusion and equation of motion

There are several tricky questions associated with the bulk or average velocity created by diffusion. Consider the following experiment being done in the absence of gravity. A very long tube is partitioned into two halves separated by a membrane. The two halves are filled with ideal gases A and B. They are at the same temperature and pressure. At some instant, the membrane is suddenly ruptured and the two gases are exposed to each other. There is no pressure gradient initially because both compartments are at the same pressure. The gases will diffuse into each other due to the concentration gradient. As the gases are ideal, one would *expect* that the pressures in both compartments will remain the same. As a result (because the temperature also is constant), the total molar concentration will remain constant. Hence, a balance of the total number of moles will yield the result that the total molar flux must be independent of the position in the tube, and hence a constant. Consequently, the molar average velocity is also a constant, and it must be zero as the tube ends are impermeable. This situation is what is normally referred to as equimolar counter diffusion: for each mole of A diffusing to one side, a mole of B diffuses to the other side. Thus, the molar density remains constant and the total molar flux is zero. However, as the molecular weights of A and B are not the same, mass average velocity will not be equal to zero. If the no-slip condition is satisfied at the tube walls, and that is expected to be valid, then there must exist a pressure drop. This contradicts our assumption that pressure must remain constant. However, apparently, no mechanism seems to exist by which pressure gradients can develop. Several such intricate questions can be found in diffusion theory[21]. Thus, simple looking problems seem to get very complex if it is insisted that average *velocity caused by diffusion alone* should also satisfy the equation of motion.

The bulk velocities created by diffusion alone are very small and hence the inaccuracies caused by the assumptions, which have to be made if we do not insist that the equation of motion be satisfied, are likely to be unimportant. *Thus, it is customary to neglect the equation of motion in solving problems involving only diffusion.* It must be once again emphasized that this pertains to a situation where only diffusion occurs and there are no other sources of motion, *i.e.,* forced convection or buoyancy driven natural convection are absent.

If we do not use the equation of motion for determining the bulk velocity, the number of equations available to solve falls short of the number of dependent variables to be determined. This is seen as follows. Take a binary incompressible system as an example. Since incompressibility is assumed, the density of the mixture ρ is treated as a known. There are two diffusive fluxes: $\mathbf{j}_A$ and $\mathbf{j}_B$. However, only one of them is independent since $\mathbf{j}_A + \mathbf{j}_B = 0$. Fick's law relates the flux to the gradients of mass fraction:

$$\mathbf{j}_A = -\rho \mathcal{D}_{AB} \nabla w_A$$

The mass conservation equation for species A in the absence of reactions can be written using Fick's law as

$$\frac{d}{dt}\int_V \rho w_A dV = -\int_A \mathbf{n}.\mathbf{v}\rho w_A dA + \rho \int_A \mathbf{n}.\rho \mathcal{D}_{AB} \nabla w_A dA$$

As $w_A + w_B = 1$, only two unknowns are there: w_A and $\mathbf{v}$. Only the above mass balance is available. Hence another equation is needed to determine $\mathbf{v}$, and equation of motion is needed to solve for this. Thus, if the equation of motion is not used, the number of equations fall short of the number of unknowns.

Ignoring the equation of motion implies that other conditions[22] are needed to solve for the bulk velocity. Sometimes, the problem posed provides scope for some approximation. The well known equimolar counter–diffusion approximation is one such and arises from energy considerations in distillation. Insoluble nature of a component provides the approximation that velocity of that component can be set to zero. These points will be illustrated in the next chapter. In the next section, a widely used condition, called *dilute solution approximation* is discussed. It is easily understood and also helps clarify the ideas discussed.

Dilute solution approximation

Consider a mixture containing n-components. Then,

$$\mathbf{n}_i = \mathbf{j}_i + w_i \rho \mathbf{v}$$

Suppose one of the components, say the nth component, is present in large excess compared to the others. That component is referred to as *the solvent*. The other components are referred to as solutes, and this mixture is called a dilute solution. Thus in a dilute solution,

$$w_i \ll 1, \;\; i = 1, 2, \ldots, (n-1), \;\; w_n \sim 1$$

In such a situation, the diffusive flux of the solutes are of interest and solvent flux is of no interest. Since $w_i << 1$, the total flux of solutes can be approximated by the diffusive flux itself:

$$\mathbf{n}_i = \mathbf{j}_i, \;\; i \leq n-1$$

As the mass fractions are small, their gradients can also be expected to be small. Thus, the fluxes would also be small. Under these circumstances, the *bulk velocity caused by diffusion alone* is negligible and one need not be concerned about the issues of satisfying the equation of motion. The mass balance equation for solutes simplifies to

$$\rho \int_A \mathbf{n}.\rho \mathcal{D}_{AS} \nabla w_A dA = \frac{d}{dt} \int_V \rho w_A dV$$

where S stands for the solvent or the nth component, and this equation can be solved for w_A.

7.8.3 Molar form of mass balance

Sometimes it is found that use of molar units of species is more convenient than the mass units. An example is a mixture of vapors at constant temperature and constant but low pressure. Here, it is advantageous to use the ideal gas law and the inference that total molar density in the vapor phase is constant. Note that, as the composition of mixture will in general vary from point to point, the mass density will not be constant. Thus, it is sometimes useful, especially when dealing with diffusion problems, to formulate balance in terms of moles rather than in terms of mass. Consider the species mass balance over a stationary control volume:

Rate of accumulation of mass of ith species in the CV = **Net rate of input of mass of ith species into the CV by convection** + **Net rate of input of mass of ith species into the CS by diffusion** + **Rate of generation of mass of ith species in the CV by homogeneous chemical reactions**

This equation can be converted into molar units by dividing by the molecular weight of species i. The left hand side of the balance is given by

$$\frac{d}{dt} \int_{V_s(t)} dV \rho_i(\mathbf{x}, t)$$

If this is divided by the molecular weight of the species, M_i, the resulting expression will be in molar units:

$$\frac{d}{dt}\int\limits_{V_s(t)} dV C_i(\mathbf{x},t)$$

where C_i is the molar concentration of species i. The first two terms of right hand side of the balance are given by

$$-\int_A \mathbf{n.v}\rho_i(\mathbf{x},t)dA - \int_A \mathbf{n.j}_i dA$$

From this, it is apparent that the total mass flux of species i at any point on the boundary is given by $\rho_i\mathbf{v} + \mathbf{j}_i$. Expressing this in terms of velocities,

$$\rho_i\mathbf{v} + \mathbf{j}_i = \rho_i\mathbf{v} + \rho_i(\mathbf{v}_i - \mathbf{v}) = \rho_i\mathbf{v}_i$$

If this equation is divided by the molecular weight,

$$\frac{\rho_i\mathbf{v}_i}{M_i} = C_i\mathbf{v}_i = \mathbf{N}_i$$

Thus, sum of the first two terms of the balance, after dividing by molecular weight of species i is given by

$$-\int_A \mathbf{n.N}_i(\mathbf{x},t)dA$$

The last term on the right hand side of the equation is given by

$$\sum_{j=1}^{N_r}\int_V \alpha_{ij} M_i\,\dot{\mathcal{R}}_j\,dV$$

After dividing by the molecular weight of species i, it is simply equal to

$$\sum_{j=1}^{N_r}\int_V \alpha_{ij}\,\dot{\mathcal{R}}_j\,dV$$

Thus, in molar units, the balance for species i is given by

$$\frac{d}{dt}\int_V C_i(\mathbf{x},t)dV = -\int_A \mathbf{n.N}_i(\mathbf{x},t)dA + \sum_{j=1}^{N_r}\int_V \alpha_{ij}\,\dot{\mathcal{R}}_j\,dV$$

This equation is also easily interpreted:

Rate of accumulation of moles of ith species in the CV = **Net rate of input of moles of ith species into the CV by convection** + **Net rate of input of mloes of ith species into the CS by diffusion** + **Rate of generation of moles of ith species in the CV**

7.8.4 Classification of mass transfer problems

Now the discussion can be summarized and mass transfer problems can be classified.

I Pure Diffusion problems

a) Dilute solutions: Only solute fluxes are of interest and for these components, $\mathbf{n}_i = \mathbf{j}_i$ and $\mathbf{v} = 0$.

b) Concentrated solutions. Fluxes of all species are of interest, However, **v** is small and, its value is not determined from equation of motion. Some condition in the problem of diffusion has to give rise to some approximation that allows determination of the bulk velocity.

II Convection problems

a) Forced convection. An external agency creates motion. Equation of motion is solved to find the bulk velocity.

b) Natural convection. Diffusion causes density gradients which in turn cause motion. Equation of motion is solved to find the bulk velocity.

Mass transfer with high fluxes

Convection problems can further be classified into those involving dilute and concentrated solutions. Concentrated solutions involve high mass fluxes. The high flux mass transfer problems are normally treated by using models and arriving at high flux corrections which can be applied to the corresponding low flux or dilute solution problems. We deal with film model in this text. Readers interested in other models of high flux corrections are referred to the text by Bird *et al.* [2]

7.8.5 Film model

As will be seen shortly, in some respects, mass transfer in concentrated solutions and in multicomponent systems, is more complex than heat transfer. It is even more so if convection is present. As a result, models will have to be used to analyze mass transfer problems for practical applications. There are two well known and commonly used models. One of them is the *film model*, commonly attributed to Hatta. The other is *surface renewal model* or *penetration theory* (or model) developed by Danckwerts.

In the film model, it is assumed that all the resistance to diffusion is concentrated in a small layer at the interface between two phases, and that forced and natural convection are absent in this layer. This layer is commonly referred to as a *film*, and hence the name film model. Convection, especially in turbulent regimes, enhances rates of diffusion or mixing, and hence it is reasonable to assume that resistance to diffusion is present where velocities are small and turbulence is absent. Usually, this assumption is valid at the interface of a liquid and a stationary solid, and probably so also at the interface between two fluids. This is the basis of film model. As convection is absent in the film, as per the assumption made, it is necessary to analyze only diffusional phenomena there.

This simplifies the problem considerably. If the problem under consideration is one of steady state, the film is also under steady state. This is the most common case that is analyzed.

The surface renewal model uses a similar physical basis and assumes that convection is absent in the vicinity of the interface between two phases. It assumes that packets of fluid arrive from the well mixed bulk of a phase and "stay" at the interface for a short time, referred to as *penetration time.* During this period, mass transfer occurs by diffusion alone. After this period, the packet returns to the bulk and gets mixed with it. A new packet will arrive from the bulk and the process repeats. The mass transfer rate is equal to the product of the renewal rate and the amount transferred to the packet per visit, averaged over its many visits to the interface. As a result, even for steady state problems, the mass transfer to the packet during the penetration period is unsteady in nature since the packet does not reside permanently at the interface and so cannot achieve steady state. This model is simpler than convective mass transfer problems, but is more complex than film model due to its unsteady nature.

The extensive use of models in solving mass transfer problems makes study of diffusion problems more important than study of heat conduction problems. This is yet another special feature of mass transfer.

7.9 ENERGY BALANCE IN A MULTICOMPONENT BODY

In section 7.2, we introduced the concept of a multicomponent body and derived equations for balance of mass of species. In the first part of chapter 8, we apply these using the approach of shell balances to look at pure diffusion problems but where temperature will be assumed to be constant. In section 3.1, energy balance equations were derived for a single component system. In this section, we derive energy balance equations for a multicomponent body. In the later part of chapter 8, we apply these equations using the approach of shell balances to simultaneous mass and heat transfer problems, but where both natural and forced convection are absent.

7.9.1 First law and multicomponent body

As we observed in section 7.2, there is considerable confusion in defining several quantities for a multicomponent body. Same is true with applying first law of thermodynamics, which needs definitions of work and heat. Once again, the texts by Woods [9] and Slattery [6] can be referred to for view points different from what is presented here. Here we follow the text by Bird *et al.* [2].

In deriving equation of motion, it is assumed that a single stress tensor represents the effects of all species. Following that, the work done by surface forces *on the multicomponent body* can be written as

$$\int_{A_s(t)} \mathbf{n}.(-P\boldsymbol{I} + \boldsymbol{\tau}).\mathbf{v}dA$$

Let the body force per unit mass acting on all the species be identical and given by $\mathbf{g}$. The work done by it *on the multicomponent body* is given by

$$\int_{V_s(t)} \mathbf{g}.\mathbf{v}dV$$

Like earlier, one of the mechanisms by which heat enters is conduction. The heat flux due to this is given by $\mathbf{q}$. There are also new mechanisms by which energy can come into a multicomponent body. It turns out, energy flux can be created in the presence of *gradients in concentration.* This is referred to as *Dufour effect.* We will ignore this in the present text. Recall that no mass is exchanged across the surface of a closed system composed of a single component. However, the surface of a multicomponent body is not so restrictive, but it moves with the local *mass average velocity.* Hence, even though no net mass is exchanged across the surface of a multicomponent body, mass of individual species can cross its surface. Therefore, energy flux can be created by species as they move across the surface and carry energy. It is *assumed* that the energy flux due to this can be written in terms of *enthalpy*. Therefore, the total energy flux is given by

$$\mathbf{q} + \sum_i \mathbf{j}_i \frac{\bar{H}_i}{M_i}$$

where $\bar{H}_i$ is the partial molar enthalpy of species i. Now the first law of thermodynamics is stated as

The rate of change in the internal energy plus the kinetic energy of a multicomponent body is equal to the rate at which heat and energy are supplied to it plus the rate at which work is done by the surroundings on it.

Let, ρ, $\mathbf{v}$, and $\hat{U}$ respectively be the density, mass average velocity and internal energy per unit mass of the system. Clearly, all these can be functions of the local composition. The kinetic energy is *assumed* to be given by $\rho v^2/2$. The total internal plus kinetic energy of a multicomponent body is given by

$$\int_{V_s(t)} \rho(\hat{U} + \frac{1}{2}v^2)dV$$

The rate of change of this is given by

$$\frac{d}{dt}\int_{V_s(t)} \rho(\hat{U} + \frac{1}{2}v^2)dV$$

and this expression is same as that given in section 3.1.

There is a difference in calculating the rate at which heat is supplied to the multicomponent body. As in section 3.1, let $\dot{Q}_m$ be the heat generated per unit volume by means *other than chemical reactions*. The internal energy is a function of composition, and as we shall see a little later, it is through this that heat of reaction enters. The rate at which heat and energy are supplied to the system is then given by

$$-\int\limits_{A_s(t)} \mathbf{n}.\left(\mathbf{q}+\sum_i \mathbf{j}_i\frac{\bar{H}_i}{M_i}\right)dA + \int\limits_{V_s(t)} \rho\,\dot{Q}_m\,dV$$

Substituting all these into the statement of the first law of thermodynamics, we get

$$\frac{d}{dt}\int\limits_{V_s(t)} \rho(\hat{U}+\frac{1}{2}v^2)dV =$$

$$\int\limits_{V_s(t)} \rho\mathbf{g}.\mathbf{v}dV + \int\limits_{A_s(t)} \mathbf{n}.\left(-P\boldsymbol{I}+\boldsymbol{\tau}\right).\mathbf{v}dA - \int\limits_{A_s(t)} \mathbf{n}.\left(\mathbf{q}+\sum_i \mathbf{j}_i\frac{\bar{H}_i}{M_i}\right)dA + \int\limits_{V_s(t)} \rho\,\dot{Q}_m\,dV$$

After applying the transport theorem to the left hand side, we can rewrite it as

$$\int\limits_{V_s(t)} \frac{\partial}{\partial t}\left(\rho\hat{U}+\frac{\rho}{2}v^2\right)dV + \int\limits_{A_s(t)} \mathbf{n}.\mathbf{v}\rho(\hat{U}+\frac{1}{2}v^2)dA =$$

$$\int\limits_{V_s(t)} \rho\mathbf{g}.\mathbf{v}dV + \int\limits_{A_s(t)} \mathbf{n}.(-P\boldsymbol{I}+\boldsymbol{\tau}).\mathbf{v}dA - \int\limits_{A_s(t)} \mathbf{n}.\left(\mathbf{q}+\sum_i \mathbf{j}_i\frac{\bar{H}_i}{M_i}\right)dA + \int\limits_{V_s(t)} \rho\,\dot{Q}_m\,dV \quad (7.11)$$

As seen in the appendix to this chapter, the equation of mechanical energy balance remains unaltered. As argued in section 3.1, as the mechanical energy balance equation is valid at all points in the domain of interest, an integral of the equation over the domain also is valid. Thus, the following equation derived in section 3.1 is also valid

$$\int\limits_{V_s(t)} \frac{\partial}{\partial t}\left(\frac{1}{2}\rho v^2\right)dV + \int\limits_{A_s(t)} \mathbf{n}.\mathbf{v}\frac{1}{2}\rho v^2 dA =$$

$$\int\limits_{V_s(t)} \rho\mathbf{g}.\mathbf{v}dV - \int\limits_{A_s(t)} P\mathbf{n}.\mathbf{v}dA + \int\limits_{A_s(t)} \mathbf{n}.\boldsymbol{\tau}.\mathbf{v}dA + \int\limits_{V_s(t)} P\nabla.\mathbf{v}dV - \int\limits_{V_s(t)} \boldsymbol{\tau}:\nabla\mathbf{v}dV \quad (3.2)$$

We subtract this from the statement of the first law of thermodynamics, and we now get

$$\int\limits_{V_s(t)} \frac{\partial}{\partial t}(\rho\hat{U})dV + \int\limits_{A_s(t)} \mathbf{n}.\mathbf{v}(\rho\hat{U})dA = \int\limits_{V_s(t)} \rho\,\dot{Q}_m\,dV - \int\limits_{A_s(t)} \mathbf{n}.\left(\mathbf{q}+\sum_i \mathbf{j}_i\frac{\bar{H}_i}{M_i}\right)dA$$

$$- \int\limits_{V_s(t)} P\nabla.\mathbf{v}dV + \int\limits_{V_s(t)} \boldsymbol{\tau}:\nabla\mathbf{v}dV \quad (7.12)$$

It is more convenient to use enthalpy for incompressible fluids. Following the procedure of section 3.1, after some rearrangement we get

$$\int_{V_s(t)} \frac{\partial}{\partial t}(\rho\hat{H})dV + \int_{A_s(t)} \mathbf{n}.(\rho\mathbf{v}\hat{H})dA =$$

$$- \int_{A_s(t)} \mathbf{n}.\left(\sum_i \mathbf{j}_i \frac{\bar{H}_i}{M_i}\right) dA - \int_{A_s(t)} \mathbf{n}.\mathbf{q}dA + \int_{V_s(t)} \rho\, \dot{Q}_m \, dV - \int_{V_s} \frac{DP}{Dt} dV + \int_{V_s(t)} \boldsymbol{\tau}{:}\nabla\mathbf{v}dV \quad (7.13)$$

Enthalpy balance for a control volume

The above equation is the enthalpy balance over a multicomponent body. We now convert it to make it applicable to a control volume following the procedure used to derive eq. 3.6. We first recognize that the left hand side of the above equation is equal to

$$\frac{d}{dt}\int_{V_s} (\rho\hat{H})dV$$

Now the transport theorem derived for *stationary control volumes*, eq. 2.6, is applied to show that the left hand side is same as

$$\frac{d}{dt}\int_{V} \rho\hat{H}dV + \int_{A} \mathbf{n}.(\rho\mathbf{v}\hat{H})dA$$

Now, recognizing that the integrals over volumes and surfaces of the system and control volume at the instant of interest are equal, we get

$$\frac{d}{dt}\int_{V} \rho\hat{H}dV = -\int_{A} \mathbf{n}.\left(\rho\mathbf{v}\hat{H} + \sum_i \mathbf{j}_i \frac{\bar{H}_i}{M_i}\right) dA - \int_{A} \mathbf{n}.\mathbf{q}dA - \int_{V} \frac{DP}{Dt} dV + \int_{V} \rho\, \dot{Q}_m \, dV + \int_{V} \boldsymbol{\tau}{:}\nabla\mathbf{v}dV \quad (7.14)$$

In eq. 7.14, the only additional term compared to what was derived in section 3.1 is the enthalpy being carried into the control volume by diffusing species. Ignoring the term involving the substantial derivative of pressure, which is a very good approximation for incompressible fluids, we can write the heat balance as follows:

Rate of accumulation of enthalpy in the CV	=	**Net rate of input of enthalpy into the CV by convection and by diffusion**	+	**Rate of input of heat through control surfaces by conduction**	+	**Rate of generation of heat in the CV except by chemical reactions, *etc.***	+	**Rate of heat generation in the CV due to viscous dissipation**

This equation has to be used for enthalpy balance. It is easy to see that this gets coupled to mass balance through diffusion terms.

7.9.2 Boundary conditions

Due to the additional term involving enthalpy, the boundary conditions involving energy balance also get modified. The boundary condition for a single component system was derived in section 3.4 by making an energy balance on an interface, and is given by eq. 3.10 . Now the same principle is applied to derive the boundary condition for a multicomponent system. Refer to figure 7.6. Note that unit normal points from phase II to phase I. The rate of energy input to the interface from phase I is given by flux balance is given by

$$-\left[\mathbf{q}^{\mathbf{I}}+\sum_i \left(\mathbf{v}_i^I-\mathbf{V}_\xi\right)\rho_i^I\frac{\bar{H}_i^I}{M_i}\right].\boldsymbol{\xi}\delta A$$

while that reaching from phase II is equal to

$$\left[\mathbf{q}^{\mathbf{II}}+\sum_i \left(\mathbf{v}_i^{II}-\mathbf{V}_\xi\right)\rho_i^{II}\frac{\bar{H}_i^{II}}{M_i}\right].\boldsymbol{\xi}\delta A$$

where subscript i on ρ indicates the *mass concentration.* There could be radiative heat flux that is absorbed, and let us denote it by $\dot{Q}_{s,rad}$. The sum of all energy and heat fluxes to the interface must equal zero, and it is so at every point on the interface. Hence we have

$$0=\boldsymbol{\xi}.\left(\mathbf{q}^{\mathbf{II}}-\mathbf{q}^{I}\right)+\dot{Q}_{s,rad}+\boldsymbol{\xi}.\sum_i\left[(\mathbf{v}_i^{II}-\mathbf{V}_\xi)\rho_i^{II}\frac{\bar{H}_i^{II}}{M_i}-(\mathbf{v}_i^{I}-\mathbf{V}_\xi)\rho_i^{I}\frac{\bar{H}_i^{I}}{M_i}\right] \tag{7.15}$$

It must be remembered that this has to be combined with the boundary condition on mass balance:

$$-\rho_i^I(\mathbf{v}_i^I-\mathbf{V}_\xi).\boldsymbol{\xi}+\rho_i^{II}(\mathbf{v}_i^{II}-\mathbf{V}_\xi).\boldsymbol{\xi}+M_i\sum_{j=1}^{N_r}\alpha_{ij}^s\,\overset{\bullet}{\mathcal{R}}{}_j^s=0 \tag{7.10}$$

Examples

Dissolution of gases into a liquid: Consider mass transfer of gaseous species into a liquid (phase II) without chemical reactions and in the absence of any radiative flux. Let the interface be stationary. Then, we have

$$\rho_i^I\mathbf{v}_i^I.\boldsymbol{\xi}=\rho_i^{II}\mathbf{v}_i^{II}.\boldsymbol{\xi}\equiv M_i\mathbf{N}_i.\boldsymbol{\xi}$$

where $\mathbf{N}_i.\boldsymbol{\xi}$ is the molar flux of species i that crosses the interface from phase II into phase I. After substituting the above result, the energy balance reads

$$-\boldsymbol{\xi}.\mathbf{q}^{\mathbf{II}}+\boldsymbol{\xi}.\mathbf{q}^{I}=-\left(\bar{H}_i^{II}-\bar{H}_i^{I}\right)\left(-\sum_i\mathbf{N}_i.\boldsymbol{\xi}\right)$$

The quantity $\bar{H}_i^{II}-\bar{H}_i^{I}$ is the difference in the partial molar enthalpy of species i when it is present in liquid phase II or in gas phase I. It is the enthalpy change on dissolution of species i from gas phase into the liquid phase. Thus, negative of that is the heat liberated upon dissolution into liquid phase. As the normal points from liquid to gas phase, negative of its dot product with flux $\mathbf{N}_i$ is the rate of dissolution of ith species. The right hand side is then the rate of heat liberation due to dissolution of all species from gas phase into the liquid. The left hand side represents the rate at which heat is conducted away from the interface into both the phases. This must equal the heat liberated due to dissolution as there is no convection and interface cannot accumulate energy.

Reaction at a catalytic surface: Consider diffusion to and reaction on a stationary monolithic catalytic surface. Let the II be the catalyst phase. Hence, velocities in phase II are zero. The boundary condition for mass balance of ith species at the interface, eq. 7.10 reads

$$-\rho_i^I \mathbf{v}_i^I.\boldsymbol{\xi} + M_i \sum_{j=1}^{N_r} \alpha_{ij}^s \overset{\bullet}{\mathcal{R}}{}_j^s = 0$$

i.e., the flux of each species to the catalyst surface must match the consumption rate. Substituting this into the energy balance, we get

$$\sum_{j=1}^{N_r} \sum_i \left(-\alpha_{ij}^s \bar{H}_i^I\right) \overset{\bullet}{\mathcal{R}}{}_j^s = -\boldsymbol{\xi}.\left(\mathbf{q}^{\mathrm{II}} - \mathbf{q}^I\right)$$

$\sum_i \left(-\alpha_{ij}^s \bar{H}_i^I\right)$ is the heat of reaction for the jth reaction. Hence, the left hand side is the rate of liberation of heat due to all reactions. The boundary condition states that this must be conducted away into either phase because interface cannot accumulate energy.

Appendix : Equations of fluid mechanics

7.A Equation of continuity

We have already shown that the balance equation for the total mass is unaltered. Hence, equation of continuity is still given by

$$\frac{\partial \rho(\mathbf{x},t)}{\partial t} + \nabla.(\rho(\mathbf{x},t)\mathbf{v}) = 0 \tag{A5.27}$$

7.B Momentum balance for a multicomponent body

According to the hypothesis made, Newton's second law is also applicable to a multicomponent body. The body forces acting on the multicomponent body are easily computed. Their magnitude is given by

$$\int_{V_s} \sum_i \rho_i \mathbf{g}_i dV$$

where $\mathbf{g}_i$ is the body force per unit volume on species i. A mass averaged body force $\mathbf{g}$ can be defined now:

$$\mathbf{g} = \sum_i w_i \mathbf{g}_i$$

where w_i is the mass fraction of species i in the mixture. In terms of the mass averaged body force, the body force acting on the multicomponent body is given by

$$\int_{V_s} \rho \mathbf{g} dV$$

It is seen that this expression is identical to that for a single component as long as the density corresponds to the density of the mixture, and the body force is the mass averaged quantity.

There is considerable discussion regarding the application of Newton's laws to multicomponent body. Some believe that all the species do not experience the same stresses, and an equation of motion should be written for each component. For view points different from what is presented here, the texts by Woods [9] and Slattery [6] can be referred to. Here we follow the text by Bird *et al.* [2]. *It is assumed that there is a single stress tensor that represents the effects of all the components.* Hence, the surface forces acting on the multicomponent body are given by

$$\int_{A_s} \mathbf{n}.\boldsymbol{\sigma} dA = -\int_{A_s} \mathbf{n} P dA + \int_{A_s} \mathbf{n}.\boldsymbol{\tau} dA$$

This is identical to what was used in a single component system. The multicomponent nature of the substance is reflected in the constitutive relationship. Thus, if Newton–Stokes law is valid for the mixture, the viscosity will be a function of the composition.

The rate of change of momentum of the multicomponent body is given by

$$\frac{d}{dt}\int_{V_s} \sum_i \rho_i \mathbf{v}_i dV = \frac{d}{dt}\int_{V_s} \rho \mathbf{v} dV$$

where the definition of mass average velocity has been used to convert the first term into the second. This expression is also identical to that derived for a single component.

Without going through all the other steps, it is easy to see that the momentum balance will be identical to that for a single component provided the velocity and body force are the mass averaged quantities, and density is the density of the mixture:

$$\rho = \sum_i \rho_i$$

$$\mathbf{g} = \sum_i w_i \mathbf{g}_i$$

$$\mathbf{v} = \sum_i w_i \mathbf{v}_i$$

The Cauchy's equation of motion remains unaltered:

$$\rho \frac{\partial \mathbf{v}}{\partial t} + \rho(\mathbf{v}.\nabla)\mathbf{v} = \rho \mathbf{g} - \nabla P + \nabla.\boldsymbol{\tau} \qquad \text{(A5.29)}$$

If the fluid is Newtonian, then

$$\boldsymbol{\tau} = \mu \left(\nabla \mathbf{v} + (\nabla \mathbf{v})^t\right) - \frac{2}{3}\mu \mathbf{I}\, \nabla.v \qquad \text{(A5.30)}$$

where μ is now a function of w_i. Navier–Stokes equations are not valid since now both density and viscosity are functions of composition.

The mechanical energy balance equation is obtained by taking a dot product with mass average velocity. It also remains unchanged from that given in chapter 2. It is reproduced here:

$$\frac{\partial}{\partial t}(\frac{1}{2}\rho v^2) + \nabla.\mathbf{v}(\frac{1}{2}\rho v^2) = \rho \mathbf{g}.\mathbf{v} - \nabla.P\mathbf{v} + P\nabla.\mathbf{v} + \nabla.\boldsymbol{\tau}.\mathbf{v} - \boldsymbol{\tau} : \nabla \mathbf{v} \qquad \text{(A5.32)}$$

Problems for Chapter 7.

7.1 A pool of *stagnant* water contained in a circular tube of diameter D is evaporating from its surface into the vapor phase above. Assume that vapor phase is also composed of water only. Let $L(t)$ be the height of the liquid level measured from the bottom of the beaker. a) What is the velocity of water in the liquid phase? b) Let dW/dt be the rate of evaporation of water at any time. Relate it to dL/dt. c) What is the velocity in the vapor phase at the interface?

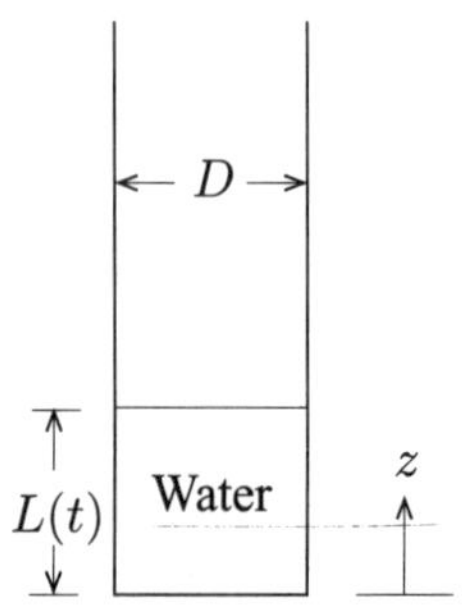

Figure for problem 7.1.

7.2 A candle is known to get extinguished slowly after lighting it when gravitational forces are absent. Why?

7.3 For the following situations, write the relevant boundary conditions.

i) A gas stream containing A ($x_{A\infty} << 1$), and at temperature T_∞ flows past a catalytic wall with a velocity V_∞. Species A reacts at the catalyst surface at a rate of $kx_{A,w}$ (moles per unit area per unit time) where $x_{A,w}$ is the mole fraction of A in the gas phase adjacent to the catalyst surface. The heat of reaction is $-\Delta H$ per mole of A consumed. The catalyst surface is insulated on the side not exposed to the gas stream.

ii) An insulated long tube is partly filled with a volatile liquid A initially at T_∞. The rest of the tube is filled with a **stagnant** gas B which is insoluble in A. Initially gas B is also at a temperature of T_∞, does not contain any A, and is separated from A by a membrane. At $t = 0$, the membrane is removed and the liquid and gas come into contact with each other. Due to vaporization, the liquid interface moves to the left. Denote the saturation vapor pressure of A by p_s and it is known that it is very small compared to P where P is the total pressure in the system. The total molar concentration c can be considered to be constant.

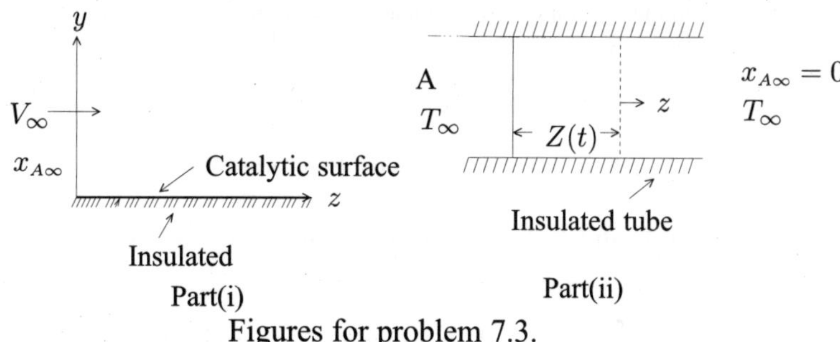

Figures for problem 7.3.

Notes

[1]A hypothesis in contradiction with the existing structures can also be proposed. Such would be a revolutionary and not an evolutionary development. Such a revolution faces stiff resistance. If and when it succeeds, it forms one of the fundamental laws of science!

[2]To avoid confusion, it is not referred to it as a closed system since it is, in a strict sense, not a closed system

[3]This is the mass concentration and should not be confused with the density of species i.

[4]Averages based on other weights, *e.g.,* mole fraction can be defined and are useful as will be seen in later chapters.

[5]Many kinds of average velocities can be defined, and there would be corresponding diffusive fluxes with respect to such average velocities. These ideas will be discussed later in greater detail.

[6]In fact, this is how it is measured. Rate of generation of each species can be measured experimentally. The intrinsic rate of reaction is obtained when this is divided by the corresponding stoichiometric coefficient.

[7]The averaged values of body and surface forces acting on it are defined in the appendix

[8]If it is assumed that the multicomponent mixture obeys Newton–Stokes law of viscosity, and that fluid properties are not a sensitive function of composition, Navier–Stokes equations will be valid.

[9]The species under consideration must be soluble in the phase, and the phase must be accessible to the species, *i.e.,* the phases cannot be separated by impermeable barriers.

[10] *Volume average velocity* is also used sometimes. It is obtained by weighting the velocities of species with respect to volume fractions. This has value in systems where volume changes due to changes in composition are negligible. This often is the case with liquid systems.

[11] Collisions between like molecules can exchange momentum and energy however.

[12] A little more exact approach is given on page 55 of the book by Present [5].

[13] This is justified for Brownian particles since they are macroscopic in size.

[14] The book by Einstein [4] also has Einstein's famous derivation of viscosity of suspensions.

[15] We have discussed some of these ideas in the context of heat transfer.

[16] Further, the solid–liquid interface will have to recede in a direction opposite to that of diffusive flux. A velocity will be created in liquid phase due to this. This will be briefly considered later.

[17] A situation analogous to a sink can arise if sugar is *consumed at a surface* for example by a catalytic reaction.

[18] In section 3.4, we have already pointed out this aspect. There we considered a single component and net mass could cross the interface due to vaporization.

[19] The word macroscopic is being used to exclude motion at molecular level, which always exists. Macroscopic motion refers to that which can be detected by the usual methods.

[20] It is called mass average velocity also because the product of density of the solution with the mass average velocity gives the total mass flux, **n**.

[21] It must be emphasized that there may be no contradiction here. In principle there are enough number of equations to find a solution for all the variables. In the particular issue being discussed, perhaps the assumptions of constancy of pressure and one dimensional diffusion may have to be abandoned. It is counter intuitive, but a solution can be found! Some do feel that the theory of diffusion in multicomponent systems is not complete! Slattery [6] refers to these ideas in his book. Please refer to our comments on progress in science made at the beginning of this chapter.

[22] The discussion presented here is similar to that presented by S. Whittaker [8].

References

[1] R. Aris. *Elementary chemical reactor analysis.* Prentice Hall, 1969.

[2] R.B. Bird, W.E. Stewart, and E.N. Lightfoot. *Transport Phenomena.* John Wiley, 2 edition, 2002.

[3] T.G. Cowling. *Molecules in motion.* Hutchinson's University library, 1950.

[4] A. Einstein. *Investigations on the theory of Brownian movement.* Dover, 1956.

[5] R.D. Present. *Kinetic theory of gases.* McGraw Hill, 1958.

[6] J.C. Slattery. *Momentum, energy and mass transfer in continua.* McGraw Hill, 1971.

[7] G.I. Taylor. Diffusion by continuous movements. *Proc. London Math. Soc., ser 2*, 20:196–211, 1921.

[8] S. Whittaker. Mass transport and reaction in catalyst pellets. *Transport in porous media*, 2:269–299, 1987.

[9] L.C. Woods. *Thermodynamics of fluid systems.* Clarendon Press, 1975.

Chapter 8

SHELL BALANCES IN PURE DIFFUSION PROBLEMS

```
We give examples of application of shell balances to solve
   problems involving only diffusion.
These illustrate identification of problem to be solved from a
   situation encountered in practice. Application of boundary
   conditions at boundaries is another concept demonstrated.
Problems illustrate analysis of gas absorption, catalytic
   reactions and distillation. The last involves simultaneous
   heat and mass transfer.
```

Analysis of mass transfer problems involving only diffusion is taken up in this chapter. We use shell balances for this purpose. As mentioned in the earlier chapter, pure diffusion problems are solved by making an assumption to avoid the solution of equation of motion. The examples considered in this chapter reflect gas absorption, catalytic reactions, and distillation. The differences between the low flux (dilute solutions) and high flux (concentrated solutions) cases will be examined to illustrate the issues discussed in the earlier chapter. Finally, the exact analogy between the low flux pure diffusive mass transfer and heat transfer by conduction is demonstrated.

8.1 EQUIMOLAR COUNTER DIFFUSION

8.1.1 Problem identification

A mixture of liquids A and B, which are completely miscible with each other at all compositions, flows past the bottom of a tube. Let A be the more volatile component. Let the mole fraction of A in the liquid be x_O. It is assumed that the mixture is ideal and follows Raoult's law. A vapor mixture of A and B is flowing past the top of the tube. Let the mole fraction of A in that vapor be y_L. The composition of the flowing vapor is different from that of the vapor phase which would be in equilibrium[1] with the liquid. Let the flowing vapor mixture be richer in the more volatile component than vapor that would have been in equilibrium with the liquid phase. Therefore, the more volatile component will diffuse from the vapor into the liquid and less volatile component will diffuse in the opposite direction. The objective of the problem is to calculate the mass flux at steady state. If the flow rates of the liquid and vapor streams are large enough, the compositions of the streams will not change due to the small diffusive flux. The physical arrangement is shown in figure 8.1.

It is assumed that thermal conductivities of both phases are sufficiently large so that the process can be considered *isothermal.* The vapor and liquid streams would then be at the same temperature, corresponding to the boiling point of the liquid mixture. This is possible because the vapor is richer in the more volatile component. Let the system be insulated so that heat is not exchanged between the system and the surroundings.

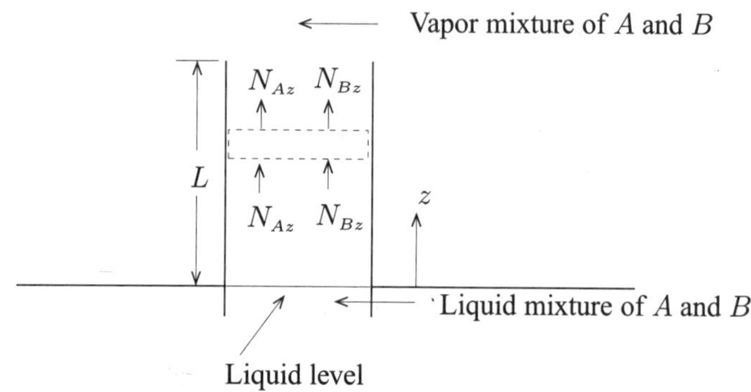

Figure 8.1. Schematic for equimolar counter diffusion. Liquid mixture of A and B flows past the bottom of a tube. A vapor mixture of the same components flow past the top of the tube. Vapor and liquid are in contact only through the tube. A and B diffuse in the opposite directions.

Simplifications and approximations

The problem is very reminiscent of distillation. In general, resistance to mass transfer is present in both liquid and vapor phases. In this section, we assume that diffusion in the vapor phase is the slower one, and we focus on it. In this problem, we expect the molar fluxes of the two components to be small but different. Hence, mass average velocity will be small, but not necessarily equal to zero. As mass average velocity is small, it can be assumed that the pressure drop required for flow is small or that the entire system is at *constant pressure.* Even if the pressure drop is small, there could be a momentum boundary layer developing along the tube wall, which would mean radial gradients in velocity will not be zero. Further, even if the flow becomes fully developed, radial velocity gradients would exist. This can lead to a composition gradient in the radial direction. However, if the radius of the tube is very small compared to the axial length, it is possible that concentration profiles in the radial direction would be evened out since mass cannot diffuse through the tube wall. In view of this, it will be assumed that radial concentration gradients can be neglected, and this is tantamount to assuming that diffusive fluxes exist only in the axial or z direction.

8.1.2 Species mass balance

As pressure and temperature are constant, the total molar concentration also remains constant. In view of this, the present example is a fit case for using molar units. We are interested in the flux of A. Since concentration variation exists only in the z direction, a thin shell of thickness Δz and area a equal to that of the tube is chosen as the control volume for making a balance of moles of A. Refer to figure 8.1. The molar balance is given by

Rate of accumulation of moles of ith species in the CV	=	Net rate of input of moles of ith species into the CV by convection	+	Net rate of input of mloes of ith species into the CS by diffusion	+	Rate of generation of moles of ith species in the CV

As the process is at steady state, the left hand side is equal to zero. As no chemical reactions are occurring in the control volume, the last term of the right hand side of the above equation is set to zero. Flux by diffusion is present, and convection caused by diffusion alone may also be present. Sum of the two is the total flux, N_{Az}. Thus, the above reduces to

$$aN_{Az}|_z - aN_{Az}|_{z+\Delta z} = 0$$

Dividing the above equation by the volume of the CV, $a\Delta z$, and taking the limit of the equation as Δz goes to zero, we get

$$\frac{dN_{Az}}{dz} = 0$$

Thus, the net flux of A per unit volume is zero.

8.1.3 Combining balance with constitutive equation

In order to solve for the concentration profiles, we need to substitute a constitutive relationship into the mass balance. It should be noticed that this procedure is similar to what was used in and heat transfer problems, where we made a shell balance for heat and substituted the constitutive relationship to determine the temperature profiles. The total flux of any species is the sum of the convective and the diffusive flux. The diffusive flux is given by Fick's law. Thus,

$$\begin{aligned} N_{Az} =& J^*_{Az} + y_A C v^*_z = J^*_{Az} + y_A(N_{Az} + N_{Bz}) \\ =& -C\mathcal{D}_{AB}\frac{dy_A}{dz} + y_A(N_{Az} + N_{Bz}) \end{aligned} \tag{8.1}$$

The above equation involves C. We assumed the gas mixture to be ideal, and C can be calculated if the pressure and temperature are known. We have assumed that the pressure drop is negligible. Hence the pressure in the tube is same as in the ambient, P. The system was assumed to be isothermal. Hence C is constant and known.

As is obvious, we cannot solve this problem till we find an expression for N_{Bz} or $N_{Az} + N_{Bz}$. This can be done only by solving the equation of motion. As mentioned in the previous chapter, we now look for a simplifying assumption to avoid solving the equation of motion.

Avoiding equation of motion

Mass balance for component B also shows that N_{Bz} is constant. Hence,

$$N_{Az} + N_{Bz} = Cv^*_z = \text{Constant}$$

We already showed that C is constant, and known. Hence the molar average velocity is constant, and, as suggested in the previous chapter, we look for a hint to calculate it but not by solving the equation of motion.

It may be pointed out that, indirectly, constancy of pressure facilitates use of these "hints" to avoid solution of the equation of motion. The conditions we use from hints are valid whether we solve the equation of motion or not. However, implementing these hints would have been very difficult if pressure is not constant. Solution of equation of motion would make everything exact, but very complex.

As the temperature *was assumed to be constant* throughout the system, we would *normally not* try an enthalpy balance. However, enthalpy balance at the interface should yield a relationship between the flux of A and B. This is done by examining the combination of mass and heat balance at the interface as indicated in section 7.9.2. As there are no reactions, and interface is stationary, eq. 7.10 indicates that the mass flux of A and B in the liquid and vapor phase are the same. So, we do not need different symbols for fluxes in the two phases. Let us denote these by N_{A_z} and N_{B_z}. Now we turn to the enthalpy balance. As the temperature in both the phases is equal and constant, conductive heat transfer in both phases may be equated to zero[2]. Further, we assumed that there is no heat exchange between the system and the surroundings. The energy balance boundary condition given by eq. 7.15 simplifies to

$$N_{Az}\left(\bar{H}_{A,v} - \bar{H}_{A,l}\right) + N_{Bz}\left(\bar{H}_{B,v} - \bar{H}_{B,l}\right) = 0$$

where we used molar units. Subscripts v and l stand for the vapor and liquid phases. But the difference between the enthalpy of the vapor and liquid phase is equal to the latent heat λ. Hence, the above equation can be rewritten as

$$N_{Az}\lambda_A + N_{Bz}\lambda_B = 0$$

Note that by using this boundary condition, a relationship between fluxes was arrived at, and it is this kind of "equation" that allows us to bypass the equation of motion. If the latent heats are equal, this implies that the net molar flux is zero or the situation corresponds to *equimolar counter diffusion*. We will now assume that the latent heats are equal. Hence[3],

$$N_{Az} + N_{Bz} = 0$$

Return to mass balance

With the *equimolar counter diffusion* simplification, the second term in eq. 8.1 is zero. Hence,

$$N_{Az} = -C\mathcal{D}_{AB}\frac{dy_A}{dz}$$

Substituting this in the balance equation

$$C\mathcal{D}_{AB}\frac{d^2y_A}{dz^2} = 0, \text{ or } \frac{d^2y_A}{dz^2} = 0 \tag{8.2}$$

Here it was assumed that the diffusion coefficient remains constant. In general it can depend upon composition, though not for ideal gases.

8.1.4 Boundary conditions

The order of presentation is changed slightly from the usual one because scaling cannot be done in this problem till boundary conditions are considered.

As with heat transfer problems, the flux and or the concentration boundary conditions can be used at the interface. At the top of the tube, the boundary condition is determined by the composition of the flowing vapors. If the flow rate of the vapors is large compared to the diffusive flux of vapors from the tube, and if the diffusive stream is assumed to mix quickly with the flowing stream, it is reasonable to assume that the composition of the vapors at the top of the tube will not be different from that of the flowing stream. Thus, the boundary condition at the top is given by

$$y_A = y_L, \quad z = L \tag{8.3}$$

The flux of A is what is to be determined and so it is not known, and consideration of the flux continuity boundary condition is not of much use. The same is true at the vapor–liquid boundary as well.

The boundary at the vapor–liquid boundary is very much akin to phase boundary in heat transfer problems. As flux is unknown, flux continuity condition is of not much help. Thus, falling back on our experience with heat transfer problems, one has to look for the condition equivalent to continuity of temperature, and that is the condition of thermodynamic equilibrium. Typical vapor–liquid equilibrium boundary conditions have been discussed in section 7.7. The vapor and liquid phases are in equilibrium and both phases were assumed to show ideal behavior. Hence Raoult's law can be applied. We assumed that diffusion in the liquid phase is fast, and hence its composition is uniform. Let the mole fraction of A in the well mixed liquid be x_o. Hence, by Raoult's law

$$y_A = \frac{P_{sat,A}}{P} x_o \equiv y_{Ao} \tag{8.4}$$

where $P_{sat,A}$ and P are the saturation vapor pressure of A and the total pressure of the system. The boundary condition then is given by

$$y_A = y_{Ao} \text{ at } z = 0$$

The two boundary conditions can be used to find the mole fraction profiles.

8.1.5 Scaling

The length of the tube forms the length scale to non-dimensionalize z. As with heat conduction problems, it is the difference in the concentration or mole fractions that drives diffusion as indicated by Fick's law. The mole fraction difference $y_{Ao} - y_{AL}$can be used to scale the mole fraction:

$$\xi = \frac{z}{L}, \quad \theta = \frac{y_A - y_{AL}}{y_{Ao} - y_{AL}}$$

Non–dimensional equations

The non-dimensional mass balance equation becomes

$$\frac{d^2\theta}{d\xi^2} = 0$$

and the boundary conditions become

$$\theta = 0, \text{ at } \xi = 1 \text{ and } \theta = 1, \text{ at } \xi = 0$$

8.1.6 Concentration profile

The solution is

$$\theta = 1 - \xi$$

The flux can be easily calculated from this.

$$N_{Az} = J_{Az} = -C\mathcal{D}_{AB}\left(\frac{dy_A}{dz}\right)_{z=0} = -C\frac{\mathcal{D}_{AB}}{L}(y_{Ao} - y_{AL})\left(\frac{d\theta}{d\xi}\right)_{\xi=0} = C\frac{\mathcal{D}_{AB}}{L}(y_{Ao} - y_{AL})$$

8.1.7 Look at the results

The flux is in the negative z direction since, as stated in the problem, mole fraction of the more volatile in the flowing vapor stream is greater than y_{Ao}.

In a binary mixture, only one mole fraction is independent. Therefore, an independent equation for the other mole fraction, in this case that of B, cannot be obtained. Thus flux of B has to be determined without solving for mole fraction of B. But of course, the flux of B is equal and opposite in sign to the flux of A. Thus, flux of B is immediately known.

The results show that as the diffusion coefficient increases, and the path length decreases, the flux increases. The flux also increases as the difference in the mole fractions at the top and at the vapor–liquid interface increases. These are expected. If the mole fraction at the top and at the interface are equal, the system is in equilibrium and there will be no mass transfer.

Similarity to heat transfer

The similarity between this problem and the heat conduction in a slab is obvious. The idea of the resistance to diffusion is relevant here and similar to that in the heat transfer. The diffusion resistance is given by $L/\mathcal{D}_{AB}$. As expected the resistance decreases with increased diffusivity and increases with an increase in the path length. These conclusions are also entirely analogous to what was learnt in conduction heat transfer.

As mentioned in section 7.8, the problem under consideration can be considered as a *film model* of the resistance to mass transfer in the vapor phase if L is considered to be the *film thickness* of the gas diffusion "film". This is the film model[4] of mass transfer and is familiar to all chemical engineers. The results of this section can be applied at a cross section of a packed bed distillation[5] column if diffusion in vapor phase controls the rate of mass transfer. In the solution of the problem being considered, we assumed that the resistance in the liquid phase was small. In a distillation column, typically both do exist. The problem can be solved when a liquid and vapor phase are put in series, and account for resistance to diffusion in both the phases. This will be a more realistic film model for a packed bed distillation column. The model developed by accounting for diffusional film resistances in both phases is referred to as the *two film theory*. This situation is also encountered when mass transfer takes place between any two immiscible fluid phases placed in series, a situation also encountered in liquid–liquid extraction. The ideas of conduction heat transfer through a series of slabs can be extended to calculate flux in such problems. The only difference in such a treatment arises in dealing with the condition of equilibrium at the boundary of phases. In case of heat transfer, this condition is equivalent to the continuity of temperature. Additionally, the flux continuity was the other condition needed. The flux continuity condition is valid in case of mass transfer as well. The condition of thermodynamic equilibrium is equivalent to equality of chemical potential and not the concentration (or mole fraction) of the same species in the two phases as seen from eq. 8.4. To solve the problem, a suitable condition of thermodynamic equilibrium, that gives a relationship between the concentration (or mole fraction) of the same species in the two phases, has to be used. In the present example, the flux could be rewritten as

$$N_{Az} = J_{Az} = C\frac{\mathcal{D}_{AB}}{L}\left(\frac{P_s}{P}x_o - y_{AL}\right)$$

and this form demonstrates the way mole fraction of the liquid phase gets incorporated.

8.2 VAPORIZATION INTO A STAGNANT GAS

8.2.1 Problem identification

Consider a liquid A which is placed in a beaker and vaporizing into a gas B. It is given that gas B is *insoluble in liquid* A. Let us assume that steady state has been reached. To make matters simple, let us assume that the liquid and gas are at the same temperature[6]. See figure 8.2. Liquid A is being

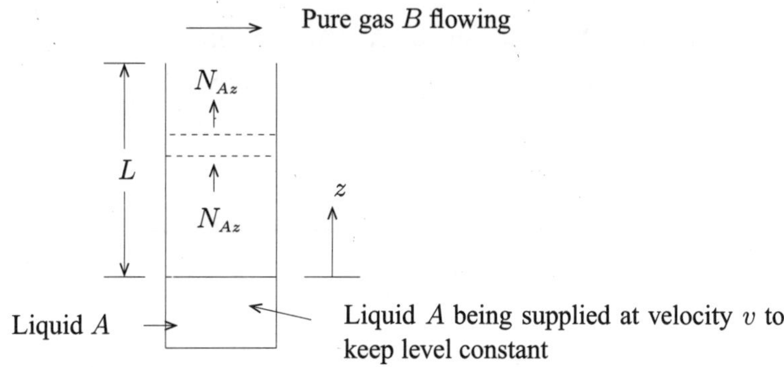

Figure 8.2. Vaporization of a volatile liquid A into a gas B insoluble in the liquid. B remains 'stagnant'.

supplied to the bottom of the beaker so that the liquid level remains constant. Its rate must be equal to the rate of vaporization, which of course is not known.

As liquid exerts its own saturation vapor pressure, the concentration of A will be more at the vapor–liquid interface. In contrast, as pure B is flowing at the top of the tube, the concentration of A will be zero there. Thus, a concentration gradient is created and A will diffuse from the liquid to the top of the tube. We want to calculate the diffusion flux of the vaporizing solute.

Simplifications and assumptions

Suppose the whole experiment is being carried out at atmospheric pressure. As the liquid vaporizes, it will move through the tube and leave at the top. Clearly mass average velocity is not zero and hence we have to solve the equation of motion to determine it. We wish to avoid solving the equation of motion for the reasons mentioned earlier, and we will return to this later. We pointed out in the previous problem, which is similar to the present one, that the radial concentration gradients may not be zero. For the same reasons mentioned there, we will assume here also that radial gradients can be neglected. Hence fluxes and concentration gradients exist only in the z direction.

We expect that the flow created by vaporization is so small[7] that there will hardly be any pressure drop due to it. Hence we assume that the pressure in the tube is atmospheric. In problems of vaporization, *e.g.*, humidification, some heat effects are involved. The central theme here is to analyze diffusional phenomena and so, as mentioned earlier, it will be assumed that temperature remains constant. Generally, vaporization problems are encountered in a low pressure environment. In view of this, it will be assumed that the gas phase is ideal.

8.2.2 Species mass balance

Once again, constancy of pressure and temperature coupled with the assumption of ideal gases makes use of molar units appropriate in this problem. Thus, we use molar fluxes, N_{Az} and N_{Bz} and mole fraction y_A. Consider a thin shell of thickness Δz, and area a equal to that of the tube, as shown in figure 8.2. As there are no reactions and we have steady state, the net molar flux of both A and B into the control volume must be zero:

$$aN_{Az}|_z - aN_{Az}|_{z+\Delta z} = 0, \quad aN_{Bz}|_z - aN_{Bz}|_{z+\Delta z} = 0$$

Dividing by $a\Delta z$ and taking the limit as Δz tends to zero,

$$\frac{dN_{Az}}{dz} = 0, \text{ and } \frac{dN_{Bz}}{dz} = 0$$

Thus, we have that both molar fluxes are constant.

8.2.3 Combining balance with constitutive equation

The constitutive relationship is the Fick's law:

$$J^*_{Az} = -C\mathcal{D}_{AB}\frac{dy_A}{dz}$$

This can be used to write an expression for the total flux

$$N_{Az} = -C\mathcal{D}_{AB}\frac{dy_A}{dz} + Cy_A v^*_z = -C\mathcal{D}_{AB}\frac{dy_A}{dz} + y_A(N_{Az} + N_{Bz}) \tag{8.5}$$

As pressure and temperature are constant and the gas phase is ideal, C is known and constant.

Avoid equation of motion

The previous equation cannot be solved unless we find an expression for N_{Bz}. The equation of motion has to be solved to find it, and we wish to avoid this. We have to look for a condition. The insolubility of gas in the liquid is what will give a clue to this. B is insoluble in liquid A, and hence is not present in the liquid phase. Thus, flux of B coming to the interface from the *liquid phase* is zero. Hence flux continuity at the interface requires that flux of B in the gas phase is zero:

$$N_{Bz} = 0, \text{ at } z = 0$$

Once again, we point out that this condition is *always* valid. But, in a binary system, we would have normally focused on the main component, A in this problem, and would not expect to examine equation or boundary condition for the other component. It is this point that has to be kept in mind.

Return to mass balance

As flux of B was shown to be constant, it can be concluded from the boundary condition that it is zero everywhere. Substituting the value for the flux of B, eq. 8.5 simplifies to

$$N_{Az} = -C\mathcal{D}_{AB}\frac{dy_A}{dz} + y_A N_{Az} \tag{8.6}$$

This equation for balance of species A can be integrated to obtain the desired result. However, to gain some more insight, we will put the mass balance in a special form. We have the following expression for N_{Az} from eq. 8.6:

$$\text{Constant} = N_{Az} = -C\mathcal{D}_{AB}\frac{dy_A}{dz} + y_A N_{Az}$$

Applying this in particular at $z = 0$,

$$N_{Az} = -C\mathcal{D}_{AB}\frac{1}{1 - y_{Ao}}\left(\frac{dy_A}{dz}\right)_{z=0}$$

Substituting this result into the right hand side of the constitutive relationship, we get

$$N_{Az} = -C\mathcal{D}_{AB}\left[\frac{dy_A}{dz} + y_A\frac{1}{1 - y_{Ao}}\left(\frac{dy_A}{dz}\right)_{z=0}\right]$$

It is convenient to differentiate it once because the boundary conditions are specified in terms of the mole fractions. Thus, the previous equation is equivalent to

$$\frac{d^2y_A}{dz^2} + \frac{1}{1 - y_{Ao}}\left(\frac{dy_A}{dz}\right)_{z=0}\frac{dy_A}{dz} = 0$$

This problem is similar to heat transfer in a slab whose opposite faces are maintained at two different temperatures. Heat balance in that problem gave only a term like the first one in the equation given. But, the previous equation is like

$$\frac{d^2T}{dz^2} - v_z\frac{dT}{dz} = 0$$

Therefore, the second term in the mass balance of A represents *convection caused by diffusion alone*. We will discuss this aspect later.

8.2.4 Boundary conditions

We need two boundary conditions to solve the balance for A, which is a second order differential equation. Two boundary conditions at $z = 0$ and $z = L$ are obvious. They constitute chemical potential equality and imposed concentration, respectively. If we assume that vapor–liquid equilibrium is given by Raoult's law,

$$y_A = \frac{P_{sat,A}}{P} \equiv y_{Ao}, \quad \text{at } z = 0$$

where $P_{sat,A}$ and P are the saturation vapor pressure of A and total pressure in the system, respectively. Because pure gas is flowing at the top of the tube,

$$y_A = 0, \quad \text{at } z = L$$

It may appear that we have not yet utilized the flux balance of A. Does it mean that the system is over determined? Continuity of the flux of A at the interface gives

$$N_{Az} = \frac{\rho v_z^l}{M_A}$$

where v_z^l is the velocity *in the liquid phase*, ρ is the density of liquid A, and M_A is the molecular weight of A. As can be seen this equation is useful to determine v_z^l, or the rate at which the liquid must be supplied for the level to remain constant. It does not constitute an additional equation for the gas phase.

8.2.5 Scaling

z can obviously be scaled with L. The mole fraction should be scaled with *mole fraction difference*, which in this problem is given by y_{Ao} itself. Let ξ and θ represent the dimensionless variables. Further let

$$\phi = -\frac{y_{Ao}}{1 - y_{Ao}} \left(\frac{d\theta}{d\xi} \right)_{\xi=0}$$

Non-dimensional equations

Substituting these into the mass balance gives

$$\frac{d^2\theta}{d\xi^2} - \phi \frac{d\theta}{d\xi} = 0$$

It may be noted that ϕ is related to the flux. Thus,

$$N_{Az} = -C\mathcal{D}_{AB} \frac{1}{1 - y_{Ao}} \left(\frac{dy_A}{dz} \right)_{z=0} = \mathcal{D}_{AB} \frac{C}{L} \phi$$

ϕ is basically a non-dimensional flux or an average velocity. The larger the flux, the greater is ϕ. Thus, it is clear that the second term in the mass balance is a "correction" due to convection caused by diffusion. The boundary conditions are given by

$$\theta = 1 \text{ at } \xi = 0, \text{ and } \theta = 0 \text{ at } \xi = 1$$

8.2.6 Concentration profiles

Solving the mass balance after implementing the two boundary conditions, we get

$$1 - \theta = \frac{e^{\phi\xi} - 1}{e^{\phi} - 1}$$

However,

$$\phi = -\frac{y_{Ao}}{1 - y_{Ao}} \left(\frac{d\theta}{d\xi}\right)_{\xi=0}$$

and substituting our solution into this we get

$$e^{\phi} = \frac{1}{1 - y_{Ao}}, \text{ or } \phi = \ln\left(\frac{1}{1 - y_{Ao}}\right)$$

We also can determine the dimensional concentration profiles using this result:

$$\ln\left(\frac{1 - y_A}{1 - y_{Ao}}\right) = \frac{z}{L} \ln\left(\frac{1}{1 - y_{Ao}}\right)$$

Note that the concentration profiles are non-linear and in particular, logarithmic in nature. Thus, the flux in dimensional terms is obtained to be

$$N_{Az} = C\frac{\mathcal{D}_{AB}}{L} \ln\left(\frac{1}{1 - y_{Ao}}\right) \tag{8.7}$$

Now we will use the dilute solution approximation to get results for the concentration and flux so that we can compare these with those obtained without using the approximation.

Dilute solutions

In solving the problem, we have not made any assumptions regarding the nature of the *composition* of the gas mixture. Suppose we have a *dilute solution*. In this example, this means that y_{A_o} is small. This will be the case with relatively non-volatile solutes. Then B is the solvent and we are not interested in the flux of B but only in the flux of A. The mass balances are unaffected by the nature of the mixture and they still give the same result:

$$\frac{dN_{Az}}{dz} = 0, \text{ and } \frac{dN_{Bz}}{dz} = 0$$

and that both molar fluxes are constant. We are not interested in B and so we focus only on A. For dilute solutions, since $y_A << 1$, the flux is given by

$$N_{A_z} = J^*_{A_z} + Cy_{scA}v^*_z \cong J^*_{A_z} = -C\mathcal{D}_{AB}\frac{dy_A}{dz}$$

This is the commonly used form of *Fick's law for dilute solutions*. Implicitly we are assuming that bulk velocity or convection caused by diffusion alone is zero. This of course implies that we need not solve the equation of motion. The pressure and molar concentration are constant because there is no bulk velocity.

It is easily noticed that the mass balance equation now reduces to

$$\frac{d^2\theta}{d\xi^2} = 0$$

We can then integrate the previous equation to find the concentration profile,

$$1 - \frac{y_A}{y_{Ao}} = \frac{z}{L}$$

and it is linear. The flux is easily found to be

$$N_{A_z} \sim J^*_{A_z} = C\mathcal{D}_{AB}\frac{y_{Ao}}{L} \tag{8.8}$$

8.2.7 Look at the results

We conclude from eq. 8.7 that the flux is in the positive z direction because the mole fraction decreases in the z direction. The flux of A is seen to increase with increased diffusion coefficient, and with increased y_{A_o} or the vapor pressure of the solute. Similarly, the flux decreases as the length of the column increases. These are expected because an increase in vapor pressure reflects an increased driving force, while an increase in L increases the resistance to diffusion. These trends are true even when the flux is low as seen from eq. 8.8.

It may be recalled that the concentration profiles are logarithmic, and not linear. Let us once again return to the analogy we drew with the heat transfer in a slab. If the analogy was perfect, the mole fraction profile should have been linear. The logarithmic terms are therefore an effect of convection caused by diffusion alone. Once the convection due to diffusion alone is negligible, the differential mass balance gives an identical equation to that obtained from heat conduction. The concentration profiles were found to be linear, similar to the temperature profiles in conduction in a slab.

The mass balance for A for dilute solutions gave a differential equation, which is equivalent to that obtained from the more exact analysis in the limit of $\phi \to 0$. But ϕ is proportional to the convective velocity and mass flux of A is proportional to ϕ. In dilute solutions, convective velocity is negligible. It then corresponds to *low flux* situations.

How is B stagnant?

The gradient in the mole fraction of B is not zero, and yet its flux is zero. It is natural to find the reason for this. From the constitutive relationship,

$$N_{Bz} = -C\mathcal{D}_{AB}\frac{dy_B}{dz} + (1 - y_B)N_{Az}$$

The bulk or the convective flux term, *i.e.,* the second term on the right hand side, is in the positive z direction since N_{A_z} is positive. However, the gradient of mole fraction of B is positive. Thus, its diffusive flux will be in the negative z direction. The convective and diffusive fluxes are in the opposite directions and are exactly balanced. The net flux is therefore zero. For A, both are in the same direction and convection adds to diffusion.

Mass transfer coefficient

The problem solved in this section can be considered as a film model for vaporization of a solute into an insoluble gas. In this context, the results obtained can be used to evaluate a mass transfer coefficient. As explained in section 7.8, mass transfer coefficient is defined as the ratio of *the flux due to diffusion* and an overall driving force. In this chapter, both natural and forced convection are absent. Hence the entire flux is due to diffusion only. Thus, *we use N_{A_z} and not J_{A_z}* to evaluate mass transfer coefficient.

Mass transfer coefficients are used with a variety of driving forces and one has to be careful to note the units! An expression for mass transfer coefficient, *defined on the basis of concentration difference* can be found from eq. 8.7, and is given by

$$k^{\bullet}_{C,A} = \frac{N_{Az}}{C\Delta y_A} = \frac{\mathcal{D}_{AB}}{L} \Bigg/ \frac{1-(1-y_{Ao})}{\ln\left(\frac{1}{1-y_{Ao}}\right)} \tag{8.9}$$

The superscript • signifies that the mass transfer coefficient includes the effect due to convective diffusive flux as well or corresponds to *high flux*. We can also use concentration profiles obtained for the low flux case. An expression for mass transfer coefficient, defined on the basis of concentration difference, can be found from those also. It is given by:

$$k_{C,A} = \frac{N_{Az}}{C\Delta y_A} = \frac{\mathcal{D}_{AB}}{L}$$

Now, we removed the superscript • to indicate that the mass transfer coefficient was calculated using the dilute solution approximation or it is the low flux limit. This is the well known expression for the mass transfer coefficient according to the film theory. *It is valid only when the fluxes are small.*

High flux correction

The numerator in eq. 8.9 is the expression for mass transfer coefficient from the usual film model, or the low flux mass transfer coefficient. The denominator is a correction for high flux. The ratio of the flux obtained by exact analysis to that obtained by neglecting convection would reflect the effect of high flux. The latter is that obtained by assuming the solutions to be dilute or that corresponding to low flux case. The ratio is referred to as correction due to high flux or simply the **high flux correction factor**, $\mathcal{E}$. Thus, the actual flux is given by multiplying the flux obtained by assuming the solution to be dilute with the high correction factor. Hence,

$$\mathcal{E} = \frac{L}{Cy_{Ao}\mathcal{D}_{AB}} N_{Az} = \frac{k^{\bullet}_{C,A}}{k_{C,A}}$$

It is easily worked out that

$$\mathcal{E} = -\frac{\ln(1 - y_{Ao})}{y_{Ao}} = 1 + \frac{y_{Ao}}{2} + \ldots$$

Since $\mathcal{E} > 1$, the flux is more[8] than that *obtained by dilute solution approximation.* Though surprising at first instance, it is understandable. A can diffuse at the "low flux rate" corresponding to a linear mole fraction gradient consistent with the imposed boundary conditions. The same gradient will make B to diffuse in the opposite direction. Hence, A must diffuse faster in order to keep B stagnant.

It should be noted that the high flux correction evaluated here is model dependent. However, the factor gives some idea as to what to expect.

Similarity to gas absorption

The expression of mass flux can be expressed in a slightly different form:

$$N_{A_z} = \frac{\mathcal{D}_{AB}C(y_{Ao} - 0)}{L} \Big/ \frac{1 - (1 - y_{Ao})}{\ln\left(\frac{1}{1 - y_{Ao}}\right)}$$

The denominator is easily recognized as the log mean of the mole fraction difference (equivalently, the difference in the partial pressure) of the stagnant component. It is the same term which appears as $(P_B)_{lm}$ in absorption of gas A from a mixture with an insoluble gas B. This is not surprising. In the gas absorption operation, a mixture of gas A and gas B are brought into contact with a *non-volatile* liquid in which only A is soluble. Clearly, the liquid does not play any role. As B is insoluble in the liquid, it is stagnant, and similarity can be expected.

Similarity to conduction heat transfer problems

Once again, consider the problem of heat transfer by conduction across a slab with thickness L and with a temperature difference maintained across it. The heat flux is constant and constancy of mass flux derived earlier is identical to the constancy of heat flux. Fick's law is *similar* to the Fourier's law of heat conduction, but is not identical to it because the former relates the diffusion flux and not the total flux to the concentration gradients. However, for dilute solutions diffusion flux is equal to the mass flux. The problem we considered for dilute solutions then is identical to that of heat transfer by conduction across a slab with thickness L and with a temperature difference maintained across it. It will be seen later that this identity between heat transfer by conduction and mass transfer by diffusion in dilute solutions holds even in convective transport.

8.3 MASS TRANSFER & CATALYTIC REACTIONS

8.3.1 Problem identification

Consider a catalyst on which the following reaction occurs:

$$2A \longrightarrow B \text{ or } B - 2A = 0$$

The apparatus can be imagined as a tube whose bottom is a catalytic surface. Let the catalyst be impervious. At the top of the tube a mixture of gases A and B with a known composition is flowing. Let its composition be given by $y_{A,L}$. See figure 8.3. The reaction is also a rate process and the rate

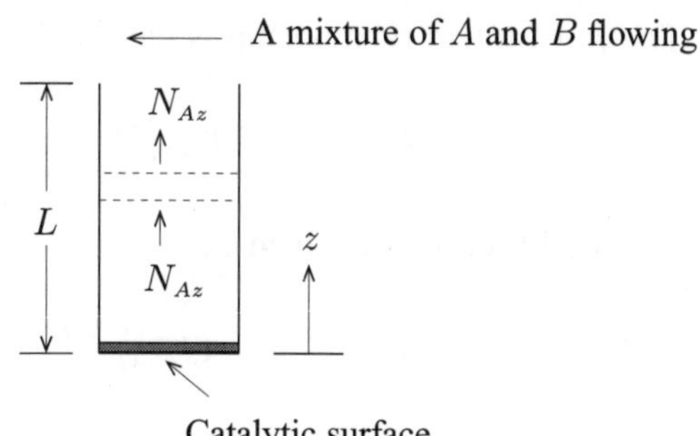

Figure 8.3. Reaction occurring on the surface of an impervious catalyst.

expression has to be specified. Let the intrinsic rate of the reaction at the surface, in moles per unit area per unit time, be given by

$$\dot{R}_s = k'' C y_A$$

As A reacts at the surface, its concentration there will fall. Hence it will diffuse towards the catalyst surface. In contrast, as B is produced at the catalyst surface, its concentration will increase there and it will diffuse away from the surface. A steady state will be established when the rate of consumption of A matches its rate of diffusion from the bulk, and similar balance is established for B also. We are interested in calculating the rate of reaction or rate of consumption of A or equivalently, rate of production of B.

Simplifications and assumptions

For reasons enumerated in the previous section 8.2, it will be assumed that diffusion is one-dimensional. Based on the discussion in section 8.2, we expect that the flow caused by the reaction at the surface to be small and hence we assume the pressure drop to be negligible. Thus, pressure can be treated as constant. It will be assumed that temperature remains constant. To keep things simple, it will be assumed that the gas phase is ideal.

8.3.2 Species mass balance

There are two components and the reaction is occurring at the catalyst surface. Generation terms are zero since reaction occurs on the surface and *not in the bulk*. Hence steady state mass balance over a differential element of unit area and thickness Δz is given by:

$$N_{Az}|_z - N_{Az}|_{z+\Delta z} = 0, \quad N_{Bz}|_z - N_{Bz}|_{z+\Delta z} = 0$$

or

$$\frac{dN_{Az}}{dz} = 0, \text{ and } \frac{dN_{Bz}}{dz} = 0$$

Thus, both molar fluxes are constant.

8.3.3 Combining balance with constitutive equation

In order to solve for the concentration profiles, we need to substitute the constitutive relationship into the mass balance. The constitutive relationship is the Fick's law,

$$J*_{Az} = -C\mathcal{D}_{AB}\frac{dy_A}{dz}$$

and the expressions for the total flux of A is given by

$$N_{A_z} = -C\mathcal{D}_{AB}\frac{dy_A}{dz} + Cy_A v_z^* = -C\mathcal{D}_{AB}\frac{dy_A}{dz} + y_A\left(N_{A_z} + N_{B_z}\right) \tag{8.10}$$

Substituting this into the mass balance for A, we get

$$\mathcal{D}_{AB}\frac{d}{dz}\left(C\frac{dy_A}{dz}\right) = \frac{d}{dz}\left[y_A\left(N_{A_z} + N_{B_z}\right)\right]$$

where we have assumed the diffusion coefficient to be constant. The balance for B after substitution of its constitutive relationship will not give an independent equation since we know that the sum of mole fractions is equal to unity.

As discussed before, we assumed pressure and temperature to be constant and that the gas phase is ideal. Thus, once the pressure and temperature of the system are known, C is constant and known. We need to determine either the sum of the fluxes or N_{B_z} to avoid solving the equation of motion.

Avoid equation of motion

Based on the previous experience, we now look towards boundary condition for B to get some information about the sum of fluxes. We do not have a concentration boundary condition at the catalyst surface. However, we do have mass flux balance. See figure 7.6. The general form of the mass flux balance at an interface in presence of a single surface reaction is given by eq. 7.10

$$-\rho_i^I(\mathbf{v}_i^I - \mathbf{V}_\xi).\boldsymbol{\xi} + \rho_i^{II}(\mathbf{v}_i^{II} - \mathbf{V}_\xi).\boldsymbol{\xi} + M_i\sum_{j=1}^{N_r}\alpha_{ij}^s\,\dot{\mathcal{R}}_j^s = 0 \tag{7.10}$$

Specializing it for a single reaction and dividing it by the molecular weight, we get

$$\left[C_i^I(\mathbf{v}_i^I - \mathbf{V}_\xi) - C_i^{II}(\mathbf{v}_i^{II} - \mathbf{V}_\xi)\right].\boldsymbol{\xi} + \alpha_i^s\,\dot{\mathcal{R}}_s = 0$$

where superscripts I and II refer to the phases, $\boldsymbol{\xi}$ is the normal pointing from phase II to phase I, $\mathbf{V}_\xi$ is the velocity of the interface between the phases, α_i^s is the stoichiometric coefficient of species i in the surface reaction and $\dot{\mathcal{R}}_s$ is the intrinsic rate of surface reaction. Since the catalytic surface is stationary, $\mathbf{V}_\xi$ is zero in that phase. Further, neither reactants nor products are present in the catalyst phase since it is impervious, and hence all concentrations will be zero. Let the fluid phase be denoted by I. Hence $\boldsymbol{\xi}$ is same as unit vector in z direction. Then the boundary condition simplifies to

$$N_{A_z} - 2\,\dot{\mathcal{R}}^s = N_{A_z} - 2k''Cy_A = 0, \text{ and } N_{B_z} + \dot{\mathcal{R}}^s = N_{B_z} + k''Cy_A = 0$$

It can be seen that the two fluxes are related to each other through the boundary condition by virtue of the stoichiometry:

$$N_{Az} = -2N_{Bz}$$

This makes physical sense because for two moles of A diffusing toward the catalyst surface, a mole of B has to diffuse away to satisfy stoichiometry. Now we use the relationship between the fluxes to find their sum

$$N_{Az} + N_{Bz} = \frac{N_{Az}}{2}$$

Thus, once again, by using the relationship between fluxes, we managed to bypass the equation of motion.

Return to mass balance

As with the previous example, since the flux of A is not known, it is more convenient to eliminate it from the mass balance. We rewrite eq. 8.10, using the relationship between fluxes as

$$N_{Az} = -C\mathcal{D}_{AB}\frac{dy_A}{dz} + \frac{y_A}{2}N_{Az}$$

Since the flux is constant, the equation is valid at all values of z and in particular at $z = 0$. Thus,

$$N_{Az} = -C\mathcal{D}_{AB}\frac{1}{1-\dfrac{y_{Ao}}{2}}\left(\frac{dy_A}{dz}\right)_{z=0}$$

where y_{Ao} is mole fraction of A at $z = 0$. Using this, the flux of A can be rewritten as

$$N_{Az} = -C\mathcal{D}_{AB}\left[\frac{dy_A}{dz} + \frac{1}{2}\frac{y_A}{1-\dfrac{y_{Ao}}{2}}\left(\frac{dy_A}{dz}\right)_{z=0}\right]$$

Substituting this into the mass balance equation and recognizing that C is constant since pressure and temperature are constant, we get

$$\frac{d^2y_A}{dz^2} + \frac{1}{2}\frac{1}{1-\dfrac{y_{Ao}}{2}}\left(\frac{dy_A}{dz}\right)_{z=0}\frac{dy_A}{dz} = 0$$

The second term of the left hand side obviously corresponds to correction due to the velocity created by diffusion.

8.3.4 Boundary conditions

The above is a second order ordinary differential equation and needs two boundary conditions. The composition of the gas at the top is known, and it forms one boundary condition:

$$y_A = y_{AL}, \quad \text{at } z = L$$

The other condition pertains to flux balance of A:

$$-C\mathcal{D}_{AB}\frac{1}{1-\dfrac{y_{Ao}}{2}}\left(\frac{dy_A}{dz}\right)_{z=0} = N_{Az} = -2k''Cy_{Ao}, \quad \text{at } z = 0,$$

8.3.5 Scaling

The length can be scaled using L. Since y_{Ao} is not known, we cannot define a mole fraction difference to scale. However, we need an estimate of the largest difference possible for scaling. If the reaction is instantaneous, the mole fraction of A at the surface will be zero. Using this argument, we scale the mole fraction with y_{AL} itself. Let ξ and θ be the corresponding non-dimensional variables. Further, let

$$\phi \equiv \frac{\dfrac{y_{AL}}{2}}{1-\dfrac{y_{Ao}}{2}}\left(\frac{d\theta}{d\xi}\right)_{\xi=0} \tag{8.11}$$

Non-dimensional equations

After substitution of the scaled variables, the mass balance equation becomes

$$\frac{d^2\theta}{d\xi^2} + \phi\frac{d\theta}{d\xi} = 0$$

The solution will be implicit because the mole fraction at the surface is not known. Let us formally write the solution however. Let us use the following boundary conditions in non-dimensional form

$$\theta = 1, \ \text{at } \xi = 1, \ \text{and } \theta = \theta_o \ \text{at } \xi = 0$$

where θ_o is the scaled mole fraction of A at the catalyst surface which is to be determined.

8.3.6 Concentration profiles

Integrating the mass balance equation once, we get

$$\frac{d\theta}{d\xi} = Ae^{-\phi\xi}$$

But from the definition of ϕ definition, *i.e.,* eq. 8.11, it follows that

$$A = \left(\frac{d\theta}{d\xi}\right)_{\xi=0} = \phi\frac{1-\dfrac{y_{Ao}}{2}}{\dfrac{y_{AL}}{2}}$$

Hence

$$\left(\frac{d\theta}{d\xi}\right) = \phi \frac{1 - \dfrac{y_{Ao}}{2}}{\dfrac{y_{AL}}{2}} e^{-\phi\xi}$$

Integrating once more and using the boundary condition that $\theta = 1$ at $\xi = 1$, the solution is found to be

$$1 - \theta = \frac{1 - \dfrac{y_{Ao}}{2}}{\dfrac{y_{AL}}{2}} \left(e^{-\phi\xi} - e^{-\phi}\right)$$

Thus the concentration profiles are non-linear.

Only an implicit expression for the flux can be found as follows. Let us evaluate the solution at $\xi = 0$:

$$1 - \frac{y_{Ao}}{y_{AL}} = \frac{1 - \dfrac{y_{Ao}}{2}}{\dfrac{y_{AL}}{2}} \left(1 - e^{-\phi}\right) \tag{8.12}$$

This equation contains ϕ, which is however related to y_{A_o} through the rate of reaction. Thus, from eq. 8.11

$$\phi = \frac{\dfrac{L}{2}}{1 - \dfrac{y_{Ao}}{2}} \left(\frac{dy_A}{dz}\right)_{z=0} = -\frac{LN_{A_z}}{2C\mathcal{D}_{AB}} = \frac{Lk'' y_{Ao}}{\mathcal{D}_{AB}}$$

where we have also used the flux boundary condition. This equation is equivalent to

$$\frac{y_{Ao}}{y_{AL}} = \frac{\phi}{y_{AL}} \frac{\mathcal{D}_{AB}}{k'' L}$$

Substituting this into eq. 8.12, we have an implicit equation for ϕ:

$$\frac{y_{AL}}{2}\left(1 - \frac{\phi}{y_{AL}} \frac{\mathcal{D}_{AB}}{k'' L}\right) = \left(1 + \frac{\mathcal{D}_{AB}}{2k'' L}\right)\left(1 - e^{-\phi}\right)$$

This equation can be solved iteratively to find ϕ. The flux is related to ϕ as seen from above:

$$N_{A_z} = -2\phi \frac{C\mathcal{D}_{AB}}{L}$$

8.3.7 Dilute solutions

We expect ϕ to be small for low fluxes. Low fluxes will occur when y_{AL} is small, *i.e.,* for dilute solutions. The flux under those circumstances can be found by taking the limit as $\phi \to 0$ of the previous implicit equation for ϕ. It is however instructive to solve the problem from the beginning again to see the principles.

In dilute solutions, we are interested in solving only for the flux of the dilute component, A. The mass balances are unaffected by the nature of the mixture and they still give the same result:

$$\frac{dN_{Az}}{dz} = 0, \text{ and } \frac{dN_{Bz}}{dz} = 0$$

or that both molar fluxes are constant. We focus only on A. For dilute solutions, since $y_A << 1$, Fick's law is given by

$$N_{Az} = J^*_{Az} + Cy_A v^*_z \cong J^*_{Az} = -C\mathcal{D}_{AB}\frac{dy_A}{dz}$$

Note that the unknown v* has been eliminated which is equivalent to knowing one flux. Hence we need not solve the equation of motion. We can assume that pressure is constant and hence C is constant. Substituting the constitutive relationship into the mass balance we get

$$\frac{d^2y_A}{dz^2} = 0$$

The solution is of course linear. Integrating once

$$\frac{dy_A}{dz} = \text{Constant}$$

But from the boundary condition that matches the flux with reaction rate at $z = 0$, we have

$$\frac{dy_A}{dz} = \frac{2k'' y_{Ao}}{\mathcal{D}_{AB}}$$

The right hand side is a constant and hence the concentration profiles are linear. Integrating once more and using the boundary condition at $z = L$, we get

$$y_{AL} - y_{Ao} = \frac{2k'' y_{Ao} L}{\mathcal{D}_{AB}}$$

or

$$y_{Ao} = y_{AL}\frac{1}{1 + \dfrac{2k'' L}{\mathcal{D}_{AB}}}$$

The flux is given by

$$N_{Az} = -2k'' C y_{Ao} = -\frac{Cy_{AL}\mathcal{D}_{AB}}{L}\frac{1}{1 + \dfrac{\mathcal{D}_{AB}}{2k'' L}}$$

An interesting way of recasting the above equation is as follows:

$$N_{Az} = -\frac{Cy_{AL}}{\dfrac{1}{2k''} + \dfrac{L}{\mathcal{D}_{AB}}}$$

Thus, we see that the driving force is the mole fraction at $z = L$, and there are two resistances to be accounted for. The first is the resistance due to diffusion. The other is due to the surface reaction. The flux is given by the ratio of driving force to the sum of the resistances.

8.3.8 Look at the results

The flux or the reaction rate increases with increasing diffusion coefficient, mole fraction in the feed ($z = L$), reaction rate constant and with decreasing L. All these are as expected. As the problem concerns diffusion and reaction, it is not customary to report a mass transfer coefficient. However, the results are reported in the form of an *effectiveness factor*, η. It is the ratio of the rate of reaction in the presence of diffusion to the rate in the absence of diffusion. If diffusion is very fast, the concentration throughout the fluid will be equal to that at the top of the tube, or y_{AL}. The consumption rate is then given by $2''Cy_{AL}$, and the flux by $-2k''Cy_{AL}$. For the low flux case, the effectiveness factor is easily calculated to be

$$\eta = \frac{1}{1 + \dfrac{2k''L}{\mathcal{D}_{AB}}}$$

As expected the effectiveness factor tends to unity as diffusion coefficient increases. As reaction rate slows down, the fluxes also decrease. Thus, it is not possible to separate the effects of high fluxes alone in a simple manner. We do not pursue this any further.

We will once again point out that the analysis is easily applicable to film model at an impervious catalyst surface, where L is equivalent to the film thickness.

8.4 SIMULTANEOUS HEAT AND MASS TRANSFER

8.4.1 Problem identification

Let us now return to the problem we considered in section 8.1 but add the complication of heat transfer as well. We will let the latent heats of the two components be different and allow heat exchange between the liquid and the vapor phases. The problem can be situated in the context of a binary packed distillation column. Our analysis is relevant at a cross section of the equipment if we use the film model. We have a binary vapor mixture brought into contact with a liquid containing the same components. Liquid becomes hotter as it descends towards the reboiler while gas cools as it rises towards the condenser. Hence, the vapor is hotter than the liquid at a given cross section. The net energy flux from vapor to the liquid is a result of both conduction and condensation. It is this we would like to include as we analyze mass transfer occurring. Refer to figure 8.4.

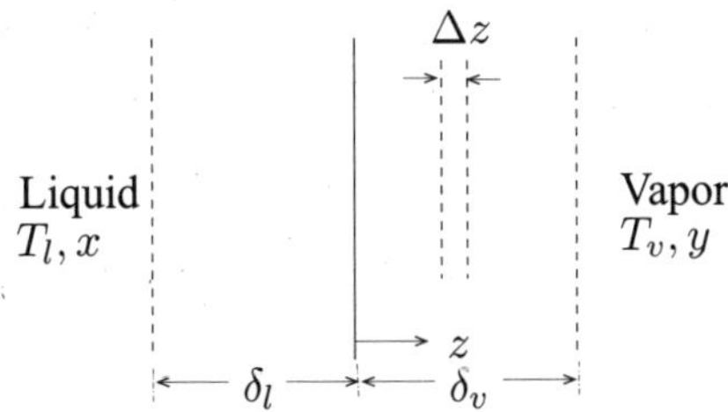

Figure 8.4. Schematic for counter diffusion of two components . The heat effects are taken into account to determine the individual fluxes of the two components instead of assuming equimolar counter diffusion or that they are in the ratio of latent heats.

Simplifications and assumptions

As the vapor–liquid equilibrium conditions are specified in terms of mole fractions, it is more convenient to use molar units. We will neglect variation in the total molar concentration due to temperature change across the film in both the phases. We analyze for steady state and will use one-dimensional film model.

8.4.2 Species mass balance

A thin shell of thickness Δz and unit area is chosen as the control volume for making a balance of A. It is unaltered from that developed in section 8.1 and gives

$$N_{Az}\big|_z - N_{Az}\big|_{z+\Delta z} = 0$$

Dividing the above equation by Δz and taking the limit of the equation as Δz goes to zero yields

$$\frac{dN_{Az}}{dz} = 0$$

Similar procedure applied to component B gives

$$\frac{dN_{Bz}}{dz} = 0$$

The mass fluxes are therefore constant. We have two phases and the above equations apply separately to both.

8.4.3 Combining balance with constitutive equation

The next step is to incorporate the constitutive equation into the mass balance. There is only one constitutive equation for a binary system and that is given by

$$\begin{aligned} N_{Az} =& J^*_{Az} + y_A C v^*_z = J^*_{Az} + y_A(N_{Az} + N_{Bz}) \\ =& - C\mathcal{D}_{AB}\frac{dy_A}{dz} + y_A(N_{Az} + N_{Bz}) \end{aligned} \tag{8.1}$$

We will not repeat the arguments given in section 8.1 here with regard to avoiding equation of motion, except reiterating that pressure is assumed to be constant across the films[9]. The mass balances will have to be written in both the phases. To simplify notation, we will first look at boundary conditions.

8.4.4 Mass transfer boundary conditions

First let us look at the interface. This is an internal boundary, and based on our experience with heat transfer, we guess that both the continuity of flux and chemical potential are of utility. As shown in section 8.1, the flux continuity specifies that the mass flux of A and B in both phases is the same.

We can then use the same symbols for fluxes in both the phases. The mass balances then simplify to

$$N_{Az} = -C\mathcal{D}_{AB,v}\frac{dy_A}{dz} + y_A(N_{Az} + N_{Bz}) \qquad 0 < z < \delta_v \tag{8.13}$$

$$= -C\mathcal{D}_{AB,l}\frac{dx_A}{dz} + x_A(N_{Az} + N_{Bz}) \qquad 0 > z > -\delta_l \tag{8.14}$$

where x and y are the mole fractions in the liquid and vapor phases. Let us assume that Raoult's law is valid. Continuity of chemical potential is equivalent to

$$y_A(z = 0) = \frac{P_{sat,A}}{P}x_A(z = 0) \tag{8.15}$$

Let us mention again that the pressure is constant across the films. The saturation vapor pressure of A has to be evaluated at the temperature of the interface. The other boundary conditions are at the ends of the mass transfer films and are given by

$$y_A = y_v, \quad z = \delta_v \tag{8.16}$$

$$x_A = x_l, \quad z = -\delta_l \tag{8.17}$$

We have two first order differential equations and two unknown fluxes. However, we have only three boundary conditions. We can therefore consider the sum of the two fluxes, $(N_{Az} + N_{Bz})$, to be an unknown that needs an equation to determine it. As mentioned in section 8.1, the enthalpy balance has to help us determine the total molar flux.

8.4.5 Enthalpy balance

We will have an energy balance in each phase. The enthalpy balance over a control volume of thickness Δz and unit area is given by

Rate of accumulation of enthalpy in the CV	=	**Net rate of input of enthalpy into the CV by convection and by diffusion**	+	**Rate of input of heat through control surfaces by conduction**	+	**Rate of generation of heat in the CV except by chemical reactions,** ***etc.***	+	**Rate of heat generation in the CV due to viscous dissipation**

We have steady state and heat generation terms are absent. Hence, we have

$$0 = \left(N_{Az}\bar{H}_A + N_{Bz}\bar{H}_B - k\frac{dT}{dz}\right)\bigg|_z - \left(N_{Az}\bar{H}_A + N_{Bz}\bar{H}_B - k\frac{dT}{dz}\right)\bigg|_{z+\Delta z}$$

for each phase. Dividing by Δz and taking limit as Δz tends to zero, we get

$$\frac{d}{dz}\left(N_{Az}\bar{H}_A + N_{Bz}\bar{H}_B - k\frac{dT}{dz}\right) = 0$$

We should note that the thermal conductivity and enthalpies are a function of composition. We will make some simplifying assumptions to illustrate the main ideas. We will assume that specific heats and thermal conductivities of both the components in both the phases are equal and are independent of temperature. We will also assume that the latent heats of the two components are different but independent of temperature. Hence, we can write in the vapor phase

$$\bar{H}_{A,v} = \lambda_A + C_p(T - T_o), \text{ and } \bar{H}_{B,v} = \lambda_B + C_p(T - T_o)$$

and in the liquid phase

$$\bar{H}_{A,l} = C_p(T - T_o), \text{ and } \bar{H}_{B,l} = C_p(T - T_o)$$

where T_o is some reference temperature. Substituting these into the energy balance, we have

$$\begin{aligned} 0 =& \frac{d}{dz}\left(N_{Az}\lambda_A + N_{Bz}\lambda_B + (N_{Az} + N_{Bz})C_p(T_v - T_o) - k_v\frac{dT_v}{dz}\right) \\ 0 =& \frac{d}{dz}\left((N_{Az} + N_{Bz})C_p(T_l - T_o) - k_l\frac{dT_l}{dz}\right) \end{aligned}$$

8.4.6 Enthalpy balance boundary conditions

As with mass transfer, we have boundary conditions specifying temperature at the ends of the films:

$$T_v = T_v(\delta_v), \quad z = \delta_v \tag{8.18}$$

$$T_l = T_l(\delta_l), \quad z = \delta_l \tag{8.19}$$

Let us turn to boundary conditions at the interface. We have the temperature continuity condition

$$T_l(0) = T_v(0) = T(0) \tag{8.20}$$

Flux continuity at the interface given by eq. 7.15 simplifies to

$$-k_v\frac{dT_v}{dz} + k_l\frac{dT_l}{dz} + N_{Az}\left(\bar{H}_{A,v} - \bar{H}_{A,l}\right) + N_{Bz}\left(\bar{H}_{B,v} - \bar{H}_{B,l}\right) = 0$$

8.4.7 Temperature and concentration profiles

Integrating the enthalpy balance equations once gives

$$e_{zv} = N_{Az}\lambda_A + N_{Bz}\lambda_B + (N_{Az} + N_{Bz})C_{pv}(T_v - T_o) - k_v\frac{dT_v}{dz} \tag{8.21}$$

$$e_{zl} = (N_{Az} + N_{Bz})C_{pl}(T_l - T_o) - k_l\frac{dT_l}{dz} \tag{8.22}$$

where e_z are constants. It is obvious that they represent energy fluxes in the z direction in the vapor and the liquid phases. Using the flux continuity boundary condition at the interface, we get

$$e_{zv} - e_{zl} = 0 \tag{8.23}$$

Now, the enthalpy balance has two first order differential equations involving two unknown energy fluxes e_{zl} and e_{zv}. But we do have four boundary conditions, namely, eqs. 8.18, 8.19, 8.20, and 8.23. The four unknowns can then be determined. However, we were short of one condition to determine the total mass flux. That is given by the condition that the temperature of the interface is a boiling point. Hence, the following condition must be satisfied:

$$\frac{P_{sat,A}\left(T(0)\right)}{P}x_A(z=0)+\frac{P_{sat,B}\left(T(0)\right)}{P}\left(1-x_A(z=0)\right)=1 \tag{8.24}$$

Liquid phase control

Due to the non-linear dependence of vapor pressures on temperature, eq. 8.24 cannot be solved in a simple way, and solutions to the whole problem cannot be displayed in a simple manner. We will present a simple case, but for a more detailed analysis, readers are referred to the paper by Ito and Asano [1]. Suppose we assume that liquid phase resistance to both heat and mass transfer controls the process. Then, we have the following simplifications:

$$y_A(0)=y_v \quad \text{and} \quad T(0)=T_v$$

where, since there is no possibility of confusion, we wrote $T_v(\delta_v)=T_v$. The above equations allow the mole fraction in the liquid phase to be calculated as

$$x_A(0)=\frac{P_{sat,A}(T_v)}{P}$$

The enthalpy balance in the vapor phase gives

$$e_{zv}=(N_{Az}\lambda_A+N_{Bz}\lambda_B)$$

Using this, the liquid phase enthalpy balance can be written as

$$e_{zv}=(N_{Az}\lambda_A+N_{Bz}\lambda_B)=e_{zl}=(N_{Az}+N_{Bz})C_p(T_l-T_o)-k_l\frac{dT_l}{dz}$$

If a further simplification is made by assuming that, in the above equation, contribution of the sensible heats can be neglected in comparison with that of latent heats, the previous equation can be integrated to obtain

$$k_l\frac{T_v-T_l}{\delta_l}=-(N_{Az}\lambda_A+N_{Bz}\lambda_B)$$

after application of the boundary conditions. A is the more volatile component. In distillation, it is expected to vaporize while B is expected to condense. We need to supply latent heat to vaporize A while heat is liberated when B condenses. The net heat liberated has to be removed. The right hand side of the previous equation is the net heat to be removed. It can only be removed through the liquid film and the left hand side represents that. By adding and subtracting $N_{Az}\lambda_B$ to the right hand side of the previous equation, it can be rearranged to get

$$N_{Az}=-k_l\frac{T_l-T_v}{\delta_l(\lambda_A-\lambda_B)}-(N_{Az}+N_{Bz})\frac{\lambda_B}{\lambda_A-\lambda_B} \tag{8.25}$$

Note that this is an equation relating N_{Az} and $N_{Az} + N_{Bz}$. This is in addition to the species mass balance eq. 8.14. Therefore, we now have enough equations and unknowns to solve the problem. Equation 8.25 can be used to solve for $N_{Az} + N_{Bz}$ in terms of N_{Az}. The result can be substituted in eq. 8.14 to obtain

$$C\mathcal{D}_{AB,l}\frac{dx_A}{dz} = -x_A\left(k_l\frac{T_v - T_l}{\delta_l\lambda_B} + \frac{\lambda_A - \lambda_A}{\lambda_B}N_{Az}\right) - N_{Az}$$

This can be solved using the two boundary conditions at the edge of the film and the interface to find the flux of A. It can be seen that transport phenomena approach allows us to analyze complicated Unit Operations such as distillation. In fact, the exact equations can be numerically integrated to avoid many assumptions we made and hence get good results.

8.5 SUMMARY AND FINAL COMMENTS

Diffusion is similar but not identical to heat conduction. Unlike conduction, diffusion alone can also generate convection. Such convective velocities however are small. Their effects are negligible for dilute solutions and pure diffusion problems in dilute solutions are identical to heat conduction problems. In general, the effects of the convective velocity can be accounted for by solving the species balance equations along with the equation of motion. However, the small values of the convective velocity allows us to assume in general that pressure drop due to them is negligible. This alone is not enough to bypass the necessity to solve the equation of motion. Some condition that allows specification of a flux or relationship between fluxes is needed to avoid simultaneous solution of the equation of motion. A few examples of this have been illustrated.

The ratio of the flux calculated by accounting for the effects of convective flux and that obtained by neglecting them is referred to as high flux correction. The setting of the problems is deliberately made similar to the classical film model. Thus, high flux corrections can be calculated for film model. Though not dealt with in this text, film model is used in this way in practice.

Problems for Chapter 8.

8.1 Suppose that the latent heats of vaporization are not equal. Let the ratio of the latent heats be ℓ. How does the analysis of section 8.1 change?

8.2 We want to illustrate issues regarding the assumptions that allow specification of the flux by the following problem. Consider vaporization of water from an aqueous solution of NaOH into a blanket of CO_2. CO_2 dissolves into aqueous NaOH, and the assumption of insolubility cannot be used. Suppose we assume that the reaction between dissolved CO_2 and Na(OH) is instantaneous and that the concentration of the alkali is large so that we need not consider its depletion. Discuss how this problem can be set up.

8.3 A very thin liquid film is suddenly exposed to equal volumes of pure gases A and B at pressure P_o and temperature T. The mass of the film is negligible, and hence it cannot support any pressure difference across it. In other words, it will move instantaneously in order to equalize pressures across it. The Henry's law constants of A and B relating their partial pressures in the gas phase to their concentrations in the liquid are H_A and H_B, respectively. The solubilities of the gases are small and hence the solutions in the liquid can be treated as dilute. Diffusion will cause movement of A and B across the liquid film. Assume that the diffusion in the liquid film can be assumed to be the controlling resistance. (What would be the criteria for testing this assumption?) Further, since the film is thin, assume that the instantaneous concentration profiles are linear. Let D_A and D_B be the diffusion coefficients of A and B in the liquid film. (a) Will the film move or not due to the diffusion of A and B? b) What will be the final position of the liquid film if gas A is insoluble in the liquid film? c) Develop an equation for the motion of the film. What will be the final position of the film when equilibrium has been reached? This experiment has been used to determine diffusion coefficient of gases in liquids. Hint: One procedure is to relate the flux through the membrane to the balance of mass in individual compartment and write an equation for the movement of the film.

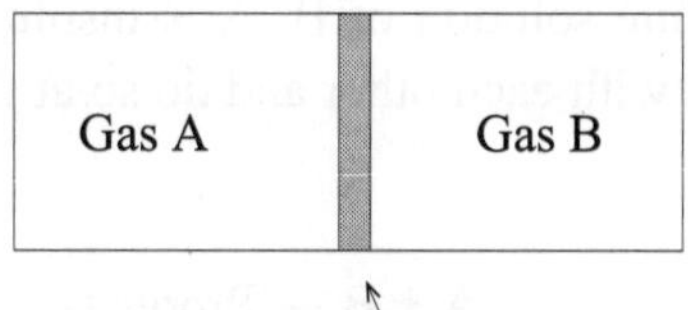

Figure for problem 8.3.

8.4 A drop of octane, suspended in a large volume of **stagnant** nitrogen, is evaporating at constant temperature and pressure. Denote the mole fraction of octane at the vapor–liquid interface by x_{Ao}, the total vapor phase density by c and the density of liquid octane by ρ_l. a) Assuming pseudo-steady state, simplify the species conservation equation for octane. What are the relevant boundary conditions? b) From the above, derive an expression for the rate of evaporation of octane. c) Assuming pseudo-steady state, derive an expression for the time required to evaporate a drop whose initial radius is R_o.

8.5 A tube contains **highly volatile** liquid C up to a height of L and it is being maintained constant. A is *sparingly soluble* in C. The equilibrium relationship between the concentration

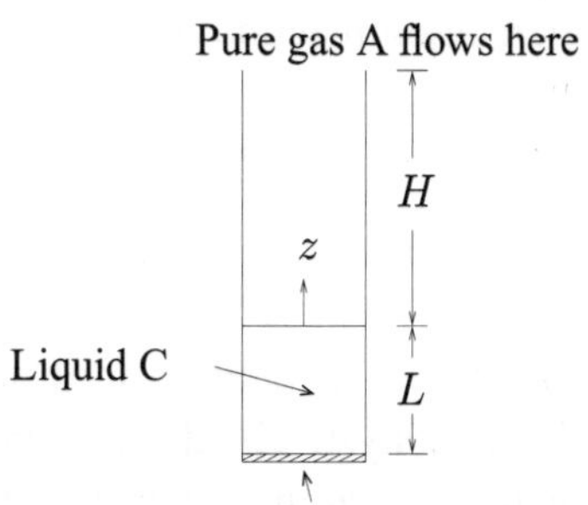

Figure for problem 8.5.

of A in the liquid phase, C_A, and the mole fraction of A in the vapor phase, x_A, is given by

$x_A = H_A C_A$ where H_A is the Henry's law constant. The bottom of the tube is made of a catalyst where A reacts irreversibly with C. Because C is in excess, the rate of reaction per *unit area* of the catalyst is given by $k'' C_A$. The reaction is exothermic and the heat liberated is $-\Delta H$ per mole of A reacted. The tube is thermally insulated. The latent heat of vaporization (per mole) of C is λ. Assume that the product formed does not influence the diffusion processes. We are interested in calculating the rate of consumption of A **at steady state**. (i) Make mass balance for species A in the liquid phase and in the vapor phase and derive the relevant differential equations. (ii) The thermal conductivity of vapors is known to be very small. As it is insulated, the heat losses through the tube are negligible. What is the mechanism through which heat of reaction is being removed? (iii) Set up the boundary conditions required. Solve the mass balances and determine the rate of consumption of A. (iv) Discuss the effect of heat of reaction and latent heat of vaporization on conversion.

8.6 Two immiscible liquid phases I and II are in contact with each other. Phase I is a dilute solution of A while II is a dilute solution of B. A is insoluble in II while B is insoluble in I. However, A and B can react with each other and do so at the **interface**.

$$\text{A} + \text{B} \rightarrow \text{Products}$$

The rate of this reaction per unit area is given by $k'' C_A C_B$ where C_A and C_B are concentrations of A and B at the interface. (a) Simplify the relevant conservation equations for steady state using film model. (b) Specify the boundary conditions. (c) Determine the concentration profiles and derive an expression for the rate of consumption of A.

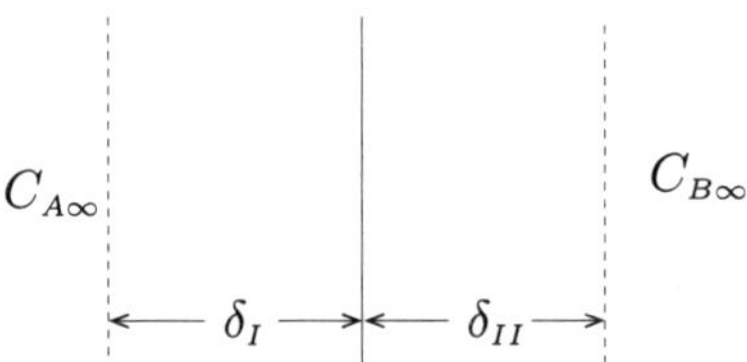

Figure for problem 8.6.

8.7 The following gas phase isomerization reaction occurs catalytically:

$$A \rightleftharpoons B$$

The equilibrium constant, K_e is a function of temperature. The reaction is endothermic and the enthalpy change upon reaction $H_B - H_A$, denoted by ΔH, is positive. Hence K_e **decreases** with decreasing temperature. A mixture of A and B is placed between two large parallel plates which are made of catalyst. The distance between the plates is δ. The isomerization reaction occurs instantaneously at the catalyst surface. One plate is maintained at T_o while the other plate is maintained at T_1 where $T_o > T_1$. The thermal conductivity, k of the gases can be taken to be equal, and constant. The diffusivity can also be taken to be constant.

Assume that neither forced nor natural convection is present. At **steady state**, calculate the energy flux at the plate which is at T_1. Is the energy flux towards the other plate or away from it?

8.8 **Photo-acoustic effect**: Consider a closed and well insulated cell. One end is a thin diaphram. At the other end, a very thin film of a volatile liquid absorbs radiation falling on it. However, its temperature is low so that it hardly emits any radiation. If the intensity of radiation falling on is varied in a periodic manner, sound is emitted by the cell. The frequency of the sound is the same as that of the intensity. (a) Explain why sound is emitted? (b) Derive the boundary conditions for mass and energy balances at the liquid-vapor interface. Alexander Graham

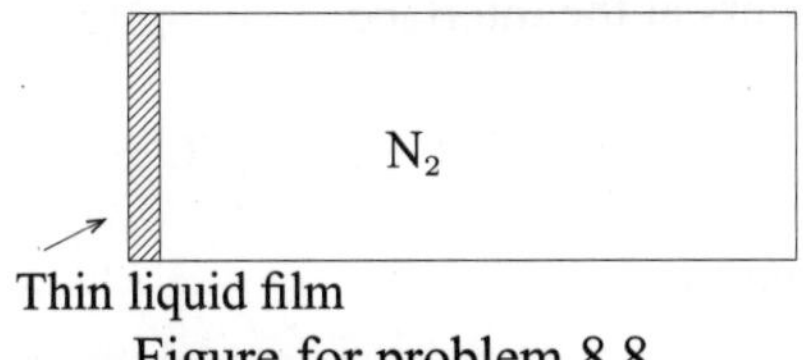

Figure for problem 8.8.

Bell made this device and referred to it as photophone. It can be used as a spectroscope to characterize the liquid used to form the film.

8.9 The following reaction occurs at a catalytic surface:

$$A \rightarrow 2B$$

The reaction is endothermic, and the heat of reaction which is nearly independent of temperature is given by ΔH. Gas A at T_f is flowing past a catalytic surface at a fast rate. The

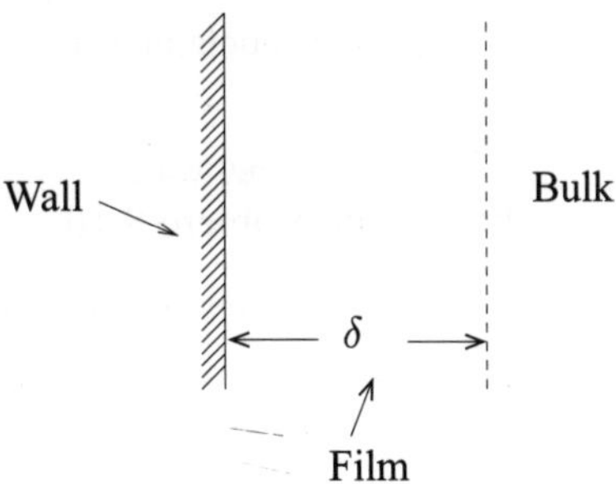

Figure for problem 8.9.

catalytic surface is at temperature T_w. We wish to calculate the rate of conversion using film theory. The rate of the reaction per unit area of the catalyst surface is given by

$$k'' x_A \, exp\left(-\frac{E}{R_g T}\right)$$

where x_A is the mole fraction of A, T is the temperature of the catalyst surface, and the rest are constants. a) Apply the film theory to derive the relevant differential equations for determining the temperature and mole fraction profiles. Assume that the total molar concentration is constant even though the temperature is varying. This would be valid if $T_w - T_f$ is not large. b) Calculate the heat flux to be supplied to the catalyst surface q_w. Is it larger than if the reaction is absent? Is it meaningful to speak of either heat or mass transfer controlling the reaction rate? c) Suppose we find that temperature at which the heat flux is zero. What would be the significance of this temperature. d) What will be the effect of having an inert gas in the system? Is it meaningful to speak of either heat transfer or mass transfer controlling the reaction rate? e) What would be the changes needed if the wall is adiabatic and $T_f > T_w$?

8.10 Liquids S_1 and S_2 are mutually insoluble. A is insoluble in S_2 while B is insoluble in S_1. The following reaction occurs at the interface

$$3A + B \rightleftharpoons 2C$$

and its intrinsic rate is given by

$$\dot{r}_s = k_{bs}C_c - k_{fs}C_aC_b$$

where C_i stand for the concentrations of the respective species in the bulk but at the interface. C is soluble in both S_1 and S_2. The solubility of C in S_1 and S_2 is C_{s1} and C_{s2} respectively. Specify all the boundary conditions that may be useful.

Channel wall

S_1 containing A

S_1 containing B

Channel wall

Figure for problem 8.10.

8.11 Consider a dilute solution of A ($NaCl$) in water (B). We are trying freeze B from a solution of concentration $C_{A,b}$ by bringing the solution in contact with plane cool wall being maintained at T_w. The melting point of B, T_m, is lowered due to the presence of A. The following

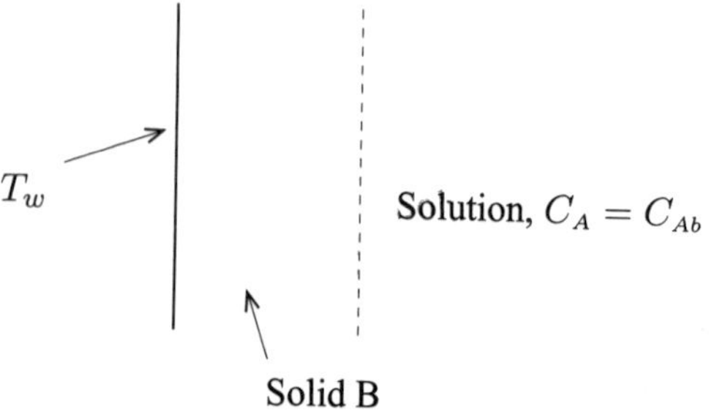

Figure for problem 8.11.

equation gives the relation between the depression in the freezing point and the concentration of A, C_A:

$$T_m = -k\,C_A$$

and upon freezing, only pure solid B forms. Let $-\Delta H_m$ be the latent heat of melting. (a) Will pure solid B formed be at a temperature higher or lower than $-k\,C_{A,b}$? (b) Use film model and pseudo-steady state assumption to determine the concentration and temperature profiles, and calculate the rate of formation of ice per unit area of the solid from the solution containing A at a bulk concentration of $C_{A,b}$ and at a temperature T_b. (c) Is this process limited by diffusion of water, salt or heat removal from solution or heat removal through ice?

8.12 Data obtained on melting of small ice spheres of radius R in a stirred vessel of pure water indicate that the Nusselt number $2hR/k$ is equal to 2. Similar ice spheres are now being melted in a stirred vessel in the same way but using 5% by weight aqueous solution of NaCl at $-1.0°$C. The following data on the solution are available. k = 1350 X 10^{-6} cal/(sec cm C), viscosity is 1.8 cp, D = 0.67 X 10^{-5}cm^2/sec, density of ice is 0.91 g/cc, and enthalpy of fusion of ice is 80 cal/g. The melting point in °C data for aqueous solution of NaCl can be approximated by $-0.6\times$ weight percent.
a) Estimate the temperature at the surface of ice spheres of size $0.2cm$ assuming that the concentration and temperature of brine does not change?
b) Calculate the time required for melting of ice spheres of initial size 0.2 cm.

Notes

[1]There will be no mass transfer if the two compositions correspond to an equilibrium state.
[2]We will look into the more general case in section 8.4.
[3]Note that $M_A N_{Az} + M_B N_{Bz} \neq 0$ and hence it follows that mass average velocity is not zero.
[4]The mass transfer coefficient corresponding to the film is easily seen to be given by $\mathcal{D}_{AB}/L$
[5]The model can also be applied to a tray column if it is assumed that the vapor and liquid phases are well mixed on each tray.
[6]This assumption can be relaxed if energy balance is incorporated.
[7]This problem is solved in many undergraduate texts and is referred to as vaporization into a *stagnant film*. The word stagnant can be interpreted to mean the velocity is small. In this particular problem, as we shall see later, the gas B remains stagnant. Reference to B is of course exact.
[8]This must not be confused with the effect of non-condensibles on condensation rate and other similar phenomena, where the introduction of non-condensibles creates a resistance that would not have been there otherwise. Here we are discussing the effect of diffusion induced convection.
[9]Note that this still permits pressure to vary across the column length.

Reference

[1] A. Ito and I. Asano. Thermal effects in non-adiabatic binary distillation. *Chem. Engg Sci.*, (4):1007–1014, 1982.

Chapter 9

CONSERVATION EQUATIONS FOR MULTICOMPONENT SYSTEMS

```
The general form of conservation equations for
   non-isothermal multicomponent systems that predict
   concentration and temperature profiles are derived.
The use of these equations is demonstrated for diffusion
   and convection problems. Calculation of concentration
   profiles in reacting systems, diffusion against
   concentration gradient, centrifugal separations, and
   diffusion in  electrolytes are new topics.
```

In chapter 8, we solved problems in mass transfer and simultaneous heat and mass transfer using shell balance approach. As was done in chapter 5, we generalize this approach and move on to derive the general balance equations for multicomponent systems. Our procedure for deriving the general balance equations is same as that followed in chapter 5. As mentioned in chapter 5, these equations form the basis for the transport phenomena approach and are also the starting point for computational fluid dynamics. We then proceed to solve problems by simplifying the general equations for specific situations.

9.1 SPECIES MASS BALANCE

We begin our effort with species balance equation. We start with eq. 7.2 derived in chapter 7

$$\frac{d}{dt}\int_{V_s(t)} \rho_i(\mathbf{x},t)dV = -\int_{A_s(t)} \mathbf{n}.\mathbf{j}_i dA + \sum_j \int_{V_s(t)} \alpha_{ij} M_i \,\dot{\mathcal{R}}_j \, dV \tag{7.2}$$

We use the transport theorem eq. 2.2

$$\frac{d}{dt}\int\limits_{V_s(t)} \phi(\mathbf{x},t) = \int\limits_{V_s(t)} \frac{\partial \phi(\mathbf{x},t)}{\partial t} dV + \int\limits_{A_s(t)} \mathbf{n}.\mathbf{v}\phi(\mathbf{x},t)dA \tag{2.2}$$

to replace the left hand side. After using the divergence theorem, we obtain the following equation:

$$\int_{V_s(t)} \left(\frac{\partial \rho_i}{\partial t} + \nabla.(\rho_i \mathbf{v}) \right) dV = \int_{V_s(t)} \left(-\nabla.\mathbf{j}_i + \sum_j \alpha_{ij} M_i \, \dot{\mathcal{R}}_j \right) dV$$

As the choice of system is arbitrary and since the equation given above is perfectly general, as was argued in chapter 5, the only way it can be valid when discontinuities are absent is by the integrands being made equal. Thus, we have the general differential equation that represents species mass balance equation:

$$\frac{\partial \rho_i}{\partial t} + \nabla.(\rho_i \mathbf{v}) = -\nabla.\mathbf{j}_i + \sum_j \alpha_{ij} M_i \, \dot{\mathcal{R}}_j \tag{9.1}$$

Noting that $\rho_i \mathbf{v} + \mathbf{j}_i = \mathbf{n}_i$, another convenient form is obtained:

$$\frac{\partial \rho_i}{\partial t} + \nabla.\mathbf{n}_i = \sum_j \alpha_{ij} M_i \, \dot{\mathcal{R}}_j \tag{9.2}$$

Another equivalent form for the mass balance is in terms of moles. If the previous equation is divided by the molecular weight we obtain the molar balance:

$$\frac{\partial C_i}{\partial t} + \nabla.\mathbf{N}_i = \sum_j \alpha_{ij} \, \dot{\mathcal{R}}_j \tag{9.3}$$

where $\mathbf{N}_i = C - i\mathbf{v}_i$. We will use either form as dictated by our convenience.

9.2 ENTHALPY BALANCE

Now let us consider the energy balance equation. We start with equation 7.13:

$$\int_{V_s(t)} \frac{\partial}{\partial t}(\rho \hat{H}) dV + \int_{A_s(t)} \mathbf{n}.(\rho \mathbf{v} \hat{H}) dA =$$

$$- \int_{A_s(t)} \mathbf{n}. \left(\sum_i \mathbf{j}_i \frac{\bar{H}_i}{M_i} \right) dA - \int_{A_s(t)} \mathbf{n}.\mathbf{q} dA + \int_{V_s(t)} \rho \, \dot{Q}_m \, dV - \int_{V_s} \frac{DP}{Dt} dV + \int_{V_s(t)} \boldsymbol{\tau}{:}\nabla \mathbf{v} dV \tag{7.13}$$

After using the divergence theorem, we get

$$\int_{V_s(t)} \left(\frac{\partial}{\partial t}(\rho \hat{H}) dV + \nabla.(\rho \mathbf{v} \hat{H}) \right) dV = \int_{V_s(t)} \left(-\nabla. \left(\sum_i \mathbf{j}_i \frac{\bar{H}_i}{M_i} \right) - \nabla.\mathbf{q} + \rho \, \dot{Q}_m - \frac{DP}{Dt} + \boldsymbol{\tau}{:}\nabla \mathbf{v} \right) dV$$

Once again, as argued earlier, the above equation can be valid in general only if the integrands are equal:

$$\frac{\partial}{\partial t}(\rho \hat{H}) + \nabla.(\rho \mathbf{v} \hat{H}) = -\nabla. \left(\sum_i \mathbf{j}_i \frac{\bar{H}_i}{M_i} \right) - \nabla.\mathbf{q} + \rho \, \dot{Q}_m - \frac{DP}{Dt} + \boldsymbol{\tau}{:}\nabla \mathbf{v}$$

Noting that $\rho\hat{H} = \sum_i \rho_i \bar{H}_i/M_i$ and that $\mathbf{n}_i = \rho_i \mathbf{v} + \mathbf{j}_i$, the previous equation is written in a readily interpretable form as

$$\sum_i \left(\frac{\partial}{\partial t}\left(\rho_i \frac{\bar{H}_i}{M_i}\right) + \nabla.\left(\mathbf{n}_i \frac{\bar{H}_i}{M_i}\right)\right) = -\nabla.\mathbf{q} + \rho\,\dot{Q}_m - \frac{DP}{Dt} + \boldsymbol{\tau}:\nabla\mathbf{v} \tag{9.4}$$

The rate of accumulation of the enthalpy of a mixture and change in the enthalpy due to convection and diffusion of species is equal to heat supplied to it by conduction and heat generation due to viscous friction as well as non-chemical reactive sources minus a small change due to change in pressure.

We derive a variant of the above equation to explicitly demonstrate the effects of heats of reaction. The left hand side of eq. 9.4 can be expanded

$$\sum_i \rho_i \left(\frac{\partial}{\partial t}\frac{\bar{H}_i}{M_i} + \mathbf{v}_i.\nabla \frac{\bar{H}_i}{M_i}\right) + \sum_i \frac{\bar{H}_i}{M_i}\left(\frac{\partial \rho_i}{\partial t} + \nabla.\mathbf{n}_i\right)$$

where we replaced $\mathbf{n}_i$ by $\rho_i \mathbf{v}_i$. Replacing the second group of terms using the mass balance for i^{th} species, eq. 9.2, the equation given above can be written as

$$\sum_i \rho_i \left(\frac{\partial}{\partial t}\frac{\bar{H}_i}{M_i} + \mathbf{v}_i.\nabla \frac{\bar{H}_i}{M_i}\right) + \sum_j \sum_i (\alpha_{ij}\bar{H}_i)\,\dot{\mathcal{R}}_j$$

But $\sum_i(\alpha_{ij}\bar{H}_i) = (\Delta H)_j$, the change in enthalpy due to j^{th} reaction. Substituting all these results into eq. 9.4, we get

$$\sum_i \rho_i \left(\frac{\partial}{\partial t}\frac{\bar{H}_i}{M_i} + \mathbf{v}_i.\nabla \frac{\bar{H}_i}{M_i}\right) = -\nabla.\mathbf{q} - \frac{DP}{Dt} + \rho\,\dot{Q}_m + \boldsymbol{\tau}:\nabla\mathbf{v} + \sum_j (-\Delta H)_j\,\dot{\mathcal{R}}_j \tag{9.5}$$

As we move along with a packet of multicomponent mixture and observe it, we will find that its enthalpy changes, first due to change in enthalpy of species and, second due to change in the amount of species contained in it. The left hand side of eq. 9.5 is the first effect. The second effect is due to heats of reactions, and the corresponding term has now been moved to the right hand side of eq. 9.5. $-\Delta H_j$ is the heat liberated due to j^{th} reaction. The total heat liberated by all reactions is obtained when $-\Delta H_j$ is multiplied by the rate of jth reaction (which causes change in the amounts of species) and summed over all reactions. That is the last term on the right hand side of eq. 9.5. If we substitute for enthalpy in terms of temperature, we will recover the form that is normally used in books on chemical reaction engineering. For example, consider ideal solutions with constant specific heats. Then

$$\sum_i \rho_i \hat{C}_{pi} \left(\frac{\partial T}{\partial t} + \mathbf{v}_i.\nabla T\right) = -\nabla.\mathbf{q} - \frac{DP}{Dt} + \rho\,\dot{Q}_m + \boldsymbol{\tau}:\nabla\mathbf{v} + \sum_j (-\Delta H)_j\,\dot{\mathcal{R}}_j$$

Further, if we have dilute solutions, the contributions made by dilute species to the convective velocity and specific heats are negligible. Hence, we can rewrite the previous equation as

$$\rho\hat{C}_p\left(\frac{\partial T}{\partial t}+\mathbf{v}.\nabla T\right)=-\nabla.\mathbf{q}-\frac{DP}{Dt}+\rho\,\dot{Q}_m+\boldsymbol{\tau}{:}\nabla\mathbf{v}+\sum_j(-\Delta H)_j\,\dot{\mathcal{R}}_j$$

This is a form that is also commonly used in reaction engineering literature. The text by Bird *et al.* [1] gives many other forms which might be more suitable for specific purposes.

9.3 CONSTITUTIVE EQUATIONS

9.3.1 Newton–Stokes law of viscosity

Generally speaking, multicomponent mixtures of simple molecules do follow Newton–Stokes law of viscosity. Thus, we can still write

$$\boldsymbol{\tau}=\mu\left(\nabla\mathbf{v}+(\nabla\mathbf{v})^t\right)-\frac{2}{3}\,\mu\,\mathbf{I}\,\nabla.v \qquad \text{(A5.30)}$$

It should be noted that viscosity will in general be a function of temperature and concentration.

9.3.2 Fourier's law

The constitutive equations for heat flux due to molecular mechanisms in multicomponent fluids are more complex than in pure fluids. Temperature gradients cause heat flux by conduction. The rate of the conductive heat flux is, as before, given by Fourier's law

$$\mathbf{q}_c=-k\nabla T$$

where subscript c stands for conduction. In addition to this, it turns out that the presence of concentration gradients also causes a heat flux. This effect is known as *Dufour effect.* Let the Dufour flux be denoted by $\mathbf{q}_d$. The total heat flux $\mathbf{q}$ appearing in eqs. 7.13 and 9.5 is therefore given by $\mathbf{q}_c+\mathbf{q}_d$. In addition to both these, as discussed in chapter 7, we have energy flux due to diffusive flux of species. Thus, the total *heat flux by molecular mechanism* is given by

$$-k\nabla T+\mathbf{q}_d+\sum_i^N\frac{\dot{\mathbf{j}}_i}{M_i}\bar{H}_i$$

The Dufour flux is generally small and we do not consider this any further. As with viscosity, thermal conductivity can also be a function of temperature and concentration.

9.3.3 Laws of multicomponent diffusion

In section 7.3, we indicated that the driving force for diffusion is the gradient of chemical potential. We also indicated there that diffusion can occur by driving forces other than concentration gradient. Chemical potential is not just a function of composition. For example, electrical potential will also influence the chemical potential of ionic species. Thus, diffusive fluxes are created by several driving forces and there are four corresponding diffusive fluxes. They are

1. Flux due to mole fraction gradient. This we were dealing with as the flux due to concentration gradient.

2. Flux due to temperature gradient. Just as heat flux is created by concentration gradients, diffusive mass flux is created due to temperature gradients. This is known as *Soret effect* or *thermal diffusion*. It turns out that this is not negligible and in fact is used in separation of radioactive isotopes. *But in this text, we will ignore this flux also.*

3. Flux due to pressure gradients. Pressure gradients cause gradients in the Gibbs free energy and create a driving force for motion. Gibbs free energy increases with pressure and the increase contributed by each component in a multicomponent mixture is proportional to its partial molar volume. Thus, when a pressure gradient is created, the gradient in Gibbs free energy experienced by each species will be different. Hence, pressure gradient causes relative movement of different species.

4. Flux due to forced diffusion or differential action of body forces on different species. The most common example of this is the diffusion of ions in electrical fields.

The above fluxes exist in binary systems also. Apart from this however, further complications are in store for multicomponent mixtures. As molecules of a species diffuse, they interact with molecules of other species and other molecules of their own species. Thus, one can expect that the rate of diffusion of a species is affected by gradients in chemical potential of other species. This makes the constitutive equations for multicomponent mixtures fairly complex.

Stefan–Maxwell equations

There are two ways of writing the constitutive equations for multicomponent mixtures. To derive a constitutive equation for diffusion in section 7.3, we used the idea that the driving force was equal and opposite in sign to the frictional force. The latter was given by the velocity due to diffusion divided by mobility. In one method, this idea is generalized to write constitutive equations for multicomponent systems. This results in the *Stefan–Maxwell form*[1]. Let the velocity of ith species be $\mathbf{v}_i$. The relative velocity between i^{th} species and j^{th}species is given by $\mathbf{v}_i - \mathbf{v}_j$. The frictional force on i^{th} species in a unit volume of mixture due to relative motion between it and j^{th} species is proportional to the relative velocity and the number of "contacts" between i^{th} and j^{th} species. The latter is proportional to $y_i y_j$ where where y is the mole fraction and subscript is the index ¿ corresponding to species. Let the proportionality constant for the frictional force between i and j species be $C\mathcal{R}T/\mathsf{D}_{ij}$, where C is the total molar concentration, $\mathcal{R}$ is the gas constant, T is the absolute temperature, and D_{ij} are known as the *Stefan–Maxwell diffusion coefficients*. Since frictional force exerted by i^{th} species on j^{th} species is equal and opposite to that exerted by j^{th} species on i^{th} species, Stefan–Maxwell diffusion coefficients must be symmetric or $\mathsf{D}_{ij} = \mathsf{D}_{ji}$. The total frictional force on i^{th} species is obtained by summing the frictional force between it and all the other species. Noting that it is opposite in sign to the relative velocity, it is given by

$$-C\mathcal{R}T \sum_j \frac{y_i y_j}{\mathsf{D}_{ij}} (\mathbf{v}_i - \mathbf{v}_j)$$

This can be rewritten in terms of the molar fluxes as

$$-\mathcal{R}T\sum_j \frac{1}{\mathsf{D}_{ij}}\left(y_j\mathbf{N}_i - y_i\mathbf{N}_j\right)$$

or

$$-\mathcal{R}T\sum_j \frac{1}{\mathsf{D}_{ij}}\left(y_j\mathbf{J}_i^* - y_i\mathbf{J}_j^*\right)$$

which is in terms of diffusive fluxes.

The driving force for creating a mass average velocity is the sum of the body forces and pressure forces.[2] The body forces on different species can in principle be different. Thus, the driving force for creating the mass average velocity per unit mass is given by

$$-\frac{1}{\rho}\nabla P + \sum_j w_j\mathbf{g_j}$$

The contribution of this average force on i^{th} species per unit mass of the mixture is obtained by multiplying it with the mass fraction of ith species. Equivalently, the same contribution *per unit volume of mixture* is obtained by multiplying it with the mass concentration of ith species. It is given by

$$-w_i\nabla P + \rho_i\sum_j w_j\mathbf{g_j}$$

The driving force[3] on i^{th} species, per unit volume of mixture, is given by the gradient of Gibbs free energy:

$$-C_i(\nabla\mu_i)_{T,P} - C_i\bar{V}_i\nabla P + \rho_i\mathbf{g}_i$$

where $\bar{V}_i$ is the partial molar volume of ith species. Note that $C_i\bar{V}_i$ is equal to ϕ_i the volume fraction of ith species. Diffusion is the motion over and above the average motion. Hence, the driving force for diffusion is the difference between the force on i^{th} species and the average driving force acting on the same species. It is given by

$$-C_i(\nabla\mu_i)_{T,P} - (\phi_i - w_i)\nabla p + \rho_i\left(\mathbf{g_i} - \sum_j w_j\mathbf{g}_j\right) \equiv C\mathcal{R}T\mathbf{d}_i \tag{9.6}$$

where we have defined $\mathbf{d}_i$ for later use. The sum of the driving force for diffusion of ith species and the frictional force experienced by i^{th} species as they move due to diffusion must be zero[4]. Thus, we get

$$-C_i(\nabla\mu_i)_{T,P} - (\phi_i - w_i)\nabla p + \rho_i\left(\mathbf{g}_i - \sum_j w_j\mathbf{g_j}\right) \quad = \quad C\mathcal{R}T\sum_j \frac{y_iy_j}{\mathsf{D}_{ij}}\left(\mathbf{v}_i - \mathbf{v}_j\right)$$

$$= \mathcal{R}T \sum_j \frac{1}{\mathsf{D}_{ij}} (y_j \mathbf{N}_i - y_i \mathbf{N}_j)$$

$$= \mathcal{R}T \sum_j \frac{1}{\mathsf{D}_{ij}} \left(y_j \mathbf{J}_i^* - y_i \mathbf{J}_j^*\right)$$

$$i = 1, 2 \ldots, N-1, N \qquad (9.7)$$

These are known as *Stefan–Maxwell* equations. It is important to note some properties of these equations. As mentioned in section 7.3, there can only be $N-1$ independent diffusive fluxes. Since D_{ij} are symmetric, when the left and right hand sides of the above equations are summed for all species, they both are found to be equal to zero. Hence, as they should be, only $N-1$ of the N Stefan Maxwell equations are independent.

Note that the equations give the driving force on i^{th} species as a function of the fluxes. *This is an inconvenient form because mass balances require explicit expressi* *n terms of mole fraction or concentration gradients.* Moreover, they do pose a probl ns but not insurmountable ones. However, Stefan Maxwell form natural of gases and hence is considered to be more fundamental in some ns, the Stefan Maxwell diffusion coefficients are found to be sar ients. This fact is of a great advantage as one need not m nts separately at least in some systems. This equality is hov nsiderable amount of work has been done to relate Stefan–M oefficients.

Fick's law form

Another way of writing a co ick's law and express the diffusive flux as a function of the driv

This is known as re known as the generalized Fick's law coefficients. As res, the Fick's law form is an explicit expression for flu ration. Therefore, they are more convenient to use in mas *l equations can be inverted* to obtain Fick's law form. Ho nly $N-1$ of the Stefan Maxwell equations are independent and h *of the entire set before inversion.* There cannot be a gener

A about Fick's law form. Consider for simplicity that only usion, and that the multicomponent mixture is ideal. Then, y to

$$-\nabla y_i = \sum_j \frac{1}{\mathsf{D}_{ij}} \left(y_j \mathbf{J}_i^* - y_i \mathbf{J}_j^*\right)$$

Suppose that Stefan–Maxwell diffusion coefficients are constants. If we invert Stefan–Maxwell equations and put them in the form of Fick's law, we will get equations like

$$\mathbf{J}_i^* = -C \sum_j \mathbb{D}_{ij} \nabla y_j$$

As can be seen from the simplified Stefan–Maxwell equations shown here, the diffusion coefficients appearing in the Fick's law form will be a function of D_{ij} *and composition.* Hence, even if Stefan–Maxwell diffusion coefficients are independent of composition, the Fick's law coefficients will not be. More over, the Fick's law coefficient, $\mathbb{D}_{ij}$ will be a function of *all* Stefan–Maxwell diffusivities and not just D_{ij}. Let us demonstrate this from the inverse of Stefan–Maxwell equations for a ternary system given in the text by Bird *et al.* [1]. For example, the inverse gives

$$\mathbb{D}_{12} = \mathsf{D}_{12}\left(1 + \frac{y_3[(M_3/M_2)\mathsf{D}_{13} - \mathsf{D}_{12}]}{y_1\mathsf{D}_{23} + y_2\mathsf{D}_{13} + y_3\mathsf{D}_{12}}\right)$$

Equivalence for binary system: We will demonstrate that Fick's law form and Stefan–Maxwell form for a binary system are equivalent, and relate the diffusion coefficients appearing in the two forms. This is directly possible because only one constitutive equation is present. Let $i = 1$ be A and $i = 2$ be B. After noting that sum of diffusive fluxes is equal to zero and sum of mole fractions is equal to unity, the right hand side of eq. 9.7 for $i = 1$ simplifies to

$$\mathcal{R}T\frac{1}{\mathsf{D}_{AB}}\mathbf{J}_A^*$$

Hence, Stefan–Maxwell equations give

$$\mathcal{R}T\frac{1}{\mathsf{D}_{AB}}\mathbf{J}_A^* = -C_A(\nabla\mu_A)_{T,P} - (\phi_A - w_A)\nabla p + \rho_A(\mathbf{g}_A - w_A\mathbf{g}_A - w_B\mathbf{g}_B)$$

But $\mu_A = \mathcal{R}T\ln a_A$ where, a_A is the activity of species A. Using this, and also the fact that sum of weight fractions is equal to unity, we will get

$$\mathbf{J}_A^* = -C\mathsf{D}_{AB}\left(y_A\nabla\ln a_A + \frac{1}{C\mathcal{R}T}(\phi_A - w_A)\nabla p - \frac{\rho w_A w_B}{C\mathcal{R}T}(\mathbf{g}_A - \mathbf{g}_B)\right)$$

We have defined Fick's law of diffusivity by

$$\mathbf{J}_A^* = -C\mathcal{D}_{AB}\nabla y_A$$

where $\mathcal{D}_{AB}$ is known as the binary diffusivity. Thus, we see that, *in a binary system,* the Stefan–Maxwell diffusivity and binary diffusivity are related by

$$\mathcal{D}_{AB} = \frac{d\ln a_A}{d\ln y_A}\mathsf{D}_{AB}$$

There is considerable confusion in the definitions and one must clearly understand, especially when looking up data, as to what was defined and measured. The relationship given shows that, in general, *only for a binary system*, the binary diffusivity is nearly the same as the Stefan–Maxwell diffusivity. Apart from the usual flux caused by concentration gradients, diffusive fluxes due to pressure gradient, and body forces that act differentially on different species, are explicitly seen in the above equation.

Special forms

The constitutive equations do look very complex. Moreover, as pointed out earlier, Stefan–Maxwell equations are inconvenient to use in species mass balance equations. One does look for cases where these equations can be conveniently converted to Fick's law forms. It is therefore good to look at some limiting approximations to get a feel for the equations. In this section, we focus on diffusion due to concentration gradients only.

1. *One component is special*: In a mixture, it is possible that there is a special component, usually the solvent. Generally speaking, we are not interested in its diffusive flux but in the diffusive fluxes of the other components. In this instance, we choose the solvent to be the component for which we do not write Stefan–Maxwell equations. This is done formally and exactly. Let us denote the solvent by subscript N. We now choose the reference velocity for defining fluxes to be $\mathbf{v}_N$:

$$\mathbf{J}_i^N = C_i(\mathbf{v}_i - \mathbf{v}_N) \quad i = 1, 2, \ldots (N-1)$$

The superscript N reminds us that the diffusive flux is defined with respect to the velocity of the solvent or the Nth component. By definition, then the diffusive flux of solvent is zero and its total flux is given by only convective flux: $C_N\mathbf{v}_N$. It is implicitly assumed that when the equation of motion is solved, the velocity determined is nearly equal to $\mathbf{v}_N$. *It is important to note that by this definition,* $\sum_i \mathbf{J}_i^N \neq 0$. The total fluxes of other species are given by $C_i\mathbf{v}_N + \mathbf{J}_i^N$. Now the right hand side of Stefan–Maxwell equations shown in eq. 9.7 are written for $i = 1, 2 \ldots N-1$ as

$$\begin{aligned} C\mathcal{R}T \sum_{j=1,\neq i}^{N} \frac{y_i y_j}{\mathsf{D}_{ij}} (\mathbf{v}_i - \mathbf{v}_j) &= \mathcal{R}T \sum_{j=1,\neq i}^{N} \frac{1}{\mathsf{D}_{ij}} \left(y_j \mathbf{J}_i^N - y_i \mathbf{J}_j^N \right) \\ &= \mathcal{R}T \left(\sum_{j=1,\neq i}^{N} \frac{y_j}{\mathsf{D}_{ij}} \right) \mathbf{J}_i^N - \mathcal{R}T \sum_{j=1,\neq i}^{N-1} \left(\frac{y_i}{\mathsf{D}_{ij}} \right) \mathbf{J}_j^N \quad (9.8) \\ &= \mathbf{B}.\mathbf{J}^N \quad (9.9) \end{aligned}$$

Note carefully the limits on the summation symbol. Here, **B** is an $(N-1) \times (N-1)$ matrix. The first term on the right hand side is its diagonal element. **J** is the vector of diffusive fluxes.

Stefan–Maxwell equations can then be written as

$$-C_i(\nabla\mu_i)_{T,P} - (\phi_i - w_i)\,\nabla p + \rho_i\left(\mathbf{g}_i - \sum_j w_j\mathbf{g_j}\right) = (\mathbf{B.J}^N)_i, \quad i = 1, 2\ldots, N-1$$

The advantage of this form is that **B** is a well defined matrix. If needed, it can be inverted and the Stefan Maxwell form can be converted to Fick's law form. In this way, it can be used in mass conservation equations. This form does allow for interaction between species.

2. *Dilute solutions*: Like earlier, we refer to the case where one component is being considered as solvent. As a further special case, let it be the major component and the rest are present to only minor extents. This is nothing but a dilute solution. In this case, for all j other than the solvent, $y_j \sim 0$ and $y_N \sim 1$. Thus, $y_j\mathbf{J}_i^N \sim 0$ except for $y_N\mathbf{J}_i^N$ which is approximately equal to $\mathbf{J}_i^N$. Thus, **B** is diagonal. We also neglect all other driving forces. Then Stefan–Maxwell equations simplify to

$$-C_i(\nabla\mu_i)_{T,P} = \mathcal{R}T\frac{1}{\mathsf{D}_{iN}}\mathbf{J}_i^N$$

or

$$\mathbf{J}_i^N = -C\mathsf{D}_{iN}y_i\nabla\text{ln}a_i = -C\mathcal{D}_{iN}\nabla y_i, \; i = 1, 2, \ldots N-2, N-1$$

and

$$\mathbf{J}_i^N = -C\mathcal{D}_{iN}\nabla y_i + C_i\mathbf{v}_N, \; i = 1, 2, \ldots N-2, N-1$$

All species obey Fick's law with a diffusivity of the species in the solvent. Thus, the diluteness of the components allows us to neglect interactions between diffusing species and the constitutive equation for a species is that of a binary system of that species and the solvent. Consequently, mass balances of all species can be treated independently, except of course if there are chemical reactions.

3. *Effective binary diffusivity*: One can define an effective binary diffusivity following the Fick's law form:

$$\mathbf{N}_i = -\mathcal{D}_{im}C\nabla y_i + y_i\sum_j\mathbf{N}_j = -\mathcal{D}_{im}\frac{d\text{ln }y_i}{d\text{ln }a_i}C_i\nabla\text{ln }a_i + y_i\sum_j\mathbf{N}_j$$

Using $\nabla\mu_i = \mathcal{R}T\nabla\text{ln}a_i$, the above expression can be recast as

$$-C_i\nabla\mu_i = \mathcal{R}T\frac{\mathbf{N_i} - y_i\sum\mathbf{N_j}}{\mathcal{D}_{im}(d\text{ln }y_i/d\text{ln }a_i)}$$

By comparing this with the Stefan–Maxwell form, we can deduce

$$\frac{1}{(d\text{ln }y_i/d\text{ln }a_i)\mathcal{D}_{im}} = \frac{\sum_j(1/\mathsf{D}_{ij})\,(y_j\mathbf{N}_i - y_i\mathbf{N}_j)}{\mathbf{N}_i - y_i\sum_j\mathbf{N}_j}$$

The effective diffusivity form is of use in computations. A special case of this is when all components except i^{th} are stationary. It could occur in absorption is a mixture of non-volatile solvents. Then, the given equation simplifies to

$$\frac{1 - y_i}{(d\ln y_i / d\ln a_i)\mathcal{D}_{im}} = \sum_{j \neq i} \frac{y_j}{\mathsf{D}_{ij}}$$

Summary: If you get the impression that the constitutive equations for diffusion in multi-component systems are complex, you are absolutely right! Generally speaking, Stefan–Maxwell form of the constitutive equations are used when it is necessary to account for the presence and diffusion of all species in a mixture. Easier to use forms are applicable to some special cases. The first of them is when we are not interested in the diffusive flux of one component, when it can be treated as the solvent. In this case, Stefan–Maxwell equations can be inverted to obtain Fick's law form and substituted into mass balance equations. Another approach is to derive effective binary diffusivity that goes along with Fick's law from Stefan–Maxwell equations for use in mass balance equations. Both these approaches however can only be used in computational approach. If the solutions are dilute, interactions between species are negligible and Fick's law for a binary system is valid for each species. That of course makes life very easy!

Let us now consider solving a few problems using the general equations.

9.4 MASS TRANSFER IN A WETTED WALL COLUMN

9.4.1 Problem identification

We start with a convection problem. A wetted wall column is a standard apparatus to determine diffusion coefficients of gaseous (or vaporous) solutes in liquids. In this apparatus, a thin film of a liquid flows down the outside or inside wall of a tube. See figure on the left side of figure 9.1. In the section where the flow is fully developed, the falling film is exposed to the desired solute,

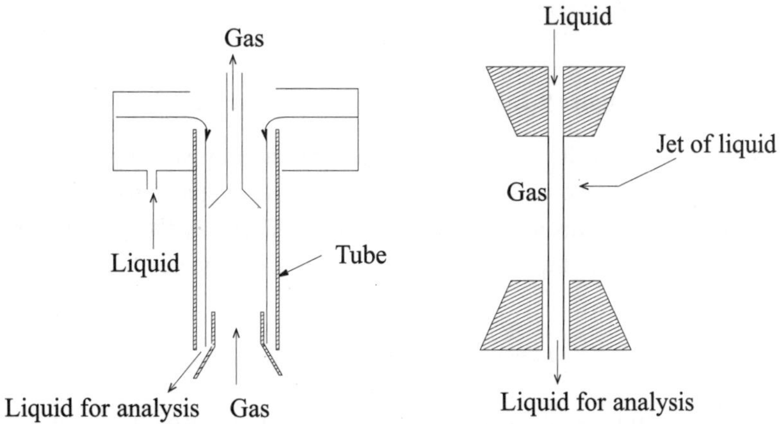

Figure 9.1. Sketch on the left is a wetted wall column. Sketch on the right is a liquid jet apparatus.

which, as we mentioned earlier is in pure[6] vapor or gaseous form. After steady state has been achieved, the liquid can be collected and the average concentration of the solute in it is measured. This measurement combined with the volumetric flow rate gives the total mass transfer rate. It is desired to calculate the diffusion coefficient of the solute in the liquid from the mass transfer rate. The flow is maintained in the laminar regime and the *time of exposure to the solute is generally short.* That should ring bells sounding "Leveque" in your mind. As we learnt from Leveque's solution in chapter 5, the depth of penetration of heat is small when contact time was short, and we expect the same here: the depth of penetration of solute into the bulk of the liquid will be small. Another common apparatus for measuring diffusion coefficients uses a jet of liquid. Here also, the jet of liquid is exposed to a vapor of or a gaseous solute for short times. One would expect that the analyses of both apparatus will follow similar lines. The difference between the Leveque solution of chapter 5 and the ones here is the following. In the heat transfer problem we considered in chapter 5, heat flows into the fluid film from the wall side, whereas in the mass transfer problems being considered now, diffusion occurs *from the free surface* or the gas-liquid interface.

Species mass balance

Let us consider that heat effects are negligible. If the film thickness is small compared to the tube diameter, we can treat the problem in rectangular coordinates as was done in treating the Leveque problem in chapter 5. Figure 9.2 shows the coordinate system. As the flow is fully developed, it

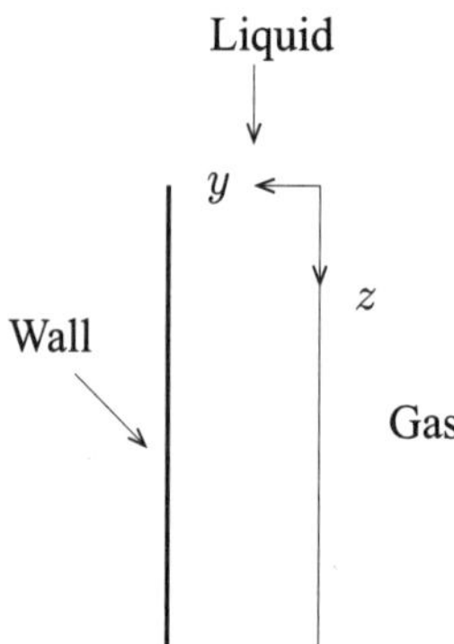

Figure 9.2. Falling film exposed to pure gas.

will be one dimensional. The velocity profile can be obtained by solving the equation of motion, and let it be denoted by $v_z(y)$. We will assume that the solute is sparingly soluble in the liquid and hence *the solutions are dilute.* This allows us to put *bulk velocity in the y direction to zero.* Let the concentration of the solute in the liquid be C. The steady state species balance equation simplifies to

$$v_z \frac{\partial C}{\partial z} = \mathcal{D} \left(\frac{\partial^2 C}{\partial z^2} + \frac{\partial^2 C}{\partial y^2} \right)$$

The axial diffusion term will be neglected in comparison with the diffusion in the y-direction while retaining the convection term in the y-direction. Detailed arguments for this have been presented in the section on Leveque solution in chapter 5. As the depth of penetration is small, only the velocity near the surface will be relevant. Thus, we can expand the velocity in the form of Taylor' series:

$$v_z(y) = v_z(0) + \left.\frac{dv_z}{dy}\right|_{y=0} y$$

Since the viscosity of gas is very small compared to the viscosity of the liquid, shear stress at the gas–liquid interface will be very small, and hence the velocity gradient at the gas-liquid interface will be zero. For the same reason, the velocity will be maximum there. As the velocity gradient is zero, the second term in the expansion for the velocity will be zero and the first term can be denoted by v_{max}. The species balance simplifies to

$$v_{max}\frac{\partial C}{\partial z} = \mathcal{D}\frac{\partial^2 C}{\partial y^2}$$

Boundary conditions

As the liquid is pure, it does not contain any solute before it is exposed to the vapor. At the gas-liquid interface, chemical equilibrium prevails and hence the concentration will be equal to the solubility of the gas in the liquid. As the depth of penetration is small, the concentration of solute in the liquid film at the wall end of the film will be zero. These constitute the boundary conditions and can written as

$$\begin{aligned} C &= 0 \quad \text{at} \quad z = 0 \quad \text{and at} \quad y = \delta \\ C &= C_s \quad \text{at} \quad y = 0 \end{aligned}$$

Since v_{max} is a constant, we can let $t = z/v_{max}$ and transform the equation into a more familiar form

$$\frac{\partial C}{\partial t} = \mathcal{D}\frac{\partial^2 C}{\partial y^2} \tag{9.10}$$

and t can be interpreted as the contact or 'penetration' time. We obtained a similarity solution to this equation for a *semi-infinite* slab in chapter 5. We can reduce our present problem to that if we can assume that the depth of penetration of the solute is very small compared to δ because we can then treat the liquid film as semi-infinite in extent. Then the boundary condition $C = 0$ at $y = \delta$ can be written as $C = 0$ as $y \to \infty$. We will make this assumption and then the boundary conditions will change to

$$\begin{aligned} C &= 0 \quad \text{at} \quad t = 0 \quad \text{and as} \quad y \to \infty \\ C &= C_s \quad \text{at} \quad y = 0 \end{aligned}$$

9.4.2 Concentration profiles

Similarity solution

Similarity solution of section 5.12 applies. All we have to do is to change the thermal diffusivity to mass diffusivity. The similarity variable for this problem is given by

$$\eta = \sqrt{\frac{y^2}{4\mathcal{D}t}} = \sqrt{\frac{y^2 v_{max}}{4\mathcal{D}z}}$$

The solution is given by

$$\frac{C}{C_s} = 1 - \text{erf}(\eta)$$

We only had to change the thermal diffusivity to mass diffusivity.

9.4.3 Look at the results

As expected concentration decreases into the film thickness, and increases with time or with axial length due absorption.

Mass transfer coefficient

We can determine the mass flux from the gradient at $y = 0$. Thus,

$$N_y = -\mathcal{D}\left.\frac{\partial C}{\partial y}\right|_{y=0} = -\mathcal{D}\left.\frac{dC}{d\eta}\right|_{\eta=0}\left.\frac{\partial \eta}{\partial y}\right|_{y=0} = C_s\sqrt{\frac{\mathcal{D}v_{max}}{\pi z}}$$

The local low flux[7] mass transfer coefficient is given by

$$k_{m,loc} = \frac{N_y}{C_s - C_b} = \sqrt{\frac{\mathcal{D}v_{max}}{\pi z}}$$

But the bulk concentration will still be zero since the depth of penetration is small. Hence,

$$k_{m,loc} = \sqrt{\frac{\mathcal{D}v_{max}}{\pi z}}\frac{C_s}{C_s - C_b}$$

The average value of mass transfer coefficient over a length Z can be calculated and, after some rearrangement, is given by

$$\frac{k_{m,avg}Z}{\mathcal{D}} = \frac{2}{\sqrt{\pi}}\sqrt{\frac{Zv_{max}}{\mathcal{D}}}$$

The total rate at which solute is absorbed per unit width, in a length of Z is given by

$$k_{m,avg}ZC_s = \mathcal{D}\frac{2}{\sqrt{\pi}}\sqrt{\frac{Zv_{max}}{\mathcal{D}}}$$

and, if it is measured, the diffusion coefficient can be calculated from it. We see from the relationship for the average mass transfer coefficient that the average Sherwood number is proportional to the square root of the product of Reynolds number and Schmidt number or Peclet number:

$$Sh_{avg} = \frac{2}{\sqrt{\pi}}\sqrt{Re_z Sc} = \frac{2}{\sqrt{\pi}}\sqrt{Pe_z}$$

In the Leveque problem we found that the heat transfer coefficient was proportional to Peclet number to the one-third power based on the characteristic length available, which was the tube diameter in that case. Here, no characteristic length is there and hence Peclet number is based on the length of the film, but the dependence on velocities and transport properties has changed from one-third power to half. As was pointed out in discussion there, convection affects the results not merely through the presence of velocity but also through the gradients of velocity. Comments made in the context of heat transfer to semi-infinite slab on penetration times and depths which is relevant here as well.

Similarity to heat transfer

Consider the corresponding heat transfer problem, though it is difficult to arrange experimentally. We imagine that a cold fluid at T_i flows down a wall. After the flow is fully developed, the free surface is exposed to hot gas at T_o. Let us assume that resistance to heat transfer in the gas phase is not important. The surface of the fluid will then be at the same temperature as the hot gas. If we neglect axial conduction, the equation of change of temperature will be given by

$$v_z \frac{\partial T}{\partial z} = \alpha \frac{\partial^2 T}{\partial y^2}$$

and the boundary conditions will be given by

$$\begin{aligned} T &= T_i \quad \text{at} \quad z{=}0 \quad \text{and as} \quad y \to \infty \\ T &= T_o \quad \text{at} \quad y{=}0 \end{aligned}$$

It is easy to see that these equations are identical to eq. 9.10 and the corresponding boundary conditions. We note that dilute solution approximation allowed us to neglect bulk velocity in the y direction, and it this that brought about total similarity between heat and mass transfer.

9.5 MASS TRANSFER WITH CHEMICAL REACTION

One of the very important problems in chemical engineering is to find ways to enhance the rates of any process. This is commonly referred to as *process intensification.* In this section we consider one method of increasing rates of mass transfer. Typically this situation arises in absorption of gases whose solubility in solvent is low, *e.g.,* CO_2 in water, and also in liquid–liquid extraction processes. One way to enhance the rates of mass transfer is to add a compound that reacts with the solute. As the solute diffuses into the solvent, it is consumed, and hence the concentration gradients are greater than when reaction is absent. Further, there will always be cases where mass transfer is accompanied by reaction. In this section we consider the general problem of mass transfer accompanied by chemical reaction.

9.5.1 Problem identification

Consider a semi-infinite body of solvent containing a reactant B present at high concentration. Let the solvent be non-volatile. Let it be exposed to a pure gaseous solute A, which reacts irreversibly with B. As the concentration of B is high, we can treat the reaction between A and B to be pseudo first order. Let the solubility of A in the solvent be C_{As}. We will consider the case where the solubility is low so that the solutions can be considered dilute. As the solutions are dilute, the convective velocities caused by diffusion alone are negligible.

Species mass balance

Based on these assumptions, mass balance for species B is not required as the decrease in its concentration can be neglected. Mass balance for species A works out to be

$$\frac{\partial C_A}{\partial t} = \mathcal{D}_{Am} \frac{\partial^2 C_A}{\partial z^2} - k_r C_A \tag{9.11}$$

where z is the depth into the semi-infinite liquid mass, and k_r is the pseudo first order rate constant.

Initial and boundary conditions

Let us assume that the solvent did not initially contain[8] any solute. As solute chemical potential in the liquid and gaseous phases are equal, the concentration of A at the gas–liquid interface will be equal to the solubility. As the body is semi-infinite, the concentration of the solute far away from the interface will be equal to the initial concentration itself. The initial and boundary conditions can be stated as

$$\begin{aligned} C_A &= 0 && \text{at} \quad t = 0 \quad \text{all } z \\ C_A &= C_{As} && \text{at} \quad z = 0 \quad \text{all } t \\ C_A &= 0 && \text{as} \quad z \to \infty \quad \text{all } t \end{aligned} \tag{9.12}$$

9.5.2 Concentration profiles

An interesting aspect of this problem is that, though the body is semi-infinite in extent, steady state can be reached. It happens when consumption by reaction exactly matches that by diffusion. Another way of looking at it is that there is a time scale of reaction, $1/k_r$, and it can be matched by a diffusion time scale over some finite length given by $\sqrt{\mathcal{D}_{As}/k_r}$. The finite time scale in combination with the diffusion coefficient creates a length scale. Existence of a finite time or length scale precludes a similarity solution and we do not attempt it.

The mass balance can be solved using Laplace transforms. However, we will show a procedure which relates the solution in presence of chemical reactions to the solution in their absence: a more general result. Laplace transform of the partial differential equation gives

$$(s + k_r)\bar{C}_A = \mathcal{D}_{Am} \frac{d^2 \bar{C}_A}{dz^2}$$

where s is the transform variable, and $\bar{C}_A$ is the Laplace transform of the concentration. The boundary conditions read

$$\begin{aligned} \bar{C}_A &= \frac{C_{As}}{s} && \text{at} \quad z = 0 \\ \bar{C}_A &= 0 && \text{as} \quad z \to \infty \end{aligned}$$

The solution of the differential equation for $\bar{C}_A$ with the given boundary condition can be written as $\bar{C}_A(s+k_r, z)$ and is given by

$$\bar{C}_A(s+k_r, z) = \frac{C_{As}}{s} e^{-\sqrt{\frac{\mathcal{D}_{Am}}{s+k_r}}z}$$

It can be rewritten as

$$\bar{C}_A(s+k_r, z) = \frac{s+k_r}{s} \frac{C_{As}}{s+k_r} e^{-\sqrt{\frac{\mathcal{D}_{Am}}{s+k_r}}z}$$

Let g be the solution of the partial differential equation *with the same boundary conditions* but in the absence of reactions. The transformed equation for g is given by

$$p\bar{g} = \mathcal{D}_{Am} \frac{d^2\bar{g}}{dz^2}$$

where wc have used p as the transform variable to avoid confusion. The boundary condition at the gas–liquid interface is given by

$$\bar{g}(p, z=0) = \frac{C_{As}}{p}, \text{ and } \bar{g}(p, z \to \infty) = 0$$

The solution for the differential equation for $\bar{g}$ with its boundary condition can be written as $\bar{g}(p, z)$. The differential equations for $\bar{C}_A$ and $\bar{g}$ can be considered as parametric, with the transform variable as the parameter. Thus, if we let $p = s + k_r$, the differential equation and boundary conditions for $\bar{g}$ becomes

$$(s+k_r)\bar{g}(s+k_r, z) = \mathcal{D}_{Am} \frac{d^2\bar{g}(s+k_r, z)}{dz^2}$$

$$\bar{g}(s+k_r, z=0) = \frac{C_{As}}{s+k_r}, \text{ and } \bar{g}(s+k_r, z \to \infty) = 0$$

where we have written the parameter explicitly. The solution for this is given by

$$\bar{g}(s+k_r, z) = \frac{C_{As}}{s+k_r} e^{-\sqrt{\frac{\mathcal{D}_{Am}}{s+k_r}}z}$$

Comparing the above with the solution for $\bar{C}_{As}$, we can infer

$$\bar{C}_A = \frac{s+k_r}{s}\bar{g}(s+k_r, z) = \bar{g}(s+k_r, z) + \frac{k_r}{s}\bar{g}(s+k_r, z)$$

This can be inverted to obtain

$$C_A = g(z,t)e^{-k_r t} + k_r \int_o^t g(z,t')e^{-k_r t'} dt'$$

It can also be written in a more compact form as

$$C_A = \int_o^t \frac{\partial g(z,t')}{\partial t'} e^{-k_r t'} dt'$$

Thus, for first order irreversible reactions, the solution for mass transfer with reaction can be obtained from the solution of mass transfer only. In this particular case, the latter is the similarity solution obtained in a previous section. Hence,

$$g(z,t) = C_{As}\left(1 - \text{erf}(z/\sqrt{4\mathcal{D}_{Am}t})\right)$$

After substituting this and considerable algebra, it can be shown that

$$\frac{C_A}{C_{As}} = \frac{1}{2}e^{-\sqrt{\frac{k_r z^2}{\mathcal{D}_{Am}}}}\text{erfc}\left(\sqrt{\frac{z^2}{4\mathcal{D}_{Am}t}} - \sqrt{k_r t}\right) + \frac{1}{2}e^{\sqrt{\frac{k_r z^2}{\mathcal{D}_{Am}}}}\text{erfc}\left(\sqrt{\frac{z^2}{4\mathcal{D}_{Am}t}} + \sqrt{k_r t}\right) \quad (9.13)$$

A more general solution which allows for non-zero initial condition as well as references to other generalizations is given in the text by Bird *et al.* [1]. As mentioned earlier, there exists a solution at steady state and is given by

$$C_A(z) = C_{As}e^{-\sqrt{\frac{k_r z^2}{\mathcal{D}_{Am}}}}$$

9.5.3 Look at the results

The concentration increases with time, and the depth to which it penetrates increases with time. This also results in the rate of diffusion slowing down. At some distance, the diffusion rate matches the reaction rate and steady state is reached. From the steady solution it can be seen that the depth is of the order of $\sqrt{\mathcal{D}_{Am}/k_r}$, confirming our arguments in the beginning of this section.

9.5.4 Mass transfer coefficient

The concentration gradient at $z = 0$, the gas–liquid interface is given by

$$\frac{1}{C_{As}}\frac{\partial C_A}{\partial z}\bigg|_{z=0} = -\frac{e^{-k_r t}}{\sqrt{\pi\mathcal{D}_{Am}t}} - \frac{2}{\sqrt{\pi}}k_r \int_o^t \sqrt{\frac{1}{4\mathcal{D}_{Am}t'}}e^{-k_r t'}dt'$$

The second term can be rearranged into an error function to get

$$\frac{1}{C_{As}}\frac{\partial C_A}{\partial z}\bigg|_{z=0} = -\frac{e^{-k_r t}}{\sqrt{\pi\mathcal{D}_{Am}t}} - \sqrt{\frac{k_r}{\mathcal{D}_{Am}}}\text{erf}(\sqrt{k_r t})$$

Hence, mass transfer coefficient defined as $N_{Az} = k_{m,r}C_{As}$ is given by

$$k_{m,r} = e^{-k_r t}\sqrt{\frac{\mathcal{D}_{Am}}{\pi t}} + \sqrt{k_r\mathcal{D}_{Am}}\text{erf}(\sqrt{k_r t})$$

where the subscript r stands for mass transfer coefficient in presence of reaction.

Enhancement factor

As stated in the beginning of this section, chemical reactions are used for process intensification or to enhance the mass transfer rates. For this purpose, we would like to compare the mass transfer rates with and without chemical reaction. Since driving force is equal to C_{As} in both cases, we can compare the mass transfer coefficients themselves. Mass transfer coefficient in the absence of reaction is given by $\sqrt{\mathcal{D}_{Am}/\pi t}$. Hence, the enhancement in the mass transfer coefficient due to reactions is given by

$$\mathcal{E} = \mathrm{e}^{-k_r t} + \sqrt{\pi k_r t}\,\mathrm{erf}(\sqrt{k_r t})$$

For $k_r t >> 1$, the error function is nearly equal to unity and the exponential function is nearly zero and hence the enhancement factor is equal to $\sqrt{\pi k_r t}$. For small times, to the order of $\sqrt{k_r t}$, the enhancement factor is given by $1 + k_r t$. As can be seen, faster reactions enhance the mass transfer rates by large factors.

Penetration model: We have referred to Danckwerts surface renewal model of mass transfer in chapter 7. This model proposes that packets of fluid reside at an interface for short times. As the time of contact is small, penetration depth is small and the packet of fluid can be considered as being semi-infinite in extent. Thus, both the similarity solution and the present solution can be thought of results for surface renewal model. We would like to compare these results with those obtained by using the film model. We will first recast the above results in a form convenient for that. The mass transfer coefficient without reaction is given by the similarity solution as

$$k_m = \sqrt{\frac{\mathcal{D}_{Am}}{\pi t}} \quad \text{or} \quad \sqrt{t} = \sqrt{\frac{\mathcal{D}_{Am}}{\pi k_m^2}}$$

Making this substitution, we can calculate the enhancement factor to be

$$\mathcal{E} = \mathrm{e}^{-\frac{k_r \mathcal{D}_{Am}}{\pi k_m^2}} + \sqrt{\frac{k_r \mathcal{D}_{Am}}{k_m^2}}\,\mathrm{erf}\left(\sqrt{\frac{k_r \mathcal{D}_{Am}}{k_m^2}}\right)$$

Film model: Results for the film model are obtained by solving the *steady state mass balance*

$$0 = \mathcal{D}_{Am}\frac{d^2 C_A}{dz^2} - k_r C_A$$

across a film of length δ with $C_A = C_{As}$ at $z = 0$ and $C_A = 0$ at $z = \delta$. The solution is given by

$$\frac{C_A}{C_{As}} = \frac{\sinh\sqrt{k_r \mathcal{D}_{Am}}(\delta - z)}{\sinh\sqrt{k_r \mathcal{D}_{Am}}\delta}$$

The mass transfer coefficient with reaction is given by

$$k_{m,r,\text{film}} = \frac{N_{Az}|_{z=0}}{C_{As}} = \sqrt{k_r \mathcal{D}_{Am}}\coth\sqrt{k_r \delta^2/\mathcal{D}_{Am}}$$

The mass transfer coefficient in the absence of reaction is simply given by $\mathcal{D}_{Am}/\delta$. The enhancement factor predicted by the film model is given by

$$\mathcal{E}_{\text{film}} = \sqrt{k_r \mathcal{D}_{Am}/k_m^2} \coth \sqrt{k_r \mathcal{D}_{Am}/k_m^2}$$

As it turns out these predictions are not very different from those of the surface renewal model. It is easy to see that in the limit of reaction rates being large, both models predict

$$\mathcal{E} = \sqrt{k_r \mathcal{D}_{Am}/k_m^2}$$

However, this coincidence is not general and breaks down for reversible reactions and other cases as pointed out by Cussler [2].

9.6 MASS TRANSFER WITH INSTANTANEOUS REACTION

9.6.1 Problem identification

In this section, we consider a special case of the topic of the previous section. Consider a semi-infinite extent of a dilute solution of B in a solvent. Let this be exposed to pure gas A which is soluble in the solvent. But A and B react *instantaneously* to form a third component. We will assume that all solutions are dilute so that we can treat diffusion of all species to be independent.

As the reaction between A and B is instantaneous, they cannot be present in the same physical zone. Thus, as A diffuses into the solvent, it consumes all B in its path. In the process, it is also consumed, and so it will not exist in the zone where B is present. Hence, the whole domain is divided into two zones: one containing only A and the other containing only B. As A continues to diffuse from the gas phase and consumes B, it continually pushes the zone containing B away from the gas–liquid interface. Thus, the boundary separating the zone containing A and the zone containing B moves away from the interface with time. Such problems involving two separate but connected zones but whose volumes are a function of time, are known as *moving boundary* problems. Moving boundary problems are also encountered in freezing or melting problems, and we encountered one such in section 6.7. The expected concentration profiles in the problem under consideration are sketched in figure 9.3.

9.6.2 Species mass balances

As solutions are dilute, convection created by diffusion alone is negligible. Since convection is absent, the mass balance for species A is given by

$$\frac{\partial C_A}{\partial t} = \mathcal{D}_A \frac{\partial^2 C_A}{\partial z^2}, \qquad 0 \le z < z_f(t)$$

Mass balance for species B is given by

$$\frac{\partial C_B}{\partial t} = \mathcal{D}_B \frac{\partial^2 C_B}{\partial z^2}, \qquad z_f(t) < z < \infty$$

In the above, $\mathcal{D}_A$ and $\mathcal{D}_B$ are, respectively, the diffusion coefficients of A and B in the solvent.

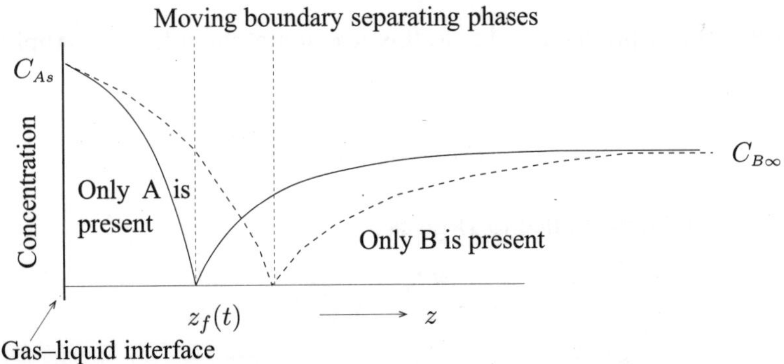

Figure 9.3. Sketch of diffusion with instantaneous reaction. A and B cannot coexist. As species A diffuses, it consumes B and creates a zone free of B. A can not enter the zone where B is present. But as A continues to diffuse and consume B, the zone containing only B moves away from the gas–liquid interface. The boundary separating the two zones is located at $z_f(t)$.

Boundary conditions

At the gas–liquid interface, chemical potential of A in the gas and liquid phases must be equal. This implies that the concentration of A in the liquid must be equal to the solubility of A in the solvent. Let it be denoted by C_{As}. As the reaction between A and B is instantaneous, the concentrations of A and B at the boundary separating the zones containing only A and only B must both be equal to zero[9]. As we move far into the zone containing only B, the concentration of B must equal the initial value. Let it be denoted by $C_{B\infty}$. These can be written as

$$C_A = C_{As} \qquad z = 0 \qquad \text{at all times} \tag{9.14}$$

$$C_A = 0 \qquad z = z_f(t) \qquad \text{at all times} \tag{9.15}$$

$$C_B = 0 \qquad z = z_f(t) \qquad \text{at all times} \tag{9.16}$$

$$C_B = C_{B\infty} \qquad z \to \infty \qquad \text{at all times} \tag{9.17}$$

$$C_B = C_{B\infty} \qquad t = 0 \qquad \text{at all } z \tag{9.18}$$

As A is not present initially in the liquid, an initial condition is not needed. While the above conditions are sufficient to solve the partial differential equation in a fixed domain, we need one more condition to determine the location of the moving boundary $z_f(t)$ in the present problem. This is obtained by making mass balance at the moving boundary. We apply eq. 7.10. Let $\boldsymbol{\xi}$ point from zone containing only A (phase II) into the zone containing only B (phase$I$), *i.e.*, it coincides with the unit vector in the z direction. Hence,

$$V_\xi = \frac{dz_f(t)}{dt}$$

Convection is absent and hence mass fluxes are given by diffusive fluxes only. Let us represent the reaction between A and B by

$$aA + bB \longrightarrow \text{Products}$$

Note that $\overset{\bullet}{\mathcal{R}}^s$ is the rate of production due to this reaction at the interface. Applying the boundary condition to species A at $z = z_f(t)$, we get

$$-\mathcal{D}_A \frac{\partial C_A}{\partial z} - a\,\overset{\bullet}{\mathcal{R}}^s = 0$$

The same boundary condition applied to B gives

$$\mathcal{D}_B \frac{\partial C_B}{\partial z} - b\,\overset{\bullet}{\mathcal{R}}^s = 0$$

Eliminating the unknown $\overset{\bullet}{\mathcal{R}}^s$ between the two, we get the boundary condition needed:

$$-\frac{1}{a}\mathcal{D}_A \frac{\partial C_A}{\partial z} = \frac{1}{b}\mathcal{D}_B \frac{\partial C_B}{\partial z} \quad \text{at } z = z_f(t) \tag{9.19}$$

This condition is easily understood. The flux of A towards the moving boundary is the $+z$ direction and it has to match the flux of B in the $-z$ direction since, according to stoichiometry, a moles of A reacts with b moles of B. It is this boundary condition that determines the movement of the boundary by matching the fluxes. It is not common that moving boundary value problems have analytic solutions, but this one does.

9.6.3 Concentration profiles

Since no characteristic length scale exist, as might be suspected, there exists a similarity solution. Further, we might even expect the solution to be an error function.

Similarity solution

We expect the similarity variable to be proportional to $z/\sqrt{\mathcal{D}t}$. However, we have two diffusion coefficients. So we might be bold and try a solution like

$$\begin{aligned} C_A &= K_1 + K_2\text{erf}\left(z/\sqrt{4\mathcal{D}_A t}\right) & \qquad 0 < z < z_f(t) \\ C_B &= K_3 + K_4\text{erf}\left(z/\sqrt{4\mathcal{D}_B t}\right) & \qquad z_f(t) < z < \infty \end{aligned}$$

where K_i are constants. We already know that error function solution satisfies the unsteady one dimensional diffusion equation. We need to only check whether this postulated solution satisfies initial and boundary conditions or not. At the moving boundary, the concentrations of A and B are zero *at all times*. Thus, we require

$$\begin{aligned} 0 &= K_1 + K_2\text{erf}\left(z_f(t)/\sqrt{4\mathcal{D}_A t}\right) \\ 0 &= K_3 + K_4\text{erf}\left(z_f(t)/\sqrt{4\mathcal{D}_B t}\right) \end{aligned}$$

This is possible while K_i are constants only if $z_f(t)/\sqrt{t}$ is also *a constant*. Thus, if similarity solution is valid, it predicts that the boundary separating zones containing only A or B will move with a speed inversely proportional to the square root of time. This is possible and hence we can pursue similarity solution further. Equations 9.15, 9.16, 9.17 and 9.18 can be implemented in a straight forward manner to find

$$\frac{C_A}{C_{As}} = 1 - \frac{\text{erf}\left(z/\sqrt{4\mathcal{D}_A t}\right)}{\text{erf}\left(z_f(t)/\sqrt{4\mathcal{D}_A t}\right)} \qquad 0 < z < z_f(t) \tag{9.20}$$

$$\frac{C_B}{C_{B\infty}} = \frac{\text{erf}\left(z/\sqrt{4\mathcal{D}_B t}\right) - \text{erf}\left(z_f(t)/\sqrt{4\mathcal{D}_B t}\right)}{1 - \text{erf}\left(z_f(t)/\sqrt{4\mathcal{D}_B t}\right)} \qquad z_f(t) < z < \infty \tag{9.21}$$

We are yet to utilize the boundary condition that matches fluxes. We have to check if it can be successfully implemented, and if it can be, we should get from it an expression for the location of the moving boundary. We find that the flux matching boundary condition can be implemented if

$$\frac{z_f^2(t)}{4t} = \gamma = \text{Constant}$$

The boundary condition then gives the following equation

$$1 - \text{erf}\left(\sqrt{\frac{\gamma}{\mathcal{D}_B}}\right) = \frac{aC_{B\infty}}{bC_{As}}\sqrt{\frac{\mathcal{D}_B}{\mathcal{D}_A}}\text{erf}\left(\sqrt{\frac{\gamma}{\mathcal{D}_A}}\right)\exp\left(\frac{\gamma}{\mathcal{D}_A} - \frac{\gamma}{\mathcal{D}_B}\right)$$

Hence, γ has to be determined from the above transcendental equation. The location of the moving boundary is given by $\sqrt{2\gamma t}$.

9.6.4 Look at the results

The solution shows that the boundary separating the two zones moves slower with increasing time. This is expected since the concentration of A falls from the solubility to zero over a length of z_f. However, the boundary moves away from the gas–liquid interface with time or z_f increases with time. Hence, the concentration gradients decrease with time. Thus, supply of A from the gas phase is slowed down and the boundary moves at a slower pace. We expect the boundary to move faster with increased solubility and the transcendental equation for γ shows that. If the initial concentration of B is increased, then concentration gradients of B increase and hence, in order for concentration gradients of A to increase so that fluxes of both components can match, the boundary between the two zones will have to stay closer to the gas–liquid interface. This is confirmed since the effect of increasing $C_{B\infty}$ is same as decreasing the solubility of A. Though more difficult to see from the equations, increasing the diffusivity of A or decreasing the diffusivity of B increases γ or the speed of moving boundary.

When a mass of warm water is exposed to a cold surface kept below the melting point of ice, a layer of ice forms and continually grows on the surface. The interface separating the ice and water moves away from the cold surface. This problem is very similar to the one we solved now.

Mass transfer coefficient

The mass flux of A is given by

$$-\mathcal{D}_A \frac{\partial C_A}{\partial z}\bigg|_{z=0} = \sqrt{\frac{\mathcal{D}_A}{\pi t}} \frac{C_{As}}{\text{erf}\left(\sqrt{\gamma/\mathcal{D}_A}\right)}$$

The enhancement factor in mass transfer coefficient is given by

$$\mathcal{E} = \frac{1}{\text{erf}\left(\sqrt{\gamma/\mathcal{D}_A}\right)}$$

This is a constant, unlike with the first order reaction, and it depends upon the diffusivities of both the components and the stoichiometry of the reaction. We will leave it to you to compare this result with that predicted by the film model.

9.7 SIMILARITY BETWEEN HEAT AND MASS TRANSFER

Now we take an interlude to emphasize the identical nature of mass and heat transfer, and the conditions when they become only similar. In all the previous problems, we neglected the convection created by diffusion. When we did this, an identical problem to what was solved could be posed in terms of heat transfer. We emphasize this point with a few more examples.

9.7.1 Mass transfer in pipe flow

Let us consider that a pure solvent flows through a tube. Suppose the wall of the tube, after the fully developed zone, is coated with a solute which is soluble in the solvent. The solute will dissolve into the flowing solvent. This problem is similar to the Leveque problem we dealt with in chapter 5. See figure 5.5. The species mass balance equation, after neglecting axial diffusion, would be given by

$$2V\left(1 - \frac{r^2}{R^2}\right)\frac{\partial w_i}{\partial z} + \boxed{v_r \frac{\partial w_i}{\partial r}} = \mathcal{D}_{is}\left[\frac{1}{r}\frac{\partial}{\partial r}\left(r\frac{\partial w_i}{\partial r}\right)\right]$$

The boxed term will be extra compared to the equation of change of temperature used in section 5.11. This will not be zero because the flux continuity boundary condition at the wall will specify that the flux of solute will create radial velocity. We will write this approximately[10] by equating the total flux of the solute to the mass flux due to the radial velocity:

$$\rho v_r(0, z) = j_i(0, z) + \rho_i(0, z) v_r(0, z)$$

The radial velocity becomes negligible only for dilute solutions when the diffusive fluxes are small. If it can be neglected, the species mass balance equation becomes identical to the equation of change of temperature for the Leveque problem. The solution we obtained there will be valid here as well. Thus, heat and mass transfer become identical.

9.7.2 Mass transfer in boundary layer

Imagine uniform flow approaching a plate coated with a soluble material. A momentum boundary layer will form. The soluble material will dissolve into the flowing fluid and a concentration boundary layer will form. See figure 6.4. This problem is similar to the thermal boundary layer problem dealt with in section 6.2. We started solving the momentum boundary layer problem by integrating the equation of continuity

$$\frac{\partial v_x}{\partial x} + \frac{\partial v_y}{\partial y} = 0$$

to eliminate the y–component of the velocity:

$$v_y = \int_0^y \frac{\partial v_x}{\partial x} da$$

where a is a dummy variable of integration. In writing this, we previously used the fact that v_y is zero at the wall. If the plate is soluble, this would not be true and we will now get

$$v_y = v_y(x, 0) + \int_0^y \frac{\partial v_x}{\partial x} da$$

By using the flux balance boundary condition, we can write that

$$\rho v_y(x, 0) = j_y + \rho w_i v_y(x, 0)$$

The y-component of velocity at the wall becomes negligible only for dilute solutions. Under those conditions, the equations for momentum boundary layer remain unaltered from what we did for thermal boundary layer. As a result the equation of change of temperature for thermal boundary layer becomes identical to the species mass balance equation.

9.7.3 Summary

The equation of change of temperature (or more accurately the equation for $\rho\hat{C}_pT$) becomes identical to species mass balance equation for dilute solutions if we assume that properties like density, diffusivity, *etc.* are constant. It is because, the convection created by diffusion is negligible for dilute solutions. Under these conditions, mass transfer and heat transfer become identical. All the results we obtained for convective heat transfer can be applied to mass transfer as well. This is the essence of *analogies between heat and mass transfer.* In view of this, I suggest that you go back to the problems we solved in convection heat transfer in chapters 4, 5, and 6, examine them and try to formulate equivalent mass transfer problems.

As we mentioned in section 7.8, mass transfer in concentrated solutions is complex since fluxes do become large. Such problems are difficult to solve except numerically. The problems become more complex in case components are more than two. For this reason, models are used to account for the effects of high flux. We have dealt with this aspect in chapter 8. We deal with one more in the following section, and move on to mass transfer involving other driving forces in the sections that follow.

9.8 UNSTEADY EVAPORATION INTO A STAGNANT GAS

9.8.1 Problem identification

In this section, we will reconsider the problem we solved in chapter 8 on finding the rate of evaporation of a liquid A into a gas B and the gas is insoluble in the liquid. The steady state version of this

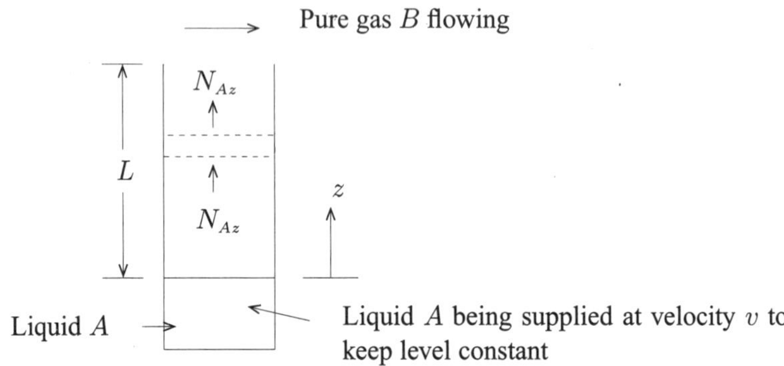

was examined there, and here we will solve the unsteady version of this problem. For convenience, figure 8.2 is reproduced here. We can imagine an experiment in which a tall beaker is partly filled with liquid, and the rate of evaporation is measured. As the beaker did not contain any vaporizing liquid or the solute, the solute content in gas above will initially be zero. We continue to blow pure gas at the top end of the beaker, and hence, the solute concentration there continues to remain at zero. As time progresses, the solute content in the gas phase builds up and steady state will be established after some time. We are interested in the unsteady state here. We will assume as we did earlier, that diffusion is one-dimensional, the pressure pressure in the tube is atmospheric and gas phase can be treated as ideal. We will also add the assumption that heat effects are negligible and temperature is therefore constant.

9.8.2 Species mass balance

Molar units are convenient to use here as well. The total mass conservation equation can be simplified to obtain

$$\frac{\partial C}{\partial t} + \frac{\partial (v_z^* C)}{\partial z} = 0$$

Since the pressure and temperature are constant, the total molar concentration or $C_A + C_B = C$ is constant. Hence, integration of the above equation gives

$$\frac{\partial v_z^*}{\partial z} = 0$$

or

$$v_z^* = \frac{N_{A,z} + N_{B,z}}{C} = \text{Function of time only}$$

But we know that since B is insoluble in A, molar flux of B at $z = 0$ is zero. Hence, the previous equation can be written as

$$v_z^* = \frac{N_{A,z}\Big|_{z=0}}{C}$$

The conservation equation of mass of species A gives

$$C\frac{\partial y_A}{\partial t} + Cv_z^*\frac{\partial y_A}{\partial z} = C\mathcal{D}_{AB}\frac{\partial^2 y_A}{\partial z^2}$$

Let us replace the molar average velocity in terms of the flux of A at the vapor–liquid interface:

$$C\frac{\partial y_A}{\partial t} + N_{A,z}\Big|_{z=0}\frac{\partial y_A}{\partial z} = C\mathcal{D}_{AB}\frac{\partial^2 y_A}{\partial z^2}$$

We will replace the mass flux of A at the gas–liquid interface using the constitutive equation to make explicit that the above is a partial differential equation for the mole fraction of A. Thus, we have

$$N_{A,z}\Big|_{z=0} = -C\mathcal{D}_{AB}\frac{\partial y_A}{\partial z}\Big|_{z=0} + y_{Ao}N_{A,z}\Big|_{z=0}$$

Solving for the mass flux of A at the interface:

$$N_{A,z}\Big|_{z=0} = -C\mathcal{D}_{AB}\frac{1}{1-y_{Ao}}\frac{\partial y_A}{\partial z}\Big|_{z=0}$$

Substituting this into the balance for A, we get

$$\frac{\partial y_A}{\partial t} - \mathcal{D}_{AB}\frac{1}{1-y_{Ao}}\frac{\partial y_A}{\partial z}\Big|_{z=0}\frac{\partial y_A}{\partial z} = \mathcal{D}_{AB}\frac{\partial^2 y_A}{\partial z^2} \tag{9.22}$$

Boundary conditions

We will state the boundary conditions first since they remain the same whether the problem is steady or unsteady. The boundary conditions are given as before by

$$y_A = 0 \quad \text{at} \quad z = L$$

$$y_A = \frac{P_{sat,A}}{P} \equiv y_{Ao} \quad \text{at} \quad z = 0$$

The initial condition is

$$y_A = 0 \quad \text{at} \quad t = 0$$

It turns out that this equation along with the boundary conditions does not have an analytic solution but does have one if the domain is semi-infinite. It is instructive to study this as it does offer a chance for high flux corrections to be evaluated under unsteady conditions at least for a model problem.

9.8.3 Concentration profiles

Similarity solution

As mentioned previously, we will assume that the boundary condition at $z = L$ are changed to $z \to \infty$ Let us restate the initial and boundary conditions

$$\begin{aligned} y_A &= 0 \quad \text{at} \quad t = 0 \\ y_A &= 0 \quad \text{at} \quad z \to \infty \\ y_A &= y_{Ao} \quad \text{at} \quad z = 0 \end{aligned}$$

Low flux case

When the vapor pressure of the liquid is small, the solutions are dilute, and the flux is small. Hence the the convective term in the balance equation can be dropped and it becomes

$$\frac{\partial y_A}{\partial t} = \mathcal{D}_{AB} \frac{\partial^2 y_A}{\partial z^2}$$

This is same as the heat transfer into a semi-infinite medium and hence we can use that solution which is also the same as that in the previous section. The similarity variable is given by

$$\eta = \sqrt{\frac{z^2}{4\mathcal{D}_{AB} t}}$$

and the solution is given by

$$\frac{y_A}{y_{Ao}} = 1 - \text{erf}(\eta)$$

The low flux mass transfer coefficient defined as $N_{A,z}|_{z=0} = k_m C y_{ao}$ is given by

$$k_m = \sqrt{\frac{\mathcal{D}_{AB}}{\pi t}}$$

Note that we did not use a superscript of • to indicate that this coefficient is for low flux.

High flux case

It turns out that the same similarity variable also reduces the partial differential equation to an ordinary differential equation! In hind sight, it is always easy to explain. As can be seen from eq. 9.22, the derivatives with respect to z on the left hand side are first order but appear twice. In terms of similarity variable this can be equivalent to taking a second derivative. Let us show this.

$$\frac{\partial y_A}{\partial z} = \frac{dy_A}{d\eta} \frac{\partial \eta}{\partial z} = \frac{dy_A}{d\eta} \frac{1}{\sqrt{4\mathcal{D}_{AB} t}}$$

and

$$\frac{\partial^2 y_A}{\partial z^2} = \frac{d^2 y_A}{d\eta^2} \frac{\partial \eta}{\partial z} = \frac{dy_A}{d\eta} \frac{1}{4\mathcal{D}_{AB} t}$$

The time derivative is given by

$$\frac{\partial y_A}{\partial t} = \frac{dy_A}{d\eta}\frac{\partial \eta}{\partial t} = -\frac{\eta}{2t}\frac{dy_A}{d\eta}$$

Substituting all these results we get

$$\frac{d^2 y_A}{d\eta^2} + 2(\eta - \mathcal{F})\frac{dy_A}{d\eta} = 0 \tag{9.23}$$

where

$$\mathcal{F} = -\frac{1}{2(1-y_{Ao})}\frac{dy_A}{d\eta}\bigg|_{\eta=0}$$

The boundary conditions are given by

$$y_A = y_{Ao} \quad \text{at} \quad \eta = 0$$
$$y_A \to 0 \quad \text{as} \quad \eta \to \infty$$

It is not difficult to work out the solution, but if you need some help, refer to the text by Bird *et al.* [1] for details of the solution. It is given by

$$\frac{y_A}{y_{Ao}} = \frac{1 - \text{erf}(\eta - \mathcal{F})}{1 + \text{erf}(\mathcal{F})} \tag{9.24}$$

However, $\mathcal{F}$ itself is unknown and a transcendental equation can be derived as follows. From the definition

$$\mathcal{F} = -\frac{1}{2(1-y_{Ao})}\frac{dy_A}{d\eta}\bigg|_{\eta=0} = \frac{y_{Ao}}{\sqrt{\pi}(1-y_{Ao})}\frac{e^{-\mathcal{F}^2}}{1+\text{erf}(\mathcal{F})}$$

This of course has to be numerically evaluated.

9.8.4 Look at the results

The solution has all the usual features of flux increasing with y_{A_o} because the driving force increases, increasing flux with diffusion coefficient as transfer rate increases, and flux decreasing with time as vaporizing solute accumulates in the gas phase.

Mass transfer coefficient

Now we will turn our attention to calculate the *high flux* mass transfer coefficient.

$$k_m^{\bullet} C y_{A0} = N_{A,z}\bigg|_{z=0} = -C\mathcal{D}_{AB}\frac{1}{1-y_{Ao}}\frac{\partial y_A}{\partial z}\bigg|_{z=0} = -C\mathcal{D}_{AB}\frac{1}{1-y_{Ao}}\frac{dy_A}{d\eta}\bigg|_{\eta=0}\frac{1}{\sqrt{4\mathcal{D}_{AB}t}}$$

Eliminating the derivative of the mole fraction, we get

$$k_m^{\bullet} = \frac{\mathcal{F}}{y_{A0}}\sqrt{\frac{\mathcal{D}_{AB}}{t}} = k_m\sqrt{\pi}\frac{\mathcal{F}}{y_{A0}}$$

The high flux correction is given by

$$\mathcal{E} = \sqrt{\pi}\mathcal{F}/y_{A0}$$

High flux corrections: Comparison of models

It is interesting to compare the high flux corrections obtained by different models. In chapter 8, we considered the steady evaporation of a liquid into a stagnant layer of an insoluble gas of a finite thickness. As we discussed earlier, such problems are prototypes of *film model.* Dankwerts proposed a model of inter phase mass transfer as an alternative to film model. It is referred to as *surface renewal model* or penetration model. We discussed this in the context of mass transfer accompanied by chemical reaction. The results of this section can be thought of as input into surface renewal model. The high flux correction calculated according to surface renewal model is found to be independent of penetration time and is given by the expression given above. In chapter 8, the high flux correction according to film model was calculated to be $-\ln(1 - y_{A0})/y_{A0}$. We compare the high flux corrections calculated according to the two models in Table 9.1. The numbers for the surface renewal theory are taken from the text by Bird *et al.* [1]. As can be seen that the two models differ but not by much. It is this type of information that provides confidence in applying models at least as far as a preliminary design and cost estimations are concerned.

Table 9.1. Comparison of high flux corrections according to film and surface renewal models

y_{A0}	0.0	0.25	0.50
Film model	1	1.15	1.38
Danckwerts model	1	1.11	1.27

9.9 DIFFUSION AGAINST CONCENTRATION GRADIENT

9.9.1 Problem identification

Now we consider a problem in multicomponent diffusion and use Stefan–Maxwell equations to solve it. We illustrate some very counter-intuitive effects that arise in multicomponent systems. We choose the simplest context of pure diffusion in one dimension at steady state to show that such effects can arise even there.

We can imagine this problem to be very similar to the gas absorption problems. Imagine three gases being absorbed into a non-volatile solvent, and it would be necessary to use constitutive equations for multicomponent systems to analyze this problem. The physical arrangement is shown in figure 9.4. A mixture of three gases and of known composition flows over the top of the tube. A non-volatile solvent is placed at the bottom of the tube. It may also contain the components in dissolved form and let us assume that the composition of the liquid is also known. An appropriate form of thermodynamic equilibrium relationship then specifies the composition in the gas phase at the gas–liquid interface. We therefore suppose that the gas phase composition at the interface is also

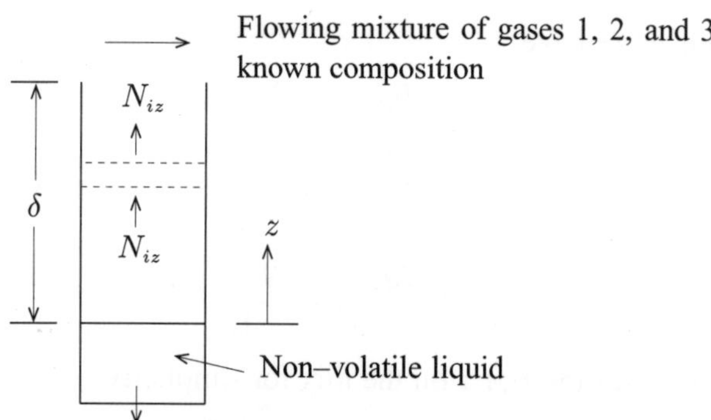

Figure 9.4. Three component gaseous mixture of known composition flows on top of a tube. They diffuse and absorb into a non-volatile solvent. The solvent may have these components also. Diffusion in the liquid phase is assumed to be fast.

known. We assume that pressure and temperature in the system is uniform and constant. We further assume that by some means the level of the liquid is being maintained constant so that the path length of diffusion is constant. To illustrate the principles of multicomponent diffusion, we assume that resistance to diffusion is concentrated in the gas phase. Let us denote the three components in the system by 1, 2 and 3.

9.9.2 Species mass balances

At steady state without chemical reactions, the mass balances simplify to

$$\frac{dN_{iz}}{dz} = 0 \quad i = 1, 2, 3$$

In other words, mass fluxes, N_{iz}, are constant and do not vary spatially.

Boundary conditions

The components are diffusing across a film of thickness δ as shown in figure 9.4. As mentioned earlier, let us assume that the mole fractions at $z = 0$ and $z = \delta$ are known. These form the boundary conditions.

Constitutive equation

Let us consider the mixture to be ideal so that we can write $\mu_i = \mathcal{R}T\ln y_i$. Let other driving forces for diffusion be absent. Stefan–Maxwell equations simplify to the following

$$-\frac{C_i}{y_i}\frac{dy_i}{dz} = -C\frac{dy_i}{dz} = \sum_j \frac{1}{\mathsf{D}_{ij}}(y_j N_{iz} - y_i N_{jz}) \quad i = 1, 2, 3$$

As temperature and pressure are constant, the total molar concentration is constant and known. For convenience we dropped the conditions of constancy temperature and pressure on the gradient operator. Hence, we have

$$-C\frac{dy_1}{dz} = \frac{y_2N_1 - y_1N_2}{\mathsf{D}_{12}} + \frac{y_3N_1 - y_1N_3}{\mathsf{D}_{13}} \tag{9.25}$$

$$-C\frac{dy_2}{dz} = \frac{y_1N_2 - y_2N_1}{\mathsf{D}_{12}} + \frac{y_3N_2 - y_2N_3}{\mathsf{D}_{23}}$$

$$-C\frac{dy_3}{dz} = \frac{y_1N_3 - y_3N_1}{\mathsf{D}_{13}} + \frac{y_2N_3 - y_3N_2}{\mathsf{D}_{23}} \tag{9.26}$$

where we dropped subscript z on the flux for simplicity.

9.9.3 Concentration profiles

We can write Stefan–Maxwell equations only for two components. The equations given however involve three fluxes, and cannot be solved in general. As the problem is one of pure diffusion, as we discussed in chapter 7.8, we have to specify some condition to avoid solution of Navier–Stokes equations.

One stagnant component

Let the condition be that one component is stagnant. This would be enforceable if one of them is insoluble in the liquid. To be concrete, let us specify that the third component is stagnant, *i.e.,* $N_3 = 0$. This condition makes the equation for the third component very simple and, eq. 9.26 becomes

$$C\frac{dy_3}{dz} = \frac{y_3N_1}{\mathsf{D}_{13}} + \frac{y_3N_2}{\mathsf{D}_{23}}$$

Since mass fluxes do not vary spatially, this can be easily integrated to obtain

$$\frac{N_1}{\mathsf{D}_{13}} + \frac{N_2}{\mathsf{D}_{23}} = \frac{C}{z}\ln\frac{y_3}{y_3(z=0)} \tag{9.27}$$

It can be noticed that the mole fractions of the third component at $z = 0$ and $z = \delta$ are not equal, and hence driving force is not zero. However, flux of the third component is zero and we encountered this in a binary system also. This was explained in the case of binary by the fact that the convective flux created by the motion of other component exactly compensates for the diffusive flux. As we shall see later, this explanation is not sufficient in multicomponent systems.

Non-stagnant components

We can choose one of the other two components for solution. Suppose we choose component 1. After substituting that flux of third component is zero in eq. 9.25, we get

$$-C\frac{dy_1}{dz} = \frac{y_2N_1 - y_1N_2}{\mathsf{D}_{12}} + \frac{y_3N_1}{\mathsf{D}_{13}}$$

Of the three mole fractions, only two are independent and hence we can replace y_2 by $1 - y_1 - y_3$. Substituting this, and eq. 9.27 into the previous equation, we get after some rearrangement

$$C\frac{dy_1}{dz} = \frac{y_1(N_1 + N_2)}{\mathsf{D}_{12}} + N_1\left(\frac{1}{\mathsf{D}_{12}} - \frac{1}{\mathsf{D}_{13}}\right) y_3(z=0)\exp\left(\frac{zN_1}{C\mathsf{D}_{13}} + \frac{zN_2}{c\mathsf{D}_{23}}\right) - \frac{N_1}{\mathsf{D}_{12}} \tag{9.28}$$

This can be also integrated along with the boundary condition at $z = 0$ to find

$$N_1 + N_2 = C\frac{\mathsf{D}_{12}}{z}\ln\left(\frac{\mathfrak{F}n}{\mathfrak{F}d}\right)$$

where

$$\mathfrak{F}n = \frac{N_1 + N_2}{N_1}y_1 - \frac{N_1 + N_2}{N_2}y_2\frac{1/\mathsf{D}_{12} - 1/\mathsf{D}_{13}}{1/\mathsf{D}_{12} - 1/\mathsf{D}_{23}} - \frac{1/\mathsf{D}_{13} - 1/\mathsf{D}_{23}}{1/\mathsf{D}_{12} - 1/\mathsf{D}_{23}}$$

and

$$\mathfrak{F}d = \frac{N_1 + N_2}{N_1}y_1(z = 0) - \frac{N_1 + N_2}{N_2}y_2(z = 0)\frac{1/\mathsf{D}_{12} - 1/\mathsf{D}_{13}}{1/\mathsf{D}_{12} - 1/\mathsf{D}_{23}} - \frac{1/\mathsf{D}_{13} - 1/\mathsf{D}_{23}}{1/\mathsf{D}_{12} - 1/\mathsf{D}_{23}}$$

The two fluxes are unknown but can be determined by using the other boundary conditions for components 1 and 3 at $z = \delta$. It may be noted that we illustrated the procedure of solving a multicomponent diffusion problem in the context of film theory.

Special case of equimolar counter diffusion

The solution given is general and we look for a further specialized case of equimolar counter diffusion of components 1 and 2 or $N_1 + N_2 = 0$. We cannot get the solution from that given, and have to start from eq. 9.28 and specialize it to the equimolar counter diffusion case. It then becomes

$$C\frac{dy_1}{dz} = N_1\left(\frac{1}{\mathsf{D}_{12}} - \frac{1}{\mathsf{D}_{13}}\right)y_3(z = 0)\exp\left(\frac{zN_1}{C}\left[\frac{1}{\mathsf{D}_{13}} - \frac{1}{\mathsf{D}_{23}}\right]\right) - \frac{N_1}{\mathsf{D}_{12}}$$

This is easily integrated to obtain

$$\frac{C}{\delta}\Big(y_1(z = \delta) - y_1(z = 0)\Big) = \frac{(1/\mathsf{D}_{12} - 1/\mathsf{D}_{13})}{(1/\mathsf{D}_{13} - 1/\mathsf{D}_{23})}\frac{C}{\delta}\Big(y_3(z = \delta) - y_3(z = 0)\Big) - \frac{N_1}{\mathsf{D}_{12}}$$

Rearranging the above equation

$$\frac{N_1}{\mathsf{D}_{12}} = \frac{C}{\delta}\Big(y_1(z = 0) - y_1(z = \delta)\Big) - \frac{\mathsf{D}_{23}}{\mathsf{D}_{12}}\frac{\mathsf{D}_{13} - \mathsf{D}_{12}}{\mathsf{D}_{13} - \mathsf{D}_{23}}\frac{C}{\delta}\Big(y_3(z = 0) - y_3(z = \delta)\Big)$$

9.9.4 Look at the results

If y_1 at $z = 0$ is greater than that at $z = \delta$, we expect N_1 to be positive. This is what is contributed by the first term, and is the effect of the gradient in the mole fraction of the first component to its own flux. However, the total flux is not just that but contributions are also made by the other components. The second term is that. Note that its sign depends upon several factors. It is always possible that $\mathsf{D}_{13} > \mathsf{D}_{12}$ and $\mathsf{D}_{13} > \mathsf{D}_{23}$[11], and $y_3(z = 0) - y_3(z = \delta)$ is also greater than zero. Under those circumstances, it is possible that the second term will dominate and N_1 will be negative even though y_1 at $z = \delta$ is less than that at $z = 0$. This will mean that the first component will diffuse against its concentration gradient!

How is the third component stagnant?

Now we focus our attention on the third component. Since $N_1 + N_2 = 0$ and N_3 is also equal to zero, the total molar flux is zero. Hence, the molar average velocity and the convective flux of all components is zero. Even then, the flux of the third component is zero. Hence, the explanation given about how a component remains stagnant in a binary is not sufficient here. It is the effect of driving forces of the other components that plays a role. This can be see from the Fick's law form:

$$\mathbf{N}_i = C \sum_j \mathbb{D}_{ij} \mathbf{d}_j + y_i \sum_k \mathbf{N}_k$$

Thus, even if the contribution to flux from the second term due to the molar average velocity is zero, it is still possible that the interaction between other components as reflected by $\mathbb{D}_{ij}$ and the driving forces $\mathbf{d}_{j \neq i}$ is such that a component can either be stagnant though gradient of its own mole fraction is not zero or can even diffuse against the direction indicated by the sign of the gradient of its own mole fraction.

These effects arise out of the interactions between three or more components and do not occur in a binary system. They have been observed and are discussed in detail by Taylor and Krishna [5].

9.10 PRESSURE DIFFUSION

We consider mass transfer due to a driving force other than concentration gradient in this section. Consider a large mass of stationary fluid of a single component. Gravitational force establishes a pressure gradient such that force due to pressure gradient opposes the weight of the fluid, and a mechanical equilibrium is established. If a particle with density different from that of the fluid is placed in the fluid, it experiences a force due to the pressure gradient. It will be equal to what would have been experienced by a packet of the fluid of the same volume, and this is Archimedes's principle. But the weight of the particle, or the force exerted by gravity on the particle, is different from that of the surrounding fluid of the same volume and hence the particle experiences a net force and moves. This can be interpreted as follows. The pressure gradient established by the surrounding fluid corresponds to the average driving force. The fluid with its density exerts a force to balance it. But a particle of density different from that of the surrounding fluid will oppose this pressure gradient but will not balance it, and the particle experiences a driving force for motion. This is the principle of pressure diffusion. We can extend this idea to a mixture of particles with different densities. When placed in a pressure gradient, particles of different densities will experience different driving forces and will move at different velocities. Hence, they can be separated using pressure diffusion. The principle applies even if the particles are of the size of molecules, and they also should separate. But we do not observe separation of molecules in a gravitational field. As separation occurs, concentration of particles increases in the direction in which they are forced to move due to pressure gradient. Concentration gradients are thus generated and diffusive motion due to this is created in the direction of lower values of concentration or in a direction that opposes separation by pressure gradient. Diffusional motion due to concentration gradients and pressure gradients oppose each other. It turns out that, in case of molecules, gravity is not sufficiently strong and only weak pressure gradients are created. Motion due to those are evened out by very small concentration gradients. As a result, no separation can be observed. However, if some other force field can be used to create large pressure gradients, it should be possible to separate molecular species. One can generate gravity-like forces in centrifuges and molecules can be separated in centrifugal force fields. Usually it is macromolecules that are commonly separated using this effect though even a lay reader of newspapers knows that the technique is used to separate radioactive isotopes.

9.10.1 Problem identification

A cylindrical tube filled with a solvent is taken and a small volume of the same solvent containing several species is placed in the middle of the tube. For convenience, we consider *dilute solutions*. The tube is rotated around z as shown in figure 9.5. The centrifugal forces establish a pressure

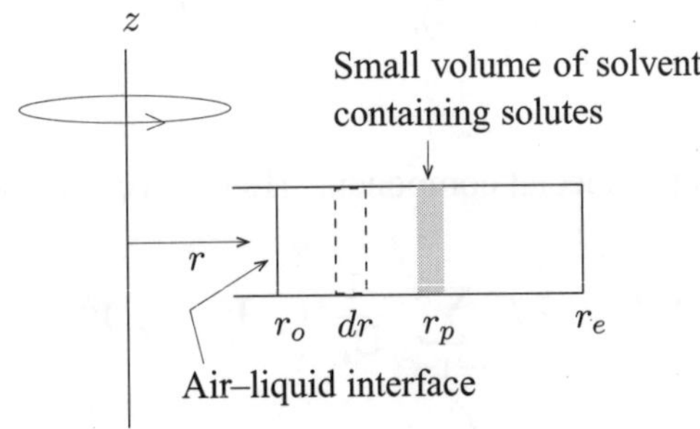

Figure 9.5. Sketch of centrifugal separation. A tube is rotated around z axis. The tube is filled with a solvent. A slug of solvent containing solutes is placed in the middle.

gradient. The pressure gradient acts differently on the dissolved species as well as the solvent and this leads to relative motion of species with respect to each other and solvent. Consequently separation of species occurs and we wish to demonstrate this principle in this section. This is commonly referred to as *centrifugal separation*.

Equation for pressure gradient

The fluid is not moving out as the bottom of the tube prevents it. Thus, the entire fluid is stationary. In the following, it is essential that you do not confuse the symbol r for the radius of the tube. As shown in figure 9.5, the r coordinate increases into the length of the tube. Force balance on a slice of stationary fluid of thickness dr and unit area[12] shown in figure 9.5 gives

$$\rho\omega^2 r dr - \frac{dP}{dr} dr = 0$$

or

$$\frac{dP}{dr} = \rho\omega^2 r$$

The pressure forces balance the centrifugal forces. Let us give some numbers to get an idea of the magnitude of centrifugal forces. Modern centrifuges used for separation of macromolecules rotate at around 70,000 rpm or about 7000 radians/sec. Thus, if the radius of the order of centimeters, the acceleration due to rotation is of the order of 50000 times as large as acceleration due to gravity on earth or 50,000 g. Hence, the forces exerted by the pressure gradients established by rotation are very large.

Species mass balance

The solvent itself is not moving and hence only mass balance of solute species is needed. Initially the species are present in the small volume introduced into the bulk and, as time elapses, they spread due to the diffusive motion. The process is unsteady. We expect the concentration profile to not vary across the cross-section of the tube because the driving forces do not vary across the cross-section. After noting that the area of the tube is constant, the mass balance for the ith species is given by

$$\frac{\partial C_i}{\partial t} + \frac{\partial N_{ir}}{\partial r} = 0$$

Constitutive equation

Let us select the solvent as the special component. Hence, we can use eq. 9.8

$$\begin{aligned} -C_i(\nabla\mu_i)_{T,P} - (\phi_i - w_i)\,\nabla P &= \mathcal{R}T \sum_{j=1,\neq i}^{N} \frac{1}{\mathsf{D}_{ij}}\left(y_j \mathbf{J}_i^N - y_i \mathbf{J}_j^N\right) \\ &= \mathcal{R}T\left(\sum_{j=1,\neq i}^{N} \frac{y_j}{\mathsf{D}_{ij}}\right)\mathbf{J}_i^N - \mathcal{R}T\sum_{j=1,\neq i}^{N-1}\left(\frac{y_i}{\mathsf{D}_{ij}}\right)\mathbf{J}_j^N, \quad i = 1,\ldots,N-1 \end{aligned} \tag{9.8}$$

where we removed the terms corresponding to forced diffusion. Now if we further specialize to *dilute solutions*, $y_i \sim 0$ and $y_N \sim 1$ the above simplifies to

$$-C_i(\nabla\mu_i)_{T,P} - (\phi_i - w_i)\,\nabla P = \mathcal{R}T\frac{1}{\mathsf{D}_{iN}}\mathbf{J}_i^N$$

It can be rearranged to get

$$\mathbf{J}_i^N = -C\mathsf{D}_{iN}\left(y_i\nabla \ln a_i + \frac{1}{C\mathcal{R}T}(\phi_i - w_i)\nabla P\right)$$

Let us assume that the solutions are ideal so that we can use the binary diffusivity in place of the Stefan-Maxwell diffusion coefficients. The solvent is stationary and hence, the total flux and diffusive flux of all species is the same. Thus, for the problem being considered, we can write

$$N_{ir} = -C\mathcal{D}_{iN}\left(\frac{dy_i}{dr} + \frac{1}{C\mathcal{R}T}(\phi_i - w_i)\rho\omega^2 r\right) \tag{9.29}$$

Let us derive expressions for the weight and volume fraction of a species in the solution. Let the partial molar volume of ith species be $\bar{V}_i$. The volume fraction is given by $y_i\bar{V}_i/\sum_j y_j\bar{V}_j$. In a dilute solution, it is equal to $y_i\bar{V}_i/\bar{V}_N$. The weight fraction of ith species in a dilute solution is given by y_iM_i/M_N. Hence,

$$\frac{1}{C\mathcal{R}T}(\phi_i - w_i) = \frac{y_i}{C_N\mathcal{R}T}\frac{\bar{V}_i}{\bar{V}_N}\left(1 - \frac{M_i}{\bar{V}_i}\frac{\bar{V}_N}{M_N}\right)$$

Partial molar volumcs are interpreted as the volume occupied by a mole of species *in solution.* The ratio of partial molar volume to molecular weight is the volume occupied by unit weight of species in solution. The term in the brackets of the above equation is unity minus the ratio of volumes occupied by unit mass of ith species and unit mass of solvent. Thus, for species which are lighter than solvent (or for species which occupy more volume per unit weight than the solvent), the term in the brackets[13] is positive. It can be seen from eq. 9.29 that such species move inward or towards smaller values of r. Conversely, heavier species move outward. This is the principle of separation according to density which we qualitatively explained in the beginning of this section.

Substituting these results into the constitutive relationship, and noting that $C_N\bar{V}_N = 1$, we get

$$N_{ir} = -\mathcal{D}_{iN}\frac{dC_i}{dr} + C_i\bar{V}_i\frac{\mathcal{D}_{iN}}{\mathcal{R}T}\left[1 - \frac{M_i}{\bar{V}_i}\frac{\bar{V}_N}{M_N}\right]\rho\omega^2 r$$

where we assumed that the total molar concentration is equal to that of molar concentration of the solvent. From Stokes–Einstein relationship, we know that the ratio of $\mathcal{R}T$ to the diffusion coefficient is the Stokes law friction factor for a mole of species. But the term

$$\bar{V}_i\left[1 - \frac{M_i}{\bar{V}_i}\frac{\bar{V}_N}{M_N}\right]\rho\omega^2 r$$

is the force on a mole of the species due to pressure gradient. This divided by the friction constant is the terminal velocity of species because inertia of species at the molecular level is small. The terminal velocity is commonly referred to in the literature on proteins as sedimentation or migration velocity. Let it be denoted by v_{ti}. It is a function of r where the particles are present since the force is a function of r. Substituting these results, we get

$$N_{ir} = -\mathcal{D}_{iN}\frac{dC_i}{dr} + C_i v_{ti}$$

Usually it is assumed that the variation of migration velocity with r can be neglected since the variation of r along the length of the tubes is not large. Thus, v_{ti} is calculated at some mean value of the radius, and is assumed to be a constant. Let it be denoted by v_{ti}^o. Substituting the constitutive relationship into the mass balance, we get

$$\frac{\partial C_i}{\partial t} = \mathcal{D}_{iN}\frac{\partial^2 C_i}{\partial r^2} - v_{ti}^o\frac{\partial C_i}{\partial r}$$

9.10.2 Concentration profiles

We now examine the nature of the solution of the previous equation.

Absence of diffusion

In the complete absence of diffusion, the molecules continue to sediment radially inward or outward depending on whether they are lighter or heavier than solvent. There will be no steady state. The lighter ones will accumulate at the air–solution (see figure 9.5) interface while the heavier ones will accumulate at the bottom of the tube. This is to be expected. We are interested in diffusion and we will not discuss solution in this limit any further.

Steady state solution

A steady state can be observed in presence of diffusion. The steady state is described by

$$\mathcal{D}_{iN}\frac{\partial^2 C_i^s}{\partial r^2} - v_{ti}^o\frac{\partial C_i^s}{\partial r} = 0$$

As explained earlier, diffusion due to concentration gradients, generated by pressure gradient, opposes the diffusive motion created by pressure gradient. Steady state is established when these two balance each other exactly. Integrating the above equation gives

$$\mathcal{D}_{iN}\frac{\partial C_i^s}{\partial r} - v_{ti}^o C_i^s = \text{Constant}$$

There are two boundary conditions at the air–solution interface and the bottom of the tube. These dictate that the flux of the solutes is zero at both ends. Thus, only one of them is useful, and using either gives

$$\mathcal{D}_{iN}\frac{\partial C_i^s}{\partial r} - v_{ti}^o C_i^s = 0$$

The concentration gradient depends upon the ratio of terminal sedimentation velocity to the diffusion coefficient, which in turn depends upon the molecular weight of the species. This principle can be used to determine the molecular weight of macromolecules. A further integration of the above equation gives

$$\ln\frac{C_i^s(r)}{C_i^s(r_o)} = \frac{v_{ti}^o}{\mathcal{D}_{iN}}\frac{r}{r_o}$$

The value of $C_i^s(r_o)$ is not known but can be determined by equating the total mass of ith species present to the initial moles of ith species that were loaded into the tube:

$$A_c\int_{r_o}^{r_e} C_i^s\,dr = \mathcal{M}_i$$

where A_c is the cross section of the tube. The equations show that, when *same* amounts are loaded, the concentration of species at a given location will be different depending upon their densities. Thus, separation has been achieved.

Unsteady solution

Solution to the unsteady equation gives further insight into the separation process. We have to solve the unsteady state mass balance

$$\frac{\partial C_i}{\partial t} = \mathcal{D}_{iN}\frac{\partial^2 C_i}{\partial r^2} - v_{ti}^o\frac{\partial C_i}{\partial r}$$

Let us assume that the small volume of solute we placed initially is like a plane source, *i.e.*, like a very thin sheet. The following will be the initial condition

$$C_i(r,0) = \frac{\mathcal{M}_i}{A_c}\delta(r - r_p)$$

where δ is the Delta function and, as shown in figure 9.5, r_p is the location where solute was placed initially. The condition that flux of all species is zero at the ends of the tube gives the two boundary conditions. However, we do not attempt to solve the problem with these boundary conditions but show the nature of separation obtained by looking at solutions at short times after centrifugation starts. Since the time elapsed is small, the solute would not have reached either end and hence we can assume the domain to be infinitely large. We can use the boundary conditions $C_i(r,t) \to 0$ as $r \to \pm\infty$. An analytical solution can be obtained with these boundary conditions. First we transform the partial differential equation by using the following variable for time: $x = r - v_{ti}^o t$. With this transformation, the partial differential equation becomes

$$\frac{\partial C_i}{\partial t} = \mathcal{D}_{iN}\frac{\partial^2 C_i}{\partial x^2}$$

The initial condition and boundary conditions are given by

$$\begin{aligned} c_i(x,t) &= \frac{\mathcal{M}_i}{A_c}\delta(x - r_p) && \text{at} \quad t = 0 \\ c_i(x,t) &\to 0 && \text{as} \quad x \to \pm\infty \end{aligned}$$

A point source spreads from its origin by diffusion. The solution for the spread of a spherical point source by diffusion in three dimensions was given in section 7.3. We do not derive[14] it, but the solution in one dimension is given by

$$\begin{aligned} C_i &= \frac{\mathcal{M}_i}{A_c}\frac{1}{2\sqrt{\pi\mathcal{D}_{iN}t}}\exp\left(-\frac{(x - r_p)^2}{4\mathcal{D}_{iN}t}\right) \\ &= \frac{\mathcal{M}_i}{A_c}\frac{1}{2\sqrt{\pi\mathcal{D}_{iN}t}}\exp\left(-\frac{(r - [r_p + v_{ti}^o t])^2}{4\mathcal{D}_{iN}t}\right) \end{aligned} \tag{9.30}$$

9.10.3 Look at the results

The concentration profile is a Gaussian function whose center moves with a speed of v_{ti}^o. Since v_{ti}^o are different for different species, the peak corresponding to different species will move to different extents. This is shown in figure 9.6. This solution of course breaks down at large times because the peaks start reaching the ends. Eventually, the steady state predicted in the previous section has to be reached.

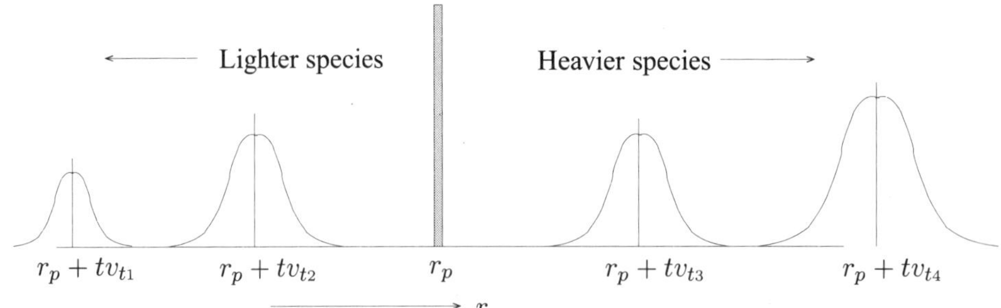

Figure 9.6. Species experience different forces due to pressure gradient. Species lighter than the solvent move to the left while the heavier ones move to the right, in the direction of centrifugal force. Both the force due to pressure gradient and the opposing drag force depend upon their size. Hence they move with different speeds, and separation occurs due to this. Figure shows a sketch of separation.

9.11 DIFFUSION IN ELECTROLYTES

9.11.1 Introduction

We use the context of electrolytes to illustrate forced diffusion. I am assuming that you have forgotten most of what you learnt about electrochemistry from your courses on physical chemistry! I am therefore providing a brief summary. If you surprise me pleasantly and remember what you read, skip this and move on to the section on problem identification. The energy of an ion is zero when it is far away from all other ions. Work has to be done to bring it closer to other ions that repel it. Conversely, work can be extracted when it comes closer to an ion that attracts it. Hence, energy of an ion is different when it is near other ions. If the electric potential at a location is ϕ, an ion present there and which has a charge $\mathcal{Q}$ will have an energy given by $\mathcal{Q}\phi$. The total energy of an ion is due to its chemical nature as well as its concentration in the solution, and that due to electrical potential. It is referred to as electrochemical potential in electrochemistry.

The force experienced by an ion of charge $\mathcal{Q}$ in any location can be obtained if ϕ there is known and is given by $-\mathcal{Q}\nabla\phi$. This is like the action of a body force. It should be noted that the force experienced by a charge depends upon its sign and magnitude. Thus, differently charged species will experience different body forces. Hence, the average body force exerted on a species and the body force experienced by the species will be different and this leads to forced diffusion.

Notation for ionic solutions

Commonly encountered ionic solutions are those of salts in water, acids in water, and so on. The compound as a whole is electrically neutral. When it is put in a solvent, it dissolves and ionizes. For example, NaCl ionizes into Na^+ and Cl^-. Strong electrolytes are those which ionize completely and the compound is not present in the solvent in unionized form. For example, NaCl is a strong electrolyte and, when it is dissolved in water, only Na^+ and Cl^- are present, and none of it is present in the form of NaCl. A compound which gives only two ions is called a binary electrolyte. We work with a simple situation of a strong binary electrolyte in this section to clearly state the principles.

Let the electrolyte be represented by

$$A^{z_A}_{\nu_A} B^{z_B}_{\nu_B}$$

Let us explain the notation. z stands for charge of an ion, and ν stands for the number of ions released when ionization occurs. When one mole of the above compound ionizes, it will form ν_A moles of ionic species A, each with a charge of z_A, and ν_B moles of ionic species B, each with a charge of z_B. Suppose that H_2SO_4 forms only[15] ionic species H and SO_4 upon ionization. ν and z of H are 2 and 1, respectively. ν and z of SO_4 are 1 and -2, respectively. Let C be the amount of the compound dissolved in a unit volume of the solvent. As it dissociates completely, the concentration of ionic species are given by

$$C_A = \nu_A C \text{ and } C_B = \nu_B C \tag{9.31}$$

Charge neutrality of the compound dictates that

$$\nu_A z_A + \nu_B z_B = 0 \tag{9.32}$$

Generally speaking, solutions of electrolytes are also electrically neutral[16]. Electrical neutrality of a solution implies

$$C_A z_A + C_B z_B = 0$$

Constitutive equation for ionic solutions

We note that electrolytic solutions are multicomponent systems because there is the solvent and then at least two ions. We have to apply Stefan–Maxwell equations and, if applicable, dilute solution formulae. First let us calculate the force due to electrical potential on the ions. The concentration of charge due to species A is given by $C_A z_A \mathcal{F}$, where $\mathcal{F}$ is the charge on a mole of electrons or the Faraday's constant. The force due to electrical potential per unit volume is therefore given by

$$-C_A z_A \mathcal{F} \nabla \phi$$

The total force due to electrical potential on a unit volume of solution is given by

$$-\left(C_A z_A + C_B z_B\right) \nabla \phi$$

But by electrical neutrality, the term in the brackets is zero, and hence the total force due to electrical potential is therefore zero. Let us now refer to eq. 9.7. The term $\rho_i \sum_j w_j \mathbf{g}_j$ is the contribution made by the total force on i^{th} species, and this term is zero for electrically neutral solutions. The term $\rho_i \mathbf{g}_i$ in eq. 9.7 is the body force on i^{th} species per unit volume. For the ionic species, this is given by

$$-C_i z_i \mathcal{F} \nabla \phi$$

Hence, the left hand side of eq. 9.7 for i^{th} species is given by

$$-C_i (\nabla \mu_i)_{T,P} - C_i z_i \mathcal{F} \nabla \phi$$

where we ignored the pressure diffusion term, which is not relevant here. We will consider solutions to be dilute[17] and take solvent as the special species. Hence, we use eq. 9.8, further specializing it to dilute solutions to obtain

$$\mathbf{J}_i^N = -\frac{\mathsf{D}_{iN}}{\mathcal{R}T}\left(C_i\nabla\mu_i + C_i z_i \mathcal{F}\nabla\phi\right)$$

or

$$\mathbf{N}_i = C_i\mathbf{v}_N - \frac{\mathsf{D}_{iN}}{\mathcal{R}T}\left(C_i\nabla\mu_i + C_i z_i \mathcal{F}\nabla\phi\right) \tag{9.33}$$

In electrochemistry literature, these are known as Nernst–Planck equations.

Consider diffusion in a dilute solution of a binary electrolyte. Let us assume that the solutions are ideal, and that the total molar concentration remains constant. Then, the constitutive relation reduces to

$$\mathbf{J}_A^N = -\mathcal{D}_{AN}\left(\nabla C_A + \frac{C_A z_A \mathcal{F}}{\mathcal{R}T}\nabla\phi\right)$$

From the view point of mass transfer, we are interested in the flux of the salt. Further, if there are any electrolytic reactions, current passes through the solution. It is also of great interest. Thus, it is desirable to develop expression for the current density.

Current density

Charge is carried by ions[18] in an electrolyte. Current is the rate of movement of charge and is a vector. Charge has a sign, *e.g.,* electrons are negatively charged. Charge moves as ionic species move, and hence current vector is related to the sign of the charge and the velocity of the species. Thus, if **I** is the current density, then

$$\frac{\mathbf{I}}{\mathcal{F}} = (\mathbf{N}_A^N z_A \mathbf{N}_B^N z_B) = (C_A z_A + C_B z_B)\,\mathbf{v} + \mathbf{J}_A^N z_A + \mathbf{J}_B^N z_B = \mathbf{J}_A^N z_A + \mathbf{J}_B^N z_B$$

since solution is electrically neutral. Hence, current density is given by

$$\mathbf{I} = -\mathcal{D}_{AN}\mathcal{F}z_A\nabla C_A - \mathcal{D}_{BN}\mathcal{F}z_B\nabla C_B - \frac{C_A z_A^2\mathcal{D}_{AN}\mathcal{F}^2 + C_B z_B^2\mathcal{D}_{BN}\mathcal{F}^2}{\mathcal{R}T}\nabla\phi$$

The factor multiplying the gradient of potential is the specific conductivity of the solution, κ

$$\kappa = \frac{C_A z_A^2\mathcal{D}_{AN}\mathcal{F}^2 + C_B z_B^2\mathcal{D}_{BN}\mathcal{F}^2}{\mathcal{R}T}$$

Using this, the previous equation can be rewritten as

$$-\nabla\phi = \frac{\mathbf{I}}{\kappa} + \frac{\mathcal{D}_{AN}\mathcal{F}z_A}{\kappa}\nabla C_A + \frac{\mathcal{D}_{BN}\mathcal{F}z_B}{\kappa}\nabla C_B$$

If concentration gradients are absent, the above is simply the Ohm's law. Conductivity of the solution can be thought of as a summation of contributions made by the two ions. The fractions contributed are denoted by *transport numbers* of the ions: t_A and t_B. Thus,

$$t_A = \frac{C_A z_A^2\mathcal{D}_{AN}}{C_A z_A^2\mathcal{D}_{AN} + C_B z_B^2\mathcal{D}_{BN}} \quad \text{and} \quad t_B = \frac{C_B z_B^2\mathcal{D}_{BN}}{C_A z_A^2\mathcal{D}_{AN} + C_B z_B^2\mathcal{D}_{BN}}$$

$$t_A = \frac{z_A \mathcal{D}_{AN}}{z_A \mathcal{D}_{AN} - z_B \mathcal{D}_{BN}} \qquad \text{and} \qquad t_B = -\frac{z_B \mathcal{D}_{BN}}{z_A \mathcal{D}_{AN} - z_B \mathcal{D}_{BN}}$$

These can be used to rewrite the equation for potential gradient as

$$-\nabla\phi = \frac{\mathbf{I}}{\kappa} + \frac{\mathcal{R}T}{\mathcal{F}}\left(\frac{t_A}{z_A C_A}\nabla C_A + \frac{t_B}{z_B C_B}\nabla C_B\right)$$

This is interpreted as follows. The applied potential gradient goes to overcome the ohmic resistance in part, and the rest of it is used to regulate diffusion of ions to ensure charge neutrality of the solution. Since $C_A = C\nu_A$ and $C_B = C\nu_B$, the given equation can be rewritten as

$$-\nabla\phi = \frac{\mathbf{I}}{\kappa} + \frac{\mathcal{R}T}{C\mathcal{F}}\left(\frac{t_A}{z_A} + \frac{t_B}{z_B}\right)\nabla C \tag{9.34}$$

where C is the concentration of the salt, were it to be present in the solution. If concentration gradients are absent, the ohmic resistance of the solution fully accounts for the potential drop. More interestingly, even if current is not flowing, the potential gradient is not zero. When current is zero, $\mathbf{N}_A/z_B = -\mathbf{N}_B/z_A$ or $\mathbf{N}_A/\nu_A = \mathbf{N}_B/\nu_B$. But the diffusivity of the two ions is different and fluxes will not be in this ratio if concentration gradient is the only driving force. Potential gradient is established suitably to ensure that current is zero.

Effective diffusivity of the salt

If the ions have different diffusivities, it will be interesting to calculate the diffusivity of the salt We can evaluate this from the constitutive relationship for either ion:

$$\mathbf{J}_A^N = -\mathcal{D}_{AN}\left(\nabla C_A + \frac{C_A z_A \mathcal{F}}{\mathcal{R}T}\nabla\phi\right)$$

We can eliminate concentration of the ion and the potential from the expression derived earlier to obtain

$$\mathbf{J}_A^N = -\mathcal{D}_{AN}\nu_A\nabla C + \frac{C_A \mathcal{D}_{AN} z_A \mathcal{F}}{\mathcal{R}T}\left(\frac{\mathbf{I}}{\kappa} + \frac{\mathcal{R}T}{C\mathcal{F}}\left(\frac{t_A}{z_A} + \frac{t_B}{z_B}\right)\nabla C\right)$$

Noting that

$$\frac{\mathcal{F}}{\kappa\mathcal{R}T} = \frac{1}{\mathcal{F}\left(C_A z_A^2 \mathcal{D}_{AN} + \mathcal{F} C_B z_B^2 \mathcal{D}_{BN}\right)} \qquad \text{and} \qquad \frac{t_A}{z_A} + \frac{t_B}{z_B} = \frac{\mathcal{D}_{AN} - \mathcal{D}_{BN}}{z_A \mathcal{D}_{AN} - z_B \mathcal{D}_{BN}}$$

the expression for the diffusive flux of A, after some algebra and rearrangement, becomes

$$\mathbf{J}_A^N = -\nu_A \frac{\mathcal{D}_{AN}\mathcal{D}_{BN}(z_A - z_B)}{z_A \mathcal{D}_{AN} - z_B \mathcal{D}_{BN}}\nabla C + \nu_A \frac{t_A}{\nu_A z_A \mathcal{F}}\mathbf{I} \tag{9.35}$$

By a similar procedure it can be shown that

$$\mathbf{J}_B^N = -\nu_B \frac{\mathcal{D}_{AN}\mathcal{D}_{BN}(z_A - z_B)}{z_A \mathcal{D}_{AN} - z_B \mathcal{D}_{BN}}\nabla C + \nu_B \frac{t_B}{\nu_B z_B \mathcal{F}}\mathbf{I}$$

Consider the case when current flow is not there. Then, as discussed earlier, $\mathbf{J}_A^N/\nu_A = \mathbf{J}_B^N/\nu_B = \mathbf{J}^N$, the diffusive flux of the salt. It is therefore given by

$$\mathbf{J}^N = -\frac{\mathcal{D}_{AN}\mathcal{D}_{BN}(z_A - z_B)}{z_A\mathcal{D}_{AN} - z_B\mathcal{D}_{BN}}\nabla C$$

The effective diffusivity of the compound is given by

$$\mathcal{D}_{eff} = \frac{\mathcal{D}_{AN}\mathcal{D}_{BN}(z_A - z_B)}{z_A\mathcal{D}_{AN} - z_B\mathcal{D}_{BN}}$$

Mass balances

Before leaving this topic, we show how the expressions derived in the previous section are used in mass balances. The mass balance of A ions is given by

$$\frac{\partial C_A}{\partial t} + \nabla.(\mathbf{v}C_A) = -\nabla.\mathbf{J}_A^N + \dot{\mathcal{R}}_A$$

The rate of reaction that appears in the above equation is the loss due to homogeneous reactions. We can replace the concentration of ions in solution with the concentration of salt, were it to be present in the solution, to obtain,

$$\frac{\partial C}{\partial t} + \nabla.(\mathbf{v}C) = -\nabla.\frac{\mathbf{J}_A^N}{\nu_A} + \frac{\dot{\mathcal{R}}_A}{\nu_A}$$

Equation 9.35 is used to substitute for the diffusive flux giving an equation for the concentration of the compound.

9.11.2 Problem identification

Let us consider a simplified example of application of forced diffusion. The process of electrolytically purifying impure metals is known as *electro-refining*. Plates of pure metal and impure metal are used as electrodes. In this process, the positive of a power source *e.g.,* a battery, is connected to the impure metal plate while the pure metal plate is connected to the negative of the power source. These connections make the potential of the impure metal more positive while the pure metal is made more negative. Due to this polarization, electrons are removed from the metal present in the impure matrix and it dissolves in the form of positively charged metal ions. The metal ions diffuse through the electrolyte to the electrode made up of pure metal. As it is more negative, the metal ions pick up electrons and deposit as metal on the pure plate. The process is shown in figure 9.7. For simplicity, we have chosen the electrolyte to be M^+X^-. We assume that only the diffusional processes are important in determining the rate[19] of the refining process.

When a potential difference is applied across the electrodes, current flows through the external circuit to or from the electrodes. As shown in figure 9.7, in the present example, electrons flow towards the positive of the power source and out from it to the negative electrode. This *electron* current exactly balances the *ionic current* created in the electrolyte by movement of ions to ensure overall charge balance. Thus, the current created matches the rate of metal deposition. Our objective in the present section is to calculate the rate of refining of the process.

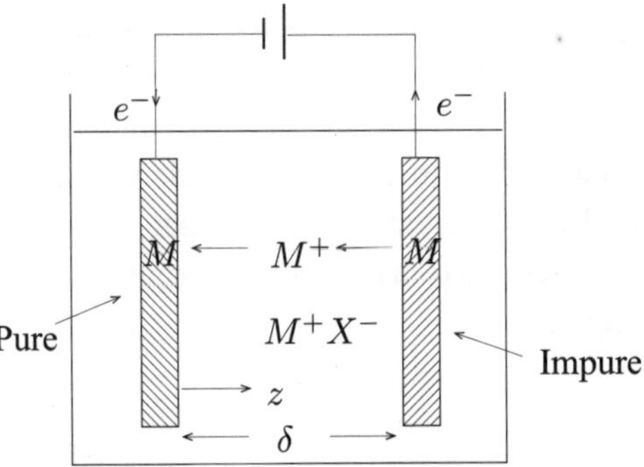

Figure 9.7. The impure metal plate is positively polarized. Hence, metal loses electrons and forms metal ions, which dissolve into the electrolyte and diffuse to the oppositely polarized plate. The electrons flow through the external circuit and reach the negative electrode. The positive metal ions that diffuse from the positive electrode gain electrons from the negative electrode and deposit as pure metal.

9.11.3 Species mass balance

The process is conducted by applying a potential difference across the electrodes. They are immersed in the electrolyte, and let us assume that it is a dilute solution. We will assume that steady state has been achieved and the process is one dimensional. Due to the applied potential difference, current will flow. Let the current density be I_z. We will assume that convection is absent.

As solutions are electrically neutral, we need to determine the concentration of only one ion. In the process, we see that M^+ moves from the positive electrode to the negative, while X^- is stagnant, and so its flux is zero. Thus, it is more convenient to write the balance of this ion. Reaction occurs only at the electrode–electrolyte interface and hence the rate of homogeneous reaction $\dot{\mathcal{R}}_X$ is zero. As solutions are dilute, we can assume that convection due to diffusion is negligible and the total flux and the diffusive flux are equal. Thus, we have

$$0 = -\frac{dJ^N_{Xz}}{dz}$$

The flux of the negative ion is constant and is equal to zero.

$$J^N_{Xz} = 0$$

Constitutive relation

The constitutive equation for the flux is given by eq. 9.35. For the electrolyte chosen $\nu_M = \nu_X = 1$ and $z_M = -z_X = 1$. Using these, the constitutive equation for the negative ion is given by

$$J^N_{Xz} = 0 = -\frac{2\mathcal{D}_{MN}\mathcal{D}_{XN}}{\mathcal{D}_{MN} + \mathcal{D}_{XN}}\frac{dC}{dz} - \frac{t_X}{\mathcal{F}}I_z = -\mathcal{D}_{eff}\frac{dC}{dz} - \frac{t_X}{\mathcal{F}}I_z$$

Combining it with the mass balance

$$-\mathcal{D}_{eff}\frac{dC}{dz} - \frac{t_X}{\mathcal{F}}I_z = 0 \tag{9.36}$$

As deposition occurs at the negative electrode, we expect concentration of the metal ion to decrease from the positive to the negative electrode. As solutions are electrically neutral, the concentration of the X^- ions also decreases from the positive to the negative electrode. This creates a concentration driving force that makes the negative ion to diffuse towards the negative electrode. The potential gradient however is positive and hence creates a force that drives the negative ions towards the positive plate. The fluxes due to these two driving forces oppose and exactly match each other so that the negative ion remains stagnant.

Charge balance

Current appears in the previous equation, and it is related to the applied potential. A charge balance is needed in order to formulate an equation for the potential. Solutions are electrically neutral and hence accumulation of charge is always equal to zero. Charge consuming reactions are not present in the bulk. Charge balance then gives

$$\frac{dI_z}{dz} = 0$$

or the current density is a constant.

9.11.4 Concentration and other profiles

Equation 9.36 can be integrated to obtain

$$-I_z = \frac{\mathcal{F}\mathcal{D}_{eff}}{t_X}\frac{C - C(0)}{z} \tag{9.37}$$

We need a condition to determine $C(0)$. Let us note that the negative ions are neither being produced nor being taken out of the apparatus. Hence, their amount and, hence the amount of the salt, must equal to what we started with at the beginning. Concentration at $z = 0$ can be obtained from this idea. If total amount of salt we put into the apparatus, per unit area, is $\delta\, C_o$, then by mass conservation

$$C_o = \frac{1}{\delta}\int_0^\delta C dz = C(0) - I_z\frac{t_x}{\mathcal{F}\mathcal{D}_{eff}}\frac{\delta^2}{2}$$

The value of $C(0)$ can be determined from this and the concentration profiles are now completely determined.

As the metal ion is monovalent in charge, a mole of metal must deposit for $\mathcal{F}$ coulombs of charge that pass through the electro-refining cell. Hence, the rate of deposition of metal is given by

$$\text{Rate of deposition of metal} = \frac{-I_z}{\mathcal{F}}$$

The rate of deposition can be immediately calculated once the current density is known.

Potential difference

Let us now calculate the potential difference that needs to be applied to achieve a given current density. Equation 9.34 simplifies in the present case to

$$-\frac{d\phi}{dz} = \frac{I_z}{\kappa} + \frac{\mathcal{R}T}{C\mathcal{F}}(t_M - t_X)\frac{dC}{dz}$$

The equation suggests that the potential gradient is different from that dictated by conductivity alone since the negative ion has to be kept stationary. The conductivity is directly proportional to concentration if we assume that pure solvent has zero conductivity and that all other properties are independent of concentration. We can therefore write it as $\kappa = \alpha C$. Substituting these into the equation for potential, and replacing the current density from eq. 9.36 we get

$$-\frac{d\phi}{dz} = -\frac{\mathcal{D}_{eff}\mathcal{F}}{\alpha t_X}\frac{1}{C}\frac{dC}{dz} + \frac{\mathcal{R}T}{\mathcal{F}}(t_M - t_X)\frac{1}{C}\frac{dC}{dz}$$

This can be integrated to obtain

$$\phi(\delta) - \phi(0) = \frac{\mathcal{D}_{eff}\mathcal{F}}{\alpha t_X}\ln\frac{2\,(C_o - C(0))}{C(0)} - \frac{\mathcal{R}T}{\mathcal{F}}(t_M - t_X)\ln\frac{2\,(C_o - C(0))}{C(0)}$$

where we used the fact that as concentration profile is linear, $C(\delta) + C(0) = 2C_o$. $C(0)$ is known from the concentration of salt put into the apparatus, and hence the potential difference that needs to be applied to obtain a given current density can be calculated.

9.11.5 Look at the results

The concentration profiles are linear and decrease from the positive to the negative electrode. The concentration gradient increases with increasing current density or increasing metal deposition rate. This is expected since the we are considering diffusion controlled process and driving force must increase to increase the deposition rate. The concentration gradient increases by redistribution of the salt. The concentration at the positive electrode goes up while that at the negative electrode decreases. The potential difference to be applied increases with current to overcome the ohmic resistance. Higher current density also implies larger concentration gradient, and hence an increased potential difference to keep the negative ion stationary. All these results are expected.

Limiting current density

One hopes to increase the rate of refining by increasing the current density, which in turn can be achieved by applying increasingly larger potential difference between the electrodes. We have noted that the rate of deposition is proportional to the current density. Equation 9.37 suggests that current density is proportional to the concentration gradient. It is not possible to increase the concentration gradient beyond that corresponding to $C(0) = 0$. Thus, it is interesting note that the equation suggests that current density cannot be increased beyond some level no matter how large a potential difference one might apply. This current density is referred to as the *limiting current density*. First we will determine its value and explain what is the physical reason for our inability to increase the current beyond some level. The limiting current density is given by

$$-I_{z,lim} = \frac{\mathcal{F}}{t_X} \frac{\mathcal{D}_{eff} C(\delta)}{\delta}$$

We mentioned that the electrolyte is not consumed during refining. Hence, the start up concentration of the electrolyte C_o, must equal the twice the average concentration of the electrolyte at steady state. As the concentration profile is linear, we obtain $C(\delta) = 2C_o - C(0)$. Hence

$$-I_{z,lim} = \frac{\mathcal{F}}{t_X} \frac{2\mathcal{D}_{eff} C_o}{\delta}$$

As current density increases, $C(0)$ decreases and the potential difference needed to maintain the current density increases. As the limiting current density is approached, the potential difference tends to infinity. From the expression for the potential difference, it can be seen that the first term blows up since solution's conductivity goes to zero as concentration goes to zero. This term would not go to infinity if solvent has some finite conductivity. The second term is the increase in potential difference required to keep the negative ion stagnant as the driving force generated by concentration gradient increases. This effect is referred to as *concentration polarization.* This blows up logarithmically and is the main physical cause for the ever-increasing potential difference required to maintain increased current densities. Concentration polarization is also observed in applications involving electrochemical power sources like batteries, fuel cells, *etc.*, and we will revisit this in the next chapter.

9.12 DIFFUSION & REACTION IN CATALYST PELLETS

9.12.1 Problem identification

Catalysts are used to enhance the rate of a chemical reaction. Catalysts can be soluble in the reaction medium, in which case the process is referred to as homogeneous catalysis. Often however, catalysts are solids while the reactants are in the fluid phase. Further, in general, the reactants and products are not soluble in the catalyst phase. Catalytic action is then interfacial in nature. It is therefore necessary to maximize the amount of area presented by the catalyst in a given volume of reactor to obtain the maximum increase in the rate of chemical reaction in the reactor. As a compromise between increased pressure drops and enhanced rates of chemical reaction, instead of fine sized catalyst particles, catalyst pellets are used in chemical processes. Catalyst pellets are made by binding the fine catalyst particles and will be porous. Consider a single pore, idealized as a cylindrical pore, of a catalyst pellet shown in figure 9.8. Reactants diffuse axially into the pore and radial gradients will be setup as they react at the wall. Thus, the situation is fairly complex where both radial and axial diffusion is coupled with reaction. However, if the radius of the pore is very small compared to the length of the pore, radial gradients can be neglected. In this sense, the situation is identical to that of heat loss from a fin. The idea can be extended to a catalyst pellet as well. As mentioned earlier, a catalyst pellet is made by agglomerating small catalyst particles. Thus, there

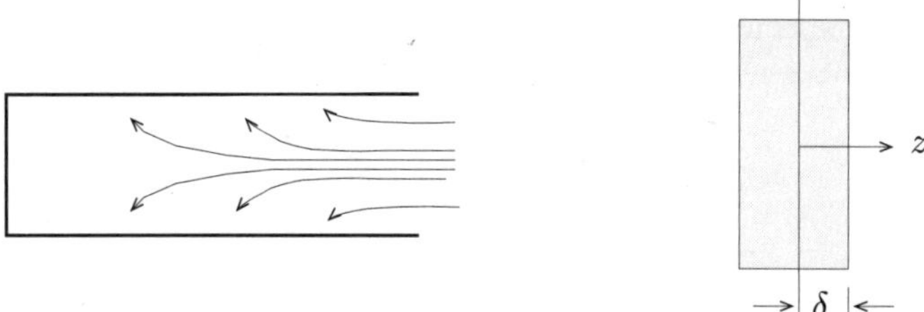

Figure 9.8. On the left hand side is a sketch of a cylindrical pore in a catalyst pellet. The walls are catalytic. Reactants diffuse axially from outside into the pore. Part of it will diffuse radially to react and another part will diffuse axially further into the pore. Right hand side is a sketch of a slab of a porous catalyst pellet.

are pores between the catalyst particles through which reactants will diffuse to the interior of the pellet. They also will have to diffuse towards the catalytic surface, and react there. If the size of the pores between catalyst particles is small compared to the radius of the pellet, which is akin to the length of the cylindrical pore, only the radial gradients in the pellet will be important and the resistance to diffusion to the surface of the particles from the middle of the pore can be neglected. It is this model that is used widely in characterizing the performance of catalyst pellets.

9.12.2 Species mass balance

Consider a catalyst pellet shaped as a thin porous slab. Refer to figure 9.8. We select this geometry keeping in mind porous electrodes, which we will consider in chapter 10. Consider the reaction

$$\text{A} \rightarrow \text{products}$$

Let us assume that the reactant is present in solution with other inert species. For simplicity, we will use dilute solution model and constant diffusivity for species A. Let us consider that the thickness in x and y directions is large and only diffusion in the z direction is important. As we discussed earlier, reactant diffuses from the surface at $z = \delta$ into the center and reacts on the catalytic surface. The resistance to diffusion from the bulk of the pores to the surface of the catalytic surface is negligible. Hence, concentration across the pore space at any z will be constant. Reaction occurs on the surface of the catalyst at a rate corresponding to this concentration. The rate of a catalytic reaction will be proportional to the surface area of the catalyst. Let the rate of *consumption of species A per unit area of the catalyst* be $\dot{\mathcal{R}}^s{}_A$. Further, let the size of the catalyst particle be very small so that a large number of particles will be present in a unit volume of the pellet. Under those conditions, the area of catalyst particles per unit volume of the pellet will be independent of volume unless the pellet itself is very small. For such large pellets[20] one can multiply the rate of surface reaction by the interfacial area per unit volume[21] to find rate of reaction per unit volume of pellet. This treatment is similar to what would have been done if the reaction occurred in the entire volume of the pellet. Such models therefore are referred to as *pseudo-homogeneous models*. Let the interfacial area per unit volume be a. The rate of consumption of A per unit volume of the pellet $\dot{\mathcal{R}}_A$ is equal to $a\,\dot{\mathcal{R}}^s{}_A$. At steady state, the mass balance for species A simplifies to

$$\mathcal{D}_A \frac{d^2 C_A}{dz^2} - a\,\dot{\mathcal{R}}^s{}_A = 0$$

Rate of reaction

The rate expression for a catalytic reaction will be fairly complex even when external mass transfer is not important since it might involve adsorption, surface reaction and desorption. For simplicity, let us assume that rate is first order with respect to the concentration of A in the bulk. Thus

$$\dot{\mathcal{R}}^s{}_A = k^s C_A$$

where k^s is the rate constant.

Boundary conditions

The outer surfaces of the pellet are at the same concentration. Hence, we have

$$C_A = C_A^o \quad \text{at} \quad z = \pm\delta$$

It may be noted that this corresponds to gradient being zero at the center of the pellet.

9.12.3 Concentration profiles

The solution is easily found to be

$$\frac{C_A}{C_A^o} = \frac{\cosh(\sqrt{ak^s/\mathcal{D}_A}\,z)}{\cosh(\sqrt{ak^s/\mathcal{D}_A}\,\delta)}$$

The quantity of interest is the rate of reaction. At steady state, all the mass diffusing reacts. Hence, the rate of consumption of A by the *entire catalyst pellet* is simply equal to the flux of A at the surface of the pellet. The consumption per unit volume of the pellet is then given by

$$\text{Rate of consumption per unit volume of pellet} = \frac{1}{\delta}\mathcal{D}_A \left.\frac{dC_A}{dz}\right|_{z=\delta}$$

Substituting the solution into the above expression, the rate of consumption is given by

$$ak^s C_A^o \frac{\tanh(\sqrt{ak^s/\mathcal{D}_A}\,\delta)}{\sqrt{ak^s/\mathcal{D}_A}\,\delta}$$

9.12.4 Look at the results

The solution shows that concentration of the reactant decreases into the depth of the catalyst pellet. It is expected because reactant gets consumed as it diffuses into the pellet. The decrease in concentration is less sharp with increase in diffusion coefficient. This is also expected as diffusion becomes faster while rate of consumption due to reaction remains unaltered as diffusion coefficient increases.

If diffusion was very fast, the concentration inside the pellet would be C_A^o, and it is confirmed by the solution. The rate of reaction per unit volume of the pellet would then be equal to $ak^s C_A^o$. The term multiplying this in the expression for the rate of reaction is then a correction that accounts for the effects of diffusion. These results are well known[22] in chemical reaction engineering. The factor

$$\phi = \sqrt{ak^s/\mathcal{D}_A}\delta$$

is known as the Thiele modulus and the correction to the reaction rate if diffusion is fast is known as the *effectiveness factor*:

$$\eta = \frac{\tanh(\sqrt{ak^s/\mathcal{D}_A}\delta)}{\sqrt{ak^s/\mathcal{D}_A}\delta} = \frac{\tanh\phi}{\phi}$$

If the effectiveness factor is small, the concentration inside the pellet is less than the bulk value and hence the reaction rate decreases. The catalyst area is not being utilized at its full potential. As can be seen, as $\phi \to 0$, diffusion is fast, Thiele modulus goes to zero and the effectiveness factor approaches unity. In the other limit, as $\phi \to \infty$, effectiveness factor approaches $1/\phi$, which is less than unity.

A very characteristic feature of chemical engineering is the analysis of phenomena involving interaction between physical and chemical processes. Diffusion and reaction in catalyst pellets is one such instance. As pellets are a composite of fine catalyst particles, in general, a two phase analysis is needed. However, under many practically important conditions where particle size is very small compared to the pellet size, one can get away with treating as if the reaction is homogeneous. Such an analysis gives an indication of estimating the relative importance of rates of diffusion into a pellet and reaction on the catalytic surface.

Problems for Chapter 9.

9.1 Consider a cylindrical pore on whose walls the following irreversible catalytic reaction occurs: $3A \to A_3$.

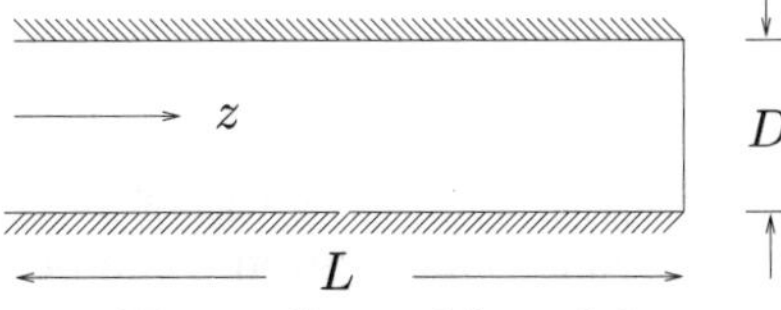

Figure for problem 9.1.

At the pore mouth, $z = 0$, pure A flows at a fast rate, i.e., $x_A = 1$, where x_A is the mole fraction of A in the mixture of gases. The intrinsic surface reaction rate per unit area of the surface is given by $k'' x_A$. As $D << L$, **gradients in the radial directions are negligible**. Consider steady state has been reached and that only A and A_3 are present in the system. Derive the differential equation and the boundary conditions needed to compute the steady state rate at which A is being consumed. Calculate the rate at which A is being consumed.

9.2 Consider a cylindrical catalyst pore of radius R and length L. The following reaction occurs at the catalyst walls: $A \rightarrow 2B$ The intrinsic rate of reaction in mole/(sec m^2) is given by

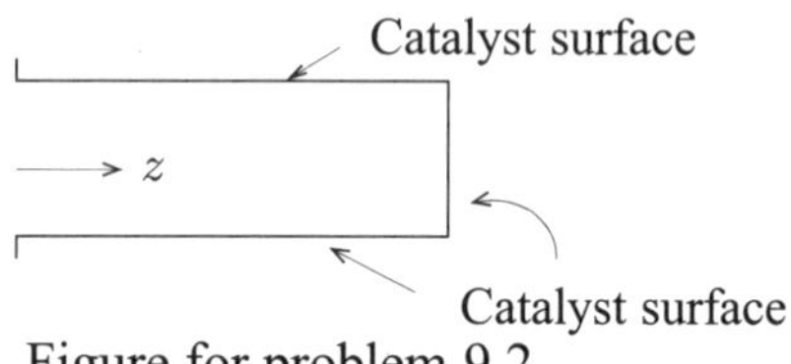

Figure for problem 9.2

$k'' C x_A$. The mole fraction of A at the pore mouth $z = 0$ is x_{Ao}. An inert C is also present in the system and the mole fraction of C at $z = 0$ is x_{Co}. As $R << L$, **gradients in the radial directions are negligible**. Consider steady state has been reached. Simplify the relevant species conservation equations to derive differential equations. Specify the boundary conditions needed to solve the differential equation. Relate $x_A(z)$ to the rate of production of B in a single pore.

9.3 Consider a porous solid with pores of very small size. The pore walls are coated with a thin film of solid A which sublimes. One end of the porous solid is sealed by attaching it to a thin and highly conductive slab, which is being maintained at a constant temperature T_o. The

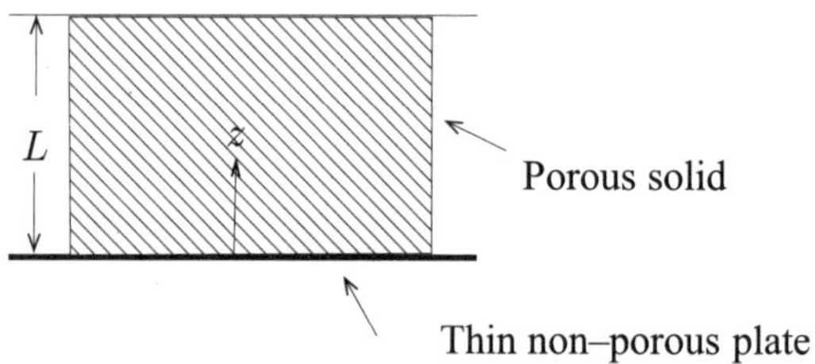

Figure for problem 9.3

other side of the porous solid is exposed to a flowing stream of gas B. The gas is at a bulk temperature of T_b and the mole fraction of A in the gas is zero. The solid sublimes into the gas since $T_o > T_b$. We wish to calculate the rate of sublimation of A into the gas stream under **steady state** conditions.

The saturation vapor pressure of A at temperature T ($T_o > T > T_b$) is given by $p_s = H_A T$. Further $p_s << P$ where P is the total pressure in the system. As the range of temperatures is small, the total molar concentration c can be considered to be constant.

Assume that temperature and mole fraction vary only in the z direction. Further, assume that the vapor in the porous space and the solid are at equilibrium. Let the latent heat of sublimation per mole of A by Q_s.

The heat and mass transfer coefficients between the gas B and the porous solid are h and k_m respectively. The effective diffusion coefficient of A in porous solid by D_e, and the effective thermal conductivity of the porous solid by k_e. Derive the differential equations that govern energy and mass balance. Specify the boundary conditions. Derive an expression for the mass flux of A into the gas B. Do you think that A might not be present in some portions of the porous solid depending on the operating conditions?

9.4 A stream of inerts containing A as a dilute component is available. A spherical porous catalyst pellet (radius = R, area per unit volume = a) is being used to convert reactant A in this stream to product B. However, A also gets converted to a side product C by a parallel reaction. Both reactions are exothermic and the heat of reactions can be taken to be given by $-\Delta H_B$ and $-\Delta H_C$. The rate of formation of B and C per unit area of catalyst are respectively given by $k''_B C_A$ and $k''_C C_A$, where C_A is the concentration of A in the pore space. The rate constants depend upon the temperature. The rates of external heat and mass transfer processes are very high. Amongst all the components, diffusion coefficient of A (D_{Ae}) is the smallest. Denote the effective thermal conductivity of the pellet by k. Outside the pellet, the temperature is T_o and the concentration of A is C_{Ao}. Derive the differential equations to find the concentration of A in the catalyst pellet at **steady** state. Specify the boundary conditions required. How can the fraction of A converted to B can be found?

9.5 a) Derive an expression for the effectiveness factor for a spherical porous catalyst pellet for the following reversible reaction:

$$A \rightleftharpoons B$$

Assume that the reaction rate expression is first order with respect to both A and B. Assume that the solutions are dilute. (b) Is the catalyst more effective when the reaction mixture is far away from equilibrium or nearer to equilibrium?

9.6 A porous spherical particle of radius R has been placed in a stream of gas B at a pressure P and temperature T. B is present in the pore space but does not adsorb on the surface. Suddenly the composition of the stream is changed, without changing the pressure and the temperature by introducing gas A into the stream. The composition is now maintained constant at a mole fraction of $x_{A\infty}$. Gas A can adsorb on the surface of the particle. The total surface area of the particle per unit volume is a. The adsorption equilibrium in the range of interest is linear. The mole fraction in equilibrium with the surface x_A^e is related to the surface concentration is given by

$$x_A^e = K_e'' C_{A,s}$$

where K_e'' is a constant and $C_{A,s}$ is the surface concentration in moles per unit area. The rate of adsorption can be assumed to be also linear:

$$\text{amount adsorbed per unit time per unit area} = k''\,(x_A - x_A^e)$$

where k'' is a constant. (a) Will the particle reach a state where nothing changes with time? What will be the mole fraction of A in the pore space of the particle? (b) Will the concentration of A on the surface of the sphere, i.e., $r = R$ change with location in general? Under what conditions can we neglect this change? (c) If the mass transfer coefficient between the gas stream and the spherical particle is large, and if the variations of composition on the surface of the sphere are negligible, what will be the boundary conditions needed for determining the concentration profiles inside the sphere? (d) Write the species balance for component A inside the sphere. Use a pseudo-homogeneous model. (e) Write the mass balance equation for species A on the surface to determine the rate of change of $c_{A,s}$ at any given position inside the sphere. (f) Specify the initial and boundary conditions needed to solve the problem. Neglect the gas phase mass transfer resistance to the surface of the sphere. (g) How will the equations simplify if $k'' >>> 1$?

9.7 Consider a porous spherical catalyst particle of radius R suspended in a large volume of a well stirred dilute solution of species A. The mass transfer coefficient between the solution and the external surface of the catalyst particle is k_m based on concentration units. Solute A diffuses **into** the catalyst particle and reacts irreversibly to form products. The reaction can be modelled as pseudo-homogeneous and to be first order with respect to concentration of A. The initial concentration of A in the solution is C_o. The mass transfer coefficient between the solution and the sphere is given by k_m. Find the rate of consumption of A.

9.8 Solute A present in a solvent decomposes irreversibly by a homogeneous reaction to yield product B:

$$\text{A} \rightarrow 2\text{B}$$

and the rate of the above reaction follows first order kinetics. Compound A also reacts *instantaneously* on a catalyst surface to yield product C:

$$\text{A} \rightarrow \text{C}$$

A solution containing A at a concentration of C_o is placed at $t = 0$ between two planar catalytic surfaces separated by distance L. Find the ratio of B to C formed for **short** contact times. Assume that solutions are dilute.

9.9 Consider a membrane containing catalytic sites where the following irreversible reaction occurs:

$$A \rightarrow C$$

The reaction can be modelled as pseudo-homogeneous and to be first order with respect to concentration of A. A solvent stream containing A at a concentration of $C_{b,l}$ flows past one face of the membrane while pure solvent flows past the other face. The mass transfer coefficients for both faces is the same and is denoted by k_m. If the membrane does not contain any A initially, find the unsteady concentration profiles.

9.10 Hydrogen and oxygen are being fed to a tube in stoichiometric ratio to form water. The average velocity of the stream entering the tube is V. The tube wall is made of a very good catalyst and oxidation of hydrogen is known to proceed irreversibly and instantaneously on the catalyst surface. The tube diameter is D while its length is L. To avoid danger of explosions, a very, very short tube is used, *i.e.*, $L/D << 1$. Correspondingly, the conversions are small. The flow is laminar. Derive an expression for the bulk concentration of water in the exit stream?

9.11 An insulated and infinitely long tube is partly filled with liquid A. The other part of the tube is filled with gas B, insoluble in A. Initially the gas and liquid are not in contact, and are initially at a temperature T_∞. They are brought into contact with each other suddenly at $t = 0$. The vapor pressure of A, p_s is dependent on temperature and is given by the Clausius–Clapeyron equation:

$$p_s(T) = C\, exp\left(\frac{-\Delta\, H}{R_g\, T}\right)$$

where C is a constant, $-\Delta\, H$ is the heat of vaporization and R_g is the universal gas constant. (a) Write appropriate balance equations needed to obtain the rate of evaporation of A. Assume that the effect of the fall in the liquid level can be neglected. (b) Specify the necessary boundary and initial conditions. (c) Sketch the profiles of the mole fraction of A in the gas phase and the temperature profiles in both the phases.

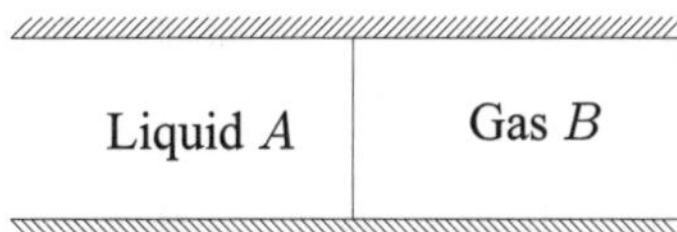

Figure for problem 9.11.

9.12 A solid sphere of radius R is placed in a uniform flow. Let us say that the uniform velocity is in the z direction and is equal to V_∞. The solubility of the solid in the fluid is very small. Let it be C_s. The fluid far away from the sphere does not contain any solute and hence the sphere slowly dissolves into the fluid. Assuming that the radius of the sphere is constant and that its radius remains constant at R, (i) specify a convenient coordinate system that you will use to solve the problem, (ii) specify the nonzero velocities, (iii) specify the coordinates on which concentration depends. (iv) simplify the mass balance equation, (v) specify the boundary conditions needed for solving the mass balance equation.

9.13 A spherical drop of hexane containing acetic acid (A) is rising at its terminal velocity in an aqueous solution of NaOH (B). A is soluble in both hexane and water. Note that solutions are dilute. The following irreversible reaction can occur:

$$A + B \rightarrow C + H_2O$$

and the rate of reaction is given by kC_AC_B. C and B are insoluble in hexane, and it can be assumed that water and hexane are mutually insoluble. We are interested in calculating the rate of loss of acetic acid from the drop. It is convenient to solve this problem from a frame located at the center of the drop and moving with the terminal velocity of the drop. Select spherical coordinates for formulating the problem. (i) Simplify the relevant equations of conservation of mass of species. (ii) Specify the boundary conditions for all the species. The concentrations of acetic acid in water and hexane at equilibrium are linearly proportional to each other. (iii) We want to investigate an important limiting case: alkali is in excess. How do the boundary conditions change if $k \to \infty$ for this case?

9.14 A mixture of benzene and toluene is evaporating from a liquid film into a stagnant nitrogen atmosphere. The temperature of the liquid film is 90 $°C$. The total pressure is 1 atm. The vapors condense at a cold wall and form a film. The cold wall is being maintained at 0 $°C$. The **partial** pressures exerted by benzene and toluene in the liquid film on the hot wall are 0.6 and 0.35 atm respectively. The vapor pressures of both benzene and toluene at 0 $°C$ are nearly equal to zero. Assume steady state prevails. (a) Specify the species conservation equations. How many boundary conditions are needed? Specify them. Using Fick's law with effective binary diffusivity, $\mathbf{N}_i = -c\,D_{im}\nabla x_i + x_i \sum_j \mathbf{N}_j$, derive expressions for the mass fluxes of benzene and toluene. b) What is the composition of the liquid condensing on the cold wall?

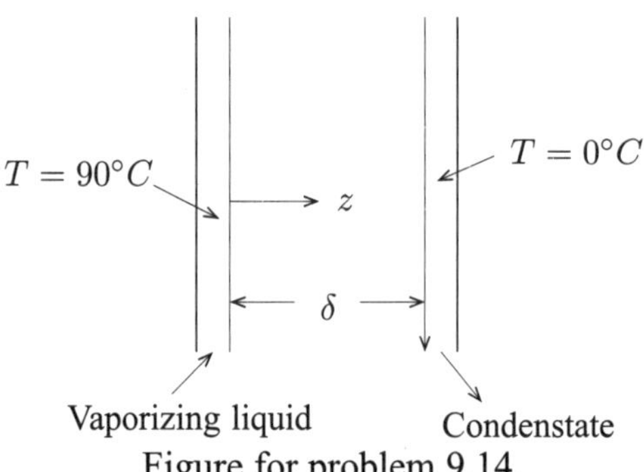

Figure for problem 9.14.

9.15 Liquid (component 1) is vaporizing into a mixture of gases (components 2 and 3). The gases

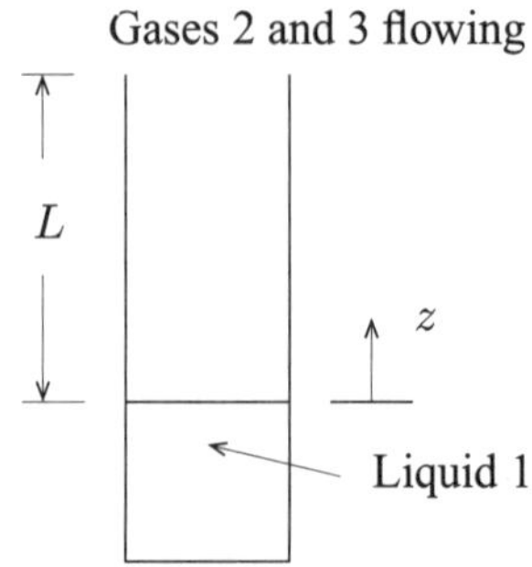

Figure for problem 9.15.

are insoluble in the liquid. An equimolar mixture of the gases is flowing past the top of the tube at $z = L$. Derive an expression for the steady state flux of component 1 using Stefan–Maxwell equations. Assume that the liquid level is constant.

9.16 A mixture of volatile liquids A and B is placed in a beaker. They form ideal solutions. The mole fraction of A in the liquid is x_{Al}. Assume that the level of the liquid and its composition are constant. Above the liquid, the beaker was filled with an inert gas C which is insoluble in the liquid mixture. The distance between the liquid level and the top of the beaker is δ. Pure C flows past the top of the beaker. As a result, A and B vaporize into the gas stream. This stream is passed through a condenser to remove A and B. (a) Using Stefan–Maxwell equations, derive an expression for the composition of the condensate. (b) Is there a possibility that the liquid composition and the condensate composition are the same exhibiting an azeotrope like behavior even though the solutions are ideal?

9.17 (a) Consider the following reaction occurring at a catalytic wall:

$$A + B \rightarrow C$$

Assume that steady state prevails. How many independent fluxes are there? Simplify the Stefan–Maxwell equations for this case assuming that diffusion occurs in only z direction. (b) It is desired that film model be used to solve the problem. Suppose both the mole fractions of A and B at the edge of the film are equal to 0.5. Suppose the reaction occurs **instantaneously** at the catalytic wall. How many boundary conditions are needed to determine the rate of production of C per unit area of the catalyst? Specify them.

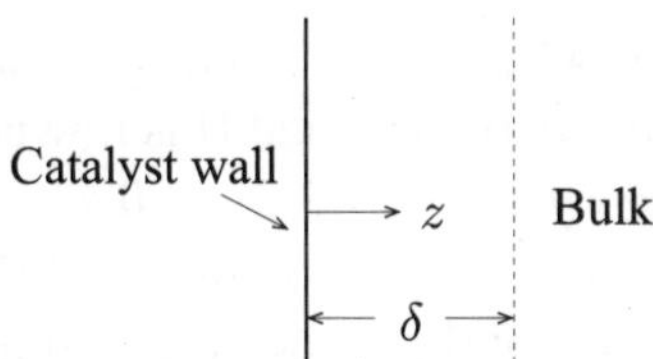

Figure for problem 9.17.

9.18 Silicon dioxide (SiO_2) is deposited on quartz in a process for making optical fibres. The deposition is achieved by flowing an **equimolar** mixture of gases $SiCl_4$ and O_2 past the hot quartz surface. Silicon dioxide grows on top of silicon, much like a layer of ash. In this problem we neglect the resistance in the ash layer and focus on the gas phase resistances. The following reaction occurs at the **hot quartz** surface:

$$SiCl_4 + O_2 \rightarrow SiO_2 + 2Cl_2$$

where the SiO_2 formed is in solid phase while the rest are in gaseous form. We want to calculate the rate of formation of the layer of SiO_2 under **steady state** conditions using film model and Fick's law with effective binary diffusivity: $\mathbf{N}_i = -c D_{im} \nabla x_i + x_i \sum_j \mathbf{N}_j$. c is the total molar concentration and can be assumed to be constant. The rate of formation of SiO_2 at the quartz surface is given by $kx_{Si,w}x_{O_2,w}$ where $x_{Si,w}$, $x_{O_2,w}$ represent mole fraction of $SiCl_4$ and O_2 in the gas phase adjacent to the hot quartz surface. (i) Simplify the relevant mass conservation equations and substitute the Fick's law into them. (ii) What are the relevant boundary conditions? (iii) Solve the equations to find the rate of increase in the thickness of SiO_2 layer if its molar density in the solid phase is ρ_{Si}.

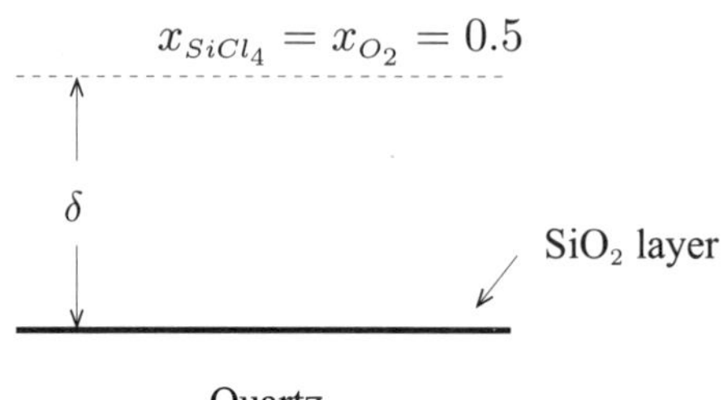

Figure for problem 9.18.

9.19 The following irreversible reaction occurring at a catalyst surface is being used to produce C from A and B.

$$\mathrm{A + B \rightarrow 4C}$$

However, the mixture of A and B also contains an impurity D, which also reacts irreversibly at the catalyst surface to produce an undesirable product E:

$$\mathrm{A + D \rightarrow E}$$

The rate of these reactions per unit area of the catalyst surface in the order listed above are given by $k_1^{''}\, x_A\, x_B$ and $k_2^{''}\, x_A\, x_D$ where x_A, x_B and x_D are mole fractions of A, B and D at the interface, respectively. A mixture of A, B and D is flowing past the catalyst at a large flow rate, and its composition is given by $x_A = 0.45$, $x_B = 0.45$ and $x_D = 0.1$. We wish to use film model to find the steady state rates of production of C and E.
a) There are five fluxes, one for each of the five species. Of them, how many are independent?
b) Use the effective diffusivity model

$$\mathbf{N_i} = -C\, D_{im}\, \nabla x_i + x_i \sum \mathbf{N_j}$$

to derive equations for determining x_i as a function of position in the film. c) Specify the boundary conditions.
d) Solve the equations to derive the necessary expressions to obtain the rate of production of D and E.

9.20 Saturated steam at 100°C is condensing at a constant wall maintained at 90°C. The heat transfer transfer coefficient corresponding to the liquid film is 1000 k cal/(m^2 hr°C). (a) What is the condensation rate per unit area if the latent heat of condensation is 10^4 kcal/kmol? (b) Look at example 18.5-1 of the first edition of the text by Bird *et al.* [1]. Choose liquid at T_o as the reference, instead of vapor at T_o chosen in the book. How does eq. (18.5-7) change?

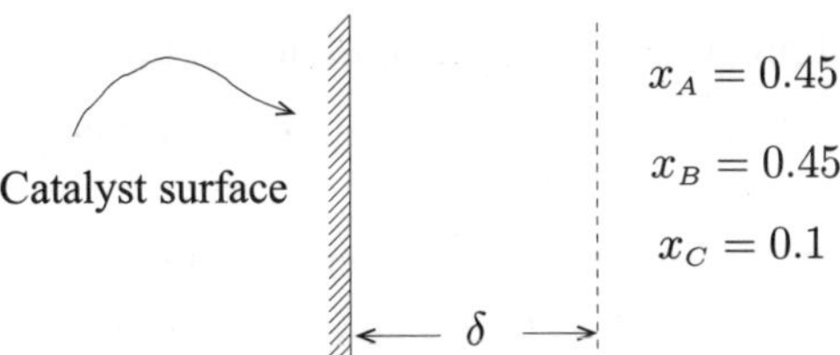

Figure for problem 9.19.

Verify if eq. (18.5-8) is still valid. c) Consider condensation in the presence of a small amount of air. The temperature of the vapor phase is still 100 C while the mole fraction of air in the vapor is 0.04. What should be the wall temperature to maintain the same rate of condensation as in part a)? (d) Can you give an **approximate** estimate of the decrease in the condensation rate compared to part a) if the wall temperature was maintained at 90 C? The following data will be of use:
Diffusion coefficient = 0.018 m^2/hr, film thickness = 10^{-4} m, concentration = 3 X 10^{-2} kmol/m^3, k = 0.025 kcal/(m hr C), c_P = 10 kcal/(kmol C). Vapor pressure of water decreases by about 35 mm Hg per degree C near 100 C.

9.21 A **thin** layer of coke has been deposited on the surface of a spherical catalyst particle of diameter D. The coke is being burnt by passing hot gaseous oxygen to regenerate the catalyst. While it is desirable to have a very high burning rate by employing high temperatures and pure oxygen, if the temperature exceeds a certain value, the catalyst sinters and such conditions have to be avoided. Thus, we wish to calculate the burning rate of coke as a function of temperature and composition of the gas using the film model. The bulk temperature of the gas is T_∞, and mole fraction of O_2 in the bulk is x_{O_2}. Assume that only CO_2 forms and the reaction occurs **only** at the **surface**. The rate of burning reaction per unit area is given by:

$$A\,exp\left(-\frac{E}{R_g T}\right)\,x_{O_2}$$

where A, E and R_g are constants, and x_{O_2} is the mole fraction of O_2 at the surface. Denote the heat of combustion of coke by $-\Delta H$.

The particle is initially at a uniform temperature of T_o before being exposed to the gas mixture. (a) Simplify the energy equation to determine the **unsteady** temperature profiles in the particle. Specify the initial and the boundary conditions. (b) Determine the temperature profiles in the solid under **pseudo-steady** conditions. (c) Simplify the species conservation equation under **pseudo-steady** conditions in the gas phase assuming that the physical properties are constant and that the total molar concentration is constant. Derive expressions for the temperature and concentration profiles in the gas phase. (d) Derive an expression for the burning rate. (e) When the coke on the catalyst particle is burnt in pure oxygen, the reaction rates are high and hence the temperature of the catalyst particle can reach high values resulting in sintering of the catalyst. To avoid this, a mixture of nitrogen and oxygen are used in place of pure oxygen. Rework the problem using Stefan–Maxwell equations.

Denote the physical properties by subscript f and of the solid by subscript s, e.g, ρ_f, ρ_s, k_f, k_s *etc*. The heat transfer coefficient between the fluid and the solid is given by $h = \frac{k_f}{\delta}$.

9.22 The unsteady temperature profile in a sphere of radius R, initially at T_o and whose surface temperature is suddenly raised to (and maintained constant at) T_s for $t > 0$ is given by:

$$\frac{T - T_o}{T_s - T_o} = 1 + \frac{2R}{\pi r} \sum \frac{(-1)^n}{n!} sin \frac{n\pi r}{R} exp \left(-\frac{n^2 \pi^2 \alpha t}{R^2} \right)$$

(a) Consider a porous spherical catalyst particle of radius R suspended in a **large volume** of a well stirred dilute solution of species A. Solute A diffuses **into** the catalyst particle and reacts irreversibly to form products. The reaction can be modelled as pseudo-homogeneous and to be first order with respect to concentration of A. The concentration of A in the solution is C_o, and mass transfer coefficient between the solution and the sphere is very large. Initially A is absent in the sphere. Determine the unsteady concentration profiles. (b) What is the steady solution for part (a)? Check this against the limit obtained from part (a). (c) Find the rate of consumption of A.

Notes

[1]What follows is to be treated as a qualitative justification rather than a derivation.

[2]The acceleration is given by the driving force minus the frictional forces. The surface forces are the viscous or frictional forces. This is the basis for deriving the Cauchy's equation of motion.

[3]As can be seen it is the negative gradient of Gibbs free energy but ignoring the dependence on temperature. As a result we have to add the thermal diffusion fluxes separately. However, please note that we are not considering Soret effect in this text.

[4]In equating the two, we are using the ideas of Brownian motion and neglecting acceleration of diffusive motion.

[5]Suppose we have components A and B in a multicomponent mixture. Then we will have D_{AB} in a multicomponent system. We can have a system where only A and B are present. The diffusion coefficient in this system is the binary diffusivity$\mathcal{D}_{AB}$. These two need not be equal and in general are not equal.

[6]The gas phase is a single component.

[7]It is a low flux coefficient since we are dealing with dilute solutions.

[8]It is realistic since the solute reacts with B.

[9]Instantaneous reaction refers to the rate constant being infinite. The rate of consumption of species is finite. Hence, the concentrations must be equal to zero.

[10] We have to really account for the fact that the velocity of the wall will also be not zero. The wall will have to recede as it dissolves. What has been written is correct if density of the solid is large compared to both the density of the solution and the concentration of solute in the solution

[11]If the components are ideal gases, this is possible if molecular weight of component 3 is smaller than that of component 2, and molecular weight of component 1 is less than that of component 2.

[12]The same result is obtained from Navier–Stokes equations in cylindrical coordinates when the mass average velocity is put to zero. However, we are making the assumption that pressure is uniform across the cross–section of the tube. This is not exact since the radial distance from the axis of rotation is not constant across the cross–section of the tube. For a more exact treatment, see text by Probstein [4].

[13]This long-winded explanation is not needed for those with greater physical feel. For species which occupy more volume per unit weight, volume fraction will be greater than the weight fraction.

[14]We encourage you to do it!

[15]It can form ionic species H and HSO_4 also.

[16]Electrical solutions are not neutral very near to charged surfaces. Such situation does arise in a zone few tens of nanometers thick near electrodes. This zone is referred to as electrical double layer. The potential gradients are large in the double layer, and this does affect charge transfer reactions. We will not consider this complication in this text. Interested readers should refer to the book by Newman and Thomas-Alyea [3].

[17]Readers interested in concentrated solutions should refer to the book by Newman and Thomas-Alyea [3].

[18]Electrons are not soluble in electrolytes and hence, unlike in solids, it the ionic species that carry current. Conversely, ions are not present in solids and it is electrons that carry current in solids. There are many exceptions to this, and solid oxides are there which conduct ions. Similarly, there are exceptions whereby solvated electrons can be present in solvents.

[19] Addition or removal of electrons at the electrode is a charge transfer reaction which can be written as $M \rightleftharpoons M^+ + e$. This reaction occurs at the electrolyte–electrode interface and requires application of some potential.

[20]This argument is very similar to those presented in justification of the continuum model.

[21]One would notice that this is also very similar to the methods used in analyzing absorption columns.

[22]A beautiful account of the early years of use of effectiveness factors is given by Aris in *Current Contents, (Eng. Tech. Appl. Sci.)* vol 26, 28, (1982). He refers to Dr. C.H. Bosanquet, who according to Aris "saved Platinum worth his weight" to ICI.

References

[1] R.B. Bird, W.E. Stewart, and E.N. Lightfoot. *Transport Phenomena.* John Wiley, 2 edition, 2002.

[2] E.L. Cussler. *Diffusion.* Cambridge University Press, 3 edition, 2009.

[3] J. Newman and K.E. Thomas-Alyea. *Electrochemical systems.* Wiley-Interscience, 2004.

[4] R.F. Probstein. *Physicochemical Hydrodynamics: An introduction.* Wiley, 1994.

[5] R. Taylor and R. Krishna. *Multicomponent mass transfer.* Wiley, 1993.

Chapter 10

ADVANCED TOPICS IN MASS TRANSFER

We consider mass transfer to a rotating disk, which creates complex convection patterns.
Natural convection is analyzed where both heat and mass transfer occurs.
We then examine typical mass transfer problem of considerable practical importance. First is Taylor dispersion, relevant to chromatographic columns and tubular flow reactors. Here, complex interplay between radial diffusion and axial convection produce a result as if axial diffusion occurs.
Second is analysis of hydrogen fuel cell, at first with planar electrodes, and then to a cell with porous electrodes.
Third is membrane separation processes illustrated by ultra-filtration.
Freezing of solvent from a solution is examined where heat is removed, and the process is influenced by mass transfer of solute.

As was already pointed out, mass transfer in dilute solutions is mathematically identical to heat transfer. The problems solved in convective heat transfer can therefore be applied directly to convective mass transfer in dilute solutions. However, there will be problems that involve special treatment and it is those that we take up in this chapter. We will also take up topics which are important applications of mass transfer but more advanced in nature than those considered in chapter 9.

10.1 MASS TRANSFER TO A ROTATING DISK

Transfer rates of a passive[1] scalar in a convective system generally vary in the direction of flow. We have seen this in the examples in chapter 5, and section 6.2. We consider mass transfer under steady state conditions to a rotating disk since it is a special case where mass transfer rate remains constant in a convective system. As mass transfer is well characterized, it can be used with effect when it is coupled to other processes, especially heterogeneous catalytic reactions. It is widely used in electrochemistry to measure rates of charge transfer reaction and is referred to as rotating disk electrode.

10.1.1 Fluid mechanics

The apparatus consists of a circular disk which is immersed in a fluid and rotated around an axis perpendicular to its plane and passing through its center. Rotational motion is also setup in the fluid due to the no-slip condition. Such a motion creates centrifugal forces, which throw the fluid radially outward. Consequently, fluid above the disk is sucked towards the disk. The apparatus and the expected flow patterns are shown in figure 10.1.

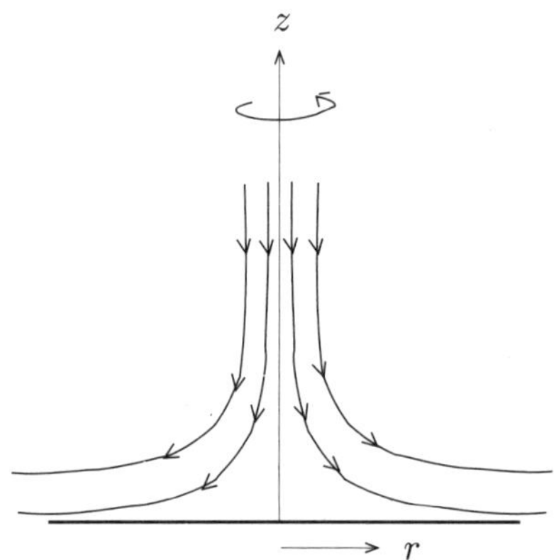

Figure 10.1. Sketch of stream lines of flow setup by a disk rotating in an otherwise stationary fluid. The rotational motion setup by the disk in the fluid creates centrifugal forces. These throw the fluid out radially which in turn creates flow from above towards the disk.

Equations of motion

We give the equations of motion to show how even such complex equations give rise to simple solvable forms. Firstly, we note that all three components of velocity are present. We do not expect them to be a function of the angle since the flow is symmetric around the z axis. When the disk rotates at a constant rotational speed, the angular velocity v_θ increases with radius, and it is expected to decrease due to viscous action as we move away from the disk or with increasing z. Hence v_θ is a function of r and z. We can present similar arguments about the other components of velocity and show that they are also functions of r and z. The equations of continuity and motion in cylindrical coordinates simplify to give:

Equation of continuity:

$$\frac{1}{r}\frac{\partial}{\partial r}(rv_r) + \frac{\partial v_z}{\partial z} = 0 \tag{10.1}$$

r Component:

$$\rho\left(v_r\frac{\partial v_r}{\partial r} - \frac{v_\theta^2}{r} + v_z\frac{\partial v_r}{\partial z}\right) = -\frac{\partial P}{\partial r} + \mu\left[\frac{\partial}{\partial r}\left(\frac{1}{r}\frac{\partial}{\partial r}(rv_r)\right) + \frac{\partial^2 v_r}{\partial z^2}\right] \tag{10.2}$$

θ Component:

$$\rho\left(v_r\frac{\partial v_\theta}{\partial r} + \frac{v_r v_\theta}{r}\right) = \mu\left[\frac{\partial}{\partial r}\left(\frac{1}{r}\frac{\partial}{\partial r}(rv_\theta)\right) + \frac{\partial^2 v_\theta}{\partial z^2}\right] \tag{10.3}$$

z Component:

$$\rho\left(v_r\frac{\partial v_z}{\partial r}+v_z\frac{\partial v_z}{\partial z}\right)=-\frac{\partial P}{\partial z}+\mu\left[\frac{1}{r}\frac{\partial}{\partial r}\left(r\frac{\partial v_z}{\partial r}\right)+\frac{\partial^2 v_z}{\partial z^2}\right] \tag{10.4}$$

Gravity was neglected in these equations. Flow was assumed to be laminar and this is valid till $\rho r^2\omega/\mu$ is less than 10^5. von Karman proposed that if the radius of the disk can be treated as infinite, some transformations can be used to convert the given partial differential equations into ordinary differential equations in z. His method is outlined below. There are no length scales available because we take the radius of the disk to be infinite. We begin with scaling of velocities. Let ω be the rotational velocity. The angular velocity should increase with radius and that is a suitable velocity scale for angular velocity:

$$v_\theta = r\omega G$$

As we described earlier, it is the centrifugal forces, which are inertial in nature, that create radial velocity. Balance of the inertial terms suggests

$$v_r = r\omega F$$

Due to viscous effects, the angular velocity decreases away from the disk. Because it drives radial motion, the radial velocity also decreases away from the plate. Hence, we expect the radial velocity to reach a maximum around a distance equal to the momentum diffusion length scale. Using the time scale offered by the rotational velocity and kinematic viscosity, we construct the following length scale of momentum diffusion

$$\ell = \sqrt{\frac{\mu}{\rho\omega}}$$

Fluid is sucked in from top to compensate for the fluid being thrown out. We therefore use mass conservation to create a velocity scale for the axial velocity. The radial flow out of a cylinder of height of ℓ must be compensated by the axial flow. Hence,

$$v_{z,ch}r^2 \sim r v_r \ell \sim r^2\omega\sqrt{\frac{\mu}{\rho\omega}}, \text{ or } v_{z,ch} \sim \sqrt{\frac{\mu\omega}{\rho}}$$

Hence, we define

$$v_z = \sqrt{\frac{\mu\omega}{\rho}}H$$

Pressure is non-dimensionalized using viscous forces

$$P = \mu\omega\mathcal{P}$$

z is non-dimensionalized using the momentum diffusion length scale

$$\zeta = z\sqrt{\frac{\rho\omega}{\mu}}$$

The functions defined along with the scalings transform the partial differential equations into

$$\left.\begin{aligned} 2F + H' &= 0 \\ F^2 - G^2 + HF' &= 0 \\ 2FG + HG' &= 0 \\ HH' + \mathcal{P}' &= H'' \end{aligned}\right\} \tag{10.5}$$

The boundary conditions are no-slip at the disk surface and both angular and radial velocities must vanish far away from the disk:

$$H = F = 0,\ G = 1 \text{ at } \zeta = 0, \text{ and } F = G = 0 \text{ as } \zeta \to \infty$$

Velocity profiles

Equations 10.5 can be solved only numerically. The solution can proceed by first solving for the velocity profiles and then integrating the last of them to find the pressure. A sketch of the velocity profiles is shown in figure 10.2. Note that the velocity gradients are confined to ζ less than about

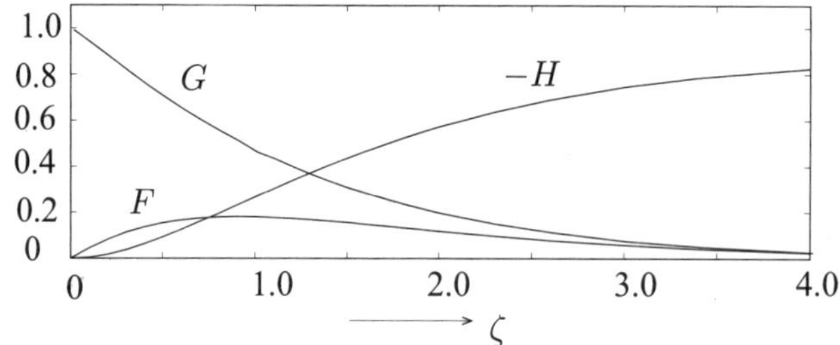

Figure 10.2. Numerically calculated velocity profiles. Data were taken from Schlichting [13].

4. Hence, the dimensional distance from the disk up to which velocity gradients exist is less than $4\sqrt{\mu/\rho\omega}$. Thus, as rotational speed increases and for liquids of low viscosities, velocity gradients are confined to decreasing distances from the disk. This distance is very much akin to thickness of a boundary layer.

10.1.2 Problem identification

Let us consider a simple example where the surface of the disk is a catalyst. Let the disk be immersed in a solvent containing a reactant A at a concentration of C_∞. Let the volume of the solution containing A be so large that it can be considered to be infinite in extent. Let A react at the surface to give products according to the reaction

$$\text{A} \rightarrow \text{products}$$

We will assume that the solutions are dilute so that we can use the binary diffusivity. We will further assume that the diffusivity is a constant. The reactant diffuses from regions far away from the disk and reacts at the surface. We are interested in determining the rate of consumption of the reactant as a function of diffusivity, rate constants, and flow parameters.

Species mass balance

The most important characteristic to note about the flow pattern is that the axial velocity is not a function of radius. It is like uniform flow towards the disk. The reactant brought towards the disk by this normal velocity can balance that which diffuses and reacts on disk. Both are proportional to the same area, and hence the concentration of solute is not expected to vary with radius[2]. The gradient of concentration at the surface of the disk is then independent of the radial position on the disk. Hence, mass transfer rates also do not vary with radius, and this is the special feature of the rotating disk. The convective diffusion equation then simplifies to

$$v_z \frac{dC}{dz} = \mathcal{D}\frac{d^2C}{dz^2}$$

where C is the concentration of A. Concentration far away from the disk is given by C_∞ and this forms the boundary condition far away from the disk:

$$C \to C_\infty \text{ as } z \to \infty$$

The boundary condition at the surface of the disk is obtained by applying flux balance. It is given by

$$\mathcal{D}\frac{dC}{dz} + \dot{\mathcal{R}}_A^s = 0 \text{ at } z = 0$$

where $\dot{\mathcal{R}}_A^s$ is the rate of *generation* of A *per unit area* of catalytic surface due to catalytic reaction. We need a rate expression for it. Let us assume that it is proportional to the concentration of A. Thus, $\dot{\mathcal{R}}_A^s = -k_s C$, where k_s is a reaction rate constant. The boundary condition at the surface of the disk will then be given by

$$\mathcal{D}\frac{dC}{dz} = k_s C \text{ at } z = 0$$

Defining a non-dimensional concentration

$$\Theta \equiv \frac{C}{C_\infty}$$

and using the non-dimensional coordinate ζ, equation of mass balance of species A can be written as

$$\text{Sc}H\frac{d\Theta}{d\zeta} = \frac{d^2\Theta}{d\zeta^2} \tag{10.6}$$

where Sc is the Schmidt number. The boundary conditions are given by

$$\frac{d\Theta}{d\zeta} = \frac{k_s}{\sqrt{\mathcal{D}\omega}}\sqrt{\text{Sc}}\Theta \text{ at } \zeta = 0, \quad \Theta \to 1 \text{ as } \zeta \to \infty$$

10.1.3 Concentration profiles

The mass balance equation can be integrated once to obtain

$$\frac{d\Theta}{d\zeta} = \Theta'(0)\exp\left(\int_0^{\zeta} dy\,\mathrm{Sc}\,H(y)\right) \tag{10.7}$$

where $\Theta'(0)$ is the derivative of non-dimensional concentration at the surface of the disk. Integrating it and using the boundary condition far away from the disk

$$1 - \Theta = \Theta'(0)\int_{\zeta}^{\infty} dx\,\exp\left(\int_0^{x} dy\,\mathrm{Sc}\,H(y)\right) \tag{10.8}$$

Applying the boundary condition at the surface of the disk to the above solution, we can solve for the gradient at the surface of the disk:

$$\Theta'(0) = \frac{1}{\dfrac{\sqrt{\mathcal{D}\omega}}{k_s\sqrt{\mathrm{Sc}}} + \displaystyle\int_0^{\infty} dx\,\exp\left(\int_0^{x} dy\,\mathrm{Sc}\,H(y)\right)} \tag{10.9}$$

Equations 10.8 and 10.9 constitute the solution to the problem. Once again, we emphasize that the flux to the surface of the disk, and hence the rate of consumption of A by catalytic reaction, is independent of r or is uniform on the entire surface of the disk.

10.1.4 Look at the results

As the velocity profiles are exactly known, various integrals can be evaluated exactly. The rate of reaction is of direct interest and can be calculated from eq. 10.9. It can then be used to find the rate constants, if needed. The ratio $\sqrt{\mathcal{D}\omega}/k_s$ reflects the ratio of resistance due to reaction and diffusion. If the reaction rate constant is small or conversely, if diffusion is very fast, concentration gradient at the surface of the disk will be zero, and concentration should equal C_∞ itself or, $\Theta = 1$ every where. Equations 10.9 and 10.8 confirm this. In this limit, the rate of reaction is given by k_sC_∞. In the opposite limit of reaction being very fast, the concentration or Θ at the surface will go to zero. Equations 10.8 and 10.9 also show this. The rate of reaction per unit area is given by the diffusive flux :

$$\text{Rate of reaction per unit area} = \mathcal{D}\sqrt{\frac{\rho\omega}{\mu}}C_\infty\Theta'(0)$$

and $\Theta'(0)$ can be evaluated from eq. 10.9 in the limit of $k_s \to \infty$. But to do this, eq. 10.9 has to be integrated numerically. However limiting forms of the integral appearing in the flux expression can be found in the limit of small and large Schmidt numbers.

Large Schmidt numbers

When Schmidt number is very large, the diffusion length scale, or equivalently the concentration boundary layer thickness, will be much smaller than the momentum boundary layer thickness.

Hence, only the velocity very near the disk surface is of importance. The boundary conditions for the equations of motion for the axial velocity indicate that both H and H' are zero at $\zeta = 0$. Hence, near the surface of the disk where ζ is very small, we expect that

$$H = -\alpha\zeta^2$$

where α is a constant. The negative sign indicates that the flow is towards the plate. Substituting this we can evaluate the integral appearing in eq. 10.9,

$$\int_0^\infty dx \exp\left(\int_0^x dy \,\text{Sc}\, H(y)\right) = \frac{(\alpha/3)^{1/3}}{\text{Sc}^{1/3}} \int_0^\infty d\beta e^{-\beta^3} = 1.612\text{Sc}^{-1/3}$$

where the constant has been numerically evaluated. Thus,

$$\Theta'(0) = \frac{1}{\dfrac{\sqrt{\mathcal{D}\omega}}{k_s\sqrt{\text{Sc}}} + 1.612\text{Sc}^{-1/3}}$$

Low Schmidt numbers

The diffusion length scale is now much larger than that of momentum diffusion length scale and hence velocity far away from the disk is relevant for finding concentration profiles. But axial velocity far away from the disk is a negative constant, $-\gamma$. Hence,

$$\int_0^\infty dx \exp\left(\int_0^x dy \,\text{Sc}\, H(y)\right) = \frac{1.131}{\text{Sc}}$$

where the constant has been obtained numerically. Hence,

$$\Theta'(0) = \frac{1}{\dfrac{\sqrt{\mathcal{D}\omega}}{k_s\sqrt{\text{Sc}}} + \dfrac{1.131}{\text{Sc}}}$$

Summary

A rotating disk sets up a very complex three-dimensional flow pattern. However, insightful analysis produces simple solutions, when the useful geometry of a finite disk is simplified by letting it extend to infinity. The solutions are expected to be valid in the central portion of a finite disk. The solutions show that mass flux to the rotating disk is independent of position. This makes the rotating disk to be a useful system to study rates of reactions and is widely used in electrochemistry.

10.2 NATURAL CONVECTION

As discussed[3] in section 6.3, temperature gradients create buoyancy forces and induce motion. The density of a solvent is affected when a solute dissolves in it. Thus, concentration gradients can also cause density gradients, and create motion. Thus, natural convection can also accompany mass transfer. In the more general case, natural convection is caused by the combined effect of concentration and temperature gradients. Such a general case has to be treated numerically. However, two limiting cases can be examined where simple scaling relationships can be found. In one limit, motion is driven mostly by density differences caused by concentration gradient or driven by mass transfer. In the other limit, it is the heat transfer driven or the density difference created by temperature gradient that is the dominant factor generating motion. Let us first attempt to derive the conditions to ascertain which of the two limits is applicable in a given situation. We will consider the case where both Prandtl and Schmidt numbers are much greater than unity, a case applicable generally to liquids.

10.2.1 Boundary layer past a vertical plate, Pr>>1, Sc>>1

Consider the natural convection boundary layer created over a vertical plate. See figure 6.6. Let the plate be at T_w while the fluid far away is at T_∞. Suppose that the plate is made up of a solute which dissolves into the solvent. Let its solubility in the solvent be C_s. Let us define the coefficient of expansion for concentration as

$$\beta_m = -\frac{1}{\rho}\left(\frac{\partial \rho}{\partial C}\right)_T$$

where C is the concentration of the solute. β_m will be positive if density of the solution decreases with increasing concentration. We have defined the coefficient of expansion for temperature as

$$\beta = -\frac{1}{\rho}\left(\frac{\partial \rho}{\partial T}\right)_C$$

Let C_∞, the concentration far away from the plate be the reference concentration while T_∞ can be used as the reference temperature. Hence, for not too large a change in concentration[4] and temperature, we can write

$$\frac{\rho}{\rho_o} = 1 - \beta_m(C - C_\infty) - \beta(T - T_\infty)$$

where ρ_o is the density at T_∞ and C_∞, β_m and β are evaluated at C_∞ and T_∞.

The equation of motion is now given by[5]

$$v_x\frac{\partial v_x}{\partial x} + v_y\frac{\partial v_x}{\partial y} = \nu\frac{\partial^2 v_x}{\partial y^2} + g\beta(T - T_\infty) + g\beta_m(C - C_\infty)$$

There are two factors which determine whether temperature difference or concentration difference dominates in generating flow. The first factor is the relative magnitudes of the buoyancy force created by the two causes. As indicated by the equation of motion, the maximum buoyancy force created due to temperature and concentration differences are given respectively by $g\beta(T_o - T_\infty)$ and $g\beta_m(C_s - C_\infty)$, and the relative magnitudes of the two is the first factor that determines the dominant one. The second factor that influences their effect in creating motion is the depth of penetration of heat and mass. If one of them is small, the volume which comes under the influence of the corresponding buoyancy force will be small, and it will be ineffective in inducing motion over a wider zone. The depth of penetration is reflected by the corresponding diffusivity. We calculate the characteristic velocity created by either if the two forces were to be present separately, and compare the two to derive the condition to predict dominance. This idea will work well as long as they are not comparable to each other. We are considering the case where both Prandtl and Schmidt numbers are greater than unity. Hence, the momentum boundary layer will be thicker than either thermal or concentration boundary layer. Hence, we have to balance the viscous forces over the thermal or concentration boundary layer with the corresponding buoyancy forces. Consider the case where we assume that buoyancy forces created by temperature differences alone. Refer to section 6.3, where using this idea we estimated that

$$V_{ch,thermal} \sim \frac{\beta g \Delta T \delta_T^2}{\nu}$$

where $\Delta T = T_o - T_\infty$. There, we also estimated the thermal boundary layer thickness thereby balancing heat transfer by convection with conduction:

$$\frac{V_{ch,thermal}}{L} \sim \frac{\alpha}{\delta_T^2} \text{ or } \delta_T^2 \sim \frac{\alpha L}{V_{ch,thermal}}$$

Using this to eliminate thickness of the boundary layer from the previous equation, we estimate the characteristic velocity as

$$V_{ch,thermal}^2 \sim g\beta\Delta T \frac{\alpha L}{\nu}$$

We can do a similar calculation to estimate the characteristic velocity created by concentration difference, if it was present alone. It is found to be

$$V_{ch,mass}^2 \sim g\beta_m \Delta C \frac{\mathcal{D} L}{\nu}$$

where $\Delta C = C_s - C_\infty$. Thus, the ratio of the characteristic velocities created by either is given by

$$\frac{V_{ch,mass}^2}{V_{ch,thermal}^2} \sim \frac{\beta_m \Delta C \mathcal{D}}{\beta \Delta T \alpha}$$

Thus, if

$$\frac{\beta_m \Delta C}{\beta \Delta T} >> \frac{\alpha}{\mathcal{D}} \equiv \text{Le}$$

the motion is mass transfer driven. If the inequality is the other way around, the flow is driven by heat transfer. The ratio of thermal diffusivity to mass diffusivity is known as *Lewis number*, Le.

Mass transfer driven flow

This calculation will be identical to the one made for heat transfer driven flow in section 6.3, and we get

$$\frac{\delta_m}{L} \sim \left(\frac{\mathcal{D}\nu}{\beta_m g \Delta C L^3}\right)^{0.25}$$

where δ_m is the thickness of the concentration boundary layer. The mass transfer coefficient is given by the ratio of the diffusivity to the boundary layer thickness. The Sherwood number is then given by

$$\frac{k_m L}{\mathcal{D}} = \text{Sh} \sim \left(\frac{\beta_m g \Delta C L^3}{\mathcal{D}\nu}\right)^{0.25} \sim \text{Ra}_\text{m}^{0.25}$$

where Ra_m is the Rayleigh number corresponding to the concentration difference. It is the analog of Rayleigh number defined earlier for heat transfer.

As mass transfer occurs, heat transfer can occur if the temperature of the plate is different from that of the fluid. The Nusselt number can be calculated from the characteristic velocity derived *for mass transfer driven flow*. We will illustrate that procedure with the calculation of Sherwood number while the flow is dominated by heat transfer.

Heat transfer driven flow

We now turn attention to the other limit where flow is driven by heat transfer, but mass transfer also occurs since the material of the plate is soluble in the solvent. As the flow is dominated by the buoyancy forces generated by temperature differences, the analysis carried out in section 6.3 applies here. We take the following results from there:

$$V^2_{ch,thermal} \sim g\beta\Delta T \frac{\alpha L}{\nu} \quad \text{or} \quad V_{ch,thermal} \sim \frac{\alpha}{L}\sqrt{\text{Ra}_T}$$

where Ra_T is the Rayleigh number based on temperature difference and the corresponding coefficient of expansion.

There are two cases possible, even when both Prandtl and Schmidt numbers are much larger than unity. Let us consider the case where Schmidt number is greater than Prandtl number or Le < 1. In this instance, the concentration boundary layer will be thinner than the thermal boundary layer. This is shown in figure 10.3. Assuming linear extrapolation, the characteristic velocity in the

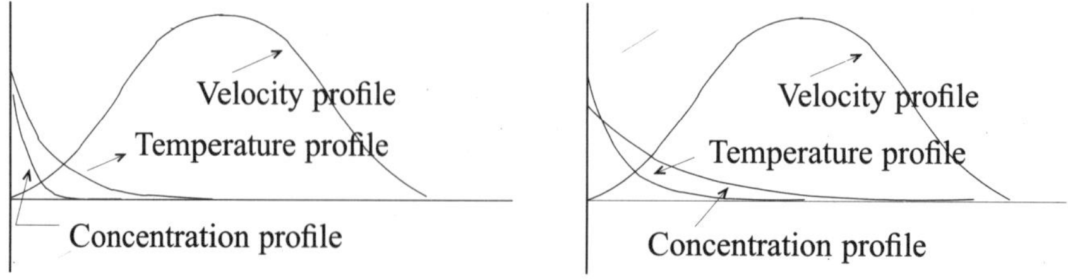

Figure 10.3. Sketch of velocity, temperature and concentration profiles in a heat transfer natural convection boundary layer. The left panel shows expected profiles when Schmidt number is larger than the Prandtl number, while the right panel shows profiles for the other way around.

concentration boundary layer will be given by $V_{ch,thermal}\delta_m/\delta_T$. But from balance of convective and diffusive transport of mass

$$\frac{V_{ch,thermal}\delta_m}{L\delta_T} \sim \frac{\mathcal{D}}{\delta_m^2}$$

Substituting for the characteristic velocity, we can solve for the concentration boundary layer thickness:

$$\delta_m^3 \sim \frac{\mathcal{D}L^2\delta_T}{\alpha\sqrt{\text{Ra}_T}}$$

We also have a result for thermal boundary layer thickness by balancing convective and conductive heat transfer:

$$\frac{V_{ch,thermal}}{L} \sim \frac{\alpha}{\delta^2{}_T} \text{ or } \delta_T \sim L\text{Ra}_T^{-0.25}$$

Substituting all these results, we get

$$\delta_m \sim \left(\frac{\mathcal{D}}{\alpha}\right)^{1/3} L\text{Ra}_T^{-0.25}$$

Thus, Sherwood number is given by

$$\text{Sh} \sim \text{Le}^{1/3}\text{Ra}_T^{0.25}$$

The other possible limit is when Schmidt number is smaller than the Prandtl number. The concentration boundary layer is thicker than the thermal boundary layer. However, as Schmidt number is still greater than unity, concentration boundary layer will still be thinner than the momentum boundary layer. As can be seen from figure 10.3, the characteristic velocity for mass transfer is V_{ch} itself. The balance between convective and diffusive mass transfer gives

$$\frac{V_{ch,thermal}}{L} \sim \frac{\mathcal{D}}{\delta_m^2} \text{ or } \delta_m \sim \left(\frac{\mathcal{D}}{\alpha}\right)^{1/2} L\text{Ra}_T^{-0.25}$$

The Sherwood number dependence now becomes

$$\text{Sh} \sim \text{Le}^{1/2}\text{Ra}_T^{0.25}$$

There are other interesting cases one can derive for other combinations, but still for heat transfer driven natural convection.

i) For Pr >>1 but Sc << 1,

$$\text{Sh} \sim \text{Le}\sqrt{\text{Pr}}\text{Ra}_T^{0.25}$$

ii) For Pr<<1 but Sc >> 1,

$$\text{Sh} \sim \text{Le}^{1/3}\text{Pr}^{-1/12}\text{Ra}_T^{0.25}$$

10.2.2 Summary

Natural convection is driven by buoyancy forces created by density gradients caused by both temperature differences and differences in the concentration of a solute. It is interesting to determine the conditions when one of the two dominates in the creation of motion. The magnitude of density changes caused by temperature or concentration gradients is not the only factor that determines this. The depth of penetration of heat or mass of the solute is also important. Simple extension of ideas covered in section 6.3 can be used to derive the condition of dominance. Further, the same ideas can be used to determine the scaling relationship of mass transfer coefficient or Sherwood number to Prandtl, Schmidt, and Rayleigh numbers.

10.3 TAYLOR DISPERSION

10.3.1 Introduction

Now we will describe an experiment and a remarkable theory for what is known as Taylor dispersion. Consider a liquid in fully developed laminar flow in a pipe. A thin slice or a plug of the same liquid but colored with a dye is introduced into it. The plug of liquid will now flow with the parabolic velocity profile. It will be stretched and will mix with the other liquid. The extent of mixedness can be measured by observing the concentration of the dye. In this experiment we are interested in the average concentration of the dye across the cross-section of the tube or *area averaged concentration*[6], and its variation along the length of the pipe. This kind of situation is encountered in chromatographic analysis and separations. It is also encountered in continuous tubular flow reactors where reaction is accompanied by axial dispersion.

Simple estimate: No diffusion

We begin by presenting a simple calculation of the average concentration assuming that molecular diffusion is absent so that the remarkable results of the above experiment can be better appreciated. Refer to figure 10.4. Let the average velocity of the fluid be $\bar{V}$. Let the thickness of the plug be

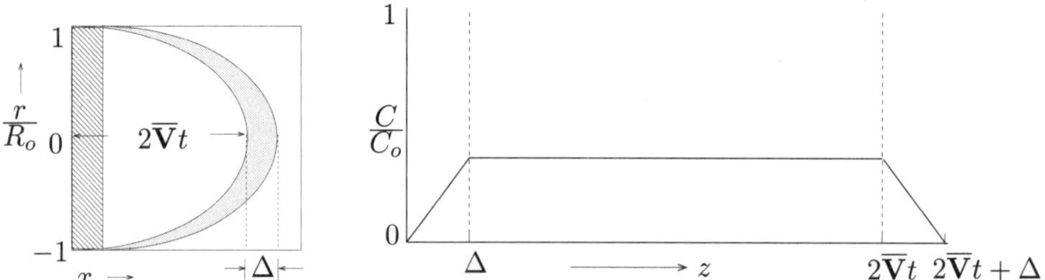

Figure 10.4. The hatched rectangle in the left panel illustrates the original dye introduced as a plug of thickness Δ. It also sketches the way the plug deforms under the influence of the laminar velocity profile in the tube if diffusion is completely absent. The right panel sketches the calculated area averaged concentration, assuming molecular diffusion is absent.

Δ. Let the concentration of the dye in the original plug be C_o. Let the length along the axis of the tube be z, where $z = 0$ is the place where the plug was introduced. After some time t, the center of the inside surface of the plug will move to $z = 2\bar{V}t$ while that of the outside surface will move to

$2\bar{V}t + \Delta$. Other points on the surfaces will move to $v_z(r)t$ and $v_z(r)t + \Delta$ as shown in figure 10.4. The two surfaces have taken the shape of a parabola. As diffusion is assumed to be absent, the concentration of the dye in the zone between the inside and outside surfaces of the distorted plug will still be C_o. The area averaged concentration of the dye at any position z is then given by

$$\bar{C} = C_o \frac{\text{Area between the two paraboloids at any } z}{\pi R^2}$$

where R is the radius of the tube. Calculation gives the following results

$$\begin{aligned}
\bar{c} &= 0, \quad z < 0 \\
\bar{c} &= C_o \frac{z}{2\bar{V}t}, \qquad 0 < z < \Delta \\
\bar{c} &= C_o \frac{\Delta}{2\bar{V}t}, \qquad \Delta < z < 2\bar{V}t \\
\bar{c} &= C_o \frac{\Delta + 2\bar{V}t - z}{2\bar{V}t}, \qquad 2\bar{V}t < z < 2\bar{V}t + \Delta \\
\bar{c} &= 0, \quad z > 2\bar{V}t + \Delta
\end{aligned}$$

As dye was introduced in the range $0 < z < \Delta$, there can be no dye for $z < 0$. Since the maximum velocity is $2\bar{V}$, there can be no dye for $z > 2\bar{V}t + \Delta$. Hence, all the dye will be contained in the zone $0 < z < 2\bar{V}t + \Delta$. The profile of the area averaged concentration is shown in the right panel of figure 10.4. If the width of the original plug introduced is nearly zero, above calculation shows that the average concentration is uniform across nearly the entire length of zero to $2\bar{V}t$. The shape is still like a plug. The original plug is being stretched without any change in the shape with the uniform concentration decreasing to $C_o\Delta/2\bar{V}t$, where it may be noted that $C_o\Delta$ is equal to the total mass of dye introduced per unit area. Now let us examine the experimental observations in light of what is expected if diffusion is absent.

Observations and controversies

It is to be noted that the observations are made at quite some distance downstream of where the dye was introduced.

1. The concentration distributions are symmetric around $z = \bar{V}t$, *i.e.*, around a plane which moves with the average velocity. The shape is Gaussian and not at all like a plug. This is illustrated in figure 10.5. One might expect that the shape is distorted due to diffusion which has a tendency to round off edges. This indicates that diffusion does play a role.

2. It is however observed that the concentration does not increase beyond zero for quite some distance beyond $z = 0$ and concentration falls to zero for z much smaller than $2\bar{V}t$. In other words, though the shape of the spread of dye indicates diffusion, *the spread occurs over a much smaller width than predicted by convection alone.* Diffusion is impeding the spread

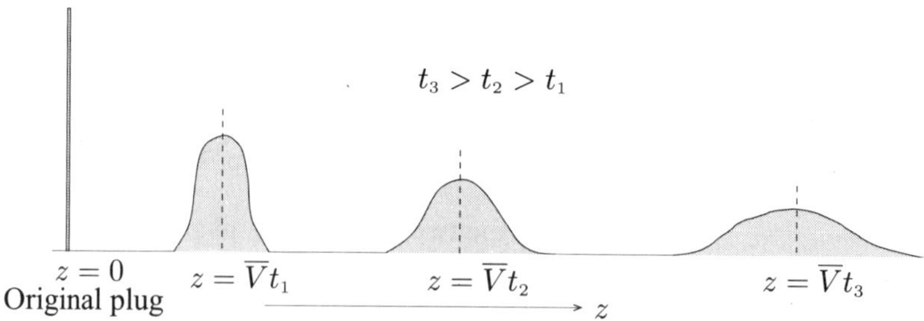

Figure 10.5. Sketches of the spreading of a plug of dye introduced in a fluid under laminar flow in a tube. The zone moves with the average velocity of the fluid. The shape is Gaussian. Spread occurs over a much smaller width than predicted by convection alone.

of dye by convection, whereas we expect diffusion to add to the width of spread caused by convection. Taylor drew attention to another very surprising feature by pointing out the following aspect. The zone occupied by dye is moving with the average velocity of the fluid. Fluid in the center of the tube moves with twice the average velocity. Thus, as concentration does not rise above zero for some distance beyond $z = 0$, pure fluid at the center, but from behind the zone containing dye, enters it, mixes with it, but because it is moving faster than the zone containing dye, it exits from there but free of the dye! It is as if fresh, faster moving fluid at the center mixes and then unmixes with the dye.

3. Another surprising fact is that the *width of the Gaussian curve decreases with increasing diffusion coefficient*! This is exactly opposite to what one would expect when diffusion plays an important role.

4. After the plug is introduced, the plug spreads by axial molecular diffusion over a width given by $\sqrt{\mathcal{D}t}$ while it spreads by convection over a width given by $2\bar{V}t$. Clearly, axial molecular diffusion is important only for very short times. However, the Gaussian spread of dye in the axial direction observed at long times, *i.e.*, at large distances downstream of the place where the plug was introduced, is as if it is by a diffusive process!

10.3.2 Taylor's theory

Taylor [14] developed a simple but heuristic theory[7] to explain these observations and hence this phenomena is known as *Taylor dispersion.* As pointed out earlier, axial diffusion is important only for very short times, which are not of much importance. But after some time, as shown in figure 10.4, the velocity profile or convection will tend to distort the plug and induce sharp concentration gradients. This causes *radial diffusion* as indicated by dashed line arrows in figure 10.6. It brings dye from slower moving areas into faster moving zones and *vice versa.* The net effective motion caused by radial diffusion and axial convection is as indicated by the curved line arrows in figure 10.6. First, and this is very important, radial diffusion makes the rear end of the plug move faster and the front end slower. Thus, radial diffusion has the effect of compressing the zone over which the dye spreads or impeding the spread due to convection. It is this remarkable insight on which Taylor's theory is based. Second, radial diffusion causes mixing across the cross-section. Taylor envisaged

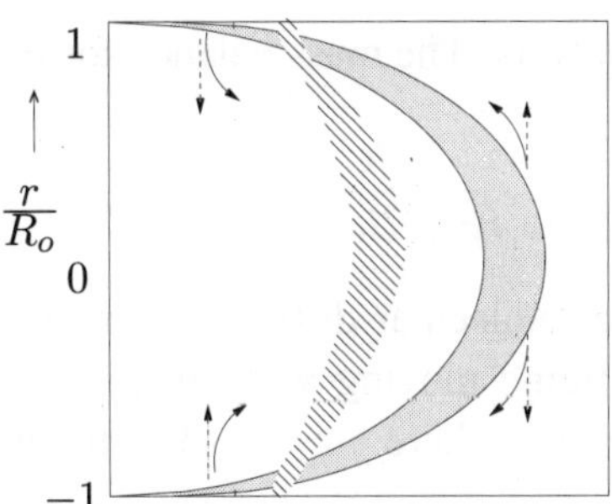

Figure 10.6. Radial diffusion is indicated by dashed arrows. It brings dye from slower moving fluid diffusing into faster moving zones and *vice versa.* The net effect of diffusion and convection is indicated by curved arrows. The original shape of paraboloids indicated by convection alone distorts into the shape indicated by hatched zone.

that at sufficiently long times[8], radial diffusion is fast compared to convection and fairly small radial gradients are able to even out the gradients caused by axial convection. Taylor's insight was that the *axial diffusion like*[9] *characteristics in the absence of axial molecular diffusion* occur under these conditions. Taylor gave an estimate of the distance downstream where this assumption is valid, and it is this that we will discuss first. The radial diffusion time scale is of the order of $R^2/\mathcal{D}$ while the time scale of convection is of the order of $z/\bar{V}$. The axial location where both are comparable occurs at

$$\frac{R^2}{\mathcal{D}} \sim \frac{z}{\bar{V}}, \quad \text{or } Pe = \frac{R\bar{V}}{\mathcal{D}} \sim \frac{z}{R} >> 1$$

As mentioned earlier, we are looking at axial distances by when radial diffusion time scale is much smaller (or radial diffusion is very fast) than convection time scale, *i.e.,* $z/\bar{V} >> R^2/\mathcal{D}$. This is same as

$$\frac{z}{R} >> Pe$$

When the fluid has reached locations which satisfy this criterion, concentrations are small, and radial gradients are also small.

Taylor's model

Let us first clearly state what is to be explained. The observations show that the area averaged concentration, defined as

$$\bar{C} \equiv \frac{1}{\pi R^2}\int_0^R 2\pi r C dr$$

behaves as if it is described by the diffusion equation in a frame moving with the average velocity or $z' = z - \bar{V}t$. Hence, it satisfies diffusion equation in that frame:

$$\frac{\partial \bar{C}}{\partial t} = D_{eff}\frac{\partial^2 \bar{C}}{\partial z'^2}$$

The analysis must therefore calculate $\bar{C}$ first and then show that it satisfies the above equation.

Now let us outline Taylor's analysis. The mass balance for the dye species is given by

$$\frac{\partial C}{\partial t} + 2\bar{V}\left(1 - \frac{r^2}{R^2}\right)\frac{\partial C}{\partial z} = \mathcal{D}\frac{\partial^2 C}{\partial z^2} + \frac{\mathcal{D}}{r}\frac{\partial}{\partial r}\left(r\frac{\partial C}{\partial r}\right)$$

First, as discussed earlier, the axial molecular diffusion is negligible compared to radial diffusion. The observations are made in a frame moving with the average velocity. Thus, we change the coordinate system from z, r, t to z', r, t where $z' = z - \bar{V}t$. Incorporating these two ideas, the mass balance becomes

$$\frac{\partial C}{\partial t} + \bar{V}(1 - 2\frac{r^2}{R^2})\frac{\partial C}{\partial z'} = \frac{\mathcal{D}}{r}\frac{\partial}{\partial r}\left(r\frac{\partial C}{\partial r}\right)$$

At the locations where observations are made, radial diffusion is very fast and is able to neutralize the gradients caused by convection. In view of this, Taylor made the following assumption. The near perfect balance between the axial convection and radial diffusion leads to pseudo steady[10] conditions. The mass balance for the dye then simplifies to

$$\bar{V}(1 - 2\frac{r^2}{R^2})\frac{\partial C}{\partial z'} = \frac{\mathcal{D}}{r}\frac{\partial}{\partial r}\left(r\frac{\partial C}{\partial r}\right)$$

Taylor integrated the above equation with respect to radius assuming that small radial concentration gradients permit treating $\partial C/\partial z'$ independent of r. The dye cannot penetrate the tube wall and hence concentration gradient at the wall must be zero, and this forms one boundary condition. This gives the result

$$C = C_o + \frac{\bar{V}R^2}{4\mathcal{D}}\frac{\partial C}{\partial z'}\left(\frac{r^2}{R^2} - \frac{1}{2}\frac{r^4}{R^4}\right)$$

where C_o is unknown and equal to the concentration at the center of the tube. The above can be used to evaluate the area averaged concentration

$$\bar{C} = \frac{1}{\pi R^2}\int_0^R 2\pi r C dr = C_o + \frac{1}{3}\frac{\bar{V}R^2}{4\mathcal{D}}\frac{\partial C}{\partial z'}$$

Eliminating the concentration at the center of the tube in terms of the average concentration, we get

$$C = \bar{C} + \frac{\bar{V}R^2}{4\mathcal{D}}\frac{\partial C}{\partial z'}\left(-\frac{1}{3} + \frac{r^2}{R^2} - \frac{1}{2}\frac{r^4}{R^4}\right)$$

We can see that if $\bar{V}R^2/4\mathcal{D}z << 1$, or $4z/R >> Pe$, then $\partial C/\partial z' \sim \partial \bar{C}/\partial z'$. Since the latter is independent of radius, we can treat $\partial C/\partial z'$ also as being nearly independent of radius, which was what was assumed to arrive at this result. $4z/R >> Pe$ is the criterion given by Taylor for the location beyond which the spread of the plug shows a Gaussian behavior. Under those conditions therefore, the concentration profile can be written as

$$C = \bar{C} + \frac{\bar{V}R^2}{4\mathcal{D}}\frac{\partial \bar{C}}{\partial z'}\left(-\frac{1}{3} + \frac{r^2}{R^2} - \frac{1}{2}\frac{r^4}{R^4}\right) \tag{10.10}$$

Now what is left is to show that the mass flux of the dye with respect to the mass average velocity follows Fick's law. The mass flux in the axial direction of the dye with respect to a frame moving with the mass average velocity is the diffusive flux, j_z. Hence,

$$j_z = \int_0^R CM\bar{V}\left(1 - 2\frac{r^2}{R^2}\right) 2\pi r dr$$

where M is the molecular weight of the dye. Substituting this into eq. 10.10, we find that

$$j_z = \frac{(R\bar{V})^2}{48\mathcal{D}} M \frac{\partial \bar{C}}{\partial z'}$$

or

$$j_z = \frac{(R\bar{V})^2}{48\mathcal{D}} \frac{\partial \bar{\rho}_d}{\partial z'}$$

where $\bar{\rho}_d$ is the area averaged mass concentration of the dye.

10.3.3 Look at the results

The diffusive flux therefore is given by Fick's law. This explains the Gaussian diffusive spread of the dye, which are the first and fourth items in the observed results we listed at the beginning of this section. But note that the diffusion coefficient is given by

$$D_{eff,ax} = \frac{(R\bar{V})^2}{48\mathcal{D}}, \quad \text{or} \quad \frac{D_{eff,ax}}{\mathcal{D}} = \frac{Pe^2}{48}$$

or the effective axial dispersion coefficient is inversely proportional to the molecular diffusivity! This explains the third item we listed in the surprising results.

A mass balance of the dye with respect to the *moving frame* is given by

$$\frac{\partial \bar{\rho}_d}{\partial t} = D_{eff,ax} \frac{\partial^2 \bar{\rho}_d}{\partial z'^2}$$

This equation was solved by Taylor and the results matched well with observations explaining the second item we listed in the surprising results. Taylor neglected molecular diffusion altogether. Aris[1] developed a more exact and beautiful theory using method of moments and showed that if molecular diffusion is also included, the result is given by

$$\frac{D_{eff,ax}}{\mathcal{D}} = 1 + \frac{Pe^2}{48}$$

The second term is the one calculated by Taylor, and is very accurate if $Pe >> 7$. Aris has also written in his inimitable style about how his paper got developed. See Citation classics in *Current Contents* of 14 January 1991. It can be accessed from the website www.citationclassics.org.

All of you know that it is this axial dispersion coefficient that is used in designing flow reactors and you would have seen correlations for it in textbooks on chemical reaction engineering.

10.4 FORCED DIFFUSION: Fuel cells

10.4.1 Introduction

Diffusion under the influence of body forces is referred to as forced diffusion. We analyze performance of a hydrogen fuel cell as an example of this. Fuel cell converts chemical energy *directly* into electrical energy. It does so through oxidation of the fuel through an electrochemical route. In this section, we discuss low temperature hydrogen fuel cells. See figure 10.7. The most simple

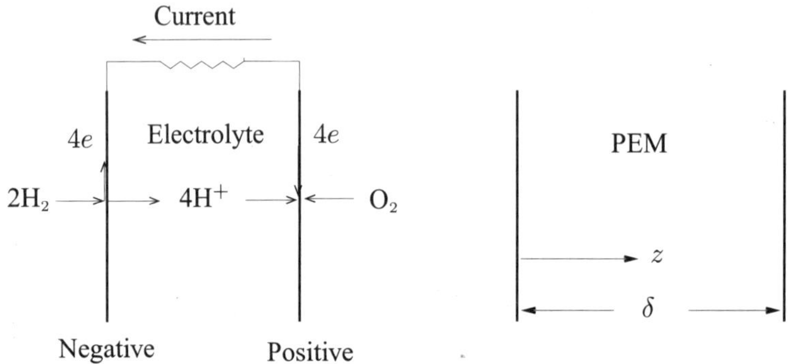

Figure 10.7. Left panel shows a schematic of a hydrogen fuel cell. Hydrogen loses electrons at the negative electrode and the protons so formed diffuse to the positive electrode through the electrolyte. Polymer electrolyte membranes (PEM) are commonly used. See text for the description. The electrons travel through an external circuit and also reach the positive electrode. There they combine with the electrons and oxygen supplied to the electrode to form water. The right panel shows the coordinate system used in the analysis.

construction of a fuel cell consists of two planar electrodes immersed in an electrolyte. Hence, they are *electronically* isolated from each other by the electrolyte. The following reaction can occur at the negative electrode to which hydrogen is supplied.

$$2H_2 \rightleftharpoons 4H^+ + 4e \tag{10.11}$$

Under some conditions, which we will discuss shortly, the negative electrode removes electrons from hydrogen to make protons, *i.e.,* the forward reaction in the scheme shown in eq. 10.11 occurs. The electrode has to be a catalyst and platinum is usually employed as the catalyst. The electrons extracted from hydrogen travel through an external circuit and reach the positive electrode while protons also diffuse towards the positive electrode through the electrolyte. Oxygen is supplied to the positive electrode and there it combines with the electrons and the protons to form water:

$$O_2 + 4H^+ + 4e \rightleftharpoons 2H_2O \tag{10.12}$$

The overall reaction, which cannot generate electrons, is given by

$$2H_2 + O_2 \rightleftharpoons 2H_2O \tag{10.13}$$

Ideal performance of the cell: Thermodynamics

Thermodynamics applies to reversible processes. The rate of a reversible process is zero. If a fuel cell is operated reversibly, the current generated will be zero. Thermodynamics predicts [10] that the potential difference[11] generated between two electrodes of a reversibly operated fuel cell is related to the free energy change of the reaction:

$$-\Delta \mathrm{G} = n\mathcal{F}U$$

where n is the number of electrons involved in the process and $\mathcal{F}$ is Faraday's constant. It is not possible to define an equilibrium potential for a reaction occurring at a single electrode. However, one can think of the equilibrium potential difference generated by any electrode if a reference electrode is combined with it. The reference electrode is a standard, and like with the choice of standard conditions, the free energy change for the reference electrode can be assigned a value of zero[12]. Then, the free energy change of the reaction occurring at the electrode of interest will also be the free energy change for the system consisting of the reference electrode and the electrode of interest. With the aid of this convention, one can associate a potential difference generated by any electrode. The potential difference so measured is the *difference* between the potential of the electrode and the fluid[13] immediately surrounding it. In this way, we can calculate the potential differences generated at the positive and negative electrodes from the free energy change for the reactions 10.11 and 10.12, respectively:

$$-\Delta \mathrm{G}_+ = n\mathcal{F}U_+, \quad -\Delta \mathrm{G}_- = n\mathcal{F}U_-$$

The potential difference calculated from free energy change is under equilibrium conditions when the net rate of the reaction is zero, and there is no flow of electrons into or out of an electrode. As we shall see shortly, when current is drawn from the cell, the potential generated is less than this value due to irreversibilities. If the fuel cell operates in a reversible manner, no current flows but the best voltage is obtained!

Operation of a fuel cell

At equilibrium, the rates of the forward and reverse reactions are balanced, and equal number of electrons are flowing in and out of the electrode. When equilibrium is disturbed, reaction occurs in one or the other direction, and current flows in the corresponding direction. Let us note that electrons are attracted towards regions of positive potential and repelled from regions at a negative potential. Suppose we apply a potential less than U_+ to the positive electrode, it will become more negative compared to equilibrium conditions. Hence, electrons will move from the electrode to the electrode–fluid interface, and combine with protons and oxygen to form water. This is the reaction that occurs in a fuel cell. Conversely, if the potential is raised above U_+, electrons will be removed from water and protons and oxygen will be generated. This is the reaction that occurs at the positive plate in the reverse reaction of eq. 10.13, *i.e.,* electrolysis of water. Similar logic applies to the negative electrode also. Negative electrode becomes more positive compared to equilibrium conditions if its potential is raised above U_-, and electrons will be extracted from hydrogen into the electrode. As a result, protons will be generated. This is the reaction that occurs in a fuel cell.

Electrolyte

We need to learn a little about the electrolyte commonly employed in fuel cells. Low temperature hydrogen fuel cells employ *polymer electrolyte membrane* or PEM as the electrolyte. We will use this in our analysis also. Polymer electrolyte membranes are made of cross-linked polymers and hence are solid in nature. Their chemical structure is like that of an ion exchange resin with the counter ions being part of the solid polymer, and the protons are bound to them by coulombic forces. The first thing to note therefore is that the concentration of the counter ions as well as the protons is constant. When the membrane is hydrated, protons become mobile. Hence, protons enter and leave the membrane under the influence of a potential gradient[14] by conduction and not by diffusion.

10.4.2 Problem identification

If the free energy change for the overall reaction is negative, the process occurs spontaneously in the thermodynamic sense. The cell potential will be positive because the free energy change is negative, and it will generate energy. Under equilibrium conditions, when the rates of the forward and backward reactions match, the cell potential or the difference between the potentials of the positive and negative electrodes is given by $U_+ - U_- \equiv U$. However, as the forward and reverse processes are matched under equilibrium conditions, no current is produced by the cell. Such a situation can be realized only when the two electrodes are not connected through an external circuit. If we connect the two electrodes with a resistor in between as shown in figure 10.7, the overall reaction occurs in the forward direction, and there will be a net flow of current through the resistor. The cell generates power. However, the process is irreversible in the thermodynamic sense, and the potential difference between the two electrodes falls below[15] U. The purpose of analysis of a fuel cell is to predict the cell potential as a function of current drawn from the cell.

Mass balance in PEM

We analyze the performance of a fuel cell under steady state conditions. The cell being analyzed is shown in figure 10.7. The membrane is very thin compared to its lateral dimensions. Hence, we assume diffusion occurs only in one dimension. As protons are the only mobile species present in the membrane, mass balance and charge balance give the same equation. Reactions do not occur in the PEM and hence at steady state, the mass balance equation simplifies to

$$\frac{dN_{H^+z}}{dz} = 0$$

where N_{H^+z} is the mass flux of protons in the z direction. The general constitutive equation is given by eq. 9.33. In the absence of convection, it simplifies to

$$N_{H^+z} = -\frac{\mathcal{D}_{H^+}}{\mathcal{R}T}\left(\frac{dC_{H^+}}{dz} + C_{H^+}z_+\mathcal{F}\frac{d\phi}{dz}\right)$$

if we assume that protons in hydrated membranes behave as an ideal solution. The first term is zero in PEM because proton concentration is constant. Thus, we have the equivalent of Ohm's law:

$$N_{H^+z} = -\frac{\mathcal{F}}{\mathcal{R}T}\mathcal{D}_{H^+}C_{H^+}z_+\frac{d\phi}{dz}$$

After integration

$$N_{H^+z} = \frac{\mathcal{F}}{\mathcal{R}T}\mathcal{D}_{H^+}C_{H^+}z_+\frac{\phi(0) - \phi(\delta)}{\delta} \tag{10.14}$$

The concentration of protons in the membrane is related to its chemical structure and is a known quantity. Thus, we only need boundary conditions for the potential to determine the mass flux. The potential is related to the rate of charge transfer reaction and hence we must connect it to the proton flux to derive the boundary conditions. The proton flux is related to the rate of charge transfer through stoichiometry. From eqs. 10.11 and 10.12 we infer that one electron must be transferred for every proton discharged by reaction with oxygen or generated from hydrogen. Hence, if I is the current density generated by the cell, we have

$$I = z^+N_{H^+z} = \frac{\mathcal{F}}{\mathcal{R}T}\mathcal{D}_{H^+}C_{H^+}\frac{\phi(0) - \phi(\delta)}{\delta} \tag{10.15}$$

where we have substituted the valence value of the proton. Charge is conserved and hence, at the electrode–fluid interface, the current density must match the rate of charge transfer. Thus, if we have a rate expression for the charge transfer reaction, the boundary conditions can be derived.

Rate of charge transfer

We discussed in an earlier section the direction of the reactions that occur at the electrodes or the electrodic reactions. Because there is a transfer of charge from the electrode to the fluid or *vice versa* in these reactions, they are referred to as charge transfer reactions. It can be anticipated that analysis of a fuel cell will involve these reactions and we will need their rates. We will give a commonly used expression for it, which is referred to as Butler Volmer equation in the electrochemistry literature. The reaction occurs at the electrode–fluid interface, and hence the rate is defined on 'per unit area' basis. The rate is considered positive if the net amount of charge transferred *from electrode to electrolyte* is positive. The rate of the charge transfer reaction is defined as the net amount of charge transferred across the interface per unit area per unit time, *i.e.,* the charge flux at the interface. From the discussion in the previous sub-section, we expect the rate to be proportional to the potential difference between the electrode and the fluid, *over and above* the equilibrium value. From the chemical reaction engineering view point, it also should be proportional to the concentrations of the reactants and the products. The equilibrium potential difference is also a complicated function of concentration. Readers have to refer to recent literature for more realistic expressions, but we will use the following simplified expression of the Butler Volmer equation for the hydrogen electrode:

$$i_- = i^o_{-,ref}\frac{P_{H_2}}{P_{H_2,ref}}\left[\exp\Big(2\mathcal{F}(\phi_s - \phi - U_-)/\mathcal{R}T\Big) - \exp\Big(-2\mathcal{F}(\phi_s - \phi - U_-)/\mathcal{R}T\Big)\right] \tag{10.16}$$

where

i_- is the flux of charge *from the negative electrode into fluid*

$i^o_{-,ref}$ is an empirical constant to be determined from experiments conducted when Hydrogen is supplied at a pressure of $P_{H_2,ref}$

$\mathcal{F}$ is Faraday's constant or charge of a mole of electrons

ϕ_s is the potential of the electrode and ϕ is the potential of fluid adjacent to the electrode

U_- is the equilibrium potential of Hydrogen electrode at the conditions at which Hydrogen is supplied to the electrode.

$\mathcal{R}$ is the gas constant and

T is the temperature.

Similarly, we will use the following expression for oxygen electrode:

$$i_+ = i^o_{+,ref} \frac{P_{O_2}}{P_{O_2,ref}} \left[\exp\left(2\mathcal{F}(\phi_s - \phi - U_+)/\mathcal{R}T \right) - \exp\left(-2\mathcal{F}(\phi_s - \phi - U_+)/\mathcal{R}T \right) \right] \quad (10.17)$$

The symbols are defined as before but stand for positive electrode. U_+ is the equilibrium potential of the electrode at the conditions oxygen is supplied to it.

Note a few features of the expressions. The potential difference between the electrode and the fluid adjacent to it can be thought of as an applied potential difference. The deviation of the applied potential difference from the equilibrium potential, namely, $\phi_s - \phi - U$ is referred to as the *overpotential*. If the overpotential is equal to zero, the rate of charge transfer reaction is zero, as it should be. The rate increases with an increase in the overpotential or as the deviation from equilibrium state increases. This is also to be expected since the difference between the applied potential and the equilibrium potential is akin to the gradient in chemical potential. The rate has been assumed to be first order with respect to concentration of reactants only, but in general it is more complex. Finally, i^o is referred to as the exchange current density in electrochemistry literature and is similar to the reaction rate constant of chemical kinetics. It may be noted that the dependence of the rate on overpotential is exponential and hence is very sensitive. If the applied potential difference is greater than the equilibrium potential, or if the overpotential is positive, the electrode is more positive compared to the state of equilibrium. Hence, electrons are expected to move from the fluid into the electrode, or equivalently, direction of flow of positive charge is from the electrode into the fluid, and the rate should be positive. The rate expression confirms this. Thus, in a fuel cell, the overpotential at the hydrogen electrode must be positive and must be negative at the oxygen electrode. This is exactly what we discussed earlier in the section on thermodynamics.

Boundary conditions

Negative plate: Charge is conserved and hence charge flowing into the electrode must match the rate of transfer of charge from the electrode into the electrolyte. The former is the current density of the cell. The rate of charge transfer reaction per unit area is given by i and is the rate at which charge moves from the plate into the fluid. Butler Volmer equation can be used to calculate this. Current density I is also the current flowing into the negative electrode. Hence,

$$I = i^o_{-,ref} \frac{P_{H_2}}{P_{H_2,ref}} \left[\exp\left(2\mathcal{F}(\phi_s(0) - \phi(0) - U_-)/\mathcal{R}T \right) - \exp\left(-2\mathcal{F}(\phi_s(0) - \phi(0) - U_-)/\mathcal{R}T \right) \right] \tag{10.18}$$

Positive plate: I is also the rate at which charge flows *out* of a unit area of the positive plate and hence

$$I = -i^o_{+,ref} \frac{P_{O_2}}{P_{O_2,ref}} \left[\exp\left(2\mathcal{F}(\phi_s(\delta) - \phi(\delta) - U_+)/\mathcal{R}T \right) - \exp\left(-2\mathcal{F}(\phi_s(\delta) - \phi(\delta) - U_+)/\mathcal{R}T \right) \right] \tag{10.19}$$

These two equations form the boundary conditions for eq. 10.15.

10.4.3 Look at the results

Mathematically speaking, there are four unknowns, $\phi_s(\delta), \phi(\delta), \phi_s(0), \phi(0)$ in eqs. 10.15, 10.18, and 10.19. Thus, we can solve for $\phi_s(\delta) - \phi_s(0)$, which is the potential developed by the cell, V_{cell}, as a function of current density. Only numerical solution is possible in general, but we will illustrate the features in limiting cases.

Low current density

As discussed earlier, the overpotential increases with current density. Thus, at low current densities, the overpotential will be small. This would also be true if the 'rate constant' for the charge transfer reaction is large. We can state a more general condition for the overpotential at the hydrogen electrode to be small:

$$\frac{I}{i^o_{-,ref}} \frac{P_{H_2,ref}}{P_{H_2}} \ll 1$$

A similar condition can be formulated for the oxygen electrode. If both these are satisfied, the over potential in both electrodes will be small, and the exponentials in the Butler Volmer expressions for the rate of charge transfer can be approximated by linear terms. Thus, eq. 10.18 can be written as

$$I = i^o_{-,ref} \frac{P_{H_2}}{P_{H_2,ref}} \frac{4\mathcal{F}}{\mathcal{R}T} (\phi_s(0) - \phi(0) - U_-)$$

and eq. 10.19 as

$$I = -i^o_{+,ref} \frac{P_{O_2}}{P_{O_2,ref}} \frac{4\mathcal{F}}{\mathcal{R}T} (\phi_s(\delta) - \phi(\delta) - U_+)$$

From eq. 10.15

$$\phi(0) - \phi(\delta) = I \frac{\mathcal{R}T}{\mathcal{F}} \frac{\delta}{\mathcal{D}_{H^+} C_{H^+}}$$

Combining the three, we obtain

$$V_{cell} = \phi_s(\delta) - \phi_s(0) = U_+ - U_- - \frac{I\mathcal{R}T}{\mathcal{F}}\left(\frac{P_{H_2,ref}}{P_{H_2}}\frac{1}{4i^o_{-,ref}} + \frac{P_{O_2,ref}}{P_{O_2}}\frac{1}{4i^o_{+,ref}} + \frac{\delta}{\mathcal{D}_{H^+}C_{H^+}}\right) \quad (10.20)$$

$U_+ - U_-$ is the equilibrium voltage corresponding to reversible operation or at zero current density and at the pressures where hydrogen and oxygen are being supplied. This is the maximum voltage a cell can develop. As current density drawn from the cell increases, the voltage decreases from the equilibrium value. The decrease increases with increasing current density. There are three resistances contributing to the decrease in the cell voltage, and they are in brackets in eq. 10.20. The first two correspond to the charge transfer reaction at the negative and positive electrodes. These terms are referred to as *activation polarization*. These correspond to the reaction resistance encountered in our analysis of catalytic reactions in chapter 9. The last one corresponds to the voltage drop in the membrane corresponding to the conductivity of the membrane. If the exchange current densities are large, the cell voltage is determined entirely by the drop due to resistance, normally referred to as ohmic loss. Conversely, if conductivity of the membrane is large, the reaction is controlled by the charge transfer reactions. This resistance can be lowered by supplying the gases at high pressure. It is generally observed that the charge transfer reaction at the oxygen electrode is sluggish. As shown by the expression, the membrane resistance can be decreased by decreasing the thickness of the membrane. This is feasible because the membranes are made of polymers, provided they are mechanically strong to seal the electrodes from each other and do not develop pin holes.

High current densities

As current density increases, or as the charge transfer reaction becomes sluggish, the overpotential increases and the linear approximation of exponentials is not valid. The condition for this for the hydrogen electrode is

$$\frac{I}{i^o_{-,ref}}\frac{P_{H_2,ref}}{P_{H_2}} \gg 1$$

and a similar expression can be written for the oxygen electrode. A different approximation, known as Tafel equation [11], has to be used here. At the negative plate, the overpotential is positive. If it is sufficiently large, the negative exponential term can be neglected, and eq. 10.18 can be written as

$$I = i^o_{-,ref}\frac{P_{H_2}}{P_{H_2,ref}}\exp\left(2\mathcal{F}(\phi_s(0) - \phi(0) - U_-)/\mathcal{R}T\right)$$

or

$$\phi_s(0) - \phi(0) - U_- = \frac{\mathcal{R}T}{2\mathcal{F}}\ln\left(\frac{I}{i^o_{-,ref}}\frac{P_{H_2,ref}}{P_{H_2}}\right)$$

At the positive electrode, the overpotential is negative. Once again, if its magnitude is sufficiently large, the positive exponential term can be neglected and eq. 10.19 can be written as

$$I = i^o_{+,ref}\frac{P_{O_2}}{P_{O_2,ref}}\left[\exp\left(-2\mathcal{F}(\phi_s(\delta) - \phi(\delta) - U_+)/\mathcal{R}T\right)\right]$$

or

$$\phi_s(\delta) - \phi(\delta) - U_+ = -\frac{\mathcal{R}T}{2\mathcal{F}} \ln\left(\frac{I}{i^o_{+,ref}} \frac{P_{O_2,ref}}{P_{O_2}}\right)$$

As before, from eq. 10.15

$$\phi(0) - \phi(\delta) = I\frac{\mathcal{R}T}{\mathcal{F}} \frac{\delta}{\mathcal{D}_{H^+}C_{H^+}}$$

Combining all the three, we get

$$V_{cell} = \phi_s(\delta) - \phi_s(0) = U_+ - U_- - \frac{\mathcal{R}T}{2\mathcal{F}}\left[\ln\left(\frac{I}{i^o_{-,ref}} \frac{P_{H_2,ref}}{P_{H_2}}\right) + \ln\left(\frac{I}{i^o_{+,ref}} \frac{P_{O_2,ref}}{P_{O_2}}\right) + \frac{I\delta}{\mathcal{D}_{H^+}C_{H^+}}\right] \tag{10.21}$$

The conclusions drawn in the context of low current densities are still valid, but the nature of the dependence is now different.

Power of cell

The power density generated by the cell is equal to $V_{cell}I$. At zero current density, the power is obviously equal to zero. However, at some current density, as can be seen from eq. 10.21, the cell voltage drops to zero and hence the power generated by the cell drops to zero once again. Thus, the power density is maximum at some intermediate current density.

10.5 POROUS ELECTRODE

10.5.1 Problem identification

The previous discussion shows that the area of the electrodes, normally referred to as the area of the cell, has to be increased to increase the power output of the cell. A plate electrode cannot accommodate significant area per unit volume of the cell. Porous electrodes can pack a large area per unit volume and hence they have to be employed to increase cell's *power density*. However, the reactants will have to diffuse into the electrode if it is made porous. An additional resistance is therefore added, very similar to what happens in a porous catalyst pellet. Construction of a porous electrode is also complex. The charge transfer reaction is interfacial in character. In a plate electrode, the electrolyte–electrode interface is planar, and the electrons flow naturally into (or out of) the electron conducting electrode while the ions flow into (or out of) the electrolyte. In a porous electrode, electrolyte–catalyst interface is present throughout the bulk of the electrode. However, current in the external circuit can only flow into or out of the outer boundaries of the electrodes. The same applies for the reactants and products as well. Hence, paths must be made from the outer boundaries of the electrode into its bulk for the conduction of ions and electrons, and diffusion of reactants and products. The porous electrode therefore is a composite made of three components: catalyst, PEM, and carbon or some other electron conducting material. See figure 10.8. The part consisting of electron conducting material forms a contiguous path to conduct electrons between the active interface and the external boundary of the electrode. The PEM part of the electrode also forms a separate contiguous path for conducting protons generated in the negative electrode to the membrane separating the two electrodes and for conducting protons from it to the

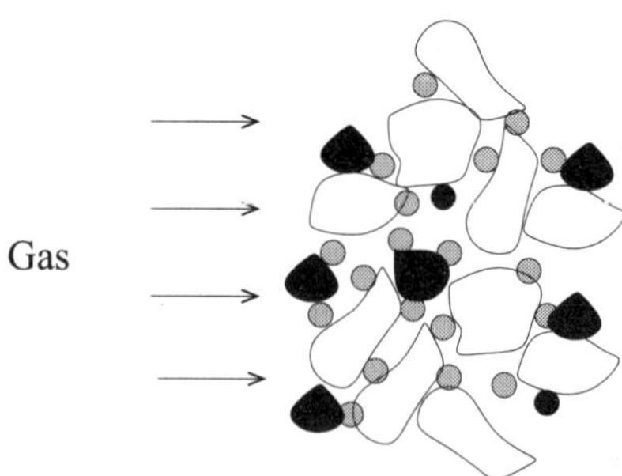

Figure 10.8. Sketch of a porous electrode using gas. The white blobs represent paste made of polymer electrolyte membrane that conduct protons. The black blobs represent electronic conductor, like carbon particles. The light colored blobs represent electrocatalyst particles, usually made of metals. The black and light colored blobs form a connected path across the entire thickness of the electrode. Electrons pass through that path. The white colored blobs form a separate connected path and it conducts protons. The pores in between all these particles allow diffusion of the gas. When the charge transfer reaction occurs on the catalyst surface, the protons and electrons will have to move into their respective conductors. Hence, charge transfer occurs at the diffuse overlapping regions of the interface where catalyst, electron conductor and PEM meet. This area is known as triphasic region or junction.

active sites in the positive electrode for reduction reaction with oxygen. There are regions in each electrode where the catalyst, PEM and electron conducting materials overlap and they are referred to as triphasic regions. The charge transfer reaction occurs in this zone, and electrons and ions flow into the respective contiguous paths. Additionally, the composite made of particles of catalyst, PEM and electron conducting materials is porous, and gaseous reactants diffuse through the pores to the surface of the catalyst. The complexity of construction of the electrode also makes its analysis more complex than for a planar electrode. We demonstrate in this section that the analysis of porous catalyst particles developed in the chapter 9 can be applied to Hydrogen fuel cells. Once again, the objective is to calculate the voltage generated by the cell as a function of the current drawn.

Mass balances

Consider a rectangular slab of an oxygen electrode shown in figure 10.9. Oxygen diffuses from the right edge of the electrode through the pores into the bulk of the electrode. Electrons also enter from the right outer edge of the electrode and are conducted to the site of reaction through the connected path of electron conducting particles. Protons come from the membrane separating the two electrodes, enter the electrode at the left edge of the electrode and diffuse through the connected regions of PEM into the bulk of the electrode. As they diffuse, they react on the catalyst surface of the triphasic zones with oxygen and electrons to produce water. We apply the pseudo-homogeneous model of a catalyst slab of chapter 9 to the porous electrode. Let a be the interfacial area per unit volume of the electrode (*i.e.,* entire porous mass) where charge transfer reaction occurs. The charge transfer reaction given by the equation

$$\mathrm{O_2 + 4H^+ + 4}e \rightleftharpoons \mathrm{2H_2O} \tag{10.12}$$

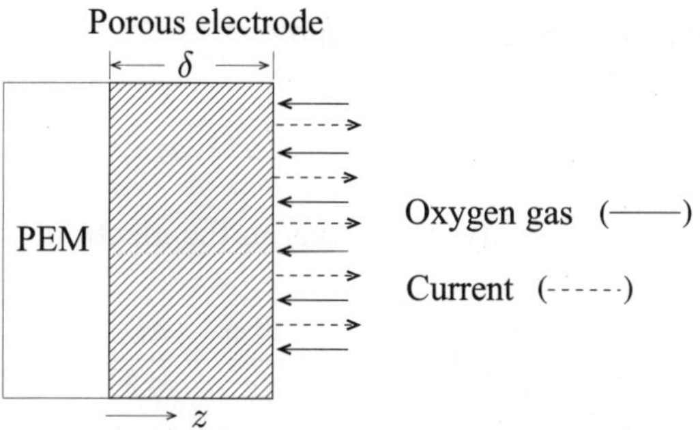

Figure 10.9. Sketch of a porous oxygen electrode using oxygen. Air may be supplied in practice. Usually there will be another porous body to the right of the electrode to ensure uniform supply of gas to the entire surface of the electrode. It is referred to as gaseous diffusion layer but is not shown in the figure. The left edge of the electrode is bonded to a slab of polymer electrolyte membrane, which separates the two electrodes. The left edge of the membrane is bonded to Hydrogen electrode, which is not shown in figure. Hydrogen electrode is similar in construction to the oxygen electrode.

is interfacial. The rate of charge transfer reaction per unit area is given by i_+, which can be obtained from eq. 10.17. Hence, from the pseudo-homogeneous model, the rate at which charge is transferred into the PEM per unit volume of electrode is given by ai_+. The reaction stoichiometry indicates that when four moles of electrons flow into the catalyst–PEM interface, a mole of oxygen and four moles of protons are consumed and two moles of water are produced. If ai_+ is the rate of charge transfer reaction, then it is equivalent to $-ai_+$ electrons flowing into the catalyst–PEM interface. Hence, the rate of *production* of various species per unit volume are given by

$$\dot{\mathcal{R}}_{O_2} = \frac{ai_+}{4\mathcal{F}}$$

$$\dot{\mathcal{R}}_{H+} = \frac{ai_+}{\mathcal{F}}$$

$$\dot{\mathcal{R}}_{H_2O} = -\frac{ai_+}{2\mathcal{F}}$$

For simplicity, we will assume that dilute solution model is applicable. Thus, only an effective binary diffusion coefficient is needed to describe diffusion. The diffusion coefficient of oxygen will be denoted by $\mathcal{D}_o$ while that of water is denoted by $\mathcal{D}_w$. Using all this, various mass balances can be written as follows. For oxygen,

$$\frac{\mathcal{D}_o}{\mathcal{R}T}\frac{d^2P_{O_2}}{dz^2} + \frac{ai_+}{4\mathcal{F}} = 0 \tag{10.22}$$

where P_{O_2} is the partial pressure of oxygen and we use ideal gas law. The mass balance for water is given by

$$\frac{\mathcal{D}_w}{\mathcal{R}T}\frac{d^2P_{H_2O}}{dz^2} - \frac{ai_+}{2\mathcal{F}} = 0 \tag{10.23}$$

As discussed earlier, the flux of protons is given by

$$N_{H^+z} = -\frac{\mathcal{F}}{\mathcal{R}T}\mathcal{D}_{H^+}C_{H^+}z_+\frac{d\phi}{dz}$$

where $\mathcal{D}_{H^+}$ is the effective diffusivity of protons in the electrode. The mass balance for protons gives

$$\frac{\mathcal{F}}{\mathcal{R}T}\mathcal{D}_{H^+}C_{H^+}z_+\frac{d^2\phi}{dz^2} + \frac{ai_+}{4\mathcal{F}} = 0 \tag{10.24}$$

Let the current density in the electronic conducting phase be i_s. This is related to the potential gradient through Ohm's law:

$$i_s = -\sigma\frac{d\phi_s}{dz}$$

where σ is the effective electronic conductivity of the electrode. The current density in the electronic conducting phase will change because charge flows into the PEM phase. Thus, charge balance in the electron conducting phase gives

$$0 = \frac{di_s}{dz} - ai_s$$

Substituting Ohm's law into it gives

$$\sigma\frac{d^2\phi_s}{dz^2} + ai_+ = 0 \tag{10.25}$$

10.5.2 Concentration profiles

It is obvious that the model for a single electrode itself is fairly complex. The model for fuel cell can be arrived at by combining the above with a model for PEM and the hydrogen electrode. The entire set of equations can be solved only numerically. For example, see Bernardi and Verbrugge [4]. The result will be a prediction of decrease of cell voltage from the thermodynamic value due to various losses. In the previous section, we have already encountered ohmic loss and loss due to the sluggishness of the charge transfer reactions. In this section, we illustrate the limitations due to diffusional resistance by taking a special case. We will make several simplifying approximations for this purpose. We list them below.

Diffusion controlled performance

1. If the conductivity of the electronic and ionic conductors is large, the potential drop in both phases across the electrode will be small. Therefore, the potentials in both phases will be constant but not equal to each other. Let them be denoted by $\phi_s(+)$ and $\phi(+)$.

2. The equilibrium potential is a function of concentration of oxygen and will vary spatially in the electrode. But to demonstrate our solution, we will assume that it can be approximated by the value at the pressure of oxygen being supplied to the electrode. Let it be denoted by U_+. With these assumptions, the overpotential is a constant throughout the electrode and is equal to $\phi_s(+) - \phi(+) - U_+$.

3. We will assume that the overpotential in the hydrogen electrode and the ohmic losses in the membrane are negligible. The former implies that $\phi(-)$, the potential in the fluid phase in the negative electrode, is equal to $\phi_s(-)$, the potential in the electron conducting phase in the negative electrode, minus U_-, the equilibrium potential in the negative electrode. Thus, $\phi(-)$ is equal to $\phi_s(-) - U_-$. As ohmic losses in PEM are also negligible, it implies that $\phi(-) = \phi(+)$. Thus, we have the result that

$$\phi_s(+) - \phi(+) - U_+ = \phi_s(+) - \phi_s(-) - (U_+ - U_-) = V_{cell} - (U_+ - U_-)$$

We will also assume that eq. 10.17 is still valid and water does not influence the rate of the charge transfer reaction. With these assumptions, the mass balance for water and oxygen become decoupled. Let us look at the oxygen balance. Combining eqs. 10.22 and 10.17, we obtain

$$\frac{\mathcal{D}_o}{\mathcal{R}T}\frac{d^2 P_{O_2}}{dz^2} + \frac{1}{4\mathcal{F}} a i^o_{+,ref} \frac{P_{O_2}}{P_{O_2,ref}} \times \left[\exp\Big(2\mathcal{F}(V_{cell} - U_+ + U_-)/\mathcal{R}T\Big) - \exp\Big(-2\mathcal{F}(V_{cell} - U_+ + U_-)/\mathcal{R}T\Big)\right] = 0 \quad (10.26)$$

We need boundary conditions to solve the above second order differential equation. Let us take the pressure at which oxygen is being supplied at the reference pressure. Let us assume that the permeability of oxygen in PEM is zero. The boundary conditions are then given by

$$\frac{dP_{O_2}}{dz} = 0 \text{ at } z = 0, \text{ and } P_{O_2} = P_{O_2,ref} \text{ at } z = \delta$$

Making note that in the oxygen electrode the overpotential is negative, the solution is easily found for this and is given by

$$\theta = \frac{P_{O_2}}{P_{O_2,ref}} = \frac{\cosh\left(z\sqrt{ak^s/\mathcal{D}_{eff}}\right)}{\cosh\left(\delta\sqrt{ak^s/\mathcal{D}_{eff}}\right)}$$

where

$$k^s = \frac{i^o_{+,ref}}{4\mathcal{F}}\left[\exp\Big(2\mathcal{F}(U_+ - U_- - V_{cell})/\mathcal{R}T\Big) - \exp\Big(-2\mathcal{F}(U_+ - U_- - V_{cell})/\mathcal{R}T\Big)\right]$$

and

$$\mathcal{D}_{eff} = \mathcal{D}_o\frac{P_{O_2,ref}}{\mathcal{R}T}$$

Now we need to connect the flux of oxygen to the current density. All the oxygen entering the electrode must react as none enters the membrane. Since four moles of electrons are consumed for every mole of oxygen, we have

$$I = -4\mathcal{F}N_{z,O_2} = 4\mathcal{F}\mathcal{D}_{eff}\left.\frac{d\theta}{dz}\right|_{z=\delta}$$

$$= a\delta i^o_{+,ref}\left[\exp\left(2\mathcal{F}(U_+ - U_- - V_{cell})/\mathcal{R}T\right) - \exp\left(-2\mathcal{F}(U_+ - U_- - V_{cell})/\mathcal{R}T\right)\right]\eta \quad (10.27)$$

where

$$\eta = \frac{\tanh\left(\delta\sqrt{ak^s/\mathcal{D}_{eff}}\right)}{\delta\sqrt{ak^s/\mathcal{D}_{eff}}} \quad (10.28)$$

10.5.3 Look at the results

If diffusional resistance was absent, the oxygen pressure would have been equal to $P_{O_2,ref}$ throughout the electrode, and the term multiplying η in eq. 10.27 would have been the current density. It only accounts for activation polarization or voltage drop required to drive the charge transfer reaction. η defined in eq. 10.28 is the effectiveness factor of the electrode, which accounts for the decrease in current density due to the diffusional limitations. It is indeed difficult to miss the similarity between this solution and the one derived for the performance of a porous catalyst!

Equations 10.27 and 10.28 may be viewed as an implicit equation for the cell voltage for a given current density. As current density increases, $(U_+ - U_- - V_{cell})$, the overpotential, has to increase to meet the demand for oxygen consumption. This corresponds to a decrease in the cell potential from the equilibrium value. The maximum value the overpotential can reach is the equilibrium potential itself when the cell potential becomes zero. It occurs at the maximum current density that can be drawn from the cell. At this current density, the concentration of oxygen is zero everywhere in the electrode. Diffusion is unable to supply oxygen demand for current densities beyond this value. The electrode's performance is limited by diffusion of oxygen.

10.5.4 Summary

As we mentioned, a complete model for a unit[16] of a fuel cell must incorporate both the electrodes and the PEM separator. The general characteristics are shown in fig. 10.10. The curve is referred

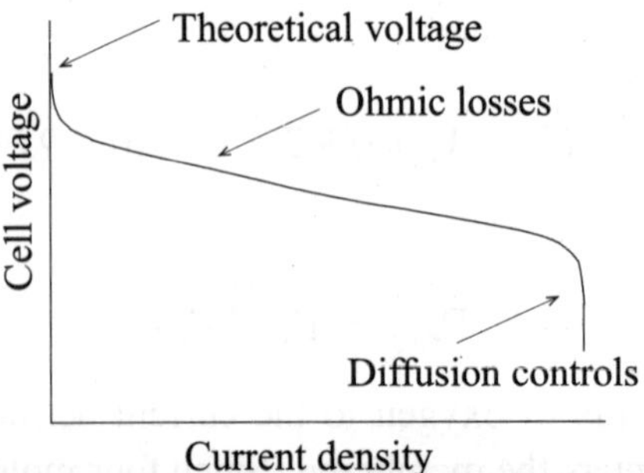

Figure 10.10. Typically observed cell voltage as a function of current density drawn from the fuel cell. The initial drop is controlled by the rate of the charge transfer reactions. The next to control the decrease in cell voltage is the ohmic resistance. The final controlling step is diffusion of the reactants.

to as the polarization curve. In general, at low current densities, the potential drop is entirely due to charge transfer reaction or is the activation polarization. As current density is increased, the overpotentials increase and hence the rate of charge transfer reaction increases, and other steps become the limiting ones. Once again, generally speaking, at moderate current densities, oxygen and hydrogen concentrations in the electrode do not decrease from the surface values significantly. Hence, decrease in cell potential at intermediate values of current density is due to ohmic losses. At even higher current densities, diffusion becomes the limiting factor.

We make one comment in passing. We did not solve the water mass balance. Such a solution can suggest whether PEM parts remain hydrated are not. It turns out that this is very important as protons cannot diffuse through if PEM is not hydrated. We did not attempt it here because a realistic solution of this is fairly complex as water may condense, and is also affected by temperature profiles. Interested readers may refer to a review by Young [16] on fuel cells for more advanced material.

10.6 MEMBRANE SEPARATION PROCESSES

Membranes are thin sheets, which can withstand mechanical stresses when suitably supported. Membranes can be polymeric and non-porous or ceramic and microporous. Due to their structural features, solutes diffuse through them at different rates. In case of polymeric membranes, they also dissolve to different extents. Selectivity in separations can be achieved due to these features. More detailed descriptions can be found in the text by Cussler [7] and other more advanced books cited in the text by Bird *et al.* [5]

We consider ultra-filtration as an example here. It is a process used to filter proteins from aqueous solutions or in general filter macromolecular solutes from solvents. The ultra-filtration membranes may be considered to offer large resistance to permeation of solutes through them. Such membranes are referred to as semi-permeable membranes because they mostly permit the solvent to pass through them. Reverse osmosis, used to separate water from brackish solutions, also works on similar principles.

10.6.1 Problem identification

We present a simple analysis of ultra-filtration using *film model*. See figure 10.11. The feed side of the membrane is the one on which the solution to be filtered is placed. The side where the filtrate is collected is the permeate side. Suppose that pure solvent and a solution are respectively

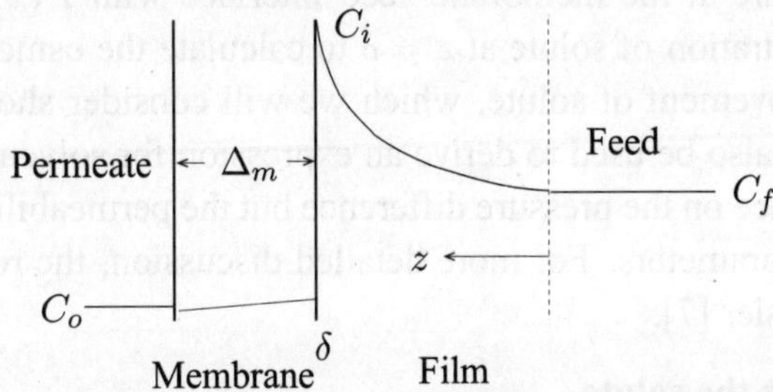

Figure 10.11. Sketch of a ultra-filtration membrane. The right side is the feed side while the left side is where permeate is collected. The membrane permits mostly solvent to permeate while a small amount of solute also does diffuse through the membrane. The curve shows the concentration profiles of the solute. Notice the very tiny gradient in the membrane.

placed on the permeate and feed sides of a membrane. Since the chemical potential of the solvent on the permeate side is greater than on the feed side, solvent will diffuse to the feed side. This is referred to as the back flow. Therefore, in order to achieve filtration, a forward driving force must be applicd to overcome the back flow. The chemical potential of both pure solvent and solvent in a solution increases with pressure. Therefore, by increasing the pressure on feed side above that on the permeate side, the chemical potential of solvent in a solution can be brought up to equal that of a pure solvent. The two sides of the membrane will be in equilibrium if such a pressure difference is applied across the membrane. This pressure difference is called the *osmotic pressure*. Thus, referring to figure 10.11, net flow of solvent across the membrane will be zero if the difference in the pressure on the feed side and that on the permeate side equals the osmotic pressure corresponding to the feed concentration. Under this condition, the forward flow of solvent from the feed side to permeate side due to the applied pressure difference is matched exactly by the back flow caused by the concentration difference. Hence, in order to achieve filtration, the pressure on the feed side must exceed the osmotic pressure. Osmotic pressure for dilute solutions can be calculated by van't Hoff's law, and is given by

$$\pi = C\mathcal{R}T$$

where C is the molar concentration of the solute. In concentrated solutions however, the dependence of osmotic pressure on concentration is exponential rather than linear. The objective of the present analysis is to calculate the filtration rate as a function of the applied pressure difference.

Movement of solvent

Many models are used for the movement of solute and solvent through the membranes. We will use hydraulic permeability model for solvent. The solvent is assumed to flow through the membrane much like in a porous medium. Let the permeability of the membrane to solvent be K_p. Referring to figure 10.11, the velocity of solvent through the membrane is given by

$$v_z = K_p\Bigg(P(z=\delta) - \Big[\pi(z=\delta) - \pi(\text{permeate side})\Big]\Bigg)$$

where the pressure on the permeate side is being taken as the reference value. Usually, resistance to flow of solvent in the membrane dominates over the resistance to flow through the 'film'. Hence, we can replace the pressure at the membrane–feed interface with $P(z = 0)$, the pressure in the bulk. We need the concentration of solute at $z = \delta$ to calculate the osmotic pressure there, and this needs a model for the movement of solute, which we will consider shortly. It may be mentioned that diffusion models can also be used to derive an expression for solvent flux. As it turns out, they predict the same dependence on the pressure difference but the permeability shows model dependent relationship to different parameters. For more detailed discussion, the readers should refer to texts by Bird *et al.* [5] and Cussler [7].

Constitutive equation for the solute

Feed side: Solute is brought to the membrane–feed interface by convection of the solvent. However, most of the solute is retained by the membrane while the solvent passes through it. As a result, solute starts accumulating near the feed–membrane interface. Therefore, the concentration of the solute increases and it begins to diffuse back towards the feed side. Steady state will be reached when the difference between the convective and diffusive flux of the solute equals the flux of solute through the membrane. We need models for movement of solute in the membrane and on the feed side to analyze this. We will use diffusion models for both these. First let us consider the feed side. The flux of solute can be written as

$$N_z = -\mathcal{D}\frac{dC}{dz} + v_z C$$

Here we approximated the bulk velocity by the solvent velocity in view of our assumption that solutions are dilute.

Membrane: At steady state, the flux of solute in the feed phase, N_z, is equal to that in the membrane phase. Diffusion of solute through the membrane can be written as

$$N_z = -\mathcal{D}'\frac{dC'}{dz} + \frac{C'}{C'_{total}}(N_z + \rho_s v_z)$$

where primed symbols are quantities in the membrane phase, C'_{total} is the total molar concentration in the membrane, and ρ_s is the molar density of the solvent. Generally, membranes are used only if they are relatively impermeable to solutes and this is possible only if the partition coefficient is small. Then, the concentration of solute in the membrane will be very small. In view of this, the convective term is neglected in the above expression. Finally we need to relate the concentration of the solute in the feed and membrane sides. It is customary to define $C'/C = m$ as the partition coefficient of the solute between the membrane and feed phase.

Solute mass balance

See figure 10.11. At steady state,

$$\frac{dN_z}{dz} = 0$$

or the flux is a constant. Concentration of solute on both sides of the membrane are known. The constitutive equation in the membrane can be integrated to obtain

$$N_z = m\mathcal{D}'\frac{C_i - C_o}{\Delta_m} \tag{10.29}$$

The constitutive equation in the feed phase can also be integrated to obtain

$$\ln\frac{v_z C_i - N_z}{v_z C_f - N_z} = \frac{v_z}{\mathcal{D}}\delta \tag{10.30}$$

Note that the concentration of the solute at the feed–membrane interface is greater than the feed concentration. This is to be expected because most of the convective flux of solute is balanced off by the opposing diffusive flux. The increased concentration at the interface increases the value of osmotic pressure. As a result, the net driving force for solvent flux decreases, or equivalently, back flow increases. This effect is called *concentration polarization*, a phenomenon similar to what we observed in electroplating. Finally, we have an expression for the velocity of solvent flux:

$$v_z = K_p\left(P(z=\delta) - \left[\pi(z=\delta) - \pi(\text{permeate side})\right]\right) = K_p\left(P_f - (C_i - C_o)\mathcal{R}T\right) \quad (10.31)$$

The three equations 10.29, 10.30 and 10.31 can be used to solve for the three unknowns, *i.e.*, C_i, v_z and N_z. They are non-linear and can only be solved numerically.

10.6.2 Look at the results

We look at a special case to get a feel for the behavior. A special case is when the solute is completely excluded, *i.e.*, $N_z = 0$ and $C_o = 0$. In this limit, eq. 10.30 reduces to

$$\ln\frac{C_i}{C_f} = \frac{v_z}{\mathcal{D}}\delta$$

Equation 10.31 can be solved along with this to obtain the following relationship between applied pressure and velocity

$$P_f - C_f\mathcal{R}T = \frac{v_z}{K_p} + C_f\mathcal{R}T\left(e^{\frac{v_z\delta}{\mathcal{D}}} - 1\right) \quad (10.32)$$

where P_f is the pressure on the feed side taking pressure on the permeate side as the reference.

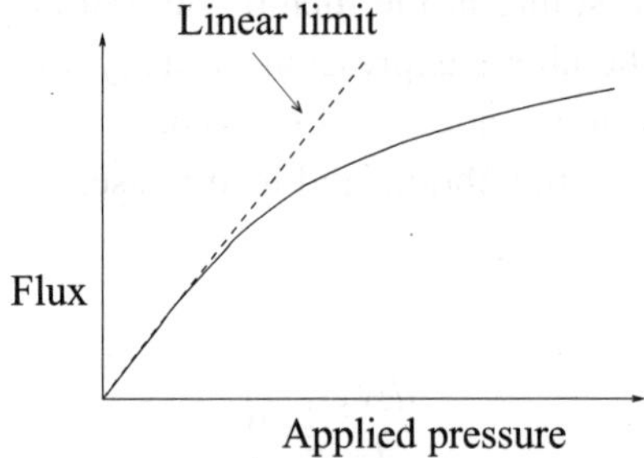

Figure 10.12. Sketch of dependence of solvent flux through a semi-permeable membrane on the difference between the applied pressure and the osmotic pressure. The increase levels off as concentration near the feed–membrane interface increases and consequently increases back flow.

Left hand side of the above equation is the driving force for the solvent flux. As expected, flux increases as the driving force increases. When the applied pressure is only marginally larger than the osmotic pressure, flux will be small, and the second term on the right hand side of eq. 10.32 will be small compared to the first. The flux in this regime will increase linearly with the applied pressure. However, as applied pressure increases, concentration polarization sets in. The osmotic pressure will increase and the back flow increases. The increase in flux will be less than linear. It will be logarithmic. The general trend is shown in figure 10.12.

It must be pointed out that if the more realistic exponential dependence of osmotic pressure on the concentration of solute is used, levelling off of the flux is even more pronounced than predicted by the linear model for the osmotic pressure.

10.7 FREEZING OF SOLUTIONS

10.7.1 Problem identification

In section 6.7 we considered solidification of a pure solvent. There we encountered a moving boundary value problem involving only heat transfer. In this section we consider freezing of solutions. In general, the solid phase created due to freezing would not have the same composition as that of the liquid except if it is a eutectic mixture. As a result, as freezing occurs, components will have to move between the two phases, and hence phase change is accompanied by diffusion as well. Problems involving both heat conduction and diffusive mass transfer are referred to as *double diffusion problems*. In this section we consider freezing of solvent from a solution, *e.g.*, water from an aqueous solution of salt. The objective is to calculate the rate of freezing as a function of the temperature difference between the freezing point of the solution and the cooling surface or *sub-cooling*.

Freezing point diagram

Solutions of different compositions will freeze at different temperatures. Generally speaking, addition of a solute depresses the freezing point. We will consider a simple freezing behavior where the freezing point decreases linearly with concentration of solute, A:

$$T_f = T_o - \Gamma C_A \tag{10.33}$$

where T_f is the freezing point of the solution while T_o is the freezing point of pure solvent, B. We will further assume that the frozen solid does not contain any solute. The freezing point diagram is shown in figure 10.13. As solute cannot be present in the frozen solvent, it has to diffuse away from

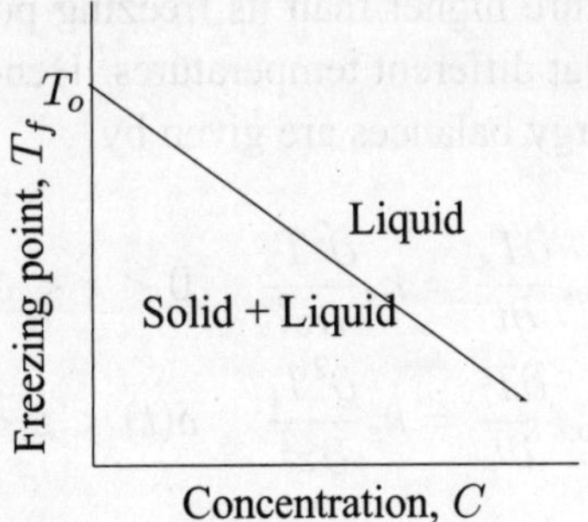

Figure 10.13. Sketch of freezing point diagram. The freezing temperature decreases linearly with increasing concentration. The two phase region is bounded by the freezing point line and the temperature axis. Therefore, the concentration of solute in the concentration is zero.

the solid–solution interface as freezing proceeds due to heat removal.

Energy & mass balances

Consider freezing of a semi-infinite block of solution. Let the solution be at T_∞ and let the concentration of solute in it be C_∞. Because it is a liquid, T_∞ has to be greater than $T_o - \Gamma C_{A,\infty}$. At $t = 0$, let the surface of the solution at $z = 0$ be brought down to T_b, a temperature below the freezing point of the solution, and be maintained there. Thus, $T_b < T_o - \Gamma C_{A,\infty} < T_\infty$. Refer to figure 10.14. Freezing will begin at $z = 0$ and will proceed deeper into the solution. As discussed in section 6.7,

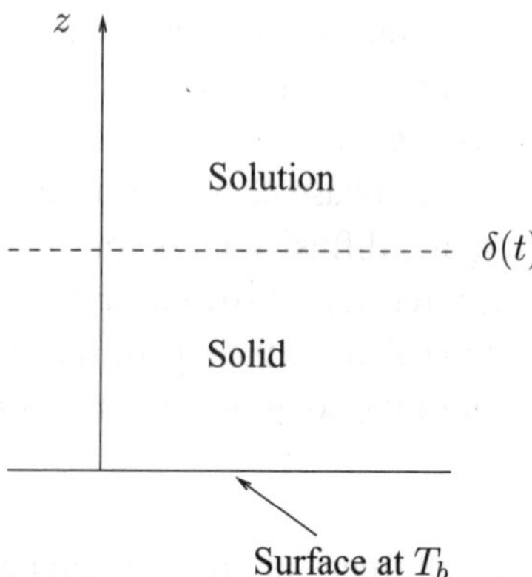

Figure 10.14. Sketch of the geometry. Solution in the range $0 < z < \infty$ is initially at T_∞ and C_∞. The bottom surface is maintained at temperature below the freezing temperature. Freezing begins at $z = 0$ and the freezing front moves away from the bottom surface. It is located at $\delta(t)$.

the solid and the solution phases will be separated by a sharp front located at $\delta(t)$. In section 6.7, we have pointed out that convection may be created due to freezing since the densities of the solid and fluid are not the same. *Here we neglect that convection.* Hence, conduction is the only mechanism of heat transfer and diffusion the only mechanism of movement of solute away from the freezing front. Here, unlike in the problem considered in section 6.7 where the liquid was at its melting point itself, the solution is at a temperature higher than its freezing point. Therefore, the freezing front and liquid far away from it will be at different temperatures. Hence, heat conduction occurs both in the solid and the solution. The energy balances are given by

$$\rho_s C_{p,s} \frac{\partial T_s}{\partial t} = k_s \frac{\partial^2 T_s}{\partial z^2} \qquad 0 < z < \delta(t) \tag{10.34}$$

$$\rho_l C_{p,l} \frac{\partial T_l}{\partial t} = k_s \frac{\partial^2 T_l}{\partial z^2} \qquad \delta(t) < z < \infty \tag{10.35}$$

Mass balance is relevant only in the solution phase. Mass balance for the *solute* is given by[17]

$$\frac{\partial C_A}{\partial t} = \mathcal{D} \frac{\partial^2 C_A}{\partial z^2} \qquad \delta(t) < z < \infty \tag{10.36}$$

Initial and boundary conditions

The initial condition is given by

$$T_l = T_\infty \quad 0 < z < \infty \tag{10.37}$$

and initial condition in the solid phase is not needed as it does not exist initially. We have two second order partial differential equations for temperature and one for concentration. Thus, we need six conditions and one more because the location of the freezing front is not known. The boundary conditions are given by

$$T_s = T_b \quad \text{at} \quad z = 0 \tag{10.38}$$

$$T_s = T_l \quad \text{at} \quad z = \delta(t) \tag{10.39}$$

$$T_l \to T_\infty \quad \text{at} \quad z \to \infty \tag{10.40}$$

$$C_A = \frac{T_o - T_l}{\Gamma} \quad \text{at} \quad z = \delta(t) \tag{10.41}$$

$$C_A \to C_{A,\infty} \quad \text{at} \quad z \to \infty \tag{10.42}$$

The first, third, and last of the above boundary conditions are self explanatory. The second boundary condition follows from the continuity of temperature. Thermodynamic equilibrium is assumed to prevail at the solid–solution interface. The fourth condition is therefore relating the freezing temperature to the concentration of the fluid adjacent to it. We need two more conditions to fully determine the solution and these are specified by the mass and energy balance at the interface. Let us use the unit vector in the z direction as $\boldsymbol{\xi}$. Thus, phase II is solid and I is liquid. The z component of the velocity of the interface is given by

$$V_\xi = \frac{d\delta}{dt} = \dot{\delta}\,(t)$$

Recall that we assumed that convection is absent. Hence, only diffusion and heat conduction are present. Flux of solute in the solid phase is zero. The mass balance equation at the interface is given by eq. 7.10. Its application to the present case then gives

$$-N_{Az} + C_A\,\dot{\delta}\,(t) = 0 \quad \text{at } z = \delta(t)$$

The volume of solution frozen per unit area in time Δt is given by $\Delta t\,\dot{\delta}\,(t)$. Hence, the amount of solute that must move out of frozen solvent per unit area is therefore given by $C_A \Delta t\,\dot{\delta}\,(t)$. This divided by Δt must therefore equal the mass flux, and this is the interpretation of the boundary condition. Substituting Fick's law into it gives

$$C_A\,\dot{\delta}\,(t) = -\mathcal{D}\frac{\partial C_A}{\partial z} \quad \text{at } z = \delta(t) \tag{10.43}$$

The energy balance is given by eq. 7.15. Its application gives for the present case

$$-k_s\frac{\partial T_s}{\partial z} + k_l\frac{\partial T_l}{\partial z} - \rho_s\,\dot{\delta}\,(t)\hat{H}_{s,B} + \rho_l\,\dot{\delta}\,(t)\hat{H}_{l,B} = 0 \quad \text{at } z = \delta(t)$$

where we used the assumption that the density of the pure solvent and solution are equal. But, $\hat{H}_{l,B} - \hat{H}_{s,B} = \mathcal{L}$, the latent heat of fusion. Hence, the above condition can be written as

$$\rho_s\,\dot{\delta}\,(t)\mathcal{L} = k_s\frac{\partial T_s}{\partial z} - k_l\frac{\partial T_l}{\partial z} \quad \text{at } z = \delta(t) \tag{10.44}$$

This boundary condition is also easily interpreted. Both the latent heat of fusion released when solvent freezes and the heat coming by conduction from the hot liquid have to be removed through the solid phase.

10.7.2 Concentration and temperature profiles

The remarkable aspect of this problem is that there exists a similarity solution for even this complex problem. What is given below is a logic of how the solution might have been arrived at, with the enormous benefit of having seen the solution! We have examined several similarity solutions. You will recall the similarity solution for conduction heat transfer to a semi-infinite slab. One important aspect of that solution is that the surface temperature is constant. The mass transfer part of the present problem is like heat transfer to semi-infinite slab if the surface concentration can remain constant. You will also recall that in chapter 9, we presented a similarity solution for mass transfer with an instantaneous chemical reaction. If you look back at it, you will see that it is similar to the heat transfer part of this problem with the dividing surface of that problem being similar to the solid–solution interface here. Again, the important point to note from that problem is that the concentration at the dividing surface was constant. The instantaneous reaction solution is applicable to the heat transfer part of this problem, if the temperature at the solid–solution can remain constant. However, if temperature remains constant, concentration also remains constant! And, the mass transfer part can also have a similarity solution. Thus, if we make a bold hypothesis that the interfacial conditions remain independent of time, we might have a similarity solution. This is the spirit of the similarity solution to the present problem. We follow the solution procedure outlined by Worster [15]. The similarity variable is given by

$$\eta = \frac{z}{\sqrt{4\mathcal{D}t}}$$

and that the interface location is given by

$$\delta(t) = \lambda\sqrt{4\mathcal{D}t}$$

where λ is a constant to be determined. This relationship is what one might expect on the basis of the solutions to the problem of mass transfer with instantaneous chemical reaction and freezing of pure solvent in section 6.7. If temperature and concentration are a function of the similarity variable only then their values at $z = \delta(t)$ will correspond to the constant value of $\eta = \lambda$, and hence will remain constant. Let us write them as $T(\lambda)$ and $C_A(\lambda)$. Worster gave the following solution to the system of partial differential equations

$$T_s(z,t) = T_b + \frac{(T(\lambda) - T_b)\,\mathrm{erf}(\epsilon_s\eta)}{\mathrm{erf}(\epsilon_s\lambda)} \qquad 0 < \eta < \lambda \tag{10.45}$$

$$T_l(z,t) = T_\infty + \frac{(T(\lambda) - T_\infty)\,\mathrm{erfc}(\epsilon_l\eta)}{\mathrm{erfc}(\epsilon_l\lambda)} \qquad \eta > \lambda \tag{10.46}$$

$$C_A(z,t) = C_{A,\infty} + \frac{(C_A(\lambda) - C_{A,\infty})\,\mathrm{erfc}(\eta)}{\mathrm{erfc}(\lambda)} \qquad \eta > \lambda \tag{10.47}$$

where ϵ is the ratio of mass diffusivity to the thermal diffusivity, and subscripts s and l refer to solid and solution phases. The solutions presented satisfy the partial differential equations and four boundary conditions given by eqs. 10.38, 10.39, 10.40, and 10.42. There are three unknowns in the solutions: $C_A(\lambda), T(\lambda)$ and λ. These are determined by using the three remaining boundary conditions, eqs. 10.41, 10.43, and 10.44. The solution space is too complex to sketch, but there is one very important result that has come out of this work which we will describe now.

Mush formation

The rate of freezing depends upon two temperature differences for a given value of latent heat of fusion. The first is the super-heating of the fluid: $T_\infty - T_f(C_\infty)$. The second is the sub-cooling of the cooling surface at $z = 0$: $T_f(C_\infty) - T_b$. The other important parameter is the concentration itself. These three determine the extent of heat to be removed through cold surface, and the extent of solute to be removed from the frozen solvent. Generally mass diffusion is slower than heat conduction. This can result in a steeper decrease in concentration away from the interface than in the temperature. The former implies faster increase in the freezing point than the temperature. Worster [15] found that, under some conditions, the freezing temperature at the local concentration does rise more quickly from the solid–solution interface than the temperature. This is shown in figure 10.15. As a result, there will be a zone where the local temperature is lower than the freezing temperature corresponding to the local concentration producing thermodynamically unstable conditions. Solidification must occur in this region also. Hence, a sharp front cannot exist. Under these

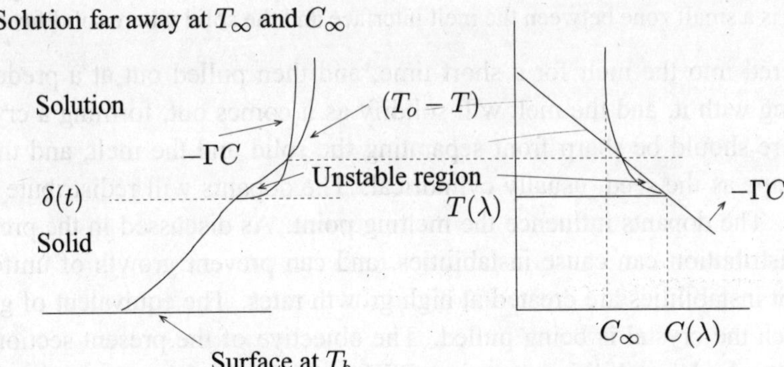

Figure 10.15. Sketch of development of thermodynamically unstable region. As temperature increases more slowly than the freezing point due to slower diffusion of mass than heat, there is a zone where freezing point is more than the local temperature.

conditions, the interface develops instabilities and an intimate mixture of solid and solution phases was found to form. This is referred to as *mush*. A patch of mushy phase separates the solution and the solid phases. Formation of mushy phase has been experimentally demonstrated. For details, readers may consult the article by Worster in the book by Batchelor *et al.* [2]. Mush formation has important implications to solidification of alloys.

10.8 Crystal growth

Formation of crystals is a very important operation in many industries. While small crystals are formed in making many products, including sugar and salt, growing large-sized single crystals is a challenge. Growing long single crystals of silicon, which are sliced subsequently to produce wafers, is an important step in the manufacture of transistors. Typically, the diameter of these can be anywhere between 0.1 and 0.3 m, and they can be as long as 2 m. We discuss *Czochralski crystallizer* which is commonly used for this purpose. A schematic of it is shown in figure 10.16. In this process, silicon doped with desired elements is placed in a crucible, and melted. A seed

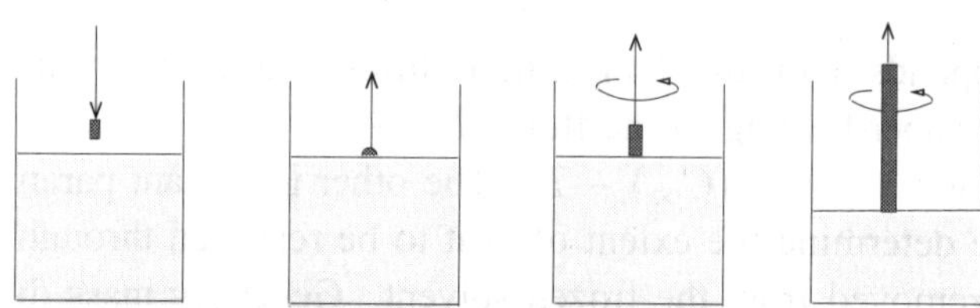

Figure 10.16. Schematic of Czochralski process. A melt is taken in a heated crucible, shown in the first panel. Typically, in a semiconductor industry, it is molten silicon containing dopants. A seed crystal of the solid is then immersed into the melt as shown in the second panel. The seed crystal is then slowly pulled out while rotating it. This is shown in the third panel. Usually, the operation is more complex than shown. The diameter of the seed crystal and the crystal that is grown on it are not the same, and the latter is larger. Adjustment of rotational speed makes this possible. There is also a thinner zone in between the two to introduce crystalline structure. The rotation induces better transport characteristics. To facilitate crystallization, the melt will be at a higher temperature than the melting point while the solid will be at a temperature lower than the melting point. As a result, there will be a temperature gradient across the crystal. There is a small zone between the melt interface and the solid where solidification occurs.

crystal is lowered into the melt for a short time, and then pulled out at a predetermined rate. It drags melt along with it, and the melt will solidify as it comes out, forming a crystal. Under ideal conditions, there should be sharp front separating the solid and the melt, and the solid should be of the same shape as the seed, usually cylindrical. The dopants will redistribute between the melt and the crystal. The dopants influence the melting point. As discussed in the previous section, the process of redistribution can cause instabilities, and can prevent growth of uniform crystals. We found there that instabilities are created at high growth rates. The equivalent of growth rate here is the rate at which the crystal is being pulled. The objective of the present section is to predict the conditions under which instabilities can arise. CFD simulations of the process have been extensively carried out in view of the importance of the process. We use an ultra simplified set of equations to make the principles apparent. We have used the texts by Davis [9], Dantzig and Rappaz [8], and the article by Burton and Slichter [6] in preparing this material.

10.8.1 Problem identification

In order to produce crystals, the top end of the crystal will have to be at a temperature lower than the melting point while the melt will be at a temperature higher than the melting point. As we are pulling the crystal out, some melt adheres to it, and solidifies when it comes out of the melt. The pulling and rotation[18] of the crystal induces forced convection in the melt. The melt is hotter than the crystal and this induces natural convection! All this influences both mass and heat transfer. This is too complex for us to handle at this level. We follow Burton and Slichter [6] and introduce the following simple model.

Film model

We use film model to describe the mass transfer processes. As the crystal is being pulled out, the melt adhering to it loses heat to the cooler surroundings and solidifies shortly after it rises above the melt. As conditions are being maintained constant, the length required to solidify will remain constant. Thus, the solidification front will lie above the surface of the melt and will remain at a constant height above the surface of the melt. We lump this zone and the concentration boundary layer in the melt into a *film* of fluid where resistance to mass transfer is concentrated. Above the solidification front, the temperature will decrease into the solid. The latent heat and the sensible heat of the melt above the melting point will be lost to the surroundings through the solid. We will assume that conduction is the mechanism of heat loss through the solid. Generally, radiation is very important in view of the high temperature of the process, but we will not consider it here. The heat loss will require a certain length of the solid to attain the temperature of the surroundings and we can again approximate that it will also remain constant. The picture presented is shown in figure 10.17 from a coordinate system whose origin is located at the solidification front. We assume that only a single dopant is present and use a one-dimensional model.

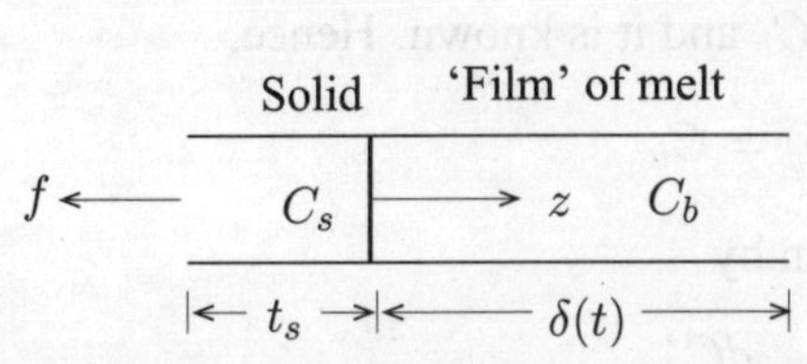

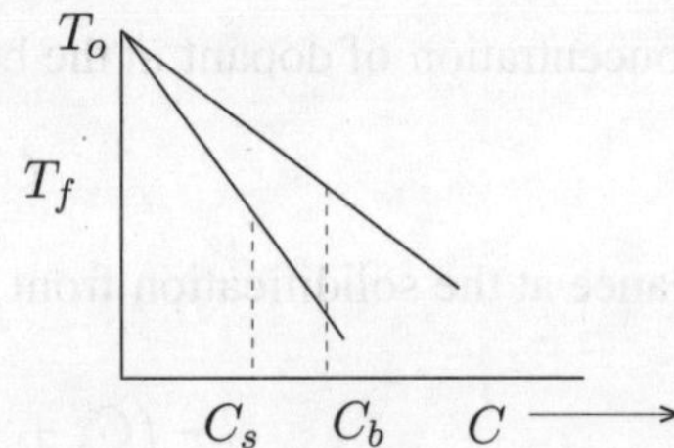

Figure 10.17. The left panel shows a schematic of the film model of Czhochralski process. The coordinate system is located at the solidification front. The mass transfer resistance is lumped in a film of melt of thickness δ. The heat transfer resistance in the solid is assumed to be contained in a length of t_s. The crystal is pulled up, that corresponds to the left in the figure, with a speed f. The right panel shows a simple phase diagram assuming a single dopant is present. C_b is the concentration of the dopant in the melt. C_s is its concentration in the crystal. Note that C_b and C_s may not correspond to equilibrium condition due to resistance to mass transfer.

Mass balance of dopant

Silicon is the major component and so its diffusion is not of any interest. Note that we are using a coordinate system located at the freezing front. To an observer in that coordinate system[19], the melt would appear moving towards the origin of the coordinate system while the solid appears to move away. The steady state mass balance for the dopant reads

$$\mathcal{D}\frac{d^2C}{dz^2} - v_z\frac{dC}{dz} = 0$$

We need a total mass balance to relate the velocity in the melt to the speed of pulling of the crystal. The dopants are very small in concentration, typically of the order of tens of ppm. Hence, if we neglect the density difference between melt and solid, balance of the total mass will dictate that the velocity of the melt and velocity of the solid are the same. The mass balance of dopant is then given by

$$\mathcal{D}\frac{d^2C}{dz^2} + f\frac{dC}{dz} = 0 \tag{10.48}$$

where f is the pulling speed of the crystal. Note it is also the production rate of the process.

Enthalpy balance

We shall shortly explain that, in order to ascertain conditions for stability, we need not write an enthalpy balance in the melt phase. Assuming that conduction dominates in the solid, the temperature profile will be linear. In particular, the gradient, G_s will be given by

$$G_s = \frac{T_i - T_a}{t_s}$$

where T_i is the temperature at the solidification front and T_a is the temperature of the surroundings of the solid.

Boundary conditions

Denote the concentration of dopant in the bulk as C_b and it is known. Hence,

$$C(z = \delta) = C_b$$

The mass balance at the solidification front is given by

$$-fC_s + fC_i + \mathcal{D}\frac{dC}{dz}\bigg|_{z=0} = 0 \tag{10.49}$$

where C_i is the concentration in the fluid phase at $z = 0$. We also have the equilibrium relationship between the dopant concentrations in the crystal and the melt.

$$C_s = mC_i \tag{10.50}$$

and m is called the distribution coefficient.

Concentration profiles

Equation 10.49 can be solved to obtain

$$\mathcal{D}\frac{dC}{dz}\bigg|_{z=0} = f(C_s - C_i)$$

Equation 10.48 can be integrated once, and the given boundary condition can be used to obtain

$$\frac{dC}{dz} = \frac{f}{\mathcal{D}}(C_s - C_i)\exp\left(-\frac{fz}{\mathcal{D}}\right)$$

One more integration can be done using the boundary condition at $z = 0$ to obtain

$$\frac{C - C_s}{C_i - C_s} = \exp\left(-\frac{fz}{\mathcal{D}}\right)$$

This can be rewritten using the equilibrium relationship between C_i and C_s as

$$\frac{C - mC_i}{C_i(1-m)} = \exp\left(-\frac{fz}{\mathcal{D}}\right) \tag{10.51}$$

C_i is still an unknown, but is determined using the boundary condition in the bulk or at $z = \delta$ to get

$$\frac{C_i}{C_b} = \frac{1}{m + (1-m)\exp\left(-\frac{f\delta}{\mathcal{D}}\right)}$$

This is used to express the concentration of the dopant in the crystal in terms of the bulk concentration as

$$\frac{C_s}{C_b} = \frac{m}{m + (1-m)\exp\left(-\frac{f\delta}{\mathcal{D}}\right)} \tag{10.52}$$

Temperature gradients

Finally, the temperature at the interface can be calculated from the phase diagram:

$$T_f(z=0) = T_i = T_o - \Gamma C_i$$

Hence, the temperature gradient in the solid can be calculated

$$G_s = \frac{T_o - \Gamma C_i - T_a}{t_s} \tag{10.53}$$

We use the energy balance at the solidification front to relate the temperature gradients in the solid and the melt. It is given by

$$k_l G_l = k_s G_s - \mathcal{L}\rho f \tag{10.54}$$

where G_l is the temperature gradient in the melt at $z = 0$, and $\mathcal{L}$ is the latent heat of melting.

10.8.2 Look at the results

Dopant concentration in the crystal

A few things can be noticed from eq. 10.52. If the film thickness is large, then the concentration of the dopant in the crystal is same as that in the bulk of the melt. If the film thickness is zero, then the concentration in the melt, but at the solidification front, is same as C_b and hence $C_s = mC_b$. The film thickness is a function of the rotational speed of the crystal. The speed of rotation influences the dopant concentration in the crystal and an increase in the speed of rotation changes it from C_b to mC_b.

Instability

Let us consider the more common case where the distribution coefficient m is less than unity. In this instance, the crystal will reject solute into the melt. Hence, the concentration decreases from the front into the bulk of the melt. This establishes a diffusive flux from the front into the melt[20], and the concentration variation is confined to the thickness of the diffusion film. We know that heat diffuses faster than mass or the absolute value of the temperature gradient in the melt is much smaller than that of the concentration gradient. Hence, Burton and Slichter [6] argue that the temperature gradient in the diffusion film of the melt can be taken as constant given by eq. 10.54. Thus, from this we can calculate the temperature increase in the melt from the freezing front. But from eq. 10.51 and the phase diagram, we can calculate the way melting point corresponding to the local value of the concentration increases from the solidification front into the melt. If the temperature in the melt increases more rapidly than the local melting point, freezing will not occur or instability does not arise. The gradient of the local melting point is calculated to be

$$\left.\frac{dT_f}{dz}\right|_{z=0} = -\Gamma\left.\frac{dC}{dz}\right|_{z=0} = \frac{mfC_b}{\mathcal{D}}\frac{1-m}{m+(1-m)\exp\left(-\frac{f\delta}{\mathcal{D}}\right)}$$

Thus, instability is not caused if

$$\frac{k_s G_s - \mathcal{L}\rho f}{k_l} \geq \frac{mfC_b}{\mathcal{D}}\frac{1-m}{m+(1-m)\exp\left(-\frac{f\delta}{\mathcal{D}}\right)}$$

It is seen that as f increases, the left hand side decreases and hence instability will result at some critical value of f. We have looked at instability caused only due to redistribution of dopants. In literature on silicon crystal growth, this is referred to as instability due to constitutional supercooling. There are other causes, *e.g.*, surface instabilities in the zone between the melt and the solidification front. As we mentioned earlier, this subject is widely investigated and if you are interested, you have to refer to literature.

Problems for Chapter 10.

10.1 A polymer membrane which is permeable to oxygen but **impermeable to nitrogen** is available. It is desired to use this membrane to make pure oxygen from air. Normally thin membranes are used and hence only flux in the direction perpendicular to the membrane is important. The mass flux through this membrane is given by

$$N = K\Delta p_{ox}$$

where Δp_{ox} is the difference in the *partial pressure of oxygen* across the membrane. Suppose air at pressure P_f is supplied to one side of the membrane. Assume that air consists of only oxygen and nitrogen with oxygen mole fraction equal to 0.21. Suppose we maintain the pressure on the other side of the membrane at P_d. Use the film model to derive an equation which can be used to predict the flux of oxygen through the membrane.

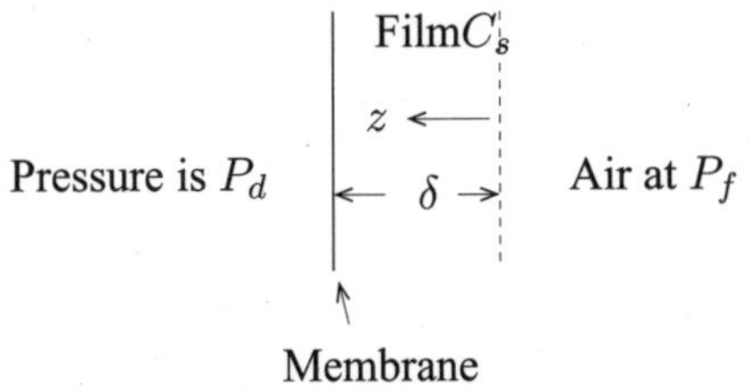

Figure for problem 10.1.

Notes

[1]A passive scalar is one that does not react with the medium. Temperature is one such!

[2]The same can occur with a disk that is soluble in the solvent. The solvent coming from far away will dilute the solute diffusing from the disk, and both can balance each other and the concentration of the solute can become independent of radius.

[3]As mentioned there, this section is also paraphrased from the excellent book by Bejan [3]

[4]This corresponds to low solubility and this also permits us to use constant diffusivity.

[5]We cancelled the pressure gradient with the body force term as explained in section 6.6

[6]Optical detection can be used to measure this value. A beam can be passed across the cross-section at any location downstream and the absorbance can be measured. Absorbance of the original plug can also be measured. The ratio of the two will give the average concentration.

[7]This section is a summary of the very lucid but longer presentation in the text by Probstein [12].

[8]At times even larger than this, *i.e.,* at distances very far from the place where the plug was introduced, radial diffusion will quickly even out all radial gradients and spread from there on will be like a plug.

[9]That is why this is referred to as *dispersion* and not diffusion.

[10]I must admit that this is really hard to grasp, and I do not feel that I have digested it!

[11]This is applicable for a closed system. A fuel cell is not a closed system. But we will assume that the supply of reactants and removal of products are also carried out reversibly.

[12]This in turn means that the potential difference between the reference electrode and the fluid surrounding it is zero

[13]At equilibrium, the potential in the fluid is constant. But, the potential of the fluid surrounding the reference electrode is same at that of the reference electrode. Hence, the potential of the fluid surrounding the electrode of interest is also the same as the reference electrode. Therefore, the potential difference measured between the electrode of interest and the reference electrodes is that between the electrode of interest and the fluid around it. Readers are referred to Newman and Thomas-Alyea [11] for a more detailed explanation.

[14]We should qualify it with the word 'mostly' since there is another mechanism known as electro-osmosis, which we will ignore in this text.

[15]If we apply a potential greater than U across the electrodes, the reactions are reversed and electrolysis occurs.

[16]Several such units are connected in series to make a stack. Several such stacks may be arranged in series and parallel to meet practical demand for power supply.

[17]We assume that the solutions are dilute and hence convection created by diffusion is neglected.

[18]Refer to our discussion on flow to a rotating disk.

[19]As viewed from the laboratory frame, the solidification front moves towards the melt.

[20]Unlike with growth from a semi-infinite body considered in the previous section, steady state is possible here. As you will notice, the situation is very much like that in ultra-filtration. Due to rejection of the dopant, its concentration at the solidification front build up, and due to this its backward diffusive flux increases. The diffusive flux reduces the convective forward flux of the dopant. At some stage, the net forward flux matches the uptake of dopant by the crystal, and steady state is reached.

References

[1] R. Aris. On the dispersion of a solute in a fluid flowing through a tube. *Proc. Roy. Soc.*, A235:67–77, 1956.

[2] G.K. Batchelor, H.K. Moffatt, and M.G. Worster, editors. *Perspectives in Fluid Mechanics*. Cambridge University Press, 2002.

[3] A. Bejan. *Convection heat transfer*. Wiley, 2 edition, 1984.

[4] D.M. Bernardi and M.W. Verbrugge. Mathematical model of a gas diffusion electrode bonded to a polymer electrolyte. *A.I.Ch.E. Journal*, 37:1151–1164, 1991.

[5] R.B. Bird, W.E. Stewart, and E.N. Lightfoot. *Transport Phenomena*. John Wiley, 2 edition, 2002.

[6] J.A. Burton and W.P. Slichter. *Transistor Technology*, volume 1, chapter 5 and 6. van Nostrand, 1958.

[7] E.L. Cussler. *Diffusion*. Cambridge University Press, 3 edition, 2009.

[8] J.A. Dantzig and M. Rappaz. *Solidification*. EPFL Press, 2009.

[9] S.H. Davis. *Theory of solidification*. Cambridge University Press, 2001.

[10] K.G. Denbigh. *The principles of chemical equilibrium*. Cambridge University Press, 3 edition, 1971.

[11] J. Newman and K.E. Thomas-Alyea. *Electrochemical systems*. Wiley-Interscience, 2004.

[12] R.F. Probstein. *Physicochemical Hydrodynamics: An introduction*. Wiley, 1994.

[13] H. Schlichting. *Boundary layer theory*. McGraw Hill, 1960.

[14] G.I. Taylor. Dispersion of soluble matter in solvent flowing slowly through a tube. *Proc. Roy. Soc.*, A219:186–203, 1953.

[15] M.G. Worster. Solidification of an alloy from a cooled boundary. *J. Fluid Mech.*, 167:481–501, 1986.

[16] J. B. Young. Thermofluid modeling of fuel cells. *Ann. Rev. Fluid Mech.*, 39:193–215, 2007.

Chapter 11

TRANSPORT PROCESSES IN TURBULENT FLOWS

```
Turbulent flows are inherently unsteady, and appear random in
   character. Probabilistic description is most suited and
   is described.
Flow quantities are broken into an average and fluctuation.
   Equations derived for correlations between fluctuations
   cannot be closed and models have to be used.
Kolmogorov proposed a model of how energy supplied into a
   system cascades through several length scales and dissipated
   into heat.
These ideas form the basis for turbulence  models and one of
   them is derived.
```

We begin with a few quotes:

It takes a shrewd fluid dynamicist to avoid turbulence for long. Quote from P.A. Davidson, *J. Fluid Mech.*,vol 429, 410 (2001).

I had less difficulty in the discovery of the motion of heavenly bodies in spite of their astonishing distances, than in the investigation of the movement of flowing water before our very eyes. From Galileo Quoted by R. Narasimha, *J. Ind. Inst. Sci.*, vol 64(a), 1-59 (1983).

It remains to call attention to the chief outstanding difficulty of our subject. Quote on turbulent flow from the text *Hydrodynamics* by H. Lamb, p 663 (1932).

The comments, the essence of which is by–and–large true even now, should give a glimpse of the difficulty in dealing with turbulent flows! We give a brief introduction to selected topics in turbulence. In my opinion, you should understand that exact analytical or computational results are not available for turbulent flows. In this sense, turbulent flows are not deterministic. One has to use language of probability much like in describing results of prediction of weather, *etc.* and we first cover these ideas. Kolmogorov developed a very important idea of energy flow in turbulence and this is the next concept you must pay attention to. We focus on these selected topics because study of turbulent flows is complex and quite advanced in nature. References are given at the end of the chapter for those interested in pursuing this subject further.

11.1 INTRODUCTION

It is often observed that the orderly streamlined motion or laminar flow observed at low Reynolds numbers gives way rather suddenly when a critical value of Reynolds number is exceeded, and the motion becomes apparently random. To quote Batchelor [1],

> ...some of these motions are such that the velocity at any given time and position in the fluid is not found to be the same when it is measured several times under seemingly identical conditions. In these motions, the velocity takes random values which are not determined by the ostensible, or controllable, or 'macroscopic', data of the flow, although we believe the *average* properties of the motion are uniquely determined by the data. Fluctuating motions of this kind are said to be turbulent.

More often than not, flows in many applications are turbulent. As these motions are 'wasteful' from the view point of desired and directed motion, extra energy is spent when the flow is turbulent. However, turbulence is accompanied by strong mixing action, and hence rates of transport of heat and mass are greatly enhanced. This is a beneficial phenomena compensating for the extra energy spent in flow. Though turbulent flows are known for long, prediction of their various characteristics from a fundamental view point is still not possible. Computations are extensively used for this purpose and they are based not just on fundamental equations but also on theories and models developed over the last several decades. In this chapter, we review these and the equations commonly used for computational predictions in applications. We refer you to many interesting introductions, *e.g.*, by Corrsin [3], Liepmann [5], and L'Vov and Procaccia [6]. An excellent book is by Tennekes and Lumley [8], and we use this extensively in this chapter. Another nice book is by Davidson [4].

11.2 PHENOMENOLOGICAL DESCRIPTION

Let us make the description of turbulence given more concrete by taking one quantity, say x component of the velocity, v_x. If it is measured at a given location in a turbulent flow field as a function of time, one would find it to be a strongly varying function of time. In some flows, it may be found that the average of the observations over a long enough time period is constant. *We would refer to such flows as steady*, even though it is a function of time! It is because, complexity of turbulent flows is such that one has to be satisfied with knowledge of time averaged or mean values. Consider such a steady flow. A typical velocity record is shown in figure11.1. It must be emphasized that the

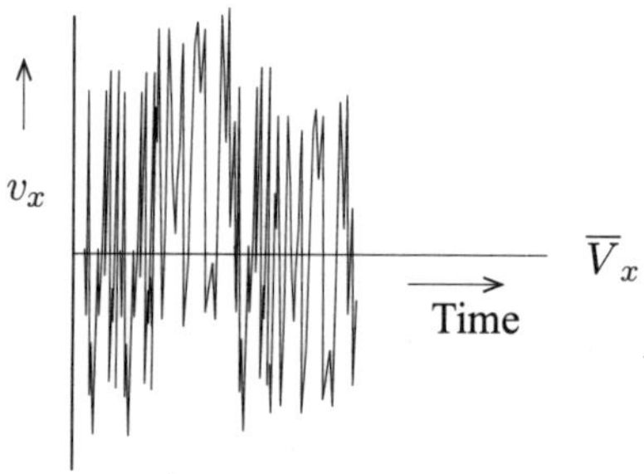

Figure 11.1. Typical record of observations of velocity at a given point.

fluctuations are not due to errors in measurement, but are inherent to the flow itself. Thus, turbulent flows are irregular or random, both in space and time.

11.3 CHARACTERISTICS OF TURBULENT FLOW

There are several characteristics of turbulent flows. An objective of theories of turbulence is to predict these. Let us consider two of these.

11.3.1 Indeterministic nature of turbulent flows

As the equations of motion of fluids rest upon well-established physical foundations, it is expected that such complex and apparently random motion can still be predicted by solving, numerically if not analytically, the Navier–Stokes equations (NSE). Though there is no evidence to doubt such a belief, solutions to NSE at high Reynolds numbers have not been found[1] so far due to limitations on speed and size of computers. Further, uniqueness of three-dimensional solutions of NSE is yet to be established.

Let us look at the situation from a theoretical or analytical view point. Though it has not been proved, suppose that unique solutions to NSE exist. Then it would imply that if the input is precisely known, turbulent flow is also uniquely determined, and an experiment must give the *same* variation in time and space every time it is repeated. Observations of turbulent flow do not indicate such reproducibility and may have to be attributed to some uncontrolled variations entering the system through inputs. It would be possible to put this to experimental test only if the input to the system can be controlled to *arbitrarily specified accuracy*. However, recent studies on dynamical systems, broadly referred to as *chaos*, indicate that even when the solutions are determined uniquely, they could be very sensitive to initial conditions, and that tiny changes in initial conditions would make the solutions look random or chaotic or turbulent. Besides, there could be minute but uncontrolled external factors which also might influence the flow. Both these factors imply that accuracy demanded of control of experimental conditions might not be achievable. Thus, turbulent flows seem to be out of reach of *precise* description at present, both mathematically and experimentally.

This comment applies equally to computational efforts also. Let us illustrate this more concretely. Usually turbulence seems to produce variations on fine length scales. It would be of the order of 0.1 mm or even less. Thus, if we want to compute velocities of fluid of volume as small as even 1 cm^3, it would require one million grid points. At each grid point we have to keep track of three components of velocity and pressure. Thus, we need to store 4 million quantities and manipulate them. As Reynolds number increases, the variations occur on an even finer length scale and hence the computational effort becomes even more difficult. For this reason, exact computations of turbulent flows in a domain of size of some practical utility have not made much progress.

Thus, turbulent flows do not appear amenable to exact description and modeling seems to be necessary. An objective of researchers in the field of turbulence is to develop models for description of characteristics of turbulence.

11.3.2 Enhanced diffusive power of turbulence

As stated earlier, turbulent flows appear to be irregular, or random, in space and time. The random motions are like the random Brownian motion. Hence, just as random molecular motions have diffusive power, random turbulent motions also create diffusion, but even more intense than molecular motions do. We have shown earlier that diffusivity by random motions is given by the product of a characteristic length and velocity. Because these scales of turbulent motion are larger in magnitude than the corresponding ones at the molecular level, turbulence causes enhanced rates of diffusion.

An example of this is already known to you. Enhanced diffusion rates lead to enhanced mixing. Now consider the differences between velocity profiles in laminar and turbulent flow in a pipe. Momentum diffuses from the center of the pipe to the walls in the direction of decreasing momentum density or equivalently decreasing velocity. The velocity gradients will be smaller if the diffusivity or extent of mixing is larger. Thus, *where turbulence prevails*, the velocity gradients in turbulent flow should be smaller than in laminar flow. Turbulence prevails in the central portion of the pipe, but is curbed by the presence of wall. A small region near the wall does not have turbulence. Hence, for a given flow rate, velocity gradients in most part of the tube are smaller for turbulent flow than in laminar flow. Thus, in the central portion, velocity profile is flatter in turbulent flow than in laminar flow. However, the no-slip condition dictates that velocity must fall to zero at the wall. Hence, for a given average velocity, the velocity gradients near the wall in turbulent flow are greater in turbulent flow than in laminar flow. This of course implies greater resistance to flow and ties in with the fact that dissipation of energy in turbulent flow is greater than in laminar flow.

Let us illustrate this a bit more quantitatively with an example. A refrigerator has a tube bank behind it to dissipate heat into the room. It does so by natural convection[2]. Suppose the length of the tube bank is 1 m, and that the temperature difference between the tubes and room is about 10 K, while the room temperature is of the order of 300 K. The buoyancy force that accelerates the fluid element, per unit mass of it, is of the order of $(g)(10/300)$. The velocity attained by the fluid element as it rises, at the end of its contact with one meter long tube bank, assuming that viscous forces are negligible, is of the order of $\sqrt{(g)(10/300)1}$ or about 0.8 m/s. If we assume that the magnitude of the random fluctuations in velocities is about 10% of the characteristic velocity, they would be of the order of 0.08 m/s. Similarly if we assume that magnitude of the length scales of fluctuations are also 10% of the largest length scale available, it turns out to be of the order of 0.10 m. Thus, diffusivity will be of the order of 0.01 m^2/s. This value is about 100 times greater than the molecular diffusivities, which are of the order of 0.0001 m^2/s. It is this enhanced diffusivity which makes turbulent flow desirable in heat and mass transfer. For the same reason, unfortunately, this also implies more dissipation of mechanical energy.

An objective of modeling of turbulent flows is to predict the enhanced diffusive power of turbulence for various conditions.

11.4 MECHANISMS AND APPROACHES

As mentioned earlier, energy dissipation is greater in turbulent flows. From this view point, it appears that controlling, if not avoiding, turbulence is desirable. Hence, it is natural to ask as to how turbulence arises. The 'routes' to turbulence are not completely charted. It is known that some laminar flows become unstable. Thus, minor perturbations involving some length and time scale will grow to some extent and probably stabilize into a flow more complex than the original one. The resulting flow would then have the main flow and a flow of a finer length and time scale superimposed on it. As Reynolds number is increased further, this flow itself can become unstable and generate an even more complex flow involving another finer length and time scale, and this process can repeat many times. This 'route' was proposed by the famous Russian physicist Landau. The resulting flow would involve many length and time scales and would look turbulent. It is like the sound produced when several musicians owning many kinds of instruments, tuned to different frequencies, play them simultaneously. However, no one has been able to show this by calculations.

In this approach, flow is imagined to be occurring on several length and time scales, and that flow can be decomposed into, perhaps, infinitely many time and length scales. It is possible to think of statistical characterization of the resulting flow, and we will consider this a little later.

Another proposed approach is to model turbulence by a combination of several non-linear oscillators. This will give rise to 'chaos', which is closely connected to the sensitivity to initial conditions we briefly described in the last section. It has been shown that a few such oscillators put together can *simulate* flow patterns similar to that of turbulent flows. This approach, referred to as dynamical systems approach, hopes to find 'signatures' of a few non-linear dynamical systems, which when combined will simulate turbulent flow. Of course this approach is also yet to be established. This approach will not be considered any further in this text.

11.5 STATISTICAL THEORY OF TURBULENCE

As mentioned earlier, the Navier–Stokes equations cannot be solved to understand the characteristics of turbulence or a deterministic approach[3] will not be successful. In fact, several other phenomena of science seem to be out of reach of precise theoretical determination. These are referred to as *stochastic*, and the precise value of a stochastic variable during a given observation is dictated by chance. The statistical theory of turbulence proposes that velocity and pressure fields in turbulent flow be treated as stochastic variables. Thus, one does not hope to predict the exact behavior of a stochastic variable but to predict the probability that the variable takes on a particular value. A familiar example is forecasting the monsoon. One can only predict what is the expected value of the rainfall, what is the reliability of such a prediction and so on. Thus, in dealing with turbulent flows, one does not aim at predicting precise time dependence of velocities, *etc.* in a given flow situation, but only try to predict the probability with which a value is attained by these quantities. We therefore take a small detour into the general methods of statistical description of any variable before focusing on turbulence.

11.5.1 Statistical description

In this chapter, as far as possible, we use the following notation. Italic letters will be used to denote the instantaneous value of the time dependent variable. Its time averaged or mean value will be denoted by the same letter but with upper case, and with a bar on top. The instantaneous value of the deviation from the mean will be denoted by the same letter but in Roman script. Thus, for the time dependent instantaneous value, we use v, $\bar{V}$ for its time averaged or for simplicity mean, value, and v for the deviation of the instantaneous value from the mean.

Probability distribution

The usual approach adopted in describing stochastic processes is aimed at predicting the probability of occurrence of a variable taking a certain value. For example, in experiments involving fifty tosses of a fair coin, one can predict the probability of getting thirty heads. But in turbulence, the variables we deal with are *continuous*. For such variables, a probability distribution is defined. If $f(v_x)$ is the probability distribution of x component of velocity, then $f(v_x)\,dv_x$ is the probability that the value of v_x lies between v_x and $v_x + dv_x$. The mean value of v_x can be computed from

$$E(v_x) \equiv \bar{V_x} = \int_{-\infty}^{\infty} f(v_x) v_x \, dv_x$$

In the literature on probability, the mean value is often referred to as the expected value and hence the symbol E. Since $f(v_x)$ is the probability distribution, its integral must be equal to unity:

$$1 = \int_{-\infty}^{\infty} f(v_x)\, dv_x$$

Another statistical quantity of interest is the variance;

$$\sigma^2(v_x) = E\left[(v_x - \bar{V_x})^2\right]$$

The statistical properties can be measured and verified against the stochastic models for the probability distributions. For example, one can measure v_x as a function of time and determine the mean, and verified against a stochastic model for the same.

Steady turbulent flows are simpler to deal with. As stochastic processes are inherently unsteady, a more precise classification of steady state processes is used. Stochastic processes are classified as *strictly stationary or weakly stationary. All* the statistics of the former process are unaffected if the time t is replaced by $t + \tau$. Thus,

$$f(v_x, t) = f(v_x, t + \tau)$$

is true for a strictly stationary stochastic process. Thus, we can treat the probability distribution to be independent of time in taking averages, *etc*. Here it will be assumed that a steady turbulent flow is a strictly stationary process.

Measurement of probability distribution

Let us examine the process of measuring[4] the probability distribution of any quantity, v. We first acquire a time record of v over some sufficiently long time T. We then mark a window of width dv around some value v_1 as shown in figure 11.2. We now measure all time intervals (marked by Δt_i in the figure) for which the value of v was between v_1 and $v_1 + dv$. The probability that v lies

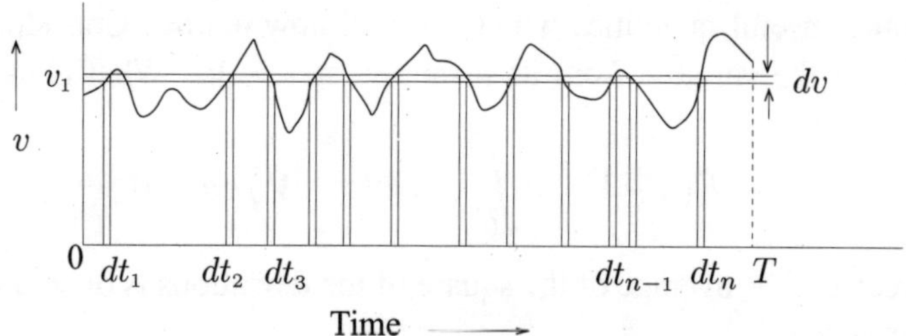

Figure 11.2. Experimental determination of probability distribution. Take a value v_1 and mark a small window of width dv around it. Measure all the time intervals in a long enough time period of T when the measured value of v fell in this band around v_1. The ratio of the sum of the time intervals to T gives the probability distribution.

between v_1 and $v_1 + dv$ is equal to sum of all the time intervals divided by T or

$$f(v_1)dv = \lim_{T \to \infty} \frac{\sum_{i=1}^{n} \Delta t_i}{T}$$

We can do this for all values that v can assume and hence we have measured the probability distribution. Thus, if a long time record of any random variable is available, its probability distribution function can be measured.

11.5.2 Fluctuations around the mean

It is also seen that the averages that we normally define coincide with the definitions that use the probability distribution. For example, from the time record of v, we will think of its average to be

$$\bar{V} = \lim_{T \to \infty} \frac{1}{T} \int_0^T v(t)dt$$

If the integral is discretized, we will write it as

$$\bar{V} = \lim_{T \to \infty} \frac{1}{T} \sum v(t)\Delta t$$

But if we slot the values of v into bins v_i, then this equation is same as

$$\bar{V} = \sum_i v_i \left(\lim_{T \to \infty} \frac{\sum_{j=1}^{j=n(i)} \Delta t_{j(i)}}{T} \right)$$

where $n(i)$ is the total number of times and $\Delta t_{j(i)}$ is the duration of jth time interval, when the value of v fell between v_i and $v_i + dv$. Thus

$$\bar{V} = \sum_i v_i f(v_i) dv$$

or in the limit of $dv \to 0$, we get

$$\bar{V} = \int_{-\infty}^{\infty} v f(v) dv$$

We have a few other useful quantities which we will now define. Consider the instantaneous value of the deviation of the variable from its mean: $\mathrm{v} \equiv v - \bar{V}$. What is its expected value or mean?

$$\bar{\mathrm{v}} = E(v - \bar{V}) = \int_0^\infty f(v)(v - \bar{V})\, dv = 0$$

This of course is expected. The average of the square of the deviations is of course not equal to zero but is equal to the variance of v:

$$\bar{\mathrm{v^2}} = E\left([v - \bar{V}]^2\right) = \int_0^\infty f(v)(v - \bar{V})^2 dv = \sigma^2(v)$$

In this brief introduction to statistical methodology, we have placed emphasis on the concepts and also have given an indication of how the quantities of statistical significance can be measured.

11.6 REYNOLDS AVERAGED NAVIER–STOKES EQUATIONS (RANS)

Observe the motion of the
water surface, which
resembles that of hair, that
has two motions: one due to
the weight of the shaft, the
other to the shape of the
curls; thus, water has
eddying motions, one part of
which is due to the principal
current, the other to the
random and reverse motion.

Leonardo da Vinci, ca. 1510

It is clear that if we could predict the probability distribution of all possible quantities of interest, we could predict expected outcomes of turbulent flows. However, this has not been achieved. It was hoped that the fluctuating properties of turbulence will follow the ubiquitous Gaussian distribution, because if they did, measurement of mean and variance would have been sufficient to describe the entire probability distribution. However, this hope has been belied. Hence, the next best thing to do is to examine only a few averaged quantities. Thus, one attempts to solve for quantities of interest with the help of equations of motion. We can derive equations, for *steady* turbulent flows, which should be obeyed by velocity fluctuations by substituting[5]

$$\boldsymbol{v} = \mathbf{v} + \bar{\mathbf{V}}, \;\; p = \mathrm{p} + \bar{P}$$

into the various equations, and averaging them.

Consider the equation of continuity for an incompressible fluid first. We get

$$0 = \overline{\frac{\partial v}{\partial t} + \nabla.v} = \overline{\frac{\partial}{\partial t}(\mathbf{v} + \bar{\mathbf{V}}) + \nabla.\left(\mathbf{v} + \bar{\mathbf{V}}\right)} = \overline{\frac{\partial v}{\partial t}} + \overline{\frac{\partial \bar{\mathbf{V}}}{\partial t}} + \overline{\nabla.\mathbf{v}} + \nabla.\bar{\mathbf{V}}$$

The average values of fluctuations will vanish and at steady state we obtain

$$\nabla.\bar{\mathbf{V}} = 0$$

We note in particular that

$$\overline{\nabla.\mathbf{v}} = 0$$

11.6.1 Closure problem

Let us follow the same procedure with Navier–Stokes equations. After substituting for the instantaneous value by the sum of mean value and deviation from it, we have

$$\frac{\partial \mathbf{v}}{\partial t} + \left(\mathbf{v}.\nabla + \bar{\mathbf{V}}.\nabla\right)\left(\mathbf{v} + \bar{\mathbf{V}}\right) = -\frac{1}{\rho}\nabla(\mathrm{p} + \bar{P}) + \nu\nabla^2(\mathbf{v} + \bar{\mathbf{V}})$$

where for simplicity we have neglected the body forces. We can average these equations and get

$$\overline{\mathbf{v}.\nabla\mathbf{v}} + \bar{\mathbf{V}}.\nabla\bar{\mathbf{V}} = -\frac{1}{\rho}\nabla\bar{P} + \nu\nabla^2\bar{\mathbf{V}}$$

for *steady* turbulent flow. Noting that

$$\overline{\nabla.\mathbf{v}} = 0$$

the time averaged equation of motion can be rewritten as

$$\nabla.\overline{\mathbf{v}\mathbf{v}} + \bar{\mathbf{V}}.\nabla\bar{\mathbf{V}} = -\frac{1}{\rho}\nabla\bar{P} + \nu\nabla^2\bar{\mathbf{V}}$$

Thus, in order to solve for the mean velocity, we need information about $\overline{\mathbf{v}\mathbf{v}}$ and their derivatives. If we try to derive an equation for $\overline{\mathbf{v}\mathbf{v}}$, though it is not shown here, then we find that we would need information about $\overline{\mathbf{v}\mathbf{v}\mathbf{v}}$ and so on. In other words, we can never derive a self-contained equation for any fluctuation, and would require information about products of fluctuations of higher order. This is called a *closure problem* because the set of equations being derived never become self-contained or "closed". Thus, we can not even solve for averaged quantities exactly. Hence, we need to make some hypothesis or develop models to solve the equations for averaged quantities. This will be considered later.

11.6.2 Reynolds stresses

The equations derived in the previous section are referred to as the Reynolds averaged Navier–Stokes (RANS) equations in honor of Osborne Reynolds who derived these for the first time. The higher level product term that arises, *viz.* $\overline{\mathbf{v}\mathbf{v}}$, can be interpreted. Consider a term like $\overline{\mathrm{v}_x\mathrm{v}_y}$. Suppose for the moment that the average velocity in y direction is zero, and that the average velocity in the

x direction is not zero. Then v_y is the y component velocity itself and hence, due to it, a fluid particle will travel in the y direction. When it does so, it takes along with it the other components of momentum, namely x and z components. In particular, it will carry with it x momentum, over and above the average value, corresponding to v_x. Thus, $\overline{\mathrm{v}_x \mathrm{v}_y}$ is the averaged transfer of x momentum in the y direction due to fluctuations. These terms therefore represent momentum transfer due to velocity fluctuations. Thus, they are equivalent to stresses, and are called **Reynolds stresses**:

$$\rho\overline{\mathrm{v}_j \mathrm{v}_i} \equiv -\overline{\tau^t_{ij}}, \quad \text{or} \quad \rho\overline{\mathbf{v}\mathbf{v}} \equiv -\overline{\boldsymbol{\tau}^t}$$

Here, we added superscript t to indicate that they are turbulence related stresses and will vanish in laminar flows. Hence, we can rewrite RANS as

$$\rho\left(\bar{\mathbf{V}}.\nabla\right)\bar{\mathbf{V}} = -\nabla\bar{P} + \nabla.\overline{\boldsymbol{\tau}^l} + \nabla.\overline{\boldsymbol{\tau}^t}$$

where we have indicated the stresses calculated using the averaged velocities and Newton–Stokes law of viscosity by superscript l. Those would correspond to stresses created if laminar flow corresponding to the average motion prevailed.

One of the important ideas arising out of this development is that averages of quantities like $\overline{\mathrm{v}_x \mathrm{v}_y}$ are very important to theory of turbulence, and need to be modeled to circumvent the closure problem. The interpretation that Reynolds stresses arise due to momentum transfer by *random* velocity fluctuations on a macroscopic scale also gives a clue that they can be treated as diffusive processes occurring due to turbulence. This idea is used extensively in turbulence modeling. This will be considered later.

11.6.3 Experimental measurements

We have already mentioned the mean and variance as a few quantities amenable to measurement. A few other quantities are also important as indicated by RANS, and also can be measured. We discuss one of them, the velocity correlation.

Cross correlation functions

Let us examine the Reynolds stress terms as they appear in the RANS a little bit more. A typical term is

$$\overline{\mathrm{v}_x \frac{\partial \mathrm{v}_y}{\partial x}}$$

It can be rewritten as

$$\lim_{\Delta x \to 0} \overline{\mathrm{v}_x \frac{(\mathrm{v}_y)\,|_{x+\Delta x} - (\mathrm{v}_y)\,|_x}{\Delta x}}$$

If we denote the values at $x + \Delta x$ by primed quantity, then, to evaluate the above, we must measure $\overline{\mathrm{v}'_y \mathrm{v}_x}$ as a function of x coordinate between from a fixed location. Here v'_y and v_x are two random variables. The average of product of two random variables is called **cross correlation**. It indicates whether the fluctuations in the two variables are related to each other or not. Thus, if the velocity fluctuations *at the same location* in various directions are independent of each other, correlations of the type then $\overline{v_i v_j}$ will vanish or the off diagonal components of Reynolds stress tensor would be zero[6]. Thus, it is important to know how the velocity fluctuations at the same and different locations are correlated. We of course expect them to be uncorrelated as the distance between the two points increases. But the decay with distance separating them is important.

11.6.4 Spectrum

The spatial dependence of any cross correlation is usually expressed in terms of Fourier transforms. Suppose there is a wave of velocity fluctuation moving through the field. Then the correlation of velocity disturbance between two points will also appear as a periodic function of the distance. Thus, Fourier transform will help in visualizing the correlation as consisting of fluctuations correlated over some length or loosely speaking as an 'eddy'. If the fluctuations were totally periodic in space, a finite number of sine or cosine functions will be sufficient to represent the correlation. However, if there is no periodicity, or in other words, if an infinite number of wavelengths exist, then a continuous distribution of wavelengths is needed to represent the cross correlation. In turbulence, there seems to be no apparent periodicity. Hence, the correlation is expressed as[7],

$$E_{xx}(k_x) \equiv \frac{2}{\pi} \int_0^\infty \overline{v_x(x+r)v_x(x)} \cos(k_x r) dr$$

where r is distance along the x axis. Batchelor in his book *Homogeneous Turbulence* shows that $E_{xx}(k_x)$ can be interpreted as the kinetic energy contained in a 'wave' of wave length equal to $2\pi/k_x$. The function $E_{xx}(k_x)$ is called the spectrum as it represents the variation of the magnitude[8] of the energy with wave number, k_x.

Spectrum is an important experimental quantity. It can be measured by feeding the two velocity signals to an integrator. The average of the integral over several time intervals or a sufficiently long interval gives the correlation. When the correlation is measured as a function of spatial distance between the locations, the spectrum can be calculated. Since the spectrum is a Fourier transform, it can be inverted to calculate the correlation:

$$\overline{v_x(x+r)v_x(x)} = \int_0^\infty E_{xx}(k) \cos(kx) dk$$

Thus, if we measure spectrum over sufficiently large range of wave numbers, the correlation function can be obtained from it. An interesting relationship is a special form of the correlation for $r = 0$:

$$\overline{v^2}_x = \int_0^\infty E_{xx}(k) dk$$

It is useful when the cross correlation is independent of spatial coordinates. Thus, in this instance, the kinetic energy contained in the fluctuations is equal to the integral of the spectrum, and is location independent. Measurements of spectrum serve to verify theories of turbulence.

As was indicated in the discussion on RANS, the equations describing turbulent flows are not closed and cannot be solved directly. Modeling is necessary. Two approaches are described here to give a flavor of the very extensive work.

11.7 KOLMOGOROV'S ENERGY CASCADE

```
Big whirls have little whirls,
    Which feed on their velocity;
And little whirls have lesser whirls,
    And so on on to viscosity.
                                Richardson (1922)
```

```
Big fleas have little fleas
    upon their backs to bite them,
and little fleas have lesser fleas,
    and so on ad infinitum.
                        "The Siphonaptera": a nursery rhyme
```

As Reynolds number increases[9], the effects of viscosity are expected to become unimportant. This implies that a flow once started on a large length scale, and if wall effects are not there, should continue to exist [10] in its state without any supply of power. Thus, if a fluid is pumped through a wire mesh, far away downstream from the mesh and also far away from the walls, the fluid should continue to have the same kinetic energy. Such an experiment generates turbulence. However, it is observed that turbulence decays away from the mesh due to viscous effects. Kolmogorov resolved this paradox by postulating the *cascade theory* of turbulent energy. The theory is set in an idealized view of turbulence. We will first review these concepts.

11.7.1 Homogeneous and isotropic turbulence

As we just mentioned, the theory has been developed in the context of absence of wall effects. Though it sounds restrictive, the results have wide applicability, and Kolmogorov's theory has proved to be of great utility. In view of the assumed absence of wall effects, certain simplifications are made in the theory.

The first approximation that comes to mind is to assume that average characteristics of turbulence *i.e.,* correlations, *etc.*, are independent of the position in space along a direction. Let us examine this in more detail. Consider a correlation between x component of velocity fluctuation at one point and y component of velocity fluctuation at another point, *i.e.,* $\overline{\mathrm{v}'_{\mathrm{x}}\mathrm{v}_{\mathrm{y}}}$. Take any point as reference. In general, the correlation would depend upon the vector separating the two points and position of the reference point. Thus, if this correlation does not change when the position of the reference point is changed, the turbulence is said to be **homogeneous**. Moving the reference point, or the origin, is equivalent to translating a coordinate system without rotation.

A second reasonable assumption to make is that turbulence is **isotropic**: the characteristics of turbulence are independent of direction, *i.e.,* they are insensitive to rotation of coordinate system and reflection of the flow on any plane [11]. Consider the correlation between two components of velocity, *e.g.,* $\overline{\mathrm{v}'_x\mathrm{v}_y}$. Let us rotate or reflect the coordinate frame, and measure the velocity fluctuations *with respect to the new orientation* of the coordinate system. Let them be represented by u. Once again consider the correlation between x and y components of the velocities between the same points:

$\overline{u'_x u_y}$. If the correlation is independent of the rotation of coordinates along with the configuration, *i.e.*, $\overline{v'_x v_y} = \overline{u'_x u_y}$, turbulence is called isotropic[12].

In the appendix, we show that in isotropic and homogeneous turbulence, there exists only one function correlating velocity fluctuations between two points, and that it depends only on the distance between the points. Thus, we have

$$\mathrm{f}(r) \equiv \frac{\overline{\mathrm{v}_x(\mathbf{x}+r)\mathrm{v}_x(\mathbf{x})}}{\overline{\mathrm{v}^2}}$$

We can also have

$$\mathrm{g}(r) \equiv \frac{\overline{\mathrm{v}_y(\mathbf{x}+r)\mathrm{v}_y(\mathbf{x})}}{\overline{\mathrm{v}^2}}$$

and a similar quantity between z component of velocity fluctuations. However, we show in the appendix that it is related to $\mathrm{f}(r)$. Hence, in isotropic turbulence, there is one characteristic value for velocity correlation, $\sqrt{\overline{\mathrm{v}^2}}$. Further, there is only one spectrum corresponding to $\overline{\mathrm{v}^2}\mathrm{f}(r)$. It is represented by E_{11}. Thus, experimental measurements on E_{11} in flow behind a wire mesh were used to test Kolmogorov's theory. Let us now outline the theory itself.

11.7.2 Generation of many length scales

Kolmogorov suggested that the rate of energy or power input *per unit mass*, ε, to the system is at large length scales as indicated by the large value of Reynolds number based on the length scale of the apparatus. The energy supplied creates motion on large length scales. The motion becomes perhaps unstable and motions of smaller length scales are created. This process occurs without loss of energy since the Reynolds number is large and hence viscous effects are unimportant. However, as this process of creation of motions on smaller length scales continues, Reynolds number at the corresponding length scales decreases. Eventually, motion will be created on a small enough length scale where Reynolds number becomes of the order of unity and viscous effects become important. Viscous action is due to molecular diffusion of momentum, and is reflective of friction. At length scales of this order, the energy supplied is dissipated into heat by the action of viscosity. This is schematically shown in figure 11.3.

11.7.3 Kolmogorov length scale

The range of size of length scales, where viscous effects are not important but is smaller than the range of sizes where energy is being supplied, is called **inertial–subrange.** Let ℓ be a length scale lying in the inertial–subrange. Let $U'(\ell)$ be an estimate of cross correlation of velocity[13] on length scale of the order of ℓ. The turn over time or the time required for motion on this length scale to become unstable can be estimated to be ℓ/U'. The instability is destroyed by viscous effects. The time required for viscous effects to propagate over ℓ is ℓ^2/ν. Thus, the length scale where the two time scales are about equal would be a good estimate of the length scale where inviscid transmission of energy ends and energy dissipation begins. *At this length scale, and at even smaller length scales, molecular diffusive processes become dominant.* Such a length scale, η, is called

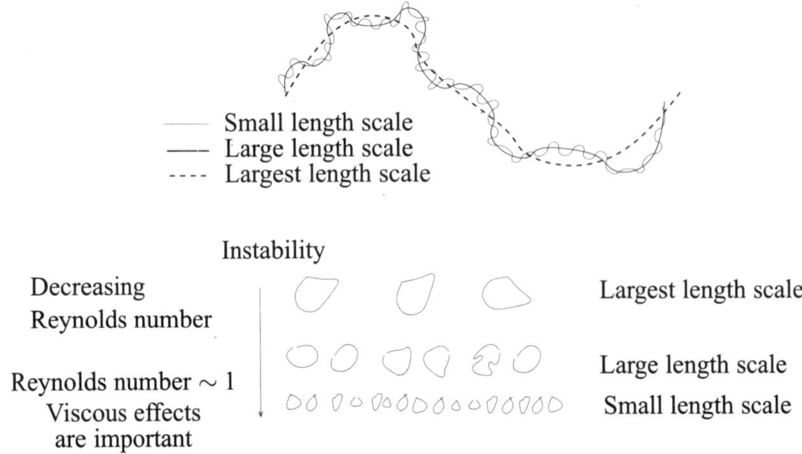

Figure 11.3. Generation of many length scales by instability.

Kolmogorov length scale, in honor of Kolmogorov. As is easily worked out, Reynolds number at this length scale is equal to unity:

$$\eta/U_K \sim \eta^2/\nu \text{ or } \frac{\eta U_K'}{\nu} = 1$$

where the symbol U_K' has been used to denote the velocity fluctuation corresponding to the Kolmogorov length scale. We can also equate an estimate of the rate at which energy is dissipated per unit mass by viscous action to the power being supplied per unit mass to maintain the flow at steady conditions:

$$\varepsilon = \nu \frac{(U_K')^2}{\eta^2}$$

Combining the above with the idea that Reynolds number at the Kolmogorov length scale is unity, we find that

$$\eta = \left(\frac{\nu^3}{\varepsilon}\right)^{1/4}$$

and

$$U_K' = (\nu\varepsilon)^{1/4} = \frac{\nu}{\eta}$$

Kolmogorov length scale is very important for all transfer processes since diffusive action begins only at this or smaller length scales. For example, chemical reactions can occur only when mixing has occurred at least at this length scale. Usually mass diffusion is slower than momentum diffusion and hence mixing has to occur at even smaller length scales for reactions to occur.

Now it is easy to understand how Kolmogorov explained the decay of turbulence behind a wire mesh. The power supplied to flow past a wire mesh generates velocity fluctuations on the length scale corresponding to the size of wires in the mesh. Due to the energy cascade, velocity fluctuations are generated at ever decreasing smaller length scales. When these length scales reach a level where Reynolds number is of the order of unity, energy is dissipated into heat through them. The dissipation occurs *everywhere* in the fluid and turbulence decays. Another way to think is that a part of the energy supplied does not go to enhancing flow, but goes into generating these wasteful motions!

Let us put some numbers so that you can get a feel for them. Consider turbulent flow in a pipe of $0.1\ m$ diameter at a Reynolds number of 10,000. The average velocity is equal to $0.1\ m/s$. Power dissipation per unit mass, ε is given by friction factor times the cube of the average velocity divided by density. Thus, ε is equal to $10^{-7}\ W/kg$. Thus, Kolmogorov length scale is of the order of a mm. It will be smaller at higher Reynolds numbers.

Kolmogorov's theory is a picture. It "explains" how turbulence decays[14] behind a wire mesh. But it is more general, and is a description of what happens in any turbulent flow. According to the energy cascade theory, in any turbulent flow, energy supplied to create flow is supplied at large length scales. Motion at large length scales creates motion at ever decreasing length scales. The energy is conserved as long as Reynolds number at the corresponding length scales is large. When motion corresponding to small Reynolds numbers is generated, molecular diffusive processes begin to dominate. In particular, due to molecular diffusion of momentum or due to viscous action, motions at small scales are dissipative and convert kinetic energy into heat. There is yet another important conclusion that can be drawn about turbulence based on this "story".

11.7.4 Velocity fluctuations and length scale

One of the objectives of statistical theory of turbulence is to predict the scale and size of fluctuations. Such a relationship is very important since the product of the velocity fluctuation and the corresponding length scale is an estimate of diffusivity due to turbulence. A concrete quantity in this direction is the velocity correlation or the spectrum, and Kolmogorov's cascade theory is able to predict it.

Suppose that the scale at which energy is being supplied, L_e, is very large. Let us suppose that Reynolds number of the flow is very large. Hence, estimating the characteristic velocity at this scale by the non-dissipative power transmission, we have

$$\varepsilon \sim \frac{U'(L_e)}{L_e}(U'(L_e))^2$$

or

$$Re \sim \frac{L_e(L_e\varepsilon)^{1/3}}{\nu}$$

Hence, we would estimate

$$\frac{\eta}{L_e} \sim Re^{-3/4}$$

Thus, the dissipative length scale and the length scale at which power is being supplied are widely separated for large Reynolds numbers. Returning to the numerical example we considered earlier, this ratio is expected to be of the order of one thousandth at a Reynolds number of 10,000. As η is the smallest length scale in the inertial range, we can say that the inertial range and the length scale at which power is being supplied are also widely separated for large Reynolds numbers.

Hence, at very high Reynolds numbers, one does not expect that velocity fluctuations corresponding to the length scale on which energy is being supplied, $U(L_e)$, to be a suitable characteristic velocity fluctuation on smaller length scales, U'. In other words we would not expect the former to be suitable for non-dimensionalizing the latter, or, to use the modern linguo, U' does not scale with U_{L_e}. One would expect the velocity fluctuations typical of the inertial–subrange to be a more suitable quantity with which U' can be scaled. We know that U'_K is one suitable choice, since it is a value of velocity fluctuation typical of inertial–subrange, but which occurs at the least size of the inertial–subrange. In a similar manner, we can expect a suitable non-dimensional length in the inertial size to be ℓ/η. Hence, we expect

$$\frac{U'(\ell)}{U'_K} = CF\left(\frac{\ell}{\eta}\right)$$

or

$$U'(\ell) = C(\nu\varepsilon)^{1/4}F\left(\frac{\ell}{\eta}\right)$$

However, we do not expect $U'(\ell)$ to depend upon ν because it is a quantity characteristic of inertial range. Knowing that $\eta \sim \nu^{3/4}$, we can conclude that the function F has to be proportional to $(\ell/\eta)^{1/3}$ so that $U'(\ell)$ is independent of ν. Thus,

$$U'(\ell) = U_K\left(\frac{\ell}{\eta}\right)^{1/3} \sim (\nu\varepsilon)^{1/4}\ell^{1/3}\left(\frac{\varepsilon}{\nu^3}\right)^{1/12}$$

Thus, Kolmogorov's theory predicts that

$$U'(\ell) \sim (\varepsilon\ell)^{1/3}$$

The last relationship could have been derived in a different way also. If a motion on the length scale ℓ having a characteristic velocity U' dies down in a turn over time of ℓ/U', the power it would have transmitted to the lower length scales non-dissipatively would be equal to its kinetic energy divided by the turn over time: $(U')^3/\ell$. But this must also be equal to the power being supplied, ε, and we recover the above relationship.

Returning to our numerical example of flow in a pipe, we can estimate that the characteristic value of velocity fluctuations across a length scale of 0.1 m is about a mm/s. The turbulent diffusivity is then of the order of $10^{-4}\, m^2/s$.

11.7.5 Prediction of spectrum of velocity correlation

Since Kolmogorov's theory is able to make a prediction of the relationship between the velocity fluctuation between two points and the distance separating them in the inertial range, it can be used to predict the spectrum of f(r) in that range. Thus,

$$E_{11}(k) = \frac{2}{\pi}\int_0^\infty \overline{\mathrm{v}_x(x+r)\mathrm{v}_x(x)}\cos(kr)dr$$

$$= \frac{2}{\pi}\int_0^\infty \overline{\mathrm{v}^2}\mathrm{f}(r)\cos(kr)dr$$

$$= \frac{2}{\pi}\eta C^2 U_K^2 \int_0^\infty F^2\left(\frac{r}{\eta}\right)\cos\left(\frac{r}{\eta}k\eta\right)d\left(\frac{r}{\eta}\right) \tag{11.1}$$

The integral can only be a function of $k\eta$. Hence,

$$E_{11}(k) \equiv U_K^2\eta\mathcal{F}(k\eta)$$
$$\sim (\varepsilon\nu)^{1/2}\left(\frac{\nu^3}{\varepsilon}\right)^{1/4}\mathcal{F}(k\eta)$$
$$\sim \varepsilon^{1/4}\nu^{5/4}\mathcal{F}(k\eta)$$

where $\mathcal{F}(k\eta)$ is a universal function of $k\eta$. From arguments similar to those used to derive the dependence of velocity fluctuations on length scale, it follows that the spectrum in the inertial range should depend only upon energy dissipation rate and k. Hence, $E_{11}(k)$ must be independent of viscosity. Since $\eta \sim \nu^{3/4}$

$$\mathcal{F}(k\eta) \sim (k\eta)^{-5/3}$$

and hence

$$E_{11}(k) \sim \varepsilon^{2/3}k^{-5/3}$$

These has been experimentally verified and is considered as a great success of Kolmogorov's theory.

We presented one approach to modeling of turbulence. Here one thinks of simplifications of turbulence possible and generates information regarding its statistical properties. Kolmogorov's theory is an outstanding success, but a lone instance, of this approach. Though very little success has been achieved with this type of approach regarding more complex turbulent flows, it turns out that the concepts generated by it have found use in other approaches to modeling of turbulence. Now we consider another typical and very successful modeling effort. As you will see shortly, this model uses many of the concepts inherent in Kolmogorov's theory.

11.8 k–ε MODEL

Practical turbulent flows are neither homogeneous nor isotropic. As mentioned earlier, in a pipe flow, turbulence will prevail in the center while it will be absent near the wall. Such complexities can only be modeled. Let us now turn to the engineering models of turbulence. Kolmogorov's theory is a qualitative but valuable picture. It has to be utilized in some more concrete models to predict characteristics of practical turbulent flows. These are done in many ways in different models. Here we give one such model developed largely by Prof. Spalding and his students.

Let us recall that a diffusion coefficient is given by a product of a velocity and length scale typical of a random process. We can interpret Reynolds stresses as momentum diffusion due to macroscopic velocity fluctuations. Hence, we can use the analogy between molecular diffusion and turbulent diffusion to write

$$-\overline{\mathrm{v}_x\mathrm{v}_y} = \overline{\tau^t} = \nu^{(t)}\left(\frac{\partial\bar{\mathrm{V}}_x}{\partial y} + \frac{\partial\bar{\mathrm{V}}_y}{\partial x}\right) \tag{11.2}$$

where $\nu^{(t)}$ is turbulent diffusivity[15] of momentum. The product $\rho\nu^{(t)}$ is referred to as eddy viscosity. Kolmogorov′s theory gives a big hint and prompts us to write

$$\nu^{(t)} \sim U'(\ell)\ell$$

From our earlier discussion as well as from this equation, we know that, unlike with molecular motion, a single value does not exist for velocity fluctuations or length scale over which velocity fluctuations are correlated. Hence, both these quantities vary as a function of position in a turbulent flow field. Thus, we can predict Reynolds stresses only if we are able to predict the local values of the velocity fluctuations and the length scales in a turbulent flow field.

Many models attempt to do this and one such model is the k$-\varepsilon$ model. The model attempts to derive equations for the kinetic energy of turbulence per unit mass, k, and the local power dissipation (due to turbulence) per unit mass, ε. Thus, local values for these quantities are obtained by solving these equations. Then, we write

$$U'(\ell) \sim \sqrt{\mathrm{k}}$$

and

$$\nu^{(t)} \sim U'(\ell)\ell \sim \frac{(U'(\ell))^4}{\varepsilon} \sim \frac{\mathrm{k}^2}{\varepsilon}$$

We will of course need proportionality constants to calculate a value for these. If the constants are "universally" valid across many types of flows, the models will be very useful. This model will work if we can calculate local values of K and ε and k–ε model attempts to do that.

11.8.1 Equation for k

Kinetic energy in fluctuations per unit mass is k:

$$\mathrm{k} = \overline{\mathrm{v}^2{}_x + \mathrm{v}^2{}_y + \mathrm{v}^2{}_z}$$

The equation for k can then be derived by taking a dot product of the equation of motion with the velocity fluctuation vector and time averaging it. We give the final result:

$$(\bar{\mathbf{V}}.\nabla)\mathrm{k} = -\rho\nabla.\overline{(\frac{\mathbf{v}.\mathbf{v}}{2} + \frac{\mathrm{p}}{\rho})\mathbf{v}} + \boldsymbol{\tau}^{(\mathrm{t})}{:}\mathbf{S} + 2\mu\nabla.\overline{(\mathbf{v}.\mathbf{s})} - \rho\varepsilon$$

where

$$s_{ij} \equiv \frac{1}{2}\left(\frac{\partial \mathrm{v}_i}{\partial x_j} + \frac{\partial \mathrm{v}_j}{\partial x_i}\right), \quad \text{or } \mathbf{s} \equiv \frac{1}{2}\left(\nabla\mathbf{v} + (\nabla\mathbf{v})^t\right)$$

and

$$S_{ij} \equiv \frac{1}{2}\left(\frac{\partial \bar{\mathrm{V}}_i}{\partial x_j} + \frac{\partial \bar{\mathrm{V}}_j}{\partial x_i}\right), \quad \text{or } \mathbf{S} \equiv \frac{1}{2}\left(\nabla\bar{\mathbf{V}} + (\nabla\bar{\mathbf{V}})^t\right)$$

where superscript t stands for transpose of the tensor. As we know from the closure problem, and we can also see this in the above equation, the equation for k involves complex products involving three velocities. These have to be *modeled.* For example, examine the first term on the right hand side, namely,

$$\nabla.\overline{(\mathbf{v}.\mathbf{v} + \frac{p}{\rho} - 2\nu\mathbf{s})\mathbf{v}}$$

The first term in this group is the divergence of $\overline{\mathrm{k}\mathbf{v}}$. Thus, it is like $\overline{(\rho\mathbf{v}\mathbf{v})}$, or Reynolds stress or turbulent diffusion of momentum flux. Thus, $\overline{\mathrm{k}\mathbf{v}}$ "looks" like turbulent diffusion of kinetic energy in fluctuations. The other terms are interpreted as turbulent diffusion of stresses. Hence it is modeled as

$$\overline{(\mathbf{v}.\mathbf{v} + \frac{p}{\rho})\mathbf{v} - 2\nu\mathbf{s}\,.\,\mathbf{v}} \equiv \frac{\nu^{(t)}}{\sigma_k}\nabla\mathrm{k}$$

where a diffusion coefficient is used for kinetic energy, but recognizing that its value is different from that for momentum. Hence, a correction factor is used, and the factor is like a Prandtl number! As discussed in the previous section, it is postulated that

$$\nu^{(t)} = C_\mu\frac{\mathrm{k}^2}{\varepsilon}$$

where C_μ is a constant. Thus, our final equation for k is given by

$$(\bar{\mathbf{V}}.\nabla)\rho\mathrm{k} = \nabla.\frac{\nu^{(\mathrm{t})}}{\sigma_{\mathrm{k}}}\nabla\mathrm{k} + \nu^{(\mathrm{t})}\mathbf{S} : \mathbf{S} - \rho\varepsilon$$

11.8.2 Equation for dissipation

An equation for ε is still needed to solve the previous equation. The power dissipation per unit mass due to turbulent fluctuations is equal to

$$\varepsilon = \nu\frac{1}{2}\overline{\sum_{i,j}\left(\frac{\partial \mathrm{v}_j}{\partial x_i} + \frac{\partial \mathrm{v}_i}{\partial x_j}\right)\left(\frac{\partial \mathrm{v}_j}{\partial x_i} + \frac{\partial \mathrm{v}_i}{\partial x_j}\right)} \equiv \nu\frac{1}{2}\overline{\nabla\mathbf{v} : (\nabla\mathbf{v})^t}$$

An equation for this can be derived by taking a dot product of the equation for vorticity with the fluctuating vorticity and time averaging it. Once again several terms will appear and have to be modeled. Without giving details we give the final equation

$$(\bar{\mathbf{V}}.\nabla)\varepsilon = \nabla.\frac{\nu^{(t)}}{\sigma_\varepsilon}\nabla\varepsilon + C_{1\varepsilon}\frac{\varepsilon}{\mathrm{k}}\nu^{(t)}S_{ij}S_{ij} - C_{2\varepsilon}\frac{\varepsilon^2}{\mathrm{k}}$$

The two equations for kinetic energy and dissipation have to be solved simultaneously with the equation of continuity and the three components of equation of motion to complete the calculations.

It can be seen that there are five constants that appear in the equations. Based on experience with computational results from several flows, these five constants are taken as: $C_\mu, C_{1\varepsilon}, C_{2\varepsilon}, \sigma_k$ and σ_ε. These five constants are generally taken to be 0.04, 1.44, 1.92, 1.3 and 1.0 respectively. With these values the model is able to calculate many turbulent flows. k–ε model is widely used in many CFD packages and that is the reason why we chose to discuss it in some detail. There are other models also and interested readers are referred to more advanced texts on computational turbulent flows.

11.9 TRANSPORT OF A PASSIVE SCALAR

In this section, we will consider heat and mass transfer in turbulent flows. Once again, the concentration and temperature fields can be written as sum of an averaged value and fluctuation. We will deal with the simple case of mass transfer in dilute solutions. With this restriction, heat and mass transfer become identical. We will denote the concentration of species or energy density $\rho C_p T$ by ϕ_i. We will denote the molecular diffusivity of this variable by Γ_i.

Presence of chemical reactions introduces more complexity, and that is a subject well beyond the scope of this text. It is easy to see the source of this complication. While transport of species or heat by turbulence requires correlation of the type $\overline{\phi_i v'}$, modeling reactions between species i and j would need correlations of the type $\overline{\phi_i \phi'_j}$. The time scale on which species are being transported by turbulent velocity fluctuations depends upon the time scale of velocity fluctuations. However, the fluctuations of concentrations of species in the presence of reactions depends upon the time scale of reactions and velocity fluctuations. Hence, separate modeling is required for computing reactive flows. Besides, it is possible that chemical reactions and accompanying heat effects can influence turbulence itself.

In the absence of reactions, both heat and species are simply transported by the velocity fluctuations, free from complications arising from any other phenomenon. In this sense, they are referred to as passive scalars. The conservation equation or equation of change of a passive scalar is given by

$$\frac{\partial \phi_i}{\partial t} + \boldsymbol{v}.\nabla \phi_i = \nabla.\Gamma_i \nabla \phi_i$$

As done earlier, the passive scalar is written as sum of a mean and fluctuation:

$$\phi_i = \bar{\phi}_i + \Phi_i$$

where Φ_i is the fluctuation from the mean. At steady state, time averaging the equation of change gives

$$\bar{\mathbf{V}}.\nabla \bar{\phi}_i = \nabla.\Gamma_i \nabla \bar{\phi}_i - \nabla.\overline{\mathbf{v}\Phi_i}$$

The last term on the right hand side is the transport of the passive scalar due to turbulence. It is modeled as

$$-\overline{\mathbf{v}\Phi_i} = \Gamma_i^t \nabla \bar{\phi}_i$$

where Γ_i^t is the eddy diffusivity of the ith passive scalar.

As transport due to turbulence is through interaction with velocity fluctuations, one might expect that the eddy diffusivities of all passive scalars to be same. As it turns out this is true only if the ratios of molecular diffusivities of the respective passive scalars are of the order of unity. When this ratio becomes very large or small, more complex $k - \varepsilon$ models for passive scalars have to be used. It is because usually, spatial variation of cross correlations exists, and in the zones where turbulence is not very intense, both diffusion and turbulent motions influence transport.

Appendix

11.A Properties of isotropic turbulent flow

Consider a simple application of these ideas when the two points are the same. Consider a correlation like $\overline{v_x v_y}$ at any point. If we now rotate the coordinate system around the y axis by 180 degrees. Then the old $-x$ axis has become the new x axis. Thus, the correlation between x and y components of the velocity is equal to $\overline{u_x u_y}$ in the new system and would be equal to $-\overline{v_x v_y}$ in the old system. If turbulence is isotropic then

$$\overline{v_x v_y} = \overline{u_x u_y} = -\overline{v_x v_y}$$

The first equality arises from the definition of isotropy while the latter follows from the argument we just gave. Hence, both must be equal to zero. The argument applies to other such correlations also. Thus, for isotropic turbulence, we then find that

$$\overline{v_x v_y} = \overline{v_x v_z} = \overline{v_z v_y} = 0$$

Similarly, it can be shown that

$$\overline{v^2}_x = \overline{v^2}_y = \overline{v^2}_z \equiv \overline{v^2}$$

Further, following similar arguments about derivatives, it can be shown that the spatial derivatives of these averages is zero. Thus, isotropic turbulence is also homogeneous.

Consider a more complex situation involving two points P and P′. There are three directions involved here: the direction of the velocity vectors and the direction of the vector separating the two points. The two points form a configuration of interest. Let the two points P and P′ lie at two different locations but along the y axis. Examine a correlation like $\overline{v_x v'_y}$, where v_x is at P and v'_y is at P′. Rotate the coordinate system and the configuration around y axis by 180 degrees clockwise. Then using arguments similar to what was used before, the correlation between x and y components of the velocity is equal to $\overline{u_x u'_y}$ in the new system and would be equal to $-\overline{v_x v'_y}$ in the old system. Thus, if turbulence is isotropic then

$$\overline{v_x v'_y} = \overline{u_x u'_y} = -\overline{v_x v'_y}$$

Hence, both must be equal to zero. With use of more complex arguments, it can be shown that there are only two types of cross correlations[16] that do not vanish:

$$\overline{v_x(\mathbf{x}+x)v_x(\mathbf{x})}, \text{ and } \overline{v_y(\mathbf{x}+x)v_y(\mathbf{x})}$$

where x is the difference in any coordinate between the two points. The first is a cross correlation of velocity components directed along the line joining the two points, or a longitudinal correlation, while the second is a cross correlation of velocity components directed perpendicular to the line joining the two points, or a transverse correlation. In view of the isotropy, it is also clear that the cross correlation must depend upon only the distance between the points of measurement:

$$f(r) \equiv \frac{\overline{v_x(\mathbf{x}+r)v_x(\mathbf{x})}}{\overline{v^2}}$$

and

$$g(r) \equiv \frac{\overline{v_y(\mathbf{x}+r)v_y(\mathbf{x})}}{\overline{v^2}}$$

It turns out that due to equation of continuity, the two are related. This simplifies our considerations a lot since we have to deal with a single characteristic velocity fluctuation, and a single function of cross correlation depending upon distance.

Let us also mention that, because only one independent cross correlation exists, we have only one spectrum corresponding to $\overline{v^2}f(r)$. It is represented by E_{11}. Thus, experimental measurements on E_{11} in flow behind a wire mesh were used to test Kolmogorov's theory.

11.B Dispersion and diffusion

We have considered the differences between dispersion and diffusion in section 7.3. It will be helpful if you can recall or refer to those ideas. There we were considering the effects of random motion of Brownian or insoluble particles. We can think of dispersion of particles made of soluble species, let us say salt. As we stir particles of salt in water, turbulent motion will disperse the particles randomly and the particles also dissolve simultaneously. The dissolution process that leads to homogenization at a molecular level is accompanied by random distribution of particles in the flow field. We now imagine that the particles also can break while moving in a flow field. Then we have three processes occurring simultaneously: breakup, dispersion, both due to turbulence, and molecular diffusion of dissolved molecules. These three processes describe how heat and mass transfer occurs in turbulent flow fields. Taylor's theory of turbulent dispersion is concerned with the second process.

Before considering Taylor's theory, let us make a few more comments to complete our discussion on dispersion and diffusion. Suppose a blob of fluid containing a soluble dye (or which is hotter) is introduced into the surrounding medium. These blobs of fluid containing species (or heat) move from one place to another place due to eddy diffusion on a coarse scale. If the solution is stirred, the blobs will be seen to continually break into smaller blobs while they move in random directions. We have discussed in the context of Kolmogorov's theory, the generation of motion on small length scales from large length scales. These can be considered as breakup of a large eddy into smaller eddies. If we imagine a blob to be an eddy, the turbulent velocity fluctuations can be thought of as the cause for the breakup of the big blobs into smaller and smaller blobs. It is as if a collection of small blobs were initially present in the big blob, and the smaller ones are formed due to the breakup process. Blobs move in a manner very reminiscent of the motion of Brownian particles. However, along with this breakup into small blobs and their dispersion, dissolution and diffusion of dye also occurs to create a molecularly homogeneous state. The larger the length scale is, smaller are the gradients, and the larger is the time scale of molecular diffusion. Thus, as long as the blob size is large, molecular diffusion will not be able to smear out the dye on a molecular scale in a reasonable time scale. Breakup and dispersion takes small blobs into regions of different concentration, and hence creates sharp gradients. Hence, breakup and dispersion of big blob only enhances the number of regions where concentration gradients are sharp. As the number of such regions increases, or as the blob size becomes smaller, diffusion becomes effective, and molecular homogenization dominates. This is similar to the ideas in the energy cascade theory. There, motion is created on smaller and smaller length scales. The processes in the inertial–subrange are *non-dissipative*, while they are *dissipative* due to viscous friction on Kolmogorov length scale. The similarity becomes apparent once we recognize that dissipation due to viscous action is same as due to molecular diffusion of momentum.

The breaking up of the initial lump into smaller ones is the result of movement due to macroscopic velocity fluctuations. Eddy diffusion disperses the blobs as they break-up. As length scales or size of the blobs decrease, a length scale is reached where the concentration gradients become sufficiently large, and the speed of molecular diffusion becomes comparable with the dispersion process. This length scale is the equivalent of Kolmogorov length scale for diffusion of species. In chemical engineering nomenclature, the dispersal process is referred to as macro mixing while the molecular diffusion process is referred to as micro mixing. It is easy to think of analogous process for dispersal of thermal energy.

As it turns out, the dispersion process is generally fast while diffusion leading to molecular homogeneity is slow. Thus, in many instances, it is good to think that the dye blob first disperses and then the dye molecules diffuse from these smaller blobs. Thus, the concepts of Taylor's dispersion in turbulent flow is of value even in the context of soluble substances.

11.B.1 Taylor's theory of turbulent dispersion

Let us return to the equation 7.6

$$\overline{ru} = 3D_t \tag{7.6}$$

relating diffusivity to the correlation between position and velocity of a Brownian particle. We have a very important result here. If the correlation between position and velocity is measured, eq. 7.6 can be used to calculate the diffusivity. Taylor [7] showed how this concept can be used to obtain an expression for fluxes due turbulence, *i.e.,* eq. 11.2. If there are no heat sources or chemical reactions, the species balance is given by

$$\bar{\mathbf{V}}.\nabla\bar{C} + \overline{\mathbf{v}.\nabla\mathrm{c}} = D\nabla^2\bar{C}$$

and the equation of change of temperature is given by

$$\bar{\mathbf{V}}.\nabla\bar{T} + \overline{\mathbf{v}.\nabla\mathrm{T}} = \frac{k}{\rho C_p}\nabla^2\bar{T}$$

We therefore have the turbulent fluxes given by $\overline{\mathbf{v}\mathrm{c}}$ for species and $\overline{\mathbf{v}\rho C_p\mathrm{T}}$ for thermal energy. Taylor showed that these can be written as the product of a gradient and a turbulent or eddy diffusivity. He further showed how the concept of correlation can be used to measure the eddy diffusivity. This is what we wish to describe here.

In an ingenious way, typical of Taylor, he proposed the following "thought experiment" to focus on dispersion or eddy diffusion *alone.* Consider *non-conducting* tiny particles suspended in a turbulent fluid. For simplicity consider velocity as well as fluctuations exist in only one dimension. Thus, they move along a line. Then if we consider all particles crossing a plane at a given time, they

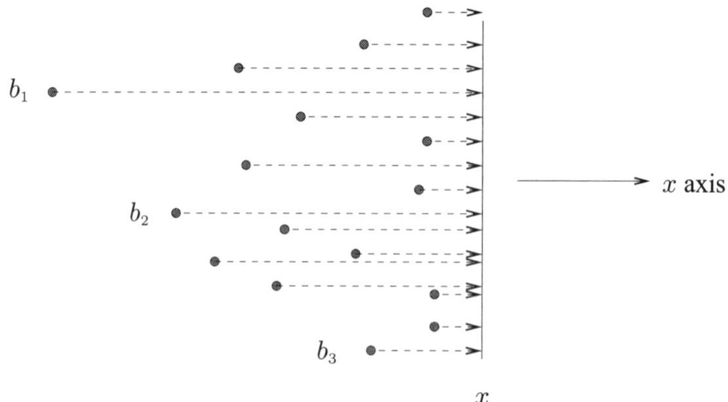

Figure 11.4. Particles reaching a given location at the same time come from different places due to velocity fluctuations.

all would have come from different locations due to the fluctuations in velocity. See figure 11.4. Let the initial location of ith particle reaching the plane at x at time t be b_i.

Thermal energy of particles can be dispersed only if they originally had different thermal energies. Hence, when the experiment started there will be a temperature gradient in the flow field or the particles would be at different temperatures depending on their location. Let the temperature gradient be linear. Thus, taking the plane at x as the reference point, the particle reaching x from b_i would have started with a temperature given by

$$T_i(0) = \bar{T}(x) - (x - b_i)\frac{d\bar{\mathrm{T}}}{dx}$$

where $\bar{T}(x)$ is the mean temperature. As the particles are non-conducting, their temperature does not change. Hence $T_i(0)$ would still be its temperature when i^{th} particle reaches location x. The heat flux at time t crossing plane at x due to the motion of particles is given by sum of the energy being carried by particles crossing the plane at x:

$$\sum_i \rho C_p \mathrm{v}_i(t) T_i(t)$$

As we just argued, because the particles are non-conducting, $T_i(t) = T_i(0)$. Hence, the heat flux at time t crossing plane at x is given by

$$\begin{aligned}\sum_i \rho C_p \mathrm{v}_i(t) T_i(t) &= \sum_i \rho C_p \mathrm{v}_i(t) T_i(0) \\ &= \sum_i \rho C_p \mathrm{v}_i(t) \left(\bar{T}(x) - (x - b_i)\frac{d\bar{\mathrm{T}}}{dx} \right)\end{aligned}$$

The summing over particles of course is the same as the averaging process over the plane located at x. The term containing $\bar{T}(x)$ will vanish since it is a constant and $\mathrm{v}_i(t)$ is a random quantity. Hence,

$$\sum_i \rho C_p \mathrm{v}_i(t) T_i(t) = -\sum_i \rho C_p \mathrm{v}_i(t)(x - b_i)\frac{d\bar{\mathrm{T}}}{dx}$$

Let us denote $x - b_i$ by X, the distance traveled by the particle. The heat flux due to random motion of particles is therefore given by

$$-\sum_i \rho C_p \mathrm{v}_i(t) X \frac{d\bar{\mathrm{T}}}{dx}$$

Therefore, the heat flux in the x direction due to random motion of particles, $q_x^{(t)}$ is given by

$$q^{(t)} = -\rho C_p \overline{\mathrm{v}_i(t) X} \frac{d\bar{\mathrm{T}}}{dx}$$

and the eddy diffusivity is given by the same type of expression for molecular diffusion,

$$\epsilon^{(t)}(t) = \overline{\mathrm{v}(t) X}$$

where $\epsilon^{(t)}$ is the eddy diffusivity of thermal energy. The difference is that the velocity fluctuations are due to turbulence and not due to molecular motion.

Taylor rewrote this equation in a different way to make it more suitable for measurements. Since all particles have the same position at time t, we can write

$$x - b_i = X_i = \int_0^t \mathrm{v}_i(t')dt'$$

Hence,

$$\epsilon^{(t)}(t) = \overline{\mathrm{v}(t) X} = \overline{\mathrm{v}_i(t) \int_0^t \mathrm{v}_i(t')dt'}$$

where we explicitly show that X and v should belong to the *same* particle by indicating that the averaging involves the velocity of the *same* particle but at different times.

Thus, diffusivity can be found from the average of the product of the velocity of a particle now and its velocity at earlier times. This is called auto correlation of velocity. For isotropic and homogeneous turbulence, this is equivalent to measuring velocity at the same point at different times and averaging it. Taylor proposed that this is a good estimate for many turbulent flows as long as the correlation dies reasonably quickly. Taylor calculated dispersion of smoke from stacks in atmosphere using this hypothesis and showed that it worked well.

It can be seen that Reynolds stresses, turbulent heat fluxes and mass fluxes of species can all be related to turbulent velocity fluctuations in this manner, and this model would suggest that all eddy diffusivities are equal;

$$\nu^{(t)} = \alpha^{(t)} = D_i^{(t)}$$

where α is the thermal diffusivity, and D_i is the species diffusion coefficient. As it turns out, this prediction is not accurate when Prandtl or Schmidt numbers deviate a lot from unity. One reason for this is the fact that turbulence in practical flows is neither homogeneous nor isotropic. Stationary walls do damp turbulence and hence the cross correlations vary with position in the flow field. The net flux due to eddy transport depends upon this variation as well. However, Taylor's theory is based on isotropic and homogeneous turbulence which predicts a single value for eddy diffusivity.

Notes

[1]Solutions to simple flows, like flow in a pipe, have been computed.

[2]This material follows that given in Tennekes and Lumley[8] very closely.

[3]The motion is completely "determined" by the equation of motion and boundary conditions. Thus, the approach of solving the equation of motion is called the deterministic approach.

[4]This material follows very closely that given by Tennekes and Lumley [8].

[5]I am sorry that in this chapter I have to deviate from the nomenclature used in earlier chapters as far as pressure is concerned.

[6]The diagonal elements would not be zero since they are averages of square of quantities *viz.* v_x^2

[7]We should write both sine and cosine functions, but we have just written for simplicity only cosine transform. For real variables, and when the spectrum is symmetric in wave number, only positive wave numbers need be considered, and cosine transform is sufficient.

[8]The nomenclature is same in IR, UV and other spectra.

[9]This material is a summary of a part of the chapter by J. Jiménez in the book *Perspectives in Fluid Mechanics* [2].

[10]Another implication of this is that drag forces should go to zero. As discussed earlier, this paradox was resolved by the boundary layer theory, which postulates that viscous forces are concentrated in a thin layer near the wall.

[11]These assumptions sound contradictory to the resolution of the paradox which we just mentioned because if there is dissipation, turbulence must decay in the direction of flow. But the decay can be sufficiently slow to allow such an assumption to be made. Similarly, in some local sense, the flow could be isotropic.

[12]See page 40 of book by Batchelor [1].

[13]From now on, we simply refer to this as velocity fluctuation.

[14]Some aspects of science are very interesting. Usually, the "first fact" a theory explains is smuggled in as a hypothesis. It is the other aspects that it is able to explain that give credence to it. A nice example is Darwin's theory of survival of the fittest. Is it not obvious that the fittest survive? It is the utility of the theory in explaining other features and its consistency with the revolution brought about by the discovery of DNA that lend credibility to Darwin's theory.

[15]A "derivation" of this kind of expression for eddy or turbulent diffusion of heat is presented in the appendix.

[16]See page 40 of the book by Batchelor [1]

References

[1] G.K. Batchelor. *Theory of homogeneous turbulence.* Cambride University Press, 1953.

[2] G.K. Batchelor, H.K. Moffatt, and M.G. Worster, editors. *Perspectives in Fluid Mechanics.* Cambridge University Press, 2002.

[3] S. Corrsin. Turbulent flows. *American Scientist*, 49:300, 1961.

[4] P.A. Davidon. *Turbulence: An introduction for scientists and engineers.* Oxford university press, 2004.

[5] W. Liepmann. The rise and fall of ideas in turbulence. *American Scientist*, 67:221, 1979.

[6] V. L'Vov and I. Procaccia. Turbulence: A universal problem. *Physics World*, page 35, August 1996.

[7] G.I. Taylor. Diffusion by continuous movements. *Proc. London Math. Soc., ser 2*, 20:196–211, 1921.

[8] H. Tennekes and J.L. Lumley. *A first course in turbulence.* MIT Press, 1972.

Chapter 12

COMPUTATIONAL TRANSPORT PROCESSES

```
Computational approach to solving problems in transport
  processes begins with division of domain of interest
  into smaller subdomains, and converting the partial
  differential equations of change into algebraic equations.
A grid point is associated with each subdomain and values
   of dependent variables are assigned to the grid points.
The main step in the conversion is discretization:
  representing derivatives by ratios of differences in the
  dependent variables  and the corresponding differences in
  location of the grid points.
An essential difference arises in the way diffusion and
  convection has to be discretized because of the non-random
  character of convection.
Algebraic equations are solved to obtain results. A few
  examples are used to illustrate the approach.
```

At the outset, we must say that though our title is more accurate, this subject is almost universally known as Computational Fluid Dynamics or **CFD**. What is in a name?! Fluid mechanics is more wide in its reach than heat and mass transfer. Hence, considerable effort has been spent on solving equations of motion and a large body of knowledge has been created using the computational approach. That body has come to be known as CFD, and almost all of it is needed and applicable in computing results for problems involving diffusion and convection in heat and mass transfer. In fact, though one uses the acronym CFD, it encompasses all these problems and not just fluid mechanics. For this reason, though we title this chapter as CTP, we will use the more common name CFD during our discussion.

12.1 WHAT IS CFD?

We live in a world where most of its behavior can, *in principle*, be predicted by three laws. They are (i) conservation of mass of species, (ii) Newton's laws of motion, and (iii) first law of thermodynamics. As we have shown earlier, *assuming that matter is continuous*, these laws can be combined *with some empirical knowledge of material properties* to derive *general partial differential equa-*

tions that predict behavior of engineering systems. It however turns out that it is difficult to find exact or even approximate solutions to these equations for realistic engineering systems and under complex conditions of operation. In recent times, computing power has increased enormously and is available at low cost. As a result, efforts have been under way to solve practically important problems using computers. This area is referred to as **Computational Fluid Dynamics** or CFD for short. Though analytical mathematics, at least in some limited way, can be done using computers, in general however, computers do arithmetic operations on numbers. Thus, the partial differential equations, have to be solved using only arithmetic operations. This is the import of the word *computational* in the topic. The subject we will discuss deals with phenomena occurring in fluids and hence the word *fluid* in the topic. The phenomena could involve flow, heat and mass transfer, and of course chemical reactions. These are of interest in general when streams flow in and out of equipment, or in dynamical conditions, and that explains the occurrence of the word *dynamics* in the subject.

12.2 WHY CFD?

As numerical methods are to be used anyway, one might ask: why apply these methods to the equations of motion. Why not apply them to molecules straight away? Matter is made up of molecules. However, molecules are very tiny in size, of the order of a few Angstroms. Thus, a m^3 of a liquid contains 10^{28} molecules and, the average distance between them is of the order of $5 \times 10^{-10} m$. Normal instruments are too coarse to measure anything on this *length scale* and can only sense the average of the effect created by several thousands of molecules. Molecules move very fast. Typically, their speeds are of the order of 100 m/s. Therefore, they will be "colliding" and changing directions every 10^{-12} s or every pico second. Therefore, the *time scale* of change is of the order of a pico second, and on this scale changes are "jerky". This is too fast for normal instruments to respond and this is the reason as to why we cannot sense the graininess and jerkiness of molecular phenomena occurring in matter. We of course are not in general interested in such small length or time scales. Yet a basic question does remain. Can motion be simulated by writing equations of motion for molecules? Some investigators do this and this area is referred to as *Molecular Dynamics*. As mentioned above, the time scale over which we must do arithmetic is of the order of pico seconds while the length scales are of the order of Angstroms. It is easily seen that to perform calculations over a time period of interest, like hours, over lengths like a meter, would require enormous computing power and is not available at the present. Hence, CFD that uses continuum models is the normal choice for calculations.

12.3 WHY NOT ONLY CFD?

If CFD can solve practical problems, why study the subject of Transport Phenomena (too much hard work!), with all the attendant analytical mathematics, like similarity solutions, separation of variables, *etc*? This is the next question that needs to be answered! It turns out that there are several things that CFD cannot do[1].

12.3.1 Turbulent flows

Efforts to solve the equations of motion to predict turbulent flows by using only numerical methods are referred to as Direct Numerical Simulation or DNS. We have learnt that turbulent flows are complex, being three-dimensional and unsteady in nature. DNS is limited by the available computing power to only very simple turbulent flows. Therefore, some models, like $k - \varepsilon$, have to be used to make calculations for complicated flows. Thus, when a CFD software is used, it usually employs models for turbulence. Some theoretical background is needed to understand these models, to select the most appropriate one, and to improve them, as you would have already seen from chapter 11.

The restriction applies to other aspects of turbulent flow as well. Thus, issues of mixing and reactions in turbulent flow are still out of scope of DNS, and some models are employed in CFD.

12.3.2 Multiphase flows

The equations of change are written for a single phase. The boundary conditions at the interface between phases are clearly spelt out. Thus, in principle, equations of motion can be used to describe multiphase systems. However, direct numerical solution of these equations, except for very simple cases like stratified flows, is not feasible at the current time. CFD therefore uses some models to make computations of multiphase flows. Thus, areas like fluidized beds, liquid–liquid dispersions, *etc.* have to be modeled. Once again, study of transport processes is needed to understand and further develop these models.

From here on, when the word CFD is used in this text, it refers to solution of equations of balance or equations of change along with some models for turbulence and not to DNS.

12.4 OVERVIEW OF CFD

CFD has three components. The first one is a description of the boundaries of any space, *i.e.,* the *domain*, in which computation is to be made. For example, it could be as simple as a tube through which a fluid flows or a stirred tank with baffles and a complicated stirring arrangement. In the former, we have to simply specify the location of the cylindrical boundary. In the latter, we have to specify the location of the tank walls, of the surfaces of the baffles, and all the surfaces that constitute the stirrer. This job is referred to as *preprocessing*, and needs a CAD like package. Many CFD packages have a preprocessor and also can interface with standard CAD packages. We will not discuss this aspect in this text as it is specific to softwares. As we shall shortly see, before computations can be made, the domain has to be sub-divided, and *grid* points have to be placed. The computed values of various quantities are assigned to the grid points. The preprocessor also does the sub-division and placement of grid points. In this chapter, we will discuss the process of dividing the domain into smaller volumes and specifying grid points.

The second step is to specify the equations and boundary conditions that dictate the solution. This is referred to as specifying the *physics* of the problem. Specification of physics is the central part of CFD. The present chapter concentrates only on this aspect. If wrong physics is specified, absurd but accurate results are obtained!

The last step is to visualize the results in terms of aids such as graphs, animations, *etc.* For example, stream lines are a good way of visualizing flow and they have to be constructed from the results. Similarly, in a heat transfer problem, isotherms give a good idea of temperature distributions, and they have to be drawn based on the results. This step is called *post processing*. It is post processing that yields all the beautiful color graphics[2] which impress industrialists! We will not discuss any of the post processing operations.

One has to be proficient in all the three aspects to be an expert user of any CFD package.

12.5 EQUATIONS AND DISCRETIZATION

We have paraphrased the material that follows from here on till the end of the chapter from the brilliant book by Patankar [4]. We also recommend the book by Versteeg and Malasekera [5].

12.5.1 Domain

CFD aims to compute, in some equipment, values for several *dependent variables* such as velocities, pressures, temperature and concentrations as a function of position and time[3], given what is being done at its boundary or the boundary conditions. The volume enclosed by the equipment is the control volume or **domain** of interest. The domain will have *inlets* and *outlets* in general. When an analytic representation of the solution is available, the values of the dependent variables can be calculated at every point of the domain as a function of time. There are infinite number of points in the domain and obviously no computer can offer the capacity to calculate the values of the variables of interest at infinite number of points like a closed form analytical solution can. One has to settle for obtaining values at some finite number of points in the domain. The points selected for obtaining solution are referred to as **grid points**. Therefore, the numerical solution we obtain is *discrete*, and not continuous. One can use the discrete solution and some scheme of interpolation to obtain the values at any point of interest lying in between the grid points, but interpolation does involve some error. Grid points can be selected in several ways. The domain can be divided into **sub-domains**. The sub-domains will be bound by *faces* and the faces are bound by *edges*. In one method, points of intersection of edges are selected as the grid points. In another method, a grid point is placed inside each of the sub-domains. Physical insight should guide the division of domain into sub-domains. More sub-domains should be created where variables are expected to vary rapidly. Thus, in general, the sub-domains need not be equal in volume, the faces of the sub-domains need not have equal area, and the distance between grid points can be different. Further, it is also possible that the shape of the domain itself may not permit division into equal sized sub-domains. It is possible to use methods of interpolation to deal with unequal volumes, but that is a matter of detail, though an important detail. However, in the present text, grid spacing will be assumed to be equal to place emphasis on

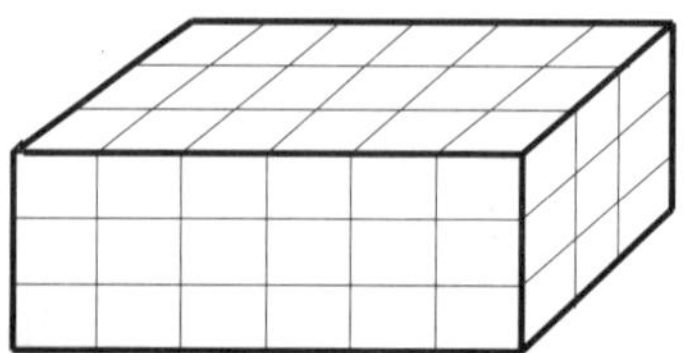

Figure 12.1. Division into sub-domains of equal volume. The original domain is shown by dark lines.

principles. A simple example is shown in figure 12.1 where a parallelepiped is divided into equal sized cubes.

The discrete solution will approach the continuous one more accurately if the number of grid points is increased. However, limitations on the computing power and the time of computation are also important factors in determining the number of sub-domains employed in calculation.

12.5.2 Equations

In general, numerical solutions use Cartesian[4] coordinates. For this reason, we give equations in the rectangular coordinates. For the sake of simplicity of writing, we use the indicial notation or the customary x, y, z notation as convenience dictates. The translation is as follows: $x \rightarrow x_1$, $y \rightarrow x_2$, $z \rightarrow x_3$.

The balance equations are displayed in a *conservative* form in CFD. Let ϕ represent any conserved intensive variable. The conservative form is same as the classical chemical engineering balance law:

Rate of accumulation of ϕ in the CV	=	**Net rate of input of ϕ into the CV by convection**	+	**Net rate of input of ϕ through the CS by diffusion**	+	**Rate of generation of ϕ in the CV by homogeneous means**

The control volume could be a full domain of interest or a differentially small volume, *i.e.,* a sub-domain. If CV is a sub-domain, this facilitates converting the partial differential equations into discretized versions. However, the rate of generation need not be "physical" in nature. It is just a mathematical arrangement and it will be seen soon that terms which have property variation will fall into this category! The generation term is normally referred to as the *source* term. The convective and diffusive inputs have a different mathematical character and hence are kept separately. These differences play a crucial role in the numerical solution and have to be dealt with carefully.

We give the balance equations for *dilute solutions of Newtonian fluids and which follow Fourier's law of heat conduction, and Fick's law of diffusion.* We permit variation in physical properties. We have the equation of continuity:

$$\frac{\partial \rho}{\partial t} + \sum_i \frac{\partial (\rho v_i)}{\partial x_i} = 0, \quad i = 1, 2, 3$$

The Newton–Stokes law of viscosity is given by

$$\tau_{ij} = \mu \left(\frac{\partial v_j}{\partial x_i} + \frac{\partial v_i}{\partial x_j} \right) - \frac{2}{3} \mu \delta_{ij} \nabla . \mathbf{v}$$

where δ_{ij} is Kronecker's delta. The equation of x component of motion is given by

$$\frac{\partial}{\partial t}(\rho v_i) + \sum_j \frac{\partial}{\partial x_j}(\rho v_j v_i) = -\frac{\partial P}{\partial x_i} + \sum_j \frac{\partial}{\partial x_j} \mu \frac{\partial v_i}{\partial x_j} + S_i, \quad i = 1, 2, 3$$

$$S_i = \rho g_i + \sum_j \left(\frac{\partial \mu}{\partial x_j} \frac{\partial v_j}{\partial x_i} \right) + \frac{\mu}{3} \frac{\partial}{\partial x_i} \nabla . \mathbf{v} - \frac{2}{3} \frac{\partial \mu}{\partial x_i} \nabla . \mathbf{v}$$

Note that the source terms contain expressions arising out of variation in properties. We can see that if the fluid is incompressible, the last two terms drop out and the term that is left is purely due to variation in viscosity. The equation of change of temperature is:

$$\frac{\partial}{\partial t}(\rho\hat{C}_pT) + \nabla.(\rho\mathbf{v}\hat{C}_pT) = \sum_j \frac{\partial}{\partial x_j}k\frac{\partial T}{\partial x_j} + \nabla.\left(\sum_i \mathbf{j}_i\frac{\overline{H}_i}{M_i}\right) + S_T$$

where

$$S_T = \dot{Q}_m + \boldsymbol{\tau}:\nabla\mathbf{v} - \frac{DP}{Dt}$$

Here , $\dot{Q}_m$ is the volumetric heat source from sources other than chemical reactions. We restrict ourselves to dilute solutions in this text. Hence,

$$\frac{\partial}{\partial t}(\rho w_k) + \nabla.(\rho\mathbf{v}w_k) = \sum_j \frac{\partial}{\partial x_j}\left(\rho D_{km}\frac{\partial w_k}{\partial x_j}\right) + S_k, \quad k = 1, 2, \cdots \neq m$$

where w_k is the weight fraction of species k, and S_k is the volumetric source of species k. D_{km} is an effective diffusivity of species k in the medium, and the subscript m stands for the solvent or the main component. Thus,

$$\mathbf{j}_k = -\sum_j D_{km}\frac{\partial w_k}{\partial x_j}$$

General conservative form

As mentioned earlier, all the equations are written in the conservative form and hence all equations are expressed in the form

$$\frac{\partial}{\partial t}(\alpha\phi) + \nabla.(\alpha\mathbf{v}\phi) = \sum_j \frac{\partial}{\partial x_j}(\Gamma\frac{\partial\phi}{\partial x_j}) + S_\phi \tag{12.1}$$

where α is some multiplying factor to the dependent variable. All equations can be recovered from this general form. For example, if $\alpha = \phi = 1$, and $S_\phi = \Gamma = 0$ are zero, equation of continuity for an incompressible fluid is recovered. Therefore, this general form is used in formulating the discretization schemes.

12.5.3 Discretization methods

A version of the general eq. 12.1 that involves only the discrete values of the variables *at the grid points* has to be produced to obtain numerical solutions. The discretized equations are solved to find the values of the variables of interest at the grid points. Broadly speaking, there are two procedures and these are briefly reviewed in the appendix. In the first procedure, referred to as **finite difference methods** (FDM), approximations for the derivatives are developed in terms of the values at the grid points, and these approximations are substituted into the partial differential equations. In the second method, an approximate form, *e.g.*, a polynomial, is assumed for the solution, and the form would have unknown constants. Since assumed form is never exact, there will be some error, and the constants that appear in the assumed form are evaluated using some criteria about reducing the error. These methods are known as **weighted residual methods**. Finite element methods (FEM) in general and finite volume method (FVM) in particular, are examples of this. In this text, we emphasize the finite volume method as it is widely used in the commonly used CFD softwares.

12.5.4 Boundary conditions

Boundary conditions needed to solve problems in transport phenomena have been discussed earlier. So far however, we have encountered relatively simple situations, and we did not face any difficulty in specifying the boundary conditions. It turns out that the exact number and nature of the boundary conditions to be specified for momentum balance is still being debated [3]. Special difficulty arises because conditions at the outlets and inlets of an equipment are difficult to specify. The most general statements one can make for flow of an incompressible fluid are the following:

1. At solid–fluid boundaries, no-slip condition is relevant,

2. At outlets, specification of shear and normal stresses is relevant. If the outlet is away from the region of interest, a commonly specified boundary condition is that dependent variables do not change in the direction of flow. These are known as "far field" boundary conditions. An example will clarify the notion. Suppose we want to compute flow around a sphere immersed in a long and wide stream. The stream itself is bounded but those boundaries, if situated far away from the sphere, will have little influence on the flow near the sphere. Thus, we might use the condition that pressure and velocities do not change far away from the sphere.

   Difficulty arises if the boundaries are not away by far enough distances from the object to permit making the above assumption. Under such circumstances, one has to examine the physical arrangement of a domain of flow, *larger than that of immediate interest*. The computational domain should in principle include what is of immediate interest as well as all that up to the boundaries where *specification can be made with certainty*. Consider an example to clarify this. Suppose we have a pump lifting water from a stream. The geometry of interest should ideally be the pump itself. However, it is easily seen that conditions at the inlet will be very difficult to specify. On the other hand, conditions far away from the inlet are those of the undisturbed stream, and can be specified. Thus, one might include more volume into the computational domain to gain accuracy in specifying boundary conditions. Increase in the computational effort is obviously the penalty of this procedure, and an optimum is to be sought.

3. In general, there are four dependent variables of interest in flow: three components of velocity and the pressure. Three out of four of these are to be specified at the inlet. Typically, for two-dimensional flows, the inlet boundary conditions are specification of pressure and one velocity.

4. The boundary conditions for heat and mass transfer are easier to specify at the inlets since the "state" of the fluid is generally known. At the outlet, the same difficulty discussed previously

arises, and it is handled in the same manner. It is easy to recognize the similarity between Danckwerts boundary conditions at the exit of a reactor, and the specification at the outlets.

5. In case of heat and mass transfer, the flux continuity and conditions of equilibrium are to be enforced at the boundaries between phases.

It can be seen that considerable experience is required to specify boundary conditions in complex cases.

12.6 FINITE VOLUME METHOD: Overview

The finite volume method (FVM) places emphasis on the implementation of the conservation properties of the equations of change. It is done as follows. The domain is divided into smaller sub-domains. The equations of change are required to be satisfied **on the average** in each sub-domain, irrespective of the form assumed for the solution. This is equivalent to equating the integral of the equations of change to zero on each sub-domain for the assumed form of solution.

The balance equations or the equations of change are derived by implementing the conservation principles on a small volume ΔV, dividing the resulting equation by ΔV, and taking the limit as ΔV approaches zero. This procedure is being reversed in the finite volume method, and hence it is a **direct implementation** of conservation principles on the sub-domains. Thus, FVM *ensures* conservation if an accurate solution of the resulting equations is obtained. If the sub-domains are sufficiently small, the procedure would accurately mimic solution of the differential equations.

12.6.1 Balance on each sub-domain

We write on each sub-domain the appropriate balance law. Thus, momentum balance is written as

$$\begin{matrix}\textbf{Rate of accumulation of}\\ x\textbf{ momentum in the CV}\end{matrix} = \begin{matrix}\textbf{Net rate of input of}\\ x\textbf{ momentum into}\\ \textbf{the CV by convection}\end{matrix} + \begin{matrix}\textbf{Sum of the } x\textbf{ component}\\ \textbf{forces acting on the CV}\end{matrix}$$

The enthalpy balance is written as

$$\begin{matrix}\textbf{Rate of accumulation}\\ \textbf{of enthalpy in the CV}\end{matrix} = \begin{matrix}\textbf{Net rate of input}\\ \textbf{of enthalpy into}\\ \textbf{the CV by convection}\end{matrix} + \begin{matrix}\textbf{Rate of input of}\\ \textbf{heat through}\\ \textbf{control surfaces}\\ \textbf{by conduction}\end{matrix} + \begin{matrix}\textbf{Rate of generation}\\ \textbf{of heat in the CV}\\ \textbf{due to chemical}\\ \textbf{reactions, } etc.\end{matrix} + \begin{matrix}\textbf{Rate of heat}\\ \textbf{generation in}\\ \textbf{the CV due to}\\ \textbf{viscous dissipation}\end{matrix}$$

We neglected the small contribution from the substantial derivative of pressure in writing this. Species mass balance is written as

$$\begin{matrix}\textbf{Rate of accumulation of}\\ \textbf{mass of } i^{th}\textbf{ species in the CV}\end{matrix} = \begin{matrix}\textbf{Net rate of input of}\\ \textbf{mass of } i^{th}\textbf{ species into}\\ \textbf{the CV by convection}\end{matrix} + \begin{matrix}\textbf{Net rate of input of}\\ \textbf{mass of } i^{th}\textbf{ species into}\\ \textbf{the CS by diffusion}\end{matrix} + \begin{matrix}\textbf{Rate of generation of}\\ \textbf{mass of } i^{th}\textbf{ species in the CV}\\ \textbf{by homogeneous chemical reactions}\end{matrix}$$

Obviously, the same equations can also be obtained if the equations of change are integrated over the sub-domain.

12.6.2 Assumed form of solution

The equations obtained from the above balances will contain both algebraic expressions as well as first order derivatives arising out of integrals of the diffusion terms. Some representation for the variables has to be assumed to evaluate the derivatives. In the finite volume method, *the variables are assumed to vary linearly in space over each of the sub-domain.* When dealing with unsteady state problems, small time increments are considered for computation, and once again a linear profile is assumed with time over the small increment of time. When the assumed form of solutions is substituted, the balance equations reduce to *non-linear* algebraic equations. Non-linearity arises from convective terms, the variation of properties, *e.g.,* density, viscosity *etc.*, due to changes in dependent variables, *e.g.,* concentration, temperature, *etc.*, and from generation terms, *e.g.,* dependence of reaction rate on concentration.

12.6.3 Method of solution

The non-linear equations are usually linearized and solved by some iterative method of solution. Typically, one starts with a guessed solution and some iterative procedure is used. A commonly used iterative procedure is discussed in the appendix.

12.6.4 Plan of presentation

From the view point of solution of equations, the species and enthalpy balances fall in one category while the momentum balances fall in a different category. The former, as you know, are referred to as equations for balance of a *passive scalar.* Passive scalar balances involving only diffusion are the most simple ones from the view point of solution of equations. The complexity increases by one level when convection is introduced, even assuming that velocity profiles are known. The complexity goes up by one further level when Navier–Stokes equations are to be solved to obtain the velocity profiles. Therefore, we proceed by considering diffusion of a passive scalar at first, and then graduating to the solution of convection and diffusion of a passive scalar where velocity profiles are known. In this text, we will not consider the solution of the momentum balance equations to determine the velocity profiles, as it belongs in a text on fluid mechanics. However, you can refer to the excellent text by Patankar [4] for this. Here, at first we deal with steady one dimensional problems and then consider generalization to unsteady multi-dimensional problems.

12.7 DIFFUSION OF A PASSIVE SCALAR

We begin with steady state one-dimensional diffusion problems. As this is the most simple case, all details can be discussed without any distractions. Consider heat conduction in a slab with heat generation. See figure 12.2. Let the faces perpendicular to the y and z directions be insulated. Let the length of the slab in x direction be L. Let the area of cross section be A. Let the face at $x = 0$ be maintained at T_o. Further suppose that the face at $x = L$ loses heat to the surroundings through convection. In view of the uniformity of boundary condition on the x faces, and insulated y and z faces, conduction in x direction is therefore the only mechanism of heat transfer. The equation to be solved is

$$\frac{d}{dx}k\frac{dT}{dx} + \dot{Q}_v = 0 \tag{12.2}$$

and the boundary conditions are

$$T = T_o, \ \text{at}\, x = 0, \ \text{and} - k\frac{dT}{dx} = h(T - T_a), \ \text{at}\, x = L \tag{12.3}$$

where T_a is the ambient temperature.

It is easy to see that this problem is similar to absorption of a sparingly soluble[5] and reactive solute into a solvent contained in a beaker of length L. Let the solvent also contain another species but at a high concentration. Suppose that the solute reacts with that species in an irreversible way. The rate of this reaction can usually be represented by a pseudo-first order rate expression. The solute reacts as it diffuses into the solvent, and the equation that describes this process is given by

$$\frac{d}{dx}\mathcal{D}_A\frac{dC_A}{dx} - kC_A = 0$$

and the boundary conditions are

$$C_A = C_{Ao}, \ \text{at}\, x = 0, \ \text{and} \ \mathcal{D}_A\frac{dC_A}{dx} = 0 \ \text{at}\, x = L$$

This is also similar to the pseudo-homogeneous model of reaction in a slab of catalyst pellet considered in chapter 9.

12.7.1 Grid generation

The first step in CFD is to divide the domain into sub-domains or regions with a finite volume. Then grid points are located in the sub-domains. It is not necessary that all the sub-domains be of equal volume. Similarly, it is not necessary that the grid points be located in the "center" of the sub-domain. In the most general case, the distances between the grid points will be different and hence evaluation of derivatives[6] will need to take this into account. We divide the domain into five sub-domains as shown in figure 12.2. In this chapter, for the sake of simplicity we will consider the sub-domains to be of equal volumes, and place the grid points at the center of the sub-domain. Let the length of sub-domain be Δx. The sub-domains and the grid points are shown in figure 12.2.

Grid points can also be located to start with and sub-domains can be drawn such that the surfaces pass through them. This is more akin to finite difference technique. In general, one of the grid points would be on the boundary if this procedure was followed. Here, in contrast, notice that the sub-domains were generated at first, and grid points were located inside the domains. Either procedure can be followed in formulating the equations and the finite volume technique is independent of the method of marking sub-domains.

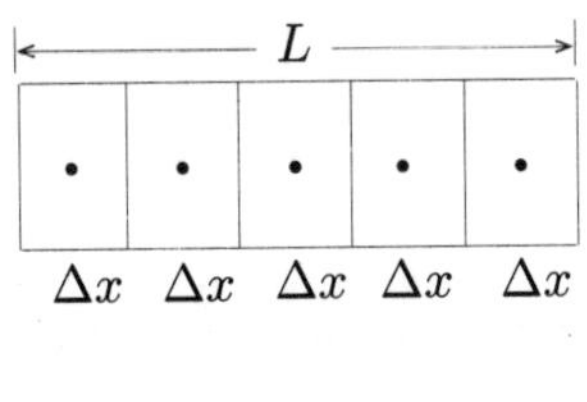

Figure 12.2. Sub-domains and grid points for one-dimensional conduction. A typical control volume is shown below with the commonly employed notation for grid points. P is the grid point in a sub-domain of interest. Point E is to the east of the grid point while point W is to the west of the grid point. The surfaces of the sub-domain volume to the east and west of the grid point are denoted by e and w, respectively. If the dimensionality is more, north and south, and front and back can be used to denote the sides and faces.

12.7.2 Conservation on sub-domains

In the finite volume method, the conservation principle is emphasized on each sub-domain[7]. As mentioned earlier, this is equivalent to writing balance on the volume of the sub-domain. Heat balance over a typical sub-domain shown in figure 12.2 results in the following equation:

$$-\left(kA\frac{dT}{dx}\right)\bigg|_w + \left(kA\frac{dT}{dx}\right)\bigg|_e + A\Delta x\,\dot{Q}_v = 0$$

12.7.3 Assumed form

Now we make an assumption for the profile of the dependent variable. As mentioned earlier, linear dependence is most commonly assumed. According to central difference scheme, the derivative at the west face is therefore given by

$$\left(\frac{dT}{dx}\right)\bigg|_w = \frac{T_P - T_W}{\Delta x}$$

while that at the east face is given by

$$\left(\frac{dT}{dx}\right)\bigg|_e = \frac{T_E - T_P}{\Delta x}$$

12.7.4 Source terms

The source term can be a complex function of the dependent variables, and in such a case, one has to linearize the expression. Alternatively, it can be factored into an iterative scheme as will be shortly discussed. Here, we proceed by assuming that the expression itself is linear. The resulting equations are similar to those obtained by linearization. Thus,

$$\dot{Q}_v\,(T_P) = \dot{Q}_c + \dot{Q}_v'\,T_P$$

Note this suits the typical first order reaction rate expression.

12.7.5 Balance equation

Substituting the above into the balance equation, and solving it for T_P results in the following equation:

$$\left(\frac{k_w A}{\Delta x} + \frac{k_e A}{\Delta x} - A\Delta x\, \dot{Q}_v'\right) T_P = \frac{k_w A}{\Delta x} T_W + \frac{k_e A}{\Delta x} T_E + A\Delta x\, \dot{Q}_c$$

The following coefficients *associated with the grid points* are commonly defined in the literature on finite volume method:

$$a_E = \frac{k_e A}{\Delta x};\ a_W = \frac{k_w A}{\Delta x};\ a_P = a_E + a_W - A\Delta x\, \dot{Q}_v';\ S_c = A\Delta x\, \dot{Q}_c$$

Using this notation, the balance equation is written in the following form:

$$a_P T_P = a_E T_E + a_W T_W + S_c \tag{12.4}$$

With the nomenclature used, this is a standard algebraic form for all balance equations. The balance equations for all the grid points forms a system of non-linear algebraic equations and has to be solved. They are non-linear because the coefficients may depend on the dependent variables. They are solved using an iterative technique, which in effect is equivalent to linearization.

12.7.6 Linearization

Now the dependence of physical properties, in this example, the thermal conductivity, on temperature has to be accounted for. There are many possibilities. It is possible to take k at the west face to be the mean of the values at the surrounding grid points:

$$k|_w = \frac{k(T_P) + k(T_W)}{2}$$

or to evaluate it at the mean temperature:

$$k|_w = k\left(\frac{T_P + T_W}{2}\right)$$

or any other from[8]. All these will make the coefficients, a_P, a_E, *etc.* dependent on temperatures and the equations become non-linear. They are solved by an iterative technique described in the appendix. The solution starts with "guess" values at all the grid points, and the *coefficients* are evaluated using them. Denoting the coefficients so evaluated by a superscript star, eq. 12.4 can be written as

$$a_P^* T_P = a_E^* T_E + a_W^* T_W + S_c$$

These are linear and hence can be solved, and commonly, by using an iterative technique.

It is possible to incorporate the non-linearity in the source term also using the same procedure. Thus, we can write

$$\dot{Q}_v\,(T_P) = \dot{Q}_c\,(T_P^*) + \dot{Q}_v'\,(T_P^*)(T_P - T_P^*)$$

and hence

$$S_c = A\Delta x\left(\dot{Q}_c\,(T_P^*) - \dot{Q}_v'\,(T_P^*)T_P^*\right)$$

The values obtained for the dependent variables by solving the equations form the "next guesses". Values for the dependent variables are obtained once again, and the procedure is repeated in this manner till some *convergence criteria* is met. Such a criterion is usually based on the magnitude of the difference between the values of the dependent variables in two successive iterations.

12.7.7 Some rules of formulation

There are certain rules that must be followed in formulating the finite volume equations. Let us briefly discuss them.

Conservativeness

The major advantage of the finite volume technique is its emphasis on conservation. This is achieved through implementing balances of conserved quantities directly on sub-domains. *Even though conservation is satisfied on each sub-domain, it is automatically satisfied on the entire domain only when common faces of sub-domains are treated in a consistent manner.* Thus, in the one-dimensional problem being considered, the east face of one control volume will also be the west face of an adjoining control volume. Thus, one must ensure that the values calculated for the fluxes crossing this face should be identical when one considers either sub-domain. Such is ensured when the gradients are calculated using central difference approximation, and might not be ensured when a higher order approximation is used for derivatives.

Convergence

Engineering sense dictates that if the temperature at a grid point increases, the effect of this would be to increase the temperature of the neighboring grid points. This is ensured only when *all the coefficients* (a_E, *etc.*) *are positive*. This is also related to the convergence of the iteration scheme used.

Scarborough Criterion

The Scarborough criterion is a mathematical requirement for the convergence of the iteration scheme. Let the coefficient a_P' be coefficient at grid point P *in the absence of source*. If a_{nb} are the coefficients of the neighboring grid points, the criterion of convergence is given by

$$\frac{\sum a_{nb}}{a_P'} < 1$$

at least at one grid point and

$$\frac{\sum a_{nb}}{a_P'} \leq 1$$

at all grid points. In this criterion, only the coefficients of neighbors where dependent variable is *unknown* are to be included. It is easily seen that from the balance equation that equality sign is satisfied at all internal points. Later on we will see that values at grid points lying on the boundary are known and it is this that meets the "less than" part of the criterion.

The iterative methods have to be used with caution and an example when the method fails is given in appendix.

12.7.8 Boundary conditions

The final part of problem is to specify the boundary conditions. As the domain has been split into sub-domains, some sides of some of the sub-domains will form the boundaries. It is on those sides that values of dependent variables or functions of them will be known. Typical boundary conditions are

1. specification of the dependent variable itself (Dirichlet condition)
2. specification of derivative of the dependent variable (Neumann condition)
3. specification of a relationship between the dependent variable and derivative of the dependent variable (Roberts condition)

In terms of heat transfer, these are equivalent to specification of temperature, flux, and heat loss by convection, respectively. A sub-domain on the boundary for a one-dimensional problem is shown in figure 12.3. We will consider that the boundary is on the left side of the control volume, and

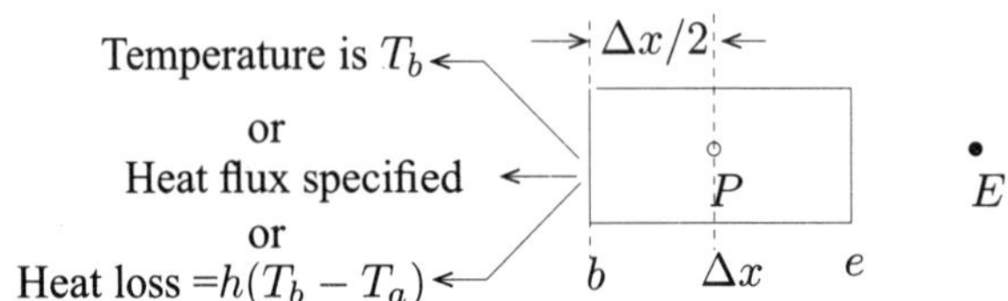

Figure 12.3. Sub-domain at a boundary for one-dimensional conduction.

the case where the boundary is on the right can be treated identically. The main difference here is that a grid point is not present to the left of the sub-domain, and its west surface coincides with the boundary. Let us denote the boundary by b. A balance on the sub-domain now gives

$$Aq_x\bigg|_b - Aq_x\bigg|_e + A\Delta x\,\dot{Q}_v = 0$$

The last two terms can be evaluated as done before. The first term requires modification because a grid point to the west is absent. It is done as follows.

1. If Dirichlet boundary condition is to be implemented on b, then, in keeping with the linearity assumption, we can write

$$q_x\bigg|_b = -k\frac{T_P - T_b}{\Delta x/2}$$

The boundary condition then is given by

$$T_P\left(\frac{k_bA}{\Delta x/2}+\frac{k_eA}{\Delta x}-A\Delta x\,\dot{Q}_v'(T_P)\right)=\frac{k_eA}{\Delta x}T_E+\frac{k_bA}{\Delta x/2}T_b+A\Delta x\,\dot{Q}_c$$

2. Heat flux q_x at b itself is specified if Neumann condition is to be employed. The boundary condition is then given by

$$T_P\left(\frac{k_eA}{\Delta x}-A\Delta x\,\dot{Q}_v'(T_P)\right)=\frac{k_eA}{\Delta x}T_E+q_x\Big|_b A+A\Delta x\,\dot{Q}_c$$

3. In case of Roberts boundary condition, heat loss is through convection, and hence

$$q_x\Big|_b = h(T_a - T_b) = k_b\frac{T_b - T_P}{\Delta x/2}$$

where h is the heat transfer coefficient and T_a is the ambient temperature. Eliminating T_b,

$$q_x\Big|_b = \frac{T_a - T_P}{1/h + \Delta x/(2k_b)}$$

The boundary condition then becomes

$$T_P\left(\frac{1}{1/h+\Delta x/(2k_b)}+\frac{k_eA}{\Delta x}-A\Delta x\,\dot{Q}_v'(T_P)\right)=\frac{k_eA}{\Delta x}T_E+\frac{T_a}{1/h+\Delta x/(2k_b)}+A\Delta x\,\dot{Q}_c$$

Notice that in all the examples, $\sum a_{nb}/a_P'$ is less than unity, and it is this that ensures that the Scarborough criterion of it being less than unity at a minimum of one grid point is obeyed.

Now let us consider an example. *In the examples, for the sake of simplicity we will assume constant properties* though the non-linearity can be handled as discussed previously.

12.7.9 Heat loss from a fin

A fin is thin in cross-section and hence, temperature gradients across the cross section are negligible. Refer to figure 12.4. Therefore, the heat loss through the surface is lumped into the balance equation itself. The balance equation is given [9] by

$$\frac{d}{dx}kA\frac{dT}{dx} - hp(T - T_a) = 0$$

where p is the perimeter. The boundary conditions are given by

$$T = T_b, \text{ at } x = 0, \text{ and } q_x = h(T - T_a) \sim 0, \text{ at } x = L$$

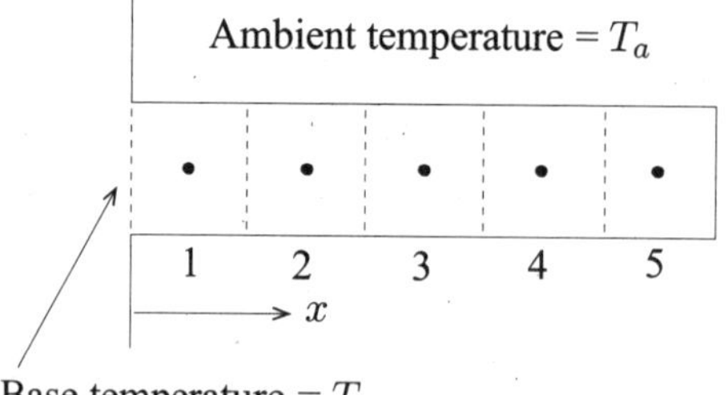

Figure 12.4. Heat transfer from a fin. The problem is one-dimensional conduction. The fin is divided into five control volumes.

Analytical solution

This equation permits an analytical solution, and is given by

$$\frac{T - T_a}{T_b - T_a} = \frac{\cosh[n(L - x)]}{\cosh nL}, \quad n^2 = \frac{hp}{kA} \tag{12.5}$$

Balance on interior control volumes

Let us turn to the numerical solution. Let us divide the fin into five control volumes. See figure 12.4. Heat balance on the interior sub-domains is given by

$$kA\frac{T_W - T_P}{\Delta x} - kA\frac{T_P - T_E}{\Delta x} - \Delta x hp(T_P - T_a) = 0$$

k is being assumed to be constant, and for one-dimensional problems, A is constant. Dividing the above equation by kA, and rearranging it,

$$a_P T_P = a_E T_E + a_W T_W + S_c \tag{12.6}$$

where

$$\begin{aligned} a_E &= \frac{1}{\Delta x} \\ a_W &= \frac{1}{\Delta x} \\ a_P &= a_E + a_W + \frac{hp}{kA}\Delta x \\ S_c &= \frac{hp}{kA}\Delta x T_a \end{aligned} \tag{12.7}$$

These equations and balance are valid for $P = 2$ to 4.

Balance on boundary control volumes

Now consider making a balance on the boundary control volumes. See figure 12.5. It can be noticed that point W is absent for point 1 in the CV that contains the left boundary. Further, we have temperature specified at a distance on $\Delta x/2$ from point 1. Thus, the balance is given by

$$kA\frac{T_b - T_1}{\Delta x/2} - kA\frac{T_1 - T_2}{\Delta x} - \Delta x hp(T_1 - T_a) = 0$$

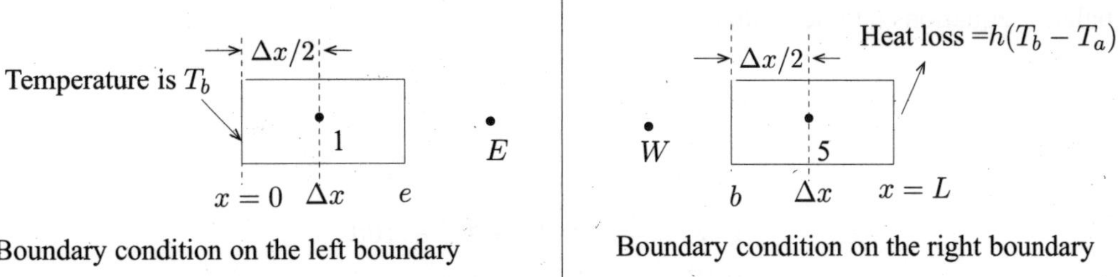

Figure 12.5. Boundary conditions on the left and right boundaries of a fin.

where we are extending the assumption of linear temperature profile on the left boundary. The equation can be rearranged to take the same form as before but with the following values for the coefficients:

$$\begin{aligned} a_E &= \frac{1}{\Delta x} \\ a_W &= 0 \\ a_P &= a_E + a_W + \frac{hp}{kA}\Delta x + \frac{2}{\Delta x} \\ S_c &= \frac{hp}{kA}\Delta x T_a + \frac{2T_b}{\Delta x} \end{aligned} \tag{12.8}$$

Similarly let us make a balance on the right boundary. The features are similar except that the heat loss on the right boundary is given by convection and in this problem it is equal to zero. Thus, balance around point 5 that contains the right boundary is given by

$$kA\frac{T_4 - T_5}{\Delta x} - 0 - \Delta x h P(T_5 - T_a) = 0$$

where zero in the equation stands for the insulation boundary condition. The equation can be rearranged to take the same form as before but with the following values for the coefficients:

$$\begin{aligned} a_E &= 0 \\ a_W &= \frac{1}{\Delta x} \\ a_P &= a_E + a_W + \frac{hp}{kA}\Delta x \\ S_c &= \frac{hp}{kA}\Delta x T_a \end{aligned} \tag{12.9}$$

Numerical solution

Take the following specific values:

$$n^2 = \frac{hp}{kA} = 25\,m^{-2},\ L = 1\,m,\ \Delta x = 0.2\,m,\ T_b = 100,\ T_a = 20$$

The balance equations can be written as

$$
\begin{aligned}
20\,T_1 &= 5\,T_2 + 1100 \\
15\,T_2 &= 5\,(T_1 + T_3) + 100 \\
15\,T_3 &= 5\,(T_2 + T_4) + 100 \\
15\,T_4 &= 5\,(T_3 + T_5) + 100 \\
10\,T_5 &= 5\,T_4 + 100
\end{aligned}
$$

The equations are easily solved by inverting a matrix. However, we will illustrate Gauss–Siedel

Table 12.1. Numerical solution of the problem of heat transfer from a fin.

Position	Analytical	Initial	First	Second	First	Second
0.1	68.5	92	74	67.8	86.9	83.3
0.3	37.9	76	51.3	42.1	70.2	65.3
0.5	26.6	60	38.4	30.3	55.5	51.6
0.7	22.5	44	28.8	24.9	41.1	38.6
0.9	21.2	28	24.4	22.4	26.7	27.6

method. Let linear temperature profile form the initial guess. We iterate by moving from point 1 to 5 in that order. Second, fourth and fifth columns of Table 12.1 show the results computed from the exact solution and for two iterations. It can be seen that the results are not very good. The value at the first grid point is already lower than the exact value, and it is true of the converged value [5] as well. This is because the gradient at the left edge of the domain is the largest, and the grid spacing is too large to capture this. Results can be improved if we increase the number of sub-domains, *i.e.,* make the grid spacing smaller. In the last two columns of the table, we show results obtained by using 15 sub-domains, which allows us to get values at the same location. Though not shown, accuracy improves. As can be seen however, convergence slows down. It is because, the rate at which the influence of the boundaries percolates into the domain is larger for larger grid spacing. This illustrates another angle to specification of grid spacing.

12.8 CONVECTION & DIFFUSION OF A PASSIVE SCALAR

The next level of complexity is introduced by convection. As mentioned earlier, we begin with a case where velocity profiles in the domain are known. Diffusion is a random phenomenon because molecules which are the carriers of "properties" move randomly. In contrast, convection transports a scalar in a biased manner. This causes bias to be introduced in discretization as well. *This is an important point and has to be understood clearly.* Once again, we begin with one-dimensional problem for simplicity.

12.8.1 Conservation equation

The equation of continuity obeyed in one-dimensional (x) takes the simple form:

$$\frac{d}{dx}(\rho u) = 0$$

where we have used symbol u for the x component of the velocity. The steady one-dimensional convection diffusion equation takes the form

$$\frac{d}{dx}(\rho u \phi) = \frac{d}{dx}\Gamma\frac{d\phi}{dx} + \dot{Q}_\phi$$

Note that the units of Γ/ρ are same as that of diffusivity. Hence, a Peclet number can be defined in terms of characteristic length and velocity as

$$Pe = \frac{\rho U L}{\Gamma} = \frac{\rho \hat{C}_p U L}{k} = \frac{UL}{D_{im}} \tag{12.10}$$

and it determines the relative strengths of convection and diffusion.

Let use use Dirichlet boundary conditions for our illustration:

$$T = T_o, \text{ at } x = 0, \text{ and } T = T_L, \text{ at } x = L \tag{12.11}$$

12.8.2 Conservation on sub-domains

Refer to figure 12.6. Application of the equation of continuity over the sub-domain gives

$$(\rho u)|_w - (\rho u)|_e = 0$$

In writing this we assumed that area remains constant because otherwise, flow cannot be one-dimensional. Usually, the mass flux is given the symbol F, and the previous equation can be

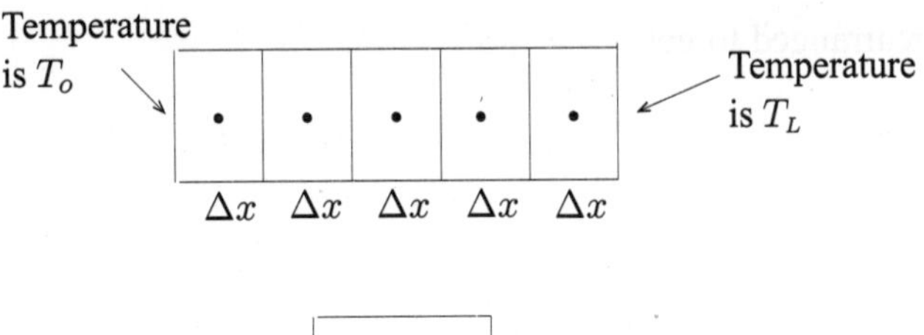

Figure 12.6. Discretization for convection problem.

rewritten in terms of the new symbol as

$$F_w - F_e = 0$$

or that F is a constant. Writing a balance of scalar ϕ on the sub-domain results in the following equation:

$$(F\phi)|_w - (F\phi)|_e - \left(\Gamma\frac{d\phi}{dx}\right)\Big|_w + \left(\Gamma\frac{d\phi}{dx}\right)\Big|_e + \Delta x\, \dot{Q}_\phi\,(P) = 0$$

12.8.3 Assumed form

We again assume a linear profile for the dependent variable. Thus,

$$\left(\frac{d\phi}{dx}\right)\bigg|_w = \frac{\phi_P - \phi_W}{\Delta x}$$

while that at the east face is given by

$$\left(\frac{d\phi}{dx}\right)\bigg|_e = \frac{\phi_E - \phi_P}{\Delta x}$$

By the same logic

$$\phi|_w = \frac{\phi_P + \phi_W}{2}$$

and

$$\phi|_e = \frac{\phi_P + \phi_E}{2}$$

The balance equation then can be rewritten as

$$F_w \frac{\phi_P + \phi_W}{2} - F_e \frac{\phi_P + \phi_E}{2} - \Gamma_w \frac{\phi_P - \phi_W}{\Delta x} + \Gamma_e \frac{\phi_E - \phi_P}{\Delta x} + \Delta\, \dot{Q}_\phi\,(P) = 0$$

The ratio $\Gamma/\Delta x$ is given the symbol D. As before, let us assume that

$$\dot{Q}_\phi\,(P) = \dot{Q}_c + \dot{Q}_\phi^{'}\,\phi_P$$

This equation can be rearranged to get

$$a_P \phi_P = a_W \phi_E + a_E \phi_E + S_c \tag{12.12}$$

where

$$\begin{aligned} a_E &= D_e - \frac{F_e}{2} \\ a_W &= D_w + \frac{F_w}{2} \\ a_P &= a_E + a_W + F_e - F_w - \Delta x\, \dot{Q}_\phi^{'} \\ S_c &= \Delta x\, \dot{Q}_c \end{aligned} \tag{12.13}$$

This form is identical to what we had earlier, except that the coefficients now have convective transport represented by F and also diffusion represented by D. We have to keep in mind that all the discussion regarding the rules obeyed by coefficients applies directly here as well. Further *notice the asymmetry in the coefficients introduced by convection.*

12.8.4 Numerical example

The formulation given can be combined with boundary conditions and solved in the same way as discussed earlier. However, the asymmetry introduced by convection leads to certain problems and that is the topic of this subsection. Let us consider a simple problem to illustrate the difficulty. Imagine a fluid flowing at a constant velocity U through an insulated duct of length L. Let it enter at a temperature T_o while the end of the duct is maintained at constant temperature T_L. The governing equations are

$$k\frac{d^2T}{dx^2} - \rho\hat{C}_pU\frac{dT}{dx} = 0$$

and the boundary conditions are

$$T = T_o, \text{ at } x = -\frac{L}{2}, \text{ and } T = T_L, \text{ at } x = \frac{L}{2}$$

For the sake of using this solution in future, the origin of the coordinate system was located in the middle of the duct.

Exact solution

There is an analytical solution[10] and is given by

$$\frac{T - T_o}{T_L - T_o} = \theta = \frac{e^{Pe(\xi+1)} - 1}{e^{2Pe} - 1} \tag{12.14}$$

where

$$\xi = \frac{2x}{L}, \; Pe = \frac{\rho\hat{C}_pUL}{2k}$$

If $Pe \rightarrow 0$, conduction is the dominant mechanism and the temperature profile is linear. The solution confirms it. If the velocity is large and in the positive x direction, $Pe >> 0$, and the temperature profile is approximated by $e^{Pe(\xi-1)}$. Hence, the temperature will nearly be equal to the inlet value over most of the domain and conduction brings it to the exit value only very near the exit as imposed by the boundary condition. In other words, conduction is confined to a small zone near the outlet. The situation is reversed if the flow is in the opposite direction. The solution is highly skewed in favor of the direction of convection when Pe is large. Figure 12.7 shows the trends qualitatively. The finite volume method however assumes linear profiles and this would go wrong in describing convection problems. Let us illustrate the failure through a numerical example. If we let $\phi = \hat{C}_pT, \Gamma = k/\hat{C}_P$, we can apply eq. 12.12 using eq. 12.13. Let us take some specific numerical values.

Case of low Peclet number

Let $\hat{C}_PT_o = 1$, $\hat{C}_PT_L = 0$, $L = 1$, $\Delta x = 0.2$, $k/(\hat{C}_P\Delta x) = 0.5$, $\rho U = 0.1$. The 'grid' Peclet number is therefore equal to 0.2. Further, generation is equal to zero, and hence $S_c = \dot{Q}'_\phi = 0$. The balance equations for the internal nodes are given by

$$\phi_P = 0.55\phi_W + 0.45\phi_E, \; P = 2, 3, 4$$

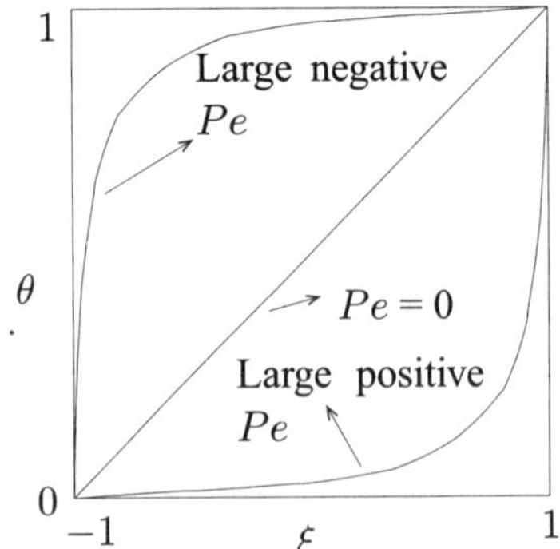

Figure 12.7. Qualitative sketch of temperature profiles in the presence of convection.

The balance at the left boundary is given by

$$F(1) - \Gamma\frac{\phi_1 - (1)}{\Delta x/2} - F\frac{\phi_1 + \phi_2}{2} - \Gamma\frac{\phi_1 - \phi_2}{\Delta x} = 0$$

Rearranging this equation after substituting the numerical values, we get

$$1.55\phi_1 = 0.45\phi_2 + 1.1$$

Similarly the balance on the right boundary is give by

$$F\frac{\phi_4 + \phi_5}{2} + \Gamma\frac{\phi_4 - \phi_5}{\Delta x} - F(0) - \Gamma\frac{\phi_5 - (0)}{\Delta x/2} = 0$$

Rearranging this after substituting the numerical values, we get

$$1.45\phi_5 = 0.55\phi_4$$

Table 12.2 shows the results computed from the analytical solution and for two iterations. As before, a linear profile has been used for initial guess. It is seen that the solution is good, and it is to be expected since convection does not dominate.

Case of high Peclet number

Let $\hat{C}_P T_o = 1, \hat{C}_P T_L = 0$, $L = 1$, $k/(\hat{C}_P \Delta x) = 0.5$, $\rho U = 2.5$. The 'grid' Peclet number is therefore equal to 5. As before, $S_c = \dot{Q}'_\phi = 0$. The balance equations for the internal nodes are given by

$$\phi_P = 0.55\phi_W + 0.45\phi_E, \; P = 2, 3, 4$$

while those for the boundaries are given by

$$2.75\phi_1 = -0.75\phi_2 + 3.5$$

and

$$0.25\phi_5 = 1.75\phi_4$$

Table 12.2. Results for the effect convection for small Peclet number.

Analytical	Initial	First	Second
0.94	0.9	0.912	0.9206
0.8	0.7	0.7266	0.75
0.63	0.5	0.5346	0.56
0.42	0.3	0.339	0.37
0.16	0.1	0.139	0.16

First notice that the Scarborough criterion is violated. Hence, Gauss–Siedel technique will not give a converged solution. This is illustrated in Table 12.3. Linear profile is used as initial guess: Instability is obvious. The equations however *do have* a solution. The solution can be obtained by inverting the matrix. The inverted solution obtained by inversion is shown[11] along with a comparison with the exact solution in Table 12.4. Clearly, the method failed when the Peclet number is high. *The error arises from using linear average for the dependent variable.*

Table 12.3. Results showing lack of convergence with Gauss–Siedel technique.

Iteration	Variable				
	ϕ_1	ϕ_2	ϕ_3	ϕ_4	ϕ_5
Initial	0.9	0.7	0.5	0.3	0.1
1	1.01	1.52	2.43	4.18	29.26
2	0.86	-0.32	-3.7	-28.41	-200
3	0.084	2.94	26.4	196	1373.7

Table 12.4. Numerical solution showing poor results for large Peclet number.

	Variable				
	ϕ_1	ϕ_2	ϕ_3	ϕ_4	ϕ_5
Exact	1.0	0.9999	0.9999	0.9994	0.92
Numerical	1.04	0.87	1.26	0.35	2.46

The cause is explained in terms of an analogy to the well known stirred tanks, and this is given in the book by Patankar [4]. The value of the dependent variable at a grid point is representative of the sub-domain. Convection 'carries' the property from one sub-domain to the other and to represent this, we can use the analogy of three stirred tanks connected in series. See figure 12.8. Normally,

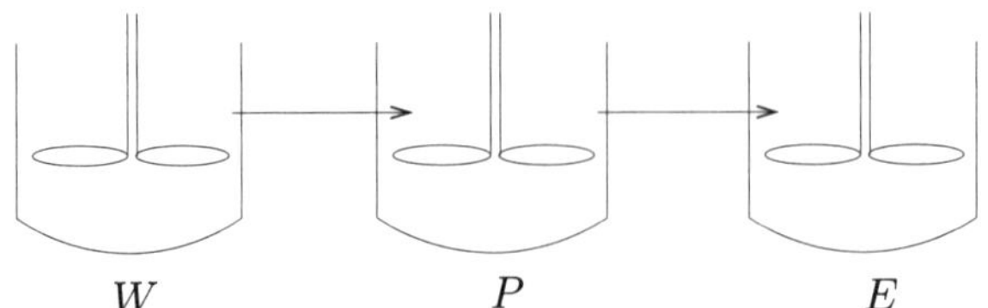

Figure 12.8. Qualitative explanation of defect in using the averaged values at surfaces in presence of convection.

for this example, we would write the balance on P, due to convection as

$$F\phi_W - F\phi_P = 0$$

under steady conditions. This is done since convection is assumed to fully dominate over diffusion, and the property convected belongs to *upstream*. In contrast, *we have assumed the property to be the average of the upstream and downstream values. Since diffusion is a random phenomena, this assumption is a good one, and is not valid for convection.*

Upwinding

If we assume that well stirred assumption is a good one, then we should be writing the balance on P as

$$F_w\phi_W - F_e\phi_P - \Gamma_w \frac{\phi_P - \phi_W}{\Delta x} + \Gamma_e \frac{\phi_E - \phi_P}{\Delta x} + \Delta x\, \dot{Q}_\phi\,(P) = 0$$

for $Pe > 0$ and

$$F_w\,\phi_P - F_e\phi_E - \Gamma_w \frac{\phi_P - \phi_W}{\Delta x} + \Gamma_e \frac{\phi_E - \phi_P}{\Delta x} + \Delta x\, \dot{Q}_\phi\,(P) = 0$$

for $Pe < 0$. Solving these for ϕ_P, they can be written as

$$(D_w + F_w + D_e + F_e - F_w - \Delta x\, \dot{Q}'_\phi)\phi_P = (D_w + F_w)\phi_W + D_e\,\phi_E - S_c$$

for $Pe > 0$ and

$$(D_w + D_e - F_e + F_e - F_w\,\Delta x\, \dot{Q}'_\phi)\phi_P = D_w\phi_W + (D_e - F_e)\phi_E - S_c$$

for $Pe < 0$. It is seen that the formulae for the coefficients have the same form as used before if we write

$$\begin{aligned} a_E &= D_e + \text{Max of}\,(-F_e, 0) \\ a_W &= D_w + \text{Max of}\,(F_w, 0) \\ a_P &= a_E + a_W + F_e - F_w - \Delta x\, \dot{Q}'_\phi \\ S_c &= \Delta x\, \dot{Q}_c \end{aligned} \qquad (12.15)$$

This is known as **upwinding** scheme.

12.8.5 Weighted upwinding

As its basis lies in assuming that convection dominates, the upwinding scheme can be expected to be wrong *in case Peclet number is not large.* We shall now examine upwind scheme for errors at small Peclet numbers. Let us examine the upwinding formula with the simple one-dimensional model being considered. $Pe > 0$ in this example. Thus,

$$(D_w + F_w + D_e)\phi_P = (D_w + F_w)\phi_W + D_e\,\phi_E$$

or in non-dimensional form

$$(2 + Pe)\phi_P = (1 + Pe)\phi_W + \phi_E$$

or

$$\frac{\phi_P - \phi_W}{\phi_E - \phi_W} = \frac{1}{2 + Pe}$$

For $Pe < 0$, it is given by

$$\frac{\phi_P - \phi_W}{\phi_E - \phi_W} = \frac{1 - Pe}{2 - Pe}$$

The balance equation for the usual linear profile assumption is given by

$$(a_E + a_W)\phi_P = a_W\phi_W + a_E\phi_E$$

or

$$\frac{\phi_P - \phi_W}{\phi_E - \phi_W} = \frac{a_E}{(a_E + a_W)} = \frac{1}{2}\left(1 - \frac{Pe}{2}\right)$$

We do have an exact formula available for the simple one dimensional problem. It can be specialized for one grid volume, say the one in the middle, by letting $L = 2\Delta x$ in eq. 12.14. The exact solution is given by

$$\frac{\phi - \phi_W}{\phi_E - \phi_W} = \frac{e^{Pe(\xi+1)} - 1}{e^{2Pe} - 1}$$

where Pe is now the grid Peclet number. In particular, $\phi = \phi_P$ at the center of the domain. Thus,

$$\frac{\phi_P - \phi_W}{\phi_E - \phi_W} = \frac{e^{Pe} - 1}{e^{2Pe} - 1}$$

The three solutions are plotted in figure 12.9. First note that the value of ϕ at P must be between those for E and W. Hence, the ordinate in the figure must always lie between zero and one. Results that assume linear profile give unrealistic results when Peclet number is less than -2 and more than 2, and this is as expected. In those ranges, upwind scheme is better than those based on assuming linear profile. The upwind scheme does worse than using the linear approximation for magnitudes of Pe smaller than around 1.5. Several hybrid schemes are proposed to get a uniformly valid expression. A simple one uses the assumption of linear profile for $-2 \leq Pe \leq 2$ and upwind scheme otherwise.

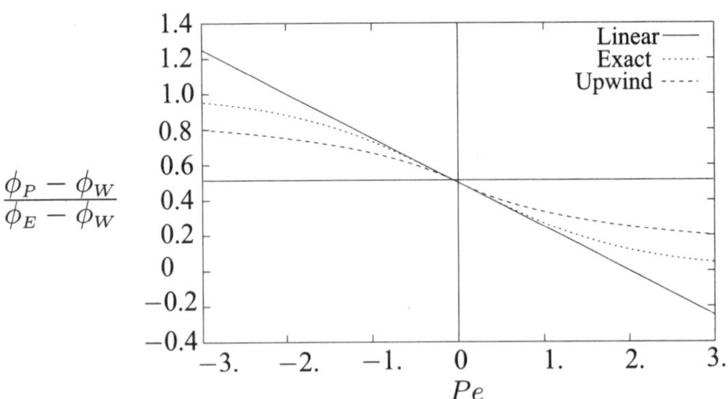

Figure 12.9. Comparison of the upwind scheme and linear profile scheme with exact solution.

Let us examine the efficacy of upwinding scheme for high Peclet numbers by returning to our numerical example for the high Peclet number case. The upwind scheme is used because the Peclet number is 5. It is easy to show that the balance equations for the internal nodes are given by

$$7\phi_P = 6\phi_W + \phi_E, \; P = 2, 3, 4$$

while those for the boundaries are given by

$$8\phi_1 = \phi_2 + 7$$

and

$$8\phi_5 = 6\phi_4$$

The solution is given in the text by Versteeg and Malasekera [5], and is shown in Table 12.5 It can

Table 12.5. Results with upwinding scheme large Peclet number.

	Variable				
	ϕ_1	ϕ_2	ϕ_3	ϕ_4	ϕ_5
Exact	1.0	0.9999	0.9999	0.9994	0.9179
Numerical	0.9998	0.9887	0.9921	0.9524	0.714

be seen that the solution does still fail at the right boundary. Thus, more complex hybrid schemes have been developed to account for this defect. You are advised to refer to textbooks on CFD for more advanced schemes.

12.9 FLOW FIELD COMPUTATION: Pressure field specified

Now we go on to the next level of complexity, but not to the full extent! The problem of determining velocity field given pressure is a task similar to what we have been discussing. This is easily seen. The equations to be solved are

$$\frac{\partial}{\partial t}(\rho) + \nabla.(\rho \mathbf{v}) = 0$$

$$\frac{\partial}{\partial t}(\rho v_i) + \nabla.(\rho \mathbf{v} v_i) = -\frac{\partial P}{\partial x_i} + \sum_j \frac{\partial}{\partial x_j}\left(\mu \frac{\partial v_i}{\partial x_j}\right) + S_i$$

where

$$S_i = \rho g_i + \sum_j \frac{\partial \mu}{\partial x_j}\frac{\partial v_j}{\partial x_i}$$

Here i or j = 1,2,3 correspond to x, y, z. The density and the three components of the velocity are the four unknowns. If the equation of state is known, the density is also known. Thus, assuming that the pressure field has been specified correctly, one of the equations is redundant. One can therefore ignore the equation of continuity and solve the three components of the equation of motion. In those equations, pressure gradient is known because pressure field is known. Thus, it can be treated as a source term. That makes the equations identical to those for diffusion of a passive scalar.

The only point that is different is that the convective terms are non-linear. This can be handled in the same way as non-linearity arising out of property variation in the conduction and convection of a passive scalar. Recall that linearization was effected in the iterative procedure. Thus, we solve the following set of equations:

$$\frac{\partial}{\partial t}(\rho v_i) + \nabla.(\rho \mathbf{v}^* v_i) = \sum_j \frac{\partial}{\partial x_j}\left(\mu \frac{\partial v_i}{\partial x_j}\right) + S_i$$

where

$$S_i = \rho g_i + \sum_j \frac{\partial \mu}{\partial x_j}\frac{\partial v_j}{\partial x_i} - \frac{\partial P}{\partial x_i}$$

and the superscript * indicates that it is the value calculated in the previous iteration. Thus, we make an initial guess for the velocity field, solve the above *linearized* equation and iterate till convergence is reached. In unsteady state problems, iteration is carried out for each time step.

For the sake of concreteness, consider a simple example of fully developed flow in a thin and wide rectangular channel. Let the direction of flow be x, and y be the direction in which the channel is thin. The equation to be solved is

$$0 = -\frac{dP}{dx} + \rho g_x + \mu \frac{d^2 v_x}{dy^2}$$

It is easily seen that this equation is identical to that solved for conduction in a fin except that the source term is a constant here whereas there it was dependent on temperature. As we mentioned in the beginning of this chapter,we will not consider the most complex problem of simultaneous determination of pressure and velocity fields.

12.10 FURTHER GENERALIZATION

So far, we have considered steady flows, and only one-dimensional problems of convection and diffusion of a passive scalar. Now we very briefly touch upon generalization to unsteady and multi-dimensional problems.

12.10.1 Steady convection and diffusion of a passive scalar in 2D

Let us now consider convection and diffusion of a passive scalar at steady state in two dimensions. We will encounter one new idea and that is the reason for including this in this chapter. *It is assumed that velocity profiles are known.* The conservation equation for steady diffusion and convection of a passive scalar in two dimensions is given by

$$\frac{\partial}{\partial x}(\rho u\phi) + \frac{\partial}{\partial y}(\rho v\phi) = \frac{\partial}{\partial x}\Gamma\frac{\partial\phi}{\partial x} + \dot{S}_\phi$$

Let us consider a control volume, which is bound by solid lines around point P shown in figure 12.10. The balance equation for the passive scalar reads,

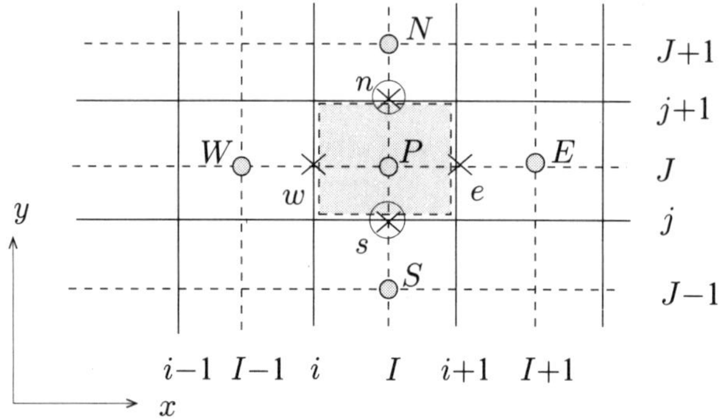

Figure 12.10. Figure shows a staggered grid. u is determined at crosses and v at crosses inside a circle. Passive scalar at grid points marked by circles.

$$(\rho u_w\phi_w)\Delta y - (\rho u_e\phi_e)\Delta y + (\rho u_s\phi_s)\Delta x - (\rho v_n\phi_n)\Delta x$$
$$-\left(\Gamma\frac{\partial\phi}{\partial x}\right)\Delta y\bigg|_w + \left(\Gamma\frac{\partial\phi}{\partial x}\right)\Delta y\bigg|_e - \left(\Gamma\frac{\partial\phi}{\partial y}\right)\Delta x\bigg|_s + \left(\Gamma\frac{\partial\phi}{\partial y}\right)\Delta x\bigg|_n + \Delta x\Delta y\ \dot{S}_\phi\,(P) = 0 \tag{12.16}$$

The values of the derivatives are evaluated by central differences as before. Thus,

$$\left(\Gamma\frac{\partial\phi}{\partial x}\right)\bigg|_w = \Gamma_w\frac{\phi_P - \phi_W}{\Delta x},\quad \left(\Gamma\frac{\partial\phi}{\partial x}\right)\bigg|_e = \Gamma_e\frac{\phi_E - \phi_P}{\Delta x}$$

and

$$\left(\Gamma\frac{\partial\phi}{\partial y}\right)\bigg|_s = \Gamma_s\frac{\phi_P - \phi_S}{\Delta y},\quad \left(\Gamma\frac{\partial\phi}{\partial y}\right)\bigg|_n = \Gamma_n\frac{\phi_N - \phi_P}{\Delta y}$$

Now let us look at evaluation of the convection terms. We need to obtain values for products of $u\phi$ and $v\phi$ at the faces bounding the control volume, *i.e.,* at e, w, n and s faces. The values of ϕ are evaluated as the average of the values at the grid points:

$$\phi_e = \frac{\phi_E + \phi_P}{2},\quad \phi_w = \frac{\phi_W + \phi_P}{2},\quad \phi_n = \frac{\phi_N + \phi_P}{2},\quad \phi_s = \frac{\phi_S + \phi_P}{2},$$

The velocities at the *faces* have to be known. This is indicated diagrammatically as follows. See figure 12.10. The control volume of interest is bound by solid lines. Hence, the faces are indicated by solid lines. Grid points lie in the control volume, and they lie on the dashed lines. Thus, while the values of the passive scalar are known on grid points marked by intersection of dashed lines, the velocities are to be known at the intersection of the solid and dashed lines. It turns out this kind of shifting of grids for different variables has to be used in computing flows in general and this scheme is known as *staggered grids*. When a flow is computed along with diffusion of a passive scalar, staggered grids have to be used. As we are assuming that velocities are known in this discussion, grids for passive scalar have to be appropriately drawn. A numbering scheme is used to indicate staggered grids. The dashed lines use capital letters as index: I in the x direction and J for the y direction. Small letters are used as index for solid lines. Refer to figure 12.10. ϕ_P is same as $\phi(I, J)$. Similarly, u_e is same as $u(i+1, J)$. Summarizing, results of computation of flow would determine $u(i, J)$ at points marked by crosses and $v(I, j)$ at points marked by crosses placed inside circles.

With this notation, the left hand side of the balance equation for the passive scalar reads,

$$v(i,J)\frac{\phi(I,J)+\phi(I-1,J)}{2}\Delta y \;-\; v(i+1,J)\frac{\phi(I,J)+\phi(I+1,J)}{2}\Delta y$$
$$+\; u(I,j)\frac{\phi(I,J-1)+\phi(I-1,J)}{2}\Delta x \;-\; u(I,j+1)\frac{\phi(I,J)+\phi(I-1,J+1)}{2}\Delta x \quad (12.17)$$

The right hand side reads

$$-\,\Gamma_w\frac{\phi_P-\phi_W}{\delta x}\Delta y + \Gamma_e\frac{\phi_E-\phi_P}{\delta x}\Delta y$$
$$-\,\Gamma_s\frac{\phi_P-\phi_S}{\delta y}\Delta x + \Gamma_n\frac{\phi_N-\phi_P}{\delta y}\Delta x, + \Delta x\Delta y\;\dot{S}_\phi\,(I,J) \quad (12.18)$$

These equations have to be solved using an iterative technique. Obviously, this is more complex, but no more new principles are involved.

12.10.2 Unsteady diffusion of passive scalars

Now we move on to consider unsteady state problems. This involves more new concepts and in order to get the principles right, we will consider only one-dimensional unsteady diffusion. Generalization to multi-dimensional problems and convection does not require any new ideas. The conservation equation takes the form

$$\frac{\partial}{\partial t}(\alpha\phi) = \frac{\partial}{\partial x}(\Gamma\frac{\partial\phi}{\partial x}) + \dot{S}_\phi$$

As an example, $\alpha = \rho\hat{C}_p$ and $\phi = T$ gives enthalpy balance for incompressible fluids, and $\alpha = 1$ and $\phi = C_i$ gives the equation of mass conservation of ith species. Consider a sub-domain of length Δx. Let the grid point in the domain be denoted by P. Balance on unit area of the sub-domain gives

$$\left.\frac{\partial\phi}{\partial t}\right|_P \Delta x = -\,\Gamma_w\frac{\phi_P-\phi_W}{\Delta x} + \Gamma_e\frac{\phi_E-\phi_P}{\Delta x} + \dot{S}_\phi\,(P)\Delta x$$

In the previous equation, both the left and right hand sides are to be evaluated at the same instant of time.

The numerical calculation starts from some known state called the *initial condition.* For convenience, the time at that instant can be written as $t = 0$. The problem is then to use the above balance equation to determine the values of ϕ after a time interval Δt. This can be seen more generally as the problem of determining the values of the dependent variable at $t + \Delta t$ given its values at t.

If we wish to use central difference scheme for time derivative also, we would need values at $t \pm (\Delta t/2)$. In particular, if we start from the initial state, we need a value at $-\Delta t/2$. This is not feasible because we do not know values prior to the initial state. Hence, we can either express the time derivative either by a forward difference scheme

$$\frac{\phi_P(t+\Delta t) - \phi_P(t)}{\Delta t} = \left.\frac{\partial \phi}{\partial t}\right|_t = \left.\left(\frac{\partial}{\partial x}(\Gamma \frac{\partial \phi}{\partial x})\right)\right|_t + \dot{S}_\phi\,(t,x)$$

or by a backward difference scheme

$$\frac{\phi_P(t) - \phi_P(t-\Delta t)}{\Delta t} = \left.\frac{\partial \phi}{\partial t}\right|_t = \left.\left(\frac{\partial}{\partial x}(\Gamma \frac{\partial \phi}{\partial x})\right)\right|_t + \dot{S}_\phi\,(t,x)$$

When the forward difference scheme is used over the sub-domain, we get

$$\Delta x \frac{\phi_P(t+\Delta t) - \phi_P(t)}{\Delta t} = -\Gamma_w \frac{\phi_P(t) - \phi_W(t)}{\Delta x} + \Gamma_e \frac{\phi_E(t) - \phi_P(t)}{\Delta x} + \dot{S}_\phi\,(t,P)\Delta x \quad (12.19)$$

It is seen that calculation of values after a time interval Δt given its values at any time t is very straight forward because the right hand side is known. In particular, if we let $t = 0$, values at Δt can be calculated, and use the values at Δt to calculate values at $2\Delta t$ and so on. This scheme is referred to as *explicit scheme* as the values at the next time step can be calculated explicitly without any iteration from the values at the previous time step. One simply 'marches' from one time to the next time. This scheme is simple but is prone to instabilities and inaccuracies.

When the backward difference scheme is used over the sub-domain, we get

$$\Delta x \frac{\phi_P(t) - \phi_P(t-\Delta t)}{\Delta t} = -\Gamma_w \frac{\phi_P(t) - \phi_W(t)}{\Delta x} + \Gamma_e \frac{\phi_E(t) - \phi_P(t)}{\Delta x} + \dot{S}_\phi\,(t,P)\Delta x \quad (12.20)$$

These form a set of simultaneous non-linear algebraic equations for $\phi(t, P)$ and these have to be solved to obtain a solution. Explicit calculation from the values at the previous time step is not possible. For this reason, this scheme is called *implicit scheme.* Implicit scheme is stable but involves iterative, and hence, time consuming procedure.

It is easy to see that an optimum has to be struck between simplicity and stability, and for more details, you are advised to refer to advanced texts on CFD. However, we will discuss one special case when properties are constant and source term is linear in ϕ.

Tridiagonal form

When properties are constant and the source term is linear in ϕ, the explicit scheme takes the form:

$$\frac{\phi_P(t) - \phi_P(t - \Delta t)}{\Delta t} = -\Gamma\frac{\phi_P(t) - \phi_W(t)}{(\Delta x)^2} + \Gamma\frac{\phi_E(t) - \phi_P(t)}{(\Delta x)^2} + \dot{S}_\phi + \dot{S}'_\phi\,\phi_P$$

It can be rearranged to read

$$-\frac{\Gamma}{(\Delta x)^2}\phi_W + \left(\frac{2\Gamma}{(\Delta x)^2} + \frac{1}{\Delta t} - \dot{S}'_\phi\right)\phi_P - \frac{\Gamma}{(\Delta x)^2}\phi_E = \dot{S}_\phi + \frac{\phi_P(t - \Delta t)}{\Delta t}$$

As can be seen, the equation for the grid point involves only its previous and next neighbor. If these linear algebraic equations are written in the form of a matrix equation, it will have a special form. Let the grid points be denoted by the index $k = 1, N$. In this new notation, if $P \equiv k$, then $W \equiv k - 1$ and $E \equiv k + 1$. The previous equation can be written as

$$a_{k,k-1}\phi_{k-1} + a_{k,k}\phi_k + a_{k,k+1}\phi_{k+1} = b_k, \quad k = 2, N - 1$$

$k = 1$ and N are the sub-domains bounded on one side by the boundary. If you refer to the earlier discussion on boundary conditions, it can be seen that the equations at these two points would take the form

$$a_{1,1}\phi_1 + a_{1,2}\phi_2 = b_1$$

and

$$a_{N,N-1}\phi_{N-1} + a_{N,N}\phi_N = b_N$$

Thus, the coefficient matrix will have only elements on the main diagonal and one diagonal each to the left and right. This is called tridiagonal form as only three diagonals of the matrix are occupied. It turns out that Gauss's elimination can be easily employed to solve this tridiagonal form, and an algorithm, known commonly as the Thomas algorithm, can be used to find the solution. Any text on CFD will give more details.

12.11 CONCLUSION

We briefly reviewed the concepts involved in solving problems in transport processes using computational techniques. The solution can be obtained only at a finite number of points in the domain. The points are placed by dividing the domain into a finite number of sub-domains or some other suitable method. The balance equations however are partial differential equations. Some approximate methods have to be used to substitute for the derivatives in terms of the geometric properties of the sub-domains and the values of the dependent variables stored at the chosen points. In this way, the partial differential equations are converted into non-linear algebraic equations which are solved by some iterative technique. Diffusion terms are treated keeping in mind their random character while the biased nature of convection requires special techniques, commonly referred to as upwinding. It was also seen that solving the convection–diffusion equation needs staggered grids where the velocities and passive scalars are stored at different points.

CFD is a very valuable and complex engineering tool. It has great depth and you should be warned not to be carried away by the simplicity reflected in this text which was obtained by placing undue emphasis on ideas. At the same time, you should not be carried away by the great volume of precise numbers, not to mention the beautiful graphics, computers produce since those come out of the physics and chemistry you have provided. Remember that the purpose of computing is not to generate numbers but to gain insight. Intelligent use of CFD based on understanding of transport phenomena is the real key to solving engineering problems.

Appendix : Brief Notes on Numerical Methods

In this appendix, we briefly outline the basics of the numerical methods. There are two key steps in numerical methods. The first is to convert the balance equations, which are partial differential equations (PDEs), into algebraic equations. The second step is the solution of the algebraic equations.

12.A Conversion of PDEs into algebraic equations

12.A.1 Finite Difference Methods

In this method, the derivatives are approximated in terms of the values at grid points. Taylor's series forms the basis of the method. Suppose we want to derive an expression for the derivative of variable T at the grid point numbered j. We can specify the number of grid points we want to use to derive the expression. Thus, we want

$$T'_j + a_o T_j + \sum_i a_{i-j,i\neq j} T_i = \text{Error}$$

where i are the indices of the grid points chosen, and a_i are coefficients. There will always be an error in this approximation because we are using a finite number of values. We determine the values of the coefficients by minimizing the error. Taylor's series is used for this purpose. It gives the following general expansion for the variable at the $(j+1)^{st}$ point:

$$T_{j+1} = T_j + T'_j h_j + \frac{h_j^2}{2} T''_j + \ldots$$

where $h_j = x_{j+1} - x_j$, and we can write similar expression for values of T at other grid points. Suppose we want to derive an expression for the derivative at j^{th} point in terms of only the value at grid point $j+1$. The expression would now read

$$T'_j + a_o T_j + a_1 T_{j+1} = \text{Error}$$

The following table can be made using Taylor's series:

Value at Grid point	Coefficient of T_j	Coefficient of T'_j	Coefficient of T''_j
T_j	1	0	0
T_{j+1}	1	h_j	$\frac{h_j^2}{2}$

Substituting for the grid point values using these expressions, we can rewrite our equation for the derivative as

$$T'_j + a_o T_j + a_1 T_j + a_1 h_j T'_j + a_1 \frac{h_j^2}{2} T''_j + \ldots = \text{Error}$$

We want to make the left hand side as close to zero as is possible. Anticipating that the step size h is expected to be small, this is done by choosing

$$a_1 = -\frac{1}{h_j}, \text{ and } a_o = -a_1$$

The term left, or the error, is of the order of $a_1 h_j$ or of the order of h_j. Substituting the values for the coefficients, we have

$$T'_j = \frac{T_{j+1} - T_j}{h_j} + \text{ terms proportional to } h_j$$

The error is of the order of h_j. This scheme is referred to as **forward difference scheme** since we obtained the derivative at a point by taking the difference between the value at a point ahead and the value at the current point. We would have derived a similar formula if we had chosen to use only the $(j-1)^{st}$ grid point to calculate the derivative at the jth point, and we would have found that also would have an error of the order of h. That formula is referred to as the **backward difference scheme**.

The error analysis indicates that if the grid size is decreased by a factor of two, the accuracy improves by a factor of two. This indicates that grid size has to be as small as possible to obtain the best possible accuracy.

Let us illustrate the method with one more example. Now suppose we want to derive an expression in terms of values at grid points $j-1$ and $j+1$. Now the expression for derivative is

$$T'_j + a_{-1}T_{j-1} + a_o T_j + a_1 T_{j+1} = \text{Error}$$

The table using Taylor's series now looks as follows

Value at Grid point	Coefficient of T_j	Coefficient of T'_j	Coefficient of T''_j	Coefficient of T'''_j
T_{j-1}	1	$-h_{j-1}$	$\frac{h_{j-1}^2}{2}$	$-\frac{h_{j-1}^3}{6}$
T_j	1	0	0	0
T_{j+1}	1	h_j	$\frac{h_j^2}{2}$	$\frac{h_j^3}{6}$

Substituting the expressions from table into our desired expression, we have

$$(1 - a_{-1}h_{j-1} + a_1 h_j)T'_j + (a_{-1} + a_o + a_1)T_j + (a_{-1}\frac{h_{j-1}^2}{2} + a_1\frac{h_j^2}{2})T''_j = \text{Terms of the order } (h_j^3 + h_{j-1}^3)$$

The left hand side can be minimized by letting

$$a_{-1}h_{j-1} - a_1 h_j = 1; \; a_{-1} + a_o + a_1 = 0; \text{ and } a_{-1}\frac{h_{j-1}^2}{2} + a_1\frac{h_j^2}{2} = 0$$

This leaves an error of the order of h^3. These can be solved to obtain

$$a_{-1} = \frac{h_j}{h_{j-1}(h_j + h_{j-1})}; \; a_o = -\frac{h_j - h_{j-1}}{h_j + h_{j-1}}; \; a_1 = -\frac{h_{j-1}}{h_j(h_j + h_{j-1})}$$

Hence, we have

$$T_j' = -\frac{h_j}{h_{j-1}(h_j + h_{j-1})} T_{j-1} + \frac{h_j - h_{j-1}}{h_j + h_{j-1}} T_j + \frac{h_{j-1}}{h_j(h_j + h_{j-1})} T_{j+1}$$

and the error is of the order of h^2.

The method has been illustrated for the general case where the step size is not equal. If the step size is equal, then all h are equal and for this special case, $-a_o = a_1 = 1/(2h)$. Hence,

$$T_j' = \frac{T_{j+1} - T_{j-1}}{2h}$$

and the error is of the order of h^2. This scheme is referred to as **central difference scheme** since values at points immediately ahead and behind are being used to evaluate the derivative at a point at the center of the two. The error decreases by a factor of four if the grid size is decrease by a factor of two as the error is of the order of h^2. For constant grid size, the central difference scheme is obviously more accurate than the scheme derived earlier by taking only two points.

Similar procedure can be followed to derive expressions for derivatives, and higher derivatives in terms of values at the grid points. This procedure is particularly useful when derivatives at boundary grid points have to be obtained to a greater accuracy than h using interior grid points. When these expressions are substituted into the equations of change, a system of non-linear algebraic equations are obtained. The values at the grid points can be obtained by solving them. This is the essence of finite difference methods.

Finite difference method is widely investigated from a mathematical view point and plenty of information is available on its convergence properties and errors involved. However, there is no proof that all the properties of the original differential equations are retained **over the whole domain** when the approximations for the derivatives are inserted into them. For example, all the equations of change represent conservation of some quantity or the other. It is not guaranteed that conservation of these quantities is obeyed by the finite difference approximation. Quantities are conserved better and better as the grid size is decreased as per the error analysis of the method.

12.A.2 Weighted Residual Methods

An assumed form for the solution *over the whole domain* is the starting point for these methods. For example, for the dependent variable u, one can start with an approximation u^*:

$$u^* = \sum_i A_i \phi_i$$

where ϕ_i are some functions of the independent variable, say x. For example, if

$$\phi_1 = 1; \; \phi_i = x^i$$

the dependent variable is being approximated by a polynomial.

Symbolically, the partial differential equation obeyed by the dependent variable can be written as

$$L u - S = 0$$

where L is an operator. For example, fully developed and steady laminar flow between parallel plates is represented by the following equation:

$$\frac{d^2 u}{dy^2} - \frac{1}{\mu}\frac{dP}{dy} = 0$$

Thus, if $L = d^2/dy^2$ and $s = (1/\mu)dP/dy$, then the equation can be written as

$$L u - S = 0$$

The assumed form for u is obviously approximate unless we are awfully lucky. Hence, $L u^* - S$ will not be equal to zero,

$$L u^* - S = \mathcal{R}$$

and the error $\mathcal{R}$ is referred to as the residual. The weighted residual methods determine the values of the constants by using some criteria to reduce the error or the residual. To make the discussion convenient, suppose that there are A_i, $i = 1, 2 \ldots n$ constants to be determined. Then, n weighting functions, $\mathcal{W}_n$ can be chosen. The constants are determined by requiring that

$$\int_{\mathcal{V}} \mathcal{W}_n \mathcal{R}\, dV = 0$$

where $\mathcal{V}$ is the domain. These will form n equations for the n unknown constants. We show a few examples of this procedure.

Sub-domain method

In this method, the whole domain is divided into as many sub-domains as there are unknown constants. Let the sub-domains be referred to by $\mathcal{V}_n$. The constants can be determined by requiring that the average of the residual be zero over each sub-domain:

$$\int_{\mathcal{V}_n} \mathcal{R}\, dV = 0$$

This is equivalent to choosing weighting functions to be delta functions, one in each domain. Finite volume methods belong to this category.

Collocation

In this method, the residual is equated to zero at n points, referred to as *collocation points*:

$$(Lu^* - S)_i = \mathcal{R}_i = 0; \ x = x_i; \ i = 1, n$$

and these equations are used to determine the unknown constants. If functions chosen to approximate the dependent variable, ϕ, belong to a set of orthogonal polynomials up to $(n-1)^{st}$ order, and the points chosen are roots of the nth order orthogonal polynomial of the same set, the method is referred to as orthogonal collocation. It is shown in books on collocation that, for a given number of collocation points, the error is reduced considerably in orthogonal collocation.

Least square minimization

In this method, the square of the residual is minimized by appropriate choice of constants. The constants are therefore determined from the following equations:

$$\frac{\partial}{\partial A_i} \int_{\mathcal{V}_n} \mathcal{R}^2 \, dV = 0$$

This is equivalent to choosing

$$\mathcal{W}_n = \frac{\partial}{\partial A_i} \mathcal{R}$$

Galerkin technique

This technique is widely used in finite element methods. In this method, the weighting functions are chosen to be the approximating functions themselves:

$$\int_{\mathcal{V}} dV \phi_i \mathcal{R} = 0; \ i = 0, n$$

It is attempting to make the error vector orthogonal to the approximating functions.

12.B Iterative methods of solution

After discretization, the balance equations become non-linear algebraic equations. Newton–Raphson is usually the technique used to solve such equations. In general however, as the grid points used are large in number, the number of equations is also large, and the commonly used techniques are too time consuming to be employed. Thus, through some procedure, the non-linear algebraic equations are linearized, and solved. Linear algebraic equations can be solved by inverting the coefficient matrix. Even this technique, though well established, is also time consuming to be employed when the number of equations is large. Therefore, iterative techniques are commonly used to solve the set of linear algebraic equations that result from balance equations. Here we summarize Gauss–Siedel technique which is commonly employed in CFD.

The balance equations have the following form:

$$a_P \phi_P = \sum a_{nb} \phi_{nb} + S_c$$

where it is possible that the coefficients are a function of ϕ. Iterative procedure starts with a guess for all the unknowns. The coefficients appearing in the equations can be calculated as a function of the guesses. The equations are then linear. Denote the guessed values of the variables and the coefficients by putting star as a superscript. The equations to be solved are therefore given by

$$a_P^* \phi_P = \sum a_{nb}^* \phi_{nb}^* + S_c^*$$

The equations are solved, and the resulting values are used as the next guess. Iteration proceeds till a specified accuracy is attained. The linear equations themselves are not inverted as mentioned before, but solved using the guessed values in the following way. The order of solution in terms of grid points is chosen in any convenient manner. Suppose it is 1, 3, 5, 2,..., N. The solution then starts with point 1. Then, the following equation

$$a_1^* \phi_1 = \sum a_{nb}^* \phi_{nb}^* + S_c^*$$

is solved to get ϕ_1. This forms the next guess for ϕ_1 and is used in all the calculations that follow, *i.e.*, in the current iteration itself. Though it sounds arbitrary, it saves storage space and so is convenient to use. The next one to be solved for the chosen order is 3:

$$a_3^* \phi_3 = \sum a_{nb}^* \phi_{nb}^* + S_c^*$$

for all neighboring points except for ϕ_1. The final one to be solved is

$$a_N^* \phi_N = \sum a_{nb}^* \phi_{nb} + S_c^*$$

The solution proceeds in this manner by visiting each grid point once in an iteration. The values of ϕ at the end of the iteration form the guesses for the next iteration.

In the text, we have discussed the Scarborough criteria to be satisfied that produces a converged solution by this technique. Here a beautiful example given in Patankar [4] is reproduced to induce caution in using the method. Consider solution of the following equation

$$T_1 = 0.4T_2 + 0.2, \; T_2 = T_1 + 1$$

The exact solution is $T_1 = 1$ and $T_2 = 2$. Scarborough criterion is satisfied. Initial guess is taken to be zero for both the variables. The successive iterations are listed below:

Variable	Iteration						
	Initial	1	2	3	4	5	∞
T_1	0	0.2	0.68	0.872	0.949	0.98	1
T_2	0	1.2	1.68	1.872	1.949	1.98	2

However, if the equations are written as

$$T_1 = T_2 - 1 \; T_2 = 2.5T_1 - 0.5$$

and solved, the following results are obtained!

Variable	Iteration				
	Initial	1	2	3	4
T_1	0	− 1	− 4	− 11.5	− 30.25
T_2	0	−3	− 10.5	− 29.25	− 76.13

Notes

[1]In reality, there are many more! Computers and hence CFD can only do what you want it to do. It is not an autonomous result producing algorithm. CFD cannot make approximations by itself. CFD basically is doing numerical work, of course and very much faster than we can do.

[2]Continuing this line of thought we take a leaf out of the editorial written by Prof J.M. Smith in July 1995 issue of part A of *Trans. I. Chem. E.*: CFD stands for **C**olorful **F**igures and **D**iagrams; **C**on**F**use**D**; **C**leverly **F**unding **D**reams; **C**hance **F**or **D**rinks!

[3]Position and time are the independent variables.

[4]The boundaries of domains cannot always be described in Cartesian coordinates. In such instances, some interpolation techniques are used to specify boundary conditions. This procedure is used as a compromise between computational convenience and inconvenience caused in implementing boundary conditions. For more details, readers should refer to a text on CFD itself.

[5]Hence, the solution can be considered dilute.

[6]The procedure to do this is given in the appendix.

[7] In the weighted residuals method, normally a form is assumed for the solution and substituted into the differential equation, and the resultant equation is integrated over the sub-domain to minimize the error. In finite volume method, there is a slight reversal of the procedure but the end result is the same if linear approximations are used.

[8]Date [2] proposed that the averaging be done by using the concept of equivalent resistances, and it works very well when dealing with boundaries between two materials whose thermal conductivities are widely different.

[9]Derivation of the balance equation is given in the text by Bird *et al.* [1] as well as in many text books on heat transfer.

[10]You would benefit by referring to (and solving!) the exercise associated with the problem on radial reactor in chapter 8.

[11]The numbers for this example have been taken from page 108 of the text by Versteeg and Malasekera [5].

References

[1] R.B. Bird, W.E. Stewart, and E.N. Lightfoot. *Transport Phenomena.* John Wiley, 2 edition, 2002.

[2] A.W. Date. *Introduction to computational fluid dynamics.* Cambridge University Press, 2005.

[3] C.A.J. Fletcher. *Computational techniques for fluid dynamics*, volume 2. Springer, 2 edition, 1991.

[4] S.V. Patankar. *Numerical heat transfer and fluid flow.* Taylor & Francis, 1980.

[5] H.K. Versteeg and W. Malasekera. *An introduction to computational fluid dynamics.* Longman, 1995.

APPENDIX

Equations of change in different coordinate systems

Equation of continuity

Rectangular coordinates

$$\frac{D\rho}{Dt} = \frac{\partial \rho}{\partial t} + v_x \frac{\partial \rho}{\partial x} + v_y \frac{\partial \rho}{\partial y} + v_z \frac{\partial \rho}{\partial z} = -\rho \nabla.\mathbf{v} = -\rho \left(\frac{\partial v_x}{\partial x} + \frac{\partial v_y}{\partial y} + \frac{\partial v_z}{\partial z} \right)$$

Cylindrical coordinates

$$\frac{D\rho}{Dt} = \frac{\partial \rho}{\partial t} + v_r \frac{\partial \rho}{\partial r} + \frac{v_\theta}{r} \frac{\partial \rho}{\partial \theta} + v_z \frac{\partial \rho}{\partial z} = -\rho \nabla.\mathbf{v} = -\rho \left(\frac{1}{r} \frac{\partial}{\partial r}(r v_r) + \frac{1}{r} \frac{\partial v_\theta}{\partial \theta} + \frac{\partial v_z}{\partial z} \right)$$

Spherical coordinates

$$\begin{aligned} \frac{D\rho}{Dt} = \frac{\partial \rho}{\partial t} + v_r \frac{\partial \rho}{\partial r} + \frac{v_\theta}{r} \frac{\partial \rho}{\partial \theta} &+ \frac{v_\phi}{r \sin\theta} \frac{\partial \rho}{\partial \phi} = -\rho \nabla.\mathbf{v} \\ &= -\rho \left(\frac{1}{r^2} \frac{\partial}{\partial r}(r^2 v_r) + \frac{1}{r \sin\theta} \frac{\partial}{\partial \theta}(v_\theta \sin\theta) + \frac{1}{r \sin\theta} \frac{\partial v_\phi}{\partial \phi} \right) \end{aligned}$$

Equations of motion for fluids

Rectangular coordinates

Cauchy's equation of motion

x Component:

$$\rho \left(\frac{\partial v_x}{\partial t} + v_x \frac{\partial v_x}{\partial x} + v_y \frac{\partial v_x}{\partial y} + v_z \frac{\partial v_x}{\partial z} \right) = -\frac{\partial P}{\partial x} + \frac{\partial \tau_{xx}}{\partial x} + \frac{\partial \tau_{yx}}{\partial y} + \frac{\partial \tau_{zx}}{\partial z} + \rho g_x$$

y Component:

$$\rho \left(\frac{\partial v_y}{\partial t} + v_x \frac{\partial v_y}{\partial x} + v_y \frac{\partial v_y}{\partial y} + v_z \frac{\partial v_y}{\partial z} \right) = -\frac{\partial P}{\partial y} + \frac{\partial \tau_{xy}}{\partial x} + \frac{\partial \tau_{yy}}{\partial y} + \frac{\partial \tau_{zy}}{\partial z} + \rho g_y$$

z Component:

$$\rho \left(\frac{\partial v_z}{\partial t} + v_x \frac{\partial v_z}{\partial x} + v_y \frac{\partial v_z}{\partial y} + v_z \frac{\partial v_z}{\partial z} \right) = -\frac{\partial P}{\partial z} + \frac{\partial \tau_{xz}}{\partial x} + \frac{\partial \tau_{yz}}{\partial y} + \frac{\partial \tau_{zz}}{\partial z} + \rho g_z$$

Navier–Stokes equations for an incompressible Newtonian Fluid

x Component:

$$\rho\left(\frac{\partial v_x}{\partial t}+v_x\frac{\partial v_x}{\partial x}+v_y\frac{\partial v_x}{\partial y}+v_z\frac{\partial v_x}{\partial z}\right)=-\frac{\partial P}{\partial x}+\mu\left(\frac{\partial^2 v_x}{\partial x^2}+\frac{\partial^2 v_x}{\partial y^2}+\frac{\partial^2 v_x}{\partial z^2}\right)+\rho g_x$$

y Component:

$$\rho\left(\frac{\partial v_y}{\partial t}+v_x\frac{\partial v_y}{\partial x}+v_y\frac{\partial v_y}{\partial y}+v_z\frac{\partial v_y}{\partial z}\right)=-\frac{\partial P}{\partial y}+\mu\left(\frac{\partial^2 v_y}{\partial x^2}+\frac{\partial^2 v_y}{\partial y^2}+\frac{\partial^2 v_y}{\partial z^2}\right)+\rho g_y$$

z Component:

$$\rho\left(\frac{\partial v_z}{\partial t}+v_x\frac{\partial v_z}{\partial x}+v_y\frac{\partial v_z}{\partial y}+v_z\frac{\partial v_z}{\partial z}\right)=-\frac{\partial P}{\partial z}+\mu\left(\frac{\partial^2 v_z}{\partial x^2}+\frac{\partial^2 v_z}{\partial y^2}+\frac{\partial^2 v_z}{\partial z^2}\right)+\rho g_z$$

Newton–Stokes law of viscosity

$$\begin{aligned}\tau_{ii} &= 2\mu\left(\frac{\partial v_i}{\partial x_i}-\frac{1}{3}\nabla.\mathbf{v}\right) \quad i=x,y,z\\ \tau_{ij} &= \mu\left(\frac{\partial v_i}{\partial x_j}+\frac{\partial v_j}{\partial xi}\right) \quad i=x,y,z;j=x,y,z;i\neq j\end{aligned}$$

Cylindrical coordinates

Cauchy's equation of motion

r Component:

$$\rho\left(\frac{\partial v_r}{\partial t}+v_r\frac{\partial v_r}{\partial r}+\frac{v_\theta}{r}\frac{\partial v_r}{\partial \theta}-\frac{v_\theta^2}{r}+v_z\frac{\partial v_r}{\partial z}\right)$$
$$=-\frac{\partial P}{\partial r}+\frac{1}{r}\frac{\partial}{\partial r}(r\tau_{rr})+\frac{1}{r}\frac{\partial \tau_{\theta r}}{\partial \theta}-\frac{\tau_{\theta\theta}}{r}+\frac{\partial \tau_{zr}}{\partial z}+\rho g_r$$

θ Component:

$$\rho\left(\frac{\partial v_\theta}{\partial t}+v_r\frac{\partial v_\theta}{\partial r}+\frac{v_\theta}{r}\frac{\partial v_\theta}{\partial \theta}+\frac{v_r v_\theta}{r}+v_z\frac{\partial v_\theta}{\partial z}\right)$$
$$=-\frac{1}{r}\frac{\partial P}{\partial \theta}+\frac{1}{r^2}\frac{\partial}{\partial r}(r^2\tau_{r\theta})+\frac{1}{r}\frac{\partial \tau_{\theta\theta}}{\partial \theta}+\frac{\partial \tau_{z\theta}}{\partial z}+\rho g_\theta$$

z Component:

$$\rho\left(\frac{\partial v_z}{\partial t}+v_r\frac{\partial v_z}{\partial r}+\frac{v_\theta}{r}\frac{\partial v_z}{\partial \theta}+v_z\frac{\partial v_z}{\partial z}\right) = -\frac{\partial P}{\partial z}+\frac{1}{r}\frac{\partial}{\partial r}(r\tau_{rz})+\frac{1}{r}\frac{\partial \tau_{\theta z}}{\partial \theta}+\frac{\partial \tau_{zz}}{\partial z}+\rho g_z$$

Navier–Stokes equations for an incompressible Newtonian Fluid

r Component:

$$\rho\left(\frac{\partial v_r}{\partial t}+v_r\frac{\partial v_r}{\partial r}+\frac{v_\theta}{r}\frac{\partial v_r}{\partial \theta}-\frac{v_\theta^2}{r}+v_z\frac{\partial v_r}{\partial z}\right) = -\frac{\partial P}{\partial r}+\mu\left[\frac{\partial}{\partial r}\left(\frac{1}{r}\frac{\partial}{\partial r}(rv_r)\right)+\frac{1}{r^2}\frac{\partial^2 v_r}{\partial \theta^2}-\frac{2}{r^2}\frac{\partial v_\theta}{\partial \theta}+\frac{\partial^2 v_r}{\partial z^2}\right]+\rho g_r$$

θ Component:

$$\rho\left(\frac{\partial v_\theta}{\partial t}+v_r\frac{\partial v_\theta}{\partial r}+\frac{v_\theta}{r}\frac{\partial v_\theta}{\partial \theta}+\frac{v_r v_\theta}{r}+v_z\frac{\partial v_\theta}{\partial z}\right) = -\frac{1}{r}\frac{\partial P}{\partial \theta}+\mu\left[\frac{\partial}{\partial r}\left(\frac{1}{r}\frac{\partial}{\partial r}(rv_\theta)\right)+\frac{1}{r^2}\frac{\partial^2 v_\theta}{\partial \theta^2}+\frac{2}{r^2}\frac{\partial v_r}{\partial \theta}+\frac{\partial^2 v_\theta}{\partial z^2}\right]+\rho g_\theta$$

z Component:

$$\rho\left(\frac{\partial v_z}{\partial t}+v_r\frac{\partial v_z}{\partial r}+\frac{v_\theta}{r}\frac{\partial v_z}{\partial \theta}+v_z\frac{\partial v_z}{\partial z}\right) = -\frac{\partial P}{\partial z}+\mu\left[\frac{1}{r}\frac{\partial}{\partial r}\left(r\frac{\partial v_z}{\partial r}\right)+\frac{1}{r^2}\frac{\partial^2 v_z}{\partial \theta^2}+\frac{\partial^2 v_z}{\partial z^2}\right]+\rho g_z$$

Newton–Stokes law of viscosity

$$\begin{aligned}
\tau_{rr} &= 2\mu\left(\frac{\partial v_r}{\partial r}-\frac{1}{3}\nabla.\mathbf{v}\right)\\
\tau_{\theta\theta} &= 2\mu\left(\frac{1}{r}\frac{\partial v_\theta}{\partial \theta}+\frac{v_r}{r}-\frac{1}{3}\nabla.\mathbf{v}\right)\\
\tau_{zz} &= 2\mu\left(\frac{\partial v_z}{\partial z}-\frac{1}{3}\nabla.\mathbf{v}\right)\\
\tau_{r\theta}=\tau_{\theta r} &= \mu\left(r\frac{\partial}{\partial r}\left(\frac{v_\theta}{r}\right)+\frac{1}{r}\frac{\partial v_r}{\partial \theta}\right)\\
\tau_{z\theta}=\tau_{\theta z} &= \mu\left(\frac{\partial v_\theta}{\partial z}+\frac{1}{r}\frac{\partial v_z}{\partial \theta}\right)\\
\tau_{rz}=\tau_{zr} &= \mu\left(\frac{\partial v_z}{\partial r}+\frac{\partial v_r}{\partial z}\right)
\end{aligned}$$

Spherical coordinates

Cauchy's equation of motion

r Component:

$$\rho\left(\frac{\partial v_r}{\partial t}+v_r\frac{\partial v_r}{\partial r}+\frac{v_\theta}{r}\frac{\partial v_r}{\partial \theta}+\frac{v_\phi}{r\sin\theta}\frac{\partial v_r}{\partial \phi}-\frac{v_\theta^2+v_\phi^2}{r}\right)$$
$$=-\frac{\partial P}{\partial r}+\frac{1}{r^2}\frac{\partial}{\partial r}(r^2\tau_{rr})+\frac{1}{r\sin\theta}\frac{\partial}{\partial\theta}(\tau_{\theta r}\sin\theta)+\frac{1}{r\sin\theta}\frac{\partial \tau_{\phi r}}{\partial\phi}-\frac{\tau_{\theta\theta}+\tau_{\phi\phi}}{r}+\rho g_r$$

θ Component:

$$\rho\left(\frac{\partial v_\theta}{\partial t}+v_r\frac{\partial v_\theta}{\partial r}+\frac{v_\theta}{r}\frac{\partial v_\theta}{\partial \theta}+\frac{v_\phi}{r\sin\theta}\frac{\partial v_\theta}{\partial \phi}+\frac{v_r v_\theta}{r}-\frac{v_\phi^2\cot\theta}{r}\right)$$
$$=-\frac{1}{r}\frac{\partial P}{\partial \theta}+\frac{1}{r^3}\frac{\partial}{\partial r}(r^3\tau_{r\theta})+\frac{1}{r\sin\theta}\frac{\partial}{\partial\theta}(\tau_{\theta\theta}\sin\theta)+\frac{1}{r\sin\theta}\frac{\partial \tau_{\phi\theta}}{\partial\phi}-\frac{\cot\theta}{r}\tau_{\phi\phi}+\rho g_\theta$$

ϕ Component:

$$\rho\left(\frac{\partial v_\phi}{\partial t}+v_r\frac{\partial v_\phi}{\partial r}+\frac{v_\theta}{r}\frac{\partial v_\phi}{\partial \theta}+\frac{v_\phi}{r\sin\theta}\frac{\partial v_\phi}{\partial \phi}+\frac{v_r v_\phi}{r}+\frac{v_\theta v_\phi}{r}\cot\theta\right)$$
$$=-\frac{1}{r\sin\theta}\frac{\partial P}{\partial \phi}+\frac{1}{r^3}\frac{\partial}{\partial r}(r^3\tau_{r\phi})+\frac{1}{r\sin^2\theta}\frac{\partial}{\partial\theta}(\tau_{\theta\phi}\sin^2\theta)+\frac{1}{r\sin\theta}\frac{\partial \tau_{\phi\phi}}{\partial\phi}+\rho g_\phi$$

Navier–Stokes equations for an incompressible Newtonian Fluid

$$\nabla^2=\frac{1}{r^2}\frac{\partial}{\partial r}\left(r^2\frac{\partial}{\partial r}\right)+\frac{1}{r^2\sin\theta}\frac{\partial}{\partial\theta}\left(\sin\theta\frac{\partial}{\partial\theta}\right)+\frac{1}{r^2\sin^2\theta}\left(\frac{\partial^2}{\partial\phi^2}\right)$$

r Component:

$$\rho\left(\frac{\partial v_r}{\partial t}+v_r\frac{\partial v_r}{\partial r}+\frac{v_\theta}{r}\frac{\partial v_r}{\partial \theta}+\frac{v_\phi}{r\sin\theta}\frac{\partial v_r}{\partial \phi}-\frac{v_\theta^2+v_\phi^2}{r}\right)$$
$$=-\frac{\partial P}{\partial r}+\mu\left(\nabla^2 v_r-\frac{2}{r^2}v_r-\frac{2}{r^2}\frac{\partial v_\theta}{\partial\theta}-\frac{2}{r^2}v_\theta\cot\theta-\frac{2}{r^2\sin\theta}\frac{\partial v_\phi}{\partial\phi}\right)+\rho g_r$$

θ Component:

$$\rho\left(\frac{\partial v_\theta}{\partial t}+v_r\frac{\partial v_\theta}{\partial r}+\frac{v_\theta}{r}\frac{\partial v_\theta}{\partial \theta}+\frac{v_\phi}{r\sin\theta}\frac{\partial v_\theta}{\partial \phi}+\frac{v_r v_\theta}{r}-\frac{v_\phi^2\cot\theta}{r}\right)$$

$$= -\frac{1}{r}\frac{\partial P}{\partial \theta} + \mu\left(\nabla^2 v_\theta + \frac{2}{r^2}\frac{\partial v_r}{\partial \theta} - \frac{v_\theta}{r^2\sin^2\theta} - \frac{2cos\theta}{r^2\sin^2\theta}\frac{\partial v_\phi}{\partial \phi}\right) + \rho g_\theta$$

ϕ Component:

$$\rho\left(\frac{\partial v_\phi}{\partial t} + v_r\frac{\partial v_\phi}{\partial r} + \frac{v_\theta}{r}\frac{\partial v_\phi}{\partial \theta} + \frac{v_\phi}{r\sin\theta}\frac{\partial v_\phi}{\partial \phi} + \frac{v_r v_\phi}{r} + \frac{v_\theta v_\phi}{r}\cot\theta\right)$$
$$= -\frac{1}{r\sin\theta}\frac{\partial P}{\partial \phi} + \mu\left(\nabla^2 v_\phi - \frac{v_\phi}{r^2\sin^2\theta} + \frac{2}{r^2\sin\theta}\frac{\partial v_r}{\partial \phi} + \frac{2\cos\theta}{r^2\sin^2\theta}\frac{\partial v_\theta}{\partial \phi}\right) + \rho g_\phi$$

Newton–Stokes law of viscosity

$$\tau_{rr} = 2\mu\left(\frac{\partial v_r}{\partial r} - \frac{1}{3}\nabla.\mathbf{v}\right)$$
$$\tau_{\theta\theta} = 2\mu\left(\frac{1}{r}\frac{\partial v_\theta}{\partial \theta} + \frac{v_r}{r} - \frac{1}{3}\nabla.\mathbf{v}\right)$$
$$\tau_{\phi\phi} = 2\mu\left(\frac{1}{r\sin\theta}\frac{\partial v_\phi}{\partial \phi} + \frac{v_r}{r} + \frac{v_\theta\cot\theta}{r} - \frac{1}{3}\nabla.\mathbf{v}\right)$$
$$\tau_{r\theta} = \tau_{\theta r} = \mu\left(r\frac{\partial}{\partial r}\left(\frac{v_\theta}{r}\right) + \frac{1}{r}\frac{\partial v_r}{\partial \theta}\right)$$
$$\tau_{r\phi} = \tau_{\phi r} = \mu\left(r\frac{\partial}{\partial r}\left(\frac{v_\phi}{r}\right) + \frac{1}{r\sin\theta}\frac{\partial v_r}{\partial \phi}\right)$$
$$\tau_{\theta\phi} = \tau_{\phi\theta} = \mu\left(\frac{\sin\theta}{r}\frac{\partial}{\partial \theta}\left(\frac{v_\phi}{\sin\theta}\right) + \frac{1}{r\sin\theta}\frac{\partial v_\theta}{\partial \phi}\right)$$

Equation of change of temperature (for a single component Newtonian fluid with constant properties.

$\dot{Q}$ represents rate of generation of heat per unit volume. It could be due to chemical reactions, viscous heat dissipation or other sources of energy. The viscous dissipation term is written as Φ_v. It is given by $\boldsymbol{\tau}{:}(\nabla\mathbf{v})$

Rectangular coordinates

$$\rho\hat{C}_p\left(\frac{\partial T}{\partial t} + v_x\frac{\partial T}{\partial x} + v_y\frac{\partial T}{\partial y} + v_z\frac{\partial T}{\partial z}\right) = k\left(\frac{\partial^2 T}{\partial x^2} + \frac{\partial^2 T}{\partial y^2} + \frac{\partial^2 T}{\partial z^2}\right) + \dot{Q} + \Phi_v \quad \text{(I.1)}$$

Fourier's law

$$q_x = -k\frac{\partial T}{\partial x},\ q_y = -k\frac{\partial T}{\partial y},\ q_z = -k\frac{\partial T}{\partial z} \quad \text{(I.2)}$$

Cylindrical coordinates

$$\rho \hat{C}_p \left(\frac{\partial T}{\partial t} + v_r \frac{\partial T}{\partial r} + \frac{v_\theta}{r} \frac{\partial T}{\partial \theta} + v_z \frac{\partial T}{\partial z} \right) = k \left[\frac{1}{r} \frac{\partial}{\partial r} \left(r \frac{\partial T}{\partial r} \right) + \frac{1}{r^2} \frac{\partial^2 T}{\partial \theta^2} + \frac{\partial^2 T}{\partial z^2} \right] + \dot{Q} + \Phi_v \quad \text{(I.3)}$$

Fourier's law

$$q_r = -k \frac{\partial T}{\partial r}, \quad q_\theta = -k \frac{1}{r} \frac{\partial T}{\partial \theta}, \quad q_z = -k \frac{\partial T}{\partial z} \quad \text{(I.4)}$$

Spherical coordinates

$$\rho \hat{C}_p \left(\frac{\partial T}{\partial t} + v_r \frac{\partial T}{\partial r} + \frac{v_\theta}{r} \frac{\partial T}{\partial \theta} + \frac{v_\phi}{r \sin\theta} \frac{\partial T}{\partial \phi} \right)$$
$$= k \left[\frac{1}{r^2} \frac{\partial}{\partial r} \left(r^2 \frac{\partial T}{\partial r} \right) + \frac{1}{r^2 \sin\theta} \frac{\partial}{\partial \theta} \left(\sin\theta \frac{\partial T}{\partial \theta} \right) + \frac{1}{r^2 \sin^2\theta} \frac{\partial T}{\partial \phi^2} \right] + \dot{Q} + \Phi_v \quad \text{(I.5)}$$

Fourier's law

$$q_r = -k \frac{\partial T}{\partial r}, \quad q_\theta = -k \frac{1}{r} \frac{\partial T}{\partial \theta}, \quad q_\phi = -k \frac{1}{r \sin\theta} \frac{\partial T}{\partial \phi} \quad \text{(I.6)}$$

Equation of conservation of species

Molar form: $\dot{\mathcal{R}}_i$ represents rate of generation of moles of species i per unit volume.

Rectangular coordinates

$$\frac{\partial C_i}{\partial t} + \frac{\partial N_{ix}}{\partial x} + \frac{\partial N_{iy}}{\partial y} + \frac{\partial N_{iz}}{\partial z} = \dot{\mathcal{R}}_i$$

Cylindrical coordinates

$$\frac{\partial C_i}{\partial t} + \frac{1}{r} \frac{\partial}{\partial r} (r N_{ir}) + \frac{1}{r} \frac{\partial N_{i\theta}}{\partial \theta} + \frac{\partial N_{iz}}{\partial z} = \dot{\mathcal{R}}_i$$

Spherical coordinates

$$\frac{\partial C_i}{\partial t} + \frac{1}{r^2} \frac{\partial}{\partial r} (r^2 N_{ir}) + \frac{1}{r \sin\theta} \frac{\partial}{\partial \theta} (N_{i\theta} \sin\theta) + \frac{1}{r \sin\theta} \frac{\partial N_{i\phi}}{\partial \phi} = \dot{\mathcal{R}}_i$$

Equation of change of concentration for a binary system (Constant density and diffusion coefficient.)

Rectangular coordinates

$$\frac{\partial C_A}{\partial t} + v_x \frac{\partial C_A}{\partial x} + v_y \frac{\partial C_A}{\partial y} + v_z \frac{\partial C_A}{\partial z} = \mathcal{D}_{AB} \left(\frac{\partial^2 C_A}{\partial x^2} + \frac{\partial^2 C_A}{\partial y^2} + \frac{\partial^2 C_A}{\partial z^2} \right) + \dot{\mathcal{R}}_A \tag{I.7}$$

Fick's law

$$\begin{aligned}
N_{Ax} &= -\mathcal{D}_{AB} \frac{\partial C_A}{\partial x} + \left(N_{Ax} + N_{Bx} \right) \frac{C_A}{C} \\
N_{Ay} &= -\mathcal{D}_{AB} \frac{\partial C_A}{\partial y} + \left(N_{Ay} + N_{By} \right) \frac{C_A}{C} \\
N_{Az} &= -\mathcal{D}_{AB} \frac{\partial C_A}{\partial z} + \left(N_{Az} + N_{Bz} \right) \frac{C_A}{C}
\end{aligned}$$

Cylindrical coordinates

$$\frac{\partial C_A}{\partial t} + v_r \frac{\partial C_A}{\partial r} + \frac{v_\theta}{r} \frac{\partial C_A}{\partial \theta} + v_z \frac{\partial C_A}{\partial z} = \mathcal{D}_{AB} \left[\frac{1}{r} \frac{\partial}{\partial r} \left(r \frac{\partial C_A}{\partial r} \right) + \frac{1}{r^2} \frac{\partial^2 C_A}{\partial \theta^2} + \frac{\partial^2 C_A}{\partial z^2} \right] + \dot{\mathcal{R}}_A \tag{I.8}$$

Fick's law

$$\begin{aligned}
N_{Ar} &= -\mathcal{D}_{AB} \frac{\partial C_A}{\partial r} + \left(N_{Ar} + N_{Br} \right) \frac{C_A}{C} \\
N_{A\theta} &= -\mathcal{D}_{AB} \frac{1}{r} \frac{\partial C_A}{\partial \theta} + \left(N_{A\theta} + N_{B\theta} \right) \frac{C_A}{C} \\
N_{Az} &= -\mathcal{D}_{AB} \frac{\partial C_A}{\partial z} + \left(N_{Az} + N_{Bz} \right) \frac{C_A}{C}
\end{aligned}$$

Spherical coordinates

$$\begin{aligned}
&\frac{\partial C_A}{\partial t} + v_r \frac{\partial C_A}{\partial r} + \frac{v_\theta}{r} \frac{\partial C_A}{\partial \theta} + \frac{v_\phi}{r \sin\theta} \frac{\partial C_A}{\partial \phi} \\
&\quad = \mathcal{D}_{AB} \left[\frac{1}{r^2} \frac{\partial}{\partial r} \left(r^2 \frac{\partial C_A}{\partial r} \right) + \frac{1}{r^2 \sin\theta} \frac{\partial}{\partial \theta} \left(\sin\theta \frac{\partial C_A}{\partial \theta} \right) + \frac{1}{r^2 \sin^2\theta} \frac{\partial C_A}{\partial \phi^2} \right] + \dot{\mathcal{R}}_A
\end{aligned} \tag{I.9}$$

Fick's law

$$
\begin{aligned}
N_{Ar} &= -\mathcal{D}_{AB}\frac{\partial C_A}{\partial r} + \left(N_{Ar} + N_{Br}\right)\frac{C_A}{C} \\
N_{A\theta} &= -\mathcal{D}_{AB}\frac{1}{r}\frac{\partial C_A}{\partial \theta} + \left(N_{A\theta} + N_{B\theta}\right)\frac{C_A}{C} \\
N_{A\phi} &= -\mathcal{D}_{AB}\frac{1}{r\sin\theta}\frac{\partial C_A}{\partial \phi} + \left(N_{A\phi} + N_{B\phi}\right)\frac{C_A}{C}
\end{aligned}
$$

Index